DATE			

ENCYCLOPEDIA
OF GAMBLING

ENCYCLOPEDIA OF GAMBLING

Carl Sifakis

Facts On File
New York • Oxford • Sydney

Encyclopedia of Gambling

Facts On File, Inc.   Facts On File Limited   Facts On File Pty Ltd
460 Park Avenue South   Collins Street   Talavera & Khartoum Rds
New York NY 10016   Oxford OX4 1XJ   North Ryde NSW 2113
USA   United Kingdom   Australia

Library of Congress Cataloging-in-Publication Data

Sifakis, Carl.
    Encyclopedia of gambling / Carl Sifakis.
        p.   cm.
    Includes index.
    ISBN 0-8160-1638-0 (HC)
    ISBN 0-8160-2426-X (PB)
    1. Gambling—Dictionaries.   I. Title.
HV6710.S54 1990
306.4'82'03—DC20   89-33107

British and Australian CIP data available on request.

Facts On File books are available at special discounts when
purchased in bulk quantities for businesses, associations,
institutions or sales promotion. Please contact the Special
Sales Department of our New York office at 212/683-2244
(dial 800/322-8755 except in NY, AK or HI).

Jacket design by Levavi & Levavi
Composition & Manufacturing by Maple-Vail Manufacturing Group
Printed in the United States of America

10 9 8 7 6 5 4 3 2 1

CONTENTS

For Emmes Buchleither,
with whom I will not play Skat.

INTRODUCTION

Gambling is the sure way of getting nothing for something.
—*Wilson Mizner*

The contest was typical of many newspaper big-money giveaways. The New York *Daily News* offered a total of $100,000 for guessing the exact score of the 1987 Super Bowl game between the New York Giants and the Denver Broncos. The outcome was 39-20, Giants. By April 1988, with the prize money long since paid out, federal authorities had determined that there had been too many winners in the contest, and that, amazingly, $85,000 of the prize money had gone to employees of the U.S. Postal Service or their friends.

It was, according to federal officials, a gambling scam based on the postal workers' use of their post office know-how. There had been 385,000 entries and only 167 came up with the correct score. Of these, 107 were submitted by postal employees or their associates. The final winners were chosen in a random drawing from the correct entries.

The authorities discovered the scam, it was said, because of a "woman scorned"—the $50,000 first-prize winner who blew the whistle after her boyfriend, a postal worker, dumped her for another woman. According to the charges brought initially for obstruction of the mails, the postal workers postmarked empty envelopes before the contest deadline, then watched the game, filled out the entry blanks with the final score and placed the envelopes in the Nebraska mail bin so that they went directly to the contest's Omaha address without being subjected to a second postmarking.

All the alleged contest cheaters came from five different New York post offices and had worked the scam *independently* of one another.

It was a case of good old American gambling ingenuity—in a word, cheating. The fact is, gambling offers a chicken-and-egg dilemma. Who came first in the history of man, the gambler or the cheater? The conventional wisdom is that early man came up with gambling as a form of sport or play. However, nothing unearthed by archaeologists is inconsistent with the flip side of the argument, that prehistoric cheaters actually invented gambling as a method of getting something from their fellow man. The earliest form of primitive dice, dating, by various estimates, from 6000 to 3500 B.C., turns out to be *crooked* dice. Gambling may not have been born out of ancient man's desire to get something for nothing but rather, as con man, gambler, screenwriter Wilson Mizner put it in his aforementioned definition of gambling, from some crafty old timer's determination to see that his fellows got nothing for their something.

It is generally agreed that the first form of gambling, preceding dice and playing cards, was simply the early pastime of tossing a stick in the air with good fortune falling to the man it pointed to on landing—a very benign game . . . unless it was invented by a cagey character who had the foresight to place himself downwind.

Does this credit early man with too much cunning? If Bronze Age man, or his predecessors, invented the wheel with no true understanding of the laws of physics, is it too unlikely that some others would figure out that the wind could give them an edge in "playing sticks"?

These men may not have understood the laws of physics, the laws of probability, or how to gain a gambling "edge," but somehow back in prehistoric times they clearly had learned that shaving a primitive die on one side altered the likelihood that chance alone would determine the results of a roll. Thus we find crooked dice in the tombs of ancient Egypt and the Orient and in the prehistoric graves of North and

South America. In the hereafter, in whatever form it took, the ancients were determined that the dear departed would do well in gambling play even with the gods. Clearly man's concept of a sucker being born every minute even extended to the gods themselves, who could be taken by a human hustler.

Throwing sticks, we now know, evolved into both dice and playing cards. Over the centuries the sticks were decorated with symbols and pictures to indicate front from back. In some cases the sticks were broadened, then flattened, then shortened into pieces that could be held in one's hand—the origin of playing cards. In the Orient today one can still find playing cards made of long pieces of board.

The same throwing sticks also evolved in another direction, being decorated on all sides of the stick so that wood with more flattened surfaces became desirable. This eventually led to the use of the knuckle-bones of sheep or other animals, which, being imperfect in shape, were simply decorated on four sides. Eventually this was increased to six sides by smoothing off the unused rounded edges, and man was well on the way to modern dice, which are now manufactured to exacting scientific specifications for casino play.

All other forms of gambling or games of chance share this common heritage from throwing sticks to dice and cards and on to dominoes, checkers, chess, tops, and indeed even the magician's wand (itself a form of misleading or deceiving, i.e., cheating the audience).

Well before the birth of Christ, six-sided dice were common in the civilized world. (It should be emphasized that dice appear in all cultures in vastly separated areas of the globe and developed in the same basic form, always with cheating pieces among the earliest types found.) We know that in all likelihood the Roman soldiers who rolled dice for Christ's garments at His crucifixion played a three-dice game called Ten. Ten is an uneven game in which some players have an unfair mathematical edge over others (see entry) and even without grasping the rules of probability, it seems likely that some successful gamblers—the Roman scribes record the superiority of some dice players over others—figured out the advantage of avoiding being the banker.

Man's written history and his biblical heritage reveal many instances of the "drawing of lots," most often by the casting of dice. Dice were used as a means to ending disputes, distributing or dividing property, or in one way or another divining God's will. Tacitus records the gambling of property and people, including slaves, among the early Germans. At times tribal battles were concluded with a game of chance. What we don't know is how often the fix was in. It figures a tribal leader agreeing to a dice

game to settle a major dispute would be prudent enough to have some very educated bones ready for the contest. It may be that early history was altered at some point by a hustler's scam.

In any study of gambling one must always recognize that dishonesty is a key ingredient of the game. Bluffing in Poker may be considered a form of cheating, noble or benign, or a kind of skill. In other aspects the cheating qualities of gambling become more apparent, especially in "organized gambling." The early gambling houses of Europe and Asia, or typically the saloons of the American Old West, were notorious for dishonest play. The itinerant gambler traveled—and fast—because his cheating ways wore out his welcome quickly. Today the modern gambling industry has developed its own way of giving its customers nothing for something. It is called the "house edge," which essentially means paying out less than the correct mathematical odds. Some may object to characterizing the gambling casino's edge as cheating, but in principle the idea of removing some chips from the action, even when the game is honest, offers no objective difference from stealing chips from a pot.

It is of course impossible for any authority on gambling to avoid such questions as "Are American casinos honest?" or "Isn't it a fact that only organized crime knows how to run the casino business?" It is instructive that organized crime is always in the forefront of campaigns to make casino gambling legal. Clearly, the "boys" have found they can make tons more money with legalized casinos than with illegal ones, a field they have long dominated. That being so, logic has it that the mobsters would run the games honestly rather than risk anything that would kill their golden gambling goose. One authority, Jimmy "the Greek" Snyder, describes the old days in Nevada gambling up to the 1950s as a period when "cheating was rampant." He insists that in recent years the bad guys are out and gaming is conducted honestly. The late John Scarne agreed. Making an on-the-spot study of Nevada gambling, he declared later that he found all the big joints honest, with only minor cheating at some small "sawdust" joints on the fringes of Las Vegas and Reno.

However, others have said that Scarne talked differently in private. A top executive at an important weekly magazine told this writer that Scarne claimed he found widespread dishonesty in Nevada while gambling in the Caribbean was "clean." The notion that Nevada was dishonest and the Caribbean honest doesn't quite jibe with the experience of most gamblers. Of course, the executive added, "Scarne functioned as a consultant to several island casinos."

It may be reasonably concluded that Nevada gambling operates without the use of gaffed equipment.

The reason for this is the "pickup"—a technique used by the Nevada Gaming Control Board to catch casino cheating. Agents will step into a casino, pick out a table and confiscate all the gaming equipment, then subject it to meticulous inspection at the board's laboratory. This may curb the use of crooked equipment, but it doesn't eliminate cheating by dealer duplicity based on "hand" ability. Many such techniques are illustrated in this book, and one should never assume he or she is immune to such tactics. Even if this action is spotted, the casino may well escape responsibility, since the establishment is often not held responsible for the tactics of its employees, the argument being that the crooked dealer might be in business for himself.

In a sense, analysis of casino honesty is beside the point. Man's instinct to gamble is clearly unquenchable. Suspicion of dishonesty has never seemed to turn away gamblers. To alter slightly Shakespeare's meaning if not his words, "the play's the thing."

There's a story this writer—and virtually every other authority on gambling—has told and retold. It concerns Canada Bill Jones, the brilliant 19th-century gambling cheat who himself consistently lost his money at Faro. Once before the Civil War Bill was taking a beating at the game in a shady joint in a small Louisiana river town. As his losses mounted, his partner got his ear in an effort to rescue him from the game. "The game's crooked," his partner whispered.

"I know it," was Canada Bill's dry response, "but it's the only one in town."

Gambling tales are unlimited and worth repeating. If some of them are untrue, it does not mean they should not be true. A case in point is the famed "bank loan" tale, recounted in the entry on Poker Stories, in which a Denver bank in the golden days of gambling in the West made a $5,000 loan on a Poker hand consisting of four kings and an ace. This was in a era when a straight flush did not beat four of a kind.

Similar too is the well-authenticated story of the no-limit Poker game played in Bowen's Saloon in Santa Fe, New Mexico in 1889 between cattle baron Ike Jackson of Colorado City, Texas and Johnny Dougherty, one of the shrewdest and most daring professional gamblers in the Southwest. With Governor L. Bradford Prince and close to 100 prominent citizens in attendance, at stake was an early version of the "Championship Series of Poker." Soon no less than $100,000 was on the table as each man raised and re-raised the other. Running out of cash, Jackson wrote out a deed to his ranch, with its 10,000 head of cattle. Unable to call, let alone raise, as he wished to do, the frantic Dougherty demanded pen and paper. He scrawled a few lines and then handed the document to Governor Prince, producing his revolver in the same motion.

"Governor," Dougherty said, "sign this or I'll kill you."

The New Mexican governor did so without so much as a prudent look at the document. Then Dougherty tossed the paper into the pot, announcing: "I raise you the Territory of New Mexico! There's the deed."

Jackson cursed and threw in his cards.

Fabulous winner-and-loser stories are common in the exploits of Bet-A-Million Gates, Nick the Greek, Tex Rickard, Soapy Smith, and many others. Some famous men have left their mark in unique ways. The great Polish pianist-statesman Ignace Paderewski once suffered through such an unrewarding session at Roulette at Deauville, France that he moved to a piano and proceeded to play Chopin's *Funeral March*. It launched the casino's tradition of nonstop music.

Despite the long list of religious figures who have inveighed against gambling, it cannot be said that the forces of religion have been fully unleashed against gambling. When the medieval church took up its campaign against gambling, it did not do so on the basis that the practice was outright sin. What the churchmen opposed were the concomitants of the activity or, as one observer put it, "because it inclined men to sloth, encouraged them to play rather than pray and led them to haunt taverns."

Gaming and dicing per se were not regarded as evil, which in part at least explains why many churches have permitted Bingo and other games of chance in fund-raising affairs. Dicing on the altar, in fact, is permitted in some churches. All Saints Parish Church of St. Ives, Cambridgeshire, England to this day holds annual dicing on its altar. The stakes of six Bibles are given to the best of 12 child dicers of the parish. The custom has existed since 1678.

This book attempts to trace the history and play of as many gambling games as possible throughout the world. In many cases some indication of strategy or at least prudent play is suggested. Definitive advice is impossible, especially in the major games such as Bridge, Chess, Blackjack, or Poker. Entire books have been written on limited aspects of these particular games.

Perhaps, though, it would be wise just to cover a few fundamentals of strategy for the greatest American indoor pastime, Poker. The most basic rules are simple: Play with poorer players; play with opponents who don't have a substantially greater bankroll; learn to develop "tells," or behavior patterns, of different players—when they raise, when they stay with poor hands, how they react physically to a strong hidden hand. Besides that, the only thing required is an understanding of the probable odds of any play and consequently when to stay and when to fold.

Of these rules the most important is the first one. If one plays with weaker opponents one has to become king of the hill. How do you know if you are playing with weaker or better players? If you win regularly, you have found your game. If you lose consistently, what are you doing in that game?

Perhaps no writer of a book on gambling can resist recalling personal experiences. This particular story refers to the second rule mentioned, never playing with opponents who have substantially more money. I was in a big game—by my standards—with six other writers and editors. Several of them were truly lovable foes. One was so inept at handling cards that he could not even shuffle them correctly. Another viewed the game as a social affair and stayed on in almost every hand as though we were playing penny ante. Another, a magazine writer, was always impoverished and was as usual playing on borrowed money.

Unfortunately, two of the players were writers with books then on the best-seller lists. There is nothing more insufferable than Poker-playing writers suddenly drawing escalating royalty money. They bet with abandon, with annoying recklessness. This, unfortunately, is devastating to players with limited funds. That was my situation. Actually, I was and still am a better Poker player than either of them. But they had the money and in fact were able to control the game. They could bluff with big raises and efforts to bluff them only led to still greater raises.

If it had not been for the hand before the last one, I would have been a very big loser. Fortunately I drew three aces at Draw, Jacks or Better. I opened, and each of the wild raisers proceeded to raise heftily. Since we were playing three-raise limit, I countered with a very small re-raise, limiting their madness. Each of my chief opponents drew three cards, which meant they had me figured for jacks and probably raised on the basis of holding queens or kings, that is, if one or both had not simply been bluffing and trying to force me out. I held my three aces and a 4 and discarded a queen (the proper play).

I failed to fill to my aces or the 4, but three aces under the circumstances was a powerful hand. My foes obviously had to figure me for two pair and if one or both either tripled up or drew a second pair they had to figure they beat me. Fortune was with me because both of them had paired up to their respective kings and queens. Both had to figure they were top dog.

I did nothing to disabuse their deductions and opened with a small bet, indicating I intended to cut down on the raises. Everyone else had dropped out. My first remaining opponent naturally raised big and the second came back with an even bigger raise. Both

figured I was caught in the middle and would either drop or play defensively with a tiny raise to kill the betting. Instead, I hit them with my biggest bet of the evening, doubling their combined raises. I now had them. They were in too deep to drop and had to call. My three aces topped queens and jacks and kings and deuces.

Yet despite that coup I ended up the night only $7 ahead. The pair with their superior bankrolls had had me down a huge amount and all I had managed to do was get even.

That was the last time I played in that game. I play Poker regularly in one weekly game and one monthly game. I'm on the profit side in both those games and keep at it. As for my big-money friends, no way. It had taken a superior hand and superior play, I might say, to get me out even. I couldn't count on doing that regularly. There was no percentage in bucking a game with players who had almost unlimited funds.

There are of course many rules to follow in playing correct Poker and I have alluded to one of them in my one-card draw to three aces. In Draw Poker it is absolute poison to draw two cards. Take three cards or one card, but never two cards. The last is the sign of an inferior player, one who telegraphs his hand for little reason. A two-card draw tells the opposition you either have three of a kind or a pair and an ace kicker (a particularly stupid hand to hold). A one-card draw indicates a weaker hand than a two-card draw and you actually are giving up very little opportunity to improve your hand. Holding a four in my pull-out hand offered me a chance to draw to it just as well as to any other card. The queen would have been a bad card to hold since in Jacks or Better the two raisers figured to have better than jacks, and since my hand killed the aces there had to be an excellent chance that one of my opponents had queens. True, I was giving up one of two chances to draw the fourth ace, but if you play Poker on the expectations of getting four of a kind you are my kind of opponent.

The one-card draw if you are not the opener has the added advantage of concealing your hand even more. You may have two pair or an even weaker hand of a possible straight or flush. I prefer my opponents to think I may be doing that. However, I never hold four cards to a straight of any kind. It is amazing how many Poker players who trumpet the fact that they never draw to inside straights (such as ace, deuce, four, five) really just demonstrate their weakness by thus revealing that they do draw to an open-end straight (such as deuce, three, four, five). The odds on the latter are much better, but still not good enough generally to ever try to fill. In fact, drawing to a four-card flush is a better bet than drawing to any kind of a straight. Occasionally I will do that, but when I drop if I don't fill, I slam my cards down and moan that I didn't catch my straight. The guidelines here are to "play smart but pose dumb."

Moderation in gambling is the real secret. In Poker it should always be rememberd that there are very few sure things, short of a royal flush or the afore-mentioned old-days hands of four aces or four kings and an ace.

There are actually very few sure things in any kind of wagering. The more sure a bet looks, the more you should think hard about it.

In the 18th century, the 21-year-old Earl of Barry-more was noted as one of England's most profligate rakes. He was at that tender age one of the fastest and fittest men in His Majesty's kingdom. Under the circumstances he readily accepted the challenge to a foot race made by a Mr. Bullock, a wealthy middle-aged butcher of epic proportions. Bullock insisted he could beat Barrymore in a 100-yard race if he got a 35-yard head start and choice of course.

Barrymore jumped at a large bet. Then the cunning Mr. Bullock played his ace. He picked as the site of the race the town of Brighton—down Black Lion Lane. It was precisely 100 yards long and one of the narrowest streets in all of England. Some stretches were a bit wider, but much of Black Lion Lane measured only 40 inches across. The lardy butcher barely could get through the lane himself and when the lane opened a bit there was still no room for Barrymore to pass him. Bullock was puffing hard at the finish, but Barrymore was screaming and cursing—and a loser.

It is a lesson to be remembered when one sits at the Poker table. Of course at Poker some hands are obviously more sure than others. Let us pick a mar-velous situation and have you come up with a straight flush on the first deal. The odds on that are 1 in 72,193. You figure to win. But suppose you are topped by a royal flush. The odds against *that* are 1 in 649,740. Yes, a royal flush is a possibility. However, the chances of the two hands coming out at the same time are almost 47 million to 1.

If that happens, you should be aware of one sure thing: It wasn't luck; you've been set up. It will not happen honestly in your lifetime, or your next one or the one after that.

There is little now to be done. You've bet like a maniac and have been taken. Swallow your losses.

Count Leo Tolstoy once said: "A gentleman is a man who will pay his gambling debts even when he knows he has been cheated."

It is solid advice. Violence goes along with gam-bling. And generally it's the loser who suffers that violence because the other side is ready for it.

Instead, follow the most important survival axiom in gambling: "Pay up and get out."

A

ACE-DEUCE STANDOFF: Excessive House Edge for Craps

While all of the nuances of the various gambling games cannot be described in this book, some are worth special mention. Among these is the Ace-Deuce Standoff in CRAPS because it demonstrates how the gullible can be fooled about odds and gambling house gouges.

At Craps tables in Atlantic City or Las Vegas casinos a "Don't Pass" line is marked Bar 1-1 or Bar 6-6. If either double 1 or double 6 is rolled (depending which is indicated) players who bet against the shooter do not win their bets as they do in private games. Instead it is a "standoff," or no bet, and is carried over to the next roll. Since 2 (1-1) or 12 (6-6) will come out on average once in 36 rolls, this constitutes the house edge on Don't Pass bets. If the house did not set up a bar, Craps players would bet against the shooter since without the bar there is built into the game a slight mathematical disadvantage to the shooter. Out of 1,980 possible rolls there are 976 winning possibilities and 1,004 losing ones. Expressed mathematically this means the shooter figures to win 49.29 percent of the time and lose 50.71 percent. Therefore by covering a shooter's bets, the house enjoys an edge of 1.41 percent. However, if the house covered the action *against* the shooter on the same basis, it would give up that advantage and the law of averages would work against the house. To solve that point the house announces it will bar 2 or 12. It doesn't matter which since either number will come out 55 times out of every 1,980 rolls. By making these results a standoff, a bet against the shooter no longer enjoys an advantage but now has a disadvantage of 1.402. (A slightly different calculation of the house advantage shows a 1.364 percent advantage.)

Essentially no matter which way the player bets,

he is bucking approximately the same house edge. Professional gamblers accept this situation, but what they do, or at least should, find objectionable is when instead of a 1-1 or 6-6 standoff, the house instead bars 1-2. While the 2 or 12 will come up 55 times per 1,980 rolls, the 3 will appear twice as often, or 110 times. (This is so because the 1 on the first die can come up with 2 on the second die, and vice versa.)

There are, unfortunately, some casinos both in this country and abroad that offer the Bar 3 instead of Bar 2 or Bar 12. One will find this at private Casino Nights, on cruise ship casinos, and at many illegal gambling joints. There is a rule of thumb used by many gamblers that when a house edge approaches 5 percent the game is too skewed against the player and should be avoided. Therefore, although they object to the house doubling the house edge with Bar 3, they will play even though they are now bucking a percentage of about 2.8 on the Don't Pass line.

This is a case of gamblers knowing too little about true mathematical odds. The house edge is not double but *more than triple!* Erroneously, many gamblers figure what is involved is simply substituting of 110 bars to the previous 55 bars. However it must be remembered part of the 55 bars are used to bring the percentage to dead even. If you double the number of bars after that, they are all gravy for the house. Take away 110 standoffs from 1,004 bets against the shooter and there are only 894 rolls left for the wrong bettor to win at. Since the house is betting with the shooter on these bets, it has against these 894 rolls a total of 976 ways to win. The gambler betting against the shooter therefore has only a 47-151/187 percent chance of winning. The house edge is 82 rolls, or 4-72/187 percent, which decimally works out to 4.385 percent. This is triple the edge on Bar 2 or Bar 12.

If you do run into a Bar 1-2 table, you should never

bet against the shooter. The fairer shake is betting with the shooter. However, a further caveat is in order. A table with the Bar 1-2 gouge may well have other odds skewed as well. As always in any form of gambling the secret here is to think before you bet.

ACE-DEUCE-JACK: Card Hustle

Few games appear to be so much in favor of the bettor while actually stacking the odds against him than Ace-Deuce-Jack. Hustlers have worked this game around racetracks and fairgrounds for years and made a handsome living off gullible bettors who are totally fooled by the mathematical principles involved.

The bank shuffles the cards, offers them for a cut, and then removes the three bottom cards from the deck. These are put aside face down so that none of the players sees them. The dealer then cuts the remaining cards into three piles. Players bet that an ace, deuce, or jack is not the bottom card on any of the three piles. If none of the three piles has an ace, deuce, or jack as a bottom card, all the bettors are paid off at even money. If the bottom card of any of the piles is an ace, deuce, or jack, the banker wins all bets.

Gullible players are certain that the odds are greatly in their favor since there are only 12 cards in a deck of 49 cards that can beat them, and since the three original discards might also be critical cards there could be 11, ten, or just nine cards against them in the deck. So far the player's logic is correct—*as long as he is talking about one pile of cards.* He actually must beat three piles and the banker needs only one ace, deuce, or jack to sweep the board. Allowing for all the mathematical variations involved in discarding three cards from the deck, the edge in favor of the banker is about 10.85 percent, making it over the long run a surefire money gouger. Some gambling casinos have introduced the game, but most avoid it since experienced gamblers stay away from the table.

ACES: Cheat-proof Dice Game

It is said there is more cheating with dice in the Far East then even in the United States. Perhaps that explains the popularity of Aces in the Far East, especially in the Philippines. World War II GI's became addicted to the game and while it might not have replaced CRAPS in popularity, GI's came greatly to appreciate not having to worry about crooked dice.

The game's full name is Aces to the Center, Deuces to the Left, and Fives to the Right, and that mouthful practically tells it all. Each player has a dice cup and five dice which are referred to by their card identities. The first player throws his dice and passes any deuces rolled to the player on his left and any fives to the player on his right. He also passes any aces to the center of the table, these dice are out of the game. The first player continues to throw his dice until he gets rid of all of them or until he makes a roll that fails to produce an ace, deuce, or five. The player to his left then becomes the shooter. Play continues until all the dice are centered. The shooter who throws the last ace is the loser.

This is an intriguing game with considerable suspense; although a player may get rid of all his dice he has to remain in the game, and he could find his stock replenished from his left or right.

By making the final ace the loser, the possibility of cheating is eliminated. True, the shooter can slip a misspotted die with no ace on it so that he could not roll a loser. However, he would eventually have to throw a deuce or 5 and the die would be passed without the opportunity to switch it out of play. As a result the misspot would go round and round and the game would never end.

Aces can be played for drinks or cash, and it has been described as the Filipino plantation owners' favorite game for very high stakes. The knock on the game is that there is only one loser; if a player loses repeatedly, the payout can be significant. Because of this there is some tendency to switch the rules of the game to make the last ace a winning one, and the winner then collects from all other players. But this may also permit a shooter to work in a crooked die . . .

ACES TO THE CENTER, DEUCES TO THE LEFT, AND FIVES TO THE RIGHT
See ACES.

ACEY-DEUCEY: Two-card Poker Game

A longtime favorite in the armed forces, Acey-Deucey probably has separated as many soldiers, sailors, and marines from their paychecks as such old reliables as POKER and CRAPS. And it can do so faster.

After an ante each player is dealt two cards, one up and one down. He may stand with these cards or he may discard one of them and get a new card, paying one chip (usually the amount of the original ante) for the privilege. The new card is dealt up or down depending on the card it is replacing. If the player feels he can improve his hand with still another substitute card, he pays two chips and gets a second replacement; he may even take a third replacement by paying three chips (in some games, five chips).

Once all the players have completed their hands there is a final round of betting as in any game of Poker. The game is played high-low; either a pair or the highest card will take the high. Two aces is the highest pair but one ace may be played for low, so that ace-deuce is the lowest possible low hand. The winners of the high hand and the low hand split the pot.

An experienced player holding, for instance, deuce-8 will seldom draw a replacement card under penalty of as much as five chips unless the pot is very large. He will be governed by the estimated probabilities of improving his hand against the size of the pot and further investment. It will probably pay to stay loose and see the final betting (if the action does not get too heavy) on the strong possibility that his deuce-8 hand will be low or quite possibly the only low hand in the game. The sign of a foolish Acey-Deucey player is one who compulsively takes all substitute cards.

ACTION: Money Wagered by a Gambler

Misunderstanding of the term "action" has led to a considerable amount of grief on the part of novice gamblers. Action merely indicates the amount of money a gambler wagers. As come-ons many casinos make action offers to bring in customers.

For instance, Bob Stupak's Vegas World recently offered gamblers a room for two nights and $1,000 in betting action for a mere $396. Only a dreamer would not have to realize that such an offer had to have strings attached. But this did not represent fakery on the part of Stupak's casino, as the fine print made clear. What the player got for his approximately $400 was $1,000 in *nonredeemable* casino CHIPS, the chips usable only once—and not returnable.

Let us say the player took all $10 chips and bet them at CRAPS. If he lost his bet, the house simply raked in his $10 chips. But suppose he won his bet. The houseman would pay him his winnings, *but still rake in the nonredeemable chips.* This may seem eminently unfair since the player won his bet and he would normally get his winnings *plus* his original bet returned. However, that was not the promise. The player had been guaranteed $1,000 in *action*. When he bet all the nonredeemable chips, he would have gotten everything that had been offered him.

The promise of action is a lure to bring players to a casino and the room accommodations tend to keep them there long after that. Thereafter they must use the established "coin of the realm" for their wagers, the freebie play having beem completed. In theory the player should be ahead; if he bets only on even-money shots with his special chips he figures to win just slightly less than half the time (the so-called law of averages minus the house percentage), but the casinos are ready to take the risk on that. Obviously, casinos wouldn't offer action chips if they didn't expect players to continue to gamble, and on average get ground down by the eternal house edge.

The promise of action chips is like BUS JUNKETS to casinos, in which players are refunded more in quarters (often plus other minor perks) than the fare they laid out. Here again on average the casinos know they will get those quarters back in their hungry slots, plus a lot more from the average player.

An interesting switch on action chips is offered in Austrian casinos (see AUSTRIA, GAMBLING IN). Like virtually all gambling houses in Europe, those in Austria impose an admission fee, 170 schillings (about $15, subect to currency swings). But unlike the others, the Austrians give the player four 50-schilling chips with which to bet free. As in America, these chips are not refundable and must be wagered. The difference is that when a player wins a bet, say for one chip, the nonrefundable chip is picked up but it is replaced by a refundable chip, which is given to the player along with the winnings due him. This makes the Austrian action chip offer much more attractive than its American counterpart, but there is the minor matter of the carfare needed to get there.

Albert J. ADAMS: New York Numbers King

During the latter part of the 19th century, the kingpin of the numbers racket in America was Albert J. Adams (1844-1907). He came to dominate the New York gambling scene through graft, trickery, and deceit; indeed, the days his games were running honestly were few and far between.

Dishonest had been the byword of policy games long before Adams, in fact going back to their introduction in 18th-century England. But unlike his predecessors, Adams juggled the numbers not only to cheat the public but other operators as well so that he could take over their operations.

Adams came to New York from his native Rhode Island about 1870 and first tried his hand at honest labor as a railroad brakeman. Soon having enough of that, Adams became a runner for policy operator Zachariah Simmons. Appreciating Adams's talent for deviousness, Simmons made Adams a partner. Some cynics said this was just Simmons's way of trying to keep Adams from cheating him. In a short time Adams seemed to outsiders to be the main man of the operation and when Simmons died, Adams took over the entire operation. Yet even before Simmons died, Adams was already rigging the game to reduce the money paid out to winners.

During this period the policy racket was dominated by independent operators, and it was common practice for these independents to "lay off" numbers that had been bet too heavily with them. The tactic was a simple one, shifting part of the action to another operator who had light play on that number. It was much like the standard insurance practice of spreading the risk.

Adams, however, frequently would not play the game. When he was approached about heavily played numbers, he announced he too had too much action on them. Then he too would spread bets around on those numbers, even though he had little or no action on them himself. This made a number of operators very vulnerable, and Adams then put the fix in to make the numbers win. The victimized operators took heavy losses and, to make their payoffs, were forced to look to Adams for loans. Adams's price: a partnership in their games. In other cases Adams refused to make the loans and the other racket men were forced to dip into their bribe money to cover their losses. Somehow the police and politicians did not view such actions as laudable and the operations were shut down. Adams simply moved in on the vacant territories. The law had no objections; Adams never welshed on bribes.

In time Adams controlled more than 1,000 policy shops. Over the years his payments to the Tweed Ring, the corrupt political group that ruled New York City, ran into the millions. Even when the reformers toppled the Tweed Ring and took over, Adams continued to operate with the connivance of the police.

Adams even operated during the famed Lexow Committee's exposé of official corruption in 1894. Appearing before that investigative group Police Commissioner John McClave took part in this exchange:

> Q: Albert J. Adams, did you ever hear of such a man?
> A: I have heard that there was such a man in existence, but I have never yet seen him.
> Q: Do you know him as a gambler?
> A: I know of no such thing.
> Q: Has he never been raided since you were commissioner of police in any of his faro banks in this city?
> A: I don't know.

Eventually the committee concluded that Adams's graft payments to dishonest officials was at the rate of $20 a month for almost 1,100 policy shops alone. Even so Adams kept on going and it was not until 1901 that law enforcement authorities finally had to take action against him; Adams was convicted and sent to Sing Sing.

Adams served a little over a year. When he returned to New York he discovered that his empire had been chopped up, with operators becoming increasingly violent to maintain their holdings. It would have taken all-out war for Adams to take back his enterprises. This was not the Adams style, which relied primarily on bribes and trickery. So Adams, an extremely wealthy man by now, quit the racket. He went into land speculation, which he found to be equally as rewarding, especially if one knew the right officials to see about inside information.

He lived out his last few years in luxury at the Ansonia Hotel in New York City, but grieved over the fact that his family rejected him. Many of them were ashamed of his criminal past and blamed him for their inability to lead normal, respectable lives. On October 1, 1907, the man the newspapers had long labeled "the meanest gambler in New York" took his own life.

AFGHANISTAN, Gambling in

Before the incursion of Russian troops into Afghanistan in 1979, Afghanistan was known as the most Islamic of Islamic countries. Laws against all forms of gambling were rigidly enforced and the punishments severe.

Although all private gambling is also forbidden in the USSR, that country has never strictly enforced such laws. The Red Army is known to have a certain tolerance of soldiers gambling. This lenience created an additional friction in Afghanistan, with the Russian troops viewed as infidels who could only infect the country's Islamic culture.

ALL FIVES: Variation of Seven Up (All Fours)

All Fives is a variation of SEVEN UP, known in England as All Fours.

How to play: The dealing, playing, and scoring are the same as in Seven Up except that additional points are added to create a winning total of 61 rather than 7. In taking tricks, the ace of trumps scores 4 points; king 3; queen 2; jack 1; the 10 is 10 points; and the 5 is 5. These points are usually scored as the game progresses on a CRIBBAGE board, but they can be figured on paper. Then the four honor points from Seven Up—high, low, jack, and game—are added in, but with the 5 of trumps counted as 5 points toward the game category. Although it still has a following, All Fives has basically given way to some forms of PITCH, especially CALIFORNIA JACK and Shasta Sam.

ALL FOURS

See SEVEN UP.

AMARILLO: Spit Poker Variation

This game, a thinking man's OMAHA wherein the same strategies apply, is preferred by many serious gamblers. Their hands can be more individualized because players cannot make use of all five spit cards.

How to play: Players are dealt two down cards after which there is a round of betting. Then five spit (or mutual) cards are dealt face up one at a time with another round of betting following each card. When there are five cards up, players have to decide their hand but *must use both their hole cards.* Thus they can use only three of the five mutual cards.

In Omaha, up to five mutual cards may be used. As a result, when the occasional pat hand—such as a straight or flush or full house—turns up, players can discard their own hole cards, play the pat hand and divide the pot (unless one of the players uses four of the mutual cards plus a higher card to the straight or flush). Up to 23 players can be accommodated, though seven to ten is more common.

AMBIGU: French Forerunner of Poker

Ambigu is an old French gambling game in which, like BOUILLOTTE, we can see the germ of POKER. How to play: Ambigu may have from two to six players with a 40-card deck, with the kings, queens, and jacks removed. The cards rank downward in value from 10 to ace.

After the ante each player is dealt two down cards. The player may reject one or both of these cards and call on the dealer for the required replacement. Following this each player is dealt two more cards, giving each a hand of four cards. A betting round follows with successive players either calling or raising the previous bet, or folding (as in Poker). All players calling or raising the last bet are once more allowed to discard and replace one to four of their cards.

The hands are exposed, the highest one taking the pot. With each winning hand there is a bonus payoff to the winner by all the losers, over and above what is already in the pot. The ranking of winning hands is best listed from lowest to the highest:

1. **Point** consists of two cards of one suit. The total spots are added, so that the 7 and 6 of hearts would be 13 points and top a 10 and 2 of spades (which make 12). The two hearts would also beat a 10 and 3 of clubs, even though the points are equal. Ties are otherwise broken by favoring two cards in sequence, such as 7-6. (A further tiebreak applying to all hands is explained below.) The winner also collects a bonus of one chip from all losers.
2. **Prime** consists of four cards of different suits. Bonus: two chips.
3. **Grand prime** is *prime* but with the player's hand totaling more than 30 spots. Bonus: three chips.
4. **Sequence** consists of three straight flush cards with the higher hand winning. Thus 8, 7, 6 of hearts beats 6, 5, 4 of spades. Bonus: three chips.
5. **Tricon** is three of a kind, highest rank winning. Bonus: four chips.
6. **Flush** is four of the same suit, not in sequence. Bonus: five chips.
7. **Doublets** are various combinations of two winning hands from prime upward:
    - **Prime** and **tricon.** All four suits are present and there is a three of a kind. In each case the bonuses are added. In this case two plus four for six chips.
    - **Tricon** with **grand prime.** This could be three 9's and a 6 covering the four suits. Bonus: seven chips.
    - **Sequence** and **flush.** This would be a three-card straight flush plus another flush card. Bonus: eight chips.
    - **Fredon.** Four of a kind. Bonus: ten chips.
    - **Fredon** with **grand prime.** Bonus: 11 chips.

No ties are permitted in Ambigu, and if any ties exist in the winning hands, from **point** through **fredon with grand prime,** the winner is declared to be the tied player nearest to the right of the deal. It must be remembered that in France, where this game still has a following, cards are dealt counterclockwise, from right to left.

Ambigu never grew to the stature of Poker undoubtedly because of the problem of the bonus payoffs. In Poker, folding represents a way for the prudent gambler to cut his losses. In Ambigu, the losers might still have to cough up an additional payout of as much as 11 chips—enough to give a tight player second or third thoughts.

AMERICAN BRAG
See BRAG.

ANY CARD WILD: Wide-open Version of Poker
The wildest of all wild-card POKER games are those that guarantee every player at least one wild card, something that even DEUCES WILD, HEINZ, and WOOLWORTH don't offer. In Any Card Wild, each player designates any card in his hand as a wild card.

In even more hectic versions of this game all other cards of the same rank as the designated wild card in the player's hand are also wild. This means that any player with a pair has at least three of a kind—and indeed that is about the lowest expectation for a winning hand. Actually the weakness of three of a kind becomes apparent when one realizes that any four-card flush or straight is automatically filled by the wild card(s). In a six-handed game, four of a kind will be the winning hand at least half the time; any actual three of a kind or two pairs automatically become four of a kind. And five of a kind is not uncommon.

Perhaps surprisingly one may witness rather high-stakes games of Any Card Wild, but these almost always are limited to the one-wild-card-per-hand version. Any Card Wild makes for an interesting game in FIVE-CARD STUD, which is wide open with considerable opportunity for bluffing.

See also: ANY SUIT WILD.

ANY SUIT WILD: Hectic Poker

There is no other way to describe the Any Suit Wild version of POKER than incredibly hectic.

How to play: The game, in a five- or seven-card version, is played one of two ways, either of which produce astronomical hands, most easily beatable by something better. Consider that the average eight wild-card game like Deuces and Treys Wild will generally lead to winning hands of a minimum of four of a kind, and one gets an idea of how powerful hands are with 13 wild cards!

One version calls for agreement beforehand as to the wild suit. However, an even more wide-open game permits each player to stipulate the wild suit for his own hand. In such a case a three-card flush produces a minimum of four of a kind; a four-card flush five of a kind; and a flush an automatically winning five aces.

Strategy: As frantic as this game is there is considerable suspense in the FIVE-CARD STUD version. In the wide-open version all players are guaranteed three of a kind since one suit must be at least doubled. Occasionally three of a kind does steal the pot, but more commonly four of a kind is needed.

In Seven-card Stud a royal flush should not be regarded as a powerhouse hand. More often than not it will be topped by five of a kind. Some prudent gamblers will even drop out on a low five of a kind.

The hands in DRAW POKER are also extremely high, but there is still room for strategy, the key points of which undisciplined gamblers unfortunately ignore. When holding three cards to a flush and an ace and another card, too many players discard only one card, seeking another ace or flush card. It is wiser to discard the ace as well and try for two new cards since only one flush card will produce five of a kind and two flush cards and another ace and a flush card will still produce the sought-after five aces.

Any Suits Wild is seldom played in Draw or Seven-card Stud games for high stakes. However, this is not true of the Five-card Stud version. One gambler, highly successful at the game, insists chronic losers like the game because they somehow find it more comforting to lose with strong hands than to be frustrated with frequent nothing hands. It may be an odd attitude, but it is the outlook prevalent in horse racing—and Poker games.

ARGENTINA, Gambling in

The government holds a tight monopoly on all gambling in Argentina. Horse racing there is probably the best in all of South America. The Argentine government also operates a state lottery on which there is heavy action, not surprising in a country that has suffered from high inflation. Illegal gambling has been quite prevalent in the recent past despite laws that call for prison sentences of up to six months. The laws were not rigidly enforced in the era of the military junta, and it was said a great many private entrepreneurs and military officials made considerable sums of money from such operations. Furthermore illicit gambling income helped maintain the support of relatively junior military officers for the dictatorship.

ARIZONA, Lotteries

In Arizona there is legalized gambling through the state lottery, net profits from which go for improvement of local transportation. The state offers instant games with a new one every eight weeks or so. A typical version is 7-11-21, which can pay $21,000 instantly. There are three basic ways to win—by *"rub off"* numbers from the lottery ticket that total 7, 11, or 21, and the prize would be the corresponding amount shown on the right side of the ticket. Losing tickets have a premium as well; by sending five losing tickets in an envelope, players are entered into a special drawing in which the winner is awarded $1,000 a week for life.

The state's big game is called "The Pick," with the top prize often being a million dollars or more. Six-for-six correct numbers out of 36 is required for a first prize.

AROUND THE WORLD: Seven-card Poker and Spit Variation

Around the World is one of the conservative Spit Poker games.

How to play: Each player gets a hand of four cards and a mutual card is turned up in the center of the table. There is a betting round and then three more mutual cards are dealt one at a time with betting sequence after each. Thus each remaining player has four hidden cards and four common upcards from which to figure his five-card hand.

This game is somewhat like SEVEN-CARD MUTUAL and OMAHA in that it allows for a great number of players.

James ASHBY: Riverboat Gambler

In the folklore of the Mississippi riverboat gamblers a grizzled old sharper named James Ashby cut out a remarkable record among the crooked fraternity. Old Ashby took innocent victims, but he skinned the sharpers as well, although they never suspected how until he retired a very rich man in the 1830s.

Ashby worked with a young confederate, and they pretended to be father and son returning home laden with cash after taking some livestock to market. The gamblers immediately honed in on the bumpkin-appearing "son" who looked like a perfect pigeon. The young man was easily inveigled into trying his luck at cards, while Ashby pretended to be an old coot teetering on the brink of senility. While the son played cards, Ashby guzzled white lightning and played snatches of tunes on his fiddle, stopping abruptly when he forgot the notes.

Meanwhile the son proved less dim-witted than he looked, winning hand after hand in defiance of all the odds. When gamblers dealt themselves a sure hand, they were frustrated by the son who dropped out of the game, never calling their set-up big bets.

"Not for a long time," a historian of the river wrote, "did the gamblers learn that tunes were signals." By then it was too late. Ashby retired from the river to live out his golden years in bountiful fortune.

ATLANTIC CITY: Dullsville at the Seashore

Ask any visitor to Atlantic City who has also been to fabulous Las Vegas and he will tell you New Jersey gambling doesn't hold a candle to the wide-open Nevada variety—that it's Dullsville at the Seashore. To many gamblers Atlantic City is a total bust, to be patronized solely because it's the only game in town. Total bust is also a perfect description of what casino gambling has been for the citizens of Atlantic City, who had danced for joy on the Boardwalk when casino gambling won approval in 1976. It was to be their salvation with jobs, money, and housing for the poor and elderly. Instead, Atlantic City is a huge slum with a dozen-odd lavish casinos towering skyward in total indifference to the city's plight.

The Atlantic City Boardwalk has become a high-roller ghetto. Wander off the Boardwalk a mere block and visit a high-crime area. Casino action, intended to eliminate crime in Atlantic City, instead has bred more, and prostitution has soared. Housing costs have spiraled out of sight, the legions of the homeless have multiplied and 90 percent of the city's businesses have disappeared. There is only one supermarket in town and no movie houses. Total population has dipped from 45,000 to 37,000 in a few short years.

But no matter, the casinos are fat and rich and happy. By 1985, after only eight years in operation, Atlantic City's 11 hotel-casinos had reported earnings of $2.2 billion—a half billion more than the total earnings of Las Vegas's 60-odd licensed establishments. And Atlantic City was doing it with only 6,000 hotel rooms, compared to 50,000 in Vegas. The secret is that Atlantic City has had 30 million visitors, most of whom didn't stay the night, and were not hard to lure from the 100-million base to be found in what is considered its drawing area.

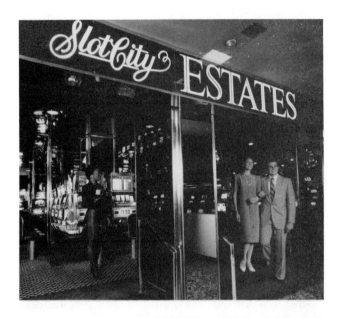

Atlantic City, stifled in part by state regulations requiring all New Jersey casinos to offer the same games at the same odds, has yet to catch on with the gambling public as has Las Vegas. The average visitor to Las Vegas stays 4½ days compared to 8 hours in Atlantic City, despite the glitter such casinos as the Tropicana offer. (Photo: Tropicana, Atlantic City)

Boasting such statistics, Atlantic City should have buried Vegas, which costs a mint for many people to reach by air, train, or auto. But Atlantic City's emphasis is on gouging. As one report put it, ". . . the prevailing attitude is 'Gouge the customers at every turn.' Rooms start at $90 a night in most places, food prices are similarly inflated and posted parking rates are as high as ten dollars for 12 hours."

The casinos have welshed on every promise they ever made to New Jersey and wrapped the Casino Control Commission around its own regulations. Early on the Commission mandated that a specific number of gaming tables had to maintain certain low minimums as a guarantee that poor players would not be forced to bet over their heads. The white flag soon went up on that one; now the casinos set their own minimums. It is hard to find BLACKJACK tables with less than a $5 minimum, compared to $1 or $2 in Nevada. On weekends or other busy times just try to find a CRAPS table with less than a $10 minimum, which essentially is too high for the average player to take what is called favorable full odds because he must now put up $20 or more to roll the cubes just once. And forget about Blackjack at $5 at peak times. There are some $10 tables, but the only open seats are usually at $25 games.

In their effort to "protect" the public, the authorities have done a better job of promoting monopoly prices and odds in Atlantic City, and come up with rules that stiffle real gambling and grind players into the dust. Compared to Vegas, the gambling variety is a joke. There is no POKER, KENO, or race-book and sports-book betting. Some of these offer some opportunities for the thinking man, and if Keno does not and is really a ripoff it does offer a low-cost respite from the hectic and expensive pace at the high-priced tables.

While certain mandated rules do help bettors, such as those on double odds in Craps, many others do not. Craps, after all, is a pure game of chance and as such allows for no skill and little real opportunity of beating the house. Blackjack too is played with six to eight decks virtually exclusively with pairs not being permitted to resplit, a very poor deal for the player.

Development of Atlantic City as a true gambling mecca will take decades mainly because the casinos want to operate on the "trickle-down" theory. Cater to the big money, the high rollers from the business field who are the world's most inept gamblers but enjoy the thrill of betting big time or are on a self-destruct binge, and forget the public, which wants to bet small. It doesn't mean ignore them totally, but bus them in and force them to dig for enough money to meet inflated minimums. After all, the rent isn't due until they're back home.

It has never occurred to the New Jersey authorities that the Casino Control Commission might benefit by having some spokesmen for the average gambler on the panel, one of whom might ask why a one-roll bet on 2 or 12 in Craps is designated to pay off at only 30 to 1 and produce an excessive house edge of 13.9 percent, when even in England, where understanding of all the ways the house profits at Craps is more limited, the gaming board has decreed a payoff of 33 to 1. The difference is enormous dropping the house edge to 5.55 percent, but as long as noncompetition between the casinos is the password it is a safe bet that players will never get a fair shake on the odds.

In Las Vegas, the boys are frightened of Atlantic City, viewing it as a threat to their business, but so far what a visit to Atlantic City tends to do is make every real gambler anxious to hop on a plane bound for that glittering mecca in the desert, where men are men and gamblers are gamblers.

See LAS VEGAS.

Further reading: *The Boardwalk Jungle* by Ovid Demaris.

AUCTION FORTY-FIVE
See FORTY-FIVE.

AUCTION PITCH
See PITCH.

AUSTRALIA, Gambling in
The down-under action in Australia is probably the best anywhere south of Las Vegas. Aussies will bet on virtually anything, including horses, lotteries, and dogs. Gambling casinos have come on strong and are at latest count available in almost all of the states. Licensed bookmaking is permitted in most places. Certain gambling games are strictly prohibited in some states and legal in others. Some states bar BINGO or BACCARAT and many bar the Chinese game of FAN TAN.

Slot-machine action may be the equal of Las Vegas percentagewise, and it is fast going high tech. Two casinos in Australia in early 1988 were among the first 11 in the world to have installed a special microcomputer-based information system made by Electronic Data Technologies in the United States that enables casinos to identify frequent slot players. The casinos provide players with a card that is "read" by the machine so that besides their normal winnings (or losings) players are rewarded with cash based on the frequency of activity—sort of like the airlines frequent-flier programs. For innovation in gambling matters, Australia is far ahead of Europe and probably the equal of the United States.

A.

B.

Austrian casino gambling (A) has been described as the most laid-back in Europe with an enlightened admission-fee policy. The casinos vary from the opulence of Baden (B)—ironically one of the last to reopen after World War II because the Russian occupation forces retained it as their headquarters—to outdoor Routlette at Velden (C). (Photos: Casinos Austria AG)

AUSTRIA, Gambling in

Casino gambling in Austria is among the best that one will find in most European countries. The super-rich are at the elegant casino in Baden's Kurpark, which in earlier times residents of Vienna had to patronize because they were not permitted in Vienna's Casino at Cercle Wiene in the Esterhazy Palace. The law, obviously intended to keep the welfare rolls from being bloated with down-and-out gamblers, is no longer in force. Austrians are dedicated casino gamblers and their casinos were the last to acknowledge there was an interlude called World War II and were the last to shut down in the "All-German Reich" (Baden finally closed its doors on August 26, 1944). The casinos started reopening in 1950—although Baden was shuttered until 1955 because it served instead as Soviet headquarters. Today, a state gambling monopoly controls the Austrian action, including the Austrian state lottery, the totalizators, football pools, as well as the organization of all other lotteries, casinos, and lesser gambling activities in the country.

Outside of Loew's Monte Carlo (which has no admission price), the Austrian casinos have the best admission policy in Europe. The cost is hefty, 170 schillings (around $15 in 1988 money) but the price includes four 50-schilling nonredeemable chips. These are like American ACTION chips, but they have full value unlike the American action chips. If a chip is bet at even money and the bet won, the nonredeemable chip is picked up and two regular 50s chips are paid. Thus, on average, players should come out ahead on the admission price, in theory losing twice, winning twice, and ending up with 200 schillings.

Austrian casinos are privately owned by Casinos Austria AG, but the government is a partner. The Austrian casinos are among the most forward-looking and innovative and were among the first to post electronically the last 20 or so results of a ROULETTE wheel so players could back-figure their "systems." Because of their professionalism Casinos Austria AG manages or provides know-how for many casinos in Holland, Turkey, Spain, Hungary, Belgium, Greece, and Spain. In addition, cruise ships under various flags are Austrian-managed.

B

BACCARAT: Famous Casino Game

Baccarat is considered one of the more glamorous casino card games, although, as played in the United States and England, it has become so highly ritualized as to be totally mindless. Players put up their chips and in effect are told by the house if they win or lose.

The game is of Italian origin but, although quite popular in that country, is regarded as a French game. Baccarat, the French word for the Italian *Baccara*, means zero—of much importance since in the game all face cards and the 10 count for zero.

Baccarat comes in numerous varieties, which will be discussed in the entries that follow. The American Game is gaining in use around the world, although it is the least interesting version. There are several varieties of play in Europe and elsewhere.

BACCARAT—American

American Baccarat has preserved many of the glamorous European trappings of the game. The Baccarat area is set apart from the rest of the casino, either roped or partitioned off. And the game is played in large measure by well-dressed men and beautiful women (mostly SHILLS to help the play get started). The American version is the more mindless of plays, since the player doesn't even have to know the rules. Play is completely proscribed, and after placing his bet a gambler can simply wait to be informed if he wins or loses. This has proved to be necessary because Americans have been traditionally frightened of the game. The European straight Baccarat and the more intriguing CHEMIN DE FER were tried in the United States in 1911 in Saratoga and Palm Beach and died a quick death. The current version in which the house/casino backs the bets originated at the Capri Casino in Havana, Cuba, in the 1950s.

In 1959 the game was introduced in America at the Dunes in Las Vegas. Although it has absolutely no strategy, American Baccarat has a devoted, and generally big-money, following since it offers one of the lowest house advantages of any casino game. It may be slower than CRAPS, but the wagers tend to be higher and the players enjoy a relaxed atmosphere and indulgent catering by dealers and hostesses that would be impossible around a crowded Craps table. Probably the greatest turnoff for some of the public is the fact that the minimum bets at Baccarat are usually $20—and one will often have to struggle to find those. More common minimums are $40 and at some casinos even $100. The maximum—forget them. They run from $2,000 to $10,000, but many casinos will even up that upon request. While on average they may not match European wagering, nevertheless it is not impossible to see the size of bets that the amazing JAMES BOND is so fond of making, although for drama these were based on Chemin de Fer.

The following are the typical house rules of American Baccarat as offered at Caesars-Atlantic City:

This ancient game of chance is played with eight (8) decks of cards. The object is to get a point count closest to 9. Picture cards and 10s, and any combination of cards totaling 10, have no value. All other cards are counted at face value. Ace is 1, Deuce is counted as 2, etc. Thus a hand containing a 9 and a 5 equals 4.

The game begins when the cards are shuffled by the croupier and placed in a dealing device called a shoe. The player acting as banker deals from the shoe. Two (2) cards are dealt to the player's hand and two (2) cards are dealt to the banker's hand. The dealer announces the point counts. If the point count of either hand is 8 or 9, it is called a natural and no

Baccarat as offered at the Las Vegas Sands. Players—usually high-stakes gamblers—can sit there doing nothing except betting their money. They will be informed if they have won or lost. (Photo: Las Vegas News Bureau)

additional cards are drawn from the dealing shoe. If neither hand has a natural, an additional card will be drawn face up for the player's and banker's hand based on the rules below, and the dealer's instruction.

There are three (3) ways to bet in Baccarat. All players including the banker can bet on the banker's hand or the player's hand, or both hands will end in a tie, i.e., neither hand wins or loses. These bets are placed before the croupier calls "no more bets" and the cards are dealt. A bet on the banker's hand wins if the banker's hand has a point count higher than the player's hand. It loses if the banker's hand has a point count lower than the player's hand. It is void if the point counts are equal. A bet on the player's hand wins if the player's hand has a point count higher than the banker's hand. It loses if the player's hand has a point count lower than the banker's hand. It is void if the point counts are equal. A winning bet on either banker's hand or the player's hand will result in a one to one payoff with winning tie bets paying out odds of eight to one. A tie bet wins if the point counts of the banker's hand and player's hand are equal and loses if the point counts are not equal.

A winning bet on the banker's hand will be assessed a 5% commission which must be paid by no later than the conclusion of each dealing shoe.

If the banker's hand is successful and wins, the participant dealing retains the dealing shoe. When the banker's hand loses, the dealing shoe passes, giving each participant a chance to handle the shoe. A participant may pass the dealing shoe at any time.

When you get right down to it, the American version of Baccarat is, as the name says, a zero. Actually it amounts to nothing more than cutting the cards two or three times and totaling the scores.

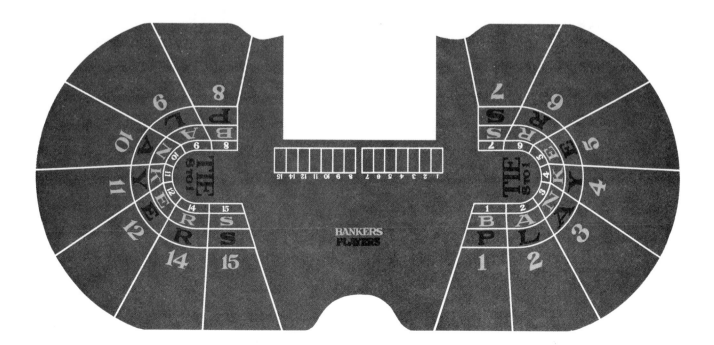

Player Hand Third Card Rule

When Player's First Two Cards Total:	Player's Hand:
0-1-2-3-4-5	Draws a Card
6-7	Stands
8-9	Natural Stands

Banker

When Banker's First Two Cards Total:	Draws When Player's Third Card Is:	Does Not Draw When Player's Third Card Is:
0, 1, 2	Banker's hand always draws on a two card total of 0, 1, 2	
3	1-2-3-4-5-6-7-8-9-0	8
4	2-3-4-5-6-7	1-8-9-0
5	4-5-6-7	1-2-3-8-9-0
6	6-7	1-2-3-4-5-8-9-0
7	Stands	
8-9	Natural Stands	

If you do play casino Baccarat, don't believe all the other players are gambling with their own money. Casinos employ a lot of shills (they prefer calling them "game starters") because few gamblers like to play alone. As the game picks up steam, the shills, the majority of them women, will fade away one at a time. Their seats at the table are too valuable to waste on staff when a high roller comes along. The shills do not lead a happy life. They are poorly paid and, amazingly, need "tokes"—tips from regular players to make out. It is an amusing phenomenon that gamblers recognize shills as a necessary part of the scene and actually tip them when they are winning. The most sophisticated gamblers know that if they are winning the casino becomes unhappy and actually chews out the female shill for the house's bad luck. If a female shill sits in games that run against the house too often, she may well be given a two-week vacation—without pay. If she returns and it happens again, she'll likely be fired. No one has ever accused casino bosses of being above superstition or too long on logic.

There is no intent here to knock American Baccarat too hard. It is no more based on chance than is Craps or ROULETTE. The 5 percent rake-off on banker bets tends to turn off many gamblers to those wagers and they bet the player instead. This is foolish because the banker wins more often than the player, and even after the rake-off, the house edge on bank bets is less—1.17 percent to 1.36. (These figures can be computed somewhat differently by other mathematical methods, but the variations remain.) Compare these edges to 5.26 for American Roulette and 1.4 in

Craps on line bets and it appears obvious that if one's bankroll can stand the pressure Baccarat is a relatively good gamble. It also is not plagued with the number of atrocious wagers connected with Craps. There is only one bad bet at Baccarat, the tie bet at 8 or 9 to 1. The house edge is over 14 percent—ties should never be bet.

BACCARAT—*Chemin de Fer*

There are many who insist the Chemin de Fer form of Baccarat is the real thing. This is the glamorous form that Hollywood always embraces. The term "Chemin de fer" means "railway" and describes the way the shoe, or "sabot," from which the cards are dealt is passed around the table. When this occurs in American Baccarat it is strictly for show. The player who is the dealer merely extracts the cards, and the game is banked by the house. In Chemmy, as Europeans call the game (Americans call it "Shimmy"), the player with the shoe actually banks the game himself. Following are the official rules as played at the lavish Casino de Deauville in France:

> Baccara - Chemin de Fer is a card game played around a table of 8 to 10 numbered places.
>
> The players do not play against the CASINO but against each other and sometimes one against the others.
>
> The aim of the game is to total 9 points or as close to 9 as possible with 2 or 3 cards. The winner being the one totaling the maximum points over his opponents. In case of a draw, the coup is void. New cards are dealt.
>
> The cards are placed in a "sabot." The "sabot" moves around to each player. He is then called the Banker. He keeps it as long as he wins, but may part from it ("passer la main") whenever he wants to.
>
> The player who asks for the "Banco" (Banker's bet or stake) is called the "Ponte." If the Banco is not taken, a player can join the other players. He then asks for the "Banco avec la table" and must participate for at least half the stake.

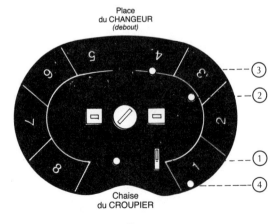

Place
du CHANGEUR
(debout)

Chaise
du CROUPIER

① BANCO
② Ponte's bet
③ A cheval bet (for half its value)
④ Player's money

Card value:
- Zero for face cards,
- 1 for Aces,
- Card value for others.

If the point value of two or three cards becomes a two-digit figure, keep the last digit.

Example: an 8 and a 5 count as 3 and not as 13 or a 7, a 6 and an 8 count as 1 and not as 21.

Any bet must be placed on the "piste."

The bet placed on the line separating the "piste" from the places is played for half its value.

The cards are therefore in the "sabot" and can only be taken out one by one, and the game can start.

At each deal, the Banker has to draw four cards from the "sabot," the first and the third for his opponent, the second and the fourth for himself. These cards are dealt face down. There are 169 deals.

The "Ponte" who gets the two cards looks at them and according to the points,

- Shows his hand if he has 8 or 9
- Does not say anything if he has 5, 6, or 7 and holds on to his cards or puts them down on the table.
- Says "Carte" if he has 5, 4, 3, 2, 1, or 0 (Baccara).

5 points allows the Ponte to draw or stand. It is advisable to use this possibility alternatively and irregularly so that Banker may never know what will be his attitude in that case.

The Banker, whatever the Ponte's move, shows his two cards and "table ainsi son point."

- At 8 or 9 shows his hand immediately.
- At 0 (Baccara), 1 or 2, he draws a card unless the "Ponte" has shown his hand.
- At 3, 4, 5, or 6 if the "Ponte" has not shown his hand, he draws a card or does not, whether his opponent has asked for a card or has not and in this latter case, according to the value of the fifth card he has received.

There is a 5% tax (Cagnotte) on the Banker's winnings.

If the Banker loses, his opponents' bets are paid from the Banker's bet, whose maximum loss is limited to what he has in the Banco.

Chemmy is clearly big-time gambling and the strategy involved with a score of 5 makes for really high-powered action. The late movie mogul Jack Warner thought nothing of setting Banco at $100,000 or more at Monte Carlo. Because the casino cannot lose at the game, they will bend regulations to cater to the whims of big Chemmy players. On a recent visit to Deauville the writer arrived near opening time and there were only two Roulette tables in operation. There was, however, a well-guarded section where a private game of Chemin de Fer was going on. Outsiders were not admitted. The play, reportedly for thousands of dollars a hand, had been running

24 hours straight and the word was it would probably run another day or two. Apparently some of the high rollers were catnapping in the area with the game never stopping.

There is one pitfall to Chemmy for a big-time player. He may lose a fortune and suddenly find the big winner deserting the game. If there are no other really big-action players in the game, the loser has no chance to get even. That hardly ever happens. Chemmy players usually appear to have money coming out their ears.

BACCARAT—Double Table

Double Table Baccarat, or more correctly *Baccarat en Banque* or *Baccarat a Deux Tableaux*, is the standard game of European Baccarat when it is banked by the house, meaning that unlike CHEMIN DE FER, the bank is not passed among the players. There is a house dealer sitting between two tables with space for six players each, and three hands are dealt instead of two. One hand is the bank's and the other two are the player hands, one on each side. However, players can bet on either or both player hands. Unlike American Baccarat, they may not bet on the bank's hand.

The action at Baccarat en Banque can get so great that frequently it becomes too heady even for the casino, so it leases out the tables to a syndicate that banks the game. The casino gets half the profits while the syndicate takes all the risks. The first syndicate was the infamous Greek Syndicate of the 1920s and the present-day syndicates still basically represent the same money. The Greek Syndicate has remained unbeaten through the decades as the world's biggest gamblers and generally it sets no limits on the wagers.

As in Chemin de Fer, the player has the option of standing or drawing when he has a total of 5. Otherwise, his reactions are limited as in Chemmy. On the other hand, the bank is not limited in any way by the rules. In practice, however, the dealer will almost always follow Chemmy procedures since this produces a hefty house edge. Remember, there is a 5 percent rake-off in Chemmy or American Baccarat on bank wins and the odds still favor the bank. In this version the syndicate has that 5 percent automatically.

There is one situation in which a player can get a slight advantage. Sometimes the bank's hand looks like it will beat one player's hand by following strict Chemmy drawing procedure, but figures to lose on the second player hand. The dealer might well have a 5 and one player draws a picture for his third card and the dealer knows that means the player has to have a total of 1, 2, 3, 4, or 5, which means the bank has a 4 to 1 chance of beating that hand. Meanwhile the second player hand draws a 4 as his third card and the dealer knows that player has a total score of 5, 6, 7, 8, or 9. Now the dealer has a decision to make on whether to draw a third card himself.

What he does is total up the betting on the two player hands and if there is much more betting on the second player hand he will opt to try to improve his score. Let us say he draws a 6, giving him a final total of 1. He will lose to the second player and it is more than likely he will lose to the first player, even though he had that hand beat going in. When playing this game the smart gambler will make his own count of the bets before deciding where to bet. He then will bet where the action isn't and gain a possible edge. There are casinos in some parts of the world where it is always prudent to do so. If, by the most amazing of circumstance, it is slightly dishonest, there is more likelihood that the house will have a greater interest in beating the higher bet hand. That at least would be a safe bet.

The game is also susceptible to other forms of cheating, which has kept it out of American play. For instance, what if the gambler playing a hand is a shill? He could be signaling the dealer what he has so that the former knows what to do about a third card.

See GREEK SYNDICATE.

BACCARAT—Mini

Mini-Baccarat is, like American Baccarat, made in the U.S.A. Baccarat upon being introduced in Nevada was bathed in an aura of opulence and wealth, the aim being to entice high rollers into a "class" game. In time, the casinos, being democratically inclined, started worrying about all the small-bettor action they might be losing (to say nothing of educating players in a smaller game to move them on to bigger action eventually). Mini-Baccarat was invented for that reason.

Mini-Baccarat is played on a table much resembling a BLACKJACK table, and in fact is generally found near the latter. Many gamblers walk right by Mini-Baccarat without noticing it is a different game. The game usually has seven seats, and before each player there are spaces for betting on the bank or the player. The player spot is put nearer the bettor since it offers a very small, fractional edge greater than the bank. Tie betting is hard to reach, and just as in the real game never should be played since the house edge climbs to a monstrous 14 percent on it.

Actually Mini is the same game as the bigger American game, the only difference being the minimums. In Atlantic City most casinos have a $10 minimum while in Nevada the game is to be found often with $2 or $5 minimums.

One dealer handles all the action involved, which frankly could be done in the bigger game except for

the fact that ritual is important for high-roller esteem. Mini, without all the show, is a faster game and that can be a disadvantage to the player since it means the small house edge grinds down the player faster than the bigger game edge does.

There is also another possible pitfall. Remember, ties do not count in the bigger game (except of course for the tie bet), and they don't in Mini either, most of the time. Unfortunately, there are some casinos that take all ties at Mini. Obviously, such games should be avoided.

BACCARAT—Mini, Cheating at

While Mini-Baccarat has proven an excellent money-making proposition for casinos, it offers special opportunities for cheating dealers working with a few players to steal from the house. As in ROULETTE it is perfectly acceptable for bettors to take copious notes on the trend of the game, for the purpose of following a system. The house is quite happy with system players and even supplies special forms for such record keeping. Players keep track of whether the player or the bank won the last several hands.

The cheaters also keep records but of different matters, namely the actual flow of cards, preferably near the end of the deal from a shoe. The player(s) in league with a crooked dealer will actually record the order of play of as many as 40 cards, which through a predetermined method the dealer makes sure to pick up in that same order.

When the cards are shuffled for the next shoe, the dealer will make sure he keeps this slug of 40 cards in one pile. He then false-shuffles the cards (see FALSE-SHUFFLE) so that the slug remains undisturbed.

The new game proceeds with the player who has been making small bets and hopefully holding his own awaiting the appearance of the first cards in the slug. He can confirm it by the first three or four cards and then knows precisely what the next 36 cards or so will be and whether the bank hand or the player hand will win. He bets big accordingly. This does not attract suspicion on the part of the floorman since he has seen the player taking copious notes earlier and merely assumes the player's screwball system just happened to catch a few games right. The house code is that the casino will eventually get its money back and the floorman is particularly mollified when he sees the player continue to play. It is assumed the house edge will eventually grind him down.

At this moment another new player or two in on the swindle will join the game and while the original winning player keeps betting high, the combined betting of the new players goes consistently the opposite way so that the betting is a wash for the house. In the meantime the dealer is setting up a new slug of cards and when the time comes all the confederate players will bet the same way and score a couple of big hits.

BACCARAT—Punto Banco

An American at a foreign casino may be put off by seeing a game labeled Punto Banco. He shouldn't be since it is nothing more than American Baccarat. Punto Banco is the most common form of Baccarat in England now and is rapidly appearing on the Continent and in Asia.

BACKGAMMON: Fastest Growing Gambling Game

Backgammon is a board game played by two opponents each of whom have 15 pieces that are put into play and then moved by throws of two dice from a cup. Descended from the ancient game of Tabula, or Table, which was a gambling game widely played in the latter period of Roman Empire, Backgammon spread quickly throughout the civilized world and is regarded as the parent of many board games, including Parcheesi, the staple game of India. But that doesn't mean the Romans played the game first. The Sumerians played a similar game that probably went back to more ancient times.

By 1750 Edmond Hoyle had written down Backgammon rules for his English constituents and the game enjoyed great acceptance with the nobility. The object of the game is to move one's own men around and off the board while setting up blocks on an opponent or hitting his tiles and forcing him back to the start.

Backgammon was always a betting game, but its popularity ebbed and flowed over the centuries. It had achieved its greatest following in this century with the adoption of a new feature, the doubling cube. With this innovation, a player may offer to double the stakes at any point, and his opponent is forced to accept this added risk or forfeit.

There is a wealth of literature on Backgammon play and strategy, likely a response to the fact that Backgammon is the fastest-growing gambling game in the world today. It cannot be estimated how many millions are won and lost in nightly games, but the stakes are undoubtedly enormous. One expert tells of a $100 game doubling and redoubling to $25,600 and since the payoff triples when an opponent is backgammoned, having some of his tiles trapped in his opponent's table, the losses mounted to $76,800 in a single game.

The Backgammon hustlers today are a fat and growing breed. Darwin Ortiz, an expert on gambling cheating, tells of several professional CRAPS hustlers who have switched entirely to Backgammon. In his book *Gambling Scams*, Ortiz takes issue with the following statement on the value of a dice cup in *Back-gammon for Blood*, Bruce Becker's definitive work on the subject: "The advantage of using a cup is that when dice are shaken and then thrown from a cup, there can be little question about the legitimacy of the roll; when dice are thrown from the hand, suspicions may—and sometimes do—arise. I, for one, will never play in a strange place without using a cup."

Becker's innocent faith in the sanitizing effect of the dice cup is typical of a great many Backgammon addicts. It is totally misplaced (see DICE CUP CHEATING). In fact, Backgammon is one of the easiest games to cheat at. First, as mentioned above, dice cups *do not* ensure fair rolls, and dice cups are always used in Backgammon. Second, a player uses his own dice exclusively. To cheat at Craps, a hustler working with gaffed dice must get them into the game and out again before they are passed to another shooter. This is not a problem in Backgammon. A player can substitute doctored dice and take them out with the greatest ease because an opponent must frequently have his eyes on the board to determine his moves. Third, the doubling cube allows a hustler to make a doubling bid when he is trailing in the play, an offer the opponent cannot refuse. Then suddenly the tide turns and the hustler becomes master of the dice. This may be through dice-cup control or the introduction of gaffed dice. Some cheats even use magnetized dice and have a small magnet strapped to their thigh. When the cheat wishes to magnetize a small portion of the table, he raises his knee under the table and throws his dice to hit that area. When he does, 6-6 comes up. The hustler will only gaff his play near the end of the game; earlier he is content to trail because that gets the doubling cube spinning.

A few key strategies a successful player should follow in an honest game: 1) Get two tiles out of the enemy's table as quickly as possible. 2) Don't crowd men on your own points; this limits your options to move. 3) Never expose a tile to risk unless hitting it exposes your opponent to greater risk. 4) Memorize the best play for each combination of the dice on your opening play, a very key move.

Recommended readings for the rules and strategy of Backgammon include: *The Backgammon Book* by Oswald Jacoby and John R. Crawfold; *Backgammon of Today* by John Longacre; *Beginning Backgammon* and *Better Backgammon*, both by Tim Holland. For the detection of crooked play, see *Gambling Scams* by Darwin Ortiz and *Scarne on Dice* by John Scarne.

BANCO: Old English Gamble and American Swindle

Banco, an old English dice game, was converted in America into an unadulterated swindle. Its very name

The *National Police Gazette* reveled in Oscar Wilde's discomfort after being swindled at Banco by New York con men. The *Gazette* pictured "the famous aesthete posing and 'mashing' on his shape" and noted he "blushed like a school girl."

was corrupted to "bunco," a term that eventually was applied to all types of confidence games.

Banco was based on the old English gambling pastime of eight-dice cloth. Cheats in America turned it into a card game using the game principles since they found cards easier to manipulate than dice.

How to play: In its card variation, banco is played on a layout of 43 spaces—42 are numbered and 13 of those contain stars. The remaining space is blank. The 29 unstarred numbers were winning ones, being worth $2 to $5,000, depending on the size of the bank and the value of the hand. Each player is dealt eight cards numbered one to six, with the total number in a hand representing the prize. However, if a number with a star comes up, the player gets no prize but can draw again by putting up a certain sum of money. The sucker is generally allowed to win at

first—with no money actually changing hands—until he is ahead a few hundred or a few thousand dollars. Then he is dealt number 27—the so-called conditional prize, meaning he has to stake a sum equal to the amount owed him and draw again or lose all his "winnings." Naturally he is dealt either a starred card or the blank and loses all.

Banco was especially heavily played in the West during the 1850s until vigilantes in California used the noose to discourage sharpers from practicing the swindle. The game was then imported to New York City about 1860 by the two greatest practitioners of the scam, Hungry Joe Lewis and George P. Miller. Both became enormously rich at it, swindling bankers, businessmen, and other prominent persons. The boys realized that if they stuck to bilking important persons, their victims were the sort who would take the loss even if they suspected they had been swindled rather than risk embarrassment by going to the police.

In 1882 Hungry Joe latched on to a likely victim, Oscar Wilde, then making a triumphant lecture tour in the United States. Hungry Joe dined with Wilde on a number of occasions and finally steered the writer to a banco game. The place was a "skinning dive," or a Big Store, common to the racket, so that everyone present—save for Wilde—was a confidence operator. All the action that took place was merely to set Wilde up.

Hungry Joe later bragged to the *National Police Gazette* that he'd "won" almost $7,000 from Wilde. Greatly chagrined Wilde tried to downplay his losses, insisting he had lost only $1,500 in cash and that he had stopped payment on a check for the balance when he discovered the game had been dishonest.

Ironically, the Wilde escapade did much to publicize the perils of Banco and the game started to decline in appeal. The con men were undeterred, simply shifting over to horse race betting capers.
See DOLLAR STORE.

BANGO: Bingo-like Card Game

For Bingo addicts, bango offers all the fun without the huge house takeout. In a gambling house the general practice is that a certain percentage, usually five percent, is taken out of the ante for the house with all the rest going to the winner in what is a dead-even game.

How to play: Generally Bango is played with two decks of cards, with different backs. The first deck is shuffled and each player, up to 10 players, are dealt five cards face up. The balance of this deck is discarded, dead for the hand.

The second deck is now brought into play, and the dealer, after shuffling the deck and offering it for a cut, turns over the top card and announces its denomination and suit. A player having the same card either turns over his card or places a marker over it. The first player to turn over all five cards yells, "Bango." He wins the pot.

In another variation of Bango, the two decks of cards are merged before the deal. This allows for more than ten players, although 12 is considered the outer limit. In this version suit doesn't matter, and if a player draws, for example, three 9's they are all cancellable when a single 9 of any suit is drawn from the remainder of the deck. Under these rules, ties can result and the pot must be split accordingly.

From the player's viewpoint Bango is better than Bingo because it is a dead-even game with no house advantage, ideal for private games. The house cut in professional games is, by Bingo standards, nominal at a relatively trifling 5 percent. While this would upset a professional gambler, that same individual would never be caught dead in a Bingo parlor where at a full game the house percentage can be as high as *200 percent*, selling, for example, $300 worth of cards and offering a prize or prizes of $100.

BANKER AND BROKER: Banking Card Game
Banker and Broker, sometimes called Blind Hookey or Dutch Bank, is a very fast-moving game in which money can be won or lost at a dizzying pace. It is popular at carnivals and "sawdust" (fly-by-night) casinos because it can be guaranteed honest—although not without its house edge.

How to play: Any number can play with a single pack of 52 cards. The deck is shuffled and then cut by one of the players. Then another player takes the deck and cuts it into as many piles as there are players, plus one pile for the banker. Players then place bets within an established minimum and maximum on any pile they wish. The leftover pile belongs to the banker.

The banker turns over his pile and the upturned bottom card becomes his point. Let us say it is a 7. He then turns over one player's pile after another, paying off all cards over 7 and collecting on 7 or less. If the banker gets an ace, there is no need to look at the bettors' cards, since the ace is an automatic winner.

The fact that the bank collects on ties at Banker and Broker gives the house a healthy percentage edge of 5.88. The game is often played as a private game and the banker is determined by a high-card draw. Thereafter the bank passes to other players when they draw an ace. However, if the banker gets an ace on the same play, he retains the deal.

Strategy: To compensate for the near 6-percent deficit bettors face, they must take the bank whenever they can. In games in which each banker is allowed to set his own minimum and maximum on

becoming the bank, he is advised to raise the minimum as high as possible. Combined with betting extremely low when not in possession of the bank, this will afford a player a bit of an edge over the long haul.

BANNING: Petitioning a Casino to Bar Oneself
In European casinos, where admissions are closely monitored, a battered gambler can request a casino to bar him from any further play. His request will be honored.

In 1972 an Italian duchess asked French casinos to bar her from stepping inside their hallowed halls for five years after her losses at Divonne at *Trente et Quartante* (THIRTY AND FORTY) exceeded 10 million francs. An American newsman stationed in Europe recently asked all European casinos to bar him for life. (He later relented but is still not allowed to get in. Occasionally, he stoops to sneaking through on another gambler's admission card.)

The European casinos have always felt honor-bound to accept such requests, but it doesn't work quite that way in America. Tell a casino executive that you are an inveterate loser and don't want to play any more and, more likely than bar you, they'll have a limo at your door to pick you up.

BAR 6-8 CRAPS PROPOSITION SCAM: Sucker Bet
It is amazing how many seasoned CRAPS players fall for the Bar 6-8 Craps Proposition, which is an outright scam. There are very few Craps players who don't think they are smarter than the next man and as such they are naturals for being taken in this bit of cubed larceny.

The hustler's pitch is to ask the so-called smart Craps player if he will bet against him shooting the dice with the 6 and 8 points "barred." In other words, when on the first roll a 6 or 8 turns up and should be the shooter's point it will be ignored and the shooter rolls again. Some victims of this scam can't believe they are hearing right, convinced that no dice shooter could be so stupid. Sometimes they even try to explain to the "dolt" that he is really stacking the odds against himself since the 6 and 8 are the easiest points for a shooter to make. They might even point out to him that will leave the shooter with just 4, 5, 9, and 10 as possible points if he doesn't win on 7 or 11 or crap out on 2, 3, or 12 on his first roll. The odds against making a 4 or 10 are 2 to 1 and on the 5 or 9 they are 3 to 2.

The hustler proves stubborn, and possibly even seems drunk, and the so-called expert finally cannot resist taking advantage of him. Sometimes the hustler does lose, but most of the time he wins with the expert-victim insisting they play more as he seeks to reverse what he regards as an incredible run of luck against himself.

Luck has nothing to do with it. In casino play the odds against the shooter is about 1.41. But under Bar 6-8 the percentages run about four times as high the other way in favor of the shooter, a situation few gamblers grasp.

What victims of the Bar 6-8 scam forget is that on the first, or come-out, roll the odds greatly favor the shooter. However, when the shooter establishes his point—4, 5, 6, 8, 9, or 10—the odds turn against him since he has much less chances of making any of these numbers before rolling a 7.

What the hustler does with Bar 6-8 is in large measure postpone moving on from the come-out roll. Since there are five ways to make a 6 and five ways to make an 8, the hustler has eliminated ten ways to establish his point out of a possible 24. *That means he frequently gets the chance to make a new first roll and keep those beautiful 2 to 1 odds in his favor!* Frequently, otherwise heady Craps shooters have gone broke fading Bar 6-8 and never suspected they are being taken.

See HARDWAYS PROPOSITION SCAM for a similar sucker bet.

BARBOOTH: Internationally Played Dice Game

Barbooth (or Barbudi) is a favorite gambling game the world over. The game, probably of Greek origin, is heavily played in the U.S. by persons of Greek or Jewish ancestry, and in much of Eastern Europe, many gaming establishments are given over completely to Barbooth.

How to play: The game, which can involve several players, essentially involves two—the shooter and the fader—who roll the dice against one another. The shooter calls the game in which 6-6, 5-5, and 3-3 are always winning combinations. At the shooter's option, 6-5 is also a winning combination. Always losing combinations are 1-1, 2-2, and 4-4. If the shooter adds 6-5 as a winner, 1-2 becomes an additional loser.

The fader then declares the amount that will be bet, and the shooter decides whether or not he wishes to accept all of the wager. If he does not, the other players around the table have the right to claim part of the action.

The shooter then rolls the dice. If none of the numbers is decisive (that is, any combination other than that listed above), the next roll is made by the fader. The dice are passed back and forth until a result is achieved. Either the shooter or the fader wins on the winning numbers or loses on the losing numbers. If the shooter loses on a throw of 1-1, 2-2, or 4-4, or the fader wins on 3-3, 5-5, or 6-6, the fader becomes the new shooter with the new fader being the player to his right. If the shooter wins or the

result is determined by a combination of 1-2 or 6-5, the shooter retains the dice and the new fader is the man to the previous fader's right.

Barbooth is a dead-even game and the house gets its cut out of the pot, deducting 5 percent of all losing bets before turning them over to the winner or winners. This means the house cut amounts to 2.5 percent of all money bet.

BARBUDI
See BARBOOTH.

BASEBALL (CARDS): Stud Poker Variations

Professional gamblers detest this game for the high element of risk in it, and they refuse to play it except when they see a poor players or two stay in when they should not and anticipate that they can be lured into building a pot.

How to play: Cards are dealt as in Seven-card Stud (although the five-card version is also playable) with the first two and the last card dealt face down. The special features are: 1) All 9's are wild. 2) A 4 dealt up entitles the player to an extra card dealt up (although in the end he may only use five of his cards to determine his hand). 3) A 3 dealt up immediately strikes the player out and he is out of the game no matter how much he has put in the pot. In many games, however—under a rule that delights the pros—a player dealt a 3 can buy his way back into the game by matching the pot. This makes all 3's in the game wild as well.

Strategy: Some players who so match the pot think picking up the wild card gives them a decided advantage, but that seldom justifies investing so much more in the pot. Basically, matching the pot should only occur near the end of the game and the decision must not be based on vague possibilities. Your hand, some experts contend, should be positively unbeatable to justify staying after a 3 calls to you.

Amateur players often foolishly stay with such weak hands as three of a kind or less. Even a straight rarely stands up, and a flush is to be regarded as a minimum good hand. A player matching the pot should have five of a kind, and high ones at that, to justify feeding the pot. The only time sharpers call for Baseball in DEALER'S CHOICE games is when not all the players are good gamblers. The smart gambler will play a game he basically hates if most of the other players have more enthusiasm than skill.
See also FIVE-CARD BASEBALL.

BASEBALL (DICE)

Baseball is a dead-even dice game for two that has become very popular in bars. All that is needed to play are a pair of dice and several counters (or markers) to represent base runners. There is also a nine-inning box-score chart. Each player gets three out per inning for a nine-inning game. Betting is done one of two ways, either a flat bet on who wins or so much per run in the difference in the score.

Scoring is quite simple, with the 3, 4, 5, 6, 7, and 8 representing outs or strikeouts by the batter. However, special exceptions apply to the 4 or 8 made the hard way (that is, 2-2 or 4-4). These are walks and put the batter on first base, with other runners, if any, advancing. The 9 is a single, 10 a double, and 11 a triple. Numbers 2 and 12 are home runs.

While this is an even game, the smart player will try to bat first if the betting is on the difference in the score. That way if he is behind after batting in the ninth inning, his opponent does not get to bat in the bottom of the inning and add to his margin of victory.

Oddly enough, dice cheaters actually work this game—not so much to win the small bets involved but rather to perfect their abilities under competitive conditions. Obviously, no cheat is going to bother with loaded dice in such a penny-ante game, but will use it as a chance to develop his techniques for playing dishonestly with honest dice. This is best performed by using the "whip shot" for throwing the dice. The dice are held with the desired number on top. In Baseball only one die needs to be controlled. If it produces a 6, an accompanying 3, 4, 5, or 6 are good numbers. Only the 1 and 2 result in an out. Thus the one die is held tight in the hand and the other die shaken and allowed to rattle against it. The dice are then thrown with a quick whiplike snap of the hand that sends them spinning. When the dice land, the one with the 6 held tight lands with the spinning motion keeping it from rolling and it settles with the 6 still on top. This particular dice throw works well in Baseball since the game is played on a hard surface, the bar or a table top in a booth. On such a hard surface a few grains of salt will actually help the die to spin and slide without turning over. Of course, it is easy enough for the cheat to spill some salt or for that matter sprinkle a few grains "for luck."

Of course, sometimes Baseball is played for substantial sums, in which case a cautious player will watch for the whip shot and the salt dodge. If his opponent spills some salt, he should blow it away.

BASEBALL BETTING: Second Only to Football in Sports Gambling

Baseball provides gamblers with their second largest form of sports-wagering action. How big? The overall figures are imprecise since most of the betting is illegal, but it is estimated that 80 to 85 percent of all betting on sports, horse racing aside, is on football and baseball. Considering the length of the season

and the number of games, the fact is that baseball should do better than it does. The World Series probably draws as much betting as a full card of Sunday professional football games. Still, the action is enormous, even without considering the private bets made among elbow benders in bars and at the ball field by bookies. Bets can include whether a particular player will get a hit, strike out, or drive in a run.

The more organized baseball bet is on the outcome of a game, but unlike FOOTBALL BETTING, which is based on a "point spread," baseball betting is done with odds, in horse-race style. A bookmaker might offer odds on a game between the Mets and Cubs at 7½-8½ Mets. This means the Mets are favorites. If you wish to bet on the Cubs you put up, for instance, 5 and if the Cubs win you get 7½ in winnings together with your money back. On the other hand, if you wish to bet on the Mets, you have to put up, in this case, 8½ in order to win 5 plus getting your 8½ back. Unless you are betting in Vegas or are a good customer you might not get such "favorable" odds, instead being offered odds of 7-9, which gives the bookie an even bigger profit margin.

The astute gambler likes to bet on baseball because it is a sport with intense loyalties among the public. It is difficult for a Met fan to bet on the Cubs and vice versa. The sharp gambler takes the odds on whichever team he thinks is getting the logical advantage with the odds. But it may well be that nobody ever wins, or at least never wins big, betting on baseball since the bookmaker's edge is so great. A good indication of this is that many newspapers run imaginary betting over the course of a season by some resident "expert." By September these experts are almost always deep in the hole in their wagering and have increased the amount of their bets to huge sums, trying to do what the average gambler is always trying to do—get even.

An example of typical casino Baseball betting rules as offered by the Las Vegas Flamingo Hilton follows:

A pointspread is generally not used in baseball wagering. Instead, players simply wager on the team of their choice. In this case, a winning straight wager will be paid in accordance with the odds of that event.

Example:

Team	Pitcher	Odds	Total
Mets	Smith	+125	6
Dodgers	Jones	−140	

WAGERING

Players lay or take money odds as noted on the wagering boards. Standardized money odds are always quoted in terms of 100. In our example the Dodgers are a −140 favorite. Therefore, if you wish to wager on the Dodgers, you must *lay* the equivalent of 140 to win 100. For example, if the Dodgers win, a $14 wager on them will win $10 for a total payback of $24. If the Mets should win, a $10 wager on them would win $12.50 for a total payback of $22.50. Sample payoffs at various odd structures are set forth below.

Admittedly, certain types of wagering can be confusing. If you need further clarification, please don't hesitate to ask a staff member.

Odds	Amount Wagered	Win	Total Payback
−155	$ 15.50	$ 10.00	$ 25.50
−120	$120.00	$100.00	$220.00
−105	$ 52.50	$ 50.00	$102.50
EV	$ 10.00	$ 10.00	$ 20.00
+110	$ 80.00	$ 88.00	$168.00
+175	$ 10.00	$ 17.50	$ 27.50

THE TOTAL

Similarly to football and basketball wagering, you may wager on whether the combined final score of both teams is *over* or *under* a stipulated number. Remember, in totals wagering it does not matter who wins the game but, instead, how many runs are scored. In this example, the *total* is 6. If you wish to wager *over* 6, you will win if the combined final score of both teams is *greater* than 6. Should you desire to wager *under* 6, you will win if the combined final score of both teams is less than 6. If the combined final score is exactly 6, all total bets would be classified as a tie, and all wagers would be refunded.

SPECIAL NOTES

When wagering on baseball, you may specify one of the following methods to apply to your wager.

ACTION—An *Action Wager* is a wager on a specific team without regard to the starting pitching matchup. Since baseball odds are dependent upon the starting pitchers, all action wagers are subject to an odds change *if* the actual starting pitchers are different from those listed on the wagering boards at the time of your wager.

LISTED PITCHERS—You may specify a team and both *Listed Pitchers*. A listed pitcher's wager only has action if *both* listed pitchers start the game. Should either or both actual starting pitchers change from those listed on the wagering boards at the time of your wager, there is no wager, and your money will be refunded.

LISTED PITCHER VERSUS OPPOSING TEAM—You may specify that *one* listed pitcher from either team must start. In the event that the specified listed pitcher does not start, there is no wager, and your money will be refunded. Your wager will be subject to an odds change should there be a change in the unspecified pitcher from that originally posted. You may specify either a listed pitcher from the team you wish to wager upon, or you may wager a team against the opposing team's listed pitcher.

NOTE: Please refer to the Sports Book House Wagering Rules and Regulations for specific wagering rules that apply in the cases of postponed, shortened, extra innings or disputed games.

BASKETBALL: Stud Poker Variation

For gamblers who do not consider PASS THE GARBAGE a wide-open enough game, Basketball is just the ticket. Actually Basketball is just Pass the Garbage with an extra passing round. Both games start off the same way. Seven down cards are dealt to each player, followed by a round of betting. Then each player picks out his three worst cards and passes them to the player to his left. This is followed by another round of betting.

In Pass the Garbage, each player then discards two of his cards to create his final five-card hand. Four cards are then turned up one at a time with betting action following each turn-up until the final showdown. In Basketball there is an additional passing of cards after the three-card shift to the left. Players study their new seven-card hands and then pass two cards to the *right*.

In this way Basketball may actually turn out to be a saner game than Pass the Garbage. Note that on the passing of three cards to the left, players only keep four of their original cards. This means that players holding a pat hand—let us say a straight or a flush—are forced to break it by passing three cards. In Pass the Garbage such an unfortunate player hopes against hope that the three cards he receives will refill his hand. However, Basketball offers a real chance at redemption. Remember the two-card pass to the right. Frequently, a busted pat hand will be restored when the player to the left passes back one or two of the same cards he had received from that player. It is a situation that adds considerable tension to the game.

When Basketball is played only for high, players having to break a pat hand should obviously pass the lowest card in their flush or straight. However, Basketball is frequently played high-low. In that case passing a deuce or 3, for instance, might be the worst thing to do since the opponent could well be going for low, in which case the card will not come back. When high-low is involved, it is best to pass on a middle-value card such as an 8 or 9, which are usually unattractive for low hands.

In any event, Basketball allows for more skill on a gambler's part than does Pass the Garbage.

BASKETBALL BETTING

Today you can get action in Las Vegas sports books on a fair number of basketball games, but overall there is no really big-time betting on basketball, certainly nothing to compare with other team sports such as football and baseball. The reason for this is the long history of "the fix" in college basketball games. Since betting on basketball must be done on a point-spread basis (betting the games on straight bets on which team will win would be like shooting fish in a barrel for the intelligent gambler), a number of fixers invaded the college basketball ranks and talked players into "shaving points." The pitch could be made to the players that they were not "betraying" their school or their teammates since they could still win the game. All the bribers wanted was that the players keep the game within the point spread. Let us say College A was favored in the betting over College B by 10 points. All the bribers asked was for the fixed player or players to see to it they only won by 9 points or less. Too many college kids proved susceptible to such a pitch, and got paid big money just to botch up on a few plays late in the game to keep the score from being a blowout.

Overall, the professional game is more acceptable to wary gamblers since the feeling is the large salaries the players receive is something of a guarantee that they will not risk being involved in a fix. But even when such games are on the level, as they overwhelmingly are, one can hear strange boos filling a basketball arena. Let us say a team is favored by 12 points and with five minutes to play it is up by 20. Gamblers who have bet on the favorite are relaxed but suddenly "garbage time" develops, as second stringers are inserted and the lead dwindles to 18, 16, 14, 12, 10 with 30 seconds left. The gamblers are booing and screaming as their sure winning bets suddenly head down the drain. It is not wise to bring a lady to such a game because of the language that will erupt from some suddenly furious losers.

The fact is, no one should bet on basketball with any degree of confidence except in the playoffs and finals in professional ball or in the final four games or so in college tournaments. Otherwise, there's no certain way to tell which way the ball will bounce.

BASSETTE: 17th-century Banking Game
For much of the 17th century Bassette dominated the leisure lives of Europe's rich. The game itself was not very complicated. Basically, a player bet that the card he had chosen would turn up in a deal before the card chosen by the dealer.

Invented about 1593 by a Venetian named Pietro Cellini, it took Italy, France, and Spain by storm and great fortunes were lost in the gaming rooms of the day. So great were the ravages of Bassette on the fortunes of the rich that Cellini came under great attack and was finally banished to Corsica. Pope Paul V and Henry of Navarre, the king of France, both

issued edicts outlawing the game—unless the banker was of noble birth, raising the suggestion that it was less the ravages of rich purses than the offense of a gambling game creating a *nouveau riche* class that was galling to the nobility.

Edicts or no, the Bassette craze continued. In England Charles II on his restoration insisted no restrictions against the game be proclaimed. In fact, Charles himself was a Bassette addict and had hit the royal treasury very hard to cover his personal losses.

By the end of the 17th century, Bassette lost favor to a new casino game, FARO (or among the more elite, Pharoah). In principle Faro was not too much different, but Bassette had developed a bad reputation because of the financial havoc it had caused. It was time for a change, although Faro did not improve the gambler's lot.

BEANSHOOTER
See PALMING CHIPS.

BEAT THE BANKER
See BEAT THE DEALER.

BEAT THE DEALER: Carnival and Small Gambling Joint Game
Known also as Beat the Shaker, Beat the Banker, Two-Dice Klondike, and High Dice, this game should not be confused with the popular bar game also called HIGH DICE. Beat the Dealer is a game popular at carnivals and "sawdust" gambling joints. The rules are simple and often the uninitiated gambler feels it is an easy game to beat. It is anything but that. Played honestly, which is not always the case, Beat the Dealer provides the bank with an advantage of 11.26 percent, an enormous edge that usually discourages a house's need to cheat.

How to play: Both the banker and the player get one roll of a pair of dice, the banker shooting first, either from a dice cup or sending the cubes down a transparent dice *chute* operated by a cord. The player has to get a higher point total than the banker to win the bet, but the banker wins all ties. This is a strictly even game except for the ties, but that exception is far greater than the average player realizes. Over the course of a mathematical total of 1,296 rolls, 2-2, 3-3, etc., in total will come out 146 times, creating the substantial house advantage of 11.26. Occasionally the rules are altered to allow the player an automatic win on a tie of 2-2, but this is basically window dressing and results in cutting the house edge only marginally, to 11.11 percent.

In some scams, operators are not satisfied with the built-in edge and gaff the game with loaded dice fixed to produce 5 or 6 on each roll. The dice can be thrown legitimately but when a big bet is on the counter the banker shakes the dice cup (whose inner surface has been slicked or polished) in an up and down movement with a slightly rotary motion that makes the dice spin around the slicked surface, and on the throw the light surfaces tend always to come up on top. This produces a score of 10, 11, or 12. If the player unwittingly controls the dice the same way, he may also get a high number, but since he loses on a tie, the odds remain heavily in favor of the crooked operation.

Players who must try Beat the Dealer, should stick to chute games only, but why anyone would try to buck 11.26 odds remains a mystery.

See also: DICE—CHEATING; DICE CUP CHEATING.

BEAT THE SHAKER
See BEAT THE DEALER.

BEAT YOUR NEIGHBOR
See ROLLOVER.

BEDSPRINGS: Poker Variation
Bedsprings is a POKER variation played fairly often in DEALER'S CHOICE games. It can be an important money-maker for the shrewd Poker player. Since there are ten betting opportunities after the ante, the pot can grow impressively. At the same time the player who gets out early with unimpressive hands will in the long run gain overproportionately when he stays the limit on a strong hand.

How to play: Each player is dealt five cards, but no draw follows. Instead ten cards are dealt face down in two rows of five. The cards on the top row are turned up one by one, with a betting round after each turn-up. The same occurs with the turn-up of each card on the bottom row. At the conclusion of the final round of betting, each player may pick a card in the top row to include in figuring his hand. Whatever card in the top row he chooses, he gets the card below it as well. Of course other players may utilize the same cards. Thus a player has a seven-card hand from which he chooses his final five cards as in Seven-card Poker. If the game is being played high-low, the player may use the same two cards for both hands or one face-up pair for high and another for low.

Strategy: It is important for good players to realize that the expectations from a seven-card hand in Bedsprings is much higher than in normal Seven-card Poker because each player gets to pick the two cards he wants. That means every player has gotten at least one card that improves his hand significantly. If he has not, he should be gone from the game unless he was dealt a pat hand. The trouble with Bedsprings for beginners is that they are hypnotized by the rapid growth of the pot and find it hard not to stay until all the cards are turned up. Conversely, the shrewd player likes the benefits involved in dropping out early.

Let us say the smart player gets five cards worth nothing on the deal. He will drop immediately, losing his ante. Depending on the number in the game, he knows that one, two, or three opponents have probably paired already and since they are just as likely to improve as he is from his lower base, he has no business bucking them. Even more important is that if he remains until the sixth turn-up he is watchful for hints that the winning hand will probably be a big one. It should be realized that two pairs, certainly below aces paired, will seldom win at Bedsprings unless there has been a big drop in the number of players early on. Three of a kind is powerful unless the turned-over cards indicate other strengths. If a top-and-bottom row produces a pair or even a paired suit—two spades, hearts, etc.—this points to hidden high power. A paired suit makes a flush fairly certain in someone's hand. A pair really raises the danger not simply of higher three-of-a-kind strength but most likely a full house. Three of a kind should not be bet with confidence if a pair or a paired suit shows. (This means that the pair produces that player's three of a kind. If it gives him a full house he can ignore any dangers coming from a paired suit, but if the open pair is a high one but represents only the pair in his full house—that is, three deuces in the hand and two queens showing—he must fear a queens' high full house.)

Much more than in ordinary Poker, Bedsprings gives the gambler with good card sense and odds sense an important edge over the less disciplined player.

See also TWIN BEDS.

BELGIUM, Gambling in
In Belgium, it is possible to gamble on almost anything. Belgians are big on all sports betting and play heavily on horse races, athletic events, cockfights, and even pigeon races. But gambling laws are rigidly enforced. Lotteries are permitted, but only those with specific state approval. Street gambling is censured; anyone caught doing so faces a possible jail term and all the money in the game will be confiscated. Private gambling games in cafes are tolerated; however, the law specifically refuses to provide redress for any unpaid gambling debts.

Casino operations were declared illegal in 1902, although enforcement of the law was less than zealous; casinos in operation prior to the legislation were allowed to stay in business, thus creating among eight such casinos a monopoly on casino gambling in the country. The casinos are in Knocke-Le Zoute,

Middlekerke, Namur, Diant, Chaudfontaine, Spa, Blankenberghe, and Ostende. All are quite large, but the showpiece and biggest is the Casino-Kursaal D' Ostende. Located but a short flying distance from Paris and London, and offering convention facilities similar to those found in Las Vegas, Ostende lures a lot of business money to the gaming tables, including its 14 BACCARAT tables (compared to two or three in other Belgian casinos). ROULETTE wheels do the steadiest business, however, and boast more players even during supposedly slow periods than any European casino, including Monte Carlo.

Perhaps because of the crowds at Ostende's Roulette, the American-style game is popular since each player gets his own individually distinctive chips. But the practical Belgians do not go in for the 0 and 00 scam. Instead American Roulette is played with just one zero, so that odds are the same as on the French wheel. Gambling books and travel guides can still be found describing Belgian Roulette as a 36-number game with no zeros and a 5 percent takeout on all winning bets. This old method gave the house an edge of 2.5 percent on all bets, and now with the use of the zero the percentages are the normal 1.35 on even-money bets and 2.70 on all others.

Like all European casinos, those in Belgium charge an admission fee, but only about a couple of dollars—compared to $10 to $15 in France and Italy. Belgian casinos also offer among the best currency exchange rates around. On a recent trip to Ostende, the dollar-exchange rate was more than 10 percent better than at the local train station or banks. Obviously, the casino wants to make it a bargain for bettors to exchange—and lose—their money there.

BELLY STRIPPERS
See STRIPPERS.

BELOTTE: France's Most Popular Two-handed Card Game
Belotte is the favorite two-handed card game in France. It is very similar to KLABERJASS as played in the United States, but the rules vary somewhat. The "schmeiss" is called "valse," or waltz. The highest-ranking melds are four jacks, worth 200 points, and four-of-a-kind of 9's, 10's, queens, kings and aces, worth 100 points. A five-card sequence is worth 50, a four-card 40, and a three-card 20. The player with the highest-ranking group scores all groups in his hand and the player with the highest-ranking sequence scores all his sequences.

If the trump maker fails to outscore his opponent, he loses his points, but the opponent only gets his own score, not the combined totals.

Otto "Abbadabba" BERMAN: Numbers Racket Fixer
The numbers racket, when run honestly, offers operators a 40 percent edge. Now that may appear ample enough margin for most racketeers, but the underworld operators see no point in charity toward those playing the game. So the numbers boys have always searched for ways to shave payoffs and give away less of what they regard as their own money.

Back in the 1930s when the mob solidified its hold on most of the numbers operations in the country, the underworld came up with its own "Einstein" to maximize its profits by fixing the results. Otto "Abbadabba" Berman (1889-1935)—whose nickname accurately depicted his magical abilities to doctor the figures so that only lightly played numbers became winners—worked for racket boss Dutch Schultz, who controlled most of the numbers racket in New York City and surrounding areas. Under Schultz's game, the winning number was derived from the betting statistics at various racetracks. It was impossible for the mob to doctor the figures at the New York tracks, but when those ovals were closed, the numbers were instead based on results from tracks the mob had successfully infiltrated.

Much has been made of the underworld trying to take over racetracks to fix races, but the real lure such tracks offered was the opportunity to alter the figures on the betting handle from which the numbers were derived. When the results came from such tracks Abbadabba, without benefit of computers developed decades later, quickly worked out how much money to pour into the mutuel machines to make sure the payoffs made by underworld numbers banks were the lowest possible. Frequently too the mob was able to wipe out independent operators by simply playing the winning number with them to the extent that they would be unable to pay off. This quickly demonstrated to the numbers-playing public the wisdom of patronizing only "connected" numbers operations.

It has been estimated that Abbadabba's manipulations added at least ten percent to the mob's enormous profits. Proof of this comes from Schultz's salary scale. The Dutchman was never noted for being loose with a dollar. He paid his top henchmen, men like Lulu Rosenkrantz and Abe Landau, about $1,200 a week while he rewarded Abbadabba at the rate of $10,000 a week.

In 1935 Dutch Schultz was murdered by the national crime syndicate, with both Lucky Luciano and Meyer Lansky agreeing that the Dutchman had to go. Schultz had developed an obsession and wanted to have prosecutor Thomas E. Dewey assassinated because the latter was pushing for his conviction. Luciano, Lansky, and their cohorts were upset by

Schultz's plan because they realized it would have serious repercussions on their own operations. A cynic might observe the boys may have been a bit less interested in saving Dewey than in the prospects of taking over the Schultz numbers empire in New York's Harlem.

The unfortunate thing about the Schultz rubout was that Abbadabba Berman was with him and met the same fate, not something the mob wanted at all. His loss was to cost the mob literally millions of dollars a year, for while others tried to imitate the technique of what Luciano's aide Vito Genovese called "the Yid adding machine," few approached even a fraction of his expertise. Don Vito was always a bit of a bigot, but in this case his use of the sobriquet was uttered in sincere mourning for the irreplaceable Abbadabba.

BEST FLUSH: Limited-rule Poker Game

In this game of Draw POKER only flushes or partial flushes are viable hands, with a draw of three cards permitted after five cards are dealt each player. Winning hands in Best Flush in descending order are: royal flush, straight flush, regular flush, four-card flush, three-card flush, and two-card flush. Ties are broken by the highest card, and if flushes are tied, by the highest card in any other suit.

Strategy: The game may seem to some gamblers to be little more complicated than flipping coins, but there are some bluffing elements. For instance, a player getting a four-card flush might well stand pat rather than draw a new fifth card and bet heavily in an attempt to force other players out of the game. Similarly, the holder of a three-card flush might only draw one card to misrepresent his power. There is excellent theory behind this. Before the discard, every player has at least a two-card flush. A three-card flush is not too powerful and in fact will have a tougher time improving than will the two-card flush. Thus a three-carder should try to bluff the two-carders out of the game with a heavy bet before the discard. Then by discarding only one card, it will appear that he has a four-card flush going in.

This is an excellent game to call in DEALER'S CHOICE since the dealer sees if anyone before him bets with strength first, and if not, he can do so. If he is trying a three-card bluff, and other players before him then surprise him by drawing only two cards, he can shift gears and do the same. To some extent Best Flush is always a dealer's edge game.

Best Flush may also be played in Stud—with no advantage to the dealer. In this game there is a tendency for gamblers to tarry a bit longer to produce more action than might ordinarily be expected. Even tight players, who will drop on the first two cards of normal FIVE-CARD STUD unless they are paired or at least have what appears to be the high card in the hand, generally await the second face card before making their departure decision. Upon the appearance of the third card in the Five-card Stud version of this game a player can stay even on three high cards in three suits provided no flush pairs are showing elsewhere already. The situation indicates that a two-card flush may well stand up and if he has an ace or two he will control those flushes.

More important, whether in the five-card or seven-card version, the Stud game allows for some wicked bluffing.

BETTING SYSTEMS: The Impossible Dreams

Albert Einstein offered two systems for winning at ROULETTE. The first was to cheat—a foolproof method as long as you don't get caught. The second was more morally and mathematically sound. It was simply to double up after every losing bet—another foolproof method. Einstein understood the laws of probability perfectly and knew the practical limitations of his suggestion—there is no such thing as a betting system that will work against a casino in Roulette or any other game. The reason is that no casino game will give a player a 50-50 chance, and any system that tries to compensate a negative situation into a positive one is attempting the impossible.

Because Roulette is possibly the biggest casino gambling game in the world (though not in the United States) and a minute or two elapses between spins of the wheel, it is an ideal game for bettors

Former Nader Raider Howard Schwartz, marketing director and resident conscience of the Gambler's Book Club, constantly writes up flaws in gambling systems being sold to the gullible for up to $5,000. (Photo: GBC)

working on systems. They have enough time to check and recheck their figures to make sure they are making the "right" bet. Thus, all the systems discussed here were probably first developed for Roulette play, but they can all be utilized in most other casino games—if unsuccessfully.

• *Martingale System.* No, Einstein was not first with it. Roulette players were losing their shirts with this one even before Einstein proposed it tongue in cheek. If his first bet is $1 and the player loses it betting red, he simply bets $2 on the next spin. (Most systems are based on winning even-money propositions, but they can be adapted to longer-shot play, with the chances of going broke increasing greatly.) If he loses that, he proceeds to bet $4 on the next spin. The grand plan behind all this is that sooner or later his color (or even or odd bet, or high or low wager) will come up and he is a winner. And he is ahead . . . $1.

There are several problems here (even putting aside the problem that arises if zero comes up). One is willpower and the other is capital. It is no major problem when a losing streak goes to three or four. It is not infeasible to put up $16 on the fifth spin to win back $16. But then the bets really start to escalate, to $32, $64, $128 by the eighth spin. Our Martingale friend is by this time nearing nervous collapse because on his next spin he must put up $256, but he figures that after so many blacks have appeared, the odds are greatly in his favor that red will now come up. Of course, nothing could be further from the truth. On every spin of the Roulette wheel the odds are 50-50 on red or black turning up. The wheel spins and it's . . . black. Our system player is now out $511. Shakily, he buys more chips and nervously places $512 on the red.

The croupier shakes his head. He motions to the plastic marker on the table. On tables where the minimum is 1 unit, the maximum is usually 500. Our bettor is now over the top. The most he can wager is $500. That means if he wins, he is still out $11. And if he loses, he is minus $1,011 and counting.

There are numerous Martingale addicts who insist they win consistently with the system, but it is not true. First of all, gamblers lie. Second, a long streak of losing bets at Roulette (or in Craps, betting Pass or Don't Pass) is hardly unusual. One of the world's most dedicated Roulette players, Paddy O'Neil-Dunne, led a team of gamblers who actually played every spin of a Roulette wheel in a Macao casino and tracked the results for 31 days. Black came up for eight or more consecutive shows *43 times*, or about 1½ times a day. There were 13 occasions when the consecutive string hit 10 or more, which may be considered the poverty line. This means a player would go broke once every two-plus days. Of course,

in theory he could come back if he proceeds to win the next 500 sequences or so in a row, but to win so many sequences would require that no other long losing streak occur, and in fact playing 500-plus sequences would take much more than two days, by which time another big losing streak or several would happen.

Yes, it is possible to win with this system for a few hours, but it would be wise to stop after you're ahead $10 or $20. Of course, you may be the sort of accursed gambler who will hit a losing streak right at the beginning. So perhaps we should forget Martingale.

• *Great Martingale System.* Believe it or not, there are those systems players who have determined that the trouble with Martingale is that you just don't win enough fast enough, and the solution is to strike quickly and get out. Instead of merely doubling the next bet, these individuals double and add a unit. Thus, a losing bet of $1 is followed by $3 and then $7. The siren call of Great Martingale is that every loss automatically means that a player's eventual profit increases by 1 unit. The mathematics is not to be faulted, but what Great Martingale does is lower the number of losses that send the bettor's wager over the maximum that much sooner. Great Martingale is highly recommended if you want to go broke quicker than with poor old Martingale. Incidentally, Martingale is named after an 18th-century English gambler named Henry Martindale. Even the name came down to us incorrectly, but that's the least of our worries if we play the system.

• *D'Alembert, or Pyramid, System.* More systems bettors use the D'Alembert System than any other. It is named after an 18th-century French mathematician who does not deserve to be remembered primarily for this application of his findings. D'Alembert formulated the law of equilibrium, which states that when two events have an equal chance of happening and one event occurs more often than the other, the second event will eventually close the gap. The key word, of course, is "eventually." Applied to Roulette, that could be days or weeks after our systems bettor has gone to the poorhouse.

What the d'Alembert players do is add a chip after each losing bet and subtract a chip after every winning bet. If they win on the first bet, they simply start what they regard as a new sequence at 1 unit. Let us say a six-spin play goes like this: Lose, lose, win, win, lose, win. After the first two spins the player is losing 3 chips. He wins them all back on the third spin, and is 2 chips ahead after the fourth spin and ends up 3 chips ahead on the sixth spin. If he stopped there he would be ahead, though the overall wins and losses are even. Thus there are times when more money results from the winning bets than the losing ones, but a small losing streak creates problems and the player can get so far behind he cannot get out, except "eventually." An additional problem is that the zero wins will sap his bankroll and hasten his defeat.

• *Trend System.* This is based on the idea that streaks do happen and that they tend to continue. This system is used on even-money and number bets at Roulette, on the assumption that the wheel is imperfect and some numbers or colors will turn up more often than others. Such players will offer charts of results that show this happening from time to time. It's true, but that's because random results will and *must* eventually include every pattern imaginable. Keep playing this and the trend stops here. (See JAGGER'S SYSTEM.)

• *Trend Reversal System.* Aha! A trend ends. So its reverse has to win. Wait at the table until black or red, or high or low, or even or odd turn up four or five times in a row and then bet against the trend. Notice that we are actually back at d'Alembert again. One has to remember that previous results mean nothing. A Roulette ball or a pair of dice for that matter have not an ounce of brainpower or memory. Just because red has turned up four times in a row that stupid ball does not know it is supposed to seek out a black slot the next time—or even three of the next five times. Essentially, what such a system player is doing is playing only some of the time. His mathematical chances are not altered if he plays 50 spins in a row or 50 spins over a span of 150. The odds for and against him, linked to each individual spin, do not shift.

• *Cancellation System.* More general magazines publish variations of this system because it seems to make sense to generalist editor types. The sales pitch is that a player can eke out small profits even when he loses two out of every three results. In theory, it works. A typical way to start this system is to set down these numbers:

1-2-3-4

Now the bettor adds and bets the two outside numbers, in this case the 1 and 4. Should he win his bet, he strikes off those numbers and his worksheet would look like this:

1̶-2-3-4̶

Now he bets the new outside numbers again—2 and 3 for a total of 5. If he wins that bet he has won 10 units and the sequence is finished, and he starts anew, with another 1-2-3-4. Let us say he loses his next bet. He places the losing amount at the right end of his figures with this result:

1-2-3-4-5

What he has done is add the total loss to the right hand end of the sequence, changing his next outside total to 6 units. Let us say he wins. Now the worksheet looks like this:

1̶-2-3-4-5̶

Now he bets the outside numbers again, 2 and 4 for 6. With a win it stands thusly:

1̶-2̶-3-4̶-5̶

On the next bet he will bet 3, and if he loses he adds the 3 to the right and will bet 6 the following game. If he wins instead he crosses off the 3's and has won another 10 units.

The lure of the Cancellation System is that a win crosses off two digits while a loss adds only one and "eventually" all the numbers will be crossed off. With a run of luck this will happen for several sequences, but once there is even a short streak the other way, the losses will escalate sharply. Actually, the Cancellation System is more deadly than the terrible Martingale. It is much more common for five losing bets to be followed by one winning bet and then three losing bets to be followed by a winning bet and then by three losing bets to be again followed by a winning bet than it is for ten losing bets to occur in a row. Thus, a bettor using this system will get in the hole much quicker and more often than with the Martingale System.

Cancel out the Cancellation System and all others. What all these systems do is imprison the player in a web of repeated and rising bets. Any system that calls for an escalation of the betting after a loss is particularly dangerous since either the player will run out of money or he will hit the casino maximum and be unable to extricate himself—except "eventually."

There are many other systems floating around, as well as variations on the aforementioned. For instance, the damaging build-up in the Cancellation System can be largely reduced by starting with a 1-1-1-1 pattern. This cuts down on the profits, but also postpones the player's final defeat for some time.

Take all systems with a grain of salt, and none more than those that appear in popular magazines or are hawked in magazine and newspaper ads. One must always ask why someone who has a surefire system is willing to part with it for $5, or $50, or $500, or even $5,000. The most ingenious pitch this writer has ever come across was made by a hustler who assured his victims that he was now a millionaire thanks to his system and had all the money he'd ever need, but that he hated the casinos so much he was willing to let others share the wealth.

Howard Schwartz, known as the resident conscience of the Gambler's Book Club, constantly ferrets out gambling system scams. Not long ago a gambler consulted Schwartz about a winning BLACK-JACK system a Las Vegas character was offering to sell for a trifling $5,000. Schwartz tried to talk the player out of buying it, and at least half succeeded. The gullible gambler still went ahead, but talked the hustler down to $2,500. It still cost the victim $4,500 because he then lost an additional $2,000 playing the system.

Or take the case of CHARLES WELLS, the immortalized "Man who broke the bank at Monte Carlo." In two fantastic runs of luck in 1891 Wells won about $400,000 at Roulette at Monte Carlo. No one could figure out his system, and for good reason. He had none, but just bet wildly on hunches.

Then the following year Wells returned to take the casino again. Instead he lost all his money, and all the money he could con from rich men who believed he had a system. Ironically, this time he *had* devised a system. He'd figured he could not expect to have another great run of luck without a disciplined betting method. Maybe he was right, but the system destroyed him just as effectively.

BEZIQUE: Forerunner of Pinochle
In its standard version, Bezique is a two-player game, it was the forerunner of Pinochle as well as two variations, RUBICON BEZIQUE and SIX-PACK (or Chinese) BEZIQUE which today are more popular than their parent. However, Bezique still has a considerable following in the United States, Canada, Great Britain, and Western Europe.

To play, the deuces through 6's in a double deck of cards are removed, leaving a total of 64 cards. The cards are then ranked according to the German sequence of ace, 10, king, queen, jack, 9, 8, 7. Eight cards are dealt to each player, with the next card turned up establishing trump suit. The turned-up card is placed partly beneath the remaining pack, which serves as a stock from which players draw cards. In Bezique the only cards that count individually for points are the aces and 10's, which are 10 points each and called "brisques." Last trick is 10 points, making a total of 170 in all. (If the dealer turns the 7 as trump card, he gets 10 points.)

Brisques, however, are not nearly as valuable as declarations, which is melding of various combinations.

These values are:

Marriage (king and queen of same suit)	20
Royal Marriage (king and queen of trump)	40
Sequence (ace-10-king-queen-jack of trump)	250
Bezique (queen of spades and jack of diamonds)	40
Double Bezique (two beziques)	500
Any four aces	100
Any four kings	80
Any four queens	60
Any four jacks	40

The nondealer starts the game by leading a card and the dealer may follow with any card he wishes. Highest card of the suit led takes the trick unless a plain lead is trumped. Upon winning a trick, a player may make a declaration by putting down a value-bearing meld face up. Only one declaration is allowed to be scored per winning trick. Other melds may be laid down, but they must wait to be scored on succeeding tricks. After declaring and before leading to the next trick, the declarer takes the top card from the deck and the loser the next, so that each hand (including the exposed declarations) still numbers eight cards. The player may lead from either his hand or from his meld, and the loser plays accordingly.

A card may not be used twice in the same declaration, but may be used for different declarations. For example, if spades are trump, the queen of spades may be used for four queens, in a marriage, sequence, and bezique. Having been played in four queens, the queen may be used elsewhere, but the player may not add a new fourth queen to the remaining three queens to score another 60 points. He would have to declare four new queens. If a sequence is played for 250 points, the player may not later declare the king and queen of trumps as 40. However, he may do the reverse, declaring the 40 points and then adding the ace, 10, jack for 250 points.

Bezique scores 40 and then a second bezique added for 500 points, but a double bezique declared at once counts only for 500 points.

When the stock gets down to only one face-down card, the previous trick taker gets it but is not permitted to declare. Instead, his opponent takes the exposed trump and the game proceeds with a different character. Thereafter, a player holding a card of the suit led must play it, and he is required to win the trick if he can. There are no more declarations and the rest of the game is designed to win brisques and the last trick.

Scores are totaled and the deal passes. The game is played usually to 1,000 or 1,500 points, and if both players go over, highest score wins. In the rare instance that the score is tied, the winning total is raised 500 points.

Bezique's strategy is most concerned with declarations, which can bring in much higher scores than brisques. Naturally, every effort is made to retain cards usable in high-count declarations. Equally important is the need to win tricks, bearing in mind that only the winner of a trick can declare. Therefore cards likely to win tricks must be retained.

Settlement is usually on the point differentials and they can be substantial if a player can strike swiftly with a double bezique in a 1,000-point game. For this reason, many gamblers prefer the 1,500-point game.

BEZIQUE—Chouette
Chouette Bezique is a form of the game that allows three or more participants. The game follows the

rules of RUBICON, SIX-PACK, or Eight-Pack Bezique. All players cut cards and the highest becomes bank, or "man in the box," while the second becomes the opponent, or the "captain." The remaining players may consult with the captain but his decisions on play are final.

The banker decides who deals, and if he wins the hand, he collects an equal sum from all the participants and continues as banker for the next hand. If however the banker loses, he must pay all the participants based on the captain's winning margin, and the captain takes over as banker. The next participant in line becomes the captain. The defeated banker goes to the bottom of the list of participants.

BEZIQUE—Cinq-cents

Cinq-cents quite possibly is the earliest form of Bezique and is played with a single 32-card deck, the rankings as in ordinary Bezique. All melds are counted as in Bezique but a nontrump sequence is added to the declaration possibilities. This would be ace, 10, king, queen, jack in any of the ordinary suits and counts 120 points. Bezique itself is called "binage," which by its very sound hints of Pinochle. High-card points are not totaled until the end of the hand.

A tricky aspect of the game is that a player believing he has accumulated 500 points in declarations and captured cards can knock, and if he had 500 points he is the winner, even if his opponents turn out to have more points. If neither player knocks and one has reached 500, he is the winner. If both are over 500, the game continues with the winning score raised to 600. If a player knocks and has less than 500 points, he loses the game.

BEZIQUE—Eight-pack

Eight-pack Bezique is actually SIX-PACK, or Chinese Bezique, enlarged with the use of a 256-card deck (a total of eight regular decks with all cards from deuces through 6's removed). Hands are 15 cards. The scoring is altered with single bezique counting for 50 points; double bezique 500; triple bezique 1,500; quadruple bezique 4,500; and quintuple bezique 9,000. In trump cards five aces count 2,000; five 10's 1,800; five kings 1,600; five queens 1,200; and five jacks 800. If the loser fails to score at least 5,000 points he is rubiconed (see BEZIQUE—Rubicon).

BEZIQUE—Four-hand

Four-hand Bezique uses a 128-card deck made up of four 32-card packs shuffled together. Each player is on his own or he may play in partnership. In the latter case, the trick taker may declare or defer to his partner to do so. Partners are also permitted to add to each other's combinations, but subject to the restrictions that the partner is under, as in the basic game of Bezique.

BEZIQUE—No-trump

No-trump Bezique is played exactly like regular Bezique except that no trump card is turned. Trump is instead determined when the first marriage is declared. There is naturally no count for the 7 of trumps.

BEZIQUE—Rubicon

Rubicon Bezique is a two-player game that introduced a number of intertwining and radical changes to the original version of Bezique, and today it enjoys more play than the basic form. The deck is 128 cards—two 64-card Bezique decks, and each player gets nine cards. No trump is established until the first marriage. The plays on declarations are far less rigid. For instance, if a player plays from a declaration he can claim the full value of that declaration by replacing the card.

In addition, there are more declarations than in straight Bezique. A "back door," or nontrump sequence, is permitted and counts for 150 points. Triple bezique earns 1,500 and quadruple bezique is worth 4,500. The trump 7 has no special value, but a player can score a "carte blanche" for 50 points if his original hand is revealed and has no face cards. Thereafter he is awarded another 50 points for each 7, 8, 9 or ace he draws from the stock before getting a picture card.

Tricks accumulate on the table until a brisque is played and the winner of that trick gets all the tricks up until that point. Taking the final trick is worth 50 points. Scores obviously mount up in this game and on completion of a deal, a player who has failed to reach 1,000 points is "rubiconed." His opponent scores all points made by both of them, plus 320 for the brisques (16 aces and 16 10's) and in addition he gets a 1,000-point bonus. This is so even if the winner also failed to achieve 1,000. All that is required is that he outscore his opponent. Scores are only figured in hundreds, so that if the player had 1,320 and the dealer 1,140, the player would win 1,300 to 1,100. In this case, the loser going over 1,000, the winner gets only a 500-point bonus. If the margin of victory is less than 100 points, the winner gets 600 points. Normally, the brisques are not counted in the score unless it is necessary to prevent a player from being rubiconed or to affect the outcome. In that case his opponent has the right to count his brisques as well.

Settlement is made on the basis of the margin of victory and the winner of the hand deals the next one.

BEZIQUE—Six-pack (or Chinese)

Six-pack (or Chinese) Bezique is today played more than its parent game. It was the favorite version for Winston Churchill who was one of the first great experts of the game. Others might even view Sir Winston as a bit of a "hustler" at the game, since inevitably visitors to the Churchill home would be guided after dinner to the Bezique table by Sir Winston and Lady Churchill. Few left the table with their purses intact.

Three 64-card Bezique decks, a total of 192 cards, are used and each player gets 12 cards. In this version the brisques are never counted and tricks are not picked up. The rubicon rule remains in place and Chinese Bezique awards 1,000 for four aces of trump; 900 for four 10's of trump; 800, four kings; 600, four queens; 400, four jacks. Carte blanche is raised to 250 points, compared to Rubicon Bezique as is the final trick.

In an unusual fillip to the play, a cut of the deck is made and the high man wins the option to decide if he wishes to deal. Almost invariably, he decides not to since the deal has a bit of a disadvantage. To compensate for this the dealer is permitted to lift a portion of cards from the pack in hope that he gets exactly 24, which gives him 250 points. Before the count (which actually represents the dealing of the two 12-card hands) the nondealer also makes a guess on the number of cards as more or less than 24. If his estimate is exact, he gets 150 points. The winning bonus is always 1,000 points and if the loser accumulates less than 3,000 points he is rubiconed.

BEZIQUE—Three-hand

Three-hand Bezique requires a 96-card deck, three of the usual 32-carders shuffled together. The player to the dealer's left leads to the first trick, and the trick taker thereafter leads to the next. All three players play to each trick and only the winner each time may declare. A triple bezique scores 1,500, and a player having counted 500 for double bezique may add the third bezique for 1,500 points. Game is usually 2,000.

BICYCLE RACE BETTING

Betting on bicycle races is almost a way of life in two countries—France, where bicycle racing is almost the national sport, and Japan. In France the action is illegal but as popular in that country as private betting on baseball and football in America.

Japan is the only country in the world with legalized betting on bicycle races and even on motorcycle and motorboat races. However, bicycle racing is the rage and more money is bet on the sport than on any other in the country. There are cycle tracks in virtually every major city and as many as 12 races are run daily on every track. Income derived from bicycle-race betting is used by local governments for housing and schools.

BIG SIX: Casino Sucker Game

Big Six is a carnival and casino gambling game that is a gold mine for the house because of its huge PC, or house percentage. The name Big Six is often ap-

plied to the casino game of Wheel of Fortune, or Money Wheel, which is explained in the following entry.

In the traditional Big Six game there are 54 equal spaces along the rim of the wheel surface, each with a picture of one side of three dice, the numbers ranging from 1 to 6. Players bet on a layout bearing the numbers 1 to 6. Let us say the player bets $1 on the 1 and the wheel stops on 1-2-3. The player wins $1 and gets his original $1 as well. Now let us say the wheel stops on 4-5-6. In this case the player loses his $1. But if the wheel stops on 1-1-2, he wins $2 plus his $1 back. And if 1-1-1 comes out he wins $3 plus his original bet back. Naturally a player is hoping for three of a kind. But the house is rooting for the same result. The casino only makes money when a pair or three of a kind appears. When different numbers come up the house must mathematically break even, paying off on three numbers and collecting on three numbers.

Thus it is hardly surprising that some Big Six wheels have no more than six slots with three different numbers. Frequently there are 24 sets with three of a kind and 24 sets with a pair and another number. Thus, when these come out some players feel they have the advantage over the house when actually it is gravy time for the house.

This is amply demonstrated by betting a dollar on each of the six numbers and continuing the process for 54 times so that mathematically at least every combination on the wheel comes up once. What happens? In six of the spins, we would break even, winning $3 and losing $3 each time. On these six bets we wagered a total of $36 and got back $36. We are dead even.

Now let us proceed to the 24 games in which a pair and another number turn up. We have put up a total of $144 on these games. Our return on the paired numbers is a total of $72 ($48 as the 2-to-1 payoff and $24 as a return on our bet). On the single number that turned up with the pair, we get back a total of $48—$24 in "winnings" and $24 on our original wager. Thus we have gotten back $72 plus $48, or $120 in all. But we bet $144 and have lost $24.

Now we consider the 24 games that come out with three of a kind, all players' fondest hope. Again we wagered $144 in these games and this time we got back our $24 on the correct number plus the profit of $72. This adds up to $96—and a net loss of $48. Together with the $24 loss on the paired results we suffered a $72 loss on a total investment of $324 ($6 × 54). This means the house advantage overall is an astounding 22.2222 percent, meaning the house keeps more than 22 cents on every dollar bet on every spin of the wheel! Other Big Six wheels have a different break of the dice numbers or a different number of slots, but the basic rule of thumb is the more paired and tripled numbers there are the more the house, not the customer, wins.

BIG SIX (Wheel of Fortune)

At all casinos in Atlantic City it is called Big Six; in Nevada it may be known by that name, Wheel of Fortune, or the Money Wheel. Nowhere is it referred to by what would be its most fitting name—the Big Sucker Game.

Let us first listen to the propaganda put out by a typical casino. This one is the Tropicana in Atlantic City, but all the others offer similar uninformative spiels:

BIG SIX

The Wheel of Fortune is probably one of the oldest games of chance in the world. On the wheel are 54 equally spaced sections containing United States currency or symbols: twenty-three sections containing $1.00 bills, fifteen sections containing $2.00 bills, eight sections containing $5.00 bills, four sections containing $10.00 bills, two sections containing $20.00 bills, one section with a joker and one section with a Tropicana flag.

Big Six allows you to bet on one or more numbers or symbols appearing on the gaming table layout. The betting layout offers you two identical areas on which you can place your bet. Each area displays various denominations of United States currency or symbols, $1.00 bills, $2.00 bills, $5.00 bills, $10.00 bills, $20.00 bills, a Tropicana flag and a joker. Bets may be placed directly on top the chosen number or symbol until the dealer announces "No more bets." Winning bets are decided by the dealer spinning a wheel with a flapper at the top which marks the winning number or symbol when the wheel comes to rest. If the flapper stops on top of a peg, the number previously passed will be the winner. The odds, stated below, are located under each bill or symbol:

Bet	Odds	Bet	Odds
$1.00	1 to 1	$20.00	20 to 1
$2.00	2 to 1	Joker	45 to 1
$5.00	5 to 1	Tropicana	
$10.00	10 to 1	flag	45 to 1

Most American casinos sport one or more Big Six wheels, and for good reason: The house take is enormous. For instance, the Trop's Big Six $5 bet gives the casino an edge of 11.1 percent—*and that's the worst deal for the house!* On the $1 bets the house PC (percentage) is 14.8; $2—16.6; $10—18.5; $20—22.2; Joker—14.8; and Tropicana (at other casinos their own logo)—14.8.

These edges of course are in the highway-robbery category, making Big Six about as attractive as the black plague. The game plays to two sucker groups. One is the loser who let us say has dropped a bundle at the BLACKJACK tables and has only a few odd bucks left. He or she might plunk down his last small bills in the hope of hitting a 20 to 1 or 45 to 1 payoff that would allow him to hustle back to the BLACKJACK table. Naturally, this seldom happens, but no casino wants a customer to leave without giving up his last loose bills.

The other sucker category is the casino newcomer who finds himself inhibited by the mysterious rules of Blackjack, CRAPS, ROULETTE, and BACCARAT. For them the simple rules of Big Six is an irresistible lure.

While obviously there is no reason ever to play Big Six, a word of caution must be added for addicts on the different payoffs in Nevada and Atlantic City. While the player in New Jersey has the best chances at the $5 bet, this is not true in Nevada, where there are only seven $5 symbols on the wheel compared to eight in Atlantic City. This little variation sends the house PC in Nevada soaring to 22.2! The Nevada casinos simply increase the $1 symbols to a total of 24 instead of 23, thus cutting the PC down to 11.1, making that wager the "best bet."

Many Big Six addicts have been brainwashed by the better odds offered on the joker and logo plays in Atlantic City, and they are convinced this makes the game a solid bet there. The truth is, it is a good bet nowhere, at no time.

BIG SIX (Wheel of Fortune)—Cheating

Cheating at various Big Six or Wheel of Fortune games is a relatively easy matter for the house, readily accomplished at crooked carnivals through the use of a foot pedal or perhaps more commonly in a "belly joint" operation. In a belly joint the operator simply presses his stomach against the counter to control the spin of the wheel. Needless to say, legitimate casinos are not about to gaff their games. It is not worth the risk when they are operating with a house edge running from 11.1 all the way up to 22.2. With legal stealing like that, cheating is unnecessary!

However, there are any number of ways players try to beat the house. The most common and frequently caught are the equivalent of past posting, in which a player tries to shift a bet to a winning position while the operator is looking at the wheel or else tries to add extra chips, bills, or coins to a winning pile.

Perhaps the most sophisticated attempts of all, if they are not fanciful tales, concern the technologically minded who turn to advanced science to bilk the casino. One of the more publicized efforts was one attributed to Prof. Edward O. Thorp, of BLACKJACK counting fame. In its March 27, 1964 issue *Life* magazine ran the following rather astonishing account:

BEATING THE WHEEL WITH THE BIG TOE

At one point, to beat the "wheel of fortune" which stands at the entrance of most casinos, he [Thorp] built a device which measured off a second with an all but inaudible click and installed it in one shoe where he could start it with his big toe. Thus armed, with his hands innocently free, he was able to time the velocity of the turning rim well enough to predict its 40 to 1 payoff and quickly enough to put down a bet almost as soon as its carny-voiced operator gave it a spin.

It is hardly necessary to cite gambling experts such as John Scarne who were rather unimpressed with the professor's big toe, to consider the technical merits of such claims. All that need be mentioned is that successful technologies are never abandoned in any field. Is the Thorp Big Toe Method still in use? The bottom line is that the money wheels of all kinds are still in place in the casinos, something that would not be the case if there was a way they were being beaten consistently. It may be noted that by the late 1980s the good professor was more concerned with stock market systems than contemplating his big toe or even the doings at the Blackjack tables.

BIG SQUEEZE: Six-card Stud Poker

Usually games of SIX-CARD STUD are best figured as having Five-card Stud probabilities in so far as winning hands are concerned. Serious gamblers know the sixth card does not generally produce the huge hands Seven-card Stud can. However, the game of Big Squeeze does offer higher expectations.

How to play: Betting occurs as in Five-card Stud when a sixth card is dealt face down. After another round of betting players may discard one card, either an up or down one, and replace it with another from the deck. There is a final round of betting and the showdown. Since the discard is generally an unneeded card, the draw qualifies as virtually the same thing as the seventh card in Seven-card Stud. Hands thus tend to be higher than in Five- or other Six-card Stud games. Big Squeeze is usually played high-low, and a sharp player can often determine whether his opponents are likely to go high or low by their discard.

BIG STORE: Fake Gambling Establishment

As portrayed in the hit movie *The Sting*, in the 19th century most gangs of gambling cheats concentrated on phony games to which were lured gullible victims. It was a good way to cheat a sucker out of hundreds or thousands of dollars, with the cheats then scattering. This was followed by the "Dollar Store," which masqueraded as a merchandise mart offering $1 bargains but making its real money from crooked gambling games on the premises. Customers who wandered in never came out with their wallets intact. Many Dollar Stores were located in the West and specialized in trimming wagon-train immigrants passing through.

Eventually, some con men figured out they could set up a "Big Store"—a completely bogus gambling parlor or horse room to trim the suckers. In such operations everyone present—the managers, bouncers, croupiers, dealers, winners and losers—were phonies, only there to impress a single well-heeled victim.

An ingenious gambler named Buck Boatwright is believed to have established the first Big Store in 1900 in Webb City, Missouri. Boatwright's operation was a slightly different gambling setup, featuring among other things fixed sporting events, generally prizefights or footraces. So convincing was the atmosphere in Boatright's establishment, which soon spawned a branch in Council Bluffs, Iowa, that a sucker almost never suspected he was losing his money in a completely play-act arena where everyone except the victim was a member of the gang.

After the sucker was roped in by being allowed to win a few small bets, he was then informed of a big fix and induced to bet thousands, only to watch as something unforeseen went wrong. In a footrace or fight the participant the victim was betting on might suddenly "drop dead," triggering a false panic since such sporting events were illegal. In other cases the victim would be kissed off when the two operators who has suckered him in, and who allegedly had lost their money along with his, got into an argument that would end with one pulling a gun and "killing" the other. In this play-acted "sting" the mortally wounded con man would slump to the floor, blood gushing from his mouth. The blood was chicken blood secreted in a pouch in the man's mouth and bitten open at the dramatic moment. It was an act that invariably put the victim "on the run" since, while he had intended only to break the law against illegal betting, he now believed he was an accessory to murder. Although the Big Store would seem to be an operation that could fleece only the most gullible, in fact it worked extremely well against businessmen and men of great wealth, men who had much to lose facing homicide charges. Few ever suspected a thing, and if they had any doubts, they were reluctant to put them to the test by going to the authorities.

The Sting accurately portrayed the Big Store in operation with perhaps only one major error of fact. Few Big Stores were one-shot deals, and were seldom disassembled after one big hit. The establishments were always set up in "protected territories," in which police and politicians would cooperate for either a flat payoff or a percentage of the take. If a doubting sucker turned to the authorities ready to reveal all, he would be informed the death he thought he had witnessed had indeed happened. The chastened sucker would then be "let off easy," usually after a bribe had been extracted from him.

The greatest of all the Big Store operatives was master fixer Lou Blonger who ran his phony gambling joints in Denver, Colorado over some four decades and made that city the "con man's capital of America."

BIMBO HIGH-LOW: Double-handed Five-card Stud

Bimbo High-Low is also known as Double-handed High-Low, which describes it most accurately.

How to play: Each player is dealt two separate hands of Five-card Stud. He must play each hand separately in turn, and if he bets one of his hands, he must cover the bet with his other hand as well. However, any player can fold one or both hands at any time. At the showdown players announce whether they are going high or low with each of their hands.

Strategy: Because the game is played high-low, players should seldom stay with both hands going one way, that is, both for high or both for low. There is some excuse for staying until the third or even fourth card when both hands are low, however, since low hands are inherently better than high; if ruined by a pair, a low hand could be catapulted into a strong high hand. Some players prefer to cut down to one hand after the third card is dealt, staying with the more promising hand based on what the opposition shows. These gamblers feel it is foolish to pay for two hands when the pot will most likely be split at the conclusion. A prudent gambler studies his opponents' style in this game and learns to identify the players who invariably cut down to one hand. When such a player holds both hands, a cautious opponent might consider folding both of his hands forthwith, since chances are the notorious "cutter" probably is holding two very strong hands.

BING-O DRAW POKER: Spit Variation

Bing-O Draw Poker is a SPIT game played much the same as CRISSCROSS, except there are more community cards from which to choose.

How to play: After players are dealt five cards, nine community cards are centered on the table in this position:

        1 2 3
        4 5 6
        7 8 9

The four corner cards are dealt up and the rest down. A betting round follows with a three-raise maximum. After that the remaining common five cards are exposed one at a time with a similar betting

interval. The last card turned up is number 5, the center card, which is wild, as are all other of the same rank.

Players then use their five-card hand and one line of three cards from the table to make their best possible high or low or high-low hand. The line may be formed horizontally, vertically or diagonally from the community square. If a line is chosen that does not pass through the number 5, the player does not benefit from that wild card, although he retains the right to any others of the same denomination as the center wild card.

Strategy: Despite the wild nature of the game, betting and raising are often on the conservative side early because players soon realize how powerful a hand has to be to win. Four of a kind is the lowest staying hand and will frequently be beat. Some tight players drop out if they have less than a straight flush. Straight flushes lose to royal flushes or five of a kind.

BINGO: Game for Addicts Only

Most books on gambling ignore Bingo or treat it disparagingly, not regarding it as a fair gamble.

Played like its predecessor LOTTO, Bingo allows for wins in various ways, covering all the numbers on a card as they are called, or filling the previously announced rows. Bingo has a total of 75 numbers compared to Lotto's 90 and a card has five rows of five numbers both vertically and horizontally, with the center space free. More than half the states permit Bingo (which is considered vital for fundraising by churches and other charities), and several allow Bingo gambling parlors, generally with a top-prize limit, but often with no limit on the cards sold (some addicts play 20 or more). Thus the house can pay out as little as a third or less of the take. As a result one should only play Bingo for charity and expect to lose money—with little risk of disappointment. See JOSEPH E. GRANVILLE; LOTTO.

BINOCHLE: Early Pinochle

In its earliest form PINOCHLE was known as Binochle, a two-handed trump game with half the pack dealt out and the remaining cards drawn during the game. As later rules were added, the name Pinochle developed along with all its interesting offshoots. Today Binochle is as dead as the dodo.

BIRD CAGE

See CHUCK-A-LUCK.

BLACK SOX SCANDAL: Fixed World Series

Can a really major sporting event be fixed? Something like the Super Bowl or the World Series? The answer is that the temptation must be there for the fix precisely because that's where the money is. Tens of millions are bet annually on these two events, which if nothing else creates motive for the crime. Self-regulation has been stiff in both professional football and baseball because of the obvious temptation. Even players found to have bet on their own teams have been subject to suspension. As a result there have been only unsubstantiated whispers about one Super Bowl game. There is, however, no question that one World Series was fixed, a scandal that so rocked baseball that it became the most-policed sporting activity in the country.

Before 1919 there had been frequent reports of tampered baseball games, many undoubtedly true, but before that year the "unthinkable" never occurred, the fixing of a World Series. Eight star players for the Chicago White Sox managed to lose the Series to the underdog Cincinnati Redlegs five games to three (the series that year was being played in an experimental nine-game set).

Full details of what was to be called the Black Sox Scandal were never entirely exposed, primarily because there was an attempted cover-up by the baseball establishment in general, and White Sox owner Charles A. Comiskey in particular. The offending players were not even suspended until almost a year later when there were only three games left in the season, and confessions by three players to a grand jury forced a reluctant Comiskey to act.

The idea for Chicago to go into the dumper apparently was first concocted by Charles Arnold "Chick" Gandil, who whispered to Boston gamblers that he could line up several teammates for such a killing if the price was right. The players Gandil "recruited" were Eddie Cicotte and Claude Williams, the team's leading pitchers, who between them had won 52 games during the regular season; left fielder Shoeless Joe Jackson; center fielder Oscar Felsch; third baseman George "Buck" Weaver; shortstop Charles "Swede" Risbergand; and utility infielder Fred McMullin.

The gamblers first approached in the plot were Joe "Sport" Sullivan of Boston and William "Sleepy Bill" Burns of New York. The pair felt they would need more capital to finance the bribes and to use for betting money, and they therefore approached the country's leading gambler, Arnold "the Brain" Rothstein. To this day it is uncertain whether or not Rothstein took part in the plot or turned the schemers down—and then blithely bet at least $60,000 on Cincinnati and collected $270,000. The theory went that since he knew the fix was in, Rothstein saw no need to pay out bribe money himself. In any event, Rothstein was not the active operative in the huge betting coup. That man was Abe Attell, the ex-featherweight boxing champion. A visitor to Attell's hotel suite in

Cincinnati later told of seeing money stacked on every horizontal surface in the room—on tables, chairs, and dresser tops—after the Redlegs' first win.

In the first game Cicotte's invincible "shine ball" lost its magic and he was knocked out in the fourth inning. In the second game Williams suffered uncharacterisic wildness and went down to defeat, 4-2. After the second game, rumors of the fix were rampant and the Redlegs were made big favorites to take the series. Bookmakers around the country would take no more action on the Redlegs, but happily took bets from the public on the White Sox. It took a year-long grand jury investigation to crack the case, with confessions being made by Jackson, Cicotte, and Williams. A reluctant Comiskey was forced to fire all the players except Gandil, who had already "retired."

Testimony showed that most of the players had gotten $5,000 for their roles in the fix (but what they may have bet is unknown), while Gandil had grabbed $35,000 for himself. How many hundreds of thousands—or millions—the gamblers made was never determined.

Perhaps the most memorable event of the entire affair concerned a group of small boys who waited outside the grand jury room while several of the players testified. When they came out, one of the boys asked Shoeless Joe Jackson, "It ain't true, is it, Joe?"

"Yes, boys," the outfielder replied. "I'm afraid it is."

That little byplay was altered in folklore to have the boy plead plaintively, "Say it ain't so, Joe."

More historical revisionism than folklore, the commonly held belief today is that the baseball establishment excised this scandalous cancer quickly and surgically. The real and forgotten truth is that the baseball magnates provided legal aid to the players and stonewalled in a fashion that would have done a Watergate plotter proud. In fact, the baseball players were acquitted by a jury and some of the players were carried on the shoulders of the jurors from the courtroom.

However, Judge Kenesaw Mountain Landis, appointed as commissioner to oversee the integrity of "the Game," was not impressed. He never let any of the players put on a White Sox—or any other—uniform again.

See ARNOLD ROTHSTEIN.

BLACKJACK: Simple Gambling Card Game

Blackjack is both a popular private and casino betting game, but while casinos have steadily increased the number of their Blackjack tables to take care of increasing business, there has been a considerable drop-off in private play. The gain of revolutionary ideas in Blackjack strategy is responsible for this. Originally, private Blackjack was a game that greatly favored the dealer for many reasons, including that the player runs the risk of busting first and that the dealer wins all ties. But since private Blackjack is played with a single deck, there are many instances when a smart player, keeping strict count of the cards, can determine that those remaining in the deck favor him, and he can increase his bet substantially and win, making up for previous small losses.

Because this is the case, we will concentrate on the casino game, recognizing the fact that some of the rules do not apply to private games. For instance, in casino Blackjack the dealer must stand on a total of 17, but in the private version the dealer has the option of drawing another card, a decision he can make according to how many opponents remain in the game, and his "read" of their possible hands.

Casino rules for Blackjack, except for very minor considerations, are the same for all casinos in Atlantic City. They can vary considerably in Las Vegas, both in opportunities of play and some other rules. The rules and odds are generally stacked against the player in casinos in northern Nevada; a survey in *Playboy* magazine concluded: "Anyone playing blackjack in Northern Nevada should be arrested for stupidity."

Here is a reprint of the official gaming guide for Caesars Atlantic City:

TRY YOUR HAND AT BLACKJACK "21"

Blackjack, or "21," is a popular game at Caesars Atlantic City. The object is to draw cards totaling closer to 21 than the dealer's cards—without exceeding 21.

You enter the game by placing a bet on the table in front of you. Please don't handle the bet after the first card is drawn from the dealing shoe. The dealer deals two face up cards for each player and two cards to himself, the first card is the dealer's face up card, the second is his "hole" card—dealt face down. Then, proceeding from his left to right, the dealer announces the total point count of each player's hand. To total the point count of your hand, use these values: any card from 2 to 10 is counted at face value. A Jack, Queen, or King is counted as 10. An Ace shall have a value of 11 unless that would give a player or the dealer a score in excess of 21, in which case, it shall have a value of 1. Also—you are re-

sponsible for correctly computing your point count for each hand. Only the dealer is permitted to handle, remove, or alter any cards used.

When the dealer announces the point count of your hand, you can make one or more of the following decisions:

Player's Blackjack: If the first two cards dealt to you total 21, the dealer will announce that you have blackjack, and, if the dealer's face up card is any card 2 through 9, you have won your bet. The dealer will pay your bet at odds of three to two and remove your cards. You can make no other bet at this time.

If you have a blackjack and the dealer's up card is an Ace or has a value of 10, no decision will be made on your hand until the dealer turns up his "hole" card. If it gives him a two (2) card total of 21, the dealer has blackjack. And you neither win nor lose your initial bet. If the dealer's "hole" card and first card do not equal 21, then your blackjack wins. Or, if the dealer has a card total of 21 in more than two (2) cards, you also win your bet. The dealer will pay your bet at odds of three to two and then remove your cards.

Insurance: Insurance is a separate bet that can be made when, and only when, the dealer's up card is an Ace. If you take insurance, you are betting that the dealer has a blackjack. To do so, place a bet not greater than one-half (½) of your initial bet on the insurance area of the blackjack table. Your insurance bet wins if the dealer has blackjack and loses if the dealer does not. Your winning insurance bet will be paid at odds of two to one. This wager is placed immediately after you receive your initial two cards.

Splitting Pairs: If the initial two (2) cards dealt to you are identical in value, you may split the pair and form two (2) hands. If you do, you must place an additional bet equal to your initial bet. You are buying the right to play two (2) hands. The dealer will deal a second card to the first of your hands, announce your point count, and respond to your decision to double down, stand, or draw before dealing to your second hand.

There are three special rules when splitting pairs. First, if you split Aces, you are dealt only one (1) additional card to each split hand and you may not take any additional cards. Second, you may not split pairs again if the second card dealt to your split is identical in value to a card of the split pair. Third, if the dealer obtains a blackjack after you have split any pair, you will lose only the amount of your initial bet and the additional amount bet will be returned to you.

Doubling Down: If your initial two (2) cards or the first two (2) cards of any split pair do not give you a blackjack, or a twenty-one (21) which is not a blackjack, you may increase your bet by making an additional bet equal to or less than the amount of your initial bet. This is known as doubling down. You can draw only one (1) additional card on the hand on which you double down. If the dealer reveals a blackjack after you have doubled down, you

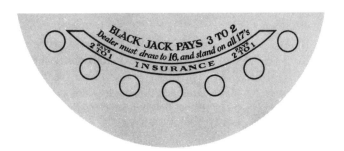

will lose only the amount of your initial bet and the additional amount bet will be returned to you.

Drawing Cards: If your initial two (2) cards do not give you a blackjack and you do not double down, or you have not split pairs, you may draw as many cards as you wish up to a point count of 21. You must stop drawing cards if your point count equals or exceeds 21. The dealer must draw additional cards if his point count totals 16 or less. If it totals 17 or more, he may not draw any additional cards.

If you have drawn additional cards and your point count exceeds 21, you lose your bet whether or not the dealer's point count exceeds 21. If you have not exceeded 21, and the dealer does, you win your bet. The dealer will pay your winning bet at odds of one to one. Once you have elected not to take additional cards and your point count has not exceeded 21, you must wait until the dealer draws all additional cards which he must draw. If your point count is then closer to 21 than the dealer's point count, you win your bet and the dealer will pay your bet at odds of one to one. If your point count is lower than the dealer's, you lose. If the dealer can't hit because his hand is 17 or more, and he and you have identical point counts, the hand is then "pushed," meaning neither you nor the dealer wins the hand. If you have 21 in more than two cards and the dealer has blackjack, you lose.

When you want an additional card or a hit, indicate with a scratching motion that you are asking to draw a card. When you have a hand where you are satisfied with the point total, a waving motion indicates to the dealer that you do not wish to draw. Dealers will only acknowledge hand signals.

We won't consider here any strategies involved in "counting" cards and indeed of what benefit they are, if any, for the average player as that subject will be covered in the succeeding entry. However, discussion of basic strategies of regular play is essential.

The basic decision players have to make is when to hit or take another card and when to stand, as well as when to double down, split, or take insurance.

Some experts vary on the specifics of when to draw or stand, but a simple effective guide is as follows:

Dealer's Hand Shows	Player Draws If Holding
2 or 3	12 or less
4, 5, 6	11 or less
7 or higher	16 or less

In All Other Instances The Player Should Stand Pat.

The above rules apply to what is called "hard hands" with no aces involved. A "soft hand" is one that consists of an ace and another card, such as ace-5, which would add up to 6 or 16, as the player wishes. When a dealer's exposed card is anything from ace to 8, the player should draw if his total

using the ace as 11 is 17 or less. If the dealer's card is 9 or higher, the player draws if his total is 18 or less. If a player's soft hand busts, he then figures the ace as 1 and proceeds in his strategy as a hard hand would warrant.

On doubling down, a player's strategy is in part determined by the casino's rules, which vary from New Jersey to Nevada. Some casinos allow doubling down only on a count of 11, and others on 10 or 11 and still others on anything. Generally, the best decision is to always double on 11, and to double on 10 if the dealer does not show an ace or a 10-point card. A 9 should only be doubled if the dealer has 6 or less. Basically, no other numbers should be doubled.

Splitting pairs is a bit more complicated and again seasoned gamblers vary on the specifics, but the most important rules are always to split aces and never to split 5's or 10's. On other options, standard advice is: if holding 2's, 3's, or 7's, split if the dealer shows 2 through 7; holding 4's, split against 5 or 6; holding 6's, split against 2 through 6, holding 8's split against 2 through 9; and with 9's, split against 2 through 9, except 7.

Insurance is generally a foolish bet to make unless the player is a counter and has determined that a dealer showing an ace very likely has a 10. In any other situation the house edge on a 2 to 1 bet is prohibitively large and the player should avoid it.

Occasionally a new version of Blackjack is offered in Nevada casinos, one recent one being "Double Exposure 21" at Vegas World in Las Vegas, under which players get to see *both* cards that the dealer is dealt before they decide what to do with their own. This, on the surface, appears to be the millennimum for Blackjack addicts. Of course, when one looks at the rest of the rules, the joy is less than unbounded.

Blackjack players will go at it for hours, but seldom can beat the house. Strategies are many but the odds very much favor the casino, although experts disagree on what the house edge is. (Photo: Las Vegas News Bureau)

Blackjack only pays even money and while a player takes all Blackjack ties, the dealer wins all other ties. There are a few other gimmicks that benefit the player, such as getting the jack and ace of spades or 6-7-8 in the same suit only; both giving a double payoff. Of course, you should not hold your breath on catching either of these hands.

Naturally, Blackjack technicians are already arguing about what the house percentage is at Double Exposure, but it is obvious that casinos are not in business to provide a winning edge to the players. It should always be assumed that when a house game works to the casino's advantage the adding of new wrinkles are seldom designed to reduce its edge, but rather to enhance it.

See also DOUBLE EXPOSURE 21.

BLACKJACK—Counting

There has been a lot written about Blackjack counting, much of it pure nonsense. Undoubtedly there is something to the various counting theories, but before we get overwhelmed by the impressive claims of a number of counters who grind out books, magazine articles, and in-person or mail-order courses on winning at the game, let us consider the bottom line.

Fact: With the appearance in 1962 of *Beat the Dealer* by New Mexico mathematics professor Edward O. Thorp the casino game of Blackjack was thrown into a state of flux. The casinos altered their rules, going from one deck of cards in a game to two, four, six, or eight packs. Counting systems were heaped on to an avid public, many guaranteeing them that the game could be turned into a money machine requiring little more than a bit of quick counting of certain cards to guarantee a steady income for life. It has been more than a quarter of a century since *Beat the Dealer* and its imitators appeared. Who won the Great Counting War?

Dr. Thorp today is still in computerized mathematical research of "sure things," but he is now concerned with looking for values in stocks and other securities. The late Ken Uston, author of numerous books on counting, was at the end of his life involved in computer work in the Middle East, helping Kuwait track billions of dollars in investments. He was not playing Blackjack in Atlantic City, although he had won a court case that barred casinos in New Jersey from refusing to let counters play. In fact, Uston,

Film actor Omar Sharif was one of the early counters advised to stay out of Las Vegas. Today he is more often seen at the more hospitable casinos of Trouville (above) and Deauville in France. (Photo: Casino de Trouville)

upon winning that case, didn't hit the Blackjack tables in Atlantic City but signed up to do TV commercials for Resorts International, the very target of his suit, touting the disguises he had used to gain access to the tables when the casinos started barring him.

And what of the casinos today? Blackjack is a much bigger game today than it was before *Beat the Dealer* appeared. More people than ever patronize the tables and *casinos today make more money from the game than ever before.* That's a pretty significant bottom line.

This doesn't mean counting is entirely "for the birds," although it is not difficult to hear disparaging words about the various systems and their advocates. One longtime gambler, Murray Friedkin, says of Thorp in *Big Julie of Vegas* by Edward Linn: "Thorp is the smartest man in the world; if you don't believe me, ask him . . . Whatever Thorp may say, I can tell you that if he has made any money on blackjack he made it by writing a book."

The late gambling expert John Scarne derided the counters and challenged Thorp to a $100,000 match at Blackjack. He later extended the challenge to other leading counting advocates. There were some nos, then yeses, then considerably more backing and filling; the Blackjack contest never came off.

Counting systems vary from advocate to advocate, so that it would be impossible to list any detailed standard version here. The principle, however, is quite simple. Since Blackjack is a nonreplacement gambling game, that is, cards that are played in a hand don't appear in later hands (until a reshuffling naturally), this makes it different from CRAPS or ROULETTE, in which the same number can reappear on the next play. In other words, the later games are replacement games with the full possibilities restored for every spin of the wheel or roll of the dice. Obviously, since cards go out of play, the situation is different in Blackjack, and certain cards favor the dealer and others the players, and there are times when it is better to increase your bet. High cards favor the player because, among other reasons, the dealer is required to hit on any score of 16 or less and if there is a preponderance of 10-point cards left in the deck, the dealer is much more likely to bust. Naturally, the same can be said of the players, but they have the ability to stand on 12 or more, especially when the dealer shows such upcards as a 5 or 6. So what a counter should do is keep track of the high card-low card ratio, and bet low when the deck is unfavorable and high when the deck is favorable to him.

Does it work? It should, and there is nothing really new about the basic concept. As long ago as the early 1900's gambling pros were counting the 10's, and John Scarne who used a sort of countdown system was himself barred from playing Blackjack in Vegas casinos in 1947, long before Professor Thorp showed up.

There is a ton of printed material on Blackjack and the usual GAMBLER'S BOOK CLUB catalog lists more than 60 books in every issue. Some of the best books with detailed discussions of counting are, besides, Thorp's main contribution: *Million Dollar Blackjack* by Ken Uston, *Playing Blackjack As a Business* by Lawrence Revere, *How to Win at Blackjack* by Stanford Wong, *Blackjack: A Winner's Handbook* by Jerry Patterson, and *Blackbelt in Blackjack* by Arnold Snyder. Several of these authors offer many more works on the subject as well. For an opposite view, however, one should also read *Scarne's Guide to Casino Gambling* by John Scarne, as well as *Scarne's New Complete Guide to Gambling.*

Studying all these books will not necessarily make you a successful counter, and indeed there is little reason to doubt one recent estimate that for every 200 Blackjack players in a casino no more than one is a real counter, and that among serious counters only one in 20 makes a success of it. The fact is that it is easy to tell people to keep track of all the cards, but doing it accurately and successfully in such a fast-moving game is another matter. Also would-be counters have little more restraint than the average gambler. "Is the dealer suspicious that I am counting?" they wonder. "Is he going to reshuffle the deck ahead of time?" Being human, they panic and bet when they shouldn't.

On a personal level I can say I play a fair amount of Blackjack at casinos, but I have never gone into counting seriously. I personally feel correct play is just about as good as any system devised. Not that it is a winning system, but you can do well with a run of luck. I do, however, count 10's to a very limited extent. I find a table with a few open seats and follow a few hands using my own version of the so-called law of averages, which admittedly really isn't there for a player. On average, 30 percent of all cards that turn up in a hand should be 10-pointers. Let's say there are five players in the game and together with the dealer 19 cards are played. If less than five cards are 10-pointers I get a little interested. I watch the next game and if it also produces a similar dearth of 10's I decide to get in for a quick hand. Admittedly, random dispersal of cards makes this not much of an edge, but I've found that when two hands in a row are short of 10-pointers the situation will tend to change in the next few games.

I sit down and play small, perhaps only $10. If I win and the 10's haven't run strong, I might try another hand. In the second game, if I lose the first hand I generally up my bet a bit and try to average it out to my advantage. In any event I don't hang

The usual rules in Blackjack in many European casinos allow non-seated players to "piggyback" their bets on other players' cards, an arrangement regarded by many counters as a gift from the gods. (Photo: Casinos Austria AG)

around long. I believe in hit and run because I consider—*I know*—Blackjack overall greatly favors the house. John Scarne estimated the house edge to be 5.9 percent, which puts it beyond the realm of acceptable gambles. Some counters insist the true house edge is only 1.5 (which of course makes it easier for them to justify a small swing of the advantage to the player by counting as proving their point). All I can say is show me that supposed low edge for the house and I'll show you some very astute Blackjack players who still go into the tank.

Along these lines, I don't understand why more Blackjack addicts, especially from the East Coast, don't head for the 21 tables in Europe rather than going to Vegas. The fare is about the same and counting is easier to get away with. The reason for this is a peculiarity in Blackjack betting that is common in many European casinos. You don't have to sit down to play the game. You can pick out another player and bet along with him, simply putting down your bet near his. This method of betting is in use in such French casinos as Deauville and Trouville in

Normandy but not in Divonne and some others. It is allowed in Baden Baden and other German casinos, in all the Austrian casinos, in Italy, in Belgium, and in England. The only limitation is that the regular player's bet and his supporters' bets all stay within the table maximum, which is seldom a problem. Some casinos, however, apply the maximums to each individual.

For a counter such a system is a positive dream. The counter does not bet *at all*, doesn't even "pay his dues," until he judges the cards to be in his favor. Then he strikes. On a recent trip I visited the casino in Baden Baden. I floated back and forth between a couple of crowded Blackjack tables until I saw a hand I couldn't believe. Twenty-five cards had been dealt out and only three were 10-pointers! I watched the next round and the ratio was only four out of 23.

I decided I'd seen enough and I had my player picked out. He was one who made the right bets, sticking when he was supposed to and drawing when it was the percentage move. I plunked down 200 marks, which happened to be the highest bet on the table. The first card my guy got was a queen and the dealer got the same. I cursed under my breath. My man and the dealer could both get 10-pointers and it would be a wash. Then my guy got an ace for Blackjack and the dealer got a 9. I won 300 marks. There were 22 cards dealt and 6 were 10's, but I decided to give it another whirl for 200 again, determined to leave the table either 500 (about $300 at the time) or 100 marks ahead. My player got 20 and the dealer busted out with 5-10-king.

As I was leaving the table I felt a hand on my arm. I had a bad feeling, but it was just a floorman informing me that another Blackjack table was opening in a moment. I nodded and told him I'd try a bit of ROULETTE, my favorite game. The Blackjack tables had seen the last of me for that night. I whiled away several hours with my wife at Roulette, winning only 85 marks all evening but deciding it had been a successful outing.

The purpose here is not to brag but to emphasize *discipline* as a way to count successfully at Blackjack. In a nonreplacement gambling game such as Blackjack the cards played in previous hands go out of play. It is different when flipping a coin for instance. If you flip it and get heads, the head is not thrown out of the game, but is "replaced" in the game. The odds do not change from 50-50 as to whether the next flip will be a head. Even after ten flips of heads in a row, the odds on the next flip are still 50-50 of another head or tail appearing. In Blackjack, the appearance of a huge and inordinate number of low-value cards makes it more probable that a larger number of high-value cards will appear in the next hand, or if they do not, then in the following hand or the one after that. This is the only time the odds turn in the player's favor and *this window of opportunity doesn't last long.* Few hustlers of counting systems inform people of this fact. Real counting of this sort is much more difficult in American casinos, where a player must sit down and play consistently. He cannot even pass up a hand to catch his breath. If he wants to do that, he has to surrender his seat. In European casinos he can play as a standee and strike when the cards turn, using a form of "the law of averages" to make a quick win. Then comes the most critical move of all—leaving the table. The odds change quickly at Blackjack, so that hit-and-run is the only system that can work.

We had our bags stashed at the train station and decided to catch a train for the Italian border with the idea of hitting San Remo, but we switched plans and kept going to Venice.

The winter casino at Venice is a nice place to visit, but I wouldn't want to play Blackjack regularly there. They have the same nonplayer betting rule, but a relatively high minimum and a very low maximum.

At the time the low was around $12 and the high ten times greater, approximately $120. Apparently this is the Italian answer to counters, and the casino must feel this keeps them away. That apparently was the reason supervision was lax, since I saw one man actually pulling a little instrument out of his pocket and working his thumb on it as the cards were played. Obviously it was a small computer of some kind, and in Vegas he would have been escorted out on the spot.

The man had some buddies with him and they had one player, a middle-aged woman playing for low stakes at one seat. She was a very good player and was winning even with the deck going against her. I decided to bet with her when the cards turned. They soon did, in accordance with my primitive technique, but the guy with the tiny computer was a bit slow getting a bet down. I had a $50 bet down with somebody's mom, I didn't know whose. Just then the guy signaled his friends to put in some bets. He was a little surprised and annoyed to see my bet in ahead of his, and mom had also upped her bet to the same amount. The guy said something to the dealer and the dealer did a very Italian yes-no routine, waved him on, and also let him bet $50. We were over the maximum and all the other spots were well covered.

Mom stood on 15 and that looked great since the Dealer's first card was a 5, but then he got a 6, for all, and the guy who had a moment ago resented me said something consoling, or maybe it was a prayer. The dealer figured to catch a 10-pointer, according to what was left in the deck, and we'd be dead. Believe it or not, he caught another 5 for 16, and then another 6 to bust out.

I took my winnings, and seeing mom turn around happily and kiss the guy who apparently was her son, I decided the chivalrous thing to do was leave. As it turned out, I didn't make another Blackjack bet that visit. I also lost about half my winnings at Roulette, but happily my wife had found a no-smoking Roulette table—do you know how hard it is to find a no-smoking spot in all of Italy?—and won so much that she wouldn't even tell me the amount.

Does Blackjack counting really work? You won't get a definitive answer from me. But honestly, using my amateurish technique, I manage to win small but pretty consistently—in almost any language.
See KEN USTON.

BLIND FIVE-CARD STUD
Players who feel Five-card Stud is too tame a game may well like Blind Five-card Stud, in which all the cards are dealt down.

How to play: After the first two cards are dealt each player looks at his cards and there is a betting round. On each round the betting is opened by the leader, the player to the dealer's left. There can be no checking—every player must cover the bet, raise, or drop out. The same procedure is followed after each round of cards is dealt. After five cards are dealt the highest hand wins.

Some professional gamblers hate this game because they are most adept at figuring out probabilities by seeing other players' upcards, but the fact remains that even in this game gambling discipline usually wins out. The successful gambler plays strictly according to the strategy that works in Five-card Stud. He drops if his first two or three cards offer him nothing. In a game of five or six players he bets two pairs aggressively because he knows he will win close to three-quarters of the time. He knows also that with the same number of opponents a pair of aces or kings will win appreciably more than they will lose. Conversely, he realizes a pair of jacks will only win a third of the time with five opponents and a quarter with six opponents. Generally, he follows the rule that if he has five opponents and he holds a pair, at least two other pairs are out there. Under those circumstances he will fold a pair of 10's or lower. Occasionally such strategy will cost him a pot, but the discipline one gains playing the percentages becomes money in the bank in the long run.

BLIND HOOKEY
See BANKER AND BROKER.

BLIND OPENING
See ENGLISH DRAW POKER.

BLIND STRADDLE
See ENGLISH DRAW POKER.

BLIND STUD: Five-card Poker Variation
While BLIND FIVE-CARD STUD is not entirely a "blind" game of POKER (players look at their own cards), Blind Stud is. Players may not look at their hole card until their hand is complete. The first is dealt down and then four cards are dealt up one at a time, with a betting sequence on each facing.

Some gamblers are frightened of this "blind" opening, thinking that the game has taken on a frantic quality. What they fail to grasp is that the game has remained virtually the same as regular Stud. The basic difference is that, in a manner of speaking, they have simply gotten their last card first.

Actually some high-stakes players love Blind Stud because it actually is a *more conservative* version of FIVE-CARD STUD, since there can be no bluffing until after the four upcards have been dealt. The game is sometimes played by simply dealing the hole card last, which is exactly the same thing.

The virtue of the game is that if a player wants to hang in on very little early, he sees exactly the opposing hands he is bucking. This blind game is so open that it is actually a good way for a novice to learn the probabilities of Five-card Stud and sharpen his general Poker skills.

BLUFF: Old Form of Poker
Bluff has been described as an obsolete form of Poker, but it is rising from the dead. Originally Poker was played as a 20-card game and 19th-century "Hoyle" guides speak of "Poker or Bluff."

How to play: the game is played with a maximum of four participants, the preferred number, who are dealt five cards from the 20-card deck limited to aces, kings, queens, jacks, and 10's. Bets, raises, and calls follow. There is no drawing of new cards, so the real action is trying to outbluff the other players. Since there are only five ranks of cards, everyone gets a hand worth something, but seasoned players realize that means "a little something is nothing."

Thus the game really revolves around the betting and the bluffing. This is an attractive situation for the competent player who knows when to bet and when to drop. It must be remembered that everyone winds up with at least a pair and at no time is any single pair, including aces, worth staying with. The usual winning hand is two pairs, and at least aces or kings up are necessary for betting with a degree of confidence. Three of a kind is a very powerful hand since by its very nature it almost eliminates the possibility of any other player having a straight. Flushes not need be feared since they are virtually impossible to draw. Actually the only flush is a royal flush and takes all. Naturally a full house and four of a kind are possibilities, but three of a kind is generally very, very good, and three aces call for strong betting.

There has been something of a comeback of Bluff, especially at those Friday night games before all the players show up. An interesting new wrinkle is playing the game as Stud, with the first two cards dealt down and three cards up and betting rounds after each upcard. This is an excellent way for the competent player to clean up, since he will drop after the first upcard and lose only his ante. Most poor players will stay on a three-card straight—the lowest possible hand at that stage in the game. A good player wants a pair to remain in the game. After the fourth card, this good player will stay only with at least a high pair so that he can be relatively sure of beating most other two-pair hands. If he holds kings and no aces are showing, he really gets worried because he fears someone has two hidden aces. If the player does not improve on his kings on the final card, his worry about the aces becomes moot because he leaves the game.

More so than in regular Poker the good player's edge comes in knowing when to drop, but with two pairs he must stay since on the last card the possible straights are dying. If a smart player draws three of a kind he proceeds on the basis that he is holding a powerhouse hand. He may be beat, but he is betting with the percentages, something most Bluff players don't do.

BOLIVIA, Gambling in

On the theory that a miner and his "gold" are soon parted, Bolivia declared all forms of gambling illegal in the mining sections of the country in 1930. Eight years later the ban was made nationwide. However, the government does run a highly successful state lottery, which has become an important source of income for the public treasury.

James BOND: World's Worst Roulette Player

Not long ago in a German casino two young men talking in a Swiss-accented German were sitting off to the side reading a French version of a James Bond novel, *Casino Royale*. They were, they were sure, going to beat the house at ROULETTE. Why not? Hadn't 007 done so? In fiction, yes.

The sad truth is that James Bond may well have been the world's worst Roulette player. Author Ian Fleming had done him wrong and in the process misled an unknown number of gambling novices. Following the reckless Bond technique these gamblers were putting great sums at risk for no reason whatsoever. They were betting 100-mark chips on the first 12 and second 12 numbers. Since the recent results were posted electronically, they were holding their heads in despair. The last ten spins had resulted in eight numbers over 24 and two zeros. This meant they were out 2,000 marks (about $1,200 at the time). Now they were doubling up on their bets and guess what came up . . . another zero!

It would have been a waste of breath to explain to them that they were making foolish bets. The will to believe is a key ingredient for a "system" bettor, and in this case the boys were following James Bond. If you can't trust 007, whom can you trust?

The sad truth is that one might trust James Bond on the elimination of enemy agents, on gourmet recipes, on drinks, and most especially on the seduction of women, but on Roulette—never.

In *Casino Royale* Bond's strategy works, but remember that it's Fleming who's spinning the wheel. In the long run Bond would have lost his shirt, betting in a way no serious Roulette gambler would. Bond decides to "play one of his favourite gambits and back two—in this case the first two dozens, each with the maximum—one hundred thousand francs. He thus had two-thirds of the board covered (less

the zero) and, since the dozens pay odds of two to one, he stood to win a hundred thousand francs every time any number lower than 25 turned up."

With Fleming telling the story, the results are remarkable. We are informed that out of seven bets Bond won six times. He lost on the last spin when 30 came up. Bond is happy because he is ahead by a half million francs. He lays off betting and naturally the zero comes up on the next spin, and we are told, "This piece of luck cheered him further . . ."

No doubt.

It's so easy to win in fiction. Bond can play stupidly and win and even dodge the zeroes. Let him try to do it in real play. (For that matter let him try to do math as he does in *Casino Royale*. Agent 007 would not have been ahead a half million francs. In a win-1, lose-2 form of betting he would have won six 1's and lost one 2, for a plus 4. However, we are not primarily concerned with Bond's lack of proficiency in basic arithmetic.)

Even if Bond's gambit of betting on 24 numbers was a good one, no serious Roulette gambler would do it 007's way, and certainly not when betting Bond-type stakes. Bond had stepped up to the table and plunked down two 100,000-franc bets on 1-12 and 13-24. A win on either of those wagers would bring a 2-to-1 payoff for 300,000 francs in all. But a serious player with more casino smarts than Bond would bet the same numbers *at considerably less risk*. If 007 had turned over his 200,000 francs to a real player, his action would have been laid down with some intelligence. First the expert would put 50,000 francs on *sixain* (*transversale simple*, or six numbers), 19-24. The payoff would be 5 to 1 on a win on any of these numbers, for a total return of 300,000 francs. Then an expert would wager the remaining 150,000 on *manque* (low numbers, 1-18). This is an even-money bet, so that the total return would also come to 300,000.

The trouble with Bond's play becomes apparent when the zero comes up. Since Bond bets on sequences of 12 numbers, his entire bet is lost when a zero appears, just as is the case when a player bets on any single number or combination of numbers. In the alternate "smart" way of betting, only the 50,000 francs on 19-24 is lost outright. The rest of the money bet on *manque* in a French or other European casino is imprisoned, meaning it is lost or released to the bettor depending on the outcome of the next spin. This is the mathematical equivalent of the player losing only one-half of his original wager. (See ROULETTE. In addition, it is a simple matter to assure the return of this half bet by wagering half the original sum the other way and putting a tiny insurance bet on zero in case it comes out twice in a row.)

The result of not betting the James Bond way is

that 75,000 francs can be saved by simply betting prudently. There are, as indicated earlier, much better bets at Roulette than covering 24 numbers. Bond is taking low odds and in Roulette the reason this is done is to get the house edge down as low as possible. Bond doesn't do that at all, producing a 2.70 percent house advantage—the highest possible in European Roulette. By comparison, betting on any even-money wager in European Roulette takes the house percentage down to 1.35. Even the way we have corrected Bond's naive play only gets the house edge down to about 1.80, meaning it is still not a smart wager.

Gambling, in short, is too serious a game to be left to amateurs like 007. Don't forget James Bond can get away with it because he's using Her Majesty's money. The average player has to use his own.

BONNETING: Robbing Gambling Houses

Throughout American history, legal and illegal gambling joints had to worry about being robbed. However, the early high-level houses in New York operated under the assumption that they were oases of refinement with no woes, and that they would need no more than their own housemen on rare occasions to handle an unruly gambler. A novice proprietor opening a new spot under that foolish assumption soon found out otherwise.

Gangs of ruffians attacked gambling joints in "bonneting" raids. Bonneting was originally a street-crime tactic whereby a gang of toughs would fall on a victim, jam his hat down over his eyes and then lift his money and valuables. If he resisted, the sightless victim was slugged into submission. When these bonneting boys took on gambling houses, they refined the technique and carried blankets, which they threw over the heads of the owner and his housemen. Moving with precision, they turned and knotted the blankets, so that the victims were almost totally incapacitated, able only to flail about and gasp for breath. The ruffians then sent the customers on the run and raided the joint's cashier booth. By the time their bonneted prisoners worked their way free, the raiders had fled with their loot.

These rowdies not only affected the house's profits but more disruptively frightened off well-behaved and well-heeled customers. The police were of little value in combating these gangs of criminals. Graft to the police only guaranteed against assaults from the forces of the law, not against such freebooting toughs whom the police were often too frightened to tackle.

The solution lay in the gambling joints matching force with force, and it was no accident that many houses soon were owned or partnered by professional boxers. Bouncers too were drawn from the pugilistic ranks, and the bonnet gangs were often waylaid even before they reached an establishment's door and given such severe beatings as to persuade them to stick to street-crime activities.

BOODLE: Variation of Michigan and Newmarket

Boodle is sometimes used as an alternate name for MICHIGAN and NEWMARKET, but it is applied by many players to cover a variation of these basic card games. Often this means adding two more Boodle cards that work the same way as the original four Boodle cards. In other cases Boodle cards in sequence are added to the game so that if, for example, the ten and jack of clubs represent a Boodle, a player must discard *both* of them to win the appropriate boodle money. This usually leads to a larger carry-over of boodle money for later deals. As a variation on that, any uncollected boodle money is simply divided among the players at the end of each hand.

Boodle rules vary greatly as there are any number of variations of play dictated by local custom.
See SPIN or SPINADO.

BOTTOM DEALING: Card-cheating Tactic

Cheating at cards does not require an entire repertoire of tricks. In fact, all that is necessary is one good gimmick. One such gimmick is bottom dealing, better known in hustler circles as "base" or "subway dealing."

Although bottom dealers will sometimes "stack" the bottom of a card deck to ensure a winning hand, a BOTTOM DECK offers about as much advantage. Still other dealers will use a confederate at the table. The dealer simply flashes the deck so that his accomplice sees the bottom cards, which he then identifies to the dealer through some sort of movement code. Three fingers extended on the left hand might indicate hearts, for instance, and a scratch on the right earlobe might indicate a card value of seven.

The two-man bottom dealing team can rake in big money—and rather inconspicuously. Let us say the boys are playing SEVEN-CARD HIGH LOW POKER. On the first deal the confederate indicates an ace on the bottom of the deck. The dealer deals it to himself, face down. Now he knows he has a good card for either high or low. The next bottom card is a king. The dealer sees an opponent with an 8. An 8 might be low, but a king will not help the opponent take a high hand. He deals out the king. Now the dealer holds an ace, 6 and 7. The new bottom card is a jack, a card the dealer doesn't want. He spots another player with a 3 showing, a possible low. He deals him the jack. Dealing himself honestly, the dealer draws a queen (which certainly does not help him). But the confederate signals that there is a deuce on the bottom. He deals himself the deuce, and he now

A.

B.

A bottom dealer moves the top card of the pack forward as though it is in the process of being dealt (A) but then drops his right thumb down to the bottom card (shown here in another design for clarity) which he has pulled forward with his remaining right fingers (B). At the same time his left thumb pulls the top card back to the deck. Bottom dealing is the easiest cheating move for a crooked dealer and requries much less dexterity than does second dealing. As a result, bottom dealing is more of a peril in low-stakes games. (Photos: E. Gerard)

has four cards to the low. The new bottom card is a 10 and his partner signals that he can use it. Since the confederate already has a 10 showing, the dealer can see why. The dealer takes an honest card himself and gets an 8, giving himself an 8 low, not a great low hand, but probably good enough because he intends to dump the next card if it is a high one on an opponent who looks like he has a chance for low. Instead a 4 appears on the bottom and the dealer wants it for himself, but his partner signals he must have the card. The dealer is not too pleased, although his 8-low appears to be good enough. With the 4 he would be 6-low and a sure-shot Jimmy. But his partner is very insistent, so he deals him the 4. His partner goes for high and the dealer for low. The eight-low is good enough and the accomplice has

10's full over 4's and takes the high. The boys take the whole pot.

Bottom dealing, according to practitioners, is much easier than dealing seconds. The dealer holds the cards in his left hand with three fingers on the side, index finger curled around the upper end, thumb almost touching the outer corner. This is known as the "MECHANIC'S GRIP" and puts professional gamblers on the alert. Few amateurs ever notice it, however. The finger and thumb of the right hand then grasp the bottom and the top card of the deck, respectively. Just as the right finger pulls out the bottom card, the right thumb drops down to it while the left thumb pulls back the top card, which has started to come off the top of the deck. It all happens in an instant and is extremely difficult to catch in a smoky room with other players more intent on the next card about to be turned over rather than on the deck itself.

BOTTOM PEEKING: Card-cheating Tactic

Bottom peeking works with BOTTOM DEALING and, sometimes eliminates the need for the bottom dealer's confederate. Instead of flashing the bottom of the deck to a second person, the dealer keeps his right hand arched over the deck as though at the ready to deal out the cards requested. The dealer's left hand seemingly holds the sides of the deck in a squared position. Then he slides his left hand back toward himself, bringing the bottom card with it. The right thumb lifts the end of the card so that he can make a quick read. If it is a card he can use, he leaves it there until his draw. If it is a card that does him no good, he bottom-deals it to another player and seeks again, continuing the process until he gets a good card. Bottom peeking is a relatively easy move

While apparently merely holding the deck the dealer is actually peeking at the bottom card and can then decide if he wants the ten of spades or if he will dish it off to an opponent in a bottom deal. (Photo: E. Gerard)

at DRAW POKER; as each player pauses to decide how many cards he wants, the dealer takes his pick.

PEEKING does not guarantee the crooked dealer a win every hand, but knowing the bottom of the deck surely tilts the odds in his favor. And because many bottom dealers adept at peeking know it is not wise to win too often on their own deal, they elect to work with a partner. Usually dealer and confederate sit next to each other so that the dealer's partner is the last to draw before the dealer. In this situation the partner can signal when he has, for instance, a four-card flush or possible straight and will indicate the card he needs. The dealer can keep bottom dealing until he finds the card. And if the dealer comes across a card that does his own hand a lot of good, he'll work his own hand and leave his partner on his own. The partner may very well fill with an honest draw, but if he does not, chances are the dealer will take the hand.

BOUILLOTTE: French Antecedent of Poker

The French game of Bouillotte is often cited as an antecedent of POKER, but it is really a quite primitive and simple form of the game now known as Poker.

How to play: Bouillotte is usually played as a four-man game with a deck of 20 cards, ranking ace, king, queen, 9, 8. All other cards are discarded. Each player is dealt three cards, and a common card, called the *retourne*, is centered on the table. Hands are bet more or less as in Poker, sometimes with a round of betting before the exposure of the *retourne* and always with a round of betting after it.

The highest possible hand would be a *brelan carre*, or four of a kind, including the *retourne*. The next highest hand is usually a *simple brelan*, three of a kind without the *retourne*. However, there is a special ranking just above the *simple brelan* called the *brelan favori*, three of a kind including the *retourne*. Thus three 9's beats three aces if the *retourne* is a nine.

Frequently no one holds a *brelan*, in which case the players expose their cards and each suit is valued in toto regardless of which players hold the individual cards. The *retourne* is counted as well. The ace is counted as 11, all face cards ten, and the others according to their spot value. The active player holding the highest card of the top-valued suit is the winner and takes the pot.

Strategy: Obviously a player holding two aces, one short of a *brelan*, would see the betting and might even press it, since if there was no *brelan* outstanding, he would hold high in at least two suits and have a 50-50 chance of winning on the two aces alone.

When only three players are available, the queens are dropped from the deck. With five players the queens stay and 7's are added to make a 24-card pack.

BOULE: "Poor Man's Roulette"

Very popular with the managements of French casinos and often called the "poor man's Roulette," Boule is more accurately referred to as "highway robbery, French style."

Boule is played in the lobbies of many French casinos, generally only a room away from genuine ROULETTE—a game in which the house percentage is a mere fraction compared to Boule. Nervous novice gamblers assume—erroneously—that because the game is played outside the casino proper, it is therefore a simpler, less risky game. Not so.

How to play: A rubber ball hurtles around a wooden bowl and comes to rest in one of 18 or 36 concavities, each marked with a number from 1 through 9. In the 18-cup version there are two positions per number. In the more common 36-cup version there are four positions to the number.

Players can bet on any of the nine numbers and winners are paid at 7 to 1. They can also make the same sort of even-money wagers that are available in Roulette, with one important variation. In French Roulette the zero results in the *en prison* rule on all even-money bets, whereby the wager is "captured" and held for another spin. If the wager then results in a win, the player gets his money back but no profit; otherwise he loses the entire wager. In Boule the number five replaces the zero on even-money wagers. Thus if a player bets on *Impair* (odd) he wins on 1, 3, 7, and 9. A player betting on *Pair* (even) wins on 2, 4, 6 and 8. In all cases the players lose on 5. Similarly, a bet on *Rouge* (red) gives a player the numbers 2, 4, 7, and 9, and a wager on *Noir* (black) covers 1, 3, 6, and 8. *Manque* (low) represents 1, 2, 3, and 4, and *Passe* (high) 6, 7, 8, and 9.

The number 5 is thus a thing of beauty for the casino, especially since Boule offers no *en prison* rule. All even-money bets are lost when the 5 wins. The result is that the house enjoys an advantage of 11.1111 percent on all bets. This compares with a 1.35 percent edge at Roulette. As a result a player can lose his money at Boule in about one-eighth the time needed

The Swiss Boule layout pays even worse odds than its French counterpart, already regarded by serious gamblers as a notorious gouge.

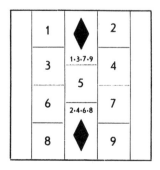

at Roulette. Clearly the rule of the house in French casinos is to get the money of the uninitiated quickly and send them on their way.

In point of fact virtually all casinos, even those sporting the lowest odds in most games, like to have one play for novices. Most American casinos lean to such gouges (aside from one-armed bandits, of course) as Big Six or various money wheels. In France generally Boule's the thing, although some establishments prefer Vingt-trois, really little more than a refinement of BOULE—with the same outrageous odds. See also VINGT-TROIS.

BOURRE: Modern Adaptation of Ecarte
Bourre is a nasty gambling game in which poor players can be suckered into losing big when they have little chance of winning.

How to play: Each of the two to seven players involved ante into the pot and are dealt five cards from a regulation 52-card desk. The cards are ranked as in POKER. After the five cards have been dealt, the next card is turned over to designate trump.

At this point players inspect their cards and can drop out if they figure their hand is too weak. Naturally the dropouts' antes are lost. The remaining players then may discard one to five cards, drawing new cards from the pack.

The player to the dealer's left leads to the first trick and others must match his card in suit. If they cannot, they must play a trump. If they are out of suit and trump, they may discard a different suit. The highest card of the suit takes the trick unless trumped, in which case the highest trump takes the trick. The winner of each trick leads to the next trick. The player or players taking the most tricks win or share the pot.

Up to this point this is a pretty simple game, but there are kickers that quickly separate the gambling men from the boys. Any player holding any of the three top trumps—ace, king, queen—*must* play them at the first opportunity. This often forces a lot of trumps out of the game early. A player who starts the game with the queen of trumps and perhaps a couple of aces may wind up not taking any of those tricks and in fact no tricks at all. In Bourre that is the road to ruin. Any player(s) who takes no tricks must add the *full* amount of that pot to the next deal's pot. This is a vicious hook because it forces some players with weak hands (or perhaps, more accurately, soft heads) to stay on into the next round when they don't have the cards to warrant doing so. However, the size of the pot sucks them in—especially if it is their money that makes up much of it—and suddenly they can be in a position of having to double again. Despite these pitfalls, it is not uncommon to see games with big pots in which players stay, draw five

new cards, and then are surprised at the awful luck of once again not catching a trick.

A good player must be heartless, know his opponents, and seek out games made up of those optimistic players who find it hard to drop and frequently make five-card draws. Given that, it's like shooting very fat fish in a barrel.

BOXING BETTING
In the 1930's and 1940's boxing was heavily bet on, probably totaling more than than $500 million annually. After that wagering on boxing took a nosedive, amounting to no more than 15 percent of that total. This was due partly to a falloff in the popularity of boxing, and moreso to a suspicion about the legitimacy of a number of prizefights both by the public and, more importantly, by most bookmakers, who refused (and many still do) to take action on most contests.

Lately there has been a pickup in betting on boxing due to the growth of the Las Vegas sports books at the major casinos. Nevertheless, overall betting is still much less than one would expect, especially allowing for inflation since the end of World War II, and most bookies limit their clients to no more than a $500 wager on any fight other than a championship bout. Many bettors follow the axiom of "always bet on the champion—he can only lose once." However, since champions tend to go off at high odds, one loss can put a dent in a bettor's bankroll and two or three can send him to the poorhouse. Also negating this system is the curious fact that some championships seem to be on a lend-lease shuttle, passing back and forth, often against the odds.

For many years organized crime had a lock on much of the boxing scene and dictated many results under the stewardship of Frankie Carbo, also known as Mr. Gray, whose other great claim to fame was that he was reputedly the gunner who popped off Bugsy Siegel (his longtime assassination buddy) on orders of top mobsters.

Only the appearance of the charismatic Muhammad Ali gave boxing a real shot in the arm in the last 2½ decades. Because he triggered so much interest in the game, some other fights have done well bettingwise, and today a big fight like Hagler-Hearns may draw more than $10 million in action. In the final analysis, boxing's heyday as a steady gambling sport is over. Bookmakers more readily place their faith in team sports and dumb horses than in boxers.

BOZENKILL RUM: Variation of 500 Rummy
A variation of 500 RUMMY geared to accommodate five or more players, Bozenkill Rum is a game in which each player is dealt hands of six cards instead of seven. However, it should be remembered that

two three-card melds with only six cards are quite hard to come by and the smart strategy in Bozenkill is to seek to feed the hand from the discard pile as rapidly as possible. The player who does so quickly will seldom do worse than his foes.

Colonel Edward Reilly BRADLEY: Florida's King of Gamblers

From 1898 to 1946, the most famous gambling entrepreneur in Florida was Edward Reilly Bradley (1859-1946), better known as Colonel Bradley. During those years Bradley ran the Beach Club in Palm Beach. Bradley always prized himself on being a professional gambler, and a successful one at that.

Born to industrious Irish immigrants in Johnstown, Pennsylvania, Bradley followed his father into the steel mills at the age of 13. A year of that was quite enough and he ran away, going west where he became a dishwasher. He always claimed he was a cowboy and a government scout in campaigns against the Apaches and that he took part in the capture of Geronimo. If Bradley lied about that it was one of the few times in his life when it could be said he had not been shooting straight.

In any event the Indian problem was settled and Bradley turned to what were to be the two great loves of his life—horses and gambling. He became a bookmaker in Arkansas and later in Memphis, Tennessee. Periodically he went stone broke and was back doing dishes until he got another stake and built up his bookmaking business again. Finally a success, he moved on to take action at bigger tracks in the Midwest and East. In 1890 he started a racing stable, Idle Hour Farm, and his horses won the Kentucky Derby four times during his lifetime.

Eventually, Bradley gave up the bookmaking business for the more lucrative field of gambling casinos. He moved to Florida and with his brother John ran the Bacchus Club for the eccentric Standard Oil millionaire and Florida hotel builder Henry Morrison Flagler. Flagler had an idiosyncrasy about hotel development. When he built one, he always erected two other buildings nearby—a house of worship and a house of chance. Presumably, one brought in the family trade and the other the monied trade. The Bacchus Club thus was a companion structure for both the Ponce de Leon Hotel and the Memorial Presbyterian Church in St. Augustine. When Flagler built the Royal Poinciana in Palm Beach, up went the Royal Poinciana Chapel and the Beach Club Casino. Four years after it was built in 1894, Bradley took over the Beach Club and turned it into the most important gaming house in the state.

Outwardly, the Beach Club was not much to look at, nothing more than a slightly large frame house. At first it had only four ROULETTE tables and one HAZARD game. But it was big enough for its clientele because Bradley restricted admission to men in evening clothes who appeared at least 25 years of age and could hold their liquor. Women and locals were strictly barred. At the end of one year, Bradley discovered he was losing money and decided he had to change his approach. Despite Flagler's opposition, the Colonel decided to admit women. Over the years Flagler became more straitlaced about gambling and is said to have offered Bradley $350,000 to close down the Beach Club and take his gambling activities elsewhere. Bradley refused and an angry Flagler brought in shrill preachers at the Royal Poinciana Chapel to castigate Bradley's activities from the pulpit.

Nothing worked, the Beach Club flourished, and by 1912 Bradley found he needed to expand his establishment. The old building was replaced by a much larger one sporting an octagonal gaming room. It may be that Bradley's new place was not quite as lavish as Richard Canfield's Saratoga Club House, but it wasn't far off and his dining room served some of the finest food to be found in the South. Many of the "400" thought it was reasonable enough to drop $50,000 at Bradley's tables after partaking of his master chef's rendition of turtle soup and Florida lobster.

The gambling was scrupulously honest and Bradley paid top dollar to his employees to guarantee that none of them would try to cheat the well-heeled clients. Staffers were paid the then unheard-of salary of $50 a day. They lived in a separate building called "the Barracks" with complete board and were not allowed to mix with the clientele even while off-duty. However, the staff drew no pay until the final day of the three-month season, when they got all their money and usually a 10 percent bonus, and were then sent home for the rest of the year. Almost all of Bradley's staffers stayed on the job for at least 25 years, so lucrative was this arrangement.

In 1923 Bradley added CHEMIN DE FER to his game roster and soon the stakes in that game proved to be greater than those offered generally at Monte Carlo. Big spenders like Harry F. Sinclair, Joshua Cosden, Harry Payne Whitney, John Studebaker, J. Leonard Replogle, and George Loft won or lost thousands in one evening. Studebaker dropped $200,000 one night at Roulette and shrugged it off.

Next to Flagler, Bradley was the best-known figure in the social history of Palm Beach. As the *New York World* was to note: "The real reason for the popularity of Palm Beach is not its climate or its hotels; it is Bradley's."

The local papers thought highly of him also. Perhaps that could be explained by the fact that Bradley owned both the *Palm Beach Post* and the *Palm Beach Times,* the former through a bankruptcy sale and the latter in payment of a gambling debt.

Bradley, like many a storied gambler—and less among most real-life ones—was generous with his money. He contributed much not only to his own Roman Catholic Church but to those of other denominations as well. After the great hurricane of 1928 he paid for the rebuilding of all battered churches in the area, including those in which he had been soundly denounced from the pulpit.

Bradley survived repeated campaigns against gambling, and when he and his brother were arrested for promoting gambling, the case was dismissed by the grand jury. After that the state turned a blind eye to activities in Palm Beach until finally in 1937 the governor ordered that gambling be terminated statewide. However, other state and local authorities simply decided that such a prohibition did not apply to the Colonel.

Bradley died in 1946, and under the terms of his will the Beach Club was torn down and the gambling equipment sunk in the Atlantic. Probably the Colonel would have mourned the fact that Flagler was no longer around to pay him a bounty. The grounds were turned over to the town of Palm Beach, which converted the property into Bradley Park.

The Beach Club had had the longest run of any illicit gambling casino in the United States, 48 years, which was said by gambling authority John Scarne to be "ample proof that he ran a percentage game, not a crooked one."

But perhaps the finest tribute to the Colonel came from former Ambassador Joe Kennedy, John F. Kennedy's father, reflecting on Palm Beach: "When Bradley went, this place lost its zipperoo."

BRAG: British Ancestor of Poker
Justifiably considered to be the British ancestor of POKER, Brag was England's most popular card game in the 16th century, and it is still widely played there today. How to play: It is a three-card-hand game played like Poker, although there are many variations. The most common does not accept straights or flushes.

Dealing and betting is the same as in DRAW POKER and only three of a kind or a pair are recognized winning hands. If no one wins, the deal rotates and the pot builds with another ante. There are three wild cards, or "braggers": the ace of diamonds, jack of clubs, and 9 of diamonds, which rank in that order in deciding ties. In hands of equal value natural three-of-a-kind of paired hands rank over those utilizing wild cards and the braggers themselves rank as listed above.

Because several deals can pass without a winner, some impatient gamblers make the black twos wild as well.

There is a variation of the game more often played in the United States called AMERICAN BRAG, in which all jacks and 9's are wild and are of equal rank. An additional difference in this game is that a pair or

three of a kind formed with wild cards outrank naturals. As a result American Brag is a more wide-open game and pots seldom build up nearly as much as in regular Brag.

BRAGGING
See PINCHING.

BRAZIL, Gambling in
Except for betting on horse races, mainly in Sao Paulo and Guanabara, gambling in Brazil is technically illegal. It is, nevertheless, widespread. For instance, a numbers game, called *bicho*, is absolutely illegal and yet bets can be placed anywhere in the country. And gambling at cards, it seems, is a national addiction—despite a ban on the importation of good-quality cards. The local products are inferior and imperfections make it easy for cheats to doctor them. As a result a prosperous industry has sprung up smuggling American cards into the country.

A true story is told about one brilliant card-smuggling plot that turned the perpetrator into a very rich man, one who later took residence in a fabulous villa atop a hill in Rio de Janeiro. He decided to shoot the works by bringing in one million packs of cards in one swoop, knowing full well that the entire shipment would be grabbed by Brazilian customs at the point of entry. All confiscated goods are then auctioned off publicly, and the government saw no reason not to do so in this case since the packs were all worthless. Each, it developed, lacked the ace of spades. The cunning smuggler had arranged for the New York supplier to remove all the aces from the consignment. Where were they? Already in Brazil, having breezed right through customs earlier. The smuggler had brought them in openly and was not challenged because aces of spades alone do not make a deck of cards. The smuggler had explained he was importing the cards to lay them in cocktail furniture tops, which would then be exported to the United States. When the incomplete decks were seized and auctioned, the smuggler entered a tiny bid for them. Not surprisingly, there were no other bids for such worthless decks. The government was pleased to get something for them. After the aces were reinserted, the cards all sold at premium black-market prices and made the ingenious smuggler a millionaire.

There are several state lotteries in Brazil, with the profits going to charity. Lotteries held on religious holidays generally have much bigger prizes.

BRIDGE: The Fashionable Gambling Game
Although there have been a great many books written about Bridge, it is far from the most-played card game in America, ranking well below POKER and RUMMY. Contract Bridge, which is now simply called

Bridge, is the most popular form and is the game played by the "ultrafashionables"—the habitues of Newport, Palm Beach, etc. But it is also played by people in every walk of life and with every sort of background. For people who take the game seriously there are Bridge clubs and tournaments and there are many who play the game at home or with friends and would be shattered if they missed their weekly game, often played only for small stakes. Bridge, however, is also played for monumental stakes and almost anyone who has wagered heavy money has undoubtedly (if unwittingly) sat at a table with a Bridge hustler or cheater. Gambling authority John Scarne held that "due to its partnership aspect, more cheating takes place at Bridge than at any other card game."

Contract Bridge evolved from Auction Bridge, a game for two two-person teams, which in turn, was derived from the centuries-old English game of WHIST. A full pack of 52 cards is dealt out, 13 to each player. The auction or bidding for the privilege of naming trump is opened by the dealer and continues until three successive players pass the bid, the trump having been established by the final bidder. The bidder plays both his own and the face-up hand of his partner (the "dummy"). Thirteen tricks of four cards each are played, the first six constituting the book, the seventh making a one-bid, the eighth a two-bid, and so on. Scoring involves a complex system of point values, bonuses, and penalties, 30 or more points are a game, two of three games a rubber, counting 250 points.

Contract Bridge developed out of Auction Bridge in the 1920s. It is similar to Auction Bridge except that: 1) only the number of tricks bid counts toward game, regardless of how many more are taken; 2) the suit count carries different point values; 3) game is 100 points; 4) winning a game makes the side vulnerable and increases its bonuses and penalties; 5) rubber counts 700 or 500 (made in two or three games); 6) tricks over the bid receive bonuses; 7) honors must be in one hand. Contract Bridge is the game used in many tournaments, some international. Bidding "systems" abound, all seeking to provide the best contract for the cards held.

In wagering, Bridge is usually played for small stakes, although there have been big bets frequently made on challenge matches. The two most famous matches, which attracted worldwide attention and could be said to have put Bridge on the map, were played by Ely Culbertson's team against teams of Sidney Lenz and Hal Sims. Culbertson won both and became the most highly regarded Contract Bridge player in the world.

Cheating at Bridge is done mainly for money, but sometimes only for prestige. Some years ago Hollywood was ripped off by a Bridge scandal in which millions were bilked from Hollywood celebrities, one movie mogul losing a quarter of a million dollars in a single year. This was a high-tech swindle making full use of the current state of the art, involving ceiling holes, telescopes, and secret listening devices. The "spy in the sky" sent messages to confederates in the game via radio transmitters strapped to their legs. It is not uncommon in international tournaments for a nation's team to accuse another of using hand signals.

The literature on Bridge strategy is huge, with hundreds of books focusing on the entire game or just certain aspects of play. It would be useless to attempt to condense their findings here, and indeed, assembling of a limited bibliography would necessarily suffer from errors of omission. Any listing of recommended readings would have to include: *Modern Auction Bridge* by Ernest Bergholt; *Compete Auction Bridge* by Wilbur C. Whitehead; *Contract Bridge and Advanced Auction Bidding* by Geoffrey Mott-Smith; *The Art of Successful Bidding* by George Reith; *Contract Bridge Made Easy* by Charles H. Goren; *Contract Bridge Complete* by Charles H. Goren; *Contract Bridge Self-Teacher* by Ely Culbertson; *Contract Bridge Complete; The Gold Book* by Ely Culbertson; *Bridge the Expert Way*, by Albert H. Morehead; *Play Bridge Tonight* by Edwin Silberstang (clear and simple for novices); *Kempson on Contract* by Ewart Kempson. For the best account on Bridge cheating, see *Scarne's New Complete Guide to Gambling* by John Scarne.

BRIDGE ADDICTS: Anything for a Game

Like POKER addicts, Bridge has its share of ardent followers. Only one story need be told to portray the "shut up and deal" instincts of Bridge addicts.

Paula, a young woman, died tragically young. At the funeral were her three grieving Bridge partners as well as another young woman, a friend of the deceased, who had accompanied one of the trio to the funeral. The four tearfully reminisced about Paula until finally one of the Bridge regulars turned to the other woman and asked, "By the way, do you play Bridge?"

"BRUSH OFF": Warning to Card Cheats

One should never assume that in a casino or legal California POKER parlor a house priority is the prevention of cheating. The fact is these houses have very little incentive for stopping cheaters, aside from stopping their establishment from getting a bad reputation. After all, when a casino or card room handles a Poker game, it is merely collecting a fee for running the game. When a cheater steals, he is not taking the house's money. So it all comes back to the house's rep, and a sad wrinkle develops. If the house makes a big deal out of catching cheaters and even goes so far as to prosecute them, it is simply advertising the fact that the establishment is rife with crooks and hustlers.

As a result, such houses prefer to get rid of the hustlers on the q.t. When a crooked player's actions get too obvious, a houseman will step up behind him and give him the "brush off" by unobtrusively brushing his thumb down the player's back. This is an age-old warning to a cheat that he has been spotted and that he should get out. Naturally the cheat takes the hint and leaves—with, unfortunately, a healthy portion of the unsuspecting players' money.

BUCK DICE: Three-dice Bar Game

A very popular bar game often played for a round of drinks instead of money, Buck Dice is a three-dice game for as many players as wish to play. Each player first rolls a single die to establish his "point" and then each takes his turn with three dice. A shooter continues to throw the dice as long as he produces his point on at least one dice on each roll. When a three-dice roll does not produce a point, the turn passes to the next player.

Each time a player makes his number he scores a point. The object is to reach a total of 15. The game continues until there is only one loser. A throw of three of a kind of the player's point automatically scores the full 15 points and is called *big buck*. Should a player roll any other three-of-a-kind number he has hit *little buck*, which is worth five points. In a common variation of the game, when a shooter reaches 13 points he is allowed to throw only two dice and when he hits 14 only one die.

The only edge a hustler can get at this game is to volunteer to shoot first, inferring the game is dead even. Actually, the first shooter enjoys a slight advantage. The fair approach is that the order of shooting be determined by the point values established at the beginning of the game.

"BUCKING THE TIGER": Faro Gambling Saying

The term "bucking the tiger" dates back to the early days of the American West when FARO was virtually the number one gambling game in the country. Western saloons and gambling joints that offered Faro signaled this by displaying a large sign featuring a picture of a tiger. Thus the term bucking the tiger described a gambler trying to beat the house at Faro— a feat, considering the general crookedness of the game, far more difficult than facing a genuine tiger. With the decline of Faro the term came to describe a compulsive or, as the gambling fraternity prefers, any "degenerate" gambler.

BULGARIA, Gambling in

As is true in most Iron Curtain countries private betting and gambling is technically illegal, but nevertheless common. Bulgaria does permit gambling casinos at its Black Sea resorts, where Western Europeans, especially Germans, enjoy betting action.

For public morale the country operates a state lottery—although the payoffs don't include million-dollar cash awards. All things considered, the lottery prizes offered are perhaps worth much more than money, consisting of such scarce consumer goods as television sets, automobiles and, perhaps best of all, apartments.

BULL POKER: Seven-card High-Low Variation

Bull Poker is a variation of SEVEN-CARD HIGH-LOW STUD that allows a player to sling a little "bull" about his hand. Unlike other Seven-card Stud games, players are given the first three cards down and they may arrange them in any order they wish. Once they have done so, however, they must leave them in that arrangement for later exposure in that order.

The next four cards are dealt up one at a time as is usual in Stud, with a betting round after each. Then the first of each player's down cards are exposed and there is more betting. This is repeated with the second down card and there is showdown betting before the final turn-up.

Each player hopes the arrangement of his three down cards has helped him bull his opponents by concealing his hand. Obviously if his three down cards contain a pair, one is played as his seventh card. More often, the three cards are arranged in such a way as to help conceal a low hand. If a player is dealt a 7, 3, 2, he will have undoubtedly arranged them in that fashion, hoping to have filled in a low hand with his face cards.

BULLFIGHTING, Gambling on

Bullfighting has been popular for millennia. The ancient Greeks and Cretans were devotees and apparently wagered heavily on the sport. The Romans imported bullfighting and it gained a great following in patrician circles. Today bullfighting commands a strong following in Spain and Mexico.

Betting—legal or illegal—is conducted with practically no attempt at subterfuge. Program and drink vendors at bullfighting arenas hustle through the crowds, offering the odds given by their respective bookmakers. Betting is usually based on which of the day's matadors will be judged to have killed his bull in the finest of styles.
See SPAIN, GAMBLING IN.

BULLOCK-TAYLOR, V.

See JEFFERSON RANDOLPH "SOAPY" SMITH.

BURNING A CARD: Protection Against Cheating

It is customary in many games to "burn a card," or take a card out of play. In BLACKJACK, for instance, after the cards are shuffled and cut, the dealer burns the top card by showing it to all players and then placing it face up on the bottom of the deck.

In high-stakes games, especially STUD POKER, burning a card has become a common occurrence. The top card is burned at the start of each turn, the saying being "you burn one and turn one." This is done as a safeguard against cheaters since, most professional gamblers insist, burning and discarding the top card cuts down on about 90 percent of all possible cheating since marked or stacked cards won't work for a scam artist when the top card is burned.

BUTTON: Casino Poker Dealing Method

In Nevada casinos, there is a house dealer for all POKER games. He does not take part in the game, but rather is there to keep the dealing honest and to see that "the *pot is right*," etc. Since he takes turns dealing for each gambler consecutively, a button is placed in front of the player to signify that he is the dealer of record. The button proceeds around the table clockwise on each succeeding game.

BUY-INS: Minimum Stake in Poker Game

As a general rule, especially in casino or card room play, a player must have a minimum stake to get into a POKER game. The amount of the stake changes according to the particular minimum and maximum betting limits of the house. Generally casinos and California card rooms require a buy-in of ten times the minimum bet. Thus in a $1-$2 game $10 is required. The Nevada casinos set low buy-ins to encourage players to enter the game. Ten times the minimum is hardly enough for sustained action. Serious Poker players seldom enter a game without at least 60 times the minimum, or at least 40 times the maximum bet permitted. The only time a serious player will go into a game with a small buy-in is when he is short of cash and is hoping to build a quick poke with a lucky first game or two.

See also TABLE STAKES.

CALABRASELLA: Italian Antecedent of Skat

Calabrasella can be considered an Italian antecedent to the German game of SKAT, with a touch of CASINO to it.

How to play: A fast game, it is for three players and uses a 40-card deck with the 8's, 9's, and 10's removed. The card rankings are unusual, going from 3 (high), deuce, ace, and then king to 4 in descending order.

The object of the game is to take tricks that contain value or "counter" cards, but there is no *trump* suit involved. Aces are worth 3 points and the 3's, deuces, kings, queens, and jacks, 1 point each, making a total of 32 points. Players are dealt 12 cards each and the remaining four cards are faced down as a *"widow."* The player to the left of the dealer looks at his cards and decides whether he can beat his two opponents' combined score in points taken. In addition to the counter cards totaling 32 points, 3 more points are gained by taking the final trick.

If the first player decides he cannot "stand," that option is passed to the next player. If all three players refuse to stand, the hand is thrown in and the deal passes. If a player stands, he must discard one to four cards from his hand and replace them from the widow. The player to the left of the stander then leads any card to the first trick, and others are required to follow suit if they can. Highest card takes the suit and leads to the next trick. The taker of the last tricks gets the discards and the remaining widow cards, if any.

The stander then adds up his points. If he has a total of 18 or more, he has won and collects the amount of difference between his score and that of the others' combined scores. For example, the stander gets 20 points, and his opponents 15. The stander collects 5 points or chips from *each* opponent, winning 10 in all. Conversely if he gets 16 points and

loses 19, he is 3 points in the hole and pays out a total of 6 points or chips. When the scoring is in points, the game is usually played to 100, with settlement made at that time. Otherwise, the payoff is made after each hand. If a stander takes all the counter points in the game as well as the final trick, he collects double or 70 points from each foe; if he takes none, he gives each 70.

Strategy: Calabrasella is not a game for the risk taker, and one should stand on his original hand, and never count on getting any support from the widow. The winner is most likely the player who best remembers the fall of the cards and thus more easily reads the hands of his opponents.

CALAMITY JANE
See HEARTS—BLACK LADY.

CALIFORNIA—Legalized Lotteries

When California joined the state lottery parade in the 1980s, there was a shudder of earth-shaking proportions in Las Vegas. The feeling was that the lottery was such a big thing and that it would siphon off so much money that the Nevada casinos would be ruined. It didn't happen, of course. In fact, the Vegas casinos went on to establish new earning marks. Lottery money and casino money were clearly shown to be poles apart. What a Californian might be willing to wager in a big payoff lottery for a dollar with a 50 percent takeout and what he lugged to Nevada for the CRAPS tables with a 1.4 percent or less takeout were two different matters. The gag in Vegas went that the casino operators were glad, perhaps even astounded, to discover that Californians could count!

At its inception California's lottery was limited to instant games (with numbers and LOTTO in the offing), with 50 percent being returned to ticket winners, 16 percent going to administration, and 5 percent for agent commissions. The remaining 34 percent was slated for public education. Because California is one of the richest and largest states, it was predicted that the lottery would produce tons of money, and it did.

Instant games, changing every two months or so, were of the rub-off type that indicates the amount won. The overall odds for winning were about 1 in 9. In the first game there were 40 million $2 winners, close to 5 million $5 winners, 100,000 $1,000 winners, and 10,000 $5,000 winners. Winners of $100 prizes are also eligible for grand-prize drawings in weekly drawings for prizes of $10,000, $50,000, $100,000, $1 million, and $3 million.

California seems to be the most zealous state in seeing to it that winners pay off back debts before collecting. One man won $1,000 and saw it all garnished by the state for back child-support payments. In the very first month of operation 60 lottery winners saw their winnings go to wipe out some $94,000 in debts.

A number of Mexicans in California who won prizes were identified as illegal aliens and were deported—along with their prize money. The same happened to an Egyptian who won $1 million. A sharp-eyed Immigration and Naturalization Service officer recognized him as an alien and out he went, but it cannot be recorded that the man left unhappily.

CALIFORNIA JACK: Two-person Gambling Game

An exciting gambling game for two with considerable skill required, California Jack, sometimes called California Loo, is played with a full pack of 52 cards.

How to play: cutting the deck determines the trump suit. Each player is dealt six cards and the rest of the deck is squared up and placed *face up* on the table. The nondealer leads with any card and the dealer must follow suit or trump the card. If he does not hold the suit, he has the option of either trumping or playing a side suit.

The winner of the trick takes the top exposed card from the pack and the loser takes the next one. The winner has the advantage here because he sees his card in advance and knows if he wants it. If he does not, he might very well lose the trick so that he will get the blind card instead. The winner of each trick leads on the next one, and play continues until all cards have been exhausted.

Points are totaled by awarding one point for high (the ace of trump), one for low (deuce of trump), one for jack (of trump), and one for game, which is determined by adding the score of the cards taken on the basis of each 10 being worth ten; each ace, four; each king, three; each queen, two; each jack,

one. Note that the total score for game is just one point in the overall score.

The game continues until one player accumulates 10 points overall (sometimes the winning total is 7). The game is usually paid on a set wager or on a point-spread difference between winner and loser.

The key to winning at California Jack is to hold both strong and weak cards in one's hand at all times. This is important when considering the exposed card on the stock. If it is valuable, a player will want to use a good card to try to take it. If it has no value, he will try to expend a losing card so as not to be stuck with it and allow his foe to take the blind card, which might well be a good one. Obviously, aside from the valuable trump cards, the most important cards in the decks are the 10's, followed by the aces, etc.

California Jack may be played by three or four players also, but it is better with just two. When three players are involved, the 3's are removed from the deck so that the hands will come out even, with a total of 48 cards.

Shasta Sam is a variation of the game, but one that is eschewed by California Jack devotees. In Shasta Sam, the remaining deck is faced down so that the winner of the trick does not know what he may get. This makes the game more one of luck than of skill.

CALL BETS: Verbal Wagers in Casino Play

It should never happen, but there are casino cheats who get away with it every once in a while, especially in smaller casinos eager for action. In some downtown Las Vegas casinos one may play quarter CRAPS and it is possible to cover all the numbers except the shooter's point by betting $6.50 if he needs a 6 or 8 ($6.75 is needed in other cases).

A player rushes over to the table and just as the shooter is about to release the dice, the newcomer yells out: "Six fifty on the numbers."

If the dealer inadvertently replies, "You're covered," the hustler has the house in a stranglehold. If the shooter on the next roll throws a 7, the newcomer loses and immediately hands over $6.50 to the dealer. However, if the next roll is any of the place numbers other than the shooter's point, the newcomer lets out a chortle as he plunks down $650 and collects on a $100 or $120 bet.

There is nothing the house can do if the dealer, caught up in the play, has replied, "You're covered," without determining the size of the wager. The bettor is entitled to collect on his "call bet." That is why Craps layouts carry the statement "NO CALL BETS." Still, despite such warnings, the house can be swindled with a call bet once in a while.

CALOOCHI: Double-deck Rummy Variant

Most popular in the eastern United States, Caloochi, sometimes called Kaluki or Kalougi, follows the basic rules of RUMMY with some important exceptions. The game is played with two 52-card decks plus four jokers by two, three, or four persons, four making the best possible game.

How to play: Players are dealt 15 cards each. The ace, which may be melded in sequence over the king and under the deuce, is worth 15 points (11 under alternative rules). Picture cards are 10 points and all other cards carry their spot value. Jokers are wild and their point value is determined by that of the card it is replacing in sets (three or four cards of the same rank such as jack-jack-jack) or in sequences (such as jack, queen, king, ace in the same suit). However, if a player is caught with an unmelded joker in his hand it counts for 25 points.

To lay down cards players must make a meld or melds totaling 51 points or more. Until he has melded, a player may not take the top discard, or lay off on an opponent's melds. However, he may take the discard if that provides him with enough for his initial meld. If a player uses a joker in a meld, another player—on his turn before he melds and discards—can claim the joker for his own hand by substituting the natural card in its place. Occasionally a player will lay down three or four jokers as a set and get credited for 15 points for each. Realistically, there is hardly a situation in which jokers played separately would not produce better results.

The game ends when a player lays down all his cards in melds or lays off a card or cards against a foe's melds. He may use a final card as a discard or in his melds, as is best for him. All the points left in opponents' hands are scored for the victor as well as his own points. If the winner scores Caloochi, which is playing down all his cards on one turn, he collects double. A Caloochi is obviously one situation in which a meld of jokers does make sense.

Because the point scores can vary greatly and produce unusually large losses, some gamblers prefer playing Caloochi with small stakes. The winner collects one chip from each player for each card still in his hand. If a player is holding jokers he must pay two chips for each. Double payoffs for scoring a Caloochi still may apply.

Caloochi can be played with five or six players as well. For five, each player gets 13 cards; for six, 11 cards. As stated previously, however, games of these sizes are not ideal and skill becomes less of a factor.

CAMBODIA, Gambling in

For several years there has been a state lottery in Cambodia, but all other forms of gambling are pro-hibited. An exception is made for casino gambling, which is restricted to foreigners, although it has been reported that wealthy locals seem to have no difficulty in crashing the action.

CANADA, Gambling in

Officially, Canada is gambling-free except for horse-race betting through totalizators and certain small-scale lotteries for charity. But anti-gambling squads have a hard time squashing all elements of illicit gambling, from bookmaking to illegal casinos and slot joints. It seems operations founded as social clubs mask a good number of Canadian gambling operations.

In recent years government-run lottery games have been started. The games are identical in each province and carry the same odds. However, the individual provinces market the tickets in the way they prefer. Lottery games in Canada are exempt from Canadian taxes, but Americans who cross the border to place bets find they are subject to those U.S. taxes.

CANADA BILL

See WILLIAM "CANADA BILL" JONES.

CANADIAN DRAW: Poker Variation

Canadian Draw is a POKER variation in which the player may open betting on a four-card flush or a four-card straight as well as the standard DRAW POKER openers. In the showdown a four-card flush beats a four-card straight and both outrank a pair but lose to two pairs. In that sense the game merely makes standard Draw Poker a little more wide open. However, serious Poker players consider CANADIAN STUD more challenging because it requires greater skill in determining the odds for staying or dropping. Canadian Stud is considered *the* game for experts only.

CANADIAN STUD: Five-card Poker Game

This game is considered by many gamblers to be the most demanding of all POKER variations, requiring more skill than any other. The rules are basically the same as those of standard FIVE-CARD STUD except that a bobtail, or open-end, straight (such as 8-9-10-Jack) beats a pair and a four-card flush tops a four-card straight. In another variation of this game, NEW YORK STUD, the flush is the only four-card hand that counts—four-card straights are out.

Canadian Stud is not a gambling-house play, but it is possible to find the game at many Caribbean island resorts, often in private games at casino hotels. Unless a player is a superb Poker player he will generally be eaten alive in such games. It takes a keen mathematical mind to determine the winning possibilities, especially those of the four-card variety.

CANASTA

See FIVE HUNDRED RUMMY.

Richard A. CANFIELD: Gambling House Operator

Some authorities described Richard A. Canfield (1855-1914) as the most successful gambler America ever produced. It was probably true because, it was said, he never gambled in his life, or at least not after he reached his majority. Canfield operated gambling houses, some perhaps the most lavish in the country, and one referred to as America's Monte Carlo. But he never gambled privately and thus always had the odds running in his favor. It was almost as though gambling bored him.

It hadn't bored him in his youth, however. He was a betting fool while working at summer jobs in resort hotels in and around his native New Bedford, Massachusetts. After five years of that, at the age of 18, he set up a small POKER joint in Providence, Rhode Island. It didn't take him long to realize that the skimming of pots by the house was so lucrative that in fact often *none* of the gamblers ended up ahead. This was when Canfield decided gambling represented a true growth field. He decided to study the phenomenon by traveling to Europe to see how the Europeans gambled—and, more important, who made money from it. In pursuit of this higher form of education, Canfield tried his luck at the gaming tables in Monte Carlo. Needless to say, he did not make a fortune. In fact, he concluded that all gambling games were profitable to the house simply because of the edge built into them, and that in the long run the edge had to make the house the winner over any gambler, no matter how skilled he was.

Returning to the United States, Canfield had big plans but still a rather limited bankroll. Complicating that was the fact that the Providence police proved as grasping as those in such "sin capitals" as New York, Chicago, and New Orleans and quickly declared themselves his silent partners. When Canfield couldn't and didn't pay since he needed all his profits as future capital, the police shut him down and he actually served a jail term.

In 1886 Canfield headed for New York, where the gambling money flowed freely, and if the police and politicians were just as grasping, there was nevertheless more money to go around. His first venture was a Poker room, started in part with borrowed capital. He soon realized this was not the road to Monte Carlo and that he would have to strive for a more opulent style. He borrowed more money—society gamblers liked him and considered him a safe investment—and moved into an exclusive area, near Delmonico's restaurant and Madison Square. Canfield hoped to draw his clients from the city's leading hotels, clustered in that downtown district. The gaming house proved an instant hit.

In 1890 Canfield bought out his partners and over the ensuing decade opened several new houses. He launched the Saratoga on East 44th Street, pumping more than $1 million into the place. The brownstone house, which in time only the elect entered through huge bronze doors, was exquisitely furnished, with valuable paintings, etchings, ancient pottery, and rich tapestries. One of the gaming rooms had teak flooring and walls lined in Spanish leather, hand-tooled in gold. Canfield employed chefs who rivaled the skills of those at Delmonico's, and every night Lucullan suppers were served with rare-vintage liqueurs and wines—all without charge to the gamblers.

In 1902 Canfield bought the Old Saratoga Club House in Saratoga, New York, and built an Italian garden around it, converting it into a glittery showplace that earned it the reputation of the Monte Carlo of America. Naturally, Canfield had greater overhead than his European counterparts, who basically just had to pay off the highest authority in their area. Canfield had to make massive payoffs to both police and politicians in order to operate. Canfield's money was probably largely responsible for the many contemporary police officials who owned yachts and large country estates. One suspected official later claimed before a government investigative body that he was not on Canfield's payroll but had accumulated his large fortune by shrewd speculation in real estate—in Japan.

Any gambler worthy of the designation had to gamble in a Canfield establishment and the Saratoga Club House probably sported the highest-stakes games (especially in ROULETTE) ever run in this country. Among the high rollers were Reggie Vanderbilt, Phil Dwyer (the "racetrack king"), and Bet-a-Million Gates. In all the play, of course, Canfield came out ahead, and he always advised clients that they could not win against his bank. He also barred from play individuals whom he determined could not afford the action—as well as never permitting any of his own employees to gamble.

Despite his unfailing payment of graft, Canfield in time found himself being prosecuted during the reform era of District Attorney William Travers Jerome. Jerome personally led a raid on the Canfield establishment next door to Delmonico's. The gambler battled the legal case for two years, until Jerome got a law passed by the state legislature that compelled witnesses to testify. Society figures until then had thought too highly of Canfield to utter a damning word about the gambling impresario. Given the new law, however, Canfield yielded to Jerome in order to prevent embarrassment to his clients. He paid a fine of $1,000 and closed down the house, concentrating thereafter on his establishment in Saratoga and another out of state in the social retreat of Newport.

In 1907 Canfield shut down the Saratoga Club as well when that community went on one of its periodic (and always short-lived) reform binges. He lived out his remaining years as a major successful Wall Street speculator and an art connoisseur. He collected an enormous number of original paintings, many by James Whistler, who also did Canfield's portrait. Following his death in 1914, Canfield was better remembered for his art activities than his gambling years, his collections being featured in numerous art publications and his Rare Sheraton and Hepplewhite exhibit appearing as a major magazine feature in *House Beautiful* in June 1916. Canfield had operated his "carpet joints" with distinction and class, and he himself went out the same way.

CANFIELD: Solitaire Gambling Game

The game Canfield is named for the fabulous gambling man RICHARD A. CANFIELD, who introduced this form of Solitaire as a gaming proposition in his Saratoga, New York establishment. In Canfield's princely house patrons could buy a deck for $52 and were paid off at $5 apiece for each card they made at the game.

To lay out the cards, the player deals out 13 cards, face down, squares them off and places them to the left as a stock, face up so that only the top card shows. The next, or 14th, card of the pile is turned up and positioned above the stock to the right. This is the first foundation. Next to the right of the stock a row of four cards are dealt face up to form the tableau.

Three additional foundations are formed when available. They are of the same rank as the first foundation. That is, if the first foundation is the jack of hearts, the other jacks are laid down next to it, as they turn up. The foundations are then built *in suit and sequence* while going "around the corner." For instance, the jack of hearts is followed in hearts by the queen, king, ace, deuce, trey, 4, and so on. The object of the game is to run all foundations to their final cards, in this case the 10's.

After the layout the rest of the pack is dealt by turning up three cards at a time, and the top card of each turn-up may be used for building. The cards underneath the turn-up card may be played once the cards above them are played. These three-card turn-ups are called the "talon" and the player can draw cards singly from the talon pile, or singly from the stock, and the cards played to the appropriate foundations or to the tableau in alternating red and black cards in descending order—that is, a 6 of spades may go on either a 7 of diamonds or hearts. Entire rows

of the tableau may be moved in the same fashion, which creates a space on the tableau. This must be filled by the top card of the stock or, if the stock has been exhausted, by the top card of the talon. Failing that, the player fills the space from the hand. When the hand is run through, the player picks up the talon pile and without shuffling starts it as a new hand. This continues as long as possible until the game is won or play comes to a standstill.

At Canfield's the $52 card buy-in was a tough nut for the player who seldom consistently got 11 or more cards to the foundations. Alas, Canfield never found the action quite as profitable as it figured to be. He had to pay an individual croupier to watch the player, not to mention others to watch the croupier.

The name of Canfield is sometimes used incorrectly for Klondike Solitaire, which is a three-card turnover game as private play and a one-card turnover as a casino gambling game. The correct version of Canfield can occasionally be found in some gambling houses, generally called either Canfield or Fascination. In Europe it may be referred to as Demon. Whatever the name, as a gambling proposition it remains a prohibitive bet because of the high buy-in price. Instead of trying to beat the game, the individual gambler would be far wiser to try to bank the game.

CARD DOMINOES

See FAN TAN.

CARD MOBS: Professional Cheats

Card mobs are professional cheaters—hustlers, shills, card manipulators, and muscle men—who work together for a living, usually traveling in search of new victims. Few of them are very good gamblers or even good cheaters. At most they have to have only one card mechanic, a man with the necessary proficiency in crooked manipulation. This is merely a technical requirement; far more important are the SHILLS or hustlers who bring in likely victims.

Once a MARK is brought to the table, he will be taken. Sometimes card manipulation is used, but often it is not necessary because the gang works with signals to indicate to one another what their hidden cards are. As a result only the high man will remain in the pot with the victim. When the gang wins they take the mark's money; when the mark wins he gets little of the gang's money.

Some card mobs seek to get into big games with several victims, but often they set up a "hot seat game" in which all the players are dishonest save for the mark. Obviously the victim is taken to the cleaners in short order.

Besides the shills, some of whom may be good-looking women who steer victims to a game after pretending to be heading for their own hotel room, there is always one muscle man who is there as a last resort to "cool off" a victim if all other cons don't work.

The general wisdom is that the only sure defense against being taken by card mobs is never to play with strangers. Some card mobs are all for that. Some card mobs of three players infiltrate a regular POKER game and avert suspicion for years. Because there are three of them, they can rotate the big winner in each game and indeed have one or both of the other two lose heavily—to themselves.

Girolamo CARDANO: Physician and Mathematician

A remarkable Italian Renaissance figure, Girolamo Cardano (1501-1576) of Milan left us the first written record of mathematical gambling problems in his *Book of Games of Chance*. In recent years many scholars have concluded that Cardano anticipated Pascal's theory of the laws of probability by about a century.

Given the fact that gambling was frowned upon in better society of the 16th century, Cardano felt obliged to justify the morality of his work. He wrote:

> Even if gambling were altogether an evil, still, on account of the very large number of people who play, it would seem to be a natural evil. For that very reason it ought to be discussed by a medieval doctor like one of the incurable diseases; for in every evil there is a least evil, in every infamy a least infamy, and similarly in loss of time and fortune. Also, it has been the custom of philosophers to deal with the vices in order that advantage might be drawn from them, as for example in the case of anger. Thus it is not absurd for me to discuss gambling, not in order to praise it but in order to point out the advantages in it, and, of course, also its disadvantages, in order that they may be reduced to a minimum.

Translation for the green-felt crowd: The good doctor kinda liked gambling. In fact, Cardano relates that once he thought of himself near death and found that constant dice playing had great therapeutic value. See also GALILEO, BLAISE PASCAL.

CARDS

The origin—or origins—of playing cards is unknown. Perhaps, as in the case of dice, many cultures developed cards independently of one another, most likely evolving them from the use of sticks and arrows and gambling on how they would fall. Thus many early Oriental playing cards really were sticks that later were widened and shortened and designed with images.

Some say the first cards turned up in Egypt, but the earliest written documentation is found in a Chinese encyclopedia written in the 17th century, which declared that playing cards were invented in 1120 as a pastime for the emperor's concubines. There are some accounts that seem to hint at the existence of cards elsewhere a few centuries previously, but historians have never been satisfied with their authenticity.

In any event, playing cards definitely turned up in southern and eastern Europe in the 1300's—about the same time as the Black Death, which may have been somewhat appropriate. No one really knows who brought cards to Europe. Some credit the Crusaders, and it seems likely the Moors imported cards into Spain and that gypsies took playing cards into eastern Europe.

Cards did not come into everyday use until the development of printing and, by the late 1400's, were very common. Columbus in his chronicles tells of cards being played by his men in 1492. In one wave of reformation, some crews took the vow against cardplaying and destroyed their decks. However, when the sailors got to the New World, they promptly plucked wide leaves from trees, marked them and started dealing. By 1500 it could be said every civilized country in the world had playing cards.

By the 18th century there was a real need to codify the rules and strategies of card games and this was done to greater or lesser extent by several "experts," most important among them being EDMOND HOYLE. Since his time the expression "according to Hoyle" has meant playing the game correctly. Less well remembered are the works of Richard Seymour, Esq., who published *The Compleat Gamester, for the Use of Young Princesses* in 1734. Seymour was much concerned with the game of WHIST as it was then played, but was not overly involved with defining the rules. His chief instructions to the young princesses involved teaching them the art of winning by fair means or foul, and he explained the techniques of peeking at other players' cards and giving hand signals to one's partner.

Why are there four suits in cards? No one really knows. The Chinese did it that way and all others followed their example. The French suits were portrayals of the social order of the time. The nobility was represented by a sword (*pique*); the merchants by a diamond (*carreau*); the clergy by a heart (*coeur*); and the peasants by a club (*trèfle*). The English word for spades comes from the Spanish *espada*, or sword. The design of the picture cards and the rankings of the king, queen, and jack have not changed since the 16th century.

In the 1930's the card makers of America and England came up with what they considered a hot idea to create a fifth suit in playing cards, which would force everybody to buy new decks. This fifth suit was called Eagle in America and Crown in England. It proved to be an idea whose time had not come—and probably never will. Card players simply ignored the new decks.

Most card historians pay little attention to a very important feature of cards—the back designs. For generations they were plain, certainly a cheater's delight. Many early back designs did not grasp the need for not being one-way pictures or images, and it must have come as a revelation to the first hustlers who discovered what a delightful situation this presented. All they had to do was arrange some card backs upside down and others upside up and know high cards from low ones, or if need be, just key cards such as aces or picture cards or whatever. Undoubtedly today there are many card hustlers bemoaning the fact that they were born a couple of centuries too late.

See EAGLES AND CROWNS; ONE-WAY PICTURES.

CARDS SPEAK (FOR THEMSELVES): Method of Determining High-low Declarations in Poker

There are many gamblers who insist the best way to play high-low poker is to eliminate the right of a player to declare which way he is going before the showdown. In fact, this is the general rule at the public poker rooms in Nevada casinos, where the game is known as High-Low Split. The casinos have found that eliminating the players' right to call his own high or low makes the game easier and less likely to provoke disputes. Players simply reveal their hands and the dealer awards half the pot to the high hand and half to the low hand. Another good reason for letting cards speak for themselves is that it cuts down on secret-partner collusion.

CASINO: Bad Gambling Game

Today Casino is not regarded as a gambling game to be played for high stakes because a skilled player can be a consistent winner. In its day it was a game in which much money changed hands, usually on a winning score of 21, with the difference in the scores of all losers being the payoff.

How to play: The game is usually played by two, three, or four, in the last case the opposite players are usually partners. It is played with a standard 52-card deck, and picture cards have no value, while all other cards from ace to 10 bear their pip value. Each player is dealt four cards and four cards are faced upon the table. Each player in turn, beginning with the first nondealer, must try to take in as many cards as possible by matching the cards in his hand with those on the table. For instance, if there is a 6 on the table and the player has a 6, he may take it. If there is more than one 6 he may take them as well. He may also take any combination of cards that adds up to six. If there is a deuce and 4 on the table, they too may be taken as a 6.

A player may also build from his hand. If there is a 5 on the table he may add an ace to it and announce he is building 6's, provided he has that card in his hand. However, he must wait until his next turn to take in such a build and risks that another player holding that card will take it first. Players may also build on a previous build either of their own or their opponents and run the same risk of losing the cards. Whenever a player cannot build or take a card, he must discard to the table pile. Players can delay taking cards, but they must take their own previous build or take another card on subsequent turns rather than discard.

After all players have used their first cards, they are dealt four more cards and play continues in this fashion until all the cards are used. When the last deal is made, the dealer must announce, "Last." The last player to take up any cards is entitled to those cards still remaining on the table.

Scoring is then done as follows:

Cards, greatest number of the 52	3
Spades, greatest number of the 13 spades	1
Big Casino, the 10 of diamonds	2
Little Casino, the deuce of spades	1
Aces (one each)	4
Total	11

The game continues in the betting version of Casino until one of the players has 21 or more points.

The decline in Casino as a betting game was due to the fact that an expert player can easily keep track of every card played and in a two-player game knows exactly which cards his opponent holds in the last hand. This memory feat is not nearly as difficult as BLACKJACK counting. Additionally, three-handed Casino is unsatisfactory since the player in the middle is at a distinct disadvantage. Four-man partnership Casino allows much opportunity for cheating and it is relatively simple for one partner to aid the other, certainly easier than in BRIDGE.

As a result, Casino is now pretty much a family or children's game and is seldom played for anything more than penny stakes. A sound way to be a consistent winner is to simply keep track of the aces, deuces, and 10's.

Variations in Casino are as follows:

• *Sweep Casino.* This is played like the standard game, but an additional point is made whenever a player takes all the cards on the table. This is especially unattractive to seasoned gamblers since it makes a precise game too undisciplined and wild. In many areas Sweep never caught on at all.

- *Royal Casino*. This makes a more interesting game in that the picture cards are given building properties since the jack is considered an 11; queen, 12; and king, 13. The ace may be considered either 1 or 14.

- *Spade Casino*. In this variation, all spades are traditionally counted as 1 point instead of merely the highest number of spades counting for 1 point. Exceptions are the deuce and jack, which have 2-point values. This means individual games total 24 points, and in this case 61 points produces a winner.

- *Draw Casino*. This is the only form of Casino that is still occasionally played for appreciable stakes. Players are dealt four cards and four cards are dealt up, with the rest of the deck becoming a stock. After each player discards he draws another card to keep his hand at four cards. The game continues in this fashion until the deck is finished, as in traditional Casino.

Some seasoned gamblers like to play Draw Casino as a "time waster." It is an excellent four-handed, no-partnership game during casino junket flights. At a dollar a point, none of the players should be so tapped out that he will be unable to patronize the tables later.

CASINO NIGHTS: Private Fund-Raising Activities

Casino Nights, or Las Vegas Nights, are fund-raising activities of various charitable or religious organizations designed to finance their activities. Since the games—and they can feature most of the games available at a legal casino—are for a worthy purpose, few people expect or even hope to win any large sum of money. They are seldom disappointed, and they chalk up their losses as a contribution to charity.

No one interested in serious gambling should tempt the fates—or more correctly the odds—offered at such affairs. The odds are so heavily skewed against the player that few can expect not to lose much more money than they thought possible. For instance, many ROULETTE wheels at Casino Nights will pay off at only 30 to 1 on a winning number instead of 35 to 1. This may not seem like much for charity, but it raises the house edge from the normal figure of 5.26 in American Roulette (already a gouge) to well over 21 percent. If you play at such a Roulette game and lose 21 percent of your bet on every spin of the wheel, it will not take long for you to go broke. All other games at these events are skewed in a similar fashion.

Remarkably, professionals who service such functions claim they never meet any opposition about the posted odds. This is a reflection on the type of gamblers who patronize these events; they are either the uninitiated or such compulsives that they will play at any lopsided odds because it offers them the chance to feed their habit in a socially approved manner. This may say something about the organizations offering such events.

There is another unwholesome footnote to all this. The charitable organizations themselves usually understand very little about gambling odds and frequently have little notion of what they should be making. Since the operators servicing the affairs understand such matters, they are in perfect position to short the charity sponsor. All that is necessary is that they use dummies to win some payoffs. The individual croupiers and dealers may have the same thoughts, and they can pay off a confederate large sums he did not win and still have their table show a handsome profit. The gullible sponsor, unfamiliar with gambling ploys, never suspects a thing.

If you are overwhelmed with a desire to give to a worthy cause, it is suggested you leave a hefty donation at the door and be on your way.

CAT RACK: Carnival Scam

This hoary old swindle is as dependable for the carnival scam operator as MILK BOTTLE TOSS. A player throws baseballs to knock stuffed cats off a shelf. Current rates generally are three baseballs for a dollar and the player must knock three cats completely off the shelf to win a big prize.

The easiest way to gaff the game is to set up four cats on a shelf, two of which are weighted; while the latter two can be knocked over, they won't go off the shelf. An accurate thrower can knock off the two light cats only and so win a minor prize, if anything. The danger in this method is that an inspection might well turn up the dirty work. Some operators therefore go in for more sophisticated deception, one with an added gimmick for preventing any of the stuffed cats from being knocked off. This involves a loose board at the back of the shelf that allows the game to proceed honestly as long as the board is right up against the shelf. However, when the board is moved back just a few inches by use of a foot pedal, the shelf is in effect widened so that the cat's center of gravity remains on the shelf and it will not fall off. Scam operators fix the game only after a sucker has knocked off two cats.

This game can at times be a relatively big-time swindle when a grifter sucks in a victim by offering a side bet of anywhere from $10 to $100 that he can't knock off more than six or seven cats with ten throws. If the victim gets up to five downed cats, the board is moved and the player's good fortune is muzzled.

CATCH THE TEN
See SCOTCH WHIST.

CENTENNIAL
See OHIO.

Jimmy CHAGRA: Las Vegas's All-time High Roller
Every once in a while a high roller hits Las Vegas and bets the roof off the place. But even Vegas—which gets its share of high-rolling kooks, including a spillover of Arab princes with seemingly unlimited cash to dump—never saw anyone quite like Jimmy Chagra. Chagra, a cocaine dealer now doing 30 years in Leavenworth, enjoys nationwide fame for, among other things, his far-ranging criminal enterprise in Texas and the fact that the day his trial was to start, the judge was shot dead. (Chagra was later charged with the judge's murder but acquitted.) None of this is why the boys in Vegas remember Jimmy.

Since Chagra knew his days of freedom were numbered, he came to Vegas determined to have a good ole time with his multi-million dollar fortune while he could. He insisted on gambling for astounding sums, which meant he had to do it at Binion's Horseshoe. The Horseshoe is the number one gambling joint for high rollers in Vegas and posts only minimums at their tables. The casino doesn't know what "maximum" means.

There have been written accounts stating how much Jimmy Chagra lost, but no one really knows the actual total. When he played POKER with Vegas's top pros, he insisted on minimum table stakes of $50,000, but everyone had to put up much more because Jimmy thought nothing of raising $20,000 at a pop on the blind. The Poker table at the Horseshoe had at least $2 million lying on it at any given time. For a while Jimmy appeared to be ahead $2 or $3 million at CRAPS and BLACKJACK, but he found ways to give it back, especially at Poker, but in more innovative ways as well. Occasionally Jimmy developed a nose for fresh desert air and ventured out to the Dunes golf course with the boys, often for a half million a round. Jimmy was a good golfer, but not that good. During a Poker session a cocktail waitress brought him a complimentary bottle of Mountain Valley water. The custom is to tip the waitress in such cases. Jimmy flipped her two packs of $100 bills—$10,000.

How many millions did Chagra drop in his weeks in Vegas before he started on the road to the slammer? Poker great Jack Strauss is quoted by A. Alvarez in *The Biggest Game in Town* as saying, "It was like that TV program *Fantasy Island*. I kept waiting for Tattoo to come on and say it was all a dream: 'Look boss! The plane! The plane!' "

If the Vegas boys went into mourning at losing Jimmy to the prison feds, some found a way to continue taking him in Leavenworth where a gambling buddy was also doing time. The gambler and Chagra were both Gin Rummy addicts and played for heavy stakes, with the payoffs to be made outside the prison. The imprisoned gambler arranged for some of the Vegas boys to back him and took Jimmy for some $50,000. Then to the bitter disappointment of his outside backers, the gambling buddy died. The boys have not figured how to get another ace player into Leavenworth.

What is the Vegas gamblers' fondest wish for Jimmy Chagra? That he wins a new trial and is released in the meantime. "The desert will turn green after that," one says.

CHASE-THE-ACE: Advanced Form of High-card Cut
Chase-the-Ace is simply a more complicated variation of HIGH-CARD CUT, with a dash of suspense and strategy added.

How to play: the players agree on a stake and divide their money into three equal piles. The dealer then offers one card face down to each player. After looking at the card, the player decides whether he wants to keep the card or exchange it with the next player. The object of the game is to avoid holding the lowest card in the hand (the ace being low). If the leader, the player to the dealer's left, decides to keep his card he announces "Stick." If he holds a king, he immediately turns it up as the high card. Otherwise he trades with the player to his left. That player in turn now decides whether to hold the card or swap it with the next player, and so on around the table. When play reaches the dealer, he turns his card face up and then decides whether to keep it or swap it for the top card of the undealt deck. All players then expose their cards and the lowest man then has to put one-third of his stake in the pot.

The deal then passes to the left and another hand is dealt. This continues until all but one player have lost their stakes. The remaining player takes the pot.

Chase-the-Ace is often played for matchsticks or candies in a children's version known as Cuckoo.

CHEATING AT GAMBLING: Growth Industry
A famous racetrack story concerns a seasoned jockey who gets the mount on a horse for the first time. The trainer tells him to break the horse last and move him up slowly until he is running fifth or so, and then to keep him in a tight hold. The jockey is also told to watch the horse's stride and determination to see how well the animal could have done if he had been turned loose.

The jock does as he is told and the horse finishes

fifth. Immediately after the race the trainer asks him, "Could he have won it?"

"Absolutely," the jockey says. "I give him a couple of cracks of the whip and he flies right past those horses."

The trainer nods. "Then we can bet him safely next week when he runs against those same horses."

"Well," the jockey says, "he'll beat them four horses in front of him, but there were a couple of horses behind me who looked like they could have beaten us all."

In gambling any story has several morals to it, and certainly this one does. But the main one is that restraint is the operating guide to gambling. There are no truly sure things—even when you cheat.

A bettor should realize there are other bettors who may be better than he, and that even if he is crooked, there may be other crooks more dishonest than himself. This pearl of wisdom becomes a worthy lesson if it teaches a bettor to stay cool, not to bet the bankroll, the bank account, or the homestead on anything ever.

There has yet to be a gambling game invented by the brain of man that did not simultaneously set other men to contemplating ways of winning at that game by any means, fair of foul. Cheating is the natural outgrowth of gambling, or perhaps it's the other way around.

If you gamble you will from time to time be cheated. You'll attend the races and bet on a logical horse without knowing it's a "boat race," with another horse already designated to be the winner. You'll play BACKGAMMON for cash with a stranger or "friend" and he'll destroy you with some dice-cup manipulation. You'll play POKER and lose as the dealer gives you your cards from the top of the deck while he takes his from the bottom. You'll go to an amusement park and see a sign saying: PULL A STRING AND WIN A PRIZE. EVERYONE A WINNER. You pay your dollar and pull a string extending through a "collar" device and win a prize worth a dime. Hard luck. You could have gotten a big prize. The operator proves it to you by grabbing all the strings and pulling them. All the prizes come up on the shelf, including that television, that VCR, that radio, that watch. And all you got was a rubber ball. Try again, maybe you'll get the biggie. You can try all day and never win anything of value. Those strings the hustler is pulling are on the feed-inside of the collar, but they don't come out on your side. In gambling, even guaranteed winners are never really guaranteed.

The late John Scarne was an honest gambler, but he could cheat the pants off anybody. Noah Sarlat, a veteran magazine editor, shaking hands with Scarne for the first time, described it as an eerie sensation; Sarlat felt he was holding Jello rather than a human hand, so supple was Scarne's. Scarne could beat anyone at cutting cards. He'd shuffle and in the process spot the aces and count the cards down to each of them. Then he'd square the deck and on his first cut get an ace, on the next cut another ace, on the third cut another ace, and on the fourth cut another ace. It was all in his hands. As his fingers slipped down the deck, Scarne actually counted the cards. The 12th card, he knew, was an ace, so he cut on the 12th card. No problem.

You love to gamble, but of course you don't want to be cheated. Bear in mind that you *may* be cheated and be watchful accordingly. When you lose a big hand in a Poker game, stare very hard at the deck hand the next time the dealer holds the cards. You might not detect a cheater's action, but if he sees you watching, he can't be sure. He's going to stop. More likely he's going to pick up his cards and leave for a "friendlier" game elsewhere.

The endless cheating scams in this book can hardly be listed in one section. They are found throughout alphabetically, and following this entry there is a listing of all cheating entries, whether they involve dice, cards, wheels, or electronic gear. Many other entries on specific games also contain information on crooked play, but unless the game itself is a total scam (such as THREE-CARD MONTE, the SHELL GAME, and even that old carnival chestnut, MILK BOTTLE TOSS) it is not listed below. You will find information on these under the specific entry on the subject.

Of course no claim can be made that the gambling scams included in this book are definitive. As their old scams are exposed, cheats stay up nights dreaming up new ones.

The following entries describe methods of cheating at gambling in general:

Baccarat—Mini, Cheating at
Banco
Bar 6-8 Craps Proposition Scam
Big Six (Wheel of Fortune)—Cheating
Big Store
Black Sox Scandal
Bottom Dealing
Bottom Peeking
"Brush Off"
Card Mobs
Cat Rack
"Chip Cut" Thefts
Chuck-a-Luck Cheating
Coin-Die Game
Cold Deck
Crossroaders
Daubing
Deck Cutting Bet
Dice—Cheating

TINTING COLORS.

⊹FOR SHADING CARDS.⊹

THESE Colors have been prepared for use on highly finished calendered, smooth and glossy Paper, Card and other surfaces. Unlike ordinary inks or paints, they do not simply LIE UPON the surface to which they are applied, but SINK INTO the material itself, and the coloring or printing on any polished or glossy surface capable of absorbing color can be *Marked, Tinted or Shaded*, in whole or in part, the surface being left in its original state. Any addition of ordinary colors to smooth and glossy surfaces always shows up and is seen at a glance, because the color rests upon the surface and gives it the appearance of having been marked or patched, while similar additions made by these Colors have the appearance of being the original work, because the Color sinks into the enamel and looks like a part of it, or as being under it. Hence they are specially adapted and used for *Tinting, Marking, Coloring or Shading* such surfaces as are presented by Enameled Paper and *CARDS*, where, with ordinary colors, the work would mar or injure the original gloss of the surface.

DIRECTIONS FOR USING THE COLORS.

1. The bottle No. 1, contains the color full strength; bottle No. 2, contains it faint.
2. One of the small bottles and one of the brushes are designed for each color. The colors can be mixed in these small bottles to obtain the shade required, and when the shade is got they can be used as wanted.
3. Before mixing, and when mixed, before using, it is always best to shake the bottles a little.
4. To mix the red color, for example, shake the bottles No. 1 and 2 red, and then take color from each of them, in small quantities or in drops, and put into the small bottle. Then try the shade, and keep on adding color from No. 1 or No. 2 until you get the shade required. The blue and green are mixed in the same way. To avoid spilling, which sometimes happens in trying to pour or drop, the liquid may be lifted out of the bottles with the brush, by repeatedly dipping the brush into them, and then pressing it against the mouth of the small bottle.
5. As you mix the colors, try them on a surface like that on which you intend to use them. In this way any shade can be got. Always bear in mind that the colors *show deeper when moist* (as is the case when they are first put on), and become fainter as they dry. Hence they must be so mixed as to leave the shade which is wanted when they become dry, no matter how much too heavy they may appear when first put on. It is only by paying proper attention to this fact that they will give satisfaction.
6. Always keep the bottles well corked when not using them. Brushes and bottles should be kept clean, and if washed in water should be dried before using, as water blisters smooth, calendered surfaces.
7. Sometimes when the brush is not properly handled, the place where the color has been put will show up. When this happens, rub the place a little with the tip of the finger or with a clean rag. When the work is finished, rubbing a little with a clean rag sometimes improves it, although not necessary.
8. When a deeper shade is wanted than one application of No. 1 will give, go over it a second time. If it is desired to apply the colors a number of times to the same spot, it should be rubbed with a rag and allowed to dry each time it is applied before applying it again. Evenness is more apt to be obtained by using a little lighter shade of color after the first few applications of the heaviest.

A little care and practice will enable any one to handle the colors satisfactorily.

Price per Set of Colors Complete, with Brushes, $5.00.

WILL & FINCK,

Manufacturers and Dealers in all kinds of Sporting Goods.

PLAYING CARDS A SPECIALTY.

769 Market Street, San Francisco.

A.

---

4   WILL & FINCK'S

Faro Dealing Cards, cut in any form, either wedges, rounds and straights, end strippers, or any other kind, ready for use............per deck $ 2 50

In ordering cards cut, always send a few cards that fit your box, or if your box is numbered, send the number, and state particularly just how you want them done.

Card Punches, coarse or fine, with small case for same.................... $ 3 00

Billiard Cloth, for covering tables, per yard, from $5 00 to 7 50

Emery Cloth, best in use, for sanding, per doz. sheets 1 00
" " " " single sheet 10

Glass Paper, best in use, for sanding, per doz. sheets 1 00
" " " " single sheet 10

Sighters, per set of four, with small case for same................... 2 50

Sighting Plate, with one sighter, (something new)...................... 2 00

Black Sighting Ink........per bottle 25

CLUB-ROOM FURNITURE.

Faro Tables................$40 00 to $ 60 00

Poker Tables, our own invention..... 150 00

Dice Tables, electric, complete, our invention...................... 150 00

Poker and Dice Table, combined, (something new).................. 250 00

Grand Hazard Dice Table, electric, complete, our own invention 175 00

Electric Dice...................each 2 50

B.

A: A 19th-century flyer put out by a leading crooked gambling supply house offers special colorings for tinting cards.

B: Catalog page from same company offers what was called "club-room furniture" and devices. Modern versions of the same items are sold underground today using the old catalogs with the prices multipled by 10 to 20 times.

C: Current newspaper ad offers marked cards for "amusement only."

C.

Dice—Honest Cheating
Dice Cup Cheating
Dollar Number Swindle
Eye Bet
Eyes in the Sky
False Cut
False Shuffle (2)
Faro—Cheating
Friars Club
Front Loaders
Gambling Supply Houses
Gin Rummy Cheating
Greek Deal
Holdout
Holdout Table
Hot Seat Game
Location Play
Luminous Readers
Mechanic's Grip
Milk Bottle Toss
Mouse Game
Nail Work
One-way Pictures
Overpaying
Palming
Palming Chips
Past Posting
Peeking
Pegging
Penny Falls
Pinching
Put and Take Dice
Put and Take Top
Sanding
Second Dealing
Shell Game
Shorting Pots
Slick Ace Desk
Slot Machine Cheating
Slot Machine Hustlers
Smack Game
Sorts
Spooking
Steer Joint
Steerer
String Game
Strippers
Subs
Switcher
Tachistoscope
Three-card Monte
Tip the Tee
Trims

CHECK AND RAISE

See SANDBAGGING.

CHECK COP

See SURE COP.

CHEESEBOX, THE: Electronic Device Used by Bookmakers

In the 1930's and 1940's, before the development of sophisticated electronic gear, the "cheesebox" was used by bookmakers in many parts of the country to keep the police off their backs. It was invented by Gerard "Cheesebox" Callahan, a rogue New York Telephone Company employee who made his major income servicing the needs of gambler Frank Costello's illicit operations.

Callahan picked up the Cheesebox monicker for inventing an electronic relay system that fit into a wooden cream-cheese box designed to help bookmakers elude police raids. The cheesebox was a masterpiece of communication, allowing the bookmaker to give a customer a phone number in the Bronx, but when dialed, the call would automatically be switched over (via the cheesebox) to a phone in Brooklyn or elsewhere. It was maddening to the police, who painstakingly traced a bookie's phone line and then staged a big raid on the apartment with the telephone. They would smash down the door to charge into an empty flat—empty, that is, except for a telephone and some mysterious gear in a cheesebox.

Naturally, the police would try to trace the lines again, but the bookie had the empty flat under observation and when it was raided, he knew it was time to move his Brooklyn operation. By the time the police got to Brooklyn, the bookmaker had a new cheesebox line—running from Queens to Manhattan.

CHESS GAMBLING

Because this book is concerned with gambling rather than with games in general there isn't space to explain Chess in any great detail. There is of course enormous literature on the subject, from the daily newspapers to books of varying degrees of expertise. The game's origin somewhere around 200 B.C. has been variously placed in India, China, and Persia. The name itself is from the Persian shah, meaning "king."

Essentially Chess is a game resembling ancient warfare and is played on a board with 64 white and black (or red) squares. Each "army" has eight pawns, two castles or rooks, two bishops, two knights, a queen, and a king. A piece is normally captured and taken from the board by another piece moving into the square it is occupying. The object of the game is not the removal of pieces but rather to move the pieces—each rank having specific and distinctive permissible moves—in such a manner that the opponent cannot prevent his king from being captured (checkmate). A draw or stalemate occurs when neither player can take the other's king without putting his own king in peril.

International Chess matches date from the 16th

century and "official" world champions are not easily determined, although Wilhelm Steinitz is generally considered to have been the first one, from 1886-1894.

It is possible to get betting action on Chess tournaments and championship play with British bookmakers and in Las Vegas. Betting on the Fischer-Spassky match was said to be huge.

The real action in Chess betting, however, involves the small wagering taking place in Chess parlors in many countries. Legend has it that actor Humphrey Bogart was a skilled Chess hustler in his down-and-out days and eked out food and rent money playing 50-cent matches in Sixth Avenue Chess parlors in New York City. Perhaps this was simply Hollywood publicity department-generated fiction, but whether Bogie was or not, the Chess hustler is a fact of life.

CHICAGO: Poker Variation
A Seven-card Stud game, Chicago turns up fairly frequently as a DEALER'S CHOICE option. It is played like standard Seven-card Stud, except that the high hand gets only half the pot. The balance goes to the player holding the highest hole-card spade. This tends to keep players with weak hands from dropping out if no high spades have appeared among the cards showing.

Cheating at Chicago: Some crooked players call Dealer's Choice "Hustler's Choice" because they can cheat in various ways according to the game called. Chicago is one of the easiest scams since all that is necessary is to palm the ace of spades at the end of a game and hold it out until someone calls for Chicago. The cheater then simply switches the ace of spades for one of his hole cards and is thereby assured of half the pot. The fact that he draws the ace directs no suspicion toward him since he did not call for the game and could hardly know that someone else would call for it. Certainly the dealer knows the hustler could not possibly have known he would call the game and is sure he is not cheating.

CHICAGO (CARDS)
See MICHIGAN.

CHICAGO (DICE)
Not to be confused with the POKER game with the same name, Chicago is a dice game that probably developed as an offshoot from the pool game of the same name. As many players as wish can play and in the first round each player tries to throw a 2 with the dice. Any who do score two points. On the next round the players try to score a 3 and making that point is worth a score of three. The rounds continue from 4 through 12, with corresponding scoring. At the end of the game the player with the highest score is the winner.

Chicago is usually played with an opening ante, and in more advanced games the high man has the option of making an additional bet after each round. The other players need not accept and if not all do, a side pot is set up for those willing to do so. The high man should increase the bet only cautiously at first since his point score in the early rounds will be fairly modest. He can also lose his lead in a single roll of the dice, especially since on each succeeding roll through 7, the chances of making a point improve for all players. After 7, the chances of making the point decrease mathematically, even though the point value climbs. Trailing players should be very cautious about matching such bets and certainly not accept supposedly attractive odds in side bets when the game reaches the 11s and 12s. The 11 will come up only twice in 36 tries and the 12 only once in 36—and the leader has as much chance of hitting these high numbers as any of his challengers.

CHICAGO FIRE
See LOUIS M. COHN.

CHICAGO PIANO: Wild Seven-card Stud Game
There are POKER players who insist Chicago Piano is the type of game that makes any other form of psychological testing needless. They say anyone who calls this game as DEALER'S CHOICE is clearly mad.

It is as zany a wild card version of Seven-card Stud as can be found. Chicago Piano crosses the line from even the standard wild games into the realm of lunacy by making every player's low hole card wild *not only for himself but for all other players*. This means in a game with seven players it is possible for 28 of the 52 cards to be wild!

The game starts with three down cards, with each player then turning up one of the cards. After a round of betting another card is dealt down followed by a turnover and another round of betting. This continues until each player has seven cards, with the last card however remaining a downcard. Since that card may create a new low for the player it can completely alter his hand.

The madness continues as everyone must sort out what all the wild cards are. It is not at all unusual for a player to end up with seven wild cards, although he of course can only use five. And not infrequently the pot may have to be split between two or more players, all holding five aces.

CHILE, Gambling in
Chile may well have more gambling than any other South American nation. Lotteries, horse-race betting, and casinos have long been popular in the country.

In 1925 the University of Concepcion was granted permission to operate a lottery, with the profits going toward the institution's general operating costs and to provide grants for students. Five years later a national lottery was created, with the profits going to the welfare system.

Chile's first casino was authorized in 1928 at the resort of Vina del Mar. Soon a number of other casinos sprang up at other resorts. Horse-race betting is also big business, with heavy betting at tracks at Valparaiso, Santiago, and a number of other cities. Only on-track betting is legal; off-track bookmaking is illegal. There are very few prosecutions under this law, however, indicating that Chileans are either very law-abiding or that the statutes are not too rigidly enforced.

CHINESE FAN TAN (BEAN VERSION): Gambling Guessing Game

There are several versions of FAN TAN. This version, played with beans, is an ancient one going back many centuries in China. It is still played today in Chinatown betting joints in America and elsewhere, and most likely in the PRC as well.

A four-cornered layout with numbers in each corner marked 1, 2, 3, and 4 is used. Bets are placed on any of these numbers and the banker proceeds to take a handful of beans from a large bowl or jar in the center of the table. He puts the beans aside four at a time until he reaches the final four (or fewer) beans. The final grouping determines the winning number: if there are four beans left, number 4 is the winner, and so on. The winning number collects all the losing bets except for a small rake-off for the house.

Played under such rules, the house must take a cut since it is otherwise a dead-even guessing game with no edge for the bank. However, some amazing scams have been pulled off in this game, frequently at carnivals or charitable or church functions. At one church affair the game was described as Fan Tan, but it was stipulated action would be taken on only the first three numbers that bettors selected in even amounts. There was no rake-off for the house. But by simply limiting action to just three numbers— which three did not matter—the house was taking an amazing 25 percent edge, *and without any risk!*

If, for example, 1, 2, and 4 were the numbers covered and one of these came up, the winner simply collected odds of 2 to 1 on his bet and was happy. The bank lost nothing. However, whenever number 3 won, the house cleared the table—and this happened 25 percent of the time.

This particular affair happened to be a church function. The game was run by a private operator who was giving the church 60 percent of the profits and keeping 40 percent. That meant he was collecting 10 percent of all the money bet with no risk. He never had to lay out a dime of his money. He didn't have to worry about a gambler hitting a lucky streak and walking away with a big chunk of the house's money—something that gambling casinos always risk. There isn't a casino management in the world that wouldn't gladly close up shop and go into this business instead if there were enough action.

CHINESE WHIST: Completely Different Whist Version

Chinese Whist is played the same way as WHIST insofar as the leading and taking of tricks goes, but there the similarity ends.

How to play: Each player is dealt a row of six face-down cards, and then six face-up cards are placed on them. Then each player is dealt a single card that he holds in his hand. The dealer announces trump and the player to his left leads any upcard to the first trick. The other players follow suits, if possible with an upcard or with the card in their hands. When an upcard is played, the downcard below it becomes the new upcard. These new upcards can alter the strategy of the contenders considerably. The winner of each trick leads to the next. Scoring is done by standard Whist rules.

Chinese Whist can be played as a three-handed game with eight downcards and eight upcards, with an odd card for each hand. In this game a player is required to take one trick more than the combined total of his opponents' tricks before he gets points for his tricks. In the two-handed version, players get 12 downcards and 12 upcards and two cards in their hands.

"CHIP CUP" THEFTS: Casino-robbing Technique

Virtually all casino security experts will agree that one of the most cunning crooked plays they have to watch out for among house dealers is chip stealing done with a "chip cup." This is a genuine $5 chip glued to the top of a hollow plastic tube closed on the top and open on the bottom, which looks like a stack of four chips.

The chip cup can work in almost any game but does best in CRAPS, mainly because there is a premium to be made in losing bets and it is easy to find losing bets in Craps. Let us say the cheat bets his phony $25 and loses. The dealer, who is in on the scam with the bettor, gathers up the chip cup with other losing bets and draws them to his bankroll where he sorts out the chips. He keeps track of the chip cup and deftly stacks it on top of four $25 chips, so that it looks like a pile of five $5 chips. Then the cheater tosses the dealer a $25 chip and requests $5 chips. The dealer passes him the chip cup, which the cheat drops into his pocket. He empties the cup, makes a legitimate bet of $5 a couple of times, and it hardly matters if he wins or loses on them, since the crooked pair has just made a $100 killing.

After a few plays, the cheat plunks down the chip cup again. Ironically, nothing is more upsetting than winning an even-money bet since that means the confederates make $25. If they lose, they will make $100. To solve this disconcerting dilemma of winning, the schemers try a quick-money tack if they are sure supervision is lax at the moment. The bettor puts his money on some one-roll bet, say on "Any 7," which means he wins or loses on the very next roll. If he wins, he is paid at 4 to 1, which on an alleged $25 means $100 profit. If the 7 doesn't come up, the bet is lost, which also means a $100 profit.

There are other ways of betting that may slow the pace of collecting but certainly attract less attention. Under this method the hustlers sometimes play honest. The player starts off putting $5 on "Any 7" and if he loses, he is out $5. If he wins, the operators are up $20. On each losing try the player bets an extra $5 chip. If he loses $5, and $10, and $15 and then wins on $20, he has a legitimate profit of $50. If he loses on $20, the schemers are out $50 and the chip cup comes into play; the result on the next roll is either a win or the change-making scam, which either way puts them up $50 in all.

Sometimes the schemers get a run of 7's and actually win several hundred dollars honestly. They stop there, figuring there's plenty of time to lose another day.

How profitable can the chip-cup scam be? Back in the 1970s one sharp gang of scam artists victimized a number of casinos over a long period and the Nevada Gaming Control Board estimated the operation had been good for somewhere between $300,000 and $400,000.

CHIPS: Private and Casino Checks
Gambling chips are the stuff of dreams. They come in two varieties. There are the chips used in private gambling games, especially POKER, in which each color has a different value. This can vary but the standard units of value are as follows: white, one unit; red, five units; blue, ten units; yellow, 25 units. The unit of course can be any sum from one cent up to $1, $10, or $100, depending on the bankrolls of the players involved.

Casino chips, more often referred to by casino personnel as "checks," can vary in different casinos but come in standard denominations and colors. The $1 chip is white; $5, red; $25, green; and $100, black. Beyond that the $500 and $1,000 chips are different colors in different casinos. In common parlance, the $1 chip is called a penny; $5, a nickel; $25, a quarter.

This is very good psychology from the casino's viewpoint, since the purpose of casino chips is to make players think they are losing less than they are really losing, along with their self-control.

A New York gambler named Big Julie Weintraub is quoted in *Big Julie of Vegas* by Edward Linn as saying, "The guy who invented gambling was bright, but the guy who invented the chip was a genius."

This gets to the nub of the situation, or as English poet and writer A. Alvarez states more directly in *The Biggest Game in Town:* "The chip is like a conjurer's sleight of hand that turns an egg into a billiard ball, a necessity of life into a plaything, reality into illusion. Players who freeze up at the sight of a fifty-dollar bill, thinking it could buy them a week's food at the supermarket, will toss two green chips into the pot without even hesitating if the odds are right."

Without the casino chip Las Vegas, Reno, Tahoe, and Atlantic City would soon go out of business. The chip makes people bet over their heads. They get caught up in their game, mesmerized by the action, and they pay their way in with a piece of plastic, not money. A man who at home would suffer heart palpitations putting down $20 in cash will bet several black chips without a second thought.

Many casinos post signs or offer brochures urging players to never bet more than they can afford to. Nice words, but they have their fingers crossed while saying them.

CHIPS—Cheating
Even in the friendliest of card games, it is advisable to take considerable care with the chips that are used. There are desperate gamblers, especially on losing streaks, who go out and try to buy the same chips that are used in a regular game and slip them into play. When it's cashing-in time, the banker suddenly discovers he has more chips than he started with but he has no way of zeroing in on a likely suspect. (Some cheats introduce the extra chips just to remain in action, and if they manage to recoup, they slip the extras back out of the game.)

The only safeguard against this duplication dodge is buying protected chips from a gambling supply house. Those chips are monogrammed and registered in a person's name and cannot be obtained by anyone else. Such chips, however, are expensive, usually 40 to 50 cents apiece.
See also "CHIP CUP" THEFTS.

CHUCK-A-LUCK: Casino and Carnival Dice Game
Chuck-a-Luck is a very old dice game, originally imported into the United States from England, where it was called Sweat-Cloth. When it first appeared in America about a decade or so after the Revolution, it was known as Sweat. Later on it was known as

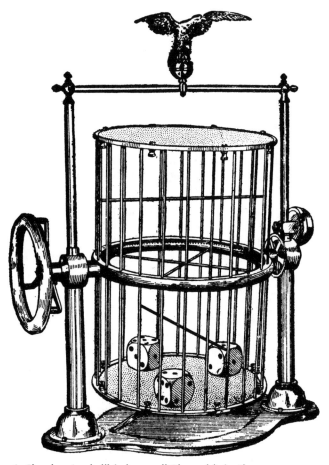

A Chuck-a-Luck "bird cage." The odds in the game even when honestly played are tremendously against the player. The late Major A. Riddle, president of the Dunes in Las Vegas, once observed that Wild Bill Hickok, Bat Masterson and other supposed western greats loved the game "probably because they never had enough upstairs to figure the odds against them."

Chuck-a-Luck or sometimes Bird Cage, since the three dice used are flipped through a cage shaped like an hourglass.

Players bet on any number from 1 to 6 and are paid off at even money if one of the three dice comes up with that number. If the number comes up on two dice, they get 2 to 1 and for all three dice the payoff is 3 to 1. Even gambling casino operators will admit that Chuck-a-Luck is a sucker's game. Major A. Riddle, president of the Dunes in Las Vegas, once noted that Wild Bill Hickok, Bat Masterson, and other supposed Western heroes loved the game "probably because they never had enough upstairs to figure the odds against them."

Many bettors are just as foolish about the game today. In fact, there are many people who actually believe the game is at worst an even-money proposition. With three dice and six numbers, obviously any number has a 50-50 chance of coming up. Since the payoff is even money and higher for two or three of a kind, many gullible bettors think the odds are actually against the house. That would be true if casinos and carnivals ever took the short end of the odds. They never do.

If a bettor really believed the odds were in his favor, all he'd have to do would be to bet all six numbers every game. What would happen? Since there are 216 different possibilities—$6 \times 6 \times 6 = 216$—he would have to bet that number of games to theoretically allow the law of averages to operate. Out of these 216 possibilities three of a kind would come up once each for each number, or six times in all. Pairs would occur 90 times. In 120 instances three different numbers would appear.

When three different numbers did appear, the player would lose $3 on the missing numbers and win three on the numbers that came up. A dead-even result. However, it is different when a pair appears. In this case the bettor would win $2 for the pair and $1 for the other die, but he would lose $1 each on the other four numbers. Net loss: $1 \times 90, or $90.

And the six times that three of a kind appears, the player would win $3 on that number but lose $5 on the five remaining numbers. Net loss: $2 \times 6, or $12.

So much for having the edge on the house! At the Chuck-a-Luck table, all the players are rooting for two or three of a kind—and so is the house. Ironically, that's where the house's profits are. Mathematically, it works out that the house holds a monstrous advantage of 7.87 percent. Most gambling establishments allow only one bettor to a number, which tends to spread out the bets on all numbers, so the house can relax and just let the money roll in—the 96 times out of every 216 games when either two or three of a kind come up.

Some operators, not satisfied with that kind of edge in a simple six-number game, offer a layout that allows for a greater variety of bets. They offer wagering on high or low numbers or odd or even, but the house collects on all bets in which three of a kind occurs, regardless of the number. The player can also bet on three of a kind and if he hits he collects at 30 to 1 (correct odds would be 35 to 1). Or he may bet on any number *total* from 4 to 17, but will automatically lose again on triplets even if his total number comes up. Payoffs vary according to the number chosen. A low total of 4 is paid off at 60 to 1, although the true odds would be 71 to 1. Payoffs on totals of 9 through 12 are paid off at 6 to 1, although the correct odds on 9 or 12 would be 8 to 1 and on the 10 or 11, 7 to 1.

If a player really wants to play a longshot, he can bet on one particular three of a kind, such as three 6's. If they come up, he collects 180 to 1, but the true odds are 215 to 1.

All these newfangled bets produce bigger profits for the house than the standard form of Chuck-a-Luck, that is, betting on a single die number. The sole exception is betting on high or low or on odd or even totals of the three dice. In these instances the house keeps only 2¾ cents out of every dollar bet—almost an act of charity on the operator's part.

Crown and Anchor, an Australian and English version, substitutes symbols for dice numbers but actually is no different from the basic game of Chuck-a-Luck.

See CROWN AND ANCHOR.

CHUCK-A-LUCK CHEATING

Although Chuck-a-Luck produces considerable profits for the operator, there are some especially greedy ones who won't stop at cheating, or "gaffing," the game. This is especially true at carnivals or at charitable fund-raisers where operators pay a fee for running the game. Since they do not appreciate a strong run against the law of averages by possible uneven betting amounts on different numbers, they are assured a real edge by fixing the game.

The most common method involves using "electric dice" and an electromagnet in the table directly under the dice cage. The dice are loaded so that they will bring up either one or two opposite sides. Let's say it is the 5 and the 2. When the magnet is on, the result will be either three 5's, three 2's, or a pair of 5's and a 2 or a pair of 2's and a 5. It doesn't much matter, since all these combinations are winners for the house.

If the form of Chuck-a-Luck being played is the more varied one, the dealer must make sure there is no action on the point totals of 9 or 12, since these total numbers may be formed by the rigged dice, requiring a payoff of around 6 to 1. When there is such action, the magnet is deactivated and the game is played honestly. (Obviously, dice fixed for 1 and 6 or 3 and 4, the other sides of the dice, will produce different combinations.)

If you are a Chuck-a-Luck addict, which is certainly not recommended here, the best chance you have to spot a rigged setup is to check the space between the floor of the cage and the table. When the table contains a magnet, the space is bound to be much smaller. The nearer the magnet is to the cage, the better—from the cheater's point of view.

Winston CHURCHILL

See BEZIQUE; BEZIQUE—SIX-PACK (or CHINESE).

CINCH: Important Pre-Bridge Game

Cinch, sometimes called High Fives or Double Pedro, was for a time one of the most popular games among serious card players, but the game lost its pull with the development of Auction Bridge and finally Contract Bridge.

How to play: Cinch was usually played by four people in partnership, but it can also be played individually by anywhere from two to six. A single 52-card deck is used and in standard four-handed Cinch each player is dealt nine cards and in turn is permitted to make one bid or pass. A new bid must overbid the previous one. The highest point number possible is 14. The high bidder then calls trump.

The cards in trumps rank from ace high down to the 6. The next ranking card is the five, which is called Right Pedro. This in turn is followed by Left Pedro, which is the 5 of the same color as trump. The remaining trump values continue down from four to deuce. In all nontrump suits, the values rank from ace down to deuce, with the exception of Left Pedro.

After the highest bidder calls trump, each player discards face up all cards in his hand that are *not* trumps and is dealt as many cards as are needed to get his hand up to six cards. The dealer does not deal himself new cards from the top of the pack but instead exercises his privilege of "robbing the pack." That is, he is allowed to look through the remaining deck cards and take whichever ones he prefers, also establishing his hand at six cards.

The high bidder then leads to the first trick and opponents may follow suit or trump the trick. The trick goes to the highest trump, or if there are no trumps to the highest card in the suit. A player who cannot follow suit may discard another suit even if he is holding a trump. The player taking a trick leads to the next one.

The purpose of taking tricks is to capture the valuable trump cards that carry the following point values: high, the ace, 1; low, the deuce, 1; jack, the game, 1; the 10, 1; Right Pedro, 5; Left Pedro, 5.

In scoring with any number of players, if the high bidder makes his bid, the player with the highest count totals his points and subtracts his opponent's total from it and is credited with the difference. Thus in partnership play if the high bid was 7 and the bidder got 8 and the opposition 6, the 6 is subtracted from 8 and the winning team is credited with 2 points. If the bidder fails to make bid, let us say by the reverse of the scores above, the opposition would score its own points plus the total of the bid. In this case that would be 8 plus 7, or 15 points. The unsuccessful bidder scores nothing.

Generally Cinch is played to a total of 51 points, but sometimes scoring is kept on a CRIBBAGE board, in which case 61 is game. Betting settlement is made on the difference in the point score.

Strategy: Cinch is a good game to play with BRIDGE addicts because they are so schooled in their favorite game that they forget that in Cinch you are not required to follow suit if you can trump instead. As a result, a long trump suit in Cinch is not necessarily as powerful as in Bridge.

When the standard version of Cinch is played by any number of players other than four, all compete individually, and if there are five or six players they receive only six cards on the deal. However, when the game has that many players, most people prefer some of the many variations of basic Cinch instead. The main variations follow this entry.

CINCH—Auction

Auction Cinch, also called Auction High Five or Razzle Dazzle, is the best of the CINCH games for five or six players. Each player is dealt six cards, with the same bidding, discarding, and restoring of hands to six cards as in Cinch. The high bidder then calls out for a card he does not have—very often it is the ace of trump—so that the holder of the card will be his temporary partner for that hand only. However, that player does not reveal his identity until he plays the called-for card. Frequently, these temporary partners are seated next to each other, which is allowable in this game. If the contract is made, each partner adds the total partnership score to his own. If the contract fails, each of the opponents scores his individual points plus the amount of the bid.

CINCH—Blind

Blind Cinch is a four-handed game, with each player dealt nine cards plus an additional four that are left face down. The highest bidder looks at his four-card packet before calling trump, and then discards seven of his 13 cards. Other players then do the same and the game is played out as in regulation CINCH.

CINCH—Sixty-three

Sixty-three is a version of CINCH with considerably more trump points. In fact, high bid is 63. The usual high-card points apply, plus 25 for the trump king, 15 for the trump 3, and 9 for the trump 9. Unlike other versions of Cinch, bidders may rebid as often as they wish. After that, the usual rules of Cinch apply, with game usually set at 150.

CINCH—Widow

Widow Cinch is for six players, with those sitting opposite each other making up three teams of two each. Each player gets eight cards, and the last four cards a face-down "widow." Bidding follows CINCH rules. The high bidder then takes the widow, calls trump, and discards six cards, so that he has the usual six cards left. Each opponent discards two cards and play is carried on and scored as in regulation Cinch.

Andre CITROEN: Automobile Magnate and Compulsive Gambler

By any standards, the French carmaker Andre Citroen stands as a spectacular example of a famous figure laid low by gambling. Citroen managed a remarkable rationalization about his gaming: It mattered not whether he won or lost or the amounts involved, he said, because the endless reports in the press about his gambling were simply good publicity for his company, enhancing the reputation of the Citroen as a fabulous car. Citroen usually paid heavily for the publicity, once dropping 13 million francs in a single session. In 1926 Madame Citroen crashed the hallowed BACCARAT room at Deauville to plead tearfully with the management to stop the game at which her husband was losing steadily. Management complied, and Madame Citroen, albeit unintendedly, had struck a blow for women gamblers' rights. Until that time women had been barred from the Baccarat room; the rules were altered following her dramatic appearance.

Had not Madame Citroen taken such a drastic step, it is very likely that Citroen would have lost his factory then and there. She was portrayed by the press as the savior of the prestigious car firm. Citroen, however, kept on gambling and losing. Some years later he managed to drop several million francs within 10 minutes at Deauville, and did lose his firm.

CLAUDIUS: Roman Emperor and Dice Addict

Among all the Roman emperors, Claudius (10 BC–AD 54) may have been the most obsessed with DICE games. He is credited with having written a book on BACKGAMMON. The emperor constantly played dice during his journeys, and he had the interior of his carriage designed so that there was no motion to interfere with the roll of the cubes. So compulsive was his addiction to dice that he often summoned Romans to shoot dice with him whom he had had had executed the day before.

The Roman dramatist Seneca wrote a play on the death of Claudius, in which the emperor heads heavenward only to be shunted away with disdain. He is sent to hell, where a new punishment is deemed necessary for a ruler who had committed so many sins. It is decided that he should get hard labor without result and desire without satisfaction. Thus the judge Aeacus decrees he has to play dice with a bottomless cup:

> For every time he rattled the bones and rolled them, both dice escaped through the hole in the base of the cup; and when he picked them up and tried to shoot again, always attempting to grab them and then to throw them, they cheated him: they dodged, and through his fingers the tricky cubes dribbled elusively away.

Seneca was on target with his punishment. A dice shooter who can get no action is truly in hell.

CLEOPATRA'S WINE WAGER
It has to stand as the greatest bar bet of all time. Cleopatra, the queen of Egypt, was entertaining her new lover, Marc Antony, on her 30th birthday and bet him she could drink the equivalent of $500,000 worth of wine at one sitting. Marc Antony unhesitantly accepted the wager.

He lost as Cleopatra proceeded to drop two pearls worth 10 million sestertia into a glass and drank them down.

COCKFIGHTING, Gambling on
A brutal, generally illegal but much-practiced sport, cockfighting was imported into the United States from the Spanish Caribbean islands and Mexico. In the antebellum South entire plantations—or at least their annual crops—were often won or lost in cockfighting wagers. By the 19th century it was a common weekend entertainment in many parts of the South and West. To add excitement and gore, cocks were sometimes fitted with steel spurs. Others were force-fed garlic to spike their hostility.

The first cockfights were established in ancient Greece by Themistocles, who was inspired by two cocks he saw fighting as he led his forces into battle with Xerxes of Persia in 480 B.C. Themistocles won the battle, and thereafter launched a cockfighting festival to honor the animals for their inspiration. In time cockfighting—and betting on its result—was popular throughout the civilized world. Today it has virtually disappeared in Italy, Russia, Germany, and England (except for some northern regions). Elsewhere cockfighting thrives with or without official sanction—Central and South America, Mexico, the West Indies, the Philippines, Belgium, France, Spain, India, and Greece.

Despite constant efforts by reformers, cockfighting has never been stamped out in the United States; clandestine matches are held in large cities for big-money purses. Not long ago, police in Los Angeles broke up a cockfighting gambling ring and freed some two dozen cocks that had fought in matches for stakes of up to $10,000. Similar arrests have been made in Chicago and New York, where vacant buildings in deserted slum areas have been turned into exhibition halls. Sudden large numbers of parked cars in such areas is frequently a tip-off to what is going on. Cockfighting has outlasted dog fighting because it is easier to maintain secrecy with fighting cocks and because most of the action takes place in barrios, where police investigation is generally unpopular.

While local laws generally ban cockfighting, proposals in Congress have called for action on a federal level. These proposals, in turn, have brought protests from congressmen representing Mexican-American areas. A Texas congressman denounced a successful House vote to ban interstate transportation of birds and the use of the mails for the promotion of cockfighting, citing "the ethnic and cultural background of some of us."

Recent stepped-up immigration of Hispanics into the United States is expected to boost the incidence of cockfighting—despite popular concern about gambling rings secretly weakening one of the birds so that it will be a sure loser.

Louis M. COHN: Craps Shooter Who Started the Chicago Fire
If this is not the real story behind the great Chicago Fire of 1871, a man named Louis M. Cohn (1853–1942) paid through the nose to buy fame in gambling folklore.

On October 8, 1871, 18-year-old Cohn was shooting CRAPS with some friends in a barn owned by a family named O'Leary. The O'Learys were great gamblers, and there was generally action at their place. On the fateful night, the game was played by the light of a lantern and at a particularly tense moment in the game, Cohn accidentally upset the lantern and hay in the barn caught fire. The fire spread uncontrollably across the entire city. Since Cohn and the O'Learys were fearful of being held responsible for the disaster, they spread the tale that Mrs. O'Leary's cow had done the dirty deed.

Cohn went on to become a rich businessman. When he died in 1942 at the age of 89, he left $35,000 to Northwestern University and, along with the gift, endowed them with his version of the Chicago Fire. True to the gambler's code, Cohn added what he regarded as an important fillip to his story: "When I knocked over the lantern," he wrote, "I was winning."

COIN-DIE GAME: Bar Hustle
Because they can stack the odds quite simply in their favor the Coin-Die game has become very popular with sharper working the saloon beat.

How to play: A coin and a die are used to play, with the usual betting unit being one dollar. Player A tosses the coin. If it comes up heads, Player A rolls the die and wins twice the number of dollars that the die shows. If the coin comes up tails, Player A pays Player B (the sharper) $4 plus the number of dollars indicated by the die. Thus on a flip of heads and a die toss of 4 Player A collects $8. On a flip of tails and a die toss of 4, Player B wins $8.

This is not an even-money game. The advantage lies with Player B, the sharper. As Northwestern

University Professor of Mathematics C. Ionescu Tulcea points out in *A Book on Casino Craps*, Player B in the long run will win 25 cents per game.

This thesis is readily demonstrated. The assumption may be made mathematically that heads will come up six times and tails six times. Thus the die will be thrown 12 times, and again mathematically it figures each number from 1 to 6 will come up twice, once favoring Player A and once favoring Player B. Charted, such results produce these dollar profits in each case:

Die roll	Player A wins	Player B wins
1	$2	$5
2	4	6
3	6	7
4	8	8
5	10	9
6	12	10
Totals:	$42	$45

The difference appears to be slight—only $3—but this works out to 25 cents for every roll on average. Player B, using this form of betting, consistently will win much more, enjoying an edge far greater than a gambling casino has on most games. It hardly takes much time to flip a coin and throw a die. What's more, stakes can be raised. Many games are played for a betting unit of $5 and even $10. Some sharpers also are successful at getting players to agree to a tails flip payoff of $5 plus the number rolled with the die. When sharpers gamble with pigeons at that rate, they end up with an edge of 75 cents a game.

On the other hand, some gamblers object to $5 or even $4. The sharper is ready with an answer: "Okay, if you think $3 is fairer, I'll be the shooter and you cover me instead." The pigeon is trapped again. The odds have now shifted in favor of Player A—the sharper, in this case—for 25 cents. A pigeon is taken coming or going in the tricky Coin-Die game.

COLD DECK: Card-cheating Technique
The "cold deck" is a technique used by card hustlers to trim a mark in a high-stakes hand. Usually this occurs in a game in which all the players except the victim are in on the scam, but sometimes a lone hustler may work the switch by himself or with the aid of a confederate not in the game.

A deck of cards of the same make and design as the one being used is rigged in advance so that there are a number of strong POKER hands. The mark gets a very powerful hand but the cheat has an even better one.

The cold deck, sometimes called a "cooler" or "package" by professional cheats, is switched into the game in a variety of ways. When several cheats work the scam together they prefer pulling it on the victim's deal. As the victim offers the deck to be cut, another player on the other side of the dealer distracts him in a variety of fashions, such as asking for change. In that moment the decks are switched and as the victim turns back, the cutter seems simply to be completing his task. Another trick is to bring in the fixed deck as a nonplayer who offers drinks on a tray, effectively covering the substitution. A good operator can fake wiping his nose with a handkerchief in which he has concealed the cold deck.

A cold deck only has to be used once in an entire session with the rest of the play being on the up and up; it hardly matters how the victim does the rest of the time. Given a hand with four aces, he will bet the farm and then lose to a straight flush. Often the switch is made just as the betting rules are altered to no-limit.

There is no defense against a cold deck other than never losing sight of the cards—and to be wary about a pat hand coming up just as the betting limits are raised.

COLD HANDS
See SHOWDOWN.

COLOR POKER: One-color-hand Game
Color Poker has grown very popular in DEALER'S CHOICE games. At first blush, winning appears to be more a matter of luck than winning at regular POKER. In one sense that is true and it encourages many players to continue in the game in the hopes of ending up with a good hand. However, a disciplined player capable of calculating the odds and knowing when to drop will inevitably do even better at Color Poker than at the more standard versions of the game. One reason for this is that poorer players tend to stay in the game to the bitter end in the hope of striking it lucky.

The winner of the game, which is played exactly like regular DRAW POKER, is determined by the highest player's hand composed *entirely* of one color, that is, either red (hearts and diamonds) or black (spades and clubs). Thus a player with two black pairs and a red card is an automatic loser, while a player who holds all black cards, even unpaired, can win the hand. Anyone holding mixed colors after the draw is out of the game. Most gamblers think it is easy to get a one-color hand, but doing so with only 26 out of 52 cards can prove rather difficult. Several hands can pass without a winner, as the pot grows considerably with a new ante on every deal. Frequently, bettors also do not stay within their color and their bets simply go to build the pot.

Naturally there is no full house or three of a kind in Color Poker and many players grieve when they must break what would be surefire openers in regular Poker. The dealer, as well as the players to his right enjoy an important advantage, learning the earlier players' draws before making their own. Let us say the dealer has an all red hand, 8 high. However, an earlier player stands pat on the draw. Obviously there is no bluffing on the draw. Drawing no cards indicates a player has a one-color hand. The dealer now must figure that player must be paired once or twice or at least has a higher card than the dealer's 8. The dealer, under the circumstances, must discard his lowest card and hope to pull another red card that will either pair him or at least give him a higher card.

Undisciplined players generally stay on the draw even when all they have is three cards of one color, hardly a smart move since every player must have at least that on his first five cards. The good player departs at that point and lets the inferior player try to fill such a hand. An exception to this rule would be if everyone before the dealer passes on openers. In that case it is worth it for the dealer to open and take a stab at filling two more cards since probably everyone will drop, thinking he has a strong hand. The odds will be against the dealer, but if he makes five color cards he probably won't have much to beat. Of course winners must expose their hands, even if everyone drops, to show that they are holding one color.

An oddity of the game is that in restricting hands to one color it is easier to make a flush than a straight. Of course the flush must still be of one suit rather than merely of matching color.

For a more wide-open version of this game see COLOR POKER WITH BLUFF.

COLOR POKER WITH BLUFF

This game is the same as COLOR POKER except that players who fail to fill a color on the draw may stay in the game and bluff it out. No bluffing (in terms of staying after the draw with mixed colors) is possible in regular Color Poker. So it is possible for a player with a mixed hand to raise on practically nothing and chase out players holding a weak one-color hand. Unlike regular Color Poker, the bettor who drives all the competition out of a game need not show his hand.

Of course, this means winning hands can consist of four of one color or even three of one color, so it is necessary to break down the rank of winning hands. In Color Poker the winning hands in descending order are: royal flush, straight flush, flush, straight, two pair, one pair, high card. When a four-of-a-color hand wins in the Bluff version, the ranks are as follows: four-royal flush, four-straight flush, four flush, four straight, two pair, one pair, high card. In three

of a color, the ranks are: three-royal flush, three-straight flush, three flush, three straight, one pair, high card.

Obviously some gamblers prefer the bluffing version of this game because it adds excitement and suspense. Sharp players, however, go for straight Color Poker since it allows them to play the percentages more to their advantage, especially when they are dealing.

COLORADO—Legalized Lotteries

Colorado's lottery games lean heavily toward instant games of the "rub out" sort. Most tickets cost $1, but Colorado has also featured rather expensive instant games like the Million Dollar Sweepstakes, with tickets costing $5. There has been criticism around the country that $5 instant-game tickets are too costly and cause some people to wager compulsively more than they should or even want to.

Revenues from Colorado lotteries are parceled out to various state endeavors, including special open-space programs, recreational facilities and parks, as well as direct payments to cities and towns.

COMET OR COMMIT: 18th-century Game Celebrating Halley's Comet

Although some gambling authorities insist Comet and Commit were two separate games and that the former, which they describe as a double-deck version, was invented to honor the appearance of Halley's comet in 1759, it is more likely that the older game called Commit deserves the honor. In fact, there are references in old game books to "Hadley's Commit," indicating that 18th-century gamblers knew more about cards than they did about spelling or astronomy. In any case the game of Comet is still called Commit by some players today.

How to play: The game accommodates three to eight players, a deck of 51 cards being used, with the 8 of diamonds removed. Cards are dealt out to the fullest extent possible for complete rounds, with at least three cards remaining over. These are put aside, face down, and are dead cards. Cards are ranked from the ace as one up to the king, according to suit.

The player to the left of the dealer leads by placing any card he wishes face up on the table. If it is the 6 of clubs, for instance, he then can continue to add more to what may be considered to be the tail of the "comet"—that is, in order, the 7 of clubs, 8 of clubs, and so on. That player is stopped when he can no longer add the next card, let us say the 9 of clubs. Whoever does hold the 9 of clubs plays it and continues on from there until he too is stopped. When the king is reached, a new sequence is started by the player who put down the king. If, however, play is halted because a needed card is in the dead pile, the player making the last play is permitted to start a new sequence. The 9 of diamonds is a wild card and can be played at any time in any way, in sequence or to start a new sequence. It could, for instance, be played after the 8 of clubs, but this would not change the fact that the 9 of clubs would still be the next playable card.

Betting is started with a pot to which all players ante at the beginning of a hand. The player who gets rid of all his cards first takes the pot. However, there are other payoffs as well. When a player discards the 9 of diamonds, he collects two chips from every player, but if he is caught with that card at the conclusion of the game, he must pay each player two chips. Usually the rules call for anyone playing a king collecting one chip from each player, as well as paying each opponent one chip for every king he is caught with. Another payoff variation includes collecting one chip from each player for starting a sequence with an ace. In this version, however, there is no penalty for being caught with an ace.

Comet is not a game without skill and whether playing the original version or any variation some gamblers are said to have won heavily at it.

In later versions, known now as Commit, two decks of cards are used alternately. However, all the aces are dropped and the two decks are separated into one consisting of all black cards and the other with all red cards, except that the 9 of diamonds is put in with the black deck and the 9 of clubs with the red deck. These are "comets" or wild cards in turn. Play is limited to two to five players and the dead hand varies according to the number of players. There are 12 dead cards in a two- or three-player game, eight with four players, and three with five players. The payoff rules become more varied. There is no ante, but two chips are paid by the others to the player discarding the comet. However, if the comet was in the dead pile in the previous hand, its value increases by two, and by two more each time that reoccurs. If it happens on three consecutive hands the comet is worth eight, but on the following hand reverts to two. If a player goes out by discarding his last card, he collects for the remaining cards in all other hands: ten chips for picture cards and all other cards according to their point value. If a player is caught with a comet, he has to pay double its value for that hand as well as double on all his other cards. If a player goes out with a comet on the last card, but not in a natural 9 position, he gets double payoffs from all. If the comet is played as a 9, however, his payoff is quadrupled.

Strategy: The first priority is to get rid of duplicated card rankings as quickly as possible, for example, to cut down from three 7's to one as soon as possible. This is more important than getting rid of a large number of cards quickly. However, as the game progresses and it appears that an opponent is close to going out, it becomes critical to run off a long string of cards starting as low as possible, but it is still fatal to be holding double or triple ranks because it will be impossible to get rid of many of the same ranked cards late in the game.

While the later refinements of Comet allowed for considerably more card sense to come into play (such as remembering which player had run out of which suits), the game eventually lost much of its popularity in England and elsewhere in the Western world to the game of Eights. It may well have been that the original Commit version, with less complicated play, might better have retained its popularity than the more complicated Comet versions that made the game too wild and made luck too dominant a factor in the payoff amounts.

COMMERCE: Old English Poker Forerunner

Despite various claims made by many experts, it really is impossible to declare one particular game as the progenitor of POKER. Many old card games contain the seeds of modern Poker, and certainly among them is the old English game of Commerce.

How to play: The game begins with an ante. Next the dealer gives each player three cards, one at a time. Each player, beginning at the dealer's left, may then return a card to the dealer who buries it at the bottom of the deck and gives the player a new card. The dealer gets one chip for this. If the player wishes to avoid this charge he can instead "barter" with the player to his left, trading a face-down card with him.

The game continues in this fashion around the table as players try to make certain combinations. "Tricon," the top hand possible, is three of a kind, with three aces being highest. The next highest hand is "sequence"—later called "sequence flush"—and today called a three-card straight flush, such as ace, king, queen of spades (the ace being high or low).

In the earliest version of Commerce the final winning hand was "point." This was the lowest value of three cards of the same suit, that is a three-card flush with point values. The ace counts for 11, face cards for ten and all others their spot value. Thus ace-6-3 is 20 points and will lose to jack-5-2 at 17 points.

Over the years Commerce was refined to add other winning combinations. Flush without point values was introduced and ranked just under sequence. Below flush was a pair, two cards of the same rank and valued as they are in Poker today. Under this refinement point, now ranking under pair, became a two-card flush and the winning score became the high, that is king-queen of clubs is 20 and beats ace-7 of diamonds at 18.

The game ends whenever a player decides to stand on his hand. When it is his turn to trade with the dealer or barter, or when offered a barter by another player, he may knock on the table instead and call the game. All hands are shown and the highest one takes the pot. The dealer, who has been collecting chips from other players, must now pay each of them one chip unless he is the winner himself. If he hasn't collected enough chips for this, he must meet the obligation from his own money.

Commerce has enjoyed a bit of a revival in recent decades, especially in Great Britain and the Commonwealth. The best strategy is to call the game as quickly as possible, especially if one of the earlier players is holding a pair or even a point of ace-picture. Chances are he can steal the pot before other players get the opportunity to improve their hands.

COMPULSIVE GAMBLING

Although the medical-psychological term for them is compulsive gamblers, people who gamble have a different, more vivid, and probably more exact name for them. They call them gambling degenerates—horse degenerates, dice degenerates, POKER degenerates, BLACKJACK degenerates, BINGO degenerates. It hardly comes as a surprise to confirmed gamblers that a degenerate gambler will cheat and steal from family, friends, employers, enemies, anyone to get more money for "action"—and that many, having finally no other recourse after destroying their careers and family life, end up "taking the gas pipe." It is viewed by confirmed gamblers as just another peril of the profession.

Estimates of the number of compulsive gamblers in the United States vary greatly, running between one and four million persons. Others say these figures are much too low. In 1976 the National Council on Compulsive Gambling estimated the number as at least six million.

However, perhaps more revealing than a nose count would be a profile of compulsive gamblers. Seventy-five percent are men. According to psychiatrist Robert Custer, medical adviser to the Council, typical compulsive gamblers are men who "are very competitive, bright, industrious, energetic and hard-driving. As adolescents, they take on adult chores such as earning money for the family. They look destined for certain success."

First they are simply attracted to social gambling for a period that may last for anywhere from one to 20 years, then they become captives to the "action." (Probably one of the best examples of a compulsive

gambler was the great Russian writer Fyodor Dostoyevsky, whose short novel *The Gambler* conveyed the mania that grips gambling addicts.) This quest for action in a gambler, says psychologist Abe Kramer of the Brooklyn Veterans Administration Medical Center, means "he craves that excitement more than sex, more than anything."

Often gamblers are hooked by a long winning streak only to be shattered by the inevitable losing phase. In this period, Dr. Custer declares, the gambler seeks "to escalate his bets to recoup. But he never does. He loses his savings and borrows. About fifty percent steal." Gambling addicts want and expect their parents, spouses, or friends to bail them out during this "desperation" phase.

Many are bailed out but when eventually the aid peters out, the gambling addict will, in the words of Robert Politzer of the Washington Center for Pathological Gambling in Washington, D.C., "bottom out" when he is emotionally and financially spent. At this time some addicts seek treatment, but the sad fact is that only four states—Maryland, New York, New Jersey, and Connecticut—fund treatment centers. Nationwide there are only about a dozen centers, compared to 2,000 for drug addicts and 4,000 for alcoholics.

Treatments vary in different centers but all are founded on the concept of total abstention from further gambling and full payment of debts. Therapy at the privately funded Washington Center seeks to "restore the gambler's self-esteem and lift him out of his depression."

One study found that 76 percent of patients who were compulsive gamblers had "major depressive disorder," and many had suicidal tendencies. Dr. Custer views addicts as potential workaholics who "are easy to treat. They work just as hard to recover as they do to gamble. You just have to get them winning at other things."

But all experts warn that gamblers in rehabilitation may start betting again. "If therapists don't take a hard-nose, confrontational approach," psychologist Kramer states, "they can be conned without even knowing it."

It is obvious that legalization of gambling activities has a direct causal relationship to the incidence of compulsive gambling. The Commission on the Review of National Policy Toward Gambling declared in a report: "Legalization of gambling increases public exposure to more types of gambling, reduces negative attitudes toward the other (illegal) types of gambling and encourages wider participation."

Most gamblers understand the dangers of going "degenerate," but agree that no law, teaching, or morality can really curb the gambling instinct.

Typical of the average gambler's attitude toward the problem was a recent incident at a Friday night POKER game, with seven regulars. One player was reflecting to another that the group had originally consisted of six players, four of whom were no longer present. One, suffering from the stress of financial difficulties, had had a fatal heart attack; another was a suicide; a third was divorced and had left town and was rumored to be in an alcoholic treatment program; and the fourth was in prison for embezzlement. The other player reflected silently on the matter for a moment and finally said, "Shut up and deal."

See also FYODOR DOSTOYEVSKY; GAM-ANON; GAMBLERS ANONYMOUS; COMPULSIVE GAMBLING—GAMBLERS ANONYMOUS'S "20 QUESTIONS."

COMPULSIVE GAMBLING—Gamblers Anonymous's "20 Questions"

GAMBLERS ANONYMOUS, the national volunteer organization for compulsive gamblers, has composed a list of 20 questions that it feels goes a long way in identifying the compulsive gambler. Everyone who gambles should from time to time ask himself these questions:

1. Do you lose time from work because of gambling?
2. Is gambling making your home life unhappy?
3. Is gambling affecting your reputation?
4. Have you ever felt remorse after gambling?
5. Do you ever gamble to get money with which to pay debts or to otherwise solve financial difficulties?
6. Does gambling ever cause a decrease in your ambition or efficiency?
7. After losing, do you feel you must return as soon as possible to win back your losses?
8. After you win, do you have a strong urge to return to win more?
9. Do you often gamble until your last dollar is gone?
10. Do you ever borrow to finance your gambling?
11. Have you ever sold any real or personal property to finance gambling?
12. Are you reluctant to use "gambling money" for normal expenditures?
13. Does gambling make you careless of the welfare of your family?
14. Do you ever gamble longer than you have planned?
15. Do you ever gamble to escape worry and trouble?
16. Have you ever committed or considered committing an illegal act to finance gambling?
17. Does gambling cause you to have difficulty in sleeping?
18. Do arguments, disappointments, or frustrations cause you to gamble?
19. Do you have an urge to celebrate any good fortune by a few hours of gambling?
20. Have you ever considered self-destruction as a result of your gambling?

According to Gamblers Anonymous, if a person answers yes to seven or more of these questions, he should be concerned he already is or could become a compulsive gambler. In a recent study of compulsive gamblers, *When Luck Runs Out* by psychiatrist Robert Custer and Harry Milt, the authors state: "Recent research on the indicators of compulsive gambling tend to show that 7 is too low a figure, that the critical figure should be 12, instead."

A recommended layman's approach might well be that an increasing number of yes answers over a period of time would certainly be a warning sign.

See also COMPULSIVE GAMBLING; GAMBLERS ANONYMOUS.

CONNECTICUT—Legalized Lotteries

In the first decade since Connecticut started lottery games in 1973, the state coffers were enriched by over $1 billion. Although not innovative in the way that would count most, higher percentage payoffs compared to true odds, the state has been a shrewd packagers of its products. In LOTTO, for example, players must pick the six winning numbers from 1 to 40 for the top prize. If some find that too taxing, they can simply ask the selling agent for a "Quick Pick," and the computer will select numbers for them. If they play more than one set of numbers the computer, if called upon, will not duplicate any of the previous numbers.

The jackpot prize represents 50 percent of all prize money and is carried over and the pot increased if there is no winner holding all six correct numbers. Odds on winning the top prize are 1 in 3,838,380. Other odds are:

Five out of six:	1 in 18,816
Four out of six:	1 in 456
Three out of six:	1 in 32. (For this prize the payoff is a flat $3.)

"Advance Action" betting on Lotto permits playing the same numbers in advance for five, ten, 26, or 52 drawings. In the numbers game, which can be played a total of 13 different ways in three- and four-digit games, advance betting is possible for up to six days.

The state also offers instant games with a top prize

of $1 million, but the odds on winning either that prize or the others of $20,000, $15,000 or $10,000 is approximately 1 in 30 million for each.

Sean CONNERY: Real-life Gambling James Bond

Most casino operators agree that the James Bond movies have been great hype for their business. Fictional Bond, the secret agent and super gambler created by British author Ian Fleming, kills spies, conquers women, and cleans up at the gaming tables (not necessarily in that order). And Sean Connery, the actor best known for portraying agent 007, struck a blow for true-life Bondian capers by proving to be an equally successful gambler.

Once at the casino at St. Vincent, Italy, Connery nonchalantly won the equivalent of about $30,000 in three spins of the ROULETTE wheel. He bet on number 17 and, amazingly, it came out three consecutive times. Mathematically, this was a 50,652 to 1 shot. This meant that theoretically if Connery had bet one dollar and simply let it ride, the original dollar would have grown to over $50,000. Connery actually bet more, skimmed off a good part of his winnings, and let the balance ride on 17. When it won again, he again took partial profits. On the third 17, Connery swept up all his profits and departed.

Some gambling writers have theorized that had he tried it again, he would have been bucking odds of 1,874,160 to 1 against the same number coming up four times running, a prospect perhaps too rich even for James Bond himself. If that was Connery's rationale for quitting, rather than simply quitting because he was ahead, he was wrong. The true odds on 17 coming up again were—as it is on every spin of a Roulette wheel—36 to 1.

See also JAMES BOND.

CONQUAIN: Mexican Predecessor of Rummy and Coon Can

Conquain is a two-handed Rummy-style game of Spanish origin that was and is much played in Mexico. In the last century it spread from Mexico to Texas and throughout the Southwest. Most card historians say that Conquain developed into COON CAN and eventually RUMMY.

How to play: Conquain is played with a 40-card pack with the picture cards removed, although sometimes the 10's, 9's, and 8's are stripped instead. The game is perhaps easiest explained by using the former deck. Ace is low and 10 high. Each player is dealt ten cards and the rest of the pack is placed face down to form the stock. The objective is to meld or lay down sequences of three or more cards in one suit, such as ace, deuce, trey of clubs, or three or

four cards of the same value such as three 7's or four 8's, etc.

The nondealer starts by turning up the top card from the stock and melding whatever he can from his hand, making use of the turned-up card. If he uses the new card, he discards an unwanted card from his hand to start the discard pile. If he cannot meld with the turned-up card, he must use it to start the discard pile. He may not, as in Rummy, take the card in his hand.

In turn, the dealer may take the top card of the discard pile. If he does not want it, he takes up the next card from the stock and makes it the new turned-up card. He has the option of taking this card in his hand (he need not meld it immediately) or leave it as a discard. If he takes the turned-up card, he must discard another card and his opponent may take that card or turn up a new card instead.

A player may lay off additional cards to his own melds as play progresses and he may also "borrow" from one to another, if both melds remain valid. He might have already laid down 7, 8, 9, 10 in diamonds, and he now adds two 10's to the 10 of diamonds to form three 10's. He cannot, however, add two 9's to the 9 of diamonds as this would break his original meld. Two 7's, on the other hand, would be valid.

Strategy: Played properly, Conquain can be very cutthroat. The sharp player will "force" an opponent when the situation warrants, especially when that player is down to two cards. Let us say the player has melded four 10's and the 4, 5, 6, and 7 of spades. He is also holding two aces. His opponent deliberately discards the 3 of spades, forcing him to add the card to his meld and discard one of his aces. Before that move, any ace would have allowed him to lay down 11 cards, but now he is forced to draw the deuce and 8 of spades, or the deuce and ace of spades, or the 8 and 9 of spades in the proper order to go out. And one or more of these cards may well be dead.

The winner is determined only when there is a complete meld of 11 cards. If neither player can go out when the stock is used up, each player antes again to the pot and the next game is for double stakes.

CONTINENTAL RUMMY: Multi-deck Version of the Basic Game

Continental Rummy is a multi-deck version of the basic game of RUMMY in which only sequences in suit matter, that is, ace, deuce, trey, 4 of spades, etc. Sets of cards of the same rank, such as three 8's or four jacks, have no value. When two to five persons play, 106 cards are used—two 52-card packs plus two jokers; for six to eight persons, three packs and three jokers; and for nine to 12, four packs and four jokers. Jokers are wild and may be used as substitutes for any card, and aces may be low below the deuce or high over the king.

How to play: each player is dealt 15 cards and the playing and drawing of cards follow the rules of Rummy. A player may not declare until he can lay all of his 15 cards down, and that must be done in certain proportions, of at least four sequences of at least three cards and not more than a total of five cards each and not more than a total of five sequences. This means there are really only three ways to meld, as follows:

5-4-3-3
4-4-4-3
3-3-3-3-3

However, continuous sequences can be broken as long as they still produce the minimum cards necessary for each; thus ace through 6 may constitute two separate sequences of three cards.

Betting settlements are handled in various ways, but the most common is for the winner to collect one chip from each losing player and another two chips for any jokers with which they are caught.

To make the game even wilder, the deuces are made wild along with the jokers. In that case the deuce does not count in sequence, so that ace, 3, 4 in spades makes an adequate meld even if a wild deuce or two is involved in making the sequence.

CONTRACT RUMMY: Multi-deck Version of the Basic Game

Like CONTINENTAL RUMMY, Contract Rummy, also called Liverpool Rummy and Progressive Rummy, is a multi-deck version of the basic game of RUMMY. As a three- or four-person game it requires two decks of 104 cards with one to four wild jokers added, according to the players' tastes. When there are five to eight players a triple deck of 156 cards is used and the wild-joker count may go as high as six. Aces count for 15 points and may be high above the king and low below the deuce. Picture cards are all 10 points, jokers 15, while all other cards carry their spot value.

How to play: the game generally calls for seven separate deals, each with its own "contract" or special melding rules for the particular deal. In the first four deals, each player gets ten cards and then 12 cards for the final three deals. After the deal, the next card is turned up to start a discard pile as in regular Rummy. Order of play and what constitutes a meld of sets or sequences in suit are the same as in Rummy, with however a major difference in the rules. If the player does not wish to take the top card of the discard pile but wishes to draw from the pack,

he must first allow the next player to his right a chance to take that discard. If the latter does so, he must also take the top card of the pack and reserve both cards in his hand, with play then reverting to the original player who takes his card from the pack. If the player to the right does not wish the discard, the privilege passes to the next player, and so on, but eventually play reverts back to the player whose turn it is.

Melds and sets are playable as in Rummy, but on the first meld each player must meet the requirements of the particular deal. These are as follows, based on three-card melds in all cases except for the seventh deal:

First deal:	Two sets (such as three kings and three 9's)
Second deal:	One set and one sequence (the latter being something like queen, king, ace of hearts)
Third deal:	Two sequences
Fourth deal:	Three sets
Fifth deal:	Two sets and one sequence
Sixth deal:	One set and two sequences
Seventh deal:	Three sequences of four cards each.

Whenever two or more sequences are required, they may be all of the same suit but not continuous (such as ace, deuce, 3 of spades and 5, 6, 7 of spades, but not ace through 6 of spades to count for two sequences).

After the initial meld requirements have been met the hand continues with players seeking to "go Rummy," or lay down all their cards. Players may lay off cards to any melds showing including those in other hands, and they may also replace a wild card (the jokers or, in some games, the deuces as well) with a natural card in sequence and shift the wild card to either end of the sequence.

In all other aspects of the deals and games are played like straight Rummy and the values left in all losers' hands are totaled against them. At the end of the seventh deal, the winner is the player with the lowest score and he collects on the difference between his score and those of each opponent. Sometimes the player with the highest score also is required to pay all opponents an additional bonus, in effect lowering the other players' losses.

See also KING RUMMY; ZIONCHECK.

COON CAN: Rummy Variation

Coon Can, sometimes called Double Rum or Two-pack Rum, is an early predecessor of RUMMY and itself is descended from the Spanish-Mexican game of CONQUAIN. Coon Can utilizes two full packs of cards along with two jokers, or 106 cards in all.

How to play: each player is dealt ten cards and the purpose of game is to play out by building sequences of three cards or more in suit, such as ace, deuce, 3 of clubs, or groups of three or four cards in rank, such as three 10's or four queens. The ace may be used as the lowest number in a sequence, meaning a one, or at the other end after a king.

The jokers are very valuable cards and may be used to represent any card the holder desires, thus it can be a third card to a group or as a part of a sequence. If the joker is melded at either end of a sequence it may be moved if the opportunity arises. Let us say a player has melded 10, jack, queen, joker as a sequence. The player then gets the king in suit. He may replace the joker with the king and figure the joker now as either an ace or 9. A joker can only be shifted once, however.

Under a variation of the game it is allowed for an opponent holding the natural card for which the joker has been substituted, to claim the joker for his own by replacing it with the natural card.

Play continues until a person has melded all his cards. This usually happens before the balance of the pack is drawn as in standard Rummy. If the stock is used up, the discard pile is shuffled and reused as the stock. Scoring for gambling purposes sets the value of jokers at 15; aces, 11; pictures, 10; and all other cards at their spot value. Losers add up the points of the cards and pay that total to the winner.

CRAPLESS CRAPS: New Casino Gouge Game
Supposedly a crapshooter's dream, Crapless Craps has reared its ugly head in some Nevada casinos. What could be more inviting on the surface than a game that doesn't cause the shooter to crap out on the first, or come-out, roll? Throw a 2, 3, or 12 and you don't lose! It's true. It is unfortunately also true that your chances of winning at this hybrid dice game—some keen gamblers disparage it by referring to it as Bastard Craps—*is almost four times worse than at standard* CRAPS.

Here are some of the kickers that makes this such a lovely game for the house: Roll a 2, 3, or 12 and you don't lose, *but* that number becomes your point, which means you must repeat that number before a 7 comes up. Since there is only one way a shooter can make either a 2 or 12 and six ways to make a 7, it becomes apparent that such numbers not being losers on the first throw generally only makes them delayed losers. The chances of hitting a 2 *twice* before a 7 appears after the first roll is, if not nil, the next thing to it. That applies as well to the 12, and the 3 is only slightly better, since it can be made two ways out of 36 compared to six ways for the 7.

The house in all its magnanimity sticks to the basic rule in Craps whereby a 7 wins on the come-out roll, but then a nasty little kicker is slipped in concerning the 11, which should also be a winner. Like the 2, 3,

and 12, the 11 does not end the game but instead becomes the shooter's point, and of course it is just as difficult to roll it again as the 3. Thus the house has created a game in which only the 7 is a winner on the first roll and in exchange for no craps on the come-out, the unlikely points of 2, 3, and 12 are converted into almost certain losers. And an initial winning 11 becomes an almost certain loser as well.

There are other minor changes in the rules that give shooters slightly improved odds on various proposition bets, but since such wagers are terrible gougers to begin with this merely turns highway robbery into mere felony robbery.

The casinos' fascination with Crapless Craps becomes apparent when one compares the house-edge differences between this game and regular Craps. In regular Craps the line bets provide a 1.4 house edge. In Crapless Craps this soars to 5.38 percent, making the game a worse deal than any of the major casino games—worse than BLACKJACK, Craps, BACCARAT, or even-money bets at Atlantic City ROULETTE. Despite this, Crapless Craps tables tend to be very crowded with players who want to avoid the let-down feeling that comes from being wiped out on the first roll of the dice. In Crapless Craps a player is guaranteed to last beyond the first roll, but when one opts this game over regular Craps he can be sure of one thing: his bankroll will dwindle much faster.

CRAPS: The Made-in-America Gambling Game
Bar none, Craps is America's No. 1 gambling game. And there is no doubt that it is history's biggest game. In America, fifty million Americans shoot Craps every year (over 10 percent are women), and more money is bet on Craps than any other game. It is the easiest private gambling game to set up. It is the biggest payday game in the armed forces. In the casinos it is the favorite game of the American "high roller"—probably to an even greater extent than ROULETTE or the various forms of BACCARAT in Europe. How much is wagered on Craps? Some gambling experts do not hesitate to make estimates, but it is impossible to measure the illegal play throughout the country. Today those estimates run to well over $200 billion a year. There seems to be no reason to dispute these figures, except perhaps to suspect they may be on the low side.

Casino BLACKJACK, as far as real wagering is concerned, does not hold a candle to Craps. True, they may post similar minimums and maximums (such as $5 and $500 and up) and indeed for special high rollers the play at Caesars Palace goes up for both to $25,000 a game, but you don't see the Blackjack bets at that level as you do in Craps. It was not at Blackjack but at Craps that a character drove in off the desert to Binion's Horseshoe Casino in downtown

Action at a Las Vegas Craps table. Note the dice in flight and perhaps more important the posted house limit, making it not particularly a high-stakes table. (Photo: Las Vegas News Bureau)

Vegas with two suitcases, one containing $770,000 in $100 bills. He changed his money into chips and under security guard headed for the Craps table.

He plunked down the entire $770,000 on a single roll—the Horseshoe basically doesn't know what the word maximum means—won, and returned to the cashier's cage with a double load of chips. The $770,000 went back into one suitcase. He opened the second suitcase, which turned out to be empty. Clearly, the man had great expectations. All he said was, "I reckoned inflation was going to eat that money up anyway, so I might as well double it or lose it all." He left and, as the people in Vegas say with some sadness, he has not returned.

There is that kind of glamour attached to Craps in America that has never rubbed off on any other gambling game.

As grandiose as it has become, Craps had humble beginnings and was and is still the greatest small-stakes gambling game played regularly. It developed out of the English dice game of HAZARD, which was imported into the New World in the 18th century. However, Hazard proved too complicated for the black slaves on the levee in New Orleans shortly

after 1800, and so they proceeded to prune back on the rules of Hazard until they ended up with a much better game, one far more mathematically equal than Hazard. The name of Craps stuck to it for no other reason than that the New Orleans French had referred to Hazard by that name. Indeed, because of the blacks' development of Craps, dice today are still referred to in slang as "African dominoes."

Craps eventually took over from FARO as the most important gambling house game, and for good reason. Faro had become so crooked and so many fortunes had been lost and lives ruined that it had to go. Still, it was not until the early part of the 20th century that Craps gained popularity beyond the black community and professional gamblers.

Today American casinos push Craps as they do no other gambling game, and for good reason. While many bettors participate in the game because of its low house edge, it nevertheless contains a great number of sucker bets that are very pleasing to a casino. Because there is very little difference between casino Craps and the private game (except that the latter offers players a better chance since there is no artificial house edge added), we can illustrate the game best in the casino format. Following is the complete description of Craps from the gaming guide of the Golden Nugget in Atlantic City. The Golden Nugget passed from the scene in 1987, but this does not alter the explanation of the rules of the game since under New Jersey law all casinos must play the game exactly the same way.

The game is played with two dice thrown by the "shooter." You may bet with the shooter or against him, or make any of the many other bets available. (see the accompanying diagram).

A) "PASS LINE"

When the shooter rolls a 7 or 11 on the first (come out) roll, you win. If 2, 3 or 12 is rolled on the come-out roll you lose. Any other number (4, 5, 6, 8, 9 or 10) becomes the "point" and you win if the "point" is repeated before a 7 is rolled. "Pass Line" bets lose if 7 is rolled before the "point" is made. Place these bets in the space marked "Pass Line" on the craps table. They cannot be removed or reduced until after they win and cannot be placed once a "Point" is established.

B) "COME LINE"

Just like betting the "Pass Line" except that "Come Line" bets are made anytime after the "point" is established. Place these bets on the "Come Line." You win on 7 or 11 and lose on 2, 3, and 12 on the roll immediately following the placement of your bet. Any other number that comes up is your "point" and your bet will be placed on that number. You win if your "point" repeats before a 7 is rolled. You lose when a 7 rolls before your "point" is made. "Come" bets can't be removed or reduced until after they win.

C) "DON'T PASS LINE"

This is the reverse of betting the "Pass Line". You win if 2 or 3 is rolled on the come-out roll, stand-off if 12 is rolled and lose if 7 or 11 is rolled. When a "point" is established, you win if 7 is rolled before the "point" is made and you lose if the "point" is repeated before a 7 rolls. Place these bets in the space marked "Don't Pass" on the craps table. "Don't Pass" bets may be removed or reduced at any time, but may not be replaced or increased until a decision on

the "point" has occurred. "Don't Pass Line" bets may be made only on the come out roll and may not be bet after the "point" is established.

D) "DON'T COME LINE"

This is the reverse of the "Come Line" bet. Place these bets on the "Don't Come Line" anytime after the "point" is established. You win if 2 or 3 is rolled, standoff if 12 is rolled, and lose if 7 or 11 is rolled on the roll immediately following the placement of your bet. Any other number becomes your "point" and your bet will be placed behind that number. You win if 7 is rolled before your "point" is rolled. You lose if your "point" is repeated before a 7 rolls. At your request, the dealer will remove or reduce your "Don't Come" bet, but it may not be replaced or increased without being re-bet on the "Don't Come Line".

"Pass", "Come", "Don't Pass", and "Don't Come" bets are all paid even money when they win.

E) TAKING AND LAYING ODDS

A player may make a wager in addition to his original or "flat" bet anytime after the "point" is established. Players may "take odds" on any "Pass Line" or "Come" bet. Players may "lay odds" on "Don't Pass Line" or "Don't Come" bets. Odds payoffs are equal to the true odds of winning or losing the bet (see the accompanying table). The odds bet wins if the flat bet wins and loses if the flat bet loses.

The dealer will be happy to explain the limits on taking and laying odds.

F) "BUY" AND "LAY" BETS

These bets pay true dice odds without requiring a "flat" bet and may be made directly on 4, 5, 6, 8, 9 or 10 at anytime. A "Buy Bet" is a wager that the number bet will roll before a 7, similar to the "Pass Line" bet. A "Lay Bet" is a wager that 7 will roll before the number wagered on, similar to the "Don't Pass Line" bet. A commission of 5% is charged on a "Buy Bet", and on the amount that could be won on a "Lay Bet." The payoff odds are shown in the accompanying table.

G) "PLACE BETS TO WIN"

These wagers can be made at anytime, directly on any, or all of the following numbers: 4, 5, 6, 8, 9 or 10. The wager on each "placed" number wins if the number rolls before a 7 and loses if 7 rolls before the

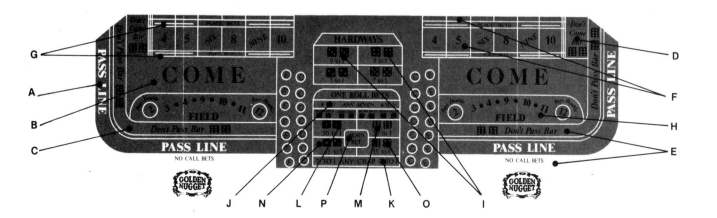

"placed" number. The "Place Bet" is similar to a "Buy Bet" but no commission is charged and the payout odds are different (see the accompanying table).

All odds, "Buy Bets" and "Place Bets" may be increased, decreased, taken back by the Player or called "off" at anytime. "Come Bet" odds, "Buy Bets" and "Place Bets" are always off on the come out roll unless designated otherwise by the Player. "Come Bet" odds, "Don't Pass" odds, "Don't Come" odds, "Buy Bets", and "Place Bets" are all given to the dealer, who places them in the proper location on the craps table. The player is responsible for placing "Pass Line" odds and keeping track of his bets.

H) FIELD BET

This is a one roll bet that may be made *on any roll. If 3, 4, 9, 10 or 11 rolls, you* win even money. If 2 or 12 *rolls, you* win, 2 to 1. *If any other number rolls, you* lose.

I) HARDWAYS

Hardway bets are located in the center of the craps table and are placed by the dealer. Hardways may be bet at any time. The four possible Hardway bets are "Hardway Six" (two 3's) and "Hardway Eight" (two 4's), which pay 9 to 1, and "Hardway Four" (two 2's) and "Hardway Ten" (two 5's)—, which pay 7 to 1. You win if the Hardway you are betting rolls before a 7. The bet loses if a 7 rolls first or if the number rolls with a non-pair combination. For example, a "Hardway Eight" wins only if two 4's are thrown before a 7 or before an "easy-way" eight (5-3 or 6-2 combination). Hardways are *off* and not working on the come out roll unless the player designates the bet to be *on*.

ONE ROLL BETS

The following bets can be made on any roll of the dice. The bets win or lose each roll depending upon the result of the throw. These bets are handed to the Dealer to be placed in the appropriate part of the craps table. Winning bets are automatically placed again for the next roll unless specifically called off by the player.

J) **Any 7:** If 7 rolls you win and are paid 4 to 1. All other numbers lose.

K) **Any Craps:** if 2, 3 or 12 rolls you win and are paid 7 to 1. All other numbers lose.

L) **Two Craps or Aces:** If 2 is rolled, you win and are paid 7 to 1. All other numbers lose.

M) **Twelve Craps or Two Sixes:** If 12 is rolled, you win and are paid 30 to 1. All other numbers lose.

N) **Three Craps or Ace-Deuce:** If 3 rolls you win and are paid 15 to 1. All other numbers lose.

O) **Eleven or Six-Five:** If eleven rolls you win and are paid 15 to 1. All other numbers lose.

P) **Horn Bet:** Is a four unit (or multiple thereof) bet whereby you are betting one-fourth of your wager on 2, 3, 11, and 12. If 3 or 11 rolls you win and are paid 3.75 to 1. If 2 or 12 rolls you win and are paid 7.5 to 1. If a number other than 2, 3, 11, or 12 rolls, you lose.

Horn High Bets: Same as a Horn Bet except that you are betting an extra unit straight up on either 2, 3, 11 or 12 as you so designate. For example: a $5.00

Horn High Aces has one dollar bet each on 3, 11 and 12 and $2.00 bet on Aces. If one of these four numbers rolls, you win, and the payoff is calculated in the same manner as a "Horn Bet". If any other number rolls, you lose.

"GOLDEN NUGGET CRAPS ODDS"

Pass Line/Come Bet	1 to 1
Don't Pass/Don't Come Bet	1 to 1
Pass Line Odds/Come Bet Odds/Buy Bets	
Numbers 4 or 10	2 to 1
Numbers 5 or 9	3 to 2
Numbers 6 or 8	6 to 5
Don't Pass Odds/Don't Come Bet Odds/	
Lay Bets	
Numbers 4 or 10	1 to 2
Numbers 5 or 9	2 to 3
Numbers 6 or 8	5 to 6
Field Bets	
3, 4, 9, 10, 11	1 to 1
2, 12	2 to 1
Place Bets	
Numbers 4 or 10	9 to 5
Numbers 5 or 9	7 to 5
Numbers 6 or 8	7 to 6
Hardways	
6 or 8	9 to 1
4 or 10	7 to 1
One Roll Bets	
Any 7	4 to 1
Any Craps	7 to 1
2 Craps or 12 Craps	30 to 1
3 Craps or 11	15 to 1
Horn Bet (3 or 11 rolls)	3.75 to 1
Horn Bet (2 or 12 rolls)	7.5 to 1

Of course, one does not expect a casino guide to point out the truth about the house edge involved in its offerings. Naturally, many of these wagers are sucker bets. Let us consider some of them after first looking at the following two charts.

The first one shows the possible variations that can result from casting a pair of dice numbered 1 to 6 a total of 36 times (6×6 being the perfect mathematical quota):

Point	Combinations to Make	Ways to Make
2	1-1	1
3	1-2, 2-1	2
4	1-3, 3-1, 2-2	3
5	1-4, 4-1, 2-3, 3-2	4
6	1-5, 5-1, 2-4, 4-2, 3-3	5
7	1-6, 6-1, 2-5, 5-2, 3-4, 4-3	6
8	2-6, 6-2, 3-5, 5-3, 4-4	5
9	3-6, 6-3, 4-5, 5-4	4
10	4-6, 6-4, 5-5	3
11	5-6, 6-5	2
12	6-6	1
	Total	36

This is the most important bit of intelligence a Craps player will ever learn about the game. The 7, of course, comes up the most, six times out of 36. Now let's look at the odds offered by the casino on whether the 7 will come up on the next roll of the dice. The payoff is 4 to 1. But if the house was willing to give the player a fair break and gave true odds the price would be 5 to 1, meaning the player would win once out of every six tries (or six out of 36). The difference between 4 to 1 and 5 to 1 works out to a house percentage of . . . 16.7 percent! That's absolutely the worst bet you can make in Craps and the worst anywhere in a casino except for that notorious money-stealer, the Big Six, or Money Wheel.

Still the pitch made by the casinos for Craps is that it offers the best odds in the house. *That* depends on you betting right all the time, something few players do. The following chart shows the bets you can make, the payoff you may get and the percentage the house takes on average on the play.

Bet	Pays	House Edge
Pass or Come	1 to 1	1.414
Don't Pass or Come	1 to 1	1.402
Place 4 or 10	9 to 5	6.7
Place 5 or 9	7 to 5	4.0
Place 6 or 8	7 to 6	1.5
Buy Bet	true odds minus 5%	4.7
Lay 4 or 10	1 or 2 minus 5%	2.4
Lay 5 or 9	2 to 3 minus 5%	3.2
Lay 6 or 8	5 to 6 minus 5%	4.0
Field	1 to 1 (double on 2 and 12)	5.5
Hardways 6 or 8	9 to 1	9.09
Hardways 4 or 10	7 to 1	11.1
Any Seven	4 to 1	16.9
Any Craps	7 to 1	11.1
2 or 12	30 to 1	13.9
3 or 11	15 to 1	11.1

It is evident that the best bets are on the Pass or Don't Pass lines, the Come and Don't Come lines, and place bets on 6 or 8. Beyond that, it's gouge time. None of the remaining bets are worth making. (There are some additional good percentage bets that can be made in a casino, which are called "odds" or "double odds" or "triple odds," but in order to make these bets a player must first make his Pass or Come line bets at the usual house edge and then may increase his bet at true odds. Most players, however, don't know how to bet odds and simply end up betting more than they wish so that the casino's total profits increase even though the house percentage decreases.) Not included in the above chart are the odds for Horn bets and High Horn bets, and for good reason. Stay away from them. All they really do is con a player into making four or five sucker bets at the same time. Consult the individual bets involved and you'll see why they are bad bets.

The essential fact is that only the even-money bets are worth making to hold the house edge down.

As soon as women show up at the Craps table the stickman will immediately start talking up the field bet, calling out that it is a great bargain bet: "You get even money betting on seven different numbers. You only lose on four numbers." The man's not lying, but add up the ways you can get the numbers—2, 3, 4, 9, 10, 11, and 12 and it totals 16, which means you lose 20 ways. Even allowing for a payoff at 2 to 1 if 2 or 12 come up (the two least likely possibilities) the house edge is a much too high 5.5 percent. Stickmen use the "bargain" pitch with women because they feel women like good buys, but the field bet is strictly a bargain for the casino.

The fact is, one must be careful how he bets Craps at different casinos. For instance, in Las Vegas one can bet on "Big 6" or "Big 8" at even money. This is the same bet that one gets at 7 to 6 odds at place bets on the 6 or 8 in Atlantic City. In fact, you can also place the 6 or 8 in Vegas and get 7 to 6 odds. But make the same bet on Big 6 or Big 8 and you get only even money. So depending on how astute the bettor is, the Vegas casinos take an edge of 1.5 or 9.09 for the same bet! A cynic might wonder if Bugsy Siegel is really dead.

Yes, Craps is America's No. 1 gambling game and that will never change because the casino won't let it. They have butchered Roulette by making it so unattractive with a zero and double zero (see ROULETTE) precisely because the house edge is too small for their liking. Roulette has a small house edge of 1.35 on even-money bets and only 2.7 on everything else including payoffs on individual numbers at 35 to 1. Let us say you wish to bet on 2 in Craps. The payoff is 30 to 1 on what is at true odds a 35 to 1 shot. Roulette pays off 35 to 1 on the 2, which at true odds is a 36 to 1 shot. At Craps the bet produces a 13.9 house edge instead of the 2.7 in Roulette. (In England where the Gaming Board sits hard on the casinos, payoffs on 2 or 12 are made at 33 to 1—not as good as they could be, but at least an attempt to give a player a fairer shake.)

Is it any wonder the Craps tables in Europe are as uncrowded (except for American tourists) as the American Roulette tables are in America? The casinos say they don't have single zero Roulette because Americans want a faster game. Actually, a game of Craps can run much longer than a spin of the Roulette wheel as the shooter may need ten or more rolls to make his point or crap out. But that isn't the point. Craps is very popular with the people who really count—the casino owners.

See ACE-DEUCE STANDOFF; DICE.

CRAPS, SIMPLIFIED

There are some casino authorities who believe a simplified form of Craps will attract more gamblers, especially women. What they say is needed is a simple game that offers bigger odds payoffs on some numbers. The following version now has some following and is also growing in popularity in private games.

The bettor places his bet and wins if the dice come up 2, 3, 4, 10, 11, or 12. The player loses on 5, 6, 7, 8, or 9. Obviously the losing numbers are ones that come up more frequently, but an adjustment is paid by increasing the odds payoff as follows:

2 pays 3 to 1
3 or 4 pays even money
10 or 11 pays 2 to 1
12 pays 5 to 1

What this does overall is give the house an advantage of 2.8 percent. This is attractive to the house of course, but will satisfy many gamblers except for high rollers who will not play against any kind of edge larger than 1.41, which they get in the basic bet in regular Craps.

Still the game is popular with hustlers and other "wrong bettors" who seek consistently to bet against the shooter. The only downer about this is paying off at high odds, which they sometimes have to do. Some hustlers therefore try to chisel down the payoffs on the 12 to 3 to 1 and anything else they can get away with. Some illegal mob joints in the New York area offer the game and up their take by cutting the 10 back to even money and paying off at 4 to 1 on the 12.

CRIBBAGE: Two-handed Card Game

Cribbage, a two-handed card game, is one of the few that can be ascribed to a single inventor, the English poet and soldier Sir John Suckling. Introduced to London in the early 17th century, Cribbage was adapted by Suckling from several earlier games, including one known as Noddy. But Cribbage is truly Suckling's invention and the rules of the game have come down to us virtually unchanged.

Cribbage is played with a full pack of 52 cards and scored with pegs on a board containing four rows of holes (two for each player). Dealt five, six (the usual today), or seven cards, each player places two in the "crib" or extra hand belonging to the dealer, and the pack is cut and the dealer turns up the top card of the lower half, which is called the "starter." This card does not figure in actual play, but it is important toward the scoring of certain points. Scoring in Cribbage is called "pegging" and is done on a Cribbage board.

If the starter is a jack, or "His Heels," the dealer pegs 2 points. If there is no jack, there is no score and the other player commences play by putting a card face up on his side of the board and calling out its count, such as "Four" for the 4 of clubs. The dealer then does the same, adding the count of his card, so that a 7 of hearts would make the running total 11. All picture cards are valued at 10 points. The play continues until the total nears 31. A player cannot go over that total, and if he therefore cannot lay down further cards, he announces, "Go." This allows his opponent the chance to continue playing cards toward reaching 31. The opponent also is entitled to peg 1 point, whether or not he himself can lay down any cards. If he can get the total to exactly 31, he is entitled to another 1-point peg.

The cards are then faced down and the player next in turn starts a new series toward 31. As play proceeds, players score other points in addition to "Go" and 31. When a card played brings the running total to 15, the player pegs 2. If a player uses a card of the same rank as his opponent's one on his last play (such as jack on jack), he gets 2 points for the pair. If a player can play a third matching card to a pair, such as a third 5 to a pair of 5's, he scores a "pair royal," which is worth 6 points. A fourth card to a set is a double pair royal and is good for 12 points. If one player lays down a 3, and the next a 4, the first player will put down a 5, if possible, scoring a sequence that entitles him to 1 point for each card in the sequence. The sequence can be of mixed suit, not necessarily all clubs, for instance. Sequences are valid even if not played in order, thus a 4, 5, and 3 still produces a sequence.

When all the cards of the hand have been played, they are turned up by both players who count their hands, the nondealer counting first. Each combination of cards totaling 15 scores 2 points. Pairs count for 2 points; triplets, 6; four of a kind, 12. Three-card sequences are 3 points and each additional card in sequence is 1 additional point. A four-card flush, which is cards of the same suit, 4 points; a five-card flush, 5 points. "His Nobs," the jack of the same suit as the starter, is 1 point. The same card or cards may be scored in unlimited number of ways and it is obviously important to catch all the variations. Under some rules "Muggins" applies, allowing an opponent to claim any points the other player fails to score. This variant is seldom employed today. After the counting of the hands, the dealer counts the scoring in the crib, using the starter card as a fifth card. He scores points just as with his hand, except that a four-card flush is not counted in the crib.

Game consists of either 61 points (once around the board) or 121 points (twice around) and the winner is the first player reaching the total. The player wins the game if he goes out first, even though the dealer would have won if he had gotten the opportunity to count his hand and crib. If a player reaches 121 before his opponent gets to 61, the loser is "lurched" and the winner is credited with a double-game victory.

Despite appearing to be complicated, Cribbage is a game of quickly learned mechanics and after a few hours a new player will feel he has learned all there is to know about the strategy involved. As he competes longer, he will discover there are many nuances that separate the successful Cribbage gambler from the rest of the players.

Cribbage has lost some popularity in recent decades, having once been perhaps the most consistently popular game in the English-speaking world. In the 1920's and 1930's it was the rage in New England, with Cribbage clubs to be found everywhere. During World War II, U.S. sailors played Cribbage aboard ship more than any other game, and almost every ship had a designated champion. Since Cribbage boards were in short supply, the boys made do with pad and pencil. Only the advent of Gin Rummy finally caused the decline of Cribbage clubs in the United States.

While Cribbage is basically a two-person game, there are variations revolving around both the cards played and the number of players. These variations follow this entry.

CRIBBAGE—Five-card

Five-card Cribbage is the earliest form of the game and proved to be less satisfying. Each player gets five cards and puts two in the crib, keeping only three. The crib therefore contains more cards than the players' hands and has more value. The nondealer must take great care about which cards he places in the crib. As compensation for the disadvantage involved of being the nondealer, he is permitted to peg 3 points on the first deal of every game. Winning score is 61, and the brevity of the game and its statistical advantages for the dealer led eventually to the advent of the six-card game.

CRIBBAGE—Partnership

Cribbage can be played in the form of two-person partnerships. Five cards are dealt to each player and each in turn puts one of the cards in the crib. At the time of counting the hands, the partners combine their hands to be scored as one. Play is to 121 points.

CRIBBAGE—Three-handed

Three-handed Cribbage follows the pattern of the two-player game but each player gets only five cards and contributes one to the crib, with an additional card dealt to the crib from the pack. Each player is on his own, and "Go" and the deal proceeds to the

left. There are larger Cribbage boards available for three-player scoring or the scores may simply be kept on paper.

CRICKET BETTING

Cricket draws high stakes gambling action in England and elsewhere, although there are Cricket purists who turn livid to see the game sullied by gambling. One 19th-century observer, Mary Russell Mitford, wrote in *English Life and Character* of her pure hatred of matches played for "money, hard money, between a certain number of gentlemen, and players, as they are called—people who make a trade of that noble sport, and degrade it into an affair of betting, and hedgings, and cheatings, it may be like boxing or horse-racing. . . ."

Ms. Mitford's opinions fell on deaf ears, and since her day betting in the British Commonwealth on international Cricket matches involves many thousands of pounds in private bets and through bookmakers. Because of the preponderance of intercounty matches in Great Britain these contests produce even more action. Lotteries are also held on the number of runs individual batsmen make in a match, etc.

CRISSCROSS: Center-card Poker Game

It is recommended that competent gamblers playing DEALER'S CHOICE often call for Crisscross, a bizarre variation of DRAW POKER—provided their opponents are the undisciplined kind who stay on weak hands.

A center-card game, Crisscross can be dealt in various ways, the most conservative and best version calling for players to be dealt two down cards. Then five cards are dealt face down in the center of the table, laid out in the following fashion:

```
      1
  4   5   2
      3
```

There is a round of betting as the dealer turns over each card in the order shown above. Card number 5, in the center of the crisscross, is exposed last and is wild, as are any other cards of the same rank. Players must choose three of the five center cards to supplement the two in their hand—either the vertical (1-5-3) or the horizontal line (4-5-2). After the center card has been revealed, players have the option of discarding one or both of their own closed cards at the draw. This is followed by a final betting round and the showdown.

Many players are fooled by Crisscross, thinking weak hands have a chance. It must be remembered that with every player having at least one wild card, three of a kind hands will be common. Seasoned gamblers drop on three of a kind, and do not even try to fill straights or flushes (although they may stay on a pat straight or flush, depending on the betting), feeling a full house is the lowest possible winning hand. Others drop if they haven't got a second wild card and hopefully more than a mere full house.

Other versions of Crisscross allow for five closed cards to be dealt to each player. They can mate anywhere from two to five cards from their hand with none to three from one of the center crosses to achieve their best hand. Of course this is a wilder game, especially with high-low as part of the action. High hands should be four of a kind at least (and a high one at that) and low hands should descend from the 6. Anything in between is almost certain to be whiplashed in the betting.

See also FIERY CROSS.

CROCKFORD'S CLUB: 19th-century English Gambling Club

The most famous English gambling club of its day, Crockford's catered from 1827 to 1844 to titled nobility and other sporting bloods such as the Duke of Wellington; Talleyrand; Prince Esterhazy; Charles, Marquess of Queensberry; Bulwer-Lytton; and Benjamin Disraeli. Fearing their expressions might betray their emotions when the cards were falling fortui-

tously for them, these dedicated gamblers sometimes wore masks to avoid the eyes of the dealer.

The club was founded by William Crockford (1774-1844), the son of a fishmonger who garnered a fortune at dice and race-horse betting, eventually owning one of England's prize racing stables and dying an extremely wealthy man. Even after his death Crockford remained the great establishment gambler. When he died in 1844, he had a number of gambling debts to collect and they would have been forfeit if his death was known. So his body was propped up in an armchair in his window and the bets were duly collected.

Crockford's closed when its owner's death was finally verified, and in 1972 a fashionable casino in London resurrected the Crockford name, though it had no real connection with the 19th century's most exclusive gaming club.

CROSSROADERS: Gambling Cheats

Originally the term "crossroader" was applied in the Old West to the thieves and cheats who pulled their dirty tricks in saloons located at the crossroads of one-horse towns. Today crossroaders are the scourge of American casinos, working card, dice, and slot machine scams that take the establishments for untold millions every year.

In its day Crockford's was the most famous English gambling club, catering to titled nobility and other sporting bloods as the Duke of Wellington, Talleyrand, Prince Esterhazy, Charles, Marquess of Queensberry, Bulwer-Lytton and Disraeli. The presentday Crockford's in London has no connection with the original. (Photo: N.Y. Public Library)

The "king of the crossroaders" in the 1950's and 1960's was Glen Grayson. He bossed a team of hustlers who spanned the globe victimizing casinos. They were particularly adept at switching dice right under the eyes of CRAPS table personnel. With fixed dice in play, a half dozen of these cheats would bet in multiple ways so that the house could be taken for thousands of dollars on every roll. The crossroaders operated only for a few games and left the table at different times, after switching the house dice back into play. It was a daring operation at the time, since so many of the casinos operated under mob control and cheaters knew that if they got caught they had reason to fear for their lives, or at the very least, their limbs.

Grayson eventually died in a plane crash, and in 1985 the story of his crossroader crew was told by a key member, John Soares, in a book called *Loaded Dice*. He related details of numerous capers in Nevada—including one at Harvey's Wagon Wheel in Lake Tahoe that netted $148,000 in a few minutes—as well as in such faraway places as London, Istanbul, and Macao. The crew had the looting of slot machines down to a science, since they had learned how to open most makes in a matter of seconds and set the wheels to produce a jackpot win on the next spin.

Soares put the crossroader credo in perspective: "I never gamble, I cheat."

CROWN AND ANCHOR: Australian Version of Chuck-a-Luck

Crown and Anchor is a three-dice casino and counter game, which is very popular in Australia, gets considerable play in Great Britain and is occasionally found in the United States. Instead of numbered pips the dice each have six symbols: heart, spade, diamond, club, crown, and anchor.

How to play: The players place their wagers on the corresponding symbols on the table layout and the dice are flipped by the banker from a dice cup. Payoffs for the player hitting one of his symbols is even money, 2 to 1 for pairs, and 3 to 1 on three of a kind. If this sounds somewhat familiar, one should compare it with CHUCK-A-LUCK; it is essentially the same game with different trappings. The house edge is exactly the same, just less than a monstrous 8 percent. If one does not play Chuck-a-Luck because of the bad odds, there is little reason to try Crown and Anchor.

CROWNS

See EAGLES AND CROWNS.

CUBA—Gambling in

Under dictator Fulgencio Batista, who was deposed by Fidel Castro in 1959, casino gambling thrived in Cuba. Under Castro it vanished.

Before Castro came to power, Cuban casinos were largely controlled by the mob and it was crime genius Meyer Lansky who brought casinos to Havana after appearing in Cuba with several suitcases stuffed with money for Batista—as a demonstration of "good faith." Lansky also personally deposited $3 million in a Zurich, Switzerland, bank for Batista and worked out a payoff scale for the ruling military junta, namely Batista, to get 50 percent of the profits thereafter.

For years Cuba was the big-money producing gambling center for the mob, perhaps even more so than Vegas, because the games did not have to be run honestly. There is a myth that says only the mob can run casinos properly and that because they are so good at it they can make a fortune running it honestly and merely skimming off part of the profits. The fact is the mob will run the games only as honestly as local conditions require. Batista was hardly the sort of individual to insist on such scruples.

As a result many knowledgeable gamblers considered Cuban casinos to be crookedly run at least part of the time. Batista's police could not be expected to sweep into a casino to check out a house for crooked devices. It was long maintained that the standard way of fixing ROULETTE was with small electromagnets under the track. Rather than being pure ivory, the balls were actually plastic with a steel slug in the center. Whenever the action got hot and heavy and certain numbers or combinations were loaded with bets, the croupier could touch a certain switch and guide the ball to a section of a wheel where the numbers were getting lesser action.

Prudent gamblers only played Cuban Roulette when the table was uniformly loaded with chips so that the fix was unworkable. Some even developed a system of simply betting lightly played numbers.

When Castro came to power in 1959, Batista, Lansky, and their cronies fled the country. Lansky did leave his brother Jake behind to see if Castro could be induced to a deal for Batista's usual share. Castro threw Jake Lansky in jail and kept him there for some time before kicking him out of the country. After that, Lansky, like several other mob figures, joined the CIA in plots to have Castro assassinated. Lansky's motivation was clear—anyone with Castro's attitude toward casinos had to be un-American.

CUCKOO

See CHASE-THE-ACE; RANTER GO ROUND.

Ely CULBERTSON: Champion Bridge Player

Freak gambling luck started champion bridge player Ely Culbertson (1891-1955) on his way to fame and fortune. Forced from his homeland by the Russian Revolution, Culbertson supported himself rather precariously for some years in Paris through card playing. Down to a mere 20 francs (about $5 at the time), he entered a gambling club and decided to bet the entire sum in one play at CHEMIN DE FER. Placing his wager, he backed off to let other players in, and as he did so a local bon vivant with whom he shared a mutual dislike stepped on his feet. Culbertson swore at the man, insults were swapped, and the pair repaired to an alley to settle things.

They wrestled for several moments before others broke up the scuffle. Out of breath and disheveled, Culbertson returned to the casino where he found turmoil at the Chemin de Fer table. His forgotten 20 francs had remained in action through 11 straight winning plays, doubling each time, and the croupier had appealed to the manager to help him locate the lucky player. Culbertson stepped forward and claimed the winnings, now over $10,000. Luckily, other players confirmed him to be the bettor. Culbertson seized his winnings and booked passage to the United States to begin his famous bridge career. Needless to say, a number of fiction writers appropriated the incident for their stories.

CURACAO STUD
See DUTCH STUD.

CUTTHROAT BRIDGE: Three-handed Game
Cutthroat or Three-handed BRIDGE is an adaptation of the basic game when only three players are available. However, a fourth hand is dealt and put aside, face down. Bidding is done by the three players, each on his own. The high bidder then turns up the odd hand, placing it between his two opponents.

This serves as the "dummy." Play follows as in Contract Bridge but scoring may be done as in Auction Bridge, if that is preferred.

The declarer scores in the usual manner if he makes his contract, but if he is beaten each opponent scores the full amount for setting him. If the opponents hold honors, each scores them in full. In contract scoring, each player can be individually vulnerable or not, as the situation demands. The first player to win two games scores 500 points for rubber, or 700 points if neither opponent has scored. In auction, the premium is 250 points.

This game is a gamble because players must bid in the hope that the cards they need will be in the dummy hand. To minimize the guesswork, a variation of the game allows for each player to be dealt 17 cards with the final remaining card laid face down as the dummy. Players study their hands and before bidding place four of their cards face down to the dummy. Thus, each player knows almost one-third of the cards in the dummy.

CZECHOSLOVAKIA, Gambling in
Private gambling is outlawed in Czechoslovakia, but the Czechs have their card games unofficially organized in private apartments for stakes not befitting a socialist country.

Bowing to the inevitable—and the desire for revenues—the government runs a lottery and various pools systems covering such sports as hockey, soccer, and horse racing. A goodly amount of these sports pools revenues are used to subsidize athletics.

D

Nicholas Andrea DANDOLOS
See NICK THE GREEK.

DARDA: Klaberjass Variation
Darda is another of the games quite close to the popular KLABERJASS, which follows many of the same general rules and uses the same 32-card deck. The rank in trumps is queen, 9, ace, 10, king, jack, 8, 7. The queen (rather than the jack, as in Klaberjass) is worth 20 and the jack just 2. In the other suits the rank is ace, 10, king, queen, jack, 9, 8, 7. Unlike Klaberjass, there is no schmeiss.

Once trump has been established and three more cards are dealt to each player, the rest of the pack is turned bottom up. If a player holds the 7 of trump he may exchange it for the card showing, or he may use the 8 if the 7 was turned up and kept as trump. If the next card that shows is a trump, the same player may exchange any card for it, and that also applies to succeeding cards that show.

Melding occurs as in Klaberjass with this alteration: Game is 10 points and the trump maker is successful if his opponents all fail to top his score. If his score is less than 100, he gets 1 point; 100-149, 2 points; 150-199, 3 points; 200 or more, 4 points. If, however, any player holds four of a kind, all play stops and the hand is over. That player scores 4 points for queens, 3 for nines, 2 for aces, kings, jacks, and 10's.

Darda has never matched Klaberjass in popularity, especially in America.

DAUBING: Method for Marking Cards During Play
Prepared *marked cards* are most often done with a form of line work or shading either bought directly from a crooked gambling supply house or painted or penned on by an artistic cheat. The danger in using previously marked cards is that the decks are trace-able back to the cheat and if they are noticed the cheat is a marked man.

A more cautious cheater, therefore, prefers to do his "daubing" during play. He carries with him a small tube of paint or paste similar in color to that of the backs of the cards in use. At a proper time, he moistens his finger and presses a very tiny spot on the card design. He may do this when he has a hand consisting of three jacks, for instance, and thereafter he knows whenever someone holds those cards. In DRAW POKER, with jacks or better, he will automatically know if an opponent has jacks or something better, a very tactical edge.

When marking the cards, he usually has a quick way of removing any leftover coloring from his finger. He might be eating a sandwich and rub it off on the bread and gulp it down, or he may stick his finger in the mustard and use that as an excuse to suck it clean.

The daub is clearly visible across the table, and yet few other gamblers (who are not looking for it) will spot it. Generally to catch such daubing it is necessary to study the card design carefully while comparing it to several other cards. The best defense against "on the job" daubing is to use several decks during a game, all with back designs in different colors or shades.

John DAVIS: America's First Casino Operator
The first true casino operator in the United States was a Louisiana entrepreneur named John Davis, who made a great deal of money as a theatrical manager in New Orleans. In 1827, he applied his funds to open an opulent casino at Orleans and Bourbon Streets. There had been other casinos throughout the South earlier, but they were all back-room operations noted for hard customers, hard liquor, and little taste. Davis's emporium served fine

A contemporary drawing of one of John Davis's class gambling casinos in New Orleans. They offered an opulence never seen before in America. (Photo: N.Y. Public Library)

French wines in place of rotgut whiskey and there were enticing offerings of free foods and cigars served from silver dishes. Davis provided expert croupiers and private rooms for "aristocractic" gamblers and among the games offered were ROULETTE, FARO, BRAG, ECARTE, BOSTON, and VINGT-ET-UN. The establishment was open 24 hours a day seven days a week, and business was so good that Davis opened a branch of equal splendor on Bayou St. John, about a mile outside the city. This establishment operated from Saturday noon to early Monday morning, and on Sunday evening an elaborate dinner was served free of charge to all players.

Davis had the gambling scene in New Orleans all to himself until 1832 when gambling was legalized and about two dozen other high-class establishments opened. All made money as the wealthy classes of Louisiana flocked to them and bet away huge sums. Individual losses of $25,000 in a night were not unheard of, and many gamblers lost $50,000 to $100,000 a year. Perhaps the highest roller to patronize Davis's casinos was Col. John R. Grymes, the lawyer who had gained great fame in his defense of the pirate Jean Lafitte. The colonel had a very lucrative law practice, but dissipated his fortune at the Davis tables and died a poor man. Legend had it that Grymes gambled at every card game available, yet had not won a single hand in a decade. Impossible, of course, but Grymes was good for losses of at least a half million dollars from 1827 to 1835.

In 1835 a reform movement in the state legislature succeeded in overturning the legalized gambling law and imposed heavy penalties on casino operators. John Davis, having become enormously wealthy, faded from the gambling scene, but many other operators continued in business illegally. New Orleans was never to be without big-time gambling from that time on.

DEAD MAN'S HAND: Aces and Eights

The Dead Man's Hand became a part of Western and gambling lore on August 2, 1876, when a saddlebum named Jack McCall walked into Carl Mann's Saloon number 10 in Deadwood, Dakota Territory, and shot the legendary Wild Bill Hickok in the back of the head. Hickok slumped over dead, still holding his POKER hand of two pairs—aces and 8's—which has been known since as the Dead Man's Hand.

Much has been made of McCall's motive in killing Hickok, ranging from his own claim that Hickok had killed his brother (of which there was no record) to a plot by crooked gamblers who had hired an assassin because they feared Hickok was going to be hired as marshal and would run them out (another silly idea since Hickok always found a way to be accommodating with gambling hustlers). Actually, there had been bad blood between Hickok and McCall for a number of days: McCall felt Hickok had cheated him out of a big pot. The amount in dispute: 25 *cents*.

DEALER'S CHOICE

Most private POKER games played in the United States are of the Dealer's Choice variety, and when properly played, they can put a smart dealer in the catbird seat. Some Dealer's Choice games are restricted by previous agreement to a few basic varieties, such as Five-card Stud, Five-card Draw, Seven-card Stud (with or without a high-low factor), and perhaps a few wild-card games. In other games greater variety is allowed, such as RED DOG, IN-BETWEEN, ENGLISH STUD, and so on.

Amazingly a great number of players—and indeed many books offering advice on gambling—fail to realize the value of Dealer's Choice for the smart player. Too many gamblers choose their games for variety instead of advantage. For instance, if the dealer observes some opponents have a tendency to stay in Seven-card High-Low games on the faintest of hopes, it becomes a good game to call because they can be counted on to contribute to the pot. On the other hand, a gambler who gets far ahead might start calling Five-card Stud because it will limit his losses. A loser should lean to Seven-card Stud, perhaps with high-low, because it will allow him to make up ground more quickly. Sometimes a gambler may want to get past an aggressive bettor sitting next to him and call Five-card Draw, Jacks or Better, if the rules call for passing the deal to the next player if there are no openers. This steals the aggressive bettor's thunder, forcing him to deal the same game rather than the one of his own choice.

When a great variety of games may be chosen the dealer should lean to the games that provide him with some sort of edge, such as BEST FLUSH or especially ENGLISH STUD. The latter game, for instance, allows the dealer to view some of the discards of all the other players before making his own decision. There are players who refuse to allow some dealer-advantage games to be called, but it never hurts to try. Typical games that offer an edge for various reasons include COLOR POKER, DOUBLE DRAW POKER, ELBOW, LEFTY LOUIE, MIKE, SKEETS, TAKE IT OR LEAVE IT, and TENS HIGH DRAW.

DEBTS, GAMBLING

Imagine the average casino gambler. He hits a lucky streak and wins a huge pile of chips. He yells for joy, flips around some chips in tips and happily heads for the cashier's window. There a hard-eyed casino executive glares at him and announces, "We ain't paying off, so buzz off." The gambler rants and raves, but is coolly informed, "If you don't like it, sue us!"

Could the gambler than go into a Nevada court and force a Las Vegas casino to pay off on its gambling debts? The answer is a flat no. A gambling debt by a private individual or by a casino is not collectible in any state in the Union. As a matter of fact, a casino can sell chips, and then refuse to reimburse gamblers for the balance. The reason: those chips were a debt based on gambling and therefore not collectible.

In actual practice, no legalized casino would ever refuse to pay off, the reason going beyond that of the good faith and credit of the casino. If this happened in Nevada, for instance, the Gaming Commission would immediately revoke the casino's license to operate.

However, the real issue is gambling debts. The laws of this country protect the welsher; he need never pay off. Often cited is the case of a man who lost a considerable sum of money in a private Poker game. He left the game, came back with a gun, counted out his losses from the chip bank and walked out. The other players yelled for the police—and got nowhere. The enraged loser had been within his rights. He had lost his money gambling, which meant it was still legally his. He had simply recovered his own property.

Very few people understand the facts of life when it comes to gambling debts. Legally, a gambler could go to a casino, establish a line of credit, run up a huge tab, and then refuse to pay. Or the welsher could pay by check and stop payment. The casino could not force such a welsher to meet his obligations under threat of having his property seized. In the bad old days when the mob influence in gambling casinos was common knowledge, it was said the mob would simply send out collectors who had very physical ways of convincing a welsher to pay. That happened far less often than imagined; today no casino would try such blatant tactics. A welsher might be subjected to the usual collection agency harassment of insulting letters, annoying telephone calls in the middle of the night, and dark threats to inform his friends or employer (which won't happen either), but the casino in the end would be left holding the bag.

This is not, however, too heavy a burden on the casinos. Although they keep their figures secret, insiders admit casino losses to welshers are not too much larger than those sustained by credit-card companies whose customers won't pay their bills. Credit-card companies can attach people's wages, homes, cars, their bank accounts. Casinos can't, but they still survive. They have the welsher over a barrel. He loves to gamble, and if he doesn't pay, he'll be blackballed by every casino in the country. Few gamblers would be able to survive such a fate.

And it should also be remembered that Las Vegas can still find a law unto itself when dealing with welshers. It is part of the town's lore that old Benny Binion, the patriarch of the family that has always owned the fabulous Horseshoe, was and is the wrong man to cross. Once, when a player received $100 in credit and refused to repay it when he lost, Binion decided the player didn't need his clothes. He had him tossed naked onto Fremont Street.

DECK-CUTTING BET: Proposition for the Gullible

On the face of it, deck-cutting bets look like even-money propositions. When a card hustler offers it at a "friendly" game, he will offer a sucker even money that he can't cut to a specific card in a 52-card deck in 26 tries. Since 26 is half of 52 it appears to the average player to be a legitimate bet.

What actually happens is that the deck is shuffled and the victim calls his card, let us say the ace of diamonds. He cuts the cards the first time and most likely does not get his card—the odds against him are 51 to 1. So the deck is squared off and reshuffled and he cuts again. After 26 times he has either won or exhausted his chances and lost. The odds, rather than being a 50-50 proposition, are far worse. The player cannot figure to get his card in 26 cuts on average but actually in 35.342 tries. This means that the hustler will win close to two out of every three bets.

If an Atlantic City casino could book this kind of action, it would buy up the state of New Jersey within a month!

DEGENERATE GAMBLERS

See COMPULSIVE GAMBLING.

DELAWARE—Legalized Lotteries

Delaware's revenues from its lottery games are on the small side in keeping with its population, but compared to other states, it tends to have games that are easier to win. The daily three-digit and four-digit numbers games are similar to those in most other states and pay off rather poorly. However, the state's "rub out" game, scratching out six spots on a ticket for a winning combination, has a better-than-average chance of producing a payoff, a rather high 1 in 4.95.

Delaware's LOTTO, at this writing, is drawn from a numbers pool of 1 to 30, and thereby offers relatively short odds for picking a winner.

DEMON
See CANFIELD.

DENMARK, Gambling in
Denmark is not known as a gambling mecca. It has no gambling casinos. The state operates a lottery and football (soccer) pools and there is horse-race betting at the track. Private dice games are allowed in wine and beer houses, but an outsider will seldom witness payoffs in any form but drinks. There are a few gambling halls with slot machines and a cheapie version of ROULETTE, with bets that require a magnifying glass to see.

DEUCES WILD: Poker Variation
The most common of all wild-card POKER games, Deuces Wild permits all 2's to be used as any other cards, even duplicating a card already in a player's hand. Therefore a hand of five of a kind becomes possible and indeed even outranks a royal flush (normally the highest possible hand). A frequent error of novice Poker players shifting from the straight version to Deuces Wild is staying with weak hands, failing to appreciate how much the addition of four wild cards alters the likely winning hands. As rule of thumb, three aces is considered the average winning hand in a game involving five or six gamblers. However, one should not be lulled into thinking three aces is all that powerful a hand if it is a "natural," consisting of three aces. Far more impressive is the same hand containing one or preferably two deuces. The latter hand reduces the chances of other players holding wild cards by 25 to 50 percent. Thus deuces should be regarded as possessing important defensive as well as offensive might.

Following this axiom, many players in Draw Poker tend to drop out if they don't have any deuces in their opening hand. It cannot be emphasized too much that wild games require an entirely different psychology of play than does straight Poker. When the number of wild cards are increased to six (say deuces and one-eyed jacks or two jokers) or eight (in many wild card games, such as HEINZ, both the 5's and 7's are wild), the generally required hand can rise to a minimum of four of a kind, and is really a powerhouse only when it includes at least two wild cards.

George DEVOL: Legendary 19th-century Riverboat Gambler
Along with Canada Bill Jones, his frequent partner, George Devol (1829-1902) was perhaps the most talented of the 19th-century Mississippi riverboat gamblers. Admittedly, part of the proof of that claim is based on Devol's 1887 autobiography, *Forty Years a Gambler on the Mississippi,* but there seems to be considerable independent evidence to support his stature.

Devol made more than $2 million from gambling, but, like most others in his profession, he couldn't keep it. Most of his winnings went in casino FARO games.

Devol capsuled his own life thusly: ". . . a cabin boy in 1839; could steal cards and cheat the boys at eleven; stack a deck at fourteen . . . fought more rough-and-tumble fights than any man in America, and was the most daring gambler in the world."

He was on target about his daring. Once while working a passenger train, Devol cheated a MARK out of all his money at THREE-CARD MONTE. The man went berserk, pressed a pistol to Devol's head and demanded his money back. Lesser gamblers would have complied. Yet, incredibly, Devol talked his way out of the situation by offering the man one more bet. The sucker complained he had no more money, but Devol offered to put up $800 against the man's shooting iron. The bet was made and the sucker handed over his piece to a member of the crowd holding the stakes. The stake holder just happened to be one of Devol's shills. As he had earlier, the sucker pointed to the wrong card, whereupon Devol grabbed the victim's gun and forced him to jump off the moving train.

On other occasions he "used his head" in more literal fashion, head-butting any poor loser who pulled a weapon; Devol's massive, dome-shaped skull made an awesome weapon. Devol won many an honest wager against various strongmen and circus performers, butting them into submission afterward.

Canada Bill was Devol's most constant partner and the pair made a perfect team. Devol dressed as a fancy dude while Canada Bill dressed and acted like a hayseed with the apparent brainpower of a cow. For a time with two other crooked gamblers, Devol ran a riverboat swindle operation that netted each of the cheats $200,000 a year.

While he wasn't quite in Canada Bill's league as a card manipulator—probably nobody was—Devol still was a master at card skullduggery. Once in a friendly game with four other gamblers he rang in a COLD DECK and on the same hand dealt each gambler four aces. (During Devol's time a straight flush did not beat four aces.) Each of the men thought they had been dealt the hand of a lifetime. Devol looked at his own hand, shook his head and dropped out, sitting back to watch the fireworks. Bets, raises, and re-raises rocked the game as each of the four put everything they had into the pot. When the hilarious showdown came, it took them three hours to sort out who owned what.

After more than 40 years of gambling on the great river and in the Wild West, Devol married and retired from the gambling tables to a quieter existence in Cincinnati. A tough wife and an even tougher mother-in-law saw to that. In 1887 he published his memoirs. Although he had forsaken the "depraved life," he managed to slip away for an occasional POKER game and to trim the suckers at Monte at the racetrack. When George Devol cashed in his chips in 1902 the *Cincinnati Enquirer* reported that he had won and lost more money than any other man in America.

For his own epitaph, Devol would have undoubtedly approved this, his description of a larcenous victim of the Three-card Monte swindle:

> The sucker feels like he is going to steal the money from a blind man, but he does not care . . . they did think he must be nearly blind, or he would have seen the mark or bent corner on the winning card. They expected to rob a blind man and got left. I never had any sympathy for them, and I would fight before I would give them back one cent. It is a good lesson for a dishonest man to be caught by some trick, and I always did like to teach it.

That sentiment has been used by card hustlers ever since as an apologia for their activities. Of course, Devol didn't really believe those self-serving words. In essence he would have concurred with Canada Bill Jones's more succinct dictum: "Suckers got no business having money."
See WILLIAM "CANADA BILL" JONES; THREE-CARD MONTE; WILSON RANGERS.

DICE: Oldest Gaming Implements Known to Man

Dice are small six-sided cubes almost always made today of cellulose or other plastic material. They are marked with spots from 1 to 6 on a side and are used in a number of games. Dice vary in size, with faces ranging from one-fifth of an inch to one inch square. The spots are cut into the faces and marked with a contrasting color, such as black on a white surface. The spots are always arranged so that the opposite faces on each die total 7, that is a 3 on one side and a 4 on the other, etc. A player casting or shooting dice holds them in his closed hand or in a dice-cup container, shakes them, and throws them out on a smooth surface. When they stop rolling, the points on the two dice are added and the result applied to the game being played. Besides CRAPS, popular dice

Dice have been developed independently in virtually all cultures. This is an illustration from *Rubaiyat of Omar Khayyam.*

games include CHUCK-A-LUCK, HAZARD, BARBOOTH, and numerous board games such as BACKGAMMON.

According to Sophocles, dice were invented by a Greek named Palamedes during the siege of Troy. Herodotus claimed they were a product of the Lydians in the days of King Atys. Both versions are discounted by historians. Archaeological finds dated variously from 6000 to 3500 B.C. prove that dice appeared in many earlier societies. In fact, because cultures throughout the world developed dice—independent of each other—it is impossible to trace their singular beginning. Early man undoubtedly tossed sticks about to see at whom they would point, and from this, dice eventually developed. So, aside from the tossing of sticks, it is safe to assert that dice are the oldest gaming implements known to man.

From the first four-sided dice made from the

A set of early bone dice used by the Arapaho Indians of North America. (Photo: N.Y. Public Library)

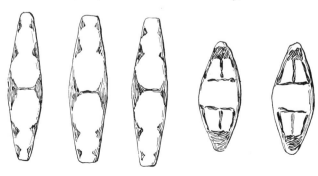

KNUCKLEBONES of sheep or other animals the manufacturing of dice has become a precise science today. This is so for what are called "perfect dice," made by hand, true to a tolerance of .0005 inch, and crafted to the exacting requirements of gambling casinos for Craps. Cheaper dice—machine-made, round-cornered, and imperfect—are referred to as "candy store dice." These are used for social and board games.

DICE—Cheating

Just as dice themselves go far back in history, so too does cheating with dice. Digs in the tombs of ancient Egypt and the Orient and even in prehistoric graves in North and South America have unearthed dice that were clearly designed for cheating. Man has obviously long been concerned about trying to control dice cheating, and one of the more unusual efforts occurred in 18th-century England when unmarked dice were thrown upon a marked board, but that form of play never caught on.

Any die that is not an absolutely perfect cube will not conform to the normal mathematical probabilities. For this reason "shapes" are the most common type of gaffed dice. The cubes are shaved down on one or more sides and as a result they will tend to settle more often on the larger surfaces. If the 1 side of a die is shaved down, this causes the surface area of the four adjoining sides to be reduced, and the 1 and 6 sides, having the larger surfaces, are more likely to come up. If the other die is shaved down on the 3 side, the 3 and 4 will be more likely to show. This is very significant in CRAPS since the chances of a 2, 3, or 12 turning up on the first throw—all losing plays for a shooter—are greatly reduced. The shooter is also less likely to crap out with a 7 after his first roll, which would also be a losing toss.

"Bevels" are another type of gaffed dice. In this case one or two sides of a die will be rounded off so that the die will tend to roll off rounded sides and come to rest on a flat side. Frequently, beveling is combined with a form of "loaded dice," which are cubes weighted to one side so that certain numbers are more likely to come up. A combination of the two forms allows either alteration to be much more

(A) skilled dice mechanic can easily substitute loaded dice for honest ones. White dice on table (A) are legitimate while dark dice in hand are loaded. When cheat picks up the honest dice he traps them between his fingers (B) and blows on them while in the process exchanging the hand hold of the two pairs of dice. He then rattles the dark dice and rolls them while holding the honest dice in his hand (C). As he rolls the loaded dice he hides the honest dice in his other hand under his money pile (D). After winning several fixed bets, he reverses the process, reintroducing the honest dice and continues shooting. (Photos: E. Gerard)

A.

B.

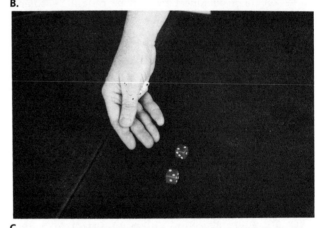

C.

D.

minute, making detection of both much more unlikely. There is a misapprehension by the public that loaded dice work every time. They do not and are not intended to. What they do is make certain numbers appear more often than others, which is still a monumental edge for a dice cheat.

Opaque dice, usually white, red, or green, are easier to load. A hole is bored into the die and the hole is filled with lead and then the hole is enameled over. This cannot be done with transparent dice—the only kind that are used in gambling casinos—but they too can be fixed by hidden loads behind some spots of the die. All that is needed is a very heavy type of load, such as gold or platinum, so that only the tiniest amount of loading is needed to affect the action of the die.

The other major type of crooked dice is called "tops and bottoms." These have one or more faces duplicated on the opposite side while other numbers are omitted. As a result certain numbers will be rolled more often. A particularly daring top and bottom, or "tee," as the dice are also known, is a die that is spotted only with 1-5-6 twice while its mate is doubled up on 3-4-5. Using such duplicated dice, a shooter cannot throw a 2, 3, 7, or 12, the only combinations by which he can lose. Tees are only used by very skillful cheats who introduce them into a game by sleight of hand and get them back out quickly. While it is true that few novice CRAPS players will spot tees because no more than three sides of a dice can be seen from any position, it is much trickier for a cheat to slip them into a casino game. Craps tables have mirrored panels around the inner edges so that housemen can see all sides of the dice. (Although I did hear an Atlantic City stickman tell an inquiring woman patron that the mirrors were there to allow the housemen to straighten their ties.) The only time cheaters use them in casino play is for one quick killing, after which they hustle the fixed dice out of the game. Even in private games with amateurs, the cheats switch back the good dice after a score since sooner or later any heavy loser will start getting suspicious.

There are such things as magnetic dice, which were formerly in great vogue. Oddly, even though they are the most high-tech form of crooked dice, they are the least used today because they are easy to spot. All that is necessary is to touch the dice to a magnet. Do Crap shooters carry magnets to check out their suspicions? They do, many in the form of a magnetized tie clip or money clip. If the die sticks to such a magnet, the shooter may have a lot of explaining to do.

All the previously mentioned gaffed dice can be spotted as well by the shrewd gambler. Suspected shapes should be placed side by side on a flat surface

A simple pivot test involves holding a suspect die between the thumb and middle finger at diagonal corners. Pressure is then relaxed on the die as it is rotated by a finger on the other hand. If the same corner swings down to the bottom each time, the die is loaded. (Photo: E. Gerard)

and one's thumb rubbed over the tops. If a "lip" is felt, the dice are shaped. Obviously, it is important to check all the sides of the dice before concluding the dice are clean.

Loaded dice may also be spotted by either a pivot or water test. In a pivot, you simply hold the die at diagonal corners between the thumb and middle finger, and relax the pressure somewhat as you rotate the die with the forefinger of your other hand. If the same corner swings down to the bottom each time, the die is loaded. The water test involves dropping a die into a full glass of water, holding a different number to the top as you release the die. If a few numbers keep showing up virtually all of the time, the dice are definitely loaded.

Of course tees are the easiest of all to spot with a quick inspection. Put the two dice together so that the total of 7 appears on the four visible sides. Then check the two outside ends of the dice. Do they make 7? Then check the inside edges where the dice have been held together. Another 7? If the answer is not a total of six 7's, you are playing with a hustler.

DICE—"Honest" Cheating

Some dice hustlers do not use gaffed dice to cheat opponents, mainly because of the possibility of exposure. These hustlers prefer to develop their skills at controlling honest dice by the way they throw them. This is called among gamblers, admittedly not too accurately, "honest" cheating.

Years of practice are necessary to be able to roll "educated" dice regularly. One of the simpler ways is the "slide shot." The cheater picks up the dice and holds the one with the number he wants to come up tightly in his pinky. He rattles the dice, but only the

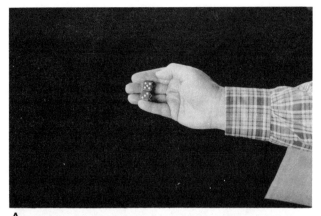

A.

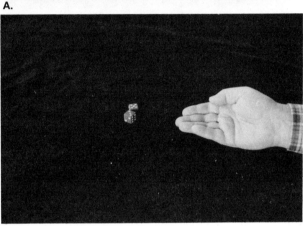

B.

The blanket roll: After placing two numbers he doesn't want against each other, the cheat gives the dice a phony rattle and locks the dice between two fingers (A). He then rolls the dice out straight (B) so that they do "cartwheels" without any spinning action. (Photos: E. Gerard)

top one is really moving in his hand. Then he flips the dice with a sort of sliding movement. The freely rolling top die hides the fact that the bottom die is sliding across the surface with the same number remaining on top. The roll is over so quickly that the action is harder to spot than you might think. The value of the slide shot is that the cheater can alter the game's mathematical odds. Let's say he is shooting CRAPS and his number is 4, a hard number to hit. If he freezes a 2 on the bottom die, however, he has eliminated five of the six ways he could lose by throwing a 7. Unless the other die comes up 5 he is safe. Of course, he has eliminated his chance of making a 4 with a 3-1. Now he can only throw a 2-2 to win. But before he immobilized the bottom die, the odds were 2 to 1 that he would crap out. He has reduced the odds so that he now has a 50-50 chance of winning, an enormous improvement.

The "drop shot" accomplishes the same end for a crooked shooter. He places the lower die the way he wants it, and he then tosses the dice straight down so that the top die lands on top of the lower die and

traps it against the table so it cannot turn over. Meanwhile the top die bounces free wildly, creating the illusion of both dice tumbling.

It will never be known how many GIs were cleaned out in military Craps games through what is known as the "blanket roll." Very often servicemen had to play the game quietly to avoid attracting the attention of the duty officer, and so they rolled the dice on a blanket to deaden sound. Instead of controlling the rolling action, a hustler would eliminate the spinning action of the dice. The point of this was to *prevent* certain numbers from appearing. Let us say the hustler has established his point and certainly doesn't want to roll a 7 and crap out. He picks up the dice and deftly places a 6 against a 1. He gives the dice a phony rattle in his hand and then rolls the dice out evenly so that they do "cartwheels." He can't control which number will come up, but he knows inside numbers will remain the 6's and the 1's virtually all the time. No craps.

There are other advanced ways of controlling dice throws such as the "whip shot," in which the dice are flipped differently than in the blanket roll. The whip shot eliminates the rolling action while maintaining the spinning action. The spinning of the dice makes it impossible to see that the dice are not rolling over at all. In that sense the whip shot is the best dishonest roll of all.

However, all these moves can be eliminated in one sure way. Once its established that the dice must be bounced against a wall or similar barrier the hustler's sleight of hand has also been eliminated. So far the cheats have not figured out a way to fix a wall so that the dice will not bounce off it randomly.

Gambling casinos require that all dice must bounce against a table side or the roll doesn't count. It's the only surefire way to eliminate controlled shooting.

Of course, if you are playing BACKGAMMON you may still have cheating problems. What? Doesn't a proper dice cup prevent controlling the dice? Well, who's to say your opponent in a big-money game has put *both* his dice into the cup? That rattling you hear could come from just one die, while he conceals the other one behind the cup. The second die will be released in a controlled slide and your opponent will be sure of at least one number.

Dice may not really be educated, but gullible gamblers will be—and pay plenty for the lessons.

DICE-CUP CHEATING
Many gamblers believe that using a dice cup eliminates cheating. As a result cheats using dice cups can have a field day at such games as BACKGAMMON, POKER DICE, BUCK DICE, HIGH DICE, and FOUR-FIVE-SIX. Dice cup hustlers will even insist that CRAPS be played with a cup.

With the use of a glass in place of a dice cup it is apparent that a "dice palmer" can control a die by the simple expedient of retaining it in his hand *behind* the dice cup. The vigorous rattle of the single die in the cup is sufficient to mask the absence of the other die. (Photo: E. Gerard)

In fact, many cheats *prefer* dice cups; loaded dice, they note, are less detectable when flipped from a dice cup than from the hand. All a cheat needs is a slick dice cup—one with a smooth, slick inner surface—loaded dice (which tend to land with their loaded sides down), and a cool technique. The same cup and dice used by an honest player will perform more or less as honest equipment.

The dice-cup cheat shakes the dice in a very special way, with an up and down and slightly rotary arm motion. As a result the loaded dice merely spin around the inside surface without rattling randomly. With a final sideward shake, the shooter gets the dice in the cup to topple over so that the loaded sides are against the cup wall. Then he throws the dice while holding the cup parallel to the table, shoving the cup forward and then jerking it back quickly. The dice slide out of the slick cup with the loads landing down. The cheat "rolls" the numbers he desires.

The beauty of the dice-cup scam is that the cheat can play honestly most of the time, thus averting suspicion, while all the other players, unaware that anything is wrong, shake the cup properly and throw the dice with the cup tilted down so that the loaded dice tend to behave normally.

An honest player's only defense against such possible cheating is to insist that the dice cup be "tripped"—that is, have a lip along the rim that causes the dice to tumble as they are flipped out of the cup. In place of a lip, cups lined with ribbed rubber are acceptable. If the only cup available is not tripped, players should insist that the cup be shaken vigorously and turned completely upside down on the tosses. When such rules are followed, the dice-cup cheat is faced with the awesome prospects of playing an honest game.

DR. PEPPER: Wild-card Poker Game

This Seven-card Stud variation goes a little nuts with wild cards—all 2's, 4's, and 10's are wild. So you can imagine what kind of hand it takes to win. Four aces would be a ho-hum hand. Even a straight flush or royal flush may not be enough. A player should have five of a kind—and high ones at that.

In a variation of this game any player dealt an up-card deuce must ante an extra two chips, four chips for a 4, and ten chips for a 10. If a player is dealt a 10 on the first upcard and has no wild cards in the hole he generally should fold rather than pay such a hefty penalty. There are very few games in which the early appearance of a wild card will cause a good player—or a foolish one, for that matter—to fold. But the fact is the game is soon going to be awash with wild cards and a player should hesitate about feeding a small pot while all he has is a single wild 10. Not all POKER addicts have the discipline to fold in this situation, which makes Dr. Pepper a surprisingly lucrative game for the serious gambler who knows how to gauge his play.

DOGFIGHTING GAMBLING

Dogfighting is an illegal gambling sport that has a long tradition in America. Although officially prohibited in every state, dogfighting contests were common in every part of the country during the 19th century, and thousands of dogs were doomed to horrible deaths. Dog stealing became a major threat as gangsters used every means possible to provide enough animals to keep up with the demand. Most top fighting dogs were imported from England or bred from that country's stock. Championship battles often generated as much wagering as did equally outlawed prizefights. Among the more infamous dogfighting arenas in the country were Bill Swan's Saloon and Rat Pit and Hanly's Dog Pit in New Orleans and Kit Burns's Sportsmen's Hall in New York.

Fights were not limited to those between dogs but were also staged with wharf rats, who were brought in to battle dogs after being starved for a considerable period of time. Most of the time the fighting terriers could handle the rodents, but occasionally a dog would try to flee after being nipped several times by the rats. The rooting of the crowd would then shift in favor of the rats, as some of the bloodthirsty audience hoped to see a canine death. Others had their money on a particular dog to get the top rat-kill score and thus wanted his competitors to take a beating. In a contest at Bill Swan's in 1879, a dog named Modoc killed 36 rats in two minutes 58 seconds. It was nowhere near a record. In 1862 a dog named Jacko killed 60 rats in two minutes 43 seconds. Later that same year Jacko established his all-time

An 1889 "sporting publication" reports the result of a big-money dog match in which losing gamblers suffered the sad fate of watching their favorite endure frightful injuries until at last its back is broken.

endurance record by disposing of 200 rats in 14 minutes, 37 seconds.

The greatest dogfight in American history was staged at the Garr farm near Louisville, Kentucky, on October 19, 1881. The canines battled under the strict revised rules as laid down by *The Police Gazette.* The purse of $2,000 was held by Richard K. Fox, the owner of that magazine. While the contest was illegal and faced the possibility of being shut down, the match attracted so much attention from coast to coast that bookmakers did a land-office business. The Ohio and Mississippi Railroad ran special excursions for dogfight gamblers from as far away as New Orleans and New York. If the authorities had stepped in to halt the fight, there would clearly have been rioting in the streets of Louisville.

Pitted against each other were New York's Cockney Charlie Loyod's brindled white dog Pilot and Louisville's "Colonel" Louis Kreiger's white battler Crib, and it had to be a fight to the death. The bloody, inhumane battle lasted an hour and 25 minutes before Pilot destroyed his opponent. Pilot became as well known and popular as the heavyweight boxing champion of the time, John L. Sullivan.

By the turn of the century, interest in dogfighting had dwindled as fans and gamblers turned to boxing instead. In recent years, however, as growing publicity and concern about pit bulls indicate, dogfighting has gotten a new lease on life. Pit-bull owners do not make their money from the purses won in these illegal fights but by betting heavily on their animals.

DOG-RACE BETTING

Dog-race or greyhound race betting has been called "America's most invisible gambling success." Legal in only 15 states, it is incredibly successful in New England, Florida, and several Western states, and today well in excess of $1 billion a year is bet on the canines. Dog racing has met strong opposition from various groups, including anti-animal-cruelty groups and, more important, the horse-race lobby, since in every head-to-head competition between the two forms, dog racing comes out on top. In New England while horse-race tracks close, dog-race tracks open and expand. One of the few places that dogs failed was at a track outside Las Vegas. It proved impossible to lure bettors away from casino tables to venture into the desert. Similarly, in England dog racing enjoyed enormous success against the horses, reaching a handle rivaling that in America with a much smaller population base, but in recent years the betting has declined with the advent of football (soccer) pools and Bingo.

There are hundreds of dog racing tracks in the world, including, besides the United States and Great Britain, Ireland, South America, Puerto Rico, France, Italy, Belgium, Holland, Spain, Australia, and China. Dog racing has been popular in Greece since at least the fifth century B.C.

In the early days the dogs chased a live hare, and efforts to produce a mechanical one in the 19th century proved a flop. In 1919 the electrical hare was introduced in California, completely revolutionizing the sport, which has thrived ever since.

In the early years dog-race betting was marked by widespread crookedness, with promoters organizing the doping and substitution of dogs. Such hankypanky is no longer viable. In the United States a racing greyhound is registered at birth, its paw prints put on file, and the dog must wear an identity disk at all times. Similar precautions are taken in England. Dog-race addicts are convinced of the innate honesty of the sport, which, after all, features man's best friend rather than jockeys whose motives may be suspect. Most important for bettors is the fact that the dogs are raced twice a week and therefore show and hold their form for a considerable period of time. Because betting pools are quite small at most tracks, crooked gamblers have found no way to stage a major coup since a sudden rush of betting on one dog would immediately be spotted.

DOLLAR POKER: Bar Game

Dollar Poker, sometimes called Liar's Poker or Money Poker, is a longtime favorite with the saloon crowd, and one of the most popular bar bets around. It can be played with just two players, but with a major variation is more popular with five or six.

As a two-man game Dollar Poker is played like POKER, with the highest Poker hand winning. The game is played utilizing the serial numbers that appear on dollar bills, consisting of two letters and eight numbers. The letters are ignored and the two players bet on what possible Poker hands they can come up with combined. In doing this, a player studies his own hand and tries to guess how much his opponent's bill can help him in that hand and bids accordingly. The number values decrease from 0 to 1, so that a pair of 0's and a pair of 4's would beat a pair of 9's and a pair of 4's.

One player starts the bidding, usually by calling a pair, and his opponent will top that bid and so on until the value bid escalates so high that one of the players does not think he can top it. He then calls. If the bidder makes the hand, he collects a dollar. If he does not, he pays the dollar. Some players try to deceive their opponent by bidding at first on a pair they don't hold, hoping their opposite number will have a pair and come back with a bid of four of a kind. The first player calls and collects, since his opponent cannot come up with four of a kind from the two bills.

This same version can by played with more than two players but the game gets too restrictive sticking to Poker hands, so play is altered to bidding on the basis of how many times a single digit appears on the bills of all the contestants. The bidding is won by the player whose bid represents the largest amount of the highest digit. Some Dollar Poker addicts operate on the principle that—with ten numbers possible in eight tries—each player on average will have .8 of any particular digit. Therefore if a player holds two 7's he will assume his five opponents will hold an average of four more 7's and he will bid as high as six 7's. This is considered a safe bet, and only if the bidding goes higher will he start to have qualms.

Dollar Poker is not a game to be played with strangers, who may ring in special bills they are holding with as many as six of the same digit. (Clark Gable, playing a con man, did this in one memorable movie scene.) Safeguards like turning in five bills to the bar's cash register and getting five bills back after four or five successive rounds are no real protection. Hustlers can still palm a special bill and dip it into the game.

As a protection, many players set an arbitrary limit of a maximum of three that will be accepted for any digit per bill. This becomes an important strategy move and many players will allow for an opponent to have three of a kind and then allow the .8 figure for other players as well as the actual count for his own hand. The ideal situation for a player is for an opponent to bid high on a three of a kind that he (the player) is holding. The latter can usually win the

bid and the game by bidding three on his hand and two or three for the other bidder's hand and average for the rest of the participants. Some players with weak hands will bid over their own expectations in hopes of driving the bidding so high that the eventual bidder will overbid. False bids are also useful in misleading opponents on how many times a certain number is present.

DOLLAR STORE: Early Gambling Swindle

During the great migrations West after the Civil War, American settlers were less concerned with Indians then with another deadly foe—crooked gamblers.

Typical was Ben Marks's Dollar Store, which opened in Cheyenne, Wyoming, in 1867. Marks was a friendly looking red-whiskered man who, so the saying went, would cheat his mother-in-law and get his wife to help him.

The Dollar Store was so named because every item in the store sold for one dollar—and most items were of solid value. Unfortunately, Marks wasn't much interested in selling his wares but used them merely as a lure to bring in potential suckers, including immigrants with their pokes for starting a new life in the West.

When a wagon-train settler stepped into Ben's establishment to pick up a sturdy shovel, he more than likely would leave without the shovel. Instead, he'd drop his stake in some of the many "gambling games" going on inside. None of Ben's games were legitimate; all were manned by confederates pretending that they were winning big money at THREE-CARD MONTE and other card games, the SHELL GAME, and other scams.

Eventually Ben Marks's idea of a Dollar Store spread and came to be known later in confidence-game circles as the BIG STORE, the fake brokerage, the bogus gambling club, or the phony horse parlor (as in the movie *The Sting*). The take from victims at such establishments rose into the many thousands of dollars.

Ironically, among the scores of dollar stores that sprang up after Ben Marks's pioneer venture was one in Chicago that grew into a prestigious modern department store. Its founder originally rented the building for a Monte swindle but discovered he could sell cheap and flashy goods at a dollar and make more than he could with a crooked gambling operation—which may tell something about how business fortunes were built in America.

DOLLAR-NUMBER SWINDLE: Sucker Bar Bet

Any regular in a tavern where bar bets are common will run into sharper offering the Dollar-number Game. The "game" should be changed to "swindle" as this is one of the hoariest cons ever worked on suckers.

The bet is that the victim can't pick three numbers that appear in the serial number on a dollar bill. If he picks the three he wins, at 2 to 1 odds on his bet. Occasionally a sharper will admit the real odds on such a bet should be 5 to 2 and sportingly offers such odds.

This is a shrewd move because some bettors may have read warnings about the game and know that 2 to 1 odds are insufficient. However, few bettors will remember what the correct odds are, although "5" will stick in their minds. The correct odds actually are more than 5 to 1, but a bettor will never find a sharper offering those odds. Many sharpers do very well betting at what is actually only half odds. And an "honest" amateur betting only for a glass of beer is certain to end up very loaded while his opponent, even with a double-beer payoff, will go home thirsty.

DOMINOES: Occasional Gambling Game

Dominoes has become to some extent a "secret" gambling game. Dominoes is actually any of several games played with oblong tiles divided into two equal spaces either blank or marked with one to six dots, or "pips." Most of the games (such as Block, Draw, Sebastopol, Bergen, Sniff, Stars, Fives-and-Threes) are played by matching spaces with the same number of dots. Generally the idea is to play out of tiles and to penalize an opponent by the number of dots he still possesses on his remaining tiles.

Dominoes is the gambling activity engaged in most often by policemen who, in most jurisdictions, are forbidden to gamble in the stationhouse with playing cards. Dice too are generally barred from the premises. Dominoes can be played and a point score kept, so that no cash need be exposed. Settlement can take place at the end of the game out of sight of any superiors.

The origin of dominoes is obscure and the subject of various theories, none entirely convincing. But it is virtually certain that the game is an offspring from dice since all the combinations of dice are found in dominoes (although not in the full mathematical range). Indeed, the earlier forms of dominoes appear to have been limited to these dice possibilities. Later, seven tiles with one or two blanks were introduced to add variety to various domino games.

A dice variation of dominoes has been used by gambling hustlers with lethal effect on the uninitiated who believe that dominoes represent exactly one half the possibilities that can be obtained with two dice, so that the odds for winning or losing remain constant. Actually this is not even remotely the case, and under the true odds in "Domino Dice" the "shooter" gets all the worst of it.

In playing the game all the dominoes are simply laid out on the table or put into a bag and a tile is drawn that becomes the shooter's point. As in CRAPS he wins with a 7 or 11 and loses with a 2, 3, or 12. Tiles with a blank are usually considered a "wash" and do not count, calling for a replay. Thus in Domino Dice the player enjoys only a 4-to-3 advantage on the first roll, compared to 2-to-1 in real Craps. From there on, the odds increase against the shooter, since generally the tile he chooses is not returned to the pack when he tries to make his point. If it were, the shooter would actually stand a 50-50 chance if his number was either a 6 or an 8, but since his point tile is now out of the game the odds against him now are 3 to 2. And the 6 and 8 remain the only numbers that look that good. The other possibilities—4, 5, 9, and 10—now suffer a 3-to-1 disadvantage.

Such odds are so outrageous that Domino Dice is not considered a legitimate game by serious gamblers—except of course if they have happened onto a sucker and victimize him by constantly betting against the shooter, or, if they themselves must shoot, greatly reducing their bet.

The sharpest Domino Dice operator this observer ever met was a uniformed officer in upstate New York who lured in players by announcing he'd pay off at "true crap odds" on all numbers, something no casino does. Thus he paid off at 6-to-5 on 6 or 8, 3-to-2, on 5 or 9, and 2-to-1 on 4 and 10. However, these are true odds only for regular Craps and hardly made a dent in the edge he had at Domino Dice.

Obviously Domino Dice is strictly a private game that casinos won't touch. Actually, professional gamblers know that it is in private games that the big scores are made since all that is necessary is finding that one sucker who does not understand true odds. Domino Dice is a good way to take him. It is almost as efficient as simply pulling a gun on him and taking his money.

FYODOR DOSTOEVSKY: Russian Writer and Compulsive Gambler

The great Russian writer Fyodor Dostoevsky (1821-1881) offers in his short novel *The Gambler* an apt portrait of the COMPULSIVE GAMBLER. It wasn't all that hard for Dostoevsky because he was describing himself. He portrays Alexey Ivanovitch's irresistible craving for risk-taking after winning a fortune in a casino. Compulsively, he must risk it all in one hand of Trente et Quarante. Should he win, he must repeat the bet until he finally loses all.

It was so for ten maniacal years for Dostoevsky in his own life. He gambled and lost so much that he was forced to borrow from friends, publishers, and other writers (he mooched considerably from Ivan Turgenev). He could not help himself, since he was overwhelmed by a great desire to bet—and lose. He wrote his wife that he actually experienced orgasm

The great Russian writer Fyodor Dostoevsky could write penetrating portraits of fictional compulsive or pathological gamblers, since he was describing himself. He wrote some of his greatest novels in desperate haste to raise money for gambling and only secondarily to feed his family. (Photo: N.Y. Public Library)

on losing a large sum of money at ROULETTE one night. Dostoevsky wrote some of his greatest novels in desperate haste to raise funds for gambling, and only secondarily to feed his family.

His second wife, Anna, recorded in her diary a typical incident of the author's behavior: "He returned, having of course lost everything, and said he wanted to talk to me. He took me on his knee and began to beseech me to give him another five louis. He said he knew that that would leave us only seven louis and that we should have nothing to live on; he knew everything, but what was to be done? In no way could he calm himself; he said that if I did not give him the money he would go off his head. . . . He begged me not to deprive him of the possibility of reproaching himself for his insane weakness, begged my pardon for heaven knows what, said he was unworthy of me, that he was a knave and I an angel, and so forth. . . . I could scarcely quiet him."

Dostoevsky was a captive of the gambling mania for a decade until 1871, when once more his wife gave him some money to travel to the casino at Wiesbaden to try to win some desperately needed money for their upkeep. As his wife writes: "I certainly did not entertain any hope of his winning at roulette, and I also was very sorry to part with a hundred thalers, which is was necessary to sacrifice, but I knew by experience of his former visits to the tables that, after receiving new and exciting impressions, after satisfying his craving for risk, for gambling, Fiodor would return home calmed, and realizing the futility of his hopes of winning at the tables would sit down with renewed strength to his novel. . . ."

The gambling expedition ended in disaster and Dostoevsky was broke within a week. When he returned home, he immediately sat down to continue work on his novel *The Devils*. But while still in Wiesbaden Dostoevsky wrote his wife a letter on April 28, 1871: "A great thing has happened to me; the filthy fancy, which has tormented me for ten years (or truer, since the death of my brother, when I found myself suddenly crushed by debts) has vanished. I kept on dreaming of winning; I dreamt seriously, passionately. Now it is all over and finished. This was actually the *last* time. Do you believe me, Anya, that now my hands are untied? Gambling was a tie on me; but now I shall think of work and shall not dream of gambling for nights on end as I used to do."

His wife later wrote in her *Reminiscences*: "I, of course, could not all at once believe in such a great happiness as Fiodor's indifference to roulette. Surely he had promised me not to play so many times before, and yet he had not found the strength to keep his word. But this time the happiness was realised, and indeed that was the *last* time he played roulette. Later on, during his travels abroad (in 1874, 1875, 1876, 1879) Fiodor never once went to a casino."

Giving a compulsive gambler money to bet is not the standard cure and hardly the one to be recommended by psychiatrists, GAMBLERS ANONYMOUS, or GAM-ANON, but in Dostoevsky's case it worked.

DOUBLE EXPOSURE 21: New Casino Version of Blackjack

In recent years Double Exposure 21 has zoomed in popularity in Las Vegas and elsewhere in Nevada. It appears to be a simple form of BLACKJACK, and—incorrectly—the surface facts of the game make it sound more advantageous for the player. But if that were so, why would casinos offer it? In fact, Double Exposure 21 is a dream game—for the house.

The key come-on to the game is that the dealer deals himself *both* cards face up. Tell that to many Blackjack players and they will automatically assume that the house is engaging in a giveaway, one that will make the average player into a sure winner.

Sadly, the truth is that what one hand giveth the other hand taketh away. Under the special rules applying to this game, the dealer, to make up for exposing both his cards, only pays off at even money for Blackjack and also wins on all ties. Only to the gullible will this be considered a minor concession. Actually it is card-table highway robbery.

It is virtually impossible to come up with a mathematical formula on what these changes mean since the odds on any game varies with the cards previously played, but research done on Double Exposure 21 shows that the average player will lose far more money at it than at the standard game of Blackjack. A gambler can clock this for himself, playing first for a couple hours at flat bets at a regular Blackjack table and then a couple of hours at Double Exposure 21. The losses at the latter will be horrendous by comparison. As a result seasoned Blackjack players avoid the game. However, the game continues to thrive in Nevada, further confirmation about that adage about a sucker being born every minute.
See also CRAPLESS CRAPS.

DOUBLE HASENPFEFFER: Partnership Game Similar to Euchre

Like HASENPFEFFER, Double Hasenpfeffer is a partnership game but it can accommodate three teams of two players as well as just two teams. It is played with double the deck used for Hasenpfeffer—actually a 48-card PINOCHLE deck—but without a joker. Cards in plain suits rank from ace-ace down to 9-9. In the *trump* suit there are two jacks (the Right Bowers) that are high followed by the two jacks of the same color (the Left Bowers) and then the remaining trumps from ace-ace down to 9-9. In a four-person game players are dealt 12 cards and in a six-person game, eight.

In the four-person game a bidder must guarantee that he and his partner (seated opposite) will take six tricks or more. If all players pass, the dealer is required to make a bid of six. In the larger game, the minimum bid is four tricks. Double Hasenpfeffer then proceeds as does the related game of EUCHRE; the bidder leads to the first trick with the high card in suit taking the trick unless it is trumped, which is optional when a player is out of suit. When two high cards of identical rank and suit are played, the first one shown wins the trick, as in Pinochle.

Scoring is the same as in Hasenpfeffer, with the bidding team scoring 1 point for each trick it takes provided it doesn't fall short of the bid. When this happens the team is penalized the number of tricks bid. If the dealer has been forced to make the minimum bid, his team is only penalized half the number. Game is 62.

If the bidder feels he can make the bid on his own,

he names trump, discards two cards, and receives what his partner considers to be his best cards. The rest of the partner's hand is discarded and he is out of the game while the bidder plays solo. If the solo makes more than his bid, he scores double.

In a less desirable variation, Double Hasenpfeffer can be played as a three-handed game as well with a minimum bid of six tricks, the high bidder playing against the other two.

DOUBLE PEDRO
See CINCH.

DOUBLE RUM
See COON CAN.

DOUBLE SIXES
See SIXES AND DOUBLE SIXES.

DOUBLE-BARREL DRAW: Lowball and Draw Poker Combination

Many POKER players don't like Draw, Jacks or Better. It can be a slow game, frequently with no openers, necessitating additional deals. The answer to their impatience is Double-barrel Draw, which combines regular Draw with LOWBALL, in which the lowest hand is the winning one.

How to play: The game starts out as normal Draw and if nobody opens with jacks or better, the game becomes Lowball. More often than not a player will open under the second circumstance and the game can continue.

While this may move things along, the gambler's strategy will alter. Normally the smart early bettors do not open on a pair of jacks, anticipating a later bettor's higher pair. In Double-barrel Draw they cannot afford the luxury of playing so tight; if the game reverts to Lowball they could conceivably have no hand at all. Because of this, serious high-stakes gamblers do not like Double-barrel Draw, but it is a nice variation in sociable games.

DOUBLE-BARRELED SHOTGUN
See SHOTGUN.

DOUBLE-DRAW POKER

A skilled player at DRAW POKER should opt to play Double Draw because, as the saying goes, "Dumb players play Double Draw twice as dumb." Best played with five players or fewer, Double Draw provides redoubled action compared to the regular game.

How to play: The game begins as standard Draw. Five cards are dealt to each player, an opening round is bet, and discards and draws of up to three cards are made. Then there is another round of betting. At this point, standard Draw ends, and in Double Draw players may discard up to three cards *again,* thus getting twice the opportunity to improve a hand. One gambling guide even goes so far as to state that players generally stay, because each player is allowed to draw twice and therefore the odds against him are reduced to half.

This is sheer nonsense. Let us say a player is dealt a 2, 5, 6, 7, and 9. He is going after an inside straight, needing the 8. To stay with this hand is a no-no for the skilled player in regular Draw. But in Double Draw, he may decide to stay, especially if the bet is small and he is a big winner. He discards the deuce and draws another 7. The unintelligent bettor, having decided that the chances of filling the inside straight are twice as good as in regular Draw, will try for the straight again, discarding the 7. While it may be argued erroneously that his chances have doubled, that was only true *before his first draw.* At that time the chances of his drawing an 8 on the first draw was at best 4 out of 47, since there is no way of telling how many 8's were dealt to other players. He did not get the 8, but that does not mean his chance of filling the straight on the second try is double. His chances of getting an 8 can only be figured to have improved to 4 out of 46. So while the undisciplined player might try for the inside straight a second time, the skilled player would not.

Some poor players can be counted on to try another tack. Having now achieved a pair of 7's, this eternal optimist switches objectives and holds the pair, drawing three new cards. This too is part of the seductive quality of Double Draw, encouraging poor players to stay with weak hands. The skilled player faced with the situation would reason that on the first deal probably two of the five players were dealt a pair of some kind. These two players have already drawn three cards each and chances are that at least one has improved his hand. The pair of 7's therefore represents a hand that is way behind in the improvement stakes—and while the hands opposing him probably have already improved, they both have another shot at improving even more. The skilled player drops, confidently and patiently waiting for another hand.

Double Draw is highly recommended in DEALER'S CHOICE when playing with undisciplined players.

DOUBLE-HANDED HIGH-LOW
See BIMBO HIGH-LOW.

DOUBTING DICE
See LIAR DICE.

DRAW POKER
See POKER.

DRAW POKER—Five-card Buy
Some experts call Draw Poker—Five-card Buy downright silly POKER. It may be, but only for silly players.

The game is played under the general rules of Draw Poker except that anything opens and a player is not limited to a three-card discard but may discard four or even five cards for new ones. Only the silly gambler takes four or five cards instead of dropping out.

In an average six-player game, three players will hold pairs in their opening hand. The chance of improving the pair with a three-card buy is significantly greater than the chance of drawing a winning hand on a five-card buy. Nevertheless, novice gamblers stay in the belief that the five-card buy will bring in winners. Expert gamblers humor the novices precisely because they build the pot. Often nobody will get anything in an opening round. In that case an expert player, if he is the dealer or a late player, will take a chance and stay with an ace or an ace, king, figuring he is high. Novice players have never grasped the idea that the standard rule of a three-card buy should protect the weak player, forcing him to drop out when he has a weak hand.

DRAW POKER HIGH SPADES
Draw Poker High Spades is a choice game for the shrewd gambler because he can learn more than he can lose by the fillip in the early betting.

The game is ordinary Draw Poker, but a side pot is set up for the high spade on the first five cards dealt. Players simply announce "I have a low spade," or "I have a middle spade" or "I have a high spade." The player who indicates he has the highest spade then reveals it and if no one is higher he takes the side pot. This is an even bet, but the smart player learns from the high spade—or high spades—revealed.

If, for instance, a jack takes the spades and the smart player is holding a pair of jacks, he knows his own hand is weak. Under no circumstances will he open on his jacks, and he might very well drop. On the other hand, a sharp player holding a pair of queens likes to know if someone else holds the king of spades. If a player has the king and subsequently drops, the pair of queens are stronger than normal. If a player is holding four spades, his try for a flush is tempered if four other players declare for spades on the opening round. (He also knows that the chances are at least one of the players is holding more than one spade.)

DRAW YOUR OWN: Seven-Card Stud Poker Variation
How to play: Each player is dealt in rotation five down cards and then three additional down cards at

which they may not look. These final three cards represent an individual deck, or stock, from which the players must draw later. There is a betting round and then players discard one card and draw one from their individual stock to replace it. Play continues in this fashion until all three replacement cards have been drawn. The winners are those with the best high and low hands with their final five cards.

Some Draw Your Own games allow players to waive a draw, but most require all three draws. Consequently, good hands can be destroyed by the forced discard. This disruptive factor alters the strategy of the game. Because good hands can be ruined, players try to keep their options open early, holding a pair while trying to accumulate low cards at the same time. Even if a player decides to break a pair to go for low, he will do so in a way that still leaves him with three cards toward a flush or straight if at all possible. Then if he gets the fourth flush or straight card, he can shift back to trying for high on the final card.

Unlike other POKER games, staying on relatively weak hands frequently pays off. Because a good early low hand may have to be broken, for instance, an opponent who sticks on a picture-high low or even a low pair can end up taking low. Players who win at Draw Your Own are those who discard in such a way as to leave as many options open as possible.

DROP DEAD: Five-dice Bar Game
Drop Dead, a popular children's game, has, like some others, been adapted in recent years into a money bar game in America and it enjoys considerable play in British pubs.

Order of play is determined by a throw of a die with the low man going first, etc. The first player rolls five dice, and if they produce no 5's or 2's, he totals up the points and gets to throw the five dice again and can add to his score if he has no 5's or 2's again. This is not too likely since the odds against throwing five dice without hitting any two specified numbers is actually about 6½ to 1 (211 to 32). If, however, the player hits any 5's or 2's, he loses those dice and keeps playing only with the remaining dice. Thus if on the first throw he gets 6-4-3-2-2, he loses the last two dice and gets no points. He now throws again with the three remaining dice. Supposed he then gets 6-1-1. He scores eight points and repeats the roll with three dice, and so on.

In a cutthroat wrinkle added to the game in the United States, each player may once during his play add another ante to the pot. Opponents who do not wish to increase their bets drop out, sacrificing their interest in the pot. Any player scoring on five or even four dice should increase the bet since such

scores frequently make him unbeatable. (The odds against scoring with four dice are about 4 to 1.) Most players will not score with five or four dice and in fact are more likely to add to their points when they have only one die.

Scores in Drop Dead are surprisingly low, and a point total of 20 is uncommon. Strangely, most gamblers prefer to shoot late in this game, as indicated by the fact that the low die thrower goes first. But it is actually preferable to shoot early because that puts the player in a position to run up a good score and force opponents to drop out or else risk building the pot for him.

Eleanor DUMONT
See MADAME MUSTACHE.

DUTCH BANK
See BANKER AND BROKER.

DUTCH STUD: Holland's Stud Poker Variation
If one plays STUD POKER in the Netherlands or the Dutch West Indies, he will find Dutch or Curacao Stud a unique version of High-Low.

Each player is dealt a face-up card. If two or more players get the same denomination, their cards are dead and are buried on the bottom of the deck by the dealer who proceeds to give out cards until all players have a starter card of a different denomination. The remainder of the deck is shuffled and the dealer proceeds to deal cards one at a time onto the center of the table. Whenever a card matches a card in a player's hand, he claims it. Following each match-up there is a betting sequence. Let us say the first matching card is a jack, giving that player the first pair. He of course bets, because high is achieved by the first player who gets four of a kind. However, let us suppose another player holds a deuce. He might well raise at this point since he is potentially low.

Play continues with betting after each matched card and continues until four of a kind appears. This winner takes half the pot. The rest goes to the low man at that time. If a player has only one card he takes low, provided no other opponent has only one card or, if he does, that it is of a higher denomination.

The player who gets the lowest starter card is top dog and should press the betting immediately. He has just as much chance of taking high as anyone else and has the best chance for low as well, since he would win any ties. Players holding higher cards should fold if they don't pair early. They may stay, however, as long as they are lagging behind players with lower-value starters.

E

EAGLES AND CROWNS: Fifth Suit Added to Playing Cards

Playing cards date back almost a millennium, and since the four-suit deck was set, cards have remained unchanged. Yet resourceful card makers, eager for a way to alter cards in their design or symbols to create a whole new market, tried any number of ways to change them. It was largely a thankless task. In the United States, France, and Russia, after those countries' revolutions, efforts were made to get rid of the references to royalty. In the United States they tried political and military figures, Indians, and the like, but all attempts in the end were duds. In later years manufacturers pushed cards using four colors rather than just two for the four suits. No luck. They tried other gimmicks, such as black backgrounds and new arrangements of the pips. Nobody bought it.

Then in 1937 the card makers made their most concerted effort to create a new market by adding a fifth suit to cards. They were called Eagles in the United States and Crowns in England and as a part of the sales pitch a five-suit Bridge game was created.

It was a wasted effort. Eagles and Crowns never really caught on. Today such original decks are probably worth more as collectors' items than anything else. Certainly gamblers made it clear they weren't going to play with them.

EARL OF COVENTRY: Fan Tan Variation

Earl of Coventry is a variation of FAN TAN and follows the same betting rules. The lone variation is that 7's do not have to be laid down first and the suits completed up to the king and down to the ace; Earl of Coventry allows the first player to lead with any card he wishes. Whatever he plays requires that the other three cards of the same rank must be played. The player who discards the last card of the rank can lead with any other card and that rank must similarly

be completed. The participant discarding his entire hand is the winner and all others must pay him one chip for each card with which they have been caught. The game is a rather simple one and unlike Fan Tan and another variation, FIVE AND NINE, Earl of Coventry is now almost exclusively a children's game. It is also sometimes called Snip Snap Snorem.

EASY GO: Even-steven Game of Chance

Easy Go is a gambling game of pure luck with no advantage for the dealer. Up to nine players can participate, using a single deck of 52 cards. The banker deals five cards face up to every player, except himself. He then turns up a card for himself, and every person holding the same rank is required to make an ante to the pot. If the card is of the opposite color the player antes one chip, but if it is of the same color he must put in two chips.

The banker will turn up five cards in all for himself, with the ante getting progressively higher. On the second card the ante is three chips for the same color and two for the opposite. On the third card: five, same; four, opposite. On the fourth card: nine, same; eight opposite. On the fifth card: 17, same; 16, opposite.

There follows a second show of cards, one at a time, and now players take out of the pot for matching cards in the same proportion that they had previously put in. If at the end of a hand there is any money left in the pot, the banker takes it as his profit. If on the other hand the pot is short, the banker makes up the difference, sustaining a loss.

As noted previously, the banker has no advantage in this game. However, when the game is banked in a gambling house, an edge is produced for the house by eliminating the color distinction during the payout round, so that it doesn't matter if the matched card is of the same or opposite color. This is enough to make the game a viable play for the house.

In private games of Easy Go the danger is gambling with a hustler adept at BOTTOM DEALING. He engages in BOTTOM PEEKING and quickly surveys the players' hands. If he sees one or more of the same card on the table, he holds it for his fifth card, guaranteeing players will have to add to the pot at the hefty 17-16 chip rate. If, however, he sees no matching card, he retains the card until the fifth card of the payout round and bottom deals it, guaranteeing he will make no big payouts.

ECARTE: Kibitzer Gambling Game

Ecarte is a two-man gambling game. Although once extremely popular in Europe, it never gained much of a following in America. In European gaming houses it was permissible for the crowd to bet on the outcome in side bets, making the game a kibitzer's delight and such bettors could frequently voice their opinions on the correct play, which the player was not bound to accept, a situation that frequently caused ill feelings when things went wrong—until fisticuffs and the like caused the game to be barred from casinos.

How to play: The game is played with a 32-card deck, with the deuces through the 6's removed. The rankings of the cards are: king (high), queen, jack, ace, 10, 9, 8, and 7 (low). Each player is dealt five cards and the next is turned up for trump. If the nondealer feels he can win three tricks, he will say "Play," which means he wishes the game to start. The non-dealer has the option of discarding as many cards from his hand as he wishes and replacing them by drawing from the remainder of the pack. If he wishes to exercise this option, he announces, "I propose." If the dealer accepts his proposal, he too has the right to draw some new cards. Otherwise the dealer can reject the proposal and force the play to begin with the original hands for both. If the proposal is accepted, both players draw and discard until one of the players calls a halt.

Before actual play starts, the player holding the king of trump may show it to score 1 point. However, some players prefer to pass up that score in hope that the highest card in the game can be more productive if kept secret. (If the king happened to be turned up to establish trump, the dealer automatically scores 1 point.)

The nondealer leads to the first trick and the dealer must follow suit if able. If he cannot follow suit, he must trump, if able. If he holds no trump, he may discard a side suit. In following a suit or trump suit if that is led, the dealer must take the suit if possible by playing a higher card. The winner of a trick leads to the next.

The object of the game is to take as many of the five tricks as possible. If a player takes three or four tricks, he scores 1 point, and if he takes all five he scores 2 points, the accomplishment being called "vole." If the nondealer plays without having made a proposal or had been refused, he gets 2 points for taking three or more tricks, but he gets no extra point for vole.

The deal passes after each hand and the game continues until one of the players wins with a total of 5 points.

The successful Ecarte player is the one who has learned the mathematical probabilities of taking three tricks in a hand. Once a player has so disciplined himself he can destroy the uninformed player, and he can ignore the urgings of his kibitzers who are very likely to goad him into drawing more cards to a sure hand in order to achieve a vole. It basically does not pay to worry about vole but to let luck operate after the three sure tricks.

EGYPT, Gambling in

Horse-race betting is big in Egypt and there is betting on pigeon shooting, held under authorized conditions. There are gambling houses as well, but Arab nationals are not admitted unless they can offer evidence of foreign nationality, although there is some indication that high-roller locals have a way of getting in. Gambling on BACKGAMMON is permitted in cafes, but BINGO, BACCARAT, and CHEMIN-DE-FER are not allowed in clubs or other establishments. Unlike many other nations in the area, gambling violations can bring very severe punishments in jail time and/or fines.

EIGHT-CARD STUD: Not-too-serious Form of Poker

Eight-card Stud is played just the same as Seven-card Stud except that an eighth card is dealt. The dealer may decide to deal it up or down and, if down, may decide to deal the seventh card up. Most serious gamblers do not approve of the game—some even considering it a children's game—because the probabilities become too uncertain. The dealing of an extra card often may not improve hands very much so that conceivably two pairs will still win quite often, but at the same time it can considerably increase the chances that a player might fill a straight or flush.

What serious players object to is that they cannot get a handle on the average minimum hand needed to win. In that sense they are more comfortable even playing games with four to eight wild cards because they can determine that they will follow a certain criteria on what constitutes the lowest likely winning hand, such as three aces in Deuces Wild and four of a kind, preferably with at least two wild cards in the hand, in games with eight wild cards. By comparison

Eight-card Stud, because of the confusing probabilities, becomes too wild a game.

EIGHTS: Gambling Game of skill

Eights, also called Swedish Rummy (which is rather odd since the game is neither Swedish nor Rummy), is an excellent test of gambling skill.

When played by two to four players, each is dealt seven cards; when played by five or six, each is dealt five cards. When played by four players, the game may be played in partnership. After the deal the top card of the pack is turned up as a starter card. The first player to the dealer's left covers it with a card of the same rank or suit if he can and wishes to. If he does not cover, he draws one card at a time from the pack until he does so. The turned-up cards are formed in a special pile.

The object of the game is to play out of cards first and to collect chips from opponents. Aiding this playing out is the fact that all 8's are wild and may be treated as any suit the player wishes. Payoffs are as follows: losers stuck with an 8 must pay the winner 50 chips, all pictures and 10's are ten chips, and all other cards pay at their point value. In case of a "block" in which no one goes out when the pack is exhausted, the player with the lowest total in his hand collects that difference from each of the others. In cases of partnerships, both partners must go out before the pair wins. In partnership games, a running point score is kept and settlement is made when the losing team hits 500.

This is an excellent "counting" game, certainly more productive and easier than BLACKJACK. It is essential to keep track of the number of cards in a suit already played and the number of 8's utilized. A good player will often be able to "corner" a suit by digging into the pack early rather than playing, especially if it means giving up an 8 early. Some sharp players automatically grab the last ten or so cards in the pack in hopes of gaining control of the game. There are games in which an expert can get rid of 20 or even 30 cards before an opponent sheds only four or five. Eights generally are too valuable to be played just for the sake of making a move. They must be held for strategic play near the end of the game, unless of course a "clear and present danger" emerges with an opponent appearing about to go out. It is also acceptable—and profitable—deliberately to cause a block by using an 8 to call a suit that is exhausted. In their haste to get rid of an extra card or two some players ignore using an 8 in this strategic fashion.

See also HOLLYWOOD EIGHTS.

ELBOW: Center-card Draw Poker Variation

Of Colombian origin, Elbow is a center-card Draw Poker game that is not too different from SPIT IN THE OCEAN and considerably tamer than games like CRISS-CROSS and TWIN BEDS.

How to play: all players are dealt two closed, or down, cards and then three cards are centered in the following elbow arrangement:

1

3   2

These cards are exposed one at a time in the numbered order with a betting round following each. These become common cards for all players. The card at the point of the elbow (number 3) is wild, as are the three other cards of the same rank.

After the elbow has been fully revealed players are permitted to discard one of their two closed cards and there is a final round of betting. A showdown follows under standard Poker rules.

If most of the players are conservative and tend to drop out on weak hands, it is possible for a pair to win occasionally. However, three of a kind should be a prudent gambler's minimum expectation for a win, and a full house and four of a kind are not uncommon.

This is an excellent game for a disciplined gambler to play against poor players, who tend to stay in on the barest expectations. The fact that three cards of all opponents are known to a good player permits him to judge pretty closely how strong his own hand really is.

ELECTION BETTING

What is likely to be the biggest bet a professional gambler will make? On a horse race, the Super Bowl, the World Series? No. As oddsmaker Jimmy "the Greek" Snyder notes: "The professionals will tell you that more money, big money, is wagered on a national election than any sports event you can name. It's the biggest Super Bowl of all."

How big are the bets? It is hard to tell. Many gamblers prefer to scatter their action around, since this tends to affect the odds less. The largest known election bet was made by a racetrack owner who lost $1.2 million against a possible profit of $1 million on Richard Nixon beating John F. Kennedy in 1960.

Another big wager: An Ohio politician who bet a quarter of a million, giving odds of 5 to 2, that FDR would defeat Willkie in 1940. Bets of $25,000 on elections are quite common in Nevada where such bets are legal, and a young Ted Kennedy bet that sum at Lake Tahoe on his brother's successful race.

There was little action on Lyndon Johnson against Barry Goldwater as several Las Vegas books took the election off the boards. Jimmy the Greek insisted the correct odds were 10 million to 1. The oddsmakers called Nixon 100-to-1 favorite against George McGovern. Action on Ronald Reagan against Walter

Mondale was light because bookmakers demanded Reagan supporters put up prohibitive odds.

Overall professional gamblers do better on predicting the outcome of elections than do political pollsters. The only time the bookmakers were wrong was in the Truman-Dewey presidential race in 1948, but there were some sharpers among them who cleaned up. Jimmy the Greek made his reputation as a political gambler by winning $170,000 on Truman. The Greek's figures made the race an absolute toss-up and, with Truman being quoted as a decided underdog, Jimmy put up $10,000 on Truman at 17 to 1. The Greek did so based on a factor that the professional pollsters disregarded—Dewey's mustache. Jimmy's research indicated that most women disliked mustaches. (A lady gambler in Pittsburgh made a hefty bet on Truman at 25 to 1. Newly arrived from Germany, she thought it inconceivable that former GI's who had lost buddies and mothers who had lost sons to the mustachioed little man in Berlin would vote for Dewey. She jumped at the huge odds and has yet to stop crowing about it.)

Most close elections are quoted by bookmakers at 6 to 5 pick 'em, meaning a bettor must put up $6 for every $5 he hopes to win. As the action comes in, the odds will rise or fall depending on which candidate gets more play. Some pundits say watching the price shifts in Vegas is the best barometer to the outcome of any election.

Late polls in 1968 showed the Nixon-Humphrey race narrowing to near even. Staffers for CBS's Walter Cronkite kept calling Las Vegas to check the odds quoted by Jimmy the Greek. Snyder called Nixon a logical 4 to 1 shot and predicted he would get 300 electoral votes. Nixon got 301.

See ARNOLD ROTHSTEIN.

ENFLE: European Card Game

More popular in Europe than in America, Enfle, also known as Schwellen and in the United States as Rolling Stone, is a game for four to six players.

How to play: A 52-card deck is used but is stripped down to eight cards a player. Cards are reduced from the lowest values, first deuces, then treys, etc. The ace is the high card, with values descending to the king, queen, jack and so on as far as the cards go. There is an ante to the pot, which is won by the first player to go out.

Tricks are taken on the basis of suits and the high-card winner of a trick leads the next card. The tricks have no value and are simply set aside in a pile. Whenever a player cannot follow suit he must "eat" all the cards on the table in the unfinished trick, but he is allowed to open the next trick. It is perfectly permissible for the player to lead right back with the suit he has just taken up.

Strategy: A good player always leads with the longest suit in hand, so as to keep cards from each suit in hand as long as possible. In addition to taking the pot (which in lower-stake games can be eliminated), the winner also collects one chip per card with which each of the remaining players are caught.

ENGLISH DRAW POKER

English Draw Poker is played exactly the same as the American Draw Poker save for the fact that the leader, or first player to the left of the dealer, is permitted to discard and draw four new cards while all others are restricted to three cards. This is hardly an advantage to the leader, since if he is drawing four cards, there is little reason for him to remain in the game.

Actually the rule is helpful to professionals. They can tab a player who makes a four-card draw as an undisciplined bettor and raise him unmercifully to build the pot.

This game of English Draw Poker is distinguished from Blind Opening or Blind Straddle, in which the leader must bet before looking at his cards and the next player must raise blind.

See OLD ENGLISH DRAW POKER.

ENGLISH HAZARD

See HAZARD.

ENGLISH ROULETTE: Private Card Game

English Roulette, frequently called Hoggenheimer, is played today solely as a private card game. It failed to make it as a casino game for a very strange reason—bettors could not be convinced the odds were not stacked against them.

The game is played with a regular card deck with a joker from which all 2's, 3's, 4's, 5's, and 6's have been removed. The banker deals out the cards face down in four rows of eight cards. This leaves only one card unplayed. For the moment this card is left undisturbed.

The top row of eight cards is considered to be spades, running down in value from left to right from ace to 7. The row below represents hearts, followed by diamonds and the bottom row is clubs. Players place bets on any card they say will turn up before the joker. The undisturbed card is now revealed and placed in its proper position. Any bets placed there are paid off and the card it replaces is then turned over, and so on. When the joker appears all bets on cards not as yet turned up are lost to the banker. In the meantime he pays off at even money for any cards that do appear. Bettors may also bet that two neighboring cards will both turn up before the joker and if correct, they win at 2 to 1 odds. This bet is made by the bettor placing his money or chips between the two cards.

The player may also bet on four cards. For instance,

if he wishes to bet that the ace and king of spades and the ace and king of hearts will all appear before the joker, he places his bet where the four corners of these cards meet. It is also possible to bet on an entire suit appearing before the joker. If a player places his stake to the right of the bottom row for example, he is betting that all the clubs from ace to 7 will turn up before the joker. If he is right he collects at 8 to 1.

At first blush, these payoffs may appear miserly, and many gamblers conclude so. For instance, let us say a player wishes to bet that both the ace and king of diamonds will appear before the joker. If he bets on each card separately, he will collect even money twice. Thus a player will reason that the payoff for getting both cards should be 3 to 1. This is not true. What these gamblers forget is that they are only concerned with three cards, the ace and king of diamonds and the joker and that on this particular bet all other cards are meaningless. All that matters is the order in which these three cards appear. This can only happen in one of six ways, as follows:

ace, king, joker
king, ace, joker
ace, joker, king
king, joker, ace
joker, ace, king
joker, king, ace

Thus, there are two ways the bettor can win and four ways the banker can win. The odds of 2 to 1 are therefore correct. Similarly, betting on all cards of the same value, four 9's, for example, is correctly paid off at 4 to 1 and the entire suit, from ace to 7, is properly paid off at 8 to 1.

However, so poisoned were gamblers' attitudes about the game that it just never caught on as a casino game with the odds either slightly reduced or a portion of all winning bets subject to a rakeoff to provide the house with some profits.

As a result English Roulette survived solely as a social game and the belief continues that the banker enjoys a big edge. As a result the prudent gambler will simply auction off his rights to the bank when it falls to him. (This may be accomplished in many fashions. Some rules call for the bank passing to the left whenever any suit from ace to 7 is completed in a game. In other games the bank is lost if four aces or four 7's appear.)

Actually, the player who sells the bank is selling nothing of value. If in the course of a long session he auctions off his rights a half dozen or a dozen times, and the bidding is often spirited, these proceeds should make him a winner—if he breaks even on all his own bets, which the law of averages says he should.

ENGLISH STUD: Combination Stud and Draw Poker

English Stud is a great game for a shrewd gambler to opt for on DEALER'S CHOICE if other players let him. The game itself is a very interesting one, combining elements of both Stud and Draw Poker. At first two down cards and one upcard are dealt each player and a betting session follows. After another upcard is dealt there is more betting. Then a fifth card is dealt face up and there is more betting.

After that each player is allowed to replace as many of his cards as he wishes, down cards replacing down cards and upcards replacing upcards. There is a final betting round and the winner is determined.

This may seem like your garden-variety game to be called in Dealer's Choice, but in truth it is more like highway robbery on the dealer's part since by playing last he gets to see everyone's discards first, giving him an enormous advantage for gauging their hands as well as his own. For instance, if a player shows deuce, 7, and king up and discards only the 7, the dealer knows he is bucking for two pairs, kings up (unless the king and deuce are of the same suit). If the dealer is holding a pair of queens and a three-card open-end straight flush, he should normally go with the pair of queens. But under these circumstances he can discard the queens and try to fill a straight or flush. The odds aren't good, but he is making the best of a bad situation. He knows only a pair of aces or a third queen would help him, and he may see some of those cards already on the table. Instead he can opt for the only chance he has. In many other situations the dealer may learn even more and place himself in a more advantageous position on his own draw.

Occasionally, some smart player will insist this game may not be called in Dealer's Choice because of the edge the dealer has. But if a gambler gets no objection he should consider calling the game whenever the circumstances permit. More often than not, another smart player will raise no objection and will also call the game himself. In that case the nondealer who knows the dealer's advantage should fold after the first three cards unless he is dealt the makings of a powerhouse hand.

E-O (EVEN-ODD)

See ROULETTE PREDECESSORS.

EUCHRE: Popular Pre-Poker American Card Game

Before the emergence of POKER, Euchre was easily the most popular card game in America, one immortalized in literature by Bret Harte.

How to play: Euchre is most suitable for two to six players, but it is best for four playing in partnerships of two. The game utilizes a "short pack," that is a regular deck from ace (high) down to 7 (low), with all lower cards removed. In trump suit the jack (Right Bower) tops all other trumps and the jack of the other suit of the same color (Left Bower) ranks as the second highest trump. (If hearts are trump the jack of hearts is the Right Bower and the jack of diamonds the Left Bower. The ace of hearts is next highest trump, and so on in hearts.)

For a time Euchre was very nearly the American national game and today it is still very popular in the Northeast—New England, New York, and especially Pennsylvania. The word "bower" is actually the Americanization of *Bauer*, German for "farmer," a name by which the jack was often known, especially in Pennsylvania Dutch country. In fact, it is sage advice that a traveler in Pennsylvania should not play Euchre with strangers, since they grow excellent Euchre players there who can eat strangers alive at the game.

There is some advantage in being the dealer in Euchre, so it is important to choose the dealer by some sort of draw, and thereafter pass the deal completely around the table. By custom the dealer must give each player five cards in bundles of threes and twos. The balance of the pack is faced down in the center of the table and the top card turned face up. This card represents potential trump, and each player to the left of the dealer in turn has the right to accept or reject it.

If all reject the trump suit, they do so by saying, "I pass." The dealer then places the card face up partly under the pack, and he deals a second round. If all four players pass again, the hand is ended and the deal passes.

If on the first round a player wishes to accept the trump suit, he announces, "I order it up." The dealer's partner then announces: "I assist." On the acceptance, the dealer picks up the turned-up trump card for his hand and discards an unwanted card face down. If there is no acceptance on the first round, the second round permits more leeway to players. This time, in turn, they may either pass or name any suit they like (other than the turned-up card) for trumps.

Once trump suit is determined, the player who named it (the maker) may decide to go it alone rather than have his partner play. Only the maker has this option. If he goes it alone and wins the "march"— taking all five tricks—he scores 4 points. If he wins three or four tricks, he scores 1 point. If he is "euchred" by failing to win three tricks, his opponents score 2 points each.

The player to the left of the dealer (or the player left of the maker, if he is going it alone) leads to the first trick. The player winning a trick leads to the next. A player must follow suit to the card led if

possible, but if he cannot do so, he may either discard or trump. Tricks are taken by the highest trump or if there are no trumps by the highest card in suit.

Should the partnership making trump suit win the march, it scores 2 points, three or four tricks score 1 point, and if they are euchred their opponents get 2 points. Scores are added after each hand and game is the first to win 5 points (by previous agreement this may be 7 or 10 points). When 5 is game it is customary to play a "rubber," so that the winner is the one who takes two out of three games.

Strategy: Because Euchre hands are very short, good players strike quickly, knowing there is little reward for patience in the game. With three sure tricks in hand, such as having the ace and both bowers, a player will opt for going it alone and hope to capture all five tricks. Most good Euchre players are prepared to accept when holding only two sure tricks, hoping their partner will provide at least one more. The 4 points for march when going it alone are very critical since they can put a team over the top. Often a team within a single point of winning and opponents 3 points away will accept the trump rather than risk letting an opponent go it alone and score a march. In such a situation it is advisable to risk being euchred instead.

There are a number of variations to Euchre. The basic ones follow this entry, but it should be noted that local rules can vary greatly.

EUCHRE—Auction

Auction Euchre is a four-handed EUCHRE variation that does not utilize a turned-up trump. Instead players in turn bid three, four, or five for the privilege of being maker. The high bidder sets trump and if that team makes the bid, it receives the amount of the bid in points. If the bidding team is euchred, the opposition gets the amount bid. Usually game is set at 15 or 20 points, with settlement on the point differential.

EUCHRE—Blind

Blind Euchre is a EUCHRE variation for two to four individual players. Hands are dealt in normal Euchre fashion but two extra cards are dealt down as a "blind." They go to the player who orders up or declares trump. He then makes the required discards and plays against all other players. When all players reject the blind, the deal passes.

EUCHRE—Call-Ace

Call-Ace Euchre is a four-handed EUCHRE variation in which a player orders up or makes trump by himself and then picks his partner by calling for the holder of an ace in a non-trump suit. If no one has the ace, the call automatically becomes that of the highest card in suit, but that partner will not be known until the hand is completed. The partners then total their tricks to see if they have won the hand. For three tricks they get 1 point each, for five tricks, 2 points. If they are euchred, all opponents score 2 points each.

The player may elect to play the hand alone. He scores 1 point for three tricks and 4 points for all five, but opponents score 2 points each if he is euchred. A 24-card pack—aces down to 9's—is used for this game.

EUCHRE—Jambon and Laps

Jambon (or Hambone) and Laps may be considered as two separate games or as one game incorporating the rules of both, or they may be played as part of the rules in other forms of Euchre, especially RAIL- ROAD. In Jambon a lone hand may offer to play with his entire hand exposed, or in some localities this may be a requirement. Under some alternate rules the opponent to the maker's left is allowed to call the first card that is played from this exposed hand. In Jambon, the march is worth 8 points, with game being 10.

Laps is a scoring variation that can be used with Jambon, Railroad Euchre, and indeed many forms of Euchre, in that when a winner exceeds the required score, the excess points are credited to the player in the next game. The Laps rule is especially valuable when a player scores a "Jamboree," which is only the five highest trump cards in a hand. The award for this is 16 points, which means if the player previously had a zero, he wins the 10-point game and has a 6-point lead in the next. Laps is something a novice should never play with a stranger. If he turns out to be an expert Euchre player, he will soar out to the lead and never look back.

EUCHRE—Joker

Joker Euchre is the same as basic EUCHRE with a joker added as "best bower," making it the highest trump. Should the joker be turned up as trump, the next card in the pack is used to establish potential trump suit, but it is the joker that is taken up by the dealer for play.

EUCHRE—Railroad

Railroad Euchre is an exceedingly fast four-person EUCHRE variation, like a speeding train, and is usually played to 10 points. Like JOKER EUCHRE it permits a joker as "best bower," and there are a number of other factors. A player may decide to go it alone, in which case he so declares. He may discard any one card he desires and in return gets his partner's best card, face down, as a replacement. The opposing team then has an option to this move, and one player may decide to oppose the bidder alone, whereupon he also discards an unwanted card and receives his partner's best card in return.

If the lone bidder wins, he gets the points award in regular Euchre, but if he is euchred by failure to take three tricks, the other team gets 4 points.

To make the game more involved, the basic rules of JAMBON AND LAPS are also added.

EUCHRE—Three-handed (or Cutthroat Euchre)

Three-handed Euchre is often referred to as Cutthroat Euchre because, under certain situations, a player may find it worthwhile to throw tricks to an opponent rather than to his partner in a hand. Play is the same as in EUCHRE except that the trump maker has to play the hand against his two opponents. If the maker wins the march he scores 3 points, and for getting three or four tricks he scores 1. If he is euchred his opponents score 2 points.

The catch in this scoring is that it is possible for two players to go over 5 in a tie that requires a tiebreaker, which can in turn produce yet another tie. More important, consider the situation that arises when the score stands as follows: Player A, 2; B, 3; C, 1. Should C make trump, player A cannot permit him to be euchred because while he would get 2 points, so would player B and he would win with 5 points. Under those circumstances, player A is forced to play cutthroat and throw tricks to player C, allowing him to take three but not more than four tricks. The subsequent score would be: A, 2; B, 3; C, 2.

There is a modern way of scoring that gets around this by awarding 1 point for three or four tricks, 2 points for a march, and when a maker is euchred, he has 2 points *deducted* from his score, none going to the other players. While this is a solution, most Three-hand Euchre players don't like it, having developed a certain fondness for cutthroat tactics.

EYE BET: Bearded Gambling Scam

A hustler betting he can bite his own eye is one of those bearded scams that has become a part of gambling folklore. Above all the Eye Bet illustrates the folly of believing there is anything like a sure bet as long as human venality can come into play.

A hustler in a bar who gives the appearance of having tippled a few too many declares he will bet $10 he can bite his right eye. Almost certainly another elbow-bender will take the bet, whereupon the hustler plops his right eye—a glass one—out of its socket and bites it.

Winner.

Most suckers accept such defeats with good grace, but few will wager on the hustler's follow-up bet, that he can also bite his left eye as well. Most have had enough and storm out of the place. On reflection, of course, a number of the other habitues of the establishment say it might well be a good bet. In Las Vegas a grizzled old gambler named Uncle Milt is noted for constantly suckering victims with this come-on. For the second wager Uncle Milt simply removes his false teeth and bites his left eye. Twenty dollars in hand, Uncle Milt is off for the nearest CRAPS table.

EYES IN THE SKY: Gambling Spy Technique

From the time the mobsters moved into gambling, fleecing suckers has been their credo. A common method used in both crooked casinos and private games is the so-called eyes in the sky scam—concealed peepholes from which spies can peer through the ceiling at card players. Meyer Lansky, one of the major operatives in organized crime, was among the foremost practitioners of the method and was said by some biographers never to have built a gambling house without "eyes." He justified the scam, claiming that management had an indispensable need to watch dealers and players to make sure there was no collusion between them.

The late mob leader Vito Genovese was involved in a number of eyes-in-the-sky scams. It is legendary how Genovese and one of his lieutenants, Mike Miranda, took a gullible businessman for $160,000, in part by getting radio signals transmitted from a spy in the room above as to what cards the victim had in his hand.

F

FALSE CARDING: Poker Strategem

Bluffing is an important part of POKER, but too many Poker novices forget that "false carding" is an important element in setting up a bluff. False carding is deliberately drawing fewer than the maximum number of cards necessary to improve one's hand so as to conceal either weakness or strength. For instance, an opener in Jacks or Better is holding a pair of aces and gets no raises. He is in an ideal position to false card by drawing only one card. This gives his opponents the impression that he holds two pair. If he comes out after the draw betting heavily, the assumption will be that he has a full house.

By and large, astute players agree there is seldom a situation in which a player at Draw Poker should ever take two cards. If he has a pair he should take one or three. If he has three of a kind, he absolutely should take just one card to indicate a weaker hand. False carding is Poker lying at its artistic best.

FALSE CUT: Card-cheating Technique

False cutting is a cheating tactic a dealer can use alone or with a confederate sitting next to him. When he has a confederate the dealer can arrange several cards in the order he wishes with an unwanted card on top. He then passes the pack to his secret partner to cut. This man grips the deck in such a way that he presses down on the top card and then pulls out the cards directly under it, leaving the top card to drop on the balance of the pack. The stacked cards remain at the top of the deck as the dealer wishes.

When the dealer is operating alone, he might try to get away with doing his own cutting, in order to ascertain an opponent's hole card in a five-card game of POKER. He simply notes a card, let us say the 7 of spades. He keeps that in position (as illustrated in the accompanying photographs with an ace of spades) atop the deck and does a false cut. The 7 of spades

is now atop the uncut portion of the pack and the dealer picks up that portion of the deck and decorously places it atop the part of the deck he cut away. Since he has put the bottom portion of the pack on top, the supposedly honest way of cutting the cards, the dealer's call for another cut often goes unheeded. He deals, and is playing against an opponent while knowing his exact power.

FALSE SHUFFLE: Cheating Technique

When a good card mechanic is at work, he can shuffle a deck of cards so that every card remains in its original position. There is more than one way for this to be done.

One way, which sounds rather bald but works because players tend to be distracted on a shuffle, involves simply leaving the corners of the two halves of the pack unmeshed as they are riffled and then sliding one half over the other as the cards are squared. An expert mechanic will do this so fast it will appear he is certainly shuffling the cards.

A more talented way is cutting the deck and then pushing one half through the other slightly so that the halves do not exactly square up. Then the dealer gives the cards what appears to be a straight cut and strips one half from the other, putting the cards back in their original order.

FALSE SHUFFLE (CASINO PLAY): Crooked Dealer Move

The False Shuffle is an important cheating method in plots to cheat a casino. This involves a crooked dealer working scams with one or more players to cheat the house, especially at Mini-Baccarat. It requires considerable dexterity on the dealer's part, but he is at an advantage in Mini-Baccarat since players can bet both with or against the bank and thus have little reason to concern themselves about a crooked

C.

Three steps to a false cut: As the cheat cuts the cards (A), he presses down on the top card (illustrated here by an upturned ace) and cuts out the portion of the pack directly under it (B). Depending on which way he restacks the two piles (C), the ace will either remain on top or is buried in the pack. If it is buried, the cutter has left the top portion of the deck in the same position minus the top card. (Photo: E. Gerard)

shuffle of the cards. The casino floorman generally concerns himself with other tables under his supervision when a dealer is involved in shuffling an eight-deck pack for a shoe.

The trick is to keep 30 or 40 cards in the same order that the player-accomplice has recorded on a pad. When the unshuffled cards start appearing the crooked player (or players) knows the order of the cards and whether the bank or the player hand will be the winner and he (they) bet accordingly.

The technique generally involved in the False Shuffle is a simple one, although performed rapidly. The dealer pulls the slug of 30 or 40 cards and fans them into a pile. He then goes through the motions of merging it with another pile but does not do so completely. Pretending to give the pile a straight cut, he strips the original 40-card slug back out and slaps it on top of the pile.

When these cards start appearing, the cheating dealer's partners swing into action and bet heavily on the next few sure bets.

See BACCARAT—MINI, CHEATING AT.

FAN TAN: Private Card Game

Although Chinese Fan Tan is a gambling joint game played with beans, the card version of Fan Tan never attracted as much appeal for gambling entrepreneurs because it doesn't offer the same kind of edge that Chinese Fan offers the house. As a result card Fan Tan, also called Sevens, Card Dominoes, or Parliament, is more of a social gambling game, but one in which a skilled professional can win a great deal.

Played by from three to eight, Fan Tan utilizes a standard 52-card deck, with all cards dealt out even when it means that some players get more cards than others. There is a one-chip ante before the deal, and those dealt one less card are usually required to add a chip to the pot to compensate for their advantage, since the object of the game is to get rid of one's cards.

The game is opened by the player to the left of the dealer who puts a 7 in the middle of the table. If he has no 7's, he must feed a chip to the pot. The next player then puts down a 7 or adds to the first player's starting 7 by either adding a card upward (an 8) or downward (a 6) in the same suit. (Actually the cards are laid sideways, high to the left, low to the right.) If he can do neither of these, he too adds to the pot. Play continues in this fashion until all the cards are played down to the ace and up to the king. New 7's may be started at any time in lieu of playing in an established row. There is considerable skill involved in deciding which of two or more cards a player should play first. There is also a penalty of three chips when a player fails to lay down a card when he is able to do so. If a player passes when holding a 7, he must give the holders of the corresponding 8 and 6 five chips each.

At the end of the game, the player who discards his hand first rakes in the entire pot after the remaining players add another chip for each card with which they have been caught.

See also FIVE OR NINE; PLAY OR PAY; EARL OF COVENTRY.

FARMER's JOY: Variation of Shoot and Red Dog

Farmer's Joy, a banking card game, is a variant of RED DOG and SHOOT. The rules of Farmer's Joy are very close to those for Shoot, with two important differences: all players (not just the dealer) contribute to the pot and players may not look at their cards before betting.

To play, the dealer turns over one card at a time from the deck until he comes up with a 7 or lower. This becomes the upcard. Then the players are each dealt three cards face down. Next players bet anything from one unit up to the total value of the pot. The object is to beat the dealer's upcard with a card of higher denomination in the same suit from one of the three cards they have been dealt. Players who win their bets take the equivalent value from the pot. If they lose, their bet is added to the pot.

This is a thinking man's game (former British Prime Minister Harold Macmillan was addicted to it), and players must remember all the cards the dealer turned up before getting a card of 7 or less. If that card is the first of its suit turned up, that means 12 others remain in the deck, and the value of the card determines how great the players' chances of winning are.

If, for example, the first card turned over is a 7, meaning the players get no hints at other cards, the odds are 7 to 4 against a player winning on his three cards. If, on the other hand, the first card turned up

is a 2, the odds favor the player, but perhaps not as much as one might assume. It is only 5 to 4 for the player since he can have at most three possible suits in his hand and perhaps only two or even one. However, if the deuce does not show until the fourth turnover, and the first three cards, all over 7, were of a different suit or suits, the odds on beating the 2 have climbed to 17 to 12.

While clearly there is an element of guesswork involved, it remains true that the better player will win over the long run because he can correctly gauge when the odds are more in his favor and when to increase the size of his wager.

FARO: One-time Top Gambling Game in America

During the 19th century, Faro was perhaps the most popular gambling game in the United States. Many a slave, a crop, or an entire plantation was won or lost on the notorious riverboats and in gambling dens, and many of the games were known to be dishonest. Even President James Buchanan was known to slip out of the White House to test his luck at Faro at Edward Pendleton's Palace of Fortune. And by 1864, in the 163 gambling houses in the nation's capital, Faro was the main game.

Called Faro in the United States and Pharaoh originally in Europe because one of the kings in an old French deck looked like an Egyptian pharaoh, the game originated in Europe and was imported first to New Orleans. From there, it spread north and west.

How to play: Any number can play and bets are

For many years Faro was the standard game used by gambling cheats to separate western miners from their gold dust. (Photo: N.Y. Public Library)

placed against a house bank or, in the case of a private game, against whoever buys the bank at auction. The game follows very strict rules, using a 52-card deck that is dealt by drawing cards face up from a special dealing box. (This box was designed to eliminate cheating and, quite naturally, became the very method of cheating.) Only *rankings* count in the game and they are represented on a felt-covered table by paintings of each card as follows:

	6	5	4	3	2	ace
7						
	8	9	10	jack	queen	king

Players put their chips on the cards they think will win or lose. If they are betting "lose," the chip is "coppered" with a special disk or a penny. The dealer discards the card showing on the pack, which is called the "soda," and then draws the next card and puts it beside the box as the loser. This means the next card showing in the box is the winner. This completes a "turn" and the banker pays off or collects on all bets settled at that time. Unsettled bets continue in action. Then new bets are made, the two cards are discarded, and a new turn begins. Players can bet on two or more cards by placing chips between them or setting chips on a corner of a card to bet on three cards at once. Bets are paid proportionally to the number of cards bet on. However, if two of the cards show on the same turn, it is a standoff and the bet does not count. However, if two cards of identical rank, such as two 7's, appear on the same turn, this is called a "split" and the banker takes half of the bet. When the box is down to the last four cards, players bet on the last pair and also try "calling the turn"—the order in which the top three cards remaining are drawn. The last card, called the "hock," is discarded. If a player guesses the correct order of the three cards, he is paid off at 4 to 1. Since there are six possible ways three cards can be arranged, the correct payoff is 5 to 1, meaning that on the last turn the banker enjoys an edge of 16.66 percent.

Some experts insist this is the only advantage the banker has, ignoring the approximate 2 percent on splits. Mathematicians are very much in dispute on the real house advantage at Faro. Some say it is at least 4 percent while others insist the real figure is nearly 15 percent. Yet one can find casino operators in Nevada who say they will not touch the game because it is "dead even." And as a matter of fact, a search for Faro throughout all of Nevada at any given time would turn it up in no more than two or three casinos.

However, the real reason for this is precisely what led to the sharp decline of Faro at the start of the 20th century—the explosive popularity of CRAPS. By that time the many losses of fortunes at Faro, thanks to the house edge and massive cheating, had astonished the public and it gladly switched to dice as inherently more honest (a debatable point). Today, STUSS, a simplified version of Faro, still enjoys some popularity.

See BUCKING THE TIGER; FARO—CHEATING; FAROBANKOPOLIS; STUSS.

FARO—Cheating

It would be hard to find a gambling game in the United States in which there was more cheating than Faro. Most of the Faro games in 19th-century Washington, D.C., were never held up as paragons of honesty. In fact, this was very convenient for the lobbyists of the day who, according to contemporary journalistic muckrakers, haunted the more fashionable gambling houses and bailed out politicos sinking in debt. By the purest of coincidences thereafter, these lobbyists won support and passage of certain special-interest bills.

If the Faro games of the national capital were of dubious integrity, that was nothing compared to the situation in the American birthplace of the game, New Orleans, or throughout the West where it became the standard way gold-rush miners were cheated of their dust and their claims. A visitor in Denver 1859 wrote of the game: "I saw the probate judge of the county lose thirty Denver lots in less than ten minutes . . . after I observed the county sheriff pawning his revolver for twenty dollars to spend in betting at Faro."

It would be safe to say that if the likes of Soapy Smith or Madame Moustache dealt Faro honestly it was a matter of pure happenstance.

The dealing box was introduced to Faro because sleight-of-hand artists had no trouble fixing the cards in hand-held games. As a result the scam artists graduated to fixing what was called the brace box, or screw box. A tiny button on the side of the box narrowed or widened the space through which the cards were dealt. With the wide slit two cards would eject at the same time. All that was necessary then was to fix the card and this was done with the "sand tell" treatment. The cards in the box had been rubbed with sandpaper. The low cards were treated on their backs and the high cards on their faces. When these two surfaces touched they could easily be made to adhere by pressure on the top card. If the dealer did not want a high or low card to show under the top cards, he simply pressed down on the top card and he was able to deal off two cards as one. Instead of sandpaper, some crooked dealers bought a special chemical preparation from a crooked chemical supply house.

With the unrestrained cheating that went on in

Faro it was inevitable that eventually the game would decline in popularity. When suckers lost, repeatedly, they inevitably lost interest in Faro; it was replaced in the gambling houses by CRAPS.

FAROBANKOPOLIS: Richmond, Virginia
Almost from its inception FARO in the United States was crooked. It was estimated that of the hundreds of Faro houses operating in Washington, D.C., during the Civil War virtually every one was dishonest. Yet in Richmond, Virginia, the opposite was the case; virtually every Faro bank and gaming establishment was considered straight. Because of this reputation, Faro thrived in Richmond as probably in no other city in the nation before or since. In consequence, Southern wits rechristened the city "Farobanko-polis."

Honesty in 19th-century gambling houses was a feature seemingly unique to the Confederacy during the Civil War. Faro had been crooked before the war, but it appears the South had a keen desire to maintain honest gambling for its morale-boosting qualities. Traditionally, food served, whether in the fine gaming establishments centered around Richmond's Exchange Hotel (every third door was an entrance to a gambling house) or in bare-walled dens on neighboring streets, was free to men in uniform whether they could afford to bet or not.

Confederate dignitaries and generals inhabited the finer establishments where each night Judah P. Benjamin, the secretary of war and later secretary of state for the Confederacy, could be found relaxing while making huge wagers. Benjamin and the others were assured of honest play since most of the housemen in the top establishments came from Virginia's first families and were eager to do their share for the war effort.

This attitude of fostering honest gaming spread to certain other Southern cities where straight operators were permitted while "blacklegs" were clamped down on, hurled into prison for months, and sometimes even forced to work on building fortifications. This novel approach to gambling died with the collapse of the Southern cause in 1865. Thereafter gambling houses in Richmond and those everywhere in the country reverted to their usual style of crooked play.

King FAROUK: Infamous Gambler
The late King Farouk of Egypt (1920-1965), was, despite several hilarious or dark-humored escapades at the gaming tables, a brilliant and much-feared gambler. Like all big gamblers, he suffered some memorable losses (such as $300,000 to film mogul Jack Warner at Monte Carlo) but his wins were more impressive. He once took the Greek Syndicate that dominated the European gambling scene for 30 mil-lion francs. That competition could be looked upon as a legitimate judge of skill because both the Greek Syndicate and Farouk had limitless funds on which to draw. A profit of $50,000 in an evening was commonplace for him.

The secret of Farouk's success at many games including his favorites—BACCARAT, CHEMIN DE FER, and POKER—was his great powers of concentration. When another gambler of the Chemmy table dropped dead of a heart attack, Farouk insisted the game go on until he decided whether to draw on five. He did and won, and was oblivious of the fact that the corpse was being carted off. He was particularly brilliant at Poker, possessing the true killer instinct and raising opponents unconscionably to drive them out. Sometimes Farouk lost but his opponents paid dearly to their nervous systems as the price of victory."

Farouk was a hard loser. He once demolished a Chemmy table when the cards ran against him. He at times threatened or attacked casino employees. When he died in exile in Rome at the age of 45, his death left a gaping vacancy in more ways than one on the gambling casino scene.

FASCINATION
See CANFIELD.

FIERY CROSS: Center-card Poker Game
Fiery Cross is an offshoot of CRISSCROSS and follows its rules, except that there are no wild cards. This version, like Crisscross, is best played under the more conservative rules with each player dealt just two downcards and then filling his hand with three upcards formed in the crossrows laid out in the center of the table as common cards:

```
        1
    4   5   2
        3
```

As each of these cards are turned up as numbered, there is the usual POKER betting sequence. Unlike Crisscross, the number 5 card is not wild. Players supplement the two cards in their hand with one of the cross rows (1-5-3 or 4-5-2) to give them five cards. Also unlike Crisscross, however, Fiery Cross can also be played high-low, with a player using one cross row for high and the other for low. However, if a player opts for going both high and low, he must win both ways or he loses both automatically.

Fiery Cross can also be played with each player getting five downcards, as the more frantic version of Crisscross allows. Since the number 5 card is not wild, the Fiery Cross version is a bit tamer—but not much.

FIFTEEN:
See QUINZE.

FINGERS: Guessing Game
Some experts insist Fingers, or *Mora,* as the Italians call it, may be just about the oldest gambling guessing game humans have played. No equipment is needed other than a hand with five fingers on it. In the United States it is particularly popular in Italian-American circles.

At a given signal, two competitors extend a hand and show a number of fingers up to five (an unopened fist is zero). At the same moment each player calls a number that he believes will be the total number of fingers displayed by both himself and his opponent.

If Player A shows two fingers and calls six and Player B holds out five fingers and calls seven, Player B wins. If, on the other hand, neither player comes up with the correct call, it is a no-game and thrown out. There is an agreed-on number of victories required for a player to win and take the pot.

The game is clearly designed for two players. If a third player wishes to participate, this is accomplished by a round-robin whereby each one plays the other two an equal number of games. When four players participate, it is best that two pairs play each other and then the two winners face each other to play for the pot.

There are many gamblers who insist they must stare into their opponent's eyes and pick up hints on his likely actions. Such concentration does not always pay off. Sometimes the action gets so intense that a player will extend four fingers and call out "three."

Fingers is regarded as the predecessor to the MATCH GAME, a very popular bar game.

FINLAND, Gambling in
Only three forms of gambling are legal in Finland—betting on horse races, football pools, and LOTTERIES. All are either run by the government or by government-sponsored groups. Half the money wagered on lotteries and football (soccer) pools is returned to winners and 20 percent goes for administrative expenses. The balance usually is divided, with 60 percent going to sports organizations and 40 percent for youth and science organizations. In certain cases the science organization share goes to artistic groups instead.

American horseplayers would undoubtedly be chagrined to learn that the state takeout on the betting pools comes to 25 percent, making profitable gambling on the nags a truly precarious occupation. However, the state is not entirely greedy; it turns over approximately half of its revenues to horse-breeding societies.

FIVE AND NINE: Variation of Fan Tan
Five and Nine follows the basic rules of FAN TAN but instead of starting with a 7, the first player has the option of opening the game with either a 5 or a 9. If he chooses a 5, all 5's in other suits open their rows and the 9's have no significance, and vice versa.

Like traditional Fan Tan this is a social gambling game that can be played penny ante or for higher stakes. There have been many tales of professional gambling operators losing their establishments after a disastrous run in private games of Five and Nine. The game allows for a bit more strategy than Fan Tan and the opener has a distinct advantage if he holds both 5's and 9's in his hand. He can decide which way to go depending on his other cards. If he holds an ace in the same suit as a 5 he leads that way just as he would start with a 9 if he holds the king.

FIVE AND TEN: Stud Poker Variation
A variation of Stud Poker, generally played in the seven-card version but also played as a five-card game, Five and Ten allows all 5's and 10's in a player's hand to be wild *provided he has at least one 5 and one 10.* A 5 without a 10 and vice versa is just an ordinary card. Anybody not holding wild 5's and 10's should drop since often four of a kind is necessary to win a hand.

WOOLWORTH is sometimes called Five and Ten, but has quite different rules.

FIVE HUNDRED RUMMY: Favorite Rummy Gambling Game
Five Hundred Rummy, also called Pinochle Rummy, is one of the oldest Rummy versions still widely played in the United States. In the 1950's, it lost popularity to Canasta, which properly should be regarded as a member of the Five Hundred family. Originating in South America, the Canasta craze caused Five Hundred Rummy gambling to virtually disappear. In time, though, gamblers deserted Canasta, which they found had more rules than it needed, and really was a game intended for friendly fun. Since this book is concerned with gambling rather than games, Canasta will get no more than passing note, with due apologies to the aficionados.

With the decline of rule-ridden Canasta, Five Hundred Rummy returned to the gaming tables and today is a favorite of many gamblers

How to play: it is best played by three or four players using a single deck. When two play, they each get 13 cards and in all other versions each player is dealt seven cards. When there are five to eight players, a double deck is used.

As in other Rummy games the object is to form melds, sets of three or four cards of the same rank (three kings or four 8's, etc.) or sequences of three or more in the same suit, such as 9, 10, jack, queen of diamonds, etc. Unlike standard Rummy the discard pile is spread out so that a player can keep track of all the discards and the unplayed cards he may need. Scoring is subject to some local variations, but generally cards are ranked from ace, king at the high on down to deuce, ace at the low. The ace counts as 15 points at all times except when it is part of a low sequence, in which case it is 1 point. All picture cards are 10 and all other cards have their pip value. Players not only meld from their own hand with new melds or onto melds they have previously made, but onto those of opponents as well. In this latter case, the player merely demonstrates where the card or cards he is melding are attached to an opponent's hand and he then places the card with his own laid-down cards.

Each player in turn takes a card from the undealt deck (the stock) into his hand. He then discards a card that may or may not be the card he has just drawn. He may, instead of drawing from the stock, take the top card from the discard pile and make a new discard. Or he may want a card far into the discard pile, in which case he must take all the cards above it as well. The player taking from the discard pile must meld the card he wanted immediately, but he need not do so with additional discards he has taken.

The hand is complete when one player melds all his cards or if no cards remain in the stock and the player whose turn it is to meld is unable to do so. (In a variation of the game, in this circumstance the other players may meld what they can. This does not apply in the case of a player laying down all his cards. In that event, the opponents are caught with those cards still in their hands.)

Players all score the points they have laid down, minus those which still remain in their hands. There is no payoff until several hands are played and one player reaches the highest score over 500. He is the winner and collects the cash value of the point differences with his opponents.

A partnership game involving four or six players paired in teams of two is also played.

Strategy: In Five-Hundred Rummy it is frequently important for a player not to concentrate on scoring points; it is sometimes more important to try to go out quickly, especially when one is behind in the score. At the beginning of the game or when a player has the lead and there is little danger of any competitor going over 500 soon, a player should strive for a big score by picking up discards liberally. Some players will take up a load of discards even if all they can lay down immediately is three deuces for 6 points. Others feel that taking too many discards is not worthwhile unless the immediate meld is at least 15 points. There is also much to be said for holding some melds in one's hands and then going out with a bang, catching other players holding many cards. Of course, there is the danger that one's opponents are working on the same idea. Strategy is what makes Five Hundred Rummy an intriguing game and one should develop "tells," as in POKER, to categorize the playing habits of opponents.

Except for the fact that Five Hundred Rummy is a weak gambling game for two, it would be the best of all Rummy games, but as it is it cannot compete against Knock Rummy or Gin.

See BOZENKILL RUMMY; MICHIGAN RUMMY; OKLAHOMA RUMMY; PERSIAN RUMMY.

FIVE ROLLS: Bar Hustler's Favorite Dice Game

This is a dice game that is a favorite of bar hustlers. Five Rolls looks like a dead-even game, and indeed a survey made of college students confirms this standard but erroneous assumption. Player A rolls a die five times. If he rolls an even number (2,4,6) three or more times, he wins. On less than three even numbers, he loses. Winners are paid off at 3 to 2.

At first glance this seems a fair bet since the chance of rolling an even number is the same as rolling an odd number and winning three times to two would seem to make 3 to 2 the correct odds.

Actually the key point is that the odds of the shooter winning or losing are dead even, so that the correct odds should be even money. Sharpers offer to shoot this game as often as they can, and in the long run will win about 25 percent of all the money bet, an enormous edge. A sharper will first suggest Five Rolls for buying the beer and then shift to $5 or $10 bets when he is the shooter.

FIVE-CARD BASEBALL: Stud Poker Variation

Unlike the more common form of BASEBALL, Five-card Baseball is played by somewhat simpler rules. The 9's and 3's are wild but a player getting either as an upcard must match the pot to stay in the game. Strategy dictates that one may match the pot if it is early in the game but never match it on the fourth or fifth card if the wild card merely gives the player a pair. As in Baseball a 4 dealt up, entitles the player to an extra face card, also dealt up.

A high three of a kind often takes the pot in this game, but the holder must beware of possible straights, flushes, and full houses, and bet conservatively when such hands look possible. A four-of-a-kind hand should be bet aggressively. Although it is a hand that turns up often, it is rare that two four-of-a-kind hands appear in the same deal.

FIVE-CARD CHARLIE: Winning Private Blackjack Hand

Five-card Charlie is a BLACKJACK hand in private games that pays double (usually) when a player utilizes five cards without busting by going over 21. The operative phrase is *private games,* for the hand is not accepted in any gambling casino anywhere in the world. Yet despite this, one will see inexperienced players in casinos trying for the hand. For some odd reason dealers seem reluctant to inform players that the Five-card Charlie hand does not pay double, doing so only after players make it. They tend to say nothing when players bust out chasing that pipe dream. But then again casinos are not in the adult education business. Casino Blackjack is strictly pay-as-you-learn.

FIVE-CARD STUD
See POKER.

FIVE-CARD STUD—FIVE BETS: Extra Betting-round Game

Five-card Stud—Five Bets is a good game for increasing the wagering in this frequently small-pot POKER game. More important, it forces a tight player—one who never stays unless he has something good or beats the board on his first two cards—to pay for the privilege of seeing a second card. The game introduces an early betting round as soon as the first card is dealt out down. This means there are five betting sequences in all, making the pot more attractive. And who knows, Mr. Tight might even have to stay a little longer because he already has money in the pot.

FIVE-CARD TURN-UP STUD
See FLIP STUD.

FLAMINGO HOTEL: Las Vegas's First Major Casino

The Flamingo, the first of Las Vegas's lavish casinos, was built with mob money under the direction of Benjamin "Bugsy" Siegel. Bugsy had come west in the late 1930's to escape a homicide investigation in New York and to manage the Eastern mobs' gambling expansion in California. Syndicate genius Meyer Lansky had assigned Siegel to investigate the potential of Las Vegas, then little more than a dusty rest spot in the desert. Siegel did and soon envisaged a new gambling empire, one that could turn the Nevada sands into gold dust. Siegel's findings backed up those of Moe Sedway, whom Lansky had sent to scout out the scene earlier.

Based on Siegel's sales pitch, several big-city mobs laid out the money to build a new casino-hotel, which was to be called the Flamingo, the nickname of Virginia Hill, Siegel's girl friend and former bedmate of a number of top mobsters.

During the Flamingo's construction, building contractor Del Webb got extremely nervous about all the hulking gangster types on the site, but Siegel assured him he had nothing to fear since "we only kill each other." At the time Bugsy had no idea how prophetic his words were. In the short run the Flamingo was a disaster. The mob's costs had soared to $6 million, triple Siegel's original estimate. Eventually, the mobsters, Lansky included, declared they wanted their money back. Siegel bought time, claiming he'd open the place in December 1946 to land-office business.

A man about Hollywood, Siegel assembled a top-flight cast to attract an expected horde of guests and bettors—George Jessel was master of ceremonies and featured stars included Jimmy Durante (always in hock to mob bookmakers), Baby Rose Marie, the Turn Toppers, Eddie Jackson, and Xavier Cugat and his band. Among the guests were some of Siegel's Hollywood friends—George Raft, George Sanders, Charles Coburn. But scores of others did not turn out. Among other errors, Siegel had staged his grand opening between Christmas and New Year's, a period considered deadly in the entertainment business. The gamblers did not show up either, and the opening was a disaster.

That sealed Bugsy's fate. He had not produced, and with good reason the mobsters had determined that Siegel had been skimming the construction money and shipping it off to a secret Swiss bank account with Virginia Hill as his bag lady. On June 20, 1947, Siegel was shot to death in the living room of Virginia Hill's Beverly Hills mansion. Hill, conveniently, was in Europe at the time.

After that Lansky appointed a new staff to run the Flamingo. It became a huge success. One casino after another, many with mob support, followed. Bugsy had been proved right about Las Vegas. Even his choice of opening time was vindicated and today it is the top period of gambling in Vegas, with headliner performers such as Frank Sinatra on hand.

Today, Vegas tries to live down its mob past, but Siegel's role is accepted with considerable esteem. Taxi drivers are loaded with Siegel lore, much of it fanciful, including the firm belief that Bugsy is buried behind the Flamingo.

FLIP STUD: Stud Poker Variation

Flip Stud, also called Mexican Stud or Five Card Turn-up Stud, is simple Five-card Stud except that the cards are dealt down. With the first two down cards each player flips over whichever card he wishes to be his upcard. Thereafter all additional cards are dealt down and the player each time flips over a card. Thus he conceals the card of his choice, but at all times is permitted only one hole card. The game allows for a greater opportunity for bluffing than ordinary Five-card. Therefore if a player has a 3 face card and then turns up another, it may indicate that he has three of a kind or that he is trying to force players out by pretending he has more than a pair of threes.

For variations of this game see SHIFTING SANDS and MONTEREY, as well as FLIP STUD WITH LOW CARD WILD.

Flip Stud can also be played in SEVEN-CARD STUD. In this version, players turn up one card each round with two down until the seventh card is dealt.

FLIP STUD WITH LOW CARD WILD

This is played the way FLIP STUD is, but it is a game filled with surprises. The player's lowest card and all others of the same value are wild. This allows for considerable skill in playing and figuring out another player's hand. Let us assume a player ends up before the turn-up of the final hole card with a pair of threes, an ace and a 7. It would appear that he holds three aces. However, if he has a deuce in the hole, the value of his hand drops to three 3's—so that another player holding a pair of 5's, and an 8, 9, and king would beat him with three kings.

FLORIDA: Legalized Lotteries and Gambling

Outside of Las Vegas and a tiny stretch along the Atlantic City boardwalk, the gamblingest spot for legalized action is to be found in Florida. In January of 1988 Florida instituted its first legal state lottery in this century, and the natives went wild, running up $13.5 million in sales on the first day tickets were available.

Yet Florida cannot be regarded as starved for legalized betting. On an average day within a 50-mile radius of Miami, an itchy bettor can choose from 10 thoroughbred races, 10 harness races, up to 52 greyhound races, and 78 Jai-alai games.

Yet, Floridians have voted down casino gambling overwhelmingly. Maybe they just wouldn't have time to cover any additional action.

FOLLOW MARY: Follow the Queen Variation

Follow Mary is a variation of Seven-card Stud, played by the standard rules for FOLLOW THE QUEEN. But, in Follow the Queen, the only wild cards are the denomination of the card dealt just after the last face queen to appear. This means there are four wild cards in that game. In Follow Mary, *all* the queens are wild and the card following the last exposed queen is also wild, as are all others of that denomination. If, however, a queen is the last exposed card played, only the queens are wild. Because this happens rarely, there are usually eight wild cards in the game.

Since the identity of the last wild card is not established until the final up round (in this version of Seven-card Stud the seventh card is usually dealt up) too many players stick around in hopes of seeing their weak hands suddenly turned strong. Unless the hand has the potential of turning not only strong but into a powerhouse hand, the player should fold. Follow Mary is seldom won by anything less than four of a kind—and a very high four of a kind at that.

FOLLOW THE COWBOY

See FOLLOW THE KING.

FOLLOW THE KING: Wild-card Stud Poker Variation

Follow the King, also known as Follow the Cowboy, is played under the rules for FOLLOW THE QUEEN except that the card appearing immediately after the *last* face-up king is wild as are all others of the same denomination. This means the wild card can change as this SEVEN-CARD STUD game progresses, but at no time are there more than four wild cards in the game.

FOLLOW THE LADY

See FOLLOW THE QUEEN.

FOLLOW THE QUEEN: Intriguing Wild-card Stud Poker Variation

Follow the Queen, known in the West more often as Follow the Lady, is a shifting wild Seven-card Stud game. The ultimate wild card is the card following the *last* queen that appears face up. All other cards of that denomination are also wild. The game can be dealt in normal fashion, the first two cards down, four up and the final card down, or, as is more common in this game, the first two down and the last five up. (The latter allows for more queens to appear.) If the last card dealt is a queen, there simply is no wild card and the game is played out as normal Seven-card.

There is betting after each round of cards, but early enthusiasm must be curbed. A queen may appear, thus designating a wild denomination, but the appearance of another queen will more than likely alter the wild card, and in the process change the players' hands. The wild card may change once, twice, or even three times. Because of this, early dropouts tend to be few and the competition will likely stay hectic until a final wild card is determined.

See also FOLLOW MARY and FOLLOW THE KING.

FOOTBALL: Seven-card Stud Poker Variation

Seven-card Football is virtually the same game as BASEBALL, but gamblers, being traditionalists, tend to play football in the winter and baseball in the summer. The wild cards vary in the two games. In Football all sixes are wild (a touchdown is six points). Threes are also wild, but if a player is dealt one face up, he must match the pot or drop out (in real football a field goal is three points, but can be missed). Any player dealt a face-up deuce gets an extra hold card (a football team getting a two-point safety also gets the ball back).

Generally a prudent player would not hope to win on less than a flush, but once in a while a straight stands up. Late in the game a player should not match the pot unless he holds five of a kind or, perhaps, four aces if there is another card or two coming.

FOOTBALL BETTING: Most Gambling of Any Sport

Forget them all—boxing, hockey, basketball, tennis, baseball—more money is bet on football than on any other team or single-man sport. The biggest gambling day in Nevada is Super Bowl Sunday when, according to the Nevada Association of Race and Sports Book Operators, the casino and smaller sports books can expect bets totaling $25 million. And that's the countable legal action on the game. Untold millions more—far greater than the legal betting—are wagered with bookmakers all around the country. Added to that are millions bet privately and in office pools. The Super Bowl is a betting extravaganza. The five biggest college bowl games on New Year's Day can be counted on for another $20 million in Nevada. A typical National Football League Sunday, in which 12 games are played, draws $10 to $15 million in action, and a football playoff game is good for $5 million.

Football brings the high-roller bettors out of the woodwork. One is a Texas oil man who bets an average of $2 million every Sunday on pro ball. Some of this action is covered in Las Vegas, but he is known to spread $50,000 to $100,000 lump sums with as many as 20 bookmakers operating in cities across the country. Many college presidents now know there is much more to football than having a winning team to satisfy their free-giving and wild-betting alumni. The college's team had better beat the "point spread" as well. Some college coaches with successful winning years still end up being fired because they did not "cover the spread." Ara Parseghian, one of the most respected coaches in Notre Dame history, once admitted his retirement from coaching was hastened by the constant pressure to beat the spread. A coach whose team wins the national championship by taking the key New Year's bowl game is a bum to fans and alumni if his team wins but does not cover the spread.

What is the point spread? It is a line set by experts (see ODDSMAKERS) who spend their entire careers gauging the differences among various teams and distill that to a point rating. This figure is a balance between the differences of the teams and an estimate of how the public will bet. If bookmakers quote one team as being 6 points better than another, a bettor wagering on the favorite is saying the team will win by more than 6 points. If the favorite wins by 7 points or more, that bettor wins. If the favorite loses or wins by less than 6 points, the better loses. If the favorite wins by 6 points, it is a standoff and the bet is canceled.

However, even if the bettor wins his bet, he does not collect even money. The bookmaker may quote the game as so many points on team A at 6 to 5 or 11 to 10. A 6 to 5 bet is a gouge by a bookie often offered only to smaller bettors. A big bettor might get action at 11 to 10. Because of the heavy competition in Las Vegas, the casinos offer action at 11 to 10. These odds are the same whichever team a gambler bets on. If the two teams are rated even, the game is quoted as "pick 'em," which means a bettor can pick either team with no point differential but must put up the 11 to win 10.

To win at football betting a sophisticated gambler must be able to gauge a vast number of variables, such as home field advantage, weather conditions, injuries to key players, differences in the kicking game, the running game, the defenses, the special squads. In addition the wagering has become more sophisticated, and more versions of betting are offered, such as over/under, teasers, and parlays. The casino football-betting card displayed here explains the betting offered by the Sands Race & Sports Book in Las Vegas.

What was perhaps the largest single wager in the history of Nevada bookmaking occurred on January 23, 1989, when the San Francisco 49ers beat the Cincinnati Bengals. Casino owner Bob Stupak of Vegas World walked into Little Caesars Gambling Casino several hours before the kickoff with two suitcases bulging with $1,050,000 in cash. He bet the entire sum on the Bengals, which were a 7-point underdog. If San Francisco won by 8 points or more, he would lose his money. San Francisco won but only by four points (20-16). So Stupak collected an even $1 million in profits, as well as his original wager.

IT'S EASY TO BET FOOTBALL

EXAMPLE	Game Time	Betting Number	Teams	Point Spread	6 Point Teaser	6½ Point Teaser	7 Point Teaser	Over/Under
	1:00	101	Chargers		+13	+13½	+14	48
		102	Raiders	7	−1	−½	EV	

STRAIGHT BETS

The point spread is always listed by the favorite. In the example above the Raiders are favored by 7 points. The Chargers are the underdog. If you wager on the Raiders, they must win the game by more than 7 points. If you wager on the Chargers, they must win the game or lose the game by less than 7 points.

The minimum bet is $10.00. The odds are 10 to 11. This means the player wagers $11.00 to win each $10.00 for a total pay back of $21.00. (Wager $22.00 to win $20.00, $55.00 to win $50.00, $110.00 to win $100.00, etc.)

In the event the Raiders win by exactly 7 points, the wager is deemed "No Action" and money will be refunded.

OVER/UNDER WAGERING

In the example above, the over/under is 48 points. You may bet that the total points scored by both teams in the game will be *over* or *under* 48 points. The odds are 10 to 11. (Same as above)

PARLAYS OVER THE COUNTER

A parlay wager is made by combining 2 to 5 teams or over/unders to make one bet. All teams must win by the listed point spread.

In the event of a tie, parlay odds reduce to the next betting bracket. For example: 2 team parlay becomes a straight bet, 3 team parlay becomes a 2 team parlay, etc.

PARLAY ODDS

#Teams	PAY
2	13 to 5
3	6 to 1
4	10 to 1
5	20 to 1

TEASERS OVER THE COUNTER

The Sands Sports Book offers 6, 6½ and 7 point teasers. Teaser bets are made by selecting 2 to 6 teams. The point spread will be *reduced on the favorite* or *increased on the underdog* by 6, 6½ or 7 points. All teams must win by the adjusted point spread.

In the event of a tie on a 2 team teaser, the bet is deemed "No Action" and money will be refunded. If there is a tie on a 3, 4, 5 or 6 team teaser the odds reduce to the next betting bracket. For example a 3 team teaser becomes a 2 team teaser, etc.

TEASER ODDS

#Teams	6 Pt. Teaser	6½ Pt. Teaser	7 Pt. Teaser
2	5 to 6	5 to 7	5 to 8
3	8 to 5	3 to 2	6 to 5
4	5 to 2	2 to 1	9 to 5
5	4 to 1	7 to 2	3 to 1
6	6 to 1	5 to 1	4 to 1

MONEY LINE WAGERS (Selected Games Only)

This type of wager is done by giving or taking money odds. In the example below the Dolphins are the favorite (-) and the Patriots are the underdog (+).

To bet on the Dolphins, the player bets $14.00 to win each $10.00 for a total pay back of $24.00. To bet on the Patriots, the player bets just $10.00 to win each $12.00 for a total pay back of $22.00. The minimum wager is $10.00.

EXAMPLE:

Game Time	Betting Number	Teams	Odds
10:00	121	Dolphins	-140
	122	Patriots	+120

*NOTE: Home team is always listed on the bottom.

The football card at the Las Vegas Sands offers several simple bets and a number of more involved or exotic plays.

FORTY-FIVE: Modern Version of Spoil Five

Forty-Five is a modern version of the old Irish game of SPOIL FIVE and is played with the "spoil," the tactic of keeping opponents from winning three tricks. Forty-Five may be played by two to five players, each playing for himself, but it is much better as a partnership game of two teams with a total of four or six players.

All tricks are taken according to the rules of Spoil Five and each is worth 5 points. Scoring is different from Spoil Five; the partners taking the most tricks subtract the point value taken by the other team. Thus if one partnership takes 20 points and the opposing partnership 5 points, the winners are credited with 15. Play continues to 45. An alternate way of scoring gives the partnership taking the odd trick 5 points and 10 points if it takes all five tricks in the hand.

Another version of this game is Auction Forty-Five in which 30 points are scored in a game, 5 points for each trick and 5 points for the team with the highest trump. Players bid by fives for the right to name trump with the low bidders always having the right to rebid. However, the dealer can take the bid merely by "holding" or matching the highest bid. Teams score what they take in tricks, but a bid of 30 becomes 60 if made. When a team fails to make bid, the amount of the bid is subtracted from its score. Game is 120 and when a team has 100 points it must bid 20 or more. Auction Forty-Five is one version of Spoil Five that made it out of Ireland, the game being especially popular in some parts of Canada.

FORWARD PASS

See TAKE IT OR LEAVE IT.

FOUR FORTY-FOUR: Eight-card Stud Variation

This is an eight-card game of Stud Poker with four cards dealt down and then four cards up. There is a betting round after each upcard is dealt. In keeping with the name of the game, all 4's are wild. In a Seven-card Stud game with four wild cards—deuces or any other—three aces generally constitutes the usual lowest possible winning hand. The eighth card alters the situation slightly, with most practitioners considering a straight as the least likely winning hand. Logically a player may stay on a straight or a flush but he should hardly bet it with unbounded confidence, although he might bet it aggressively if he gets it early and so try to drive out the competition. A slight variation of this game is THREE FORTY-FIVE.

FOUR JACKS
See POLIGNAC.

FOUR-CARD FLUSH PROPOSITION: Poker Hustler's Swindle
It is impossible to play POKER any length of time without running into hustlers offering all sorts of "proposition bets." For instance, a hustler hears a player bemoaning the fact that he is constantly dealt four cards to a flush on the opening deal and never fills it.

"Tell you what," the hustler announces. "I'll bet you 15 to 1 you don't get a four-card flush on the next deal."

Of course, few Poker players have any idea about the probabilities of being dealt a four-flush hand, but 15 to 1 looks mighty attractive since it will make the player a winner regardless of whether or not he fills. What the player doesn't realize is that the odds against being dealt such an opening hand is 22 to 1, giving the hustler almost a 31 percent advantage.

Some hustlers will bet the table on four-card flushes, offering to book all the players at the same time. The agreement generally is that he'll pay $15 to any and all players getting the four-card hand. Naturally the player has to expose his hand, collect and drop out, never drawing to his discard. In one such instance, over ten hands against five opponents the hustler paid off twice, ending up $18 ahead. But the hustler gained another uncalculated advantage. It turned out he won both the hands in which a four-card flush turned up. Both holders of the four-card flushes lost the opportunity to draw an additional card. The odds against their doing so were a relatively low 4½ to 1. Thus the hustler had gotten rid of an opponent who might have topped him with a rather small payoff.

The general rule on proposition bets is that they are only good for the propositioner.

FOUR-CARD POKER
There are many games of POKER played with just four cards, with the usual assortment of wild cards or games that are played both for high and low.

How to play: Only four cards are dealt to each player and in Draw Poker a player can draw up to four new cards. In Stud the first card is down and the remaining three up, with a betting round after each upcard.

Generally the game is played when it is felt there are too many players for five-card games, but the fact is only the same number of players can be accommodated in Draw with four cards and the standard version, which allows for three cards on the draw. Four-card Stud will of course accommodate 13 players. The drawback to the game is that pots tend to be smaller, unless there are a lot of participants.

Strategy: Some players mistakenly believe straights and flushes are easier to fill in four-card games compared to five-card games. However, four flush cards out of four is virtually as hard to get as five flush cards out of five. Thus, the hand rankings in Four-card Poker stays the same as in five-card rules, descending as follows: straight flush, four of a kind, flush, straight, three of a kind, two pair, pair, and high card.

Some good Poker players like the game because it is easier to read opponents' possible hands, and there are many occasions when three of a kind in Stud is a certain winner and can be bet without fear.

FOUR-FIVE-SIX: Gambling-house Game
Four-Five-Six has long been popular in the northwestern United States, Alaska, and western Canada, and gambling joints and tinhorns have found it a convenient way to trim miners and lumberjacks of their pay. This is a three-dice game played with a dice cup, and the banker or operator first covers the bets all the players make.

Unlike most games, the bank then plays first. If he throws three of a kind, or any pair plus a 6, or 4-5-6 he automatically wins all bets. If he throws 1-2-3 he loses and pays off all bets immediately. If he throws any pair plus a 1, he also loses. If he rolls any pair plus a 2, 3, 4, or 5, the latter becomes his point number against which the other players then compete. If he does none of the above, he simply rolls again until he achieves one of these results.

Should the banker end up with a point number, the player to his left gets the cup and then wins if he rolls a winning combination, loses if he rolls a losing combination. If he achieves a point number, he wins or loses depending on whether or not his number is higher or lower than the banker's point. Ties are usually a wash, although some hard-nosed operators insist that the house wins on a tie.

Obviously, no gambler should compete under the last stipulation. Besides, the house does not need that edge, since the banker already enjoys an advantage by going first. The fact that there are more winning numbers than losing ones gives the banker an advantage of almost 2½ percent on all monies bet. This is almost double the house edge a gambling house enjoys on the pass or don't pass line at CRAPS, so it is apparent that Four-Five-Six has to grind players into the dust at almost twice the pace of Craps table play.

Some crooked operators of course greatly improve the odds in their favor by using crooked dice-cup techniques as well.

See also DICE-CUP CHEATING.

FOURFLUSHER: Card Cheater

Today we speak of a fourflusher as a dishonest or untrustworthy person, a man who does not keep his word. However, the derivation of the term is much more specific, going back a particular type of POKER cheater. The fourflusher is a man who attempts to pass off a four-card flush as a full hand. Let us say the cheater has four spades in his hand but as his final card draws a club. He will position his cards so that the four spades show and only a portion of the black club symbol in the corner of the card. In a fast-paced game, or one in which there is a lot of drinking by the players, a fourflusher may well get away with such a deception.

However, generally Poker players are a little harder to fool than that, so *two* fourflushers are necessary for the scam. The cheater claiming the five-card flush, lays down his hand with the bogus card covered effectively, and his secret partner immediately snatches up the hand to make sure there are five spades. The action is quick-paced and the second cheater nods and slams the cards into the discards, cursing his and the other players' supposed hard luck. Confirmation that the winning hand was correct usually satisfies the remaining players who are more concerned about starting another hand and hopefully getting even.

Sometimes the act is carried out in even more dramatic fashion. As he looks at the bogus hand, the second cheater moans, "And me with a straight."

Since a straight is the next highest hand possible, the second fourflusher's words further pacify the other players, because if they lost to a flush they would most likely have lost to a straight as well. Of course, the second fourflusher has no straight, but no one ever asks to see a supposed losing hand.

FOUR-FOUR-FOUR: Eight-card Stud Variation

This is a STUD POKER game with four cards dealt up, four cards down and all 4's wild. Three cards are dealt down at the start. The four upcards are dealt, one at a time, with betting between each deal. The last card is dealt down. A full house is considered the lowest likely winning hand, but many cautious gamblers will not stay on anything less than four of a kind.

FOURTEENS: Dice Game Variation of Twenty-six

Fourteens is a ten-dice banking game played a lot like TWENTY-SIX, a popular tavern tournament game. However, Fourteens is even more stacked in favor of the house. In Twenty-six a player picks a number and rolls ten dice from a cup a total of 13 times and wins if he makes his point 26 times.

Fourteens features a special gimmick that seemingly makes it easier to win, but that is a deception. In Fourteens the player does not have to pick his number until *after* his first roll. Obviously he takes the number that turns up most. In fact, if no number comes up three times on the first roll, the player gets to pick a number and is credited with three for his first roll. He has four more rolls to make his number a total of 14 times. The guaranteed three-point minimum starter thus is clearly a come-on, since it virtually has to be maintained on average over the five rolls. Let us say a shooter's number is 6. Having scored three on the first round, he has to average 2.75 6's over the next four rolls. The average he is likely to achieve is 1.666, an enormous difference. Bettors who end up with a score of 11, 12, or 13 may console themselves they came close, but in actuality they have exceeded the law of averages and still lost. Let us even take a far-out example and assume a player rolled *seven* like numbers on the first roll. He still would have to do marginally better than average the rest of the way or he would still lose!

Of course, the game is made seemingly attractive by offering 8 to 1 odds. Other establishments quote 8 *for* 1, which is really only 7 to 1. Other places cut the odds as low as 6 for 1. An added gimmick allows that if a player fails to make his point at all in his last four tries, he is paid off at the winning odds. This is strictly a selling pitch and rarely happens.

When offered a choice between the games of Fourteen and Twenty-six, the smart *loser* will opt for the latter. He will at least lose his money more slowly.

FOUR-TWO CARD PROPOSITION SCAM: Hustler's Delight

The hustler's secret to all private bets is to gain a percentage advantage over a foe while seemingly offering a dead-even proposition or even a bet that appears to put the hustler at a distinct disadvantage. Nowhere is this more true than in the Four-two Card Proposition, a scam pure and simple, although using "logic" the victim is convinced the game is all in his favor.

Any four pictures and two aces are pulled from a deck, shuffled and dealt out in a row. The hustler bets the sucker that he cannot pick two cards from the six without pulling an ace. Immediately the victim starts reckoning, and comes up with the theory that he has the advantage, four cards to two. Many patsies jump at such a bet at even-money odds as a steal. Actually, they should be getting odds!

The fact is that very few gamblers really understand how to figure odds even on only slightly complicated propositions, such as in Four-two Card. "Common sense" is no substitute for cold mathematical reality and only "common sense" could infer that having four cards to two aces automatically gives the player the advantage.

The true mathematical formula shows that with six cards a total of 15 two-card combinations are possible. It is stated thusly:

$$\frac{6 \times 5}{1 \times 2} = 15$$

Now, taking out the two aces, we must determine how many combinations are possible by the four remaining cards. This is stated:

$$\frac{4 \times 3}{1 \times 2} = 6$$

Subtract the six from the 15 in the six-card possibilities and it becomes apparent that an ace will turn up in nine of the 15 possibilities. Nine to 6 translates to 3 to 2 *against* the proposition!

Anyone who does not believe these figures needs only take four cards from a deck—a 10, jack, queen, and king—and arrange them in the various combinations. He can mate the king with the queen, jack, and 10. The queen can only be matched with the jack and 10 (the king-queen mating has already occurred). The jack and 10 represent the final match-up. Total: Six possibilities.

Now the would-be bettor can take one of the aces and see he can match it with the king, queen, jack, and 10. He can do so with the second ace as well. This makes a total of eight possibilities with one ace. Add the instance of the two aces being matched and that makes nine possibilities.

There is no way a victim can last any length of time collecting only even money when the true odds against him are 3 to 2.

See also FREEZE-OUT PROPOSITION.

FRANCE, Gambling in

Quite a few of the average Frenchman's favorite gambling activities happen to be illegal—private card and dice games, football pools and lotteries, and in fact most gambling on sports and athletic events, as well as private bookmakers. Nevertheless, all these activities are avidly pursued through bookmakers.

There is legal on- and off-track betting on horse and dog racing. The great legalized lottery is the Loterie Nationale, and there are certain others especially authorized for charity.

There are two types of legal gambling houses, casinos (of which there are almost 200) and smaller *cercles*, which are open only to members and many of which also exclude women. The important games at the *cercles* are BACCARAT and POKER. Many of the casinos will not interest too many American gamblers since they are limited to BOULE, a game with very unfair odds. A tourist traveling in France should not show up at a lesser-known gambling establishment before checking out what it offers. Some offer only Boule, others Baccarat (also of limited interest to many Americans), and others, remarkably, only *Roulette Americaine*. Unlike several other countries in Europe that use the American format in some of their ROULETTE games but cut back to one zero, the French casinos embrace the two-zero concept and a few actually forsake the French game entirely, showing they can be as greedy as the American casinos.

On the whole, of course, the large casinos in France are the most elegant and decorous, although some do show signs of going to pot. The French casinos are more likely to enforce dress codes, but this is true most often during evening hours. During the day on the French Riviera shorts are permissible. (This is even so in staid old Monte Carlo.)

Many casinos are opulent showpieces, such as the casino in Deauville, in Normandy, which is sometimes called Paris's 21st Arrondissement. Deauville has been described accurately as "a glittering wedding cake by the sea, sumptuously decorated." It has been a playground for European royalty since the 19th century when Napoleon III's half-brother put it on the map by introducing horse racing to the area. During the August racing season, formal dress is a must in most of the casino's lavish rooms.

As inviting as Deauville is, a smaller casino in nearby Trouville is perhaps more hospitable for the relaxed gambler. The action at Roulette at Deauville, even in slow periods, is brisk and no-nonsense. It is considerably more laid back in Trouville, which can be described as the friendliest casino in France. Articulate croupiers will debate and gossip, if that is your thing, and the Roulette table is more like a family get-together, often climaxed by the appearance of actor Omar Sharif, a frequent visitor. This, needless to say, is not true on weekends or in peak season when the action is wall-to-wall.

The Deauville casino is owned by a large chain that operates other glitzy casinos in Cannes, La Baule, Le Touquet, and Juan-Les-Pins. There are a number of casinos at seaside resorts; one of the most luxurious, at Biarritz, was Somerset Maugham's favorite.

A.

C.   B.

Casino gambling in France (A) has been described as varying from the stuffy to the most relaxed in Europe. The Casino Municipal de Trouville (B) not far from the more chic and formal casino at Deauville (C) is often described as the friendliest of all Gallic gambling houses. The Roulette table is more like a family get-together with talkative croupiers who will debate and gossip if that is your thing. (Photos: Casino de Trouville; M. L. Balluff)

The most profitable money-making casinos are those near Switzerland (where the numbered account money is) and the one at Divonne, 11 miles from Geneva, takes in millions more in Roulette wagering than any casino in France. Evian, a 35-minute boat trip from Lausanne, is another top grosser, usually ranking among the top three casinos in profit. Although many stories are told about huge bets made in Cannes, Deauville, and across the so-called border in Monte Carlo, the really big wagers are made at Divonne and Evian. A high-rolling winner of one spin of the wheel at these establishments can use his profits to go right out and buy a seaside villa or a thoroughbred.

Nice has several casinos, but makes the kind of headlines European gaming institutions do not appreciate. There are tales of underworld influence, bribery, skimming, and murder. American tourists from metropolitan areas should feel right at home in Nice.

FREEZE-OUT
See TABLE STAKES.

FREEZE-OUT PROPOSITION: Hustler's Tactic
The Freeze-out Proposition is a gimmick used by gambling hustlers to tie up a sucker in a long series of bets in which the hustler has the advantage. The two sides agree that they will each put up a certain amount and bet against each other for specified amounts until one or the other loses all the money he has put up. Let us say a hustler has conned a sucker into betting on the Four-two Card Proposition, in which, say, four red cards and two black cards are constantly shuffled and the sucker wins at even money whenever he draws two red cards. Actually, the odds favor the hustler in this game at 3 to 2, something that will become apparent to the victim the more they play.

The hustler, however, has suckered his victim into betting a total of $200 at $5 a game with the understanding that the full bet is not complete until one or the other has won the entire $200. A player who drops out will forfeit that sum.

The reason hustlers work the Freeze-out is to offset possible quirks in the law of averages. While the hustler should win three out of five games, there is always a chance his opponent might have a run of extraordinary luck and win several games in a row against the true odds. The hustler doesn't want his pigeon to have a lucky streak and walk away winning, so he utilizes the Freeze-out to assure that the proper odds eventually work to his advantage. See FOUR-TWO CARD PROPOSITION SCAM.

FRENCH WHIST: Variation of Scotch Whist

Like SCOTCH WHIST, French Whist is not traditionally regarded as a true WHIST game. French Whist is played exactly like Scotch Whist save for one variation. The 10 of diamonds is counted as 10 points when captured—even when another suit is trump. This makes for a livelier game than Scotch Whist since the non-trump 10 of diamonds especially is a very vulnerable card and players' strategy alters considerably to try to catch it.

FRIARS CLUB: Fabled Gambling Site

The Beverly Hills Friars Club deserves a special salute in the history of American gambling. Some of the greatest Hollywood gambling cheats operated there, and it was within its hallowed halls that the Hollywood version of GIN RUMMY was developed, with games played for $2 a point—a murderous amount under the HOLLYWOOD GIN version of cumulative scoring. The Friars was the site of an outrageous gambling scam that its members will long remember. In 1968, Johnny Roselli—the representative of the Chicago mob and overseer of its operations in Las Vegas and the movie capital—was convicted along with four others of swindling several Hollywood personalities, including singer Tony Martin and comedians Phil Silvers and Zeppo Marx, out of $400,000 in rigged Gin Rummy games. The Chicago boys even brought in an electronics engineer to install special cheating devices. One of the cheats manned special peepholes in the ceiling and flashed information to a player in the game who wore electronic signaling devices on his leg or in a special girdle. That Roselli and his confederates were able to fool Zeppo Marx was a tribute to their abilities; Zeppo was supposedly one of the movie colony's shrewdest crooked gamblers, and like his brother Chico, noted for his use of elaborate signaling methods.

FRONT LOADERS: Blackjack Cheating

The odds in casino BLACKJACK, regardless of any so-called counting methods, are close enough so that almost any edge a player can get will give him a playing advantage over the house. One method many players try is attempting to see the dealer's down, or hole, card. The methods used for this purpose are called "hole card plays," and the safest and best of these (in the sense that it is not blatant cheating) is what is known as "front loading."

Front loaders will frequently get very upset if they are accused of doing anything dishonest. Can they help it if they just happen to catch a glimpse of the dealer's hole card? The secret is for the player somehow to get his eye level down low enough so that he sees the dealer's hole card as it is slipped under his upcard. Some dealers simply have a bad habit—from the house's viewpoint—of carelessly lifting the card too high. Front loaders will "adopt" such a dealer, memorizing his shift hours and joining his game at all times. If the dealer changes jobs, rest assured that the front loaders will eagerly turn up at his new casino.

Some dealers deal themselves downcards in such a way that the card will flash for an instant toward "first base"—the seat to their extreme left—and others toward "third base"—the seat to their extreme right—and still others to the seat directly opposite them. Front loaders learn a particular dealer's idiosyncratic style and position themselves accordingly.

There are numerous ways that players slouch themselves into the lowest possible position in their seats, some doing a tipsy or arthritic routine that sinks them low. Others, previously ambulatory, have been known to roll up to the table in wheelchairs. One of the more ingenious front-loading dodges was pulled by a high roller who brought a midget to the table and positioned him in the peeking seat. Since the midget never bet more than the minimum, he aroused no suspicions on the part of the pit boss that he might be front loading. The high roller, betting big, clearly was not guilty of any such crime since he never watched the dealer and seemed only to be studying his own hand. Actually, of course, he was periphally picking up signals from his little partner and drawing or standing on the basis of what the dealer's hole card was.

It is not easy for front loaders to find a susceptible dealer, and they may have to scour several casinos before finding a likely candidate. Reading a card that is exposed for only a split second is an art form requiring both perfect vision and long periods of training, often using mechanical and electronic aids to develop one's visual acuity.

Few front loaders will become 100 percent perfect in identifying a flashed card, but if they are right most of the time, they will hardly ever bust out by going over 21. Just as valuable is knowing when to draw on a seemingly strong hand because the dealer has a stronger one of 17 or more. Of course, front loaders have to be judicious about this and never make it obvious that they have some sort of edge. For instance, a good Blackjack player will seldom split 10's since he has a 20 and is an almost certain winner. But if the dealer shows a 7 and has a 9 in the hole, the front loader might be tempted to split his hand and try to win two hands since the dealer will most likely bust out on his next card. However, such a move, made more than once, is a sure tip-off to a pit boss, and the front loader will soon find himself being escorted out of the casino, with orders never to return. Considering that possibility, he is much better off just to take his winnings on the 20 and forget about splitting, saving his smart moves for less detectable moments.

See SPOOKING; TACHISTOSCOPE.

FRUSTRATION
See TWO-CARD POKER.

G

GALILEO: Physicist, Astronomer, Dice Expert

In between his many discoveries of astronomical phenomena and physical laws, Galileo (1564-1642) also spent considerable time on a treatise on dice problems and expectations. He counseled an Italian nobleman-patron—or, more exactly, a dice hustler—that it would be wiser for him to bet on 10 coming up more often than 9 in a three-dice game. Galileo's dice research indicated that in a head-to-head game of gamblers betting 10 against 9, the 10 would, over the long run, win 51.92 percent of the time to 48.08 for the 9, because there were two more combinations (27 to 25) for the 10 than for the 9. This worked out to an edge of almost 4 percent for the gambler betting the 10—almost three times the 1.41 edge that, today, is good enough for gambling casinos to grind crapshooters into the dust.

Besides presumably guiding his patron on the road to riches, Galileo was laying the groundwork for some of the first probability theorems.

See also: GIROLAMO CARDANO, BLAISE PASCAL.

GAM-ANON: Organization for Spouses of Compulsive Gamblers

Formed in 1960, Gam-Anon consists of hundreds of support groups around the country geared to counsel and aid spouses of compulsive gamblers. An informal organization, Gam-Anon generally meets in churches, synagogues, or community houses. There are no fees or membership requirements. Many members remain [l]ong after their own problem is [resolved to] help others through the same [straits. Tel]ephone numbers are exchanged [and members are en]couraged to call one another for [help whe]n crisis develops. Experts agree [that Gam-Anon, mu]ch like GAMBLERS ANONYMOUS [(the organization] of compulsive gamblers), has

helped hundreds of thousands of spouses and their families.

An offshoot of Gam-Anon is Gam-Ateen, a group for the teenaged children of compulsive gamblers. These teenagers are considered to be in vital need of special help and advice.

Like Gamblers Anonymous, the telephone numbers of local Gam-Anon and Gam-Ateen chapters appear in the telephone books. However, if no reference is available, the local Gamblers Anonymous can provide the address of the nearest Gam-Anon or Gam-Ateen organization.

Should that information not be available, inquiries can be sent to the National Council on Compulsive Gambling, c/o John Jay College of Criminal Justice, 444 West 56th Street (Room 3207S), New York, N.Y. 10019.

GAM-ATEEN

See GAM-ANON.

GAMBLERS ANONYMOUS

Gamblers Anonymous, or GA as it is called by members, was founded in 1957 as "a self-help fellowship designed to help the compulsive gambler to control his gambling problem." It has tens of thousands of members in 300 to 400 groups around the country. Members attend regular meetings, for which there are no dues or fees. Membership is not rigidly controlled as in some other organizations and many gamblers only show up for a few meetings. But many others stay in the organization for years and manage with GA's aid to keep their addiction to gambling under control. In addition to meetings, GA sponsors three conventions annually and publishes a monthly bulletin. In some respects Gamblers Anonymous is run like Alcoholics Anonymous although there is much less of a religious orientation.

Besides his many discoveries of physical and astronomical facts, Galileo did much research into dice theory and expectations for certain clients. It may be presumed this gave them a considerable edge at the gaming tables. (Photo: N.Y. Public Library)

"We say without hesitation that the most important step a compulsive gambler can take toward recovery is to get into Gamblers Anonymous and become a steady and active participant," say Robert Custer, M.D., chief of Treatment Services of the

Mental Health and Behavior Science Service of the U.S. Veterans Administration, and Harry Milt in their book *When Luck Runs Out*.

See also COMPULSIVE GAMBLING—GAMBLERS ANONYMOUS'S "20 QUESTIONS"; and GAM-ANON.

GAMBLER'S BELT

Part of the code of the Old West was that if a professional gambler beat the rest of the boys regularly, he was probably cheating. It was a conclusion that usually had merit, and the mind-set was such that a gambler often ended being beaten up, run out of town and sometimes killed on the spot. Although professional card sharps might be fast with cards, it did not necessarily follow they were quick on the draw. Thus one of the favorite defensive weapons on the part of the gambling brethren was a particularly lethal device called the gambler's belt, which one Western historian called "no doubt a rupture hazard, but like the broadside from a battleship when fired."

The gambler's belt actually originated in the early gambling hells of Philadelphia, Cincinnati, and Chicago but proved extremely popular on the Mississippi and then in the West. Typically, it was a body belt fitted with three small-caliber revolvers that were fired simultaneously when the wearer operated a trigger mechanism hidden on his right side. Although the wearer's trousers would be destroyed, the damage to his target was more pronounced, with three hits to the abdomen. A Nevada gambler once used such a belt to kill a miner who had taken serious objection to his method of dealing cards. Other miners in the gambling joint were duly impressed by the device and watched in wonderment as the gambler explained how it worked. On reflection they decided it did kind of give the gambler an unfair edge in the gunfight, so they took him outside and strung him up.

GAMBLER'S BOOK CLUB: "Research Institute"

It has 80,000 devoted followers in 50 states and 60 foreign nations, including some in the communist bloc, who will scour its latest catalog in hopes of finding a book with that one bit of wisdom that will make them a winner at gambling. Despite its name and subject, the Gambler's Book Club enjoys a special niche of honor in a field known for its hustlers. Founded by the late John Luckman and his wife Edna in 1964, the GBC operates under Luckman's code of being honest to the gambling public. He was never accused of being a "shill" for the gambling industry. Located in Las Vegas about seven furlongs from the strip—where else?—the GBC services a wide range of customers both through the mail and at its retail outlet at 630 S. 11th Street. At any given mo-

Late founder John Luckman of the Gambler's Book Club was known as the conscience of the gambling industry. (Photo: GBC)

ment among those present might be casino dealers, professional gamblers, agents of the FBI and the Nevada Gaming Control Board, and the local police who use the bookstore as a resource to bone up on their knowledge of the field.

Suddenly a gambler might pop into the store, his taxi's meter running, just long enough to grab a pile of books on the subject he is interested in, and then continuing post haste to his hotel to study them before hitting a casino.

Such a hit-and-run type researcher misses out on the flavor and action at the store, which one news account described as reminding visitors "of an old country store with pickle barrel, crackers and coffee." The report added, "Luckman substituted doughnuts for the pickles but the atmosphere remains the same. Gaming executives, players, magicians and visitors from around the world, all find their way to Luckman's retail shop." The Book of the Month Club was never like this.

The store atmosphere is sometimes a combination of "Damon Runyon headquarters" and academia. Bettors discuss and exchange ideas on every area of gambling right in the aisles with others or with the clerks (as well as with Luckman before his death in 1987 at the age of 63), or with GBC manager, Howard Schwartz, a former Nader raider and schoolteacher. Another man, a BLACKJACK counter, sort of a GBC resident expert on the specialty, answers the question about an unusual betting practice and whether it has ever been used in any Atlantic City casino—"Impossible, if it was, I'd know about it."

Luckman had been a dealer and floorman at several Las Vegas hotels including the Tropicana and Caesars Palace before he launched the GBC, recognizing the need for accurate, affordable, and timely information

for the novice and expert casino player, horseplayer, and sports bettor.

Today the GBC store has more than 1,000 titles in stock and in the rear of the store a used-book section of more than 2,000 titles for collectors, researchers, or librarians. Luckman clearly believed in a "gambler's freedom of information act" but constantly warned about system sellers with outrageous claims about how easy it is to become wealthy through gambling, saying it was not true. "Not one in 10,000 can consistently win at casino gambling, sports betting, parimutuels, or any game that has negative expectations."

The book club's mailing list is particularly heavy with the names of inmates of state prisons, although federal penitentiaries do not allow gambling books in their institutions. Luckman approved of that, saying, "I think they should stock up on law books." He did not think as highly of a manager of a Vegas casino who told the casino's gift shop not to carry Luckman's *Facts of Blackjack* (written under the name of W. I. Nolan) because it would "smarten up the players" too much. The book remains one of the more popular titles in the GBC's 24-year history.

Most books mentioned in this book as recommended reading can be obtained by writing the Gambler's Book Club, P.O. Box 4115, Las Vegas, NV 89127. A free 24-page tabloid-sized catalog is also available. For those wanting rush service on books ordered by credit card, telephone orders are available at 1-800-634-6243 from 9 to 5 Pacific time, Monday through Saturday.

See BETTING SYSTEMS.

GAMBLERS CAVALRY
See WILSON RANGERS.

GAMBLER'S FALLACY: Law-of-Averages Myth
It is the most basic fact of gambling that the law of averages makes the gambling casino a sure winner when a player tries to buck the odds. The fact is, however, that while there may be a law of averages for a casino, there is no such animal at work for the individual player. Even seasoned gamblers will forget this basic premise, known to experts as "gambler's fallacy." There is no "law" that says that if black has turned up five, 10, or even 15 times in a row, that the next winner will be red. The odds on any spin of a ROULETTE wheel, any toss of the dice or, for that matter, the flip of a coin never change. They remain the same no matter what happened on the previous play, the previous dozen plays, or whatever.

Let us say you are flipping a coin with a friend and have called heads five times in a row and lost every bet. Isn't it a safe bet to call heads again because the odds now are that heads will come up? The answer is that the "law of averages" is indeed in effect. What that law says, however, is not that heads will come up on the next toss but rather that the odds are 50-50 on heads—no more, no less.

For the individual gambler there simply is no other law of averages. There may be for the casino, which is booking the bets of, say, 1,000 players every minute, but the individual player simply can't bet fast enough and often enough to get any "law" going in his favor. Unknowing or undisciplined gamblers start banking on a law of averages that doesn't exist rather than on the theory of probability. This latter theory predicts what will come about mathematically on average or "in the long run." Unfortunately, this means next to nothing for the individual gambler since, as J. P. Morgan, a man noted for considerable success in stock market gambling, once put it, "In the long run we are all dead."

Any gambler can go to his grave still waiting for his luck to turn. This foolish belief in the law of averages without grasping the real meaning of the theory of probability buries unthinking gamblers more ways than one. A player who is losing consistently may increase his bets because he knows the "law" makes it mandatory that his luck must turn. Even more tragically, some gamblers don't press a winning streak because they feel they have beaten the law of averages up until then and that their luck is sure to run out.

Gambler's fallacy, in short, can convert losers into paupers and big winners into small winners.

See also "GUESSER'S DISADVANTAGE."

GAMBLER'S PRAYER: Cards as Bible

In the early days of settlement in the American West, the saddle-sore circuit preachers were more than tolerated because they did not rant and sermonize against gambling, but instead used the language of cards to spread the gospel. In fact, even the gambling saloon proprietor gladly accepted the circuit riders. His ROULETTE wheels were stilled, the FARO box covered, the POKER tables cleared of chips and the bar

Gamblers in Tombstone, Arizona, pause in their whoop-it-up gambling to hear the gospel. (Photo: N.Y. Public Library)

closed. Cowpokes and miners removed their hats and listened to the preacher's "Gambling Prayer":

If you'll listen a while, pard,
I'll show you the Bible in cards,
The ace that reminds us of one God,
The deuce of the Father and Son.
The trey of the Father and Son and Ghost,
For you see all of them three are but one. . . .

After the service the proprietor would see to it that the hat was passed to pay the padre. Then the gambling resumed.

During the Civil War a Western private, one Richard Lee, was hauled before a mayor on a charge of playing cards during religious services. In his defense Lee explained he had been on the march for six weeks, without prayer book or Bible. All he had was a deck of cards. He spread them out before the judge and proceeded to recite the "Gambler's Prayer," making only one revision. When he got to the knave, he identified it as the constable who had arrested him.

Case dismissed.

GAMBLING DEBTS
See DEBTS, GAMBLING.

GAMBLING SUPPLY HOUSES: Purveyors of Crooked Equipment

First the lie: Since it is against the law to sell crooked gambling equipment, crooked gambling-supply houses do not exist. The truth: You can find such outfits in New York, Los Angeles, and a number of other large cities. Certain "novelty" stores in many cities act as outlets for the merchandise, but the customer has to be known and trusted.

All this is a change from 15 or 20 years ago when a number of firms doing business in crooked gambling supplies advertised in men's, detective, and how-to magazines and published mail-order catalogs. To protect themselves, these publications carried the caveat that purchasers could not use these items for illegal purposes but only for entertainment and magic demonstrations. The caveat did not in time prevent a legal crackdown. In 1964 the law hit the K.C. Card Co. of Chicago (originally of Kansas City, until law-enforcement pressure forced it to leave) and confiscated the firm's mailing list, containing the names of 40,000 clients in all 50 states and 24 countries. K.C. was finally closed down due to local and federal heat.

This did not mean the end of the line for the crooked companies. They continue to produce, and if they have no catalogs of their own it doesn't mean a customer can't ask for K.C. number so-and-so, or even a number from an old Will & Finck catalog. Will & Finck was the oldest and biggest company of this kind, dating well back into the 19th century. A tinhorn in the old West could hit a town, decide what dodge the local cowmen and prospectors would fall for, and wire Will & Finck, who shipped the order immediately to the nearest express office.

Today the crooked gambling-supply makers rely on word-of-mouth to hawk their wares and sometimes use agents to locate floating Crap games and the like, passing on information about their latest offerings.

John W. "BET-A-MILLION" GATES: Fabled Gambler

John W. Gates (1855-1911), better known as Bet-a-Million Gates, was the King of the Plungers. He frequently bet other millionaires as much as $50,000 on which of two raindrops would make it down a windowpane first.

Gates, a self-made millionaire who became the world's biggest manufacturer of barbed wire, was always thinking of ways to risk money in wild bets. He was a true eccentric, but he was not a lousy gambler. Over any appreciable streak, his winnings generally topped his losings. Gates, like all successful gamblers, understood he had one great advantage in his bets. He had comeback money, the ability to double up after he lost and bet again and again. He loved betting on the horses and was said to have lost $375,000 in one day at Saratoga. On another occasion he won $600,000 on one of his own horses. Gates got his nickname when he once tried to place a $1-million bet on a horse, causing the bookmakers to run for cover.

Although it appeared that Gates let his betting get out of control, that was not really the case. He tended to bet when he enjoyed an advantage. Once Bet-a-Million was dining with wealthy playboy John Drake, whose father had founded Drake University and was a governor of Iowa. Over their coffee, Gates suggested they each dunk a piece of bread and bet on whose bread attracted the most flies—at $1,000 per fly. Gates won several thousand dollars, slyly gaining the edge by surreptitiously slipping six lumps of sugar into his coffee cup.

From the moment Gates awakened each morning he was looking for and plotting action. Once en route by train to the races at Saratoga, he needed a fourth for BRIDGE and roped in a newspaperman as his partner. "We play for five a point," he said, "but I'll guarantee your losses and you can keep what you win."

When the game ended, the reporter tallied up the score and joyfully proclaimed he was ahead $500 at five cents a point. Gates howled with laughter and wrote out a check for $50,000. They were playing, he informed the newspaperman, for $5 a point. The reporter took the money and promptly retired.

It became a matter of great prestige to place a wager against Bet-a-Million. In Kansas City, a local sport approached Gates saying a K.C. syndicate wanted to gamble with him on any sort of bet. He produced a roll of $40,000. Gates flipped a gold piece in the air. "Heads or tails," he announced. "You call it." The local gambler lost, and Gates pocketed the $40,000. The loser's consolation was his new found local celebrity—the man who lost $40,000 to Bet-a-Million Gates in less than ten seconds. (Actually, Gates had to win. If he'd lost the flip, he'd have bet $80,000 on the next toss and kept doubling the bet until he won.)

Late in life Gates announced he was through with gambling and lectured before church audiences, warning people not to play cards or dice, or bet on the horses, or speculate on the stock market. Later, he was asked if he really intended to keep his vow. "Once a gambler," he said, "always a gambler."

That seemed like a reasonable bet.

GENERAL: Puerto Rican Dice Game

General, or more correctly *Generala*, is *the* dice game of Puerto Rico, far more popular with the locals than CRAPS. It can be a party or family home game, a bar game for drinks, and a genuine gambling contest with hundreds or thousands of dollars changing hands in a single session.

Score sheets must be made up with the players' names listed across the top and the following entries placed vertically on the left:

1
2
3
4
5
6
Straight
Full House
Four of a Kind
Small General

All players get a chance to throw five dice from a cup over ten rounds. On each round the player can roll all or some of the dice up to a total of three times, in an effort to improve his hand. Hands are given in POKER values.

The highest possible score is "Big General"—five of a kind with all five dice with the same number, thrown on the first roll only. Big General automatically wins the game at any stage of the contest. The next highest score is "Small General"—five of a kind achieved on the second or third roll. For instance, on the first roll the shooter gets three 2's. On the second

roll with the remaining two dice, he gets another 2 and on the final try he also gets a 2, giving him five of a kind. This is worth 60 points and is entered on the line on the score sheet for Small General. This is the last time the player can try for Small General. On the next round he may fill in any of the remaining nine lines.

If on the first cast the shooter throws what is a pat hand in Poker—such as four of a kind, full house, or straight—he must take the score allowed and cannot try to improve on the hand with one or two more rolls. Four of a kind is worth 45 points on the first roll, and 30 points on a second or third try. A full house is 35 on the first and 30 on subsequent rolls.

A straight (1 through 5 or 2 through 6) is 25 points on the first try and 20 thereafter. The number 1, or ace, is permitted to be wild in the case of a straight only, but in limited fashion. The ace may be used for a 2 or 6 but it cannot take the place of a 3, 4, or 5.

The remaining scoring lines are point numbers, with the total being worth the total points achieved, thus three aces are only three points while five 6's would be 30 points. Of course, if a player has not scored Small General when he throws five 6's, he would more likely take the 60 points for Small General instead. Too, players failing to get much of anything on a round will likely take a zero or a low point score on the 1 line rather than close off a higher scoring possibility on later rounds. It is here that skill and strategy are involved.

As an example, a shooter gets 1-1-3-6-6. He would have two casts of a single die trying for either a 1 or 6 to get a full house. However, aces are valuable for a straight. With two aces the shooter has both the 2 and 6; if he keeps the 3, he has two dice left to get the 4 and 5 on the subsequent roll. This is a far more attractive possibility early in the game as long as he has his 1 line free to take a low score if things don't pan out. If on his second roll he gets 3-5 instead of the 4-5, he should alter strategy. He should probably give up on the straight and try for the full house, keeping 1-1-3-3 and reshoot the 5. He could still try for the 4 and a straight, but at this stage the shooter can make a straight with one number whereas he can achieve the full house with one of two numbers. Since the full house is worth 10 points more than the straight, it is clearly the preferable hand to play for.

At the end of the ten rounds all the players add up their scores and the high man is the winner, receiving the point value difference from the losing players. The payoff for Big General is agreed upon in advance. In a five-handed game this differential can easily come to 200 points or higher. Thus in a penny-a-point game the winner would garner $2. In a dollar game his winnings would be $200. The stakes are determined by the relative bankrolls of the players, however, games of $5 or $10 a point are not unheard of in private games in Puerto Rico's luxury hotels.

General is similar to a number of other games, such as Yacht (often described as the English form of General), Crag, Double Cameroon, and the trademarked dice game called Yahtzee. These tend to be more party or family fun games, and have not developed the gambling following General enjoys in Puerto Rico.

GERMAN SOLO: Modern Development of Ombre

German Solo may be regarded as a modern, and certainly less erratic development of the old Spanish game of OMBRE. Instead of the 40-card Spanish deck used for Ombre, German Solo uses a 32-card pack with rankings, with a few exceptions, going from ace high down to 7 low. Exceptions to this order are: queen of clubs, which is known as "Spadilla," is always highest trump, followed by the 7 of trump, which is "Manilla" and then the queen of spades, which is "Basta" and third highest trump. Fourth highest is the ace of trump and this continues down to the 8. Notice that red trump suits have more cards than black trump suits.

Each of four players are dealt eight cards and in order, starting with the player to the dealer's left, they bid for the privilege of calling trump. The object of the game is to take at least five tricks, which is done by the highest card in suit. If a player is out of suit, he may either trump or discard from another suit. The winner of each trick leads to the next.

Bids are made according to the type of game to be played, which are as follows in an ascending scale of value:

1. Simple Game (sometimes called Frog). The bidder proceeds to name the trump suit in other than clubs, and then he calls for a nontrump ace he does not have (or a king, if he happens to hold all the aces). The holder of that ace is his partner for this hand only, but he does not reveal his identity. The partnership is revealed only when the called ace appears in a trick. The partners must take five tricks, and each partner receives one chip from each opponent if they succeed or give each opponent one chip if they fail.
2. Simple Game in Color. This is the same game as the previous one except that the trump suit is clubs. (In a variation, a different suit may be specified, but usually it is clubs.) The bidders each win two chips from the opposition or lose two, depending on their taking five tricks.
3. Solo in Suit. In this game or hand the bidder plays alone against all three opponents, naming any trump suit other than Color (clubs). If he captures five tricks, he wins two chips from each opponent; if he doesn't he pays each opponent two chips.
4. Solo in Color. This is the same procedure as Solo in Suit but the player names Color as trump. For a five-trick win, he collects four chips instead of two from each opponent or loses four to each.
5. Solo Tout. This is a bid in which the bidder undertakes to take all eight tricks with any trump other than Color. The prize is eight chips from, or to, each opponent.
6. Solo Tout in Color. Played exactly like Solo Tout, this requires the bidder to make Color trump and he wins 16 chips from each foe with success or loses 16 to each if he fails.

GERMANY, Gambling in

The Germans spend more of their gambling money on state-run lotteries such as Lotto and football (soccer) pools than any other people in Europe. They even have a lottery where you try to pick six football games that will end in ties—an old bugaboo for American sports bettors. It isn't easy, but hit it and you are set for life.

There are thousands of betting shops where you can get down action on horse races and football matches. Germany is also quite a country for gambling casinos. But don't be fooled by signs outside of seedy little joints in big cities that call themselves casinos. These are *spielhallen* that offer slot-machine action and, in some, card games. Avoid them; the odds are greatly stacked against the player, giving nowhere near the return of American casinos.

Most genuine casinos are pretty plush affairs, even by European standards. Some visitors find German casinos heavy and gross, but actually they are extremely efficient and laid back. Unlike American casinos they don't ban clocks from the premises; they assume that they are attractive enough in what they offer not to have to keep you there by hook or by crook, and that you'll come back on your own. Among the major countries in Europe Germany has about the lowest casino admission prices to be found anywhere. Only Austria offers a better deal, giving you more in chips than the price of admission. Also enticing is a sub-rosa arrangement in some casinos that allows you to buy chips with a check written against a credit card. If you end up ahead, your check is returned to you and you get no finance charge against your card.

Baden Baden sports the oldest, richest, and most beautiful casino in Germany, and possibly all of Europe. Its gambling rooms are stunning and there is outdoor ROULETTE on a vine-covered patio in sum-

Originally built in the early 19th century, the various gambling rooms of the Baden Baden casino were decorated by theatrical designers of the Paris Opera. Closed for 60 years in an era of reform, Baden Baden was reopened in 1933 by the Nazis who needed hard currencies. (Photo: N.Y. Public Library)

mer. The casino also features a famous double-wheel table where at the height of the season betting is conducted with real gold chips. On Friday morning two master croupiers give free instruction on the casino games. It is by far the best course of the type you can get anywhere in the world. The croupiers themselves also take regular courses—the public is not admitted—and are up on all the latest scams and misunderstandings that can occur in a casino.

Other leading casinos include those in Constance (nestled in truly beautiful surroundings), Lindau, Hamburg, Travemunde, Berlin, Garmish-Parten-kirchen, Wiesbaden, and Bad Homburg. There are special buses from Frankfurt throughout the day for the latter two casinos. Bad Homburg occupies a special niche in European gambling history, since it where the brothers Blanc (who later set up gambling in Monte Carlo) cut their teeth in the business, and it was the setting for the most famous short novel

on compulsive gambling, *The Gambler* by Fyodor Dostoevsky. It is also where the Russian author ran through a very nonfictional fortune himself.

Perhaps the best pitch for casino gambling is offered on a sign in the Bad Neuenahr casino that seeks to clear the conscience of the religious. It reads: "The church has larger sins than gambling to worry about."

GET YOU ONE
See GIN POKER.

GHANA, Gambling in
In 1960, Ghana opened its first casino, the Casino Africa in Accra, under American management. The country also boasts a sweepstakes, a national lottery, and HORSE-RACE BETTING. There are also pools on overseas sports such as soccer. Card and dice games are extremely popular, although most are illegal.

GIN: Cutthroat Card Game for Two

Gin or Gin Rummy is essentially KNOCK RUMMY with tighter restrictions on knocking to give the player with poor cards more of a chance. But that capsule description does an injustice to Gin Rummy, which is a notorious cutthroat game and a rather delightful one for sticking it to an opponent one dislikes. When Hollywood and the rest of the American entertainment world discovered Gin, they turned it into a high-stakes pastime that could produce enormous winnings and losses. The game, according to most sources, was devised by Elwood T. Baker of New York's Knickerbocker Whist Club in 1909 and was first called Gin Poker. Because of its resemblance to RUMMY, later on it became known as Gin Rummy or just plain Gin. Since World War II the growth of the game has been extraordinary.

As in KNOCK RUMMY, each player is dealt ten cards. Then the dealer turns up the top card from the deck to form a discard pile. The object of the game is to meld sets, three or four cards of the same value (such as three queens or four 3's), or sequences of three or more cards in suit (such as ace, deuce, 3 of hearts or 10, jack, queen, king of clubs). The ace can only be played low in sequence below the deuce. Picture cards are worth 10 points and all others carry their pip value.

The dealer's opponent has first refusal on the up-card. He adds it to his hand and discards another in its place, or he may offer that privilege to the dealer. If the dealer also declines the card, the opponent opens play by taking the top card from the pack. He discards, and the turn is passed to the dealer. The game continues with each player taking turns either drawing from the deck or the discard pile and discarding.

No melds are made until one of the players gets his "deadwood"—cards he cannot meld—down to 10 points or less. He can then knock, bringing play to an end. The knocker lays down all his sets and sequences, makes a discard and then counts up his deadwood. Then his opponent melds all the cards he can in sets or sequences and he also has the additional privilege of laying off any cards from his hand that fit onto the knocker's melds. If, for instance, the knocker lays down three aces and the opponent has the fourth ace, he may lay it off. Similarly, if the knocker lays down 5, 6, and 7 of spades, the opponent can lay off the 4 and 8 of spades, if he has them.

In scoring, the knocker then subtracts his deadwood points from those of his opponent and scores the difference to his credit—assuming, of course, that his count is less. If however the opponent ties or beats the knocker, he has "undercut" him and wins the hand, scoring 25 points plus the difference in deadwood points, if any. If the knocker has melded all his cards so that his count is zero, he is "gin," which is the correct terminology. In this case his opponent may not lay off any cards against the knocker's melds. The knocker wins even if his opponent still is able to reduce his own count to zero. The knocker is awarded 25 points as well as the difference in counts, if any.

The game is completed when a player scores 100 points or more. For having won, he also adds 100 points bonus to his score. If his foe has failed to win a hand during the game, the winner doubles his entire score, including the game bonus. Each player then receives 25 points for every hand he has won. This is called a "line" or "box" bonus. Then the scores are totaled for each player and the higher score collects the difference from the lower one. Depending on the betting unit per point, this can be a very substantial difference.

Some experts consider Gin Rummy the cruelest game around; experienced players utilize bluffing along with card memory to mislead an opponent. "Advertising" is considered an approved way of bluffing. It involves a player discarding a card of some value, hoping to decoy his opponent into discarding other cards of the same suit or rank. Early discards set the tone of the game and reveal the player's intentions—or what he wants his opponent to believe are his intentions. The shrewd Gin player deduces much about his opponent's hand not by what he discards but rather by the cards he is *not* discarding. Through this the good player seeks to form a rapid picture of his opponent's hands. Choosing the appropriate discard is a vital part of the game, and it is generally best to discard if possible a card of the next rank but of another suit to the card an opponent discards.

The logic and strategies of Gin are the subjects of several books, including *Gin Rummy* by Oswald Jacoby; *Complete Gin Rummy* by Walter L. Richard; *Scarne on Cards* by John Scarne; and *Go with the Odds* by Charles H. Goren.

See also GIN—DOUBLE, GIN—FOUR-HAND OR PARTNERSHIP, GIN—HOLLYWOOD, GIN—OKLAHOMA and GIN CHEATING.

GIN CHEATING

An old-time sharpshooter once said that the best game to cheat at is Gin Rummy. Because it's only a two-man game, you only have to fool one person. Cheating at Gin is accomplished in a variety of ways, in addition to the usual bottom dealing, second dealing, etc. One simple operation is the "bottom stack." When it is a cheater's turn to deal, he simply gathers up the cards and keeps a previously played set of four cards, such as four 9's, together at the bottom of the pack. As he riffles the cards, he allows the four cards to fall first and remain together on the bottom of the pack. He continues to do this no matter how many riffles are made. Then he offers a cut. He lets it go through legitimately and usually the opponent cuts about half the deck, which positions the four 9's together in the middle of the pack. However, it really does not matter where they fall. Either they will be dealt to the two players initially or they will remain in the deck to be drawn by them. When the player sees he has two 9's, he knows his opponent also has two. However, his opponent does not share this knowledge. Nines are high cards and in time the disadvantaged player will probably get rid of them. Score a meld for the cheater.

Another gimmick is the "51-card deck."

A cheat simply leaves one card in the box when he takes out the cards. All he has to know is the identity of that card to have an important edge in the game. For instance, he buries a deuce in the box. He does not try for a meld in deuces because he knows the odds of getting it are 25 percent less than usual. If he holds one deuce in his hand, he can stick his opponent with two deuces that can't be melded as a set. This alone gives the cheater a sure knock advantage. The reassuring thing about such a scam is that it is rarely spotted and, if it is, most Gin players will accept the "overlooked" card as a mere oversight.

The real edge in Gin is riskier, since it involves signaling by a third party. In the famous FRIARS CLUB scandal in Hollywood in the 1960's a group of four sharpshooters took some of show business' biggest stars for $400,000 in crooked Gin games—at least, that was the sum the celebrities admitted was lost. The crooks actually drilled peepholes in the ceiling and had a spy signal a player electronically as to what the victim had in his hand. Not all signaling has to be so high tech. A kibitzer in the guise of observer could be flashing signals to the opposing player. The only defense against this is playing one's cards very close to the vest, or preferably under the vest.

Even as fabled a character as Nick "the Greek" Dandolos was taken in a spy scam for a half-million dollars. He played a two-week Gin session with a hustler at the poolside of the FLAMINGO HOTEL casino in Las Vegas. The two players wore only bathing suits, but the cheat had a radio receiver under his suit. From a hotel room above the pool, an accomplice watched with a telescope and operated a radio cue prompter. The schemers took no chances that Dandolos would shift his position out of the spy's view. The tables and chairs were riveted to the pool's concrete floor.

Later Ian Fleming appropriated the scheme for the nasty Mr. Goldfinger to use in a JAMES BOND novel.

GIN POKER: Two-handed Game

Gin Poker, a two-player game, was invented by gamblers to pass the time when there were not enough players for regular POKER. Gin Poker is a hybrid game with elements of POKER and GIN RUMMY. The object of the game is to come up with a *complete* Poker hand, that is, in descending order of best hands, a royal flush, straight flush, four of a kind, full house, flush, or straight. Note that four of a kind is technically not a "complete" five-card hand, but it qualifies as a winning hand because obviously no fifth card can improve on it. Three of a kind, two pairs, or one pair are not considered complete hands because they can be improved upon.

The pot usually consists of the opening ante, although some gamblers permit an additional bet, raise, and re-raise after both players evaluate their opening hand of five cards. Where raises are permitted at this stage a player might raise on an opening hand of two pairs, three of a kind, or a four-card flush or open-end straight. Anything less hardly warrants an additional investment.

After each player has his five cards the balance of the deck (the stock) is placed face down in the center of the table. The nondealer then takes a card from the stock and may keep it in his hand or discard it on a face-up pile next to the stock. If he keeps the card, he must discard another from his hand. The dealer then can pick his new card from the stock or from the top card of the discard pile. Play continues in similar fashion until a player announces "Gin Poker," meaning he has one of the complete hands. He must discard his unneeded card and the other player has the right to draw one additional card before play ends. On the showdown, the best complete Poker hand from straight on up wins the pot.

GIN—Double

Double Gin is a GIN variation for high flyers, but some careful gamblers are fond of the game since it is a bluffer's paradise. On any turn a player may "double," or declare the hand worth twice the usual points. A player with a truly rotten hand may actually bluff his way out of disaster by first picking up a couple of upcards to give the impression of enormous strength and then double. The opponent may fall for the ploy and fold.

At this point the hand is reckoned on the basis that the doubler has knocked and automatically gets a bonus, usually at least 10 points and in some localities 20. The resigner pays this bonus along with the difference in the deadwood count if he does not undercut the doubler. Frequently the resigner will undercut but he can collect nothing since he has resigned, and the doubler still keeps his bonus.

If the opponent does not resign but accepts the double, the game continues in the normal way with double scoring. In some areas a redouble is also permitted. This doubling rule makes the game harder to gauge, but it represents a defensive play for the gambler stuck with bad cards. Overall, Double Gin is not for the faint of heart.

GIN—Four-handed or Partnership

Four-handed or Partnership Gin is standard GIN—or, more precisely, two simultaneous games of two-player Gin. After each hand, the score of each team is combined. If one hand is completed before the other, a partner may advise the player in the game still in progress.

GIN—Hollywood

GIN was a reasonably popular game in the 1920's and 1930's, but it really caught on with the public when it became a Hollywood craze in the 1940's as movie figures adopted what became known as Hollywood Gin. Not that the unadulterated version was played nearly as much outside the movie mecca. It was such a big-money game that it hardly could be, not at $2 or $3 a point or more, which was prohibitive enough, but because almost all hands figured in three games at once!

Off the record show-business personalities will admit that individuals have lost as much as a quarter of a million dollars at the game in a few months. Certainly losses of $10,000 a night are common. It is easy to lose so heavily under Hollywood Gin scoring rules even though the game is not as complicated as it seems and is no more than pure Gin Rummy.

Score is kept in three adjoining columns. The first hand's results are credited to game 1. The score in the second hand is credited to game 2 and also becomes a second score in game 1. The third hand is tallied in games 1, 2, and 3. All subsequent hands won by a player are scored for him in all three games. Each game is scored independently and players get all the bonuses they are entitled to in that game. When a player gets 100 points in any game, he wins that game but continues competing in the remaining games. Play ends when all three games are completed. Needless to say, among addicted Hollywood Ginners, these spectaculars go on far beyond the third game.

Actually there is nothing wrong with Hollywood Gin except the stakes involved. When really big bucks are involved, cheating becomes a real peril. But even without it, high-stakes losses can put a player in the poorhouse posthaste. Yet many Gin players like to play Hollywood Gin—for, say, a tenth of a cent a point. When the action gets up in the dollars, it's ulcer time.

See FRIARS CLUB, GIN CHEATING, MARX BROTHERS.

GIN—Oklahoma

Oklahoma Gin follows the rules of GIN RUMMY, but with one important variation that drastically alters the strategy of the game. Rather than accepting a knock at 10 or fewer deadwood points, the rank of the upcard determines the maximum number of points with which a player may knock on that hand. If the upcard is a 3, he may not knock unless his deadwood count is 3 or less. Under some rules the ace allows for a knock of 1, while others hold that an ace requires that a player have gin. Another frequently invoked rule prescribes that if the upcard is a spade, the scoring for the hand is doubled.

In Oklahoma Gin, games are played to at least 150 points, with 200 or 250 preferred. The bonus for winning is raised accordingly.

GIN—Round the Corner

Round the Corner Gin is simply a variation of the standard game and may be adapted to any other version as well. The ace can be used as both a bottom (deuce-ace) or top (ace-king) card in any sequence. The key factor is that sequences may go around the corner (for instance, king-ace-deuce of hearts). An unmatched ace in the hand counts as 15 points, making it a deadly as well as valued card. Because the ace is so dangerous and makes it difficult for a player to get his deadwood count down to 10 points, it cuts down on knocks.

Under most rules, the game score is extended to 125 points, sometimes 150. In another variation, if a knocker declares gin and his opponent is able to reduce his own hand to zero, there is no scoring on that deal.

GIN—Straight

Straight Gin is the same game as GIN, but with a simplified method of scoring. This version is extremely popular among gamblers who don't care to risk their shirts on the standard game.

In Straight Gin, a stake is agreed upon in advance and is payable to the player who first gets to 100 points or more. There are no extra bonuses involved for game or box and the differences in scores is not figured in the payoff. However, most Straight Gin players do permit a double payoff in the event a player scores a shutout.

GIN—Three-handed

Three-handed Gin is more of a social game, being little more than an annoyance to some Gin gamblers. Three-handed games may be played in a number of ways, one being that each plays the other two in turn, with the partnership consulting on their play, a situation that can lead to ill feelings when big stakes are involved.

In another version a cut of the cards eliminates the low man, who will play the winner on the next round. Play may then continue in round-robin fashion so that the two players who have not faced each other play the third man, or play may continue with the winner continuing to play the odd man each time. The game ends when one player reaches 100 points and obviously, under the latter option, a player on a winning streak has the best chance of getting there.

Yet another version allows all three players to be dealt ten cards and to play in turn. The winner of each hand scores the difference between his deadwood count and the combined counts of his two opponents. There is no bonus for undercutting and if the knocker is tied, the tying player wins the hand and 20 points are deducted from the knocker's score. Layoffs are only permitted on the knocker's hand and only to the original matched sequences so that if the knocker has a sequence of 8, 9, and 10 of hearts, another player may add the 7 or jack of hearts, but the third player may not then add the 6 or queen of hearts. Going gin is worth 40 points and when the stock is down to three cards the game ends in a draw if no one knocks. Game is usually 200, with the bonuses that apply in Standard Gin added to the scores. Each player must pay the difference in scores to any player with a higher point total. This version is not played much; the round-robin form is generally preferred by most Gin players. Gin simply does not work well in genuine three-handed form.

GO BOOM

See ROCKAWAY.

GOING TO BOSTON

See YANKEE GRAB.

GOLF BETTING

It is difficult to estimate the amount of money wagered on golf. Most bookmakers will give a bettor odds on golf, including odds on a particular player in a particular tournament. The sports books in Nevada casinos put out a line on major golfing events. But the private bets between players, the nonprofessionals, can be enormous, with bets made on various aspects of play. Overall, the consensus has it that golf betting in the U.S. hits close to one billion dollars annually.

Golf, a noble sport, dates to the time of the Romans when a version known as *paganica* was played using a crooked stick and a feather-stuffed ball. By the 19th century golf was highly popular in Scotland and attracted a growing number of gamblers. Today in England bookmakers are permitted to take bets at tournaments. Unlike at the races, they are expected to dress decorously, take no cash bets and not shout out odds. The Professional Golfers' Association refused to allow the usual bookmakers action at tourneys. In America, the PGA also refused to cooperate and caused the Las Vegas Tournament of Champions to cancel its "Calcutta pool."

With variations, a Calcutta pool is set up among bettors so that the various players are "auctioned." Bids of $25,000 are not unusual. In the 1959 Calcutta pool at Las Vegas, a Los Angeles businessman named Carl Anderson collected $95,760 by backing the eventual winner, Stan Leonard.

As a tournament progresses, gamblers who "own" players will try to hedge their bets or sell off pieces of their man in order to guarantee themselves a profit. In one case in Las Vegas, a casino operator "bought" a leading golfer for $20,000 and hustled shares in him that totaled $60,000.

Critics of many golf pools contend that many can be (or are) rigged and some top pools have been canceled for this reason. In many smaller tournaments it has developed that hustlers have joined a club strictly to get into the Calcutta play. They pass themselves off as lousy golfers and are accorded a high handicap. Suddenly during the tournament they become top-shelf performers and walk off with first prize.

In private play it is common for these hustlers to take fellow golfers for small, and not so small, fortunes. A real hustler will manage to work more than one club in an area at the same time, losing several smaller matches and then taking the big ones.

GRAND HAZARD: Variation of Chuck-a-Luck

Grand Hazard is basically the same three-dice game as the more involved CHUCK-A-LUCK, with two variations. The first is in terminology. In Grand Hazard three of a kind is referred to as "Raffles." Second, in payoff rates. As a rule of thumb, most Chuck-a-Luck layouts quote payoffs at, for instance, 6 *to* 1 while most Grand Hazard layouts offer odds at 6 *for* 1. This is no minor matter. When a Chuck-a-Luck payoff on a point total of 10 or 11 is 6 *to* 1, the house edge is 12½ percent. When a Grand Hazard layout quotes 6 *for* 1 for the same points, the house edge zooms to 25 percent!

If one must play these games, it is not important to worry whether the game is called Chuck-a-Luck or Grand Hazard, and the names often are now used interchangeably, but rather which way the odds are quoted. If the key word is *"to,"* the player will lose his money fast. If the word is *"for,"* he will lose it very much faster.

Riley GRANNAN: Gambling Pioneer

Long before the mob in the 1940's saw visions of a gambling paradise in the Nevada desert, a Western gambler named Riley Grannan (1868?-1908) had the same dream. If he had been successful, gamblers today would be heading for Rawhide, Nevada, and Las Vegas today might be little more than a filling station at the crossroads. In any event, Grannan was a truly successful Western gambler, a brilliant student of horse racing (he once collected on a $275,000 bet on a horse) and the inventor of modern form-betting.

Born in Paris, Kentucky, about 1868, Grannan came to the Western frontier fairly late in the game and realized the day of the tinhorn gambler was passing. He came up instead with the idea of establishing a gambling palace that offered customers something unique in the West—honest gambling. This was in keeping with the Grannan image; he was noted for both his honesty at gambling and for his personal generosity. For the locale of this great dream, Grannan selected the wide-open spaces around Rawhide, Nevada. He plunked down $40,000 for the land in 1907 and started pouring money into building. There were many who considered it foolhardy to build a mammoth gambling center in the desert, but Grannan saw it as part of the draw. Traveling a great distance, he said, was what would make the prize all the more appealing. Grannan died suddenly in 1908, and that effectively ended his dream. His personal fortune had been drained by the cost of his project.

He was widely celebrated at his death. The Rev. W. H. Knickerbocker, who had resigned from the fashionable Methodist Trinity Church of Los Angeles to go out among the miners, gave a moving farewell sermon that brought hardened adventurers, miners, cowmen, and gamblers to tears. Many newspapers as far away as California carried the sermon in full. In part it went:

"I know that there are those who will condemn him. There are those who believe today that he is reaping the reward for a misspent life. There are those who are dominated by medieval creeds. To those I have no words to say about him. They are ruled by the skeleton of the past and fail to see the moral beauty of a character lived outside their puritanical ideas. His goodness was not of that type, but of the type that finds expression in a word of cheer to a discouraged brother; the type that finds expression in quiet deeds of charity; the type that finds expression in friendship, the sweetest flower that blooms along the dusty highway of life; the type that finds expression in manhood.

"He lived in the world of sport. I do not mince my words. I am telling what I believe to be true. In the world of sport—hilarity sometimes, and maybe worse—he left the impress of his character on this world, and through the medium of his financial power he was able with his money to brighten the lives of its inhabitants. He wasted it so the world says. But did it ever occur to you that the most sinful men and women who live in this world are still men and women? Did it ever occur to you that the men and women who inhabit the night-world are still men and women? A little happiness brought into their lives means as much to them as happiness brought into the lives of the straight and the good. If you can take one ray of sunlight into their nightlife and thereby bring one single hour of happiness, I believe you are a benefactor.

"Riley Grannan may have 'wasted' some of his money this way. . . .

"I say to you that the man who by the use of his money or his power is able to smooth one wrinkle from the brow of care, is able to change one moan or sob into a song, is able to wipe way one tear and in its place put a jewel of joy—this man is a public benefactor.

"I believe that some of Riley Grannan's money was 'wasted' in this way."

Perhaps the greatest tragedy of Riley Grannan's death was that it left gambling in Nevada open to gangster Bugsy Siegel.

See FLAMINGO HOTEL.

Joseph E. GRANVILLE: Stock Market and Bingo Guru

Most famous as a stock market tip-sheet publisher, Joe Granville (1923-   ) is something of an authority on gambling, BINGO in particular. Pundits suggest his stock market and Bingo dabbling are complimentary enterprises.

Granville is a controversial character. His predictions on stocks have not always been accurate; he once caused a monumental drop of 39 points in the market in one day by advising his readers to sell their stocks. What followed was a major up market. Among his other "expert" enterprises has been the announcing of the date, time, and epicenter of California earthquakes, dates that passed with stunning silence.

All of these, it might be argued, make Granville the ideal expert on Bingo. His 1977 book, *How to Win at Bingo,* is touted as offering "the amazing new easy-to-use GRANVILLE SYSTEM." Just how easy to use this book is, with its series of charts and graphs and tables of probabilities, can be left to the individual reader. Having actuarial training would probably be helpful.

Like other Bingo system advisers, Granville advocates that players choose their own cards, looking for those with certain different numbers or numbers with different endings. The trouble with this notion is that few players have the ability to take in a card with 25 numbers on it that quickly. They need time to compare the numbers. Very few Bingo parlors will allow players more than a few seconds to pick their own cards—if they don't simply hand out the cards helter-skelter. And in the final analysis there is no approach with a true statistical basis that will make any system better than a random selection of cards.

The crux of the problem in coming up with a winning Bingo system is connected to the house take. When the player is bucking a totally packed parlor, as for instance in the much-publicized Bingo games at Harrah's clubs in Lake Tahoe and Reno, the house edge has been estimated at 200 percent or more! One would think that if Granville's mathematical wizardry can conquer Bingo, it would be easy for him to beat the piddling 1½ to 2½ percent edges involved in many CRAPS and ROULETTE bets.

On the other hand when Granville talks about money management, he offers some good sense for Bingo addicts. He points out that only a limited number of cards should be played—in the parlors one can see addicts going mad trying to check out 21 cards at once—and that after three cards the potential for winning actually *decreases*. Of course, any system that advises investing less in a losing game becomes automatically a "winner" of sorts.

Granville on gambling can be amusing and interesting reading. But far more informative than his Bingo advice is another work: *The Book of Granville: Reflections of a Stock Market Prophet*. Although it is filled with his technical theories on the market, it becomes more fun when it gets into his personal life and specifically his wagering habits—how, nearly broke, he slept for months on the floor in his office; how he vanished on a week-long gambling jag in European casinos; and about the wild nights he spent haunting Daytona Beach Bingo joints.

Glen GRAYSON
See CROSSROADERS.

GREAT BRITAIN, Gambling in
Given the shift in exchange rates Britons spend somewhere in excess of $10 billion a year on legalized forms of gambling. There is horse-race and dog-race totalizator wagering as well as private bookmakers and betting offices where these races can be bet. There are football (soccer) pools and Bingo does a huge business throughout the British Isles. Also in evidence are numerous casinos or gambling clubs, not only the more lavish and refined ones in London, but in almost every populous city.

The English casinos are more tightly regulated by the government than those in America. As a result, bettors get a fairer shake. Take CRAPS. The casino edge on field bets is usually reduced in England by making the 5 rather than 4 a part of the field. Wherever the 4 is retained instead, 2 to 1 is paid on 1-1 and 3 to 1 on 6-6, which narrows the edge considerably. Other odds are also beefed up. Proposition bets on 6 and 8 are paid at 9½ to 1 and on the 4 and 10 at 7½ to 1. These payoffs are a hefty half-point better than the odds in Nevada or Atlantic City. Similarly, two aces or two 6's pay 33 to 1 compared to 30 to 1 (and sometimes an even more gouging 30 *for* 1) in the States.

The Gaming Board also requires casinos to post strategy hints for novices on the best way to play BLACKJACK so that they don't make foolish errors. You can just see an American dealer or stickman warning a player he's making a stupid move! The rules also protect players in other ways, such as with doubling down only permitted on 11, 10, and 9, and the splitting of 4-4, 5-5, and 10-10 strictly prohibited. The government also bars insurance bets in Blackjack, since 99.9 percent of the time these are poor wagers.

The top casinos in London bear names made famous by the James Bond novels—Crockford's, Quent's, and Metropole. Admission to such casinos requires a 48-hour waiting period during which you apply for membership. If you are England bound, have your travel agent or hotel set this up in advance and you can float right into the casino. If you know someone who is already a member, you can be admitted as his or her guest. Tipping at English casinos is strictly forbidden. Finally, don't be surprised if the American games you wish to play aren't available. Some casinos have eliminated Craps—too noisy. And don't expect as an American to be especially catered to. The big wheels among customers these days are wealthy Arabs who seem to prefer to come to London rather than anywhere else when they are in a gambling mood.

GREECE, Gambling in
The Greeks have a reputation for being dedicated gamblers and the laws of the country support this. Most cafes or clubs boast pinball machines that pay off in money prizes. Organized card games are theoretically restricted to special gambling rooms, but it is hardly unusual to see a large "sociable" game in

action in many cafes. Serious games of chance such as ROULETTE, BACCARAT, etc., are restricted to licensed casinos and clubs. There are casinos in the Grand Hotel on the island of Rhodes and a glamorous one patronized by the international set on the island of Corfu in a fantastic 19th-century palace, the Achilleon.

Athens boasts perhaps the most spectacular casino in Europe, one on Mount Parnis. It has been said that gamblers at Nevada's Lake Tahoe manage never to observe the scenery, but this would be impossible on Mount Parnis. The great casino, perched at the top of Mt. Parnis, overlooks the entire Attica plain. International gourmet dining and dancing is offered in this most glamorous of settings. And there is something very special about the black-tie international clientele riding up to the mountain top on a funicular. Entertainment is top-flight and the costs for everything are far higher than one would have to spend on the Las Vegas strip. But the crowd, or at least most of it, seems well able to afford it. For the others, presumably, it is a case of "See Greece and die."

The Greeks are also heavy bettors in football (soccer) pools, and there is a very popular national lottery. Athens has horse racing with totalizator betting as well as off-course bookmakers.

GREEK DEAL: Rare Card Cheater's Method

While card players must always be alert to possible crooked dealers—those practicing "seconds," dealing the card under the top card, or "bottoms," dealing the card on the bottom of the deck—they don't really have to worry about the so-called Greek deal. This is dealing the second card from the bottom.

Obviously, this is a gold mine of a move, especially in BLACKJACK since the dealer needs only to learn the bottom card (a simple matter) before burning the top card, which of course is aimed at preventing any bottom dealing.

Why if the Greek deal is such a good thing do gamblers need not worry about it? Ironically, because it is a very difficult maneuver and probably not more than a handful of card manipulators can master it. If they can, they are hardly likely to waste their talents on any but the most high-stakes games. There has long been a belief among gamblers that some crooked casinos use Greek dealers in their games. This too is most unlikely, for no good Greek dealer would need a casino for a partner; he can do much better on his own.

See also BOTTOM DEALING; SECOND DEALING.

GREEK SYNDICATE: Combine That Dominates Much of European Gambling

Ever since the 1920's the big-money play at BACCARAT in European casinos has usually been controlled by the so-called Greek Syndicate, the operating descriptive words assigned to it being, almost interchangeably, "famous" and "infamous." The syndicate was founded in 1920 by an Armenian, a Frenchman, and two Greeks, Anthanose Vagliano and Nicholas Zographos—Europe's Nick the Greek—the latter two becoming the most visible members. Vagliano, who had accumulated a fortune in shipping, was the chief money man of the group and Zographos was the syndicate's super player-dealer noted for his incredible memory. The so-called BLACKJACK COUNTING experts and scholars have great difficulty even with the use of computers in devising a credible system for winning at Baccarat, but Zographos could do it all from memory.

He had the ability to remember every card of the 312 (six packs) that are played in Baccarat. Thus the amazing Zographos could instantly figure his chances for drawing a card he needed, and he was so adept at it that he proved a sure winner. There never was a season that the syndicate failed to win, and the Greeks were so confident that when Zographos held the bank himself he readily announced: *"Tout va"*—the sky's the limit.

The syndicate proved such a success that eventually most of the important casinos turned over the running of the Baccarat tables to the syndicate in exchange for half the profits. The system continues to this day, with the Greek Syndicate always successful against the most determined Baccarat addict.

After Zographos's death in 1953 the syndicate kept up its winning ways. As important as his skills were, in the final analysis they were merely the topping of the pudding. If we assume that the Baccarat high roller and the bank are equal in skill—quite an assumption—the decisive factor will eventually be the size of the bankroll of the two parties. Even a multimillionaire will eventually hit a losing streak that will lay him low. The syndicate has the resources to keep coming back time after time and all the while the bank edge continues in its favor. There is a saying on the Riviera that goes, "Conquerors of the world will rise and fall but the Greeks are eternal."

Jonathan GREEN: "The Reformed Gambler"

The biggest selling books on gambling in America in the mid-19th century were not Hoyle-type manuals or even general advice on winning at various games but rather those concerned with informing a gullible public that it was being swindled. At least the books sold well to nongamblers such as religious groups and to such anti-gambling activists as journalist Horace Greeley and others who formed the New York Association for the Suppression of Gambling.

There were many reforms and reformers accomplished in the anti-gambling field and even if they tended to be short-lived, they left their mark. None contributed more to the movement than Jonathan Green, who gained national fame in the mid-1800's as "Green, the Reformed Gambler." Green wrote and lectured tirelessly and his startling exposes bore all the facility of a former gambler determined to make amends for a misspent life. His books became impressive best-sellers and one, *Gambling Unmasked*, ran through a number of editions and was reprinted in abridged form for 50 cents a copy, or 12 for $4, for those eager to spread the anti-gambling gospel.

While not many details of Green's beginnings are known, in *Gambling Unmasked* we learn something of Green's supposed early years. He was, he assured his public, left motherless at a tender age and thus ripe for being lured into misdeeds by vicious men until he found regeneration as a devout Christian. There is much to doubt about Green's tales since his writings are a curious combination of fact and humbug. Undoubtedly, however, some of his claims were accurate. As another 19th-century observer capsuled Green's charges, they were, "first, that all gamblers were thieves; secondly, that they never played on the square; thirdly, that faro had less percentage than any other banking game, and that it was twenty percent worse than stealing anyhow." There was little to quarrel about with that.

However, Green was keenly aware that his audience wanted new and ever more startling charges to keep his campaign going, and he assured the public that the criminal mind knew no limit in its ability for grand conspiracies. In 1847, he published *The Secret Band of Brothers*, which advanced one such thesis.

"We will not wonder," he wrote, "when we learn that there are men of wealth and influence in almost every town, who are sworn to aid and befriend these villains. They are sometimes lawyers and jurors, and even judges." It does seem that Green was being a little unfair blanketing the simple and time-honored practice of taking bribes with a charge of a cult-like conspiracy.

This Secret Band of Brothers was never uprooted, but Greeley and many others accepted Green's claims. Green did have a way with him for demonstrating his statements. For instance, he claimed in lectures that every deck of playing cards manufactured in America was coded by the Secret Band so that professional gamblers could readily decipher them to rob the amateur and the honest. Green astounded his audiences by having a volunteer, generally a local person of unimpeachable character, venture forth to purchase a pack of cards.

Green would open them and lay them on the table before him, face down. Then he would pick up a card and hold it turned toward his audience and left them gasping as he identified card after card by rank and suit. Professional gamblers were outraged by Green's false claims but could not disprove them;

they were reduced to the unconvincing argument that all the volunteers were in Green's employ and had simply returned with previously marked decks. Not until some years later after Green retired from the Association for the Suppression of Gambling did the gamblers discover Green's secret. The inventive reformer had simply fixed the table with a tiny "shiner," or mirror, and as he lifted a card he caught a flash of it and could identify it while ostensibly only seeing the back of the card.

Green retired from the fray in 1852 and although his books continued to sell smartly, the anti-gambling crusade faltered. Waves of reform had been touched off but eventually, despite any restrictive laws that were passed, the gamblers returned to action, once again taking up their old ties with officials. Green himself was probably sanguine about it. After all, he had proved that just as it was possible to make a handsome living through dishonest gambling it was equally possible to do so by a dishonest exposure of it.

GREYHOUND RACING
See DOG RACING.

GRUESOME TWO-SOME
See HURRICANE.

"GUESSER'S DISADVANTAGE": False Gambling Theory

The so-called Guesser's Disadvantage is, in a sense, the flip side of the GAMBLER'S FALLACY, and it is amazing how many professional gamblers believe it in varying degrees.

The Guesser's Disadvantage holds that a bettor who follows no set pattern, but rather makes his selections on sheer instinct, has to do worse than one following some sort of disciplined method. This wrong-headed theory is in a sense a restatement of the Gambler's Fallacy—that there is something in the workings of the law of averages that makes it more likely at some point for red to come up more often than black in ROULETTE or that five consecutive "head" flips of the coin somehow increase the chances of "tails" coming up on the next toss. The fact is that all 50-50 chances remain 50-50 propositions at any given moment in the play. That being so, a gambler who bets wildly with no pattern whatsoever has the same chance of being right on any particular roll of the dice, flip of the coin, or spin of the wheel.

Gambling expert John Scarne was undoubtedly correct when he theorized that the Guesser's Disadvantage idea originated back in the era when bettors couldn't figure out why operators of games always showed a profit. Not understanding house percentages, they saw that players lost consistently and attributed that to the fact that they were betting in indiscriminate fashion. In reality the house edge, however it came about, was the real answer. Roulette and CRAPS had a percentage in the house's favor no matter what the bet. In BLACKJACK the fact that players could bust out by going over 21 and lose to the house even if the dealer did the same thing was an overwhelming advantage against even the best of players.

It's the house edge and not Guesser's Disadvantage that makes the rich casino richer and the poor bettor poorer.

See GAMBLER'S FALLACY.

H

HAIRTRIGGER BLOCK: Chicago's Deadly Gambling Center

During the Civil War, there was more gambling in Chicago than in any other city, North or South, even outdoing New Orleans. Professional sharks fattened there since it was a city that almost didn't know what honest gambling was. Victims were available by the thousands, among them Army officers (especially paymasters), soldiers returning from the front with many months pay, new enlistees with their bonuses, speculators with war contracts, and so on.

The center of the gambling racket was on Randolph and Clark Streets, an area safe for gamblers because of the heavy graft paid to police. The area teemed with "skinning houses" for trimming the suckers. Naturally, with so much money won and lost so easily, shootings and killings were common, outdoing anything in the frontier towns of the so-called Wild West. Randolph Street between Clark and State was, in fact, referred to as "Hairtrigger Block" because of the many shootings that took place there.

Most of the shootings were between professional gamblers over the right to fleece a potential "mark." Sometimes too they represented matters of "honor" on the part of two gamblers. The most famous feud involved two notorious gamblers, George Trussell, the dandy of Gambler's Row, and Cap Hyman, described as "an insufferable egotist, an excitable, emotional jack-in-the-box." They could not play cards together for any length of time before bad blood flowed. Both were also heavy drinkers and if they could not tolerate each other stone sober, they could be counted on to pull guns on each other when drunk. Each probably shot at the other at least 50 times. Fortunately or unfortunately, when drunk both were horrible marksmen and the damage that ensued was to windows, bar mirrors, and street signs.

As long as the pair's shootouts took place on Hair-trigger Block, the forces of law and order turned their backs. However, when they'd been drinking the two would sometimes stagger into other areas in search of each other and continue their shooting spree. A previously tolerant *Chicago Tribune* declared, "The practice is becoming altogether too prevalent."

Once in 1862 Hyman staggered into the lobby of the Tremont Hotel, convinced that Trussell was hiding there. He fired several shots and allowed no one to leave or enter the hotel for an hour. Hyman was frequently arrested for such forays, and after paying his fine, he would meticulously deduct the amount from his next payoff to the police.

When the shooting started, it was common on Hairtrigger Block for the habitues to immediately place wagers on which one would be killed. Alas, the results were forever a standoff. Trussell was killed in 1866 by his mistress, who, it developed, was a much better shot than Hyman. Cap Hyman went insane and died in 1876.

HAITI, Gambling in

Despite all the unpleasantness in recent decades—and probably in large measure because of it—gambling has long prospered in Haiti. In the days of the iron rule of the Duvaliers gambling houses flourished in most towns and there was a large casino in Port-au-Prince. "Papa Doc" invited the mob in to run things, demanding, it was said, a huge cut for himself. Gambling junkets run by mob crime families in several big cities brought in the gamblers for action that, according to U.S. government witnesses, was frequently fixed. Certainly, there was good reason to believe this because Papa Doc's personal demands put honest profit margins under great pressure. Haiti clearly was not exactly the best place to which the trusting gambler should venture.

With the demise of Papa Doc and the toppling of

"Baby Doc" the mob action in Haiti is not what it used to be. However, the locals still take time out from political activity to play the national lottery, and private LOTTERIES flourish in many towns, providing income for hordes of street-corner ticket sellers. Prizes tell something about the economic conditions in the country, with a typical jackpot being a cow. Other awards include a pig, goat, or hen.

Gambling on cockfighting also thrives, and it has been said that any crackdown on such activities would probably lead to street rioting.

HARDWAYS PROPOSITION SCAM: Unfair Craps Bet

There is a gamblers' axiom that there is no easier mark in any game than a player with a little bit of knowledge about odds. Certainly that is truer about private proposition bets among dice players than almost any other. Many gamblers, sure that they know all about betting odds, have been taken at what is called the Hardways Proposition Scam.

At Casino CRAPS a hardway bet is one involving the combination of 4, 6, 8, and 10. The bettor wagers that one of these numbers will come up the hard way, that is, the total coming up in paired dice (e.g., 2-2, 3-3, 4-4, and 5-5). If instead the number comes up another way, such as 5-3 or 6-2 for the 8, the bettor loses. He also loses if a 7 comes up. This makes the hardway bet a long shot and the casino claims to pay off accordingly, offering at best 7 to 1 odds on the 4 or 10 and 9 to 1 odds on the 6 or 8. The true odds should be 8 to 1 and 10 to 1, respectively, meaning the house edge on 4 and 10 is 11-1/9 percent and 9-1/11 percent on the 6 and 8. These are extremely high gouges for the house and seasoned Craps players generally avoid such bets, leaving them for the amateurs.

It is this situation that sets up the scam. A hustler sails into a bar and announces happily: "Boy, did I clean up in Atlantic City today. Took the Craps table for $1,500. All on hardway bets. Man, that's the only way to beat the house. It's the only bet that gives the shooter the edge."

Such inflammatory nonsense gets the desired reaction from a seasoned gambler or two, who tries to explain about the true odds, that the house has a sure advantage and has to win.

"Baloney," the hustler replies. "I always win at Craps on hardways bets. If you don't think so, put your money where your mouth is."

One of the drinkers (actually a confederate of the hustler) suggests that they teach this loudmouth a lesson. "Let's each put up some money and bet him at regular casino odds," he whispers. "If we all put up just a little, we can't get murdered if he has a run of luck, and the odds will be way in our favor."

The boys set up a bank with $300 and the hustler put up $5 a roll. If the dice came up 2-2 or 5-5 he got 7 to 1, the standard casino payoff for 4 and 10 the hard way. If the dice came up 3-3 or 4-4, he got 9 to 1. However, if any of the four numbers—4, 6, 8, or 10—came up in any other fashion or the 7 appeared, the hustler lost.

Within 20 minutes the hustler strolled out of the bar with the patrons' $300. "Take my advice, fellows," his final advice was, "next time you go to A.C. bet hardways. You can't lose."

If any of his victims took his advice, you can bet they lost at the casinos.

Such private hardways bets are out-and-out swindles. The victims are lured into a wager that has nothing to do with true casino rules. In casino play, a gambler who puts $5 on all hardways bets (which is what the hustler was doing) not only loses the individual number bets when they come up other than hardways, or "soft," but *all* the hardways bets lose when a 7 appears. This was where the hustler was outsmarting so-called intelligent bettors. He was only paying off on a single hardways bet when he should have been paying on *four* of them! So instead of giving up a monstrous house edge the hustler had turned the hardways 4 and 10 to a 38.8 percentage edge in his favor. On the hardways 6 and 8 his advantage became 31.8. This meant he figured to win about one bet in three and got paid off double or triple that.

See BAR 6-8 CRAPS PROPOSITION for a similar scam.

Dick HARGRAVES: Mississippi Gambler

Hollywood has much to be thankful to Dick Hargraves (1824-1882) for, since his character has been the inspiration for many movies about that most romantic of characters, the Mississippi riverboat gambler.

Hargraves was more colorful than any screenwriter's imagination could have conjured up. He ordered all his clothing from his native England and his boots from Paris. He launched his professional gambling career at the age of 16 when he came to New Orleans. His first job was as a bartender—at least until he won $30,000 in a legendary POKER game. Hargraves was never again to work at anything in his life save for his long days and nights at the card table.

Hargraves became famous on the river for the next two decades as both an honest and completely pitiless gambler. Hargraves made no apology for this latter trait since at least 90 percent of all riverboat gamblers were crooked. As long as he played on the square, he felt his victims had no kick when he took their money. And he had no sympathy for any hard-luck story about a man losing all his property and facing his family now mired in poverty.

Over the course of the 1840's and 1850's Hargraves was said to have killed at least eight men who sought revenge after losing their money and often all their worldly possessions to him.

Of course the women of New Orleans were attracted to a blade of Hargrave's reputation and magnetism, and he fought several duels over women as well. He once became the lover of a banker's wife and killed the enraged husband when challenged to a duel. When the man's brother came after him, he killed him as well in a shootout in a Natchez-under-the-hill gambling den. When Hargraves returned to New Orleans, the distraught banker's widow stabbed him and killed herself. Hargraves recovered from his wounds and married a girl whose life he had saved in a fire.

Unlike most gamblers on the river, Hargraves sided with the North in the Civil War and served as an officer. After the war, wealthy but ill, Hargraves relocated in Denver, where he died in 1882.
See MISSISSIPPI GAMBLERS.

HAROLDS CLUB
See HAROLD S. SMITH, SR.

HASENPFEFFER: Euchre-like Gambling Game
Hasenpfeffer is a four-person partnership game that is considered by many to be part of the EUCHRE family. Others consider it a separate game entirely, since the scoring rules are generally quite different.

How to play: Hasenpfeffer is played with a 24-card deck (aces down to 9's) plus a joker. Players are dealt six cards each and the final card is faced down as a "widow." The joker is rated as "best bower" just as it is in several Euchre variations, making it highest trump, followed in turn by the jack of trump, then the jack of the same color. These are followed by the remaining trump cards in descending order. The nontrump suits all go from ace high to 9 low except for the jack in the nontrump color suit.

The object of play is to take tricks, which is done with the highest card in suit if it is not trumped, in which case the trick goes to the highest trump. Players must play in suit if they can. If not, they may either trump or discard from a different suit as they wish. The taker of a trick leads to the next.

Trump is named by the highest bidder who makes a point call on the number of tricks he thinks he and his partner can make. If the high bidder and his partner make their contract, they receive 1 point for each trick. Otherwise, the amount of the bid is taken from their score, even if a minus results. The defense always gets 1 point for each trick it takes. Game is set at 10 points, but if both teams go out during the same hand, the one making the bid is declared the winner.

If all players pass on the bidding round, the one holding the joker must reveal it and make a bid of 3. If the widow turns out to be the joker, there is a new deal.
See DOUBLE HASENPFEFFER.

HAZARD: Craps Forerunner
Hazard, sometimes called English Hazard, was the fore-runner of CRAPS and was apparently first played by English crusaders passing the time while besieging an Arabian castle in the 12th century. The game really came into its own in the 17th and 18th centuries in England. Basic Hazard was and is a two-dice game, not to be confused with Grand Hazard, which is a three-dice game similar to Chuck-a-Luck.

How to play: A player bets other players that he will make what eventually becomes his point.

In England the shooter was referred to as the caster and on his first roll he seeks to establish his "main" point. This has to be a 5, 6, 7, 8, or 9. If he does not get one of these main points on his first try, he continues to roll the dice until he does so. The caster then throws the dice again and if he repeats his main point he immediately wins his bets.

There are other possible ways to win or lose on this throw of the dice. For example, if he throws a 12 and his main point is 5, 6, 8, or 9, he loses. In all cases he loses if he throws a 2 or 3, which is known as "crabs." He wins his bet if he throws a 12 when his main point is 6 or 8, and he also wins on an 11 if his main point is 7.

If none of the above occur, and instead the caster throws a number from 4 to 10 but not his main point, this number becomes his "chance" point. He then continues to throw the dice and now must hit his chance point to win before his main point comes up, in which case he loses.

There are undoubtedly dice hustlers alive today bemoaning the fact that they were born a few centuries too late. Had they been born earlier—and known what man now knows—they could have really cleaned up, since Hazard players during the Middle Ages and in most cases well into the Renaissance did not grasp the principle of the law of averages and odds in relation to dice. Most bettors did not comprehend all the ways various combinations could be achieved with two dice. A hustler could indeed have made a fortune.

Great fortunes were made—and lost—at Hazard. At Crockford's, the famous 19th-century London gambling establishment, Lord Chesterfield lost the equivalent of $115,000 in a seven-hour Hazard session. Then Lords Rivers, Sefton, and Grenville really carved their way into the Hazard Hall of Fame by each dropping what was about a half-million dollars in a single evening.

One of the earliest art illustrations of Hazard (by Thomas Rowlandson) as played in an English gambling establishment. (Photo: N.Y. Public Library)

What really killed Hazard as the greatest dice game of all was the constant addition of new concepts, to compensate for new knowledge gained about gambling odds. Many of these concepts proved erroneous and as a result shrewd gamesters lost when they had determined they were bound to win. In the meantime Hazard came to America, but here it lost out to one of its refinements, in the form of Craps, a gambling game that also in large measure brought about the decline of Faro as well.

HEARTS: Very Popular Gambling Game
Hearts, a game that can be played in many variations, is most intriguing for gambling purposes. Its traditional form makes an excellent game, although it is more often played with a number of innovations, the primary examples of which directly follow this entry.

How to play: Pure Hearts is played with a 52-card deck with three to six persons, all playing solo. When there are three players, a black deuce is removed from the deck. With five, both black deuces are removed. With six, the 2 of hearts is retained but the other three deuces are stripped along with a black 3. Ace is high and deuce is low.

The entire deck is dealt, and there is no bidding and no trump. The object of the game is to avoid taking any tricks containing hearts; each heart taken counts as 1 point against that player. The tricks themselves have no value. The first player leads any card he wishes to the first trick. The other players must follow suit if possible. A player who cannot may discard any other suit including hearts. The highest card in suit takes the trick and leads to the next trick. A player may save himself from penalty if he manages to take *all* the hearts, a goal he may determine to pursue after he is saddled with several hearts and feels he can control the game to get the rest.

Scoring is done in various ways, determined in advance. One of the most common calls is for the game to terminate when a player gets a total of 50 points, at which time the player with the lowest score takes the pot.

Many authorities identify games such as POLIGNAC and SLOBBERHANNES as Hearts games, although they are not played for hearts. This book considers them as separate games and lists them separately. The games that follow are deemed to be true Hearts variations. In many respects they offer more spice to the game, but many Hearts gamblers prefer pure Hearts in the same way that many POKER addicts will not be lured away from pure Poker.

A less-than-proficient player at Hearts will be a sure loser in a game with experts since the chief skills involve counting cards, reading distribution, and visualizing possibilities. As in Poker, the only survival method when one finds oneself losing regularly to certain players is to stop competing with them.

HEARTS DUE: Special-dice Game
Originally this game had to be played with special dice lettered H-E-A-R-T-S, but gamblers have adapted it to regular numbered dice so that 1 is the H, 2 the E, and so on. How to play: Six dice are used for this game and after an ante each player throws all six dice and his score is totaled as follows:

H or 1	5
H-E or 1-2	10
H-E-A or 1-2-3	15
H-E-A-R or 1-2-3-4	20
H-E-A-R-T or 1-2-3-4-5	25
H-E-A-R-T-S or 1-2-3-4-5-6	35

If there is a duplication of letters or numbers, only one counts. The game can consist of just one round, but more commonly a score of 100 is needed to win. There is a kicker to this game, however: if a shooter throws three H's or three T's, his entire score up to that point is canceled and he has to start again from zero.

HEARTS—Auction
How to play: In this variation, players, after viewing their hands, bid for the right to call the suit that will replace hearts as the cards to be avoided. The player who offers the biggest contribution to the pot wins that right. This suit is referred to as the "minus suit" (and can be hearts if there are no bids or the highest bidder opts for hearts). Otherwise, play is the same as in Hearts.

Strategy: Some players tend to bid too recklessly. The cautious approach is to bid when one has either no cards or just one low card in a suit and good low distribution in the other suits. In the latter case the player may lead with that one-card suit and then let his opponents fight it out for the rest of the hand. Of course, some defensive bidding may be called for if a player sees he will be extremely vulnerable to a suit another player bids on. In that case he might be forced to bid higher to take the play away from that suit.

Settlement in Auction is very specific. At the end of a hand, each player pays one chip into the pot for each card he has taken in the named suit. If one or more players are "clear"—having no minus cards—the pot is his or is divided equally. If all the players are "painted"—each having some minus cards—or if one player has taken all 13 of them leaving the other players painted—the pot is declared to be a jack. There is no further bidding on a jack pot. Instead there is a new deal and the previous top bidder again names the minus suit and the game is played accordingly until there is a winner.

HEARTS—Black Lady

Black Lady, also called Black Maria, Slippery Anne, and Calamity Jane, is the most popular form of Hearts in the United States. Its popularity notwithstanding, many Hearts purists do not look upon the innovations in Black Lady as an improvement on the basic game. Their objections are also probably linked to the idea of the queen of spades as representing disaster, a carryover from the childhood pastime of Old Maid.

How to play: The queen of spades counts for 13 points as against 1 point for each of the 13 hearts, thus greatly changing the game. According to some versions, the queen must be played on a trick the first time that a player holding it cannot follow suit. Since the winner in many games is the person with the lowest score, this prevents the player holding the queen from trying to dump it on the low scorer in order to wrest that position for himself. This is one of the least defensible aspects of the game.

Another innovation of Black Lady is the pass. Before the start of play, each player examines his cards and then passes three cards face down to the left (in some regions the pass is made to the player on the right). When there are five or more players the pass is frequently limited to two cards. The pass does allow for the exercise of strategy by the astute competitor. Some players panic if they hold high spades and frequently pass them when they should not. A high spade or two, if protected by several low spades, can be a source of strength. These high spades can often control the suit in the play of tricks. Other players mistakenly get rid of all hearts regardless of their pip value—only to find that they are then saddled with high hearts on the pass. Then

when a trick is led in hearts they are forced to eat several points. By and large only high hearts should be passed, and it is much better to play to weaken one's hand in either clubs or diamonds.

Counting for wagering purposes in Black Lady is the same as in straight Hearts.

HEARTS—Cancellation

Cancellation Hearts is a game designed to allow six to ten persons to participate by using two 52-card decks shuffled together. How to play: The cards are dealt out evenly with the leftover cards forming a widow that goes to the taker of the first trick. This is not an unmixed blessing, since a player can get stuck with some hidden hearts.

The rules of Hearts are followed thereafter with one exception. When two identical cards are played on the same trick they cancel each other out and are not involved in taking the trick even if they happen to be high. If all the cards in a trick are canceled, the trick goes to the winner of the following trick. Hearts count for one point each and the queen of spades for 13. Usually Cancellation Hearts is played until a player hits 100, whereupon the lowest score takes the pot.

HEARTS—Domino

Domino Hearts is played quite differently than other versions of the game.

How to Play: Each player gets only six cards with the rest of the pack serving as a stock placed face down in the center. When a player is unable to follow suit, he must draw from the stock, one card at a time, until he can play the suit led. Only when the stock is depleted can the game be played as regular Hearts, with discards out of suit permitted.

Strategy: Previous "reads" of opponents' draws from the stock will determine a good player's strategy in the latter part of the game. Players drop out when they exhaust their cards. If a player takes a trick on his last card, the player to his left leads to the next trick. Only the 13 hearts count as points in Domino Hearts; those remaining in the hand of the last active player count against his score just as those normally taken in tricks.

The game is played until a player hits a minus score of 31, at which point the opponent with the fewest points takes the pot.

HEARTS—Draw or Two-handed

Draw Hearts, sometimes called Two-handed Hearts, is a two-person game with each player dealt 13 cards at the start. The winner of each trick draws the top card from the pack and the loser the next, with the game continuing to normal conclusion after the pack is exhausted.

HEARTS—Heartsette

The Heartsette version of HEARTS is for three to six players.

How to play: A black two is removed from the deck when three or four play, and in all other cases a full deck is used. In a three-person game each player gets 16 cards; four players, 12; five players, ten; six players, eight. The balance of the cards are left face down as a widow. Whoever takes the first trick must take the widow, and all hearts in it will count against his score. However, he also gains the advantage of being the only one to see the widow's contents.

This game is often played in the Black Lady version, in which the queen of spades costs 13 points. In that case it is absolutely vital to try to dodge the first trick.

HEARTS—Hooligan

How to play: Hooligan Hearts is an offshoot of Black Lady Hearts and is played in the same way except that the 7 of clubs costs 7 points to the player taking that trick. On the other hand, the 10 of diamonds is an asset since the player taking it is allowed to deduct 10 points from his score. Additionally, if a player captures all the hearts, the queen of spades, and the 7 of clubs, all his opponents are penalized 33 points, except for the holder of the 10 of diamonds. If the player capturing all the penalties also acquires the 10 of diamonds, his score is dropped by 43 and all opponents are penalized 33.

Sometimes the principle of the 10 of diamonds (or, sometimes, the jack of diamonds) being a plus value of 10 points is incorporated into regular Black Lady.

HEARTS—Joker

In Joker Hearts the joker is inserted into the game in place of the deuce of hearts. The joker ranks in value as a heart between the 10 and jack and thus only can fall to the jack, queen, king, or ace of hearts. However, no points are tallied for the taking of the joker. This game is particularly meaningless to HEARTS purists since it adds a change that does not affect the game's basic strategy.

HEARTS—Omnibus

There is great difficulty in agreeing on just what the exact rules for Omnibus Hearts are, since the game tends to incorporate most of the innovations in various HEARTS games as they are played in different localities. It might be described as a grab-bag version of the game, but there are those experts who say it offers "the greatest opportunity for skill among all the Hearts variants." Cynics might add that the skill involved is in remembering which rules to follow.

The rules of Black Lady apply as do those of Hooligan, except that the 7 of clubs is not a penalty card. Frequently the jack of diamonds or even the 8 of diamonds replaces the ten as the 10-point plus card. Included are the passing of cards, the third-trick rule, the tell-all-hearts rule, and the use of a widow for leftover cards instead of removing cards from the pack to make the hands come out even. Scoring is usually up to 100 instead of 50.

These are the rules of Omnibus Hearts some of the time. To paraphrase Lincoln, you can play Omnibus Hearts with some of the rules all of the time, and all of the rules some of the time—and even all of the rules all of the time. Pure Hearts, anyone?

HEARTS—Pink Lady

Some HEARTS players, not satisfied with the wide-open nature of Black Lady, play a comparatively little-known variation of the game called Pink Lady. In this version—which is at times really an extension of Hooligan Hearts with the 10 of diamonds as a plus 10 and the 7 of clubs as a minus 7—the queen of hearts is raised to a 13-pointer with other hearts continuing as 1 point each.

In many versions of this game the 7-of-clubs factor is dropped, and it must be admitted that a certain strategic subtlety is added. The total minus points are 38 and the plus points are 10. A player caught with the queen of spades can sometimes lessen the damage by saddling an opponent with a 13-point penalty as well. Additionally, a player with a particularly low score can be finessed by his opponents into taking both deadly queens, thus tightening up the competition. Thus, there is a constant shifting of alliance among the players in accordance with how the cards are running.

Because scores can move rapidly the normal game completion at 50 points is often raised to 100. In many respects, Pink Lady is a more intriguing game than Black Lady, which is too reminiscent of the childhood game of Old Maid.

HEARTS—Pip

Pip Hearts resembles pure HEARTS closely, but with one enormous difference that makes the scoring hot and heavy. The penalty for a heart is 1 point plus the pip value of the card. In addition, the picture cards are also ranked: jack, 11; queen, 12; king, 13; ace, 14. The queen of spades is never a penalty card in this game (since the penalties are wild enough already). This is rough tough game of Hearts that should be reserved for only top players because of the potential pitfalls. An amateur will be eaten alive by canny players.

HEARTS—Red Jack

In Red Jack Hearts the jack of diamonds becomes a plus card, and is worth 10 points to its captor. Those points are ultimately subtracted from the player's heart score. Red Jack Hearts therefore are easily incorporated into almost any other version of HEARTS.

HEARTS—Third Trick

Third Trick Hearts is sometimes referred to as a separate game, but it really is no more than a single rule under which no player may lead a heart until the third trick. HEARTS purists thoroughly approve of this departure since it makes for a more disciplined game. The rule is always applied in Omnibus Hearts, or at least it should be.

HEINZ

This is another one of those incredibly wild seven-card stud POKER games with too many wild cards. In this case the wild cards are the 5 and the 7. A smart player might call this game in DEALER'S CHOICE without an ante, or at most a small one, and drop if he doesn't get at least one 5 or 7, preferably as hole cards. It generally makes little sense to hang around in this game with only three of a kind after five cards since at least four of a kind is almost always needed to win. If someone is showing two wild cards, it is reasonable to assume he has four of a kind. If few or no wild cards are showing by the third up-card, it should be obvious to the smart gambler that the others probably have one or more in the hole.

HELP YOUR NEIGHBOR: Old Dice Game

In various forms Help Your Neighbor is one of the oldest dice gambling games, and it is currently enjoying something of a revival as a bar game.

How to play: This three-dicer is for two to six players. If there are six players each is assigned one number. If there are two players the first player gets numbers 1, 2, and 3 and the second 4, 5, and 6. With three players, the numbers are divided 1, 2 and 3, 4, and 5, 6. With four players each gets a number from 1 to 4 and the 5 and 6 are dead. With five players the 6 is dead.

Usually every player puts up ten coins and then each player in turn casts the three dice. Let us say the first throw produces 1-3-4. Players one, three, and four must put a coin each into the kitty. On the next throw 3-3-5 comes up. Player five antes up a coin and player three puts in two coins. At this stage player number three is in the lead since the object of the game is to feed all of one's coins to the pot. The first to do so wins the pot.

The virtue of the game is that the players whose numbers come up less frequently, and thus lag in the competition, can at least take comfort that they are losing less money. Players in contention have to keep feeding the pot, thus paying for the privilege of having a shot at winning all the money.

Wild Bill HICKOK: Welsher

There are many portraits drawn of the legendary Wild Bill Hickok (1837-1876), the great Western "shootist." It is generally agreed that Hickok was a man who made a living as a lawman, a graft-taker, and a POKER player. The first two are true; the third is a patent lie. The fact is Hickok was a lousy card player and most of his biographers admit he lost more money than he won at Poker—when he played it on the square. Generally speaking he always lost since he lacked the skills to make it as a tinhorn. Still, Hickok managed to hold his own. He did so by welshing since very few men were willing to hit the leather with a gunslinger as renowned as Wild Bill.

A story often told about Hickok in his army scouting days had him being regularly cleaned out in Poker games in Sioux City, Iowa. One night in an effort to get even Hickok played a sky's-the-limit two-handed game with a sharp gambler named McDonald. As usual the cards were going against Wild Bill and his rage built up steadily. Then with reckless abandon he started betting heavily on an apparently powerhouse hand. Undaunted, McDonald kept raising back until the pot covered most of the table.

"I've got three jacks," McDonald announced, spreading his cards.

"I have a full house," Wild Bill responded, "three aces and a pair of sixes." He tossed his cards aside, face down.

"Aces full on sixes win," McDonald conceded, turning up the hand. "Hold on!" he cried. "I see only two aces and one six."

Wild Bill produced a six-gun in his right hand and said, "Here's my other six." Then he flashed a Bowie knife in his left hand. "And here's my one spot."

McDonald needed only a brief look at Hickok's hard eyes to declare: "The hand is good. Take the pot."

Throughout his career Wild Bill made consistent use of his get-even technique. Thus it is hardly surprising that after he was shot dead from behind in a Poker game in Deadwood, Dakota Territory in 1876, even the prosecution at the trial of his cold-blooded murderer, Jack McCall, had to admit, "Bill's reputation as a gambler was bad."

As a result the miner's court trying the case set McCall free. But ultimately that trial was ruled illegal, and McCall was retried and hanged.

See also DEAD MAN'S HAND.

HIGH CARD CUT: World's Simplest Card Gamble

There are many stories told about high-stakes gambles being settled by a simple cut of the cards, but the biggest recorded single bet on a high-card cut occurred on September 9, 1928 in New York City. Two legendary gamblers, Arnold Rothstein and a West Coast character, "Nigger" Nate Raymond, wagered $40,000 at the conclusion of a long POKER session on a single cut. Raymond cut first and got a king. Rothstein then cut—and turned up a 10. It should be noted that Rothstein welshed on paying his losses that night, which came to a total of $319,000, including the $40,000 high cut. A few weeks later he was murdered.

Canada Bill Jones, the fabled 19th-century gambling cheat, supposedly died in poverty, according to some accounts, after betting $180,000 on a single cut of the cards—"the only time in his life he had gambled without cheating," according to one version. But the tale, or at least the sum involved, is generally considered to be somewhat inflated.
See also CHASE-THE-ACE.

HIGH DICE: Bar Game

There are several games that are known as High Dice. One version is a five-dice bar game, played for drinks or occasionally an ante.

How to play: Each player in turn casts the dice up to five times. After each roll he must set aside at least one die, the one with the highest score and preferably a 6. He may set aside more than one die if they are high scores. On each subsequent roll he may shoot the remaining dice and must on each cast subtract at least one die. The winner is the player who has assembled the most points, the highest possible being 30, based on five 6's.

Strategy: The error most players fall into is trying slavishly for all 6's, frequently passing up a 5 on a roll if they have also made one or more 6's. For instance, 6-6-5 on the first roll (or upon completion of the second roll) is a powerhouse position since the player has two dice to roll on the next cast and one more on the following. That makes it a 50-50 proposition that he will get one more 6 and the odds greatly favor him for getting one more 6 or a 5 on the two casts. A 6-6-5-6- or 6-6-5-5-anything is generally a winning score. The key is to hold 5's along with any 6's.

Also known as High Dice is a two-dice game called BEAT THE DEALER or Beat the Banker or Two-Dice Klondike. This is a carnival hustle or a fly-by-night or sawdust-casino operation.

HIGH DICE
See BEAT THE DEALER.

HIGH FIVES
See CINCH.

HIGH POINT: Gambling House and Carnival Dice Game

High Point is an excellent money game for the house, which explains why one can often find it at small casinos and carnivals. It can be played with one, two, or three dice and sometimes even more.

How to play: The player first rolls the dice for the house and establishes a point. Let us say it is a three-dice game and the result is 5-3-2, making a house total of 10. Now the player rolls again and must beat the 10. He rolls 4-4-3, or 11. He wins. However, if he rolls 4-3-3, his total is 10 and he loses. The house wins if the player ties or scores less than the house. To win the player must be high.

For High Point to be a dead-even game all that would be necessary would be to make all ties a wash, calling for a new roll. The house wins on ties gives it an enormous edge; in a one-die game the edge is about 17 percent. Because the take is so blatantly high, most High Point games use two or three dice. With two dice the house advantage is around 11 percent and with three dice 9 percent. When more than three dice are used the house edge drops considerably, and thus it is very difficult to find such games.

HIGH POINT CRAPS: High Point Variation

High Point Craps is a logical extension of HIGH POINT, which cuts down the huge house advantage but still produces an edge of about 2.35 percent for the house.

How to play: Under the general rules, first rolls totaling 2 or 3 do not count. Thus the numbers that apply are any number from 4 to 12. If the player throws 11 or 12, he wins even money immediately. Any other number becomes the shooter's point. He now rolls again and must beat his point. If, for example, his point is 7, he wins on 8 or more. However, if he rolls a 7 or lower, he loses. Like other newer games of simplified CRAPS, High Point Craps appeals to amateur gamblers who prefer a more simple dice game.
See also CRAPS, SIMPLIFIED.

HIGH ROLLER: Big-time Gambler

You will recognize them at the gaming tables, and away from them as well. He—or she—is the person with the biggest pile of chips (at least for a while) in front of him. He makes enormous bets and often asks that the betting limits be removed. Usually his wish is granted. And away from the tables none of his wishes are refused. The saying is that "if the doorman bows so low he scrapes his nose, that's a *real* high roller."

Casinos break their back for high rollers, or "VIP's" as they prefer calling them. They pick up the tabs for their suites. Their gourmet meal checks are canceled, and if they want to show off with a half dozen guests at their table—no problem.

Average casino customers stand in awe of such black-chip bettors. Obviously, they feel, a high roller who bets so big must know what he is doing, must be an astute gambler. Some players even follow a high roller's betting system, riding along with him. It sometimes works, too. Sometimes a high roller will walk away from the table $50,000 or $100,000 ahead. This does not dampen the casino's affection for him. In fact, the casino help will, if anything, do even more for him. Even if he ends a three-day betting spree with a pile of the casino's money, they adore him. They limo him to the airport (if he didn't come on his own wheels). And when the following week or month he wants to come back, they'll pick him up at his home, limo him to a private jet and fly him in for more royal treatment. The casino knows what it's doing. *This* time Mr. High Roller won't be a big winner. The odds are he'll take a bath and the casino will reclaim his previous winnings plus a lot more.

High rollers are the casino world's version of Wall Street's greater fool theory. Casinos love high rollers not only because they will eventually get back their money from those who have had a lucky run but because for every one who does win there are two other high rollers who are losing more than he is winning.

There was a time a few years ago when a Canadian named Brian Molony was Caesars Atlantic City's favorite high roller. They jetted him in from Toronto whenever he had the gambling itch. The transportation was free as were the luxury accommodations, the gourmet meals and drinks. Why it reached the point that the casino's big brass felt so kindly toward him that they presented him with an $8,500 Rolex. In less than two years Caesars absorbed a total tab of over $60,000 on Molony for various favors extended. The Caesars executives were clearly swell fellows. However, there is some possibility that the fact that Molony dropped over $7 million at the gambling tables had something to do with their attitude. Molony wanted the maximum lifted at BACCARAT? No problem, and he subsequently bet as high as $75,000 a hand. There was that classic two-day period when Molony dropped $2 million. There wasn't anything the boys at Caesars wouldn't do for him on that trip—that is, anything but give back his money.

It would perhaps have been judicious for Caesars to have done so, for the casino was to come under risk of losing its license. The New Jersey Casino Control Commission was to determine that the casino had been less than energetic in ascertaining the source of their windfall. They could and should have learned by the simplest of credit checks that Molony worked for the Canadian Imperial Bank of Commerce. The more Molony lost to Caesars the more he tapped the till up in Toronto. It came to light that Molony had embezzled some $10.2 million from his employer. The joke along the Atlantic City boardwalk was the poor Caesars wanted to know where the remaining $3.2 million had gone.

Eventually Molony got ten years in prison and in late 1985 Caesars was penalized by being hit with a forced 24-hour closing. It added up to the largest fine ever imposed on a casino, but there were those who regarded it as a slap on the wrist. All things considered, Caesars was believed to have been mightily relieved.

The casinos practically kiss the ground before VIP's because they represent not human beings but dollar signs. Many high rollers are people who have so much money they can afford to gamble mindlessly without fear of the consequences—that is, if one ignores those who lose their wealth, their savings, their homes, sometimes their very lives to the casinos. To be sure there are the occasional high rollers who are expert gamblers, which generally means that they will lose their money somewhat slower.

There is simply no reason for other casino players to be impressed with a high roller or to replicate his action. In *Darwin Ortiz on Casino Gambling*, the author, one of the keener and more honest observers of the gambling world today, comments: "What defines a high roller is the fact that he loses much more money than the average player. That hardly makes him an ideal role model."

HIGH-CARD POOL
See RED DOG.

HIGH-LOW
See POKER.

HIGH-LOW POKER—Five-card Stud
Although not nearly as popular as High-Low POKER in the seven-card version, High-Low Five-card Stud has built up a devoted following in recent years. There is good reason for this. Few players drop early in the five-card version because there is a good chance that a low hand up to the 9 or 10 or even a face card win low. Then too a low-looking hand that is busted by the late appearance of a pair can be turned into a solid high hand.

A special wrinkle in the rules permits a player to go both high and low with the same five cards (in the seven-card version players have the luxury of using different sets of five toward both high and low hands). Under this rule a straight or flush may be called for high or low or both. This can produce some frantic betting, and if a player holding a straight or flush becomes fearful of a possible full house, he can play it safer and declare only for low. What's more, the appearance of a four-card straight or flush on the upside gives that player the perfect chance to bluff.

Overall, the size of pots in this game tend to be much larger than one might ordinarily expect.

HIGH-SPADE SPLIT: Poker Variation with Many Versions

High-Spade Split is not so much a separate game of POKER as it is an adaptation to a great many other Poker games. With this adaptation, the person with the highest hand splits the pot with the player with the highest spade. Draw Poker is probably the best game for it, since the high spade will remain hidden and it is uncertain what kind of strength a bidder has. It is also usually played with those versions of Stud, such as Mexican or NEW GUINEA STUD, in which a player may succeed in keeping his high spade turned down.

High-spade is a good game for the astute player to call because some poor players will get sucked into staying with a weak high spade, such as a queen. Even in a six-player game of Draw it is conceivable that virtually all the cards will be taken, making it highly likely that the king or ace will be needed for high spade. A jack of spades might win if there are several dropouts, but it should never be bet with aggressiveness or even confidence.

HIJACKINGS: Gambling-game Stickups

It is one of the perils of the profession, stickups at big-money gambling games. Big-time gamblers are frequently tailed by hijackers, hoping to catch them at a big-money game. Big gamblers are always pointed out in awe wherever they go, and hijackers may look to hit them before, during, or after a game.

As fabled gambler Amarillo Slim puts it: "We get held up every once in a while. But that's just one of the hazards of this business because if we get hijacked, we don't say anything about it to the law. We're not looking to run and tell it." Slim considers himself lucky, having been held up only three times over a ten-year period.

Gamblers have developed many safeguards, few of which they will reveal. Frequently they will make reservations at one hotel and show up at another where a game is scheduled. Often they will change cabs going to a game. It is also becoming common not to play with cash at high-stake games—unless a player is regarded as a possible welsher. In that case it's cash on the barrelhead and hijackers be damned.

HOCA
See ROULETTE PREDECESSORS.

HOCKEY GAMBLING

There is almost as much betting on hockey as there is on college and professional basketball, although this observation must be tempered by recognizing that many bookmakers refuse to take much action on college basketball because of the "fix factor."

Hockey is regarded as "clean" as far as fixed games go, and betting lines on professional hockey emanate from Cincinnati, Minneapolis, Las Vegas, and Montreal. Montreal may well be the most important since so many of the fans and players come from Canada. Some years ago an official estimate was that Canadians wager some $15 million on games in the National Hockey League. That figure is undoubtedly larger now.

Hockey betting is usually based on point spreads, with a favorite rated as being one or more goals better than an underdog. For instance, team A may be established as being a favorite by 1½ goals. This means team A must beat team B by two goals for backers of team A to win their bets. Conversely, if team B wins or loses by only 1 goal, its backers collect their bets. In addition, they may also lay odds of 6 to 5 or 11 to 10, that is, put up the higher sum to win the smaller amount. Bookmakers tend to quote 6 to 5 odds if the bettor is only a casual client or the bookie's action on the sport or game is limited. To get 11 to 10 a bettor is probably a regular customer. The difference in the two sets of odds is not insignificant. Six to 5 gives the bookmaker a hefty edge of 8.33 percent while 11 to 10 cuts his advantage down to 4.54 percent. But even this smaller edge is rough on the bettor, who obviously must do much better than the odds he is bucking. If he breaks even on the games, he is an overall loser, and being right 55 or 60 percent of the time with goals spotted is something few experts can do. As a result most hockey betting is done by fans—big and small bettors—and not by true professionals.

HOGGENHEIMER
See ENGLISH ROULETTE.

HOLD 'EM: Spit Variation of Poker

Hold 'Em, a Spit variation of POKER, is a great betting game, popular especially in illegal Poker clubs in the Southwest. It is also extremely popular under slightly different rules in Las Vegas and is used in the annual Las Vegas World Series Hold 'Em tournament. Hold 'Em is a tough game and is won consistently only by the best players.

How to play: Betting starts as soon as each player

is dealt two down-cards. There can be a large number of players in Hold 'Em, but in Vegas play there are never more than 11 and tournaments are limited to nine. The best games involve two to nine players.

After an ante and the betting on the first two cards, three cards are faced up as common cards for all players. At this point all players have a five-card Poker hand, consisting of the three common cards and the two cards they hold. There is now a round of betting followed by the facing of another common card. There is further betting and then a final upcard is dealt and showdown betting follows. Surviving players make their best Poker hands using three of the upcards and the two cards in their hand.

Wild cards are not used in this game and aren't necessary. There is action enough because Hold 'Em is pretty much of a bluffing and heavy betting game. In big-money games it often happens that a nothing hand is able to steal the pot with some daring betting that drives out the other players. However, the basic strategy is to refrain from betting any large amounts on two poorly matched hole cards of low rank. It is prudent to drop out with weak openers. If one stays and the first three upcards fail to produce a good hand, it is compounding the folly to stay any longer. For an excellent discussion of strategy for Hold 'Em, see *Scarne's Guide to Modern Poker* by John Scarne and *Winning Poker Strategy* by Edwin Silberstang.

HOLDOUT TABLE: Gaffed Gambling Furniture

Prices today: $2,000 and up, way up. It's for a cheater's "holdout table" and it would be shocking to know how many (and which) people own such furniture. The average person who wants to cheat at cards lacks the ability to palm cards or use a holdout machine. So he may decide to try a holdout table that does the "palming" for him. Gamblers who buy these tables tend to be affluent and use them in high-powered "friendly" games.

With this cheater's table it is possible to secrete a wanted card in a slit that can be opened by a mechanism that can be operated by pressing one's knee on the bottom surface of the tabletop. Even fancier tables are available to gamblers who can pay the freight. Some tables have a sliding track that allows one cheat to secrete a card in the table and transfer it to his partner on the other side. Some eight-position Poker tables have a hidden lazy-susan arrangement that allows a card or cards to be transferred to any other position when properly triggered.

Technically it is illegal to transport such gambling equipment across state lines, but specialists handle these matters for "safe" customers (frequently solicited among the high rollers at casinos). They will install the table and even remain in a client's home

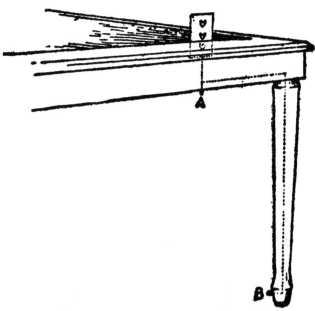

A 19th-century version of a holdout table shows a slit where a card can be hidden and then brought up to replace another in the cheater's hand. The unwanted card is slipped into the slit for concealment, the operation controlled by a foot lever. The 1888 price for a table of this sort was $150. They cost 10 times and more today.

for a few days to school them in the subtleties of its operation. A customer can proudly show off his new showpiece Poker table to unsuspecting friends—and then proceed to make them pay for its cost.

HOLDOUTS: Card-switching Machines

In the last few decades card cheaters have come to rely less and less on holdout machines, in part because gamblers have become more sophisticated about such scams. Casino personnel and professional gamblers have become more alert to spotting these devices, so that wearing one has become a dangerous practice.

However, there are still devotees of the holdout machine in its many varieties, the most common of which is an arm-pressure sleeve holdout that can slide a card back and forth under the cheat's shirt at the wrist. The contraption slides forward whenever the operator presses his arm against the side of his body. When the arm pressure is stopped, the contraption slides back under the shirt cuff. All a cheat has to do is bring the slide forward when he wants to secrete a card that will come in handy later and then retrieve it as needed.

Other holdouts include a vest model that is strapped to the chest under a vest or jacket, and since many gamblers play their cards "close to the vest," a transfer can be executed without suspicion. A more de-

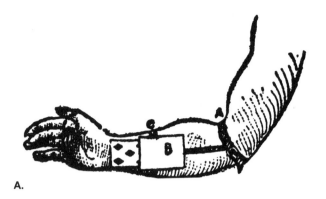

A.

B.

A Sleeve Hold Out machine (A) as exhibited in a 19th-century catalog for card cheats. A similiar vintage woodcut shows gamblers catching a holdout culprit in action (B).

ceptive holdout actually operates through a cheat's waistband and is concealed in the crotch.

It is not unusual for gamblers to use a "holdout handshake," pumping another player's hand vigorously while heartily gripping his forearm with their other hand. This allows for a thorough check for an arm holdout. Mafia hoods have the additional advantage of embracing their compatriots as a greeting and thus can check them out for chest devices. Finally, mob boys like to have women around their big games as well, and if they become suspicious of a big winner, have the female surreptitiously "cop a feel for a holdout" south of the belt line.

HOLLAND, Gambling in

Holland, like its neighbors, offers the usual Lotto and sports LOTTERIES, and a number of casinos, some more populated by natives than tourists. One reason is that tourists to the Netherlands are frequently on tours on a tight budget, which doesn't make them ideal casino clients. The most attractive of the nation's casinos is in Scheveningen in the Kurhaus, a gigantic old monument. The Kurhaus is nationally protected, but the casino players are not.

HOLLYWOOD EIGHTS: Variation of Eights

Hollywood Eights is a two-handed variation on the excellent gambling game of EIGHTS. The count in Hollywood Eights varies from the standard version and is scored as in Gin Rummy. Each 8 is worth 20; ace, 15; pictures and 10, 10; and all others bear their pip value. The winner is the first to accumulate 100 points.

Scoring is set up for three simultaneous games. The player who wins the first hand gets the score in game 1. The second hand won is scored in both games 1 and 2. The third and all subsequent hands are scored in all three games.

HONEYMOON BRIDGE: Game for Two

Honeymoon Bridge is a game for two using the regular 52-card BRIDGE deck.

How to play: Thirteen cards are dealt to each player and the nondealer leads to the first trick with the dealer following suit if he can, as in a no-trump situation in Bridge. The winner of each trick draws the top card from the remaining stock and his opponent takes the next one. The winner then leads to the next trick, and the procedure continues until the stock is exhausted.

The first 13 tricks play no role in the scoring, and once each player has his final 13 cards the two players bid as in bridge, with the dealer bidding first. Bidding continues until one player passes a bid, double, or redouble. The nonbidder leads to the first trick and the hand is played out and scored as in Contract Bridge.

HONG KONG, Gambling in

Hong Kong has no legal gambling aside from horse racing, which has achieved a sort of exalted station. The population is predominantly Chinese, and there is considerable illegal hidden and not so hidden gambling. FAN TAN parlors abound and one always hears "the twittering of the sparrows"—the sounds of shuffling tiles resounding from the back streets.

For casino gambling, residents and tourists make their way to the Portuguese island of Macao, about 40 miles across the Pearl River Estuary. The trip can be made in a luxury ferry or much faster by hydrofoil if one is impatient for action. Hong Kong funnels well over a million gamblers a year to Macao.

HOOK GAME: Casino "Rake" in Poker Games

A strong case can be made for never playing POKER at a parlor or casino for a number of reasons, but if one does, every effort should be made to avoid a "hook game." In a hook game, the casino rakes in a certain percentage of every pot, to make up for its expenses in running the game. Is the rake justified? Think about it—the casino is actually making itself *a winner in every hand*. Hooks vary anywhere from 5 to 15 percent, which at either end is pretty outrageous. It is the kind of handicap that is almost impossible to overcome. While most Vegas casinos run hook games most of the time, there are occasions when the play is based on an hourly house charge with no cutting of the pot. Figure out how much it will cost you to play for a few hours and on that basis estimate if the charge makes any sense. Strictly speaking, the only way to "beat" a hook game is never to win a pot.

HORSE-RACE BETTING

It is called the "Sport of Kings." Horse racing is at least 6,000 years old and there is no way of knowing precisely when man started betting on the outcome. Certainly by 1500 B.C. chariot racing was a way of life among the Assyrians; tablet inscriptions indicate that the racing stables of the Assyrian kings were by then already very old and elaborate. By 1000 B.C. selective breeding was under way to produce top racers, and the first mounted race on which we have written information occurred in Greece during the 33rd Olympiad around 624 B.C.

Organized racing at weekly set dates goes back to 12th-century England during the reign of Henry II. Later King John kept numerous "running horses" in the royal stables, but racing owes the most to Charles II, the first of the Restoration monarchs, who promoted the sport to such an extent that he is known as "the father of the British turf." After the grim years of Puritan rule under the Cromwells, the English were eager for some public gaiety and horse racing became a popular diversion once again. Oliver Cromwell too enjoyed horse racing, but in private.

Today thoroughbred flat racing is the top-drawing betting sport in America, despite growing competition from trotters, dog races, and jai alai. Attendance figures however are fairly meaningless since many bettors are regulars, never missing a day at the track. Still somewhere between 20 and 40 million persons bet on the horses every year. But horse racing does not get the lion's share of professional gamblers' bets or supply bookmakers and the Las Vegas sports books with most of their business. Both football and baseball get much bigger action. Many professional gamblers go light on the horses because they have difficulty picking winners. They find other sports, especially football and baseball, easier to dope out, and they will plunge more heavily on election bets than they would on the Belmont Stakes. Elections are viewed as easy bets while the horses represent too many imponderables. Even such an important gambling guru as oddsmaker Jimmy "the Greek" Snyder, who loves the track, considers it more a recreational activity than a money-making source. He defines the racetrack as a place "where windows clean you."

Naturally, horse racing is not free of cheating situations, and scandals concerning fixed races and bribed jockeys turn up fairly regularly. Some bookmakers either flatly refuse or severely limit the bets they will accept from certain tracks. Louisiana tracks have from time to time been suspect and in 1987 *Playboy* called it the worst state for horse racing in the country, adding, "The champion jockey in Louisiana is the one who spends the fewest days a year testifying before grand juries in race-fixing cases."

However, the best indication that the sport is relatively clean is attested to by the fact that bookmakers and the Las Vegas casinos accept racing action. If they were being fleeced in betting coups, they would drop racetrack betting in short order.

Even gamblers who lose regularly are addicted to horse racing, since it is a sport in which one matches wits with other humans. Unlike casino games such as CRAPS, ROULETTE, and even BLACKJACK, a bettor is not betting against the house but other players, and he is filled with an enormous sense of satisfaction when he wins a race he has handicapped. Handicapping horses is not easy. Studies of the importance of weight, previous form, class, speed ratings, track variants, and post position only scratch the surface, as do mastering the factors that allow horses that quit in six-furlong races (those of ¾ mile) to win at seven furlongs or a mile, or of quitting milers to win at a mile and an eighth.

There is a wealth of literature on betting the horses, some crammed with information, others silly and misleading. A novice can find useful introductions to the fundamentals in such books as *Ainslie's Complete Guide to Thoroughbred Racing* by Tom Ainslie and *Scarne's New Complete Guide to Gambling* by John Scarne. Perhaps equally enlightening would be the writings of such humorists as H. Allen Smith, dealing with the frustrations of unworkable betting systems.

There are thousands of "advisers" and touts at the tracks ready to offer you a winner, much in the style of Chico Marx selling Groucho a surefire system in *A Day at the Races*. (In real life Chico was always a sucker for a good tout.) A tout will circulate through a crowd and pass out as many as a half-dozen sure winners on the next race and then return to the bettors to whom he cited the actual winner, looking for a payoff.

One of the greatest swindles in the game are the "adviser services" that claim to have inside information from the stables and know about a horse that can't lose. They are so sure that they offer the gullible the horse's name for "free." All they ask is that the client put down a small wager of $10 for them and send in the profits if the horse wins. Of course, they supply every horse in a six-horse field to different victims, and invariably those winners are ripe for a second offering, but this time for a real killing at $100. (Horseplayers are the most honest people in the world. Give them a winner and the great majority will pay up—and of course want more.) One-sixth of these will win on the second scam and be set up for a $500 bet. Even the losers can be resurrected with a phony story about the horse not feeling well and they are offered the next selection really free. The one-sixth of these winners are now ripe for the regular betting scam as well.

The cruel fact is that no real tout would ever share an absolute sure thing with anyone since heavy betting on a selection will drive the payoff price down. More likely, when what appears to be a truly hot horse comes along, the touts will circulate tips on *other* horses as certain winners, which will drive up the odds on the animal they really like.

Does anyone ever really beat the races? There is a much-quoted folk myth that says, "You can't beat the races but you can beat a race." Sadly, whether one bets nine races a day or one a day over nine days, the odds remain the same, with all the imponderables of a race reappearing daily. Admittedly, though, certain systems do work *some* of the time and efforts to isolate these factors seem to reward certain players. The late sportswriter Joe Williams once estimated that 95 percent of all racegoers are steady losers and that the remaining 5 percent are steady winners. Others put the figure of successful players lower, at around 2 percent.

Of course it must be understood what a "successful" horseplayer is. He is a person who sometimes wins enormous amounts and sometimes loses just as heavily. Frequently he is totally wiped out, but this does not faze him. He will come back sooner or later for a big killing and he will be riding high for a time. This sort of persistence—or disdain for money—is something with which the average person cannot cope.

Off-track betting in New York has created a whole new crop of horseplayers. When off-track betting started it was predicted that the system would kill racetrack attendance. It undoubtedly hurt attendance to some extent, but it also created a partnership that is inseparable. New York's OTB clearly draws in a lot of bettors who never have the inclination or available time to go to a racetrack. In an odd way OTB figures demonstrate that there is such a breed as the successful horseplayer.

At the average OTB office, bettors lose 40 percent of the money they bet. This is a much higher figure than at the track, but serves to demonstrate the high percentage of novice bettors patronizing OTB. However, in some offices the losing percentage is much lower. For instance, at the Forest Hills branch in Queens—an area where a great many track figures, jockeys, owners, agents, trainers, etc. live—the loss ratio is only 20 percent. This indicates that the bettors in Forest Hills are "hot ones." It doesn't necessarily mean there are fewer unsophisticated bettors there than at any other OTB office, but that the "smart money" bet cuts down the average. Obviously there are some OTB clients at Forest Hills capable of winning consistently.

At least, that represents hope, and hope springs eternal in the horseplayer's breast.

HOT SEAT GAME: Gambling Scam

Frequently, card mobs will set up a "hot seat game," one in which there is only one honest player—the victim. This usually takes place in private games in casino hotels or even on plane junkets. Usually there are rotating players, with some dropping out and others entering the game at various stages.

Early on the pigeon may be allowed to win small amounts of money, but this is quickly taken back in the next game. All this is done to whet his appetite, to make him feel he must really hit it big when the cards are right so that he can weather losing spells. Eventually of course the victim is dealt an "unbeatable" hand and the betting gets hot and heavy. Soon everything the pigeon has is in the pot and he wants to bet more. The boys magnanimously allow him to write a check. (After all, they say, if he's on a gambling junket, the casino has already checked out his credit so they are sure the check is good.)

Naturally the pigeon sadly discovers that his hand is not quite good enough. He is crestfallen and may be out many thousands of dollars. Now what is often an integral part of the hot seat game is acted out. It is the "tear-up." The winner of the pot is very sympathetic and says the game had really gotten out of hand, that they hadn't meant to go in for such heavy stakes. "Look," he says, "let's forget all about the check. I'll take the pot and call it square."

The pigeon is much impressed by this and watches gratefully as the winner folds up his check and rips it into small pieces. The pieces are dropped into an ashtray and another player sets them on fire. The gambling debt is squared. The act serves the card mob well, since the victim is so grateful for having the check canceled that he is almost unconcerned about his heavy money losses. The card mob has also protected itself by "cooling off" the victim so that he doesn't get the idea he has been cheated and make a beef to hotel security.

Of course, within a few hours a member of the mob is on a plane bound for the victim's hometown to cash the supposedly destroyed check. Often the cheats have learned in advance the color of the victim's checks, and if not the winner, a sleight-of-hand expert, has several checks in different colors in his pockets. The confederate simply draws out the right one, switches it as he folds up the real check, which ends up in his pocket.

When a card mob works this scam they simply keep the game going until 9 o'clock in the morning, and before the game breaks up, the check has already been cashed.

Edmond HOYLE: Authority on Card Games

He is still recognized as the ultimate authority on cards of all time. The phrase "according to Hoyle" has become part of our language. POKER rules in any number of books are those set "according to Hoyle." Never mind that Hoyle never witnessed a game of Poker, no matter how many "Hoyle" books analyze the game or are devoted completely to the subject. Much the same is true of other "Hoyle" books that appear in endless editions. They too contain an enormous number of games whose rules would perplex the immortal Hoyle. No matter; Edmond Hoyle (1671 or 1672-1769) is today to gambling what Noah Webster is to dictionaries.

Hoyle was a barrister in his early years, but the facts of his life are quite sketchy until he published *A Short Treatise on the Game of Whist* in 1742, when he was about 70 years old. It is known that the old gentleman had been earning a good living for some time as an instructor in gaming, showing pupils how to win at various gambling games. Indeed, it appears that Hoyle was a bit of a hustler himself and frequently took less proficient gamblers at his favorite haunt, the Crown Coffee House in London's Bedford Row. In 1751 Hoyle published *A Short Treatise on the Game of Brag.* Actually, he was almost baited into doing so by certain younger gamblers at the Crown who insisted the old master was not up to a game that involved not only good cards and finesse but the equally important art of bluffing. Hoyle, it is said,

not only demonstrated his knowledge of BRAG but cleaned up against his detractors.

Hoyle published only two other treatises on card games, one on Quadrille and the other on PIQUET. He also wrote guides to BACKGAMMON in 1743 (his codification of the rules and strategy of the game is still largely in vogue) and Chess in 1761. In all some 13 editions of his treatise on Whist appeared before the old master died at the age of 97. In addition, there were many pirated editions of his work so that both Hoyle and his publisher took to autographing all copies they put out to attest to their genuineness. The most important aspect of Hoyle's popularity was that the British public, and eventually those in most other countries as well, refused to accept any guides that were not "Hoyles."

As a result Hoyle has become memoralized in such works as *The New Complete Hoyle* (1956) and *According to Hoyle* (1965), edited by Frey. Even Ely Culbertson, certainly a far greater contemporary expert than Hoyle, had to publish his book of games as *Culbertson's Hoyle.* And as the 20th century wears down, the phrase "according to Hoyle" has been joined by the phrase "according to Scarne." In 1974 the *London Times* devoted a long tribute to American gambling expert John Scarne, which said in part: "Edmond Hoyle passed away in 1769. He left us with a rich legacy of games and game rules. I think he would have been proud to see his mantle passed to John Scarne. According to Hoyle—not anymore. Now it is according to Scarne."

Certainly more card games are now played following Scarne's rules, but Hoyle remains immortal. In fact surveys and polls taken over the years show that many people believe Hoyle is a living person, residing in Miami or California or some other sunny clime and still issuing edicts. Publishers are not immune to this anachronistic thinking. When a writer recently attacked one of "Hoyle's laws," the publisher insisted on toning down the diatribe. He said he did not want to antagonize the illustrious old man and push him into a lawsuit.

Howard HUGHES: Las Vegas's Biggest Sucker

It was in the mid-1960's that eccentric billionaire Howard Hughes (1905-1976) blew into Law Vegas and into the hearts of so many people—the locals, the mobsters, and the betting public. Hughes started buying up hotel casinos, which sent property values soaring, and the gambling public so trusted him that they actually started to trust Las Vegas casinos. Gambling and tourist income started growing at 25 percent a year, double what it had been previously. Everybody loved Howard because they were making a buck—and the mobsters loved him because they were unloading their holdings at jacked-up prices, and they were still doing right well.

It all started because Hughes was a big gambler, and not exactly a good one. One night he took an awful bath at Moe Dalitz's Desert Inn, where he had rented an entire floor. Coming on in typical Howard Hughes style when his ego took a beating, the billionaire offered to buy the place for $30 million—cold cash, up front immediately. The owners of the Desert Inn sold out on the spot.

Actually, it was a great deal for the mob at the moment; the feds were all around them looking for evidence on skimming operations. To some it looked like the day of the skim was over, and Hughes seemed to provide a perfect escape hatch. In almost no time Hughes was on a mad casino-buying spree, both in Vegas and Reno—the New Frontier, the Silver Slipper, the Landmark, the Sands, the Castaways. Within a few years his holdings were providing the state of Nevada with 17 percent of its gambling tax revenues.

Exactly what brought on Hughes's Las Vegas fever isn't known. In fact, it could have been several things. He may have simply wanted to get back into a form of show biz. He may have thought he had such a great business sense that he could make the casinos even more profitable. He may also have liked the thought of having a state all his own. There was also the dollars-and-cents incentive that his new holdings served as a dodge to the undistributed profits tax. It was a matter of either spending the money or giving it to the government. By dealing with the underworld he was getting something tangible in return.

Hughes's investment in Vegas quickly turned sour. In part he did some unwise things, from the business viewpoint. He ordered "the girls" chased. Taking the hookers out of Vegas is like taking the novocaine out of dentistry. As the Hughes hotels turned into what Jimmy the Greek Snyder, a one-time public relations consultant for Hughes, called "Mom and Pop" joints, business started to slide. High rollers want fast action at the gaming tables and still more fast action as soon as they step away. Hughes's preoccupation with getting rid of the party girls was perhaps more astonishing coming from a man who in his heyday bragged of having deflowered no fewer than 200 virgins in Hollywood.

But if Hughes's anti-sin crusade hurt, it was nothing compared to some of his business decisions. He gullibly kept many mob employees in their casino posts, which probably explained why a large undercover seller in the Desert Inn, Johnny Roselli, bragged to later informer Jimmy Fratianno: "Right now we've got the D.I. in good hands."

Hughes was under the illusion that he could in-

crease the legally admitted profit of casinos on investment to 20 percent, but he never did better than 6 percent. By 1970, four years after he'd started, Hughes was millions in the red. The mob guys had eaten him alive.

Finally Hughes bowed out of Vegas and slowly the mob's influence returned, despite public claims that they had gone away for good. The mob's representative in Vegas in the 1970's and 1980's was Tony Spilotro until he was pink-slipped in 1986. His bludgeoned body and that of his younger brother Michael were found in an Indiana cornfield.

It is impossible to measure mob influence in Vegas in the post-Hughes era because some of the casino owners are probably fronts.

HUNDRED AND ONE RUMMY: Gamblers' Favorite Knock Rummy Variation

Hundred and One Rummy is a KNOCK RUMMY variation that is very popular with professional gamblers.

How to play: The game follows most of the rules of Knock Rummy, but is run like a tournament with players falling out of contention if their point score hits 101. The competition gets complicated as the contenders' point total rises. When a player has 92, he may only knock when his deadwood count is 8 or less. If a player has 100, he may not knock at all. His only option to win the hand is to "go Rummy," or meld all his cards. If in any hand a player has a count over the allowable limit, he is automatically out of the game and the other players' scores for the hand simply don't count.

The game is played for a pot with an ante of one chip of agreed-upon value. If a player is eliminated from the game, he may buy his way back in by making a new ante to the pot. At this point he is given the highest score outstanding among the active players and the game continues. Let us say our loser manages to go out again. He may buy in yet again, but this time he must pay a double ante. If he goes out a third time, he can buy in again by doubling his previous ante. He can either keep doing this or go to a psychiatrist, which will probably prove cheaper. A player should reenter a game only if he feels he is superior to his foes and that he was only eliminated because of a horrendous run of cards.

HUNGARY, Gambling in

The gambling instinct has always been strong in Hungary, from pre-Communist days to the present. The present government has allowed more gambling than probably any other Iron Curtain nation and football (soccer) pools called Toto and a lottery called Lotto have run since 1947 and 1957, respectively. As is true in most Red countries, the most popular prizes offered are houses, apartments, and cars. There are also several types of LOTTERIES that are worked off deposit accounts—a way of fostering savings.

Individuals are not permitted to run gambling enterprises and in all other forms of authorized lotteries, deemed to be in the public interest, no money prizes are offered. However, some cafes are permitted to run card games in which the house must enforce betting limits so that big losses do not occur.

Since 1980 Casino Austria AG, whose parent company runs all the Austrian casinos, has guided the Hungarians in establishing several casinos in order to lure in capitalist tourist money. There is the noted Budapest Casino in the Hilton Hotel and several casinos in spa areas.

HURRICANE

Under standard American rules the game of Hurricane (in Europe the game is called American Two-card Poker) is a form of two-card Stud.

How to play: Each player gets two cards as in TWO-CARD POKER or Frustration, but in this version one card is dealt up and one down. The game is most often played deuces wild and high-low, often leading to a crossfire of raising and re-raising, especially since the player holding high frequently knows he's betting a sure thing.

Strategy: An expert gambler can win a lot of money at this game if his opponents include players who like "to take a chance" on their hands. The game is also known as Gruesome Two-Some, which is fitting for those players who are consistent losers at it.

I

I DOUBT IT: Children's and Adults' Card Game

I Doubt It is a game that has been described by "Hoyle" guides as being for children from "nine to ninety." It can be a rapid-play game for children, but it has also made it in the adult gambling world because it requires some of the main skills needed for POKER, that is, having card sense and knowing when to bluff.

How to play: The game is best suited to three, four, or five players, but with more players a double deck may be used. The entire deck is dealt out and the player to the left of the dealer (eldest hand) starts by laying down one to four cards that he announces to be one to four aces. The object of the game is to get rid of all cards first and collect one chip for every card each opponent is still holding.

Thus the first player must announce at least one ace and lay down at least one card. This card may be an ace or the player may be bluffing. If any of the other players believe he is lying he or she announces, "I doubt it." If more than one player makes the challenge, the first player in sequence is regarded as the challenger. If a challenge is made, the card(s) are turned over. If the player was bluffing, he must take back his card or cards and, after the first play, any previous cards that were discarded without challenge. If, however, the leader has told the truth, the doubter must take the entire discard pile. Play then reverts to the next player, who must discard deuces. Play continues on in this progressive fashion (treys, 4's, 5's, etc.) with players announcing one to four of the required rank on their turn.

Strategy: One should get rid of cards that he will not be required to play, but hold cards needed on his next few rounds. Therefore in a three-man game, the player laying down aces knows he will also have to discard 4's, 7's, 10's, etc., and it would be foolish

for him to bluff such cards away. Early on, if a player has a poor hand he might opt be a doubter frequently and hope that he is wrong so that he can get control of the discard pile to better control the game and gauge other players' claims.

Once a sequence has been completed up to the kings, the next sequence reverts back to ace, deuce, and so on. Bluffing remains a key to the game, but a good player with good card sense can figure out when other players are vulnerable and are forced to bluff and he can stick whomever he wishes with the pile whenever he wishes.

When adults play this game they often just call it "Doubt," but it is not advisable to play it for big stakes if one is not very familiar with it. Strategies have to be absorbed and then it will be child's play to trim less knowledgeable opponents.

IDIOT'S DELIGHT: Card-tossing Game

Idiot's Delight is undoubtedly one of the oldest card games, one involving no strategy, no thinking—but considerable skill. It is the equivalent of tossing pennies, but has been a high-stakes gamble countless times. The game involves tossing cards into a receptacle of some kind (in the Old West, a trusty ten-gallon hat) from an agreed-upon distance, usually five feet or more. Competitors generally toss half a deck each, red or black cards. When there are four competitors, each will take a separate suit of 13 cards. Payoffs are made on the basis of whoever lands the most cards.

There were and still are Idiot's Delight hustlers, operating very much like pool hustlers. They practice at it so much that they generally can sink at least 95 out of 100 cards. In the days of the small dishonest circuses that traveled small-town America it was common for the outfit to have a card-tossing scam artist who would skin the rubes in betting contests, luring them in with some inept efforts and then suddenly shifting to near perfection.

ILLINOIS—Legalized Lotteries

Illinois' lottery revenues go into the state's general fund, but particularly benefit the elderly in the form of tax relief. They also go toward elementary, secondary, and higher education; to local governments in revenue-sharing; and to various human-services programs.

A typical Illinois Lotto game is 1 to 44; players must pick six correct numbers out of six to win a jackpot prize. Daily numbers are offered in both three-digit and four-digit games with a typically miserly payoff of slightly under 50 percent—less than organized crime offers for its daily numbers.

Illinois' instant games of the *"rub off"* variety tend to offer higher prizes. One, the Cool Cash Million, pays off with an instant prize of $100,000. Winners of lesser prizes are eligible for a $1-million drawing. Overall, chances for winning some prize are 1 in 4, but this could be nothing more than a free lottery ticket. The chances of winning a $100,000 prize are only 1 in 6 million, and the $1-million jackpot only 1 in 60 million.

IN-BETWEEN: Game of Luck

In-Between is a private game that most serious gamblers studiously avoid. It appeals to players who want fast action, but they often end up buying an illusion.

How to play: Players ante and then are dealt two cards face down. The object of the game is to be dealt a third card that falls between the first two cards, i.e., if the player is dealt a 4 and an 8, he must get a 5, 6, or 7 to win.

When a player is dealt his two cards he bets a minimum of the original ante up to the maximum in the pot. He lays his bet near the pot and gets his card. If he wins, he withdraws an amount equal to his bet from the pot, and if he loses, his bet is added to the pot. Pots tend to grow considerably. If a player is dealt a pair, he is of course an instant loser, as is also the case if he gets consecutive cards, i.e., 7 and 8. In this case he must contribute what was the previously agreed-upon minimum to the pot.

The pot also grows rapidly because there is an additional ante after each hand. If the pot is taken a new ante replenishes it, even in the middle of a hand.

The probabilities of In-Between, or Yablon, as it is also known, dictate that a player needs a seven-spread in cards to have an about even chance of drawing a winning hand, that is, a spread from 3 to

10, for instance. With such a hand a winning card would be any from the 4 to the 9. The bettor would lose on 2, 3, 10, jack, queen, king, ace. To get an advantage the bettor actually requires an eight-spread, and still will only have a slight edge. Even a slight edge, however, won't necessarily offset a string of losing bets.

Strategy: There are no sure winning bets in this game as in many other similar games, such as ACEY-DEUCEY. The best bet for In-Between is on a deuce-ace, which makes all cards from 3 to king a winner. The bettor can still lose on a deuce or an ace, however. A winner has to bet big when the opportunity arises, but bad luck can still lay him under. The least desirable aspect of the game is that one must bet big to win big, unlike games such as POKER where occasionally one can bet small and still catch a big pot.

It's not uncommon in In-Between games with six or seven players for only one player to end up winning big. This is usually less a question of strategy than of luck. In-Between is not exactly the thinking man's card game.

INDIA, Gambling in

Legal gambling in India has been in large measure restricted to horse racing, a sport that gained support among the rich under British rule. There are racetracks in all the major cities, and bookmakers handle bets on races. There is also some dog racing and, needless to say, considerable illegal card and dice gambling. Wagering on various forms of bird or animal fighting has been outlawed and all other forms of gambling are punishable with light sentences under a 1955 law that sets the maximum sentence for a gambling offense at six months in prison and a fine of about $170.

Nevertheless, illegal gambling is widespread and well-organized. Matka, a lottery controlled from Bombay, takes in millions of rupees in bets every day. The revenues go to a small group of organized-crime figures that the police have compared to the Mafia.

In late 1987, the government drew up plans to change the law and allow gambling casinos, with houses slated for Kashmir and Bombay, and Goa and Cochin in the south. The government is looking for ways to attract Arab money and to increase tourism in general. However, the casinos would be restricted to foreigners, and Indians would not be permitted entry. This would mean that wealthy Indians would have to continue to take their action to neighboring Nepal. However, wealthy Indians will probably get around these restrictions in the same way the super-rich do in other countries with such taboos—through the securing of dual passports.

INDIAN DICE: Recommended Bar Game

If one plays bar games and wishes to avoid being hustled, just about the best small gambling game is Indian Dice, which may be just about the most popular of all saloon games in America.

How to play: This game is for any number of players, using five dice. The object is to build the best possible POKER hand, the value of the dice varying upward from the 2 to the 6 with the 1 being wild and counting for any other number. No straights are permitted in Indian Dice and the highest possible hand is five of a kind, followed by four of a kind, full house, three of a kind, two pairs, and one pair.

Each player is allowed up to three throws of the dice and may set aside as many of the dice on each throw as he wishes. Let us say on the first throw a player rolls 4-4-2-3-5. He holds the pair and on the next roll throws 1-3-6. He most likely will hold the 1, giving him three fours. He rolls again and gets 2-2, ending up with a full house.

Strategy: Indian Dice is a dead-even game with all players having an equal chance, but this does not eliminate skill and strategy. Let us say a player gets 1-2-4-5-6 on his first roll. Many players will hold the 1-6, thus having the highest possible pair going into the second round. This, however, is usually not the right play. He would be better off simply holding the 1. The reason: On his next roll he will use four dice and the probabilities are better than even that he will throw some kind of pair with four dice (actually 720 chances out of 1,296). If this happens he will have three of a kind and still have two dice to improve on his hand on his final throw. He also has (on the second roll) an extra die working at picking up a second 1.

On the other hand, let us say a previous player ended up with two pairs—5's and 3's. In this case it would be advisable for the player to hold his 1 and his 6, since it gives him a higher pair than his opponent with two pairs and either another 1 or a 6 or another pair will win for him.

Indian Dice is usually played for small stakes or for drinks. When only two are playing, the winner is generally decided by the best of three games. When more players are involved and the play is for drinks, the low man in the first round plays the low man in the second round. The loser of this low-man final buys the drinks.

See also POKER DICE.

INDIAN GAMBLING CASINOS: The "Redskins' Vegas"

Some might see it as the Indians at last "getting even" with the white man. In the late 1980's the St. Regis Indian Reservation on the northern New York state border introduced a version of casino-type gambling. Because the courts have ruled the Mohawks are an independent "nation" the state has no authority to enforce its gambling or tax laws on Indian reservations. As a result the Mohawks have built hangar-sized bingo halls, slot machines joints, and, as an added lure for gamblers, strip joints.

Thousands of gamblers from as far away as Michigan, New Jersey, and even the western Canadian provinces travel every weekend to the big-money arcades. The lure: Instead of the $1,000-a-night winnings cap on New York state-regulated bingo parlors, the Mohawks offer payoffs that hit $100,000. In a two-year period one establishment, the Mohawk Palace, paid out more than $5 million in cash and prizes.

The reservation, with what the media has reported to be the backing of "secret outside investors," is on the way to becoming a gambling mecca, with bus tours running from the Big Apple and beyond. In the works are resort hotels, shows with top-flight entertainment, and an expanded jetport in nearby Massena, New York, to bring in more spenders. A New Jersey woman is a typical customer who drives five hours from her Trenton home to play high-stakes Bingo. "I could go to Atlantic City, spend $500 in 15 minutes, and the thrill is gone," she declared. "But on the reservation, I get a full night of entertainment—and the odds are better, too."

After a night of Bingo, unsated gamblers move on to nearby glitzy mini-casinos sporting such names as "Silver Dollar" and "Golden Nugget" to take on the slots.

Beyond the appeal of high-stakes games, gamblers like the fact that lucky bettors can walk away with millions in cash, cars, furs, and vacations, all "tax free." Experts agree that with that kind of lure, the Mohawks are masters of their fate and their world and it's only a matter of time before gambling on the reservations becomes a multi-million-dollar business.

INDONESIA, Gambling in

Indonesians are among the world's most avid gamblers, which explains why the post-Sukarno government decided in the 1960's to allow gambling casinos. The plan was to cater to foreigners, but perhaps even more important was to keep the wealthier Indonesians and their betting money home. The Indonesian super-rich were for years among the biggest gamblers in such casino world capitals as Macao, London, and Las Vegas. Some Vegas gambling executives insist that Indonesians are among the most talented BLACKJACK counters.

If there is any place in the real world to match Rick's fabulous gambling joint in *Casablanca* for foreign intrigue it is the Sarinah Casino in Jakarta, the national capital. At the tables are foreign businessmen, military officers and politicians, and diplomats of many nations. It's bet on the red and make a deal.

IOWA—Legalized Lotteries

Iowa, unlike most other states, emphasizes using its lottery profits to create more income, using revenues for projects that attract capital investment, create new jobs, and encourage research and development.

The first type of game offered by the state was of the instant variety, involving the wiping off of latex-covered spots to determine if one is a winner. Tickets cost $1, and in a special innovation Iowa collects its 4 percent sales tax out of that as well, presumably on the grounds that a 50-percent takeout is not enough of a tariff. Based on a sale of 40 million tickets, a player has 1 chance in 33 million-plus of hitting a jackpot of $5,845,000. Overall, chances of winning something are about 1 in 10.

IRAQ, Gambling in

Despite the perils of Iran-Iraq war, gambling habits in Iraq remained intact. Even when the key city of Basra was virtually under the guns of the Iranians during the late 1980's, the Iraqi citizenry kept morale high by flocking to the local racetrack "to improve the breed."

IRELAND, Gambling in

Under the Gaming and Lotteries Act of 1956, the only gambling games permitted in Ireland were those in which the banker and player had an equal chance. This eliminated slot machines and casinos in general. Small games of chance were permitted at circuses and fairs, provided the play was for very small stakes. Small lotteries for philanthropic purposes also were exempted from the prohibitions provided that the units of wagering and the prizes were quite modest.

And then of course there is the mammoth IRISH SWEEPSTAKES, which is in a class by itself and remains the biggest gambling operation of its kind in the world.

The Irish remain ardent bettors on horses and bookmaking is legal both on course and off. The same applies to dog racing.

IRISH SWEEPSTAKES

Unlike a lottery, in which numbers are generated by lot, the winning numbers in a sweepstakes are based on the results of a special event, often a horse race. That is true of the Irish Sweepstakes, which was set up in 1930 to raise money for Irish hospitals. Run three or four times a year, the Irish Sweepstakes donates 25 percent of the money received to hospitals with the remaining 75 percent after expenses going to the lucky winners.

Since the sales of Sweepstakes tickets were legal only in Ireland, the promoters had to get around various legal obstacles to sell them in other countries, where demand for tickets during the worldwide depression was enormous. The U.S. and British post offices refused to handle mail for the Irish Sweepstakes, and in 1935 alone American officials returned more than one-million letters to the senders. Irish promoters got over this hurdle by setting up secret agents in the United States and smuggling in tickets months in advance of the contest. In 1948 U.S. officials seized two-million tickets found aboard the ocean liner *America*. Still, the flow could not be staunched and Sweepstakes tickets also found their way into other countries, especially Great Britain, the Scandinavian countries, and Australia where the demand was enormous. This was true despite the fact that thousands of bogus tickets were printed and sold, leaving a number of supposed winners holding the bag. The genuine tickets warned customers to beware of forgeries, but of course so did the fakes. Sales nevertheless soared, and for a long time 96 percent of all tickets were sold outside Ireland! During this period it was estimated that somewhere between one-half and three-quarters of all sales were in the United States; this was true until the 1970's when legalization of state-run lotteries in various states resulted in a big decline in sweepstakes sales. Still, the Irish Sweepstakes thrives and continues to be the biggest operation of its kind in the world.

ISRAEL, Gambling in

Israel does not permit gambling casinos to operate and pool betting on football is rather limited. Private betting is another matter and some Israelis have put up huge satellite dishes to pick up American television; this has enabled them to bet heavily on NFL games. One visiting American declared he had no trouble getting down $5,000 bets.

On a realistic level, it is generally recognized that Israel will be the last nation in the Middle East to permit casino-style gambling. The nation is still sensitive to the controversy over the efforts of the late underworld gambling genius, Meyer Lansky, to settle in the country. That, plus the fact that previously a great number of American Jewish gangster-gamblers were let in under the "law of return," makes it even more imperative that the country not be viewed as a gambling mecca.

Some public service-type organizations can stage LOTTERIES, such as the Red Shield of David (the equivalent of the Red Cross), the Committee for the Soldier, and Mif'al Hapayis, an organization sponsored by the government and local authorities that uses net income for building schools, hospitals, and dispensaries. Usually disabled persons are employed selling the lottery tickets.

ITALIAN DECK: 40-card Deck

A great many card games popular in the United States and of course in Italy as well as in other countries with a large Italian population use what is called an Italian deck. This is a regular deck of playing cards from which the 8's, 9's, and 10's have been removed. Among the games utilizing such a 40-card deck are partnership *tressette, briscola,* CALABRASELLA, and *primiera.*

ITALY, Gambling in

There are laws in Italy that forbid gambling in any public place, in any club or private home, but don't get the idea that such activities aren't common. This is, after all, Italy.

Of course, there is plenty of the legalized brand of gambling, with totalizator betting on horses as well as a very big lottery. There are also four casinos in Italy—in San Remo (the biggest), Campione, Venice, and St. Vincent. American tourists are surprised to discover that some Italian casinos have the highest admission prices on the Continent—close to $15 in Venice, for example. Minimum bets are steep too, such as about $20 at ROULETTE—and that's for one number only. This policy dates back to when the Italian lira was approaching funny-money status, but with the nation's recent economic recovery, budget-minded gamblers find it a tough nut to crack.

However there are other compensations such as the atmosphere at Venice's Casino Municipale in the Ca Vendramin Calergi, one of the most famous palaces on the Grand Canal, where Richard Wagner died. It is perhaps fitting that the palace should become a gambling house, considering the German composer's profligate ways. And there is a certain charm when the summer betting switches to the famous Lido and one can watch croupiers bicycling to work in tuxedos.

But the real charm from a gambling viewpoint is the lack of supervision of BLACKJACK counters. I witnessed players with small computers that they popped in and out of their pockets and then watched them pounce forward to make a big bet. (In the Italian casinos it is possible to stand behind a player and bet on his card independently, although such a player has no say on his strategy.) All this goes on while TV cameras rotate ominously from the ceiling, but evidently no one is watching. It is only in an Italian casino that I've ever witnessed casino personnel undecided on which of two bettors had put down a winning chip. In perhaps typical Latin spirit, the high-chaired spotter tried to mediate an argument between the two gamblers and clearly did not know which way to rule. (In other countries, housemen have been known to rule, rightly or wrongly, but always unhesitatingly.) In Solomonic wisdom he finally suggested a compromise with each player taking half and that's how the deal was cut, the true owner of the chips apparently not being all that certain himself.

All in all, Italian casinos are fun places, but stay away from the separate rooms for slot machines (these are outside the admission area). A quick survey on Campione revealed that the returns don't warrant the investment.

J

JAGGERS'S SYSTEM: Finding Biased Roulette Wheels

There was a time at the end of the 19th century when the hallowed Monte Carlo casino thought it had had it, that it might have to shut down its ROULETTE games. An English engineer named William Jaggers had found a way to beat six Roulette tables all at the same time. It was incredible. Nothing like that had ever happened before.

Jaggers had acquired a Roulette wheel of his own in England and spent months spinning it, trying to devise a betting system. As he analyzed his figures, he discovered that many numbers were not turning up as often as they should and others much too frequently over a long length of play. Jaggers correctly concluded that the wheel was biased in favor of certain numbers.

That was all he needed to know, and he was off to Monte Carlo to study the Roulette wheels. He hired six assistants to track every spin of six wheels over a five-week period, after which Jaggers interpreted the figures. He discovered some very startling facts about each of the wheels. All had certain biases that rendered the law of averages fallible.

Then Jaggers and his assistants took on the wheels, his aides following specific patterns of betting that the engineer had devised. On their very first day they won the equivalent of $70,000, and over the next four days Jaggers's system showed an additional profit of about $300,000.

The casino, needless to say, didn't know what had hit it. Supervisors tracked the betting patterns of Jaggers and his confederates and could not detect the use of a system; indeed each bet far differently from the others. In one instance Jaggers started betting when 5 came up, staying with number 17 for ten straight spins. Only then, for the first time, did one of the directors think that there might be some-

thing wrong with the wheels. Overnight the wheels on the tables were switched.

Jaggers did not spot the switch immediately and by the time he did, he had given back two-thirds of his winnings. So it was back to the drawing board until he figured out the problem and reidentified the wheels. Once he had done so, he went back into action and the casino's losses soared once again. Not only was Jaggers winning again, but other bettors jumped in, blindly following his wagers. Famed Monte Carlo came close to closing its tables.

Finally, the manufacturer of the wheels was summoned and he concluded that the problem revolved around the immovable partitions between the numbers. If he replaced them with movable ones, they could be changed around daily so that no pattern would hold.

That decision finished Jaggers's system. The English engineer promptly spotted the change, and decided it was time to go home. After rewarding his assistants, Jaggers was thought to have profited by about a quarter of a million dollars. So far as is known Jaggers never challenged the Roulette wheels again.

Others have, needless to say. Many people firmly believe that no Roulette wheel can be perfect and although all wheels are tested every 24 hours, that the biases are still there for that day. That is why some Roulette players repeatedly play numbers that have appeared previously. Others believe in playing neighbors—that is, the numbers next to a winning number—on subsequent plays. Does this work? Well, the European casinos helpfully publish guides that show all the neighbors for every number on the wheel. Would they do this if it really worked?

JAI ALAI: World's Fastest Team Gambling Game

Jai alai, which is a big betting sport in Latin America, southern Europe, and the United States, has been

167

described as the world's fastest gambling game. The rules vary to some extent from country to country, but the fans everywhere gamble enthusiastically on the outcome.

The game originated more than two centuries ago in Spain, based on a form of handball played by the Basques. It is played by two or more players with a basket hand covering (cesta) and a ball (pelota) that is slightly larger, harder, and heavier than a golf ball. The ball, which can travel at 150 miles an hour, must hit against the wall of a specially marked playing court and bounce back in fair territory. When it is hit right, the opposition is not always able to catch it in the air or, on the first bounce, return it to the back wall.

From Spain the game went to Cuba and then after the Spanish-American War to the United States. Florida has permitted legal parimutuel betting on jai alai since the 1930's, with the betting similar to horse racing, including wagers on win, place, and show, and such exotic combinations as daily doubles, quinellas, perfectas, and the "Big Q." The Big Q involves picking two teams that you think will finish first or second. If they win, you get to make a pick of your choices for the first and second place in the second half of the wager. The top betting in America is found at Dania, Florida's finest jai alai palace.

The MGM Grand Hotel in Las Vegas introduced jai alai before the hotel was destroyed by fire. The game has not proved popular with professional gamblers and is largely played by a public that simply bets on numbers as much as anything. The professional gambler is notoriously suspicious of an athletic contest that involves humans rather than dumb animals, even boxing not getting the betting play that the public thinks.

JERSEY HIGH-LOW: Draw Poker Variation

Jersey High-Low was created by the late gambling expert John Scarne, and while it is an intriguing game there can be little doubt that Scarne himself could have won a fortune at it in high-stakes private games. So far as can be determined, no detailed analysis of the game has ever been done, but it is certain that Scarne himself understood the perverse nature of the game. (A good rule of thumb is to be wary of any new game suggested by an expert gambler, since he has mastered the ins and outs involved already.)

How to play: Players receive the standard five cards as in normal Draw Poker and then the dealer sets up four rows of three down cards in the center of the table. Players bet first on their closed hands, after which the dealer exposes one row of the centered cards. Betting rounds, generally limited to three

raises, follow the exposure of each row and on the turn-up of the final row the last betting sequence occurs.

Players must make their final hands from three cards in their hand and two cards from one of the three-card groups on the table. If a player is going for both high and low, he may use one three-card row for high and another for low. Straights and flushes cannot be considered as low.

Strategy: Few players grasp all the ramifications of Jersey High-Low. But let us peek at a game that involves some excellent players. Player A is dealt a pat full house of three queens and a pair of 9's. Disgustedly, he drops out on the first betting round, not even waiting to see any of the community three-card rows. Clearly, he is no dummy.

Player B has three 5's, a 6, and an ace. He stays. Player C has 2, 4, and jack of hearts and 7 and 3 of diamonds. He bets heavily—as he should. Player D is holding deuces and 6's paired and a 10. He is not happy but stays, vowing to himself to get out if the first three-card row does not help him.

Of course, these are mythical smart players. Average gamblers would find it difficult to behave in the disciplined way that they do.

First, any pat hand on openers—a full house or a straight or flush—must be broken since a player may ultimately only use three cards from his hand. In the case of Player A, assuming he speculated about keeping the three kings, he would have difficulty refilling to a full house again. True, he would have four tries at it, but remember that he must get a pair in a row of three, no easy matter mathematically. And if, let us say, a pair of 5's turns up in a row, all the other players can make use of them as well. What if another player already has 5's paired? Of course, Player A might also get four of a kind with his kings or 9's, but that is not too likely as there are only three cards left in the deck as possible winners and he has to assume that some of the other players may have already been dealt one or more of those cards. He is in a very bad position. And remember that he is only competing for half the pot—with his high cards there is no way he can go for low.

Player B, with three 5's, a 6 and an ace, is in better shape. He can hope for four 5's or a full house and very likely get neither, but he also has the 6, 5, and ace going for low, which is a very good start.

Player C has a three-card flush working, two different three-card straight possibilities, and with his 2, 3, 4, and 7 has alternate combinations of three cards toward the low. He should be betting the pants off his opponents.

Player D is not in good shape and probably is wrong to stick around, because he can only hope to fill his two pairs to a full house. He has a hard row to hoe since, though he doesn't know it both a deuce and 6 are already held by others. Still he is taking a shot and might pull a case deuce or 6.

Before playing out this game, the careful gambler should try to think ahead to what the likely high and low winning hands will be. For low, a seven-high is about mandatory. High is more complicated. Only under the rarest of circumstances do three of a kind stand up. The usual winning hand in this kind of game is a straight or a flush and once in a while a full house.

To stay in the game early it is necessary to hold either a three-card flush or straight, and preferably low cards at that, so that the potential for low is also there. A player with three opening 9's has a less playable hand than a player with a pair of deuces and two low cards, even if they will not make a straight with a deuce.

To be successful at Jersey High-Low it is necessary to ignore most of what one knows about virtually all other games of POKER. That's what makes this game an expert's dream.

John "Mushmouth" JOHNSON: Black Gambling King

John V. "Mushmouth" Johnson is considered the most successful black gambler America ever produced, but he was even more of a rarity as a black man becoming pretty much king of the hill in white gaming circles as well. For more than a quarter of a century until 1907 Johnson, a flamboyant figure in Chicago gambling, controlled the city's policy racket as well as scores of FARO, POKER, and CRAPS operations in the black sections. He was even a powerful presence in the Chinese quarter, where he extracted a fee for protection from all gambling enterprises. Johnson's clout derived from his ability to deliver, across party lines, a huge block of black votes at election time.

Although his birth date is unknown, Mushmouth apparently was a native of St. Louis. He turned up in Chicago in the early 1870's as a waiter in the renowned Palmer House. About a decade later he was working as a floorman in Andy Scott's gambling emporium on South Clark Street. Scott liked him so much he cut him in for a small percentage of the operation. Mushmouth soon went out on his own, however, to fill a vacuum he felt existed in the city's gambling structure. There was, he thought, no really good nickel gambling joint, and so he opened one at 311 South Clark. The gambling tables were open to all races, with bets running as low as 5 cents in all games. In 1890 Mushmouth sold out and opened a saloon and gambling hall at 464 State Street, where he operated for the last 17 years of his life without any interruption of business despite the periodic legal crackdowns that hit the city.

Mushmouth also started a new venture with two leading white gamblers, Tom McGinnis and Bill Lewis. They opened the lavish Frontenac Club on 22nd Street, which ran on a strictly whites-only basis. No one got into the place without either being known or displaying a certain amount of cash. Nor did Johnson lose popularity in the black community because he was running a whites-only gambling palace. Indeed, his success in the white world was a matter of black pride.

Johnson never gambled himself and was believed to have accumulated an estate of a quarter of a million dollars, a fortune for that day, especially for a black man. Still, Johnson insisted he had made much more money for whites than he did for himself, and shortly before he died in 1907 he told friends he had only $15,000. He said he'd paid $100,000 in fines, and several times that annually for police protection. "I have had to pay out four dollars for every one I took in," he claimed, adding that he was always hit harder than his white counterparts because of his color.

When Johnson's sentiments became known, a top police official declared his outrage, calling Johnson a "whiner," and a "damnable liar." It was clear to knowledgeable observers that the police were not reacting to the charge that they were grafters, but rather that they were bigots.

JOHNSON-WILLARD HEAVYWEIGHT CHAMPIONSHIP BOUT: Fixed Fight

One of boxing's greatest gambling coups was linked to the 1915 heavyweight title fight between Jack Johnson and Jess Willard in Havana, Cuba. It was obvious that Willard was not much more than a plodder with little grounding in scientific boxing and could not really beat the crafty black champion, even though at age 37 he was past his prime. Yet there was very heavy betting on Willard, which suggested that the fix was in. Johnson won the early rounds but was knocked out in the 26th.

Johnson later admitted that he threw the fight, and purists might say this was never proved. However, that shrewd gambler Wilson Mizner, puzzled by the inexplicable betting, decided to go to the source. So a few days before the fight Mizner wired Johnson: "What Shall I Do?"

Johnson and Mizner were close friends, and the latter reasoned that if the fight was on the level, Johnson would wire back that Mizner should bet on him. Mizner waited, and when he got no response, he understood. He bet several thousand dollars, every cent he could raise, on Willard, and collected.

William "Canada Bill" JONES: Three-card Monte Gambling Cheat

He cut a shabby figure along the Mississippi during the middle of the 19th century, but William "Canada Bill" Jones (?-1877) was without doubt the most talented Three-card Monte cheat who ever operated in this country. George Devol, second to Canada Bill as the gambler-con man of the century, described him in his autobiography *Forty Years a Gambler on the Mississippi* as:

> . . . a character one might travel the length and breadth of the land and never find his match, or run across his equal. Imagine a medium-sized, chicken-headed, tow-haired sort of a man with mild blue eyes, and a mouth nearly from ear to ear, who walked with a shuffling, half-apologetic sort of a gait, and who, when his countenance was in repose, resembled an idiot. His clothes were always several sizes too large, and his face was as smooth as a woman's and never had a particle of hair on it.
>
> Canada Bill was a slick one. He had a squeaking, boyish voice, and awkward gawky manners, and a way of asking fool questions and putting on a good natured sort of grin, that led everybody to believe that he was the rankest kind of sucker—the greenest sort of country jake. Woe to the man who picked him up, though. Canada was, under all the hypocritical appearance, a regular card shark, and could turn monte with the best of them. He was my partner for a number of years, and many are the suckers we roped in, and many the huge roll of bills we corralled.

He was a Gypsy born in Yorkshire, England, and grew up in that society of pan menders, fortune tellers, and horse traders, and he developed flim-flams in many areas. He practiced with cards almost around the clock and became so adept at cheating that finally other Gypsies refused to gamble with him. He was believed to have been about 20 when he emigrated to Canada where he learned the tricks of bent-card Three-card Monte from Dick Cady, the top practitioner of the craft north of the border. Cady discovered that young Jones was much more adept at maneuvering the cards than he himself was so he let Canada Bill run the game while he acted as his shill. Eventually, Bill was lured south by tales of great gambling kills to be made on the Mississippi riverboats. Cady refused to go, warning him that Americans were a different breed of suckers, apt to get violent when trimmed, unlike the more docile Canadians. Cady proved to be correct, but Canada Bill was too smooth a cheat not to be able to work his way out of any tight spot.

Normally, Three-card Monte favors the dealer 2 to 1, but Canada Bill seldom gave a sucker such a decent break. He manipulated cards with such dexterity that he could show a victim two aces and a queen and then, in the act of throwing the cards, palm the queen and substitute a third ace so that the sucker had no chance at all.

Around 1850 Jones formed a partnership with Devol and two other talented gamblers, Tom Brown and Holly Chappell. The larcenous quartet operated on the Ohio and Mississippi rivers for nearly a decade. When the partnership was dissolved, each man's share of the profits was running at more than $200,000 a year.

As quickly as both he and Devol made their money, however, they found ways of squandering it, both being suckers for FARO. Canada Bill, who was addicted to gambling for its own sake, was the coiner of what was to become a classic gamblers' comment, later attributed to many others. Marooned in a small Louisiana river town, Canada Bill diligently hunted up a Faro game where he proceeded to lose consistently. His partner of the moment tried to get him to stop. "The game's crooked," the partner whispered.

"I know it," Canada Bill replied, "but it's the only one in town."

When river traffic dwindled and then virtually disappeared by the start of the Civil War, Canada Bill shifted his operations to the rails. The railroads, however, did not exhibit the tolerance for gamblers that the riverboats had, and Three-Card Monte players were rousted and dropped off in the middle of nowhere. In 1867 Canada Bill wrote to one of the Southern lines offering to pay $25,000 a year for the right to operate without being molested. He also made the Union Pacific a tempting offer he was sure they could not refuse. For $10,000 per annum he wanted the sole right to run Three-card Monte games on the line and as an added inducement he promised to restrict his cheating to Chicago commercial travelers and Methodist preachers. The hard-hearted railroad rejected his overtures and Jones was forced to look elsewhere for suckers.

He found them at fairs and race courses throughout the Midwest. In 1874 Canada Bill brought his act to Chicago, where with two other old-time gambling rogues, Jimmy Porter and "Colonel" Charlie Starr, he established four crooked gambling joints after, according to detective Allan Pinkerton, he "secured an understanding" with the police. His partners ran all the crooked games except for Monte, which was Canada Bill's specialty, and soon most of Chicago's top bunco men were steering victims to him.

Within six months Jones had accumulated $150,000, but he soon lost it all to other gamblers at Faro and CASINO. Canada Bill moved on to Cleveland where the same easy-come, easier-go routine continued. In poor health, Canada Bill finally wound up in Reading, Pennsylvania, noted then as a refuge for gamblers. Almost broke, he was admitted to Charity

Hospital, where he died in 1877. He was buried there, the burial costs being provided by the mayor who later was reimbursed by Chicago gamblers, many of whom came east for the funeral.

John Quinn, in his 1892 history of gambling called *Fools of Fortune,* relates that at the funeral Canada Bill "was recognized as a general all-round confidence operator, and so distrustful were those who knew him of appearances which he put forth that . . . as the coffin was being lowered into the grave one of his friends offered to bet $1,000 to $500 that 'Bill was not in the box.' The offer found no takers, for the reason, as one of his acquaintances said, 'that he had known Bill to squeeze through tighter holes than that.' "

See GEORGE DEVOL; THREE-CARD MONTE.

K

KALOUGI
See CALOOCHI.

KALUKI
See CALOOCHI.

KANKAKEE SEVEN-CARD STUD: Wild-Card Game

How to play: In this variation of Seven-card Stud POKER there is a betting round, beginning with the player to the dealer's left immediately after the two downcards are dealt. Then each player is dealt an upcard that is wild, as are all others like it thereafter, but to *that player only*. Thus everyone has at least a pair after the first three cards. The game then proceeds like normal Seven-card Stud.

Strategy: Like most wild games, Kankakee favors the experienced player who does not chase cards on outlandish hopes. The key to the game is to forget playing for lesser hands like straights or flushes, which rarely win. Even full houses aren't usually strong enough since most hands are won by four of a kind, and a good number by straight flushes or five of a kind.

Basically, a player should drop if he doesn't have three of a kind after four cards or, at the very least, three cards toward a straight flush. Additionally, many professionals drop if another player pairs his wild card, unless they also have a powerhouse hand going.

This is an excellent game to call in DEALER'S CHOICE if one is playing against undisciplined players who tend to stay on a mere glimmer of hope.

Honest John KELLY: Trusted Gambler

For a quarter of a century until the early 1920's, John Kelly (1856-1926) was regarded as the most honest gambling house proprietor in the country. That made him extremely popular with the gaming public, but not with the police, to whom he refused to pay graft.

He believed that if money had to be expended for police protection, the house edge would be destroyed and that the only way a gambling house could then stay in business would be to run crooked games. Kelly opted for simply dealing the minions of the law out.

Honest John earned his nickname in 1888 when, following a baseball career, he turned to umpiring. He refused a $10,000 payoff to shade his decisions favorably toward the Boston team in a crucial Boston-Providence series that decided a pennant race. Learning about Kelly's refusal, League president Nick Young dubbed him "Honest John" and the sobriquet stuck. Honest John became the darling of the big-time gamblers, and he was trusted to deal in card games involving tens of thousands of dollars a hand.

Kelly's reputation for honesty earned him enough of a stake that he was able to open a gambling house of his own in New York. At times Kelly had several establishments running simultaneously. His most famous place was a brownstone at 156 West 44th Street, where he fought many highly publicized battles with police. He always claimed his biggest expense came from replacing doors and windows wantonly smashed by indignant detectives. The most notorious raid took place in 1912, when the police ran amok with crowbars and fire axes, destroying doors, windows, expensive furniture, and gambling equipment. The raid boomeranged on the police; public sentiment was with Kelly, who was seen as a hero and an incorruptible gambler. In the aftermath of all the publicity Kelly opened a new gaming house called the Vendome Club on West 114th Street, which was an instant success. When Kelly shut the West 44th Street brownstone, the frustrated police were convinced he was still in business there and stationed a uniformed officer at the front door. Sightseeing buses took visitors past it, and guides pointed out the gambling house that wouldn't pay off the police. The guides described how Kelly's patrons supposedly used to slip into the brownstone through secret passageways connected to other buildings. The ever-frustrated police subsequently raided the brownstone repeatedly, but never found any signs of gambling.

In the early 1920's Kelly sold the brownstone to the Republican Party and closed his other establishments. He relocated for a time in Miami Beach, Florida, where he also refused to pay for police protection. When Honest John Kelly died in March 1926, the staid *New York Times* thought his death important enough to run his obituary on its front page.

KENO: Casino Lottery Game

Keno is a lottery game offered by most casinos in Nevada, and for very good reason: the casinos love potential gold mines. On the other hand, the game is not permitted by the Casino Control Commission

Most Nevada casinos eagerly offer Keno since it represents a gold mine for the house. A & B: Some of the odds payoffs and betting patterns as played at a typical casino. C: A losing Keno ticket, the easiest souvenir to accumulate in Nevada.

HOLIDAY CASINO'S COMBINATION SPECIAL

MARK 4 GROUPS OF 2
$15.00 TICKET — $1.00 A WAY
4 Way 2 6 Way 4 4 Way 6 1 Way 8

Catch	Ticket Pays
1100	1.00
1110	4.00
1111	10.00
2000	15.00
2100	20.00
2110	28.00
2111	49.00
2200	148.00
2210	249.00
2211	417.00
2220	1,947.00
2221	3,628.00
2222	31,640.00

Ask Our Friendly Keno Writers About Combination and Way Tickets

Three ways or more can be played for .50 a way.

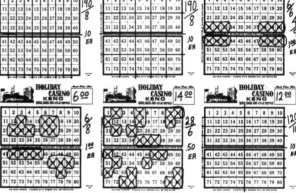

B.

HOLIDAY CASINO

Center Strip — Across from Caesars Palace

$1.00 KENO RATE

$50,000 KENO

Limited to Aggregate Players Each Game

PICK 1 NUMBER

Winning Number	Bet $1.00 Ticket Pays	Bet $5.00 Ticket Pays	Bet $100.00 Ticket Pays
1	3.00	15.00	300.00

PICK 2 NUMBERS

Winning Numbers	Bet $1.00 Ticket Pays	Bet $5.00 Ticket Pays	Bet $100.00 Ticket Pays
2	12.00	60.00	1,200.00

PICK 3 NUMBERS

Winning Numbers	Bet $1.00 Ticket Pays	Bet $5.00 Ticket Pays	Bet $10.00 Ticket Pays
2	1.00	5.00	10.00
3	42.00	210.00	420.00

PICK 4 NUMBERS

Winning Numbers	Bet $1.00 Ticket Pays	Bet $5.00 Ticket Pays	Bet $10.00 Ticket Pays
2	1.00	5.00	10.00
3	4.00	20.00	40.00
4	112.00	560.00	1,120.00

PICK 5 NUMBERS

Winning Number	Bet $1.00 Ticket Pays	Bet $5.00 Ticket Pays	Bet $10.00 Ticket Pays
3	2.00	10.00	20.00
4	20.00	100.00	200.00
5	480.00	2,400.00	4,800.00

PICK 6 NUMBERS

Winning Numbers	Bet $1.00 Ticket Pays	Bet $5.00 Ticket Pays	Bet $10.00 Ticket Pays
3	1.00	5.00	10.00
4	4.00	20.00	40.00
5	88.00	440.00	880.00
6	1,480.00	7,400.00	14,800.00

PICK 7 NUMBERS

Winning Numbers	Bet $1.00 Ticket Pays	Bet $5.00 Ticket Pays	Bet $10.00 Ticket Pays
4	1.00	5.00	10.00
5	20.00	100.00	200.00
6	350.00	1,750.00	3,500.00
7	8,500.00	42,500.00	50,000.00

PICK 8 NUMBERS

Winning Numbers	Bet $1.00 Ticket Pays	Bet $5.00 Ticket Pays	Bet $10.00 Ticket Pays
5	9.00	45.00	90.00
6	80.00	400.00	800.00
7	1,500.00	7,500.00	15,000.00
8	25,000.00	50,000.00	50,000.00

PICK 9 NUMBERS

Winning Numbers	Bet $1.00 Ticket Pays	Bet $5.00 Ticket Pays	Bet $10.00 Ticket Pays
4	.50	2.50	5.00
5	2.50	12.50	25.00
6	43.00	215.00	430.00
7	280.00	1,400.00	2,800.00
8	4,000.00	20,000.00	40,000.00
9	25,000.00	50,000.00	50,000.00

PICK 10 NUMBERS

Winning Numbers	Bet $1.00 Ticket Pays	Bet $5.00 Ticket Pays	Bet $10.00 Ticket Pays
5	2.00	10.00	20.00
6	20.00	100.00	200.00
7	132.00	660.00	1,320.00
8	960.00	4,800.00	9,600.00
9	3,800.00	19,000.00	38,000.00
10	25,000.00	50,000.00	50,000.00

PICK 11 NUMBERS

Winning Numbers	Bet $2.00 Ticket Pays	Bet $5.00 Ticket Pays	Bet $10.00 Ticket Pays
5	2.00	5.00	10.00
6	14.00	35.00	70.00
7	140.00	350.00	700.00
8	720.00	1,800.00	3,600.00
9	3,600.00	9,000.00	18,000.00
10	25,000.00	50,000.00	50,000.00
11	50,000.00	50,000.00	50,000.00

PICK 12 NUMBERS

Winning Numbers	Bet $2.00 Ticket Pays	Bet $5.00 Ticket Pays	Bet $10.00 Ticket Pays
6	10.00	25.00	50.00
7	58.00	145.00	290.00
8	466.00	1,165.00	2,330.00
9	1,572.00	3,930.00	7,860.00
10	3,280.00	8,200.00	16,400.00
11	24,000.00	50,000.00	50,000.00
12	50,000.00	50,000.00	50,000.00

PICK 13 NUMBERS

Winning Numbers	Bet $2.00 Ticket Pays	Bet $5.00 Ticket Pays	Bet $10.00 Ticket Pays
6	4.00	10.00	20.00
7	30.00	75.00	150.00
8	140.00	350.00	700.00
9	1,350.00	3,375.00	6,750.00
10	7,140.00	17,850.00	35,700.00
11	12,000.00	30,000.00	50,000.00
12	40,000.00	50,000.00	50,000.00
13	50,000.00	50,000.00	50,000.00

YOU CAN PLAY AS MANY TICKETS ON EACH GAME AS YOU WISH.
TICKETS CAN BE PLAYED FOR ANY MULTIPLE OF RATES SHOWN.

A.

BARBARY COAST

LIMIT
$50,000 KENO
(Each Game To Aggregate Winners)

FIRST GAME	NO. OF GAMES	PRICE
66		
LAST GAME	1	$1.00

1/4   1.00

1	2	3	4	5	6	7	8	9	10
11	12	13	14	15	16	17	18	19	20
21	22	23	24	25	26	27	28	29	30
31	32	33	34	35	36	37	38	39	40

Winning Ticket Must Be Cashed Before Start Of Next Game

41	42	43	44	45	46	47	48	49	50
51	52	53	54	55	56	57	58	59	60
61	62	63	64	65	66	67	68	69	70
71	72	73	74	75	76	77	78	79	80

WRITER	DATE	TIME	STA.	SERIAL NO.
SHARON	12/15/87	11:58	7	8142

C.

in New Jersey and, say the cynics, also for a very good reason. The state prefers a game with such terrible odds (for the player) to be offered by its own state lotteries. Why cut the casinos in on such a good thing?

Keno is nothing more than a gussied-up version of Bingo. The player gets a card with 80 numbers on it and marks from one to 15 of them. If those he chooses turn up in the 20 numbered balls selected by one or another mechanical methods, the player wins. It is possible to win $25,000, or perhaps even $50,000, for an investment of as little as 70 cents or one dollar. Of course, winning the jackpot is something like a 2 million to 1 chance, so the odds are not exactly wonderful, even considering the fact that having less than all the numbers correct still may entitle the player to a lesser prize. The fact is that, everything considered, the house edge runs between 20 and 25 percent. Gambling authority Allan Wilson says that Keno's odds are so heavily stacked against the player that "It is positively the worst sucker game in the house."

Well, true and false.

In a matter of speaking, it might be the best game in the world for some amateur gamblers. They are of course seduced by the concept of risking little and winning much, a goal almost never achieved. Still, there is something to be said for the game as a respite from the other casino games. It is possible to last an hour at Keno and go for less than $10. One can lose that and much more on one roll of the dice at CRAPS.

If the game is played in a Keno lounge, the chairs will be very comfortable and a player can usually get a complimentary drink or two from the cocktail waitress. (The drink is free, but custom requires that the waitress be tipped.) Overall, Keno comes closer to recreational gambling than any other casino game. The danger is that it can become addictive, and instead of betting 70 cents, a player increases his bets to $5, $10, or $20 a game, chasing that illusory jackpot. Keno addicts often develop a morbid fear that if they skip just one game, *that* will be the one that would have made them rich. This attitude can pile up heavy losses.

Few serious gamblers play Keno except during breaks from other action, especially if they want a quiet drink away from the tables. One might wonder if the Keno setup is worth all the trouble for the casinos if it detracts big gamblers from their main activity, but the fact is that the lopsided odds merit the house action. Additionally, consider the case of the tapped-out gambler who has dropped every bill he has on him. He is down to his last 70 cents. He doesn't want to go to the slots—indeed he might not find one available and, besides, winning a few quarters won't help him recoup. What about Keno? He

could try marking 10 spots for 70 cents. The payoff numbers read:

5 Pays	$1.40
6 Pays	$14.00
7 Pays	$98.00
8 Pays	$700.00
9 Pays	$2,660.00
10 Pays	$12,500.00

The player's fantasies run amok. Ten wins and he's on Easy Street. Considering the state of his finances, 8 or 9 wins amount to the same thing. With 6 or even 7 wins he could get back to the tables. Why even 5 wins would give him two more flings at Keno to build a stake.

The player eagerly marks his card—and loses. He can rationalize the loss more than most others. He took a negligible risk on the chance of a big payoff.

The casino has a rationale of its own: wouldn't it have been careless to let a player leave without cleaning him out of his last 70 cents?

KENYA, Gambling in
There may be less gambling in Kenya than in most other African nations. There is horse-race wagering but the season is rather short. Some years ago both football (soccer) pools and dog racing were outlawed. Lotteries run by charitable or youth organizations are allowed, but the prizes are kept small. However, it is legal for foreign lotteries to be sold in the country and the Irish Sweepstakes enjoys considerable popularity.

KING RUMMY: Variation of Contract Rummy
Although King Rummy is considered an alternate name for CONTRACT RUMMY, it is more correctly its own game with its own rules and many gamblers feel it is superior to the latter.

How to play: Like Contract Rummy there are several deals requiring certain opening melds before each player tries to play out his hand. The game is limited to four players using two regular decks, ten-card hands, and four jokers that are the only wild cards permitted. The opening contracts on melds are as follows:

First deal: One set of three cards (such as three aces) and one sequence in suit of four or more cards (such as 3, 4, 5, and 6 of clubs)

Second deal: Three sets of three or more each

Third deal: Two sequences of four or more each

Fourth deal: Two sets of three each, plus a sequence of four.

On the fourth deal, the opening meld is enough for the player to go out of the game, unless he has collected extra cards as in Contract Rummy. On the previous deals players need not finish with their opening meld but may lay off their remaining cards on their own melds or those of their opponents. Whenever a joker is melded, the player's discarding of a card is suspended while the other players are in turn given an opportunity to replace the joker with the natural card it is being used for. That player who does so retains the joker in his hand for later use. Once this option has been offered, play resumes from the interruption.

In scoring, jokers count for 25 points; aces, 15 (whether used high or low); pictures, 10; and all others for their pip value.

KINGS IN THE CORNER: Card-building Betting Game

How to play: Kings in the Corner is a game for two to six players, each of whom is dealt a hand of five cards. Then the dealer deals a layout of four cards in a diamond-shaped arrangement with the pack of cards placed in the middle of the diamond. The corners of the layout are left free for the kings that will be played in the course of the game. The layout follows (with four sample cards used for demonstration purposes):

(king)	8 of hearts	(king)
4 of clubs	(pack)	7 of spades
(king)	jack of clubs	(king)

Starting with the player on the dealer's left, each player in turn may build on the cards showing in descending order and in alternate colors (e.g., on the table itself, the 7 of spades may be put on the 8 of hearts). A player may build either from the table (as in this case) or from his hand. If, in the layout above, he has a red 10 in his hand he would also play that on the jack of clubs. He may also fill any holes that open up on the table, such as when the 7 of spades (above) is placed on the 8 of hearts he may replace it with any card from his hand.

The first player continues to lay down cards as long as he can. If he has any kings, he lays them down in the corners as indicated, and they too can be built upon with a queen of the opposite color, and so on.

When the player can no longer lay down cards he draws a card from the pack and plays it if possible, which may then allow him to lay down still more cards from his hand. If not, he may draw another card from the pack. However, whenever a drawn card produces no further builds, the play passes to the next player.

The game and a pre-antied pot is won by the first person to get rid of all his cards. If, as happens occasionally, an early player goes out before the later players and the dealer get to play, a complete series of games are required so that all players deal and lead first.

Strategy: This is not the world's greatest gambling game, but there is some strategy involved in how one plays his hand to create additional openings and builds. Poor players will not always make the proper moves and may even miss a chance to lay down cards, giving a competent player something of an edge.

KLABERJASS: Two-handed Card Game

Klaberjass is a two-handed card game that once was very "in" along New York's Great White Way. It was shilled enthusiastically by Damon Runyon, whose guys and dolls characters were addicted to the game. It is not an American game in origin, although it enjoyed its greatest popularity here. Some say the game, also known as Klob and by various other names elsewhere, is of Swiss, Dutch, French, or Hungarian origin. Considering its great popularity in Jewish goulash joints (translation: card rooms), the Hungarian origin is probably correct, at least as to which group of gamblers brought the game to the New World.

The game is played with a 32-card pack, from 7 up through the ace. Cards in the trump suit rank high to low as follows: jack, 9, ace, 10, king, queen, 8, 7. Both players are dealt six cards, three at a time. The next card is turned up and the rest of the pack placed partially over it, face down. The nondealer bids first and he has three options. He can "take it," meaning accept the turned-up card as trump suit; he can "pass," refusing to accept the turned-up card as trump suit; or he can "schmeiss," offering to play with the card as trump suit or throw in the hand, as the dealer prefers. A "yes" response from the dealer leads to a new deal and a "no" means the hand is to be played with the turned-up card as the trump suit.

If the nondealer passes, the dealer has the option of taking the card, passing, or schmeiss. If the dealer also passes, there is a new round of bidding with first the nondealer and then the dealer naming one of the other three suits as trump. If both decline, there is a new deal.

When a trump is called, each contestant is dealt three more cards. If either holds the 7 of trump, he can exchange it for the faced trump. Either the 7 or the turned-up card is then put on the out-of-play pile. Before the first trick is played, both players meld the sequences in their hands. Melding, unlike the scoring, follows natural rankings, with ace high. Sequences must be in consecutive rank and of the same suit. A three-card sequence is worth 20 points, and a four-card sequence 50 points. A higher four-card sequence beats a sequence of equal length. If both players hold sequences that tie as to high card, the trump sequence wins or if neither sequence is trump, the nondealer's beats the dealer's.

If the nondealer holds a sequence, he announces its point value, 20 or 50. The dealer then announces "Good" or "Not good," according to whether or not he has a higher score. If the dealer's sequence is of the same value, he asks his opponent how high his sequence goes to determine whose is higher. The high sequence is not shown until after the first trick has been played, and then it is laid down along with any other sequences the player may have.

The nondealer plays first. He may lead any card, and it is necessary to follow suit if one is able to and to trump when not able to follow suit if one has a trump, and to win a trump lead when possible. The higher trump wins any trick containing a trump, and the higher card of the suit led wins all other tricks. The winner of a trick leads to the next. After the first trick has been played, the higher-ranking meld shows and scores all sequences in his hand, while his opponent does not count any sequences.

If a player holds the king and queen of trumps he can score 20 points for them by announcing "Bella" as soon as he plays the second of them to a trick. If a player holds king, queen, and jack of trumps he may score a sequence and Bella as well.

The object of the game is to take tricks in which there are counting cards. These are: *jasz* (trump jack), 20 points; *menel* (trump nine), 14 points; any ace, 11 points; any 10, 10 points; any jack, 2 points; any queen, 3 points; any king, 4 points.

In addition, 10 points are scored for taking the final trick of the hand. Scores are then totaled—melds, points in tricks, Bella, and final trick.

If the trump maker has the higher score, each player records his full score; if they are tied, only the trump maker's opponent gets his score, and the trump maker gets nothing. If the nonmaker has the higher score, he is credited not only with his points but those of the trump maker as well. When the trump maker sees that his opponent is going to outscore him, he can strategically cut his losses by not claiming Bella. Game is at 500 points and if both are over 500, the highest score wins.

KLOB

See KLABERJASS.

KLONDIKE: Carnival and Casino Game

Klondike is a five-dice game that one will run across at carnivals and the like, and it can be found in some casinos as well. Generally at carneys the dice are released through a chute. The counter banker plays first and then the customers try to beat his POKER score. Straights don't count in this game and the

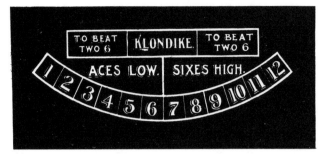

A sample Kondike layout, this one ranking 6's as high.

value, working upward, goes one pair (with aces ranking over 6's), two pairs, three of a kind, full house, four of a kind, and five of a kind. The banker's hand stands against all the players who put up money against him, and they all take turns trying to beat him. The banker wins on ties; numbers not paired do not count. Therefore one pair of aces ties another, and it does not matter what the remaining dice show.

In the casino version of Klondike, players can bet either that their hand will beat the banker or lose to him. Placing the money on a "win" space means the player must beat the banker's hand, while putting chips on a "lose" space means the gambler must get a lower score to win. In addition, a player can bet Beat Two Aces, which means he automatically wins if he makes two pairs or more.

On win and lose bets the bank's winning-all-ties edge results in a house advantage of 5.195 overall. Bear in mind that an unpaired hand is an automatic loser and will come up quite often. The Beat Two Aces bet is strictly a sucker bet, more than doubling the odds against the bettor with an edge of 11.11 percent in favor of the house.

The chute is not used in casino games. Instead the banker shoots from one dice cup and leaves his dice hand in view while the other players, one at a time, use a second dice cup and another set of dice. This avoids any argument as to what the banker's hand was.

The use of separate dice by the banker and players allows for the possibility of a rigged game, but considering the big house advantage, no legitimate casino would take the risk. This is not necessarily so of carnival or fly-by-night operators. Some of these sharpers will ring in electric dice that allow the banker to throw a high hand whenever he wishes, which will be when the betting gets steep. For a time saw-dust joints in Ohio, Kentucky, and Louisiana were known by insiders to use electric dice fairly often.

KLONDIKE SOLITAIRE

Klondike Solitaire, which can be played as a betting game, is dealt out in the normal table solitaire manner. The first card is dealt face up, followed by six down cards placed in the same row to the right. Then a face-up card is placed partially over the first down-card next to the first face-up card, followed by another series of downcards to the right, completing a second row. The procedure is continued with one fewer card laid out each round, until there are seven piles with one, two, three, four, five, six, and seven cards in order from left to right. The top card on each pile is face up and those under it are downcards.

The remaining deck is then turned over, one card at a time, and each may be added to any face-up card on the layout that is one value lower and of the opposite color. Face-up cards on the layout may also be moved to another higher-ranking open card of the next higher rank and opposite color. When a face-up card and the units covering it are moved, the top downcard on the pile is turned face up.

An exposed ace is placed above the layout and can be added to as succeeding cards in the same suit are exposed. If a turned-over card from the remaining cards cannot be played it is laid down next to the deck in a waste pile and the next card in the deck is turned over. If that card is playable it is played, and the top card (and subsequent cards) of the waste pile may now also be playable. When the waste pile is again dead, another card from the deck is turned over, and either played or placed on the waste pile. The deck may be gone through only once; when the last top card on the waste pile is unplayable the game is over. The purpose of the game is to transfer as many cards from the deck, waste pile, and layout to the four ace foundations, which can be added to in suit to the king.

In a betting game, the player buys the deck for 11 units and is paid one unit for each card placed on an ace foundation. It is possible to place the entire 52 cards on the foundations, in which case the player earns a profit of 41 units. It is impossible to work out a mathematical banker advantage for Klondike because the player's prospects in any given game are determined by the face-up cards and the possibilities that result. However, over the long run a banker selling the deck for 11 units will come out on top.

KNOCK POKER: Rummy and Poker Mix
A game combining elements of both POKER and RUMMY, Knock Poker is quite similar to KNOCK RUMMY though the hands are ranked as in Poker. It can be played by from two to six players, but is best with three to five.

How to play: Following a one-chip ante, each player is dealt five cards as in Draw Poker. The remaining cards are placed in the center to form the stock. The first player draws the top card from the stock and can keep it or discard it. Subsequent players can draw cards either from the stock or the discard pile, as in Rummy.

Any player after drawing a card and before discarding can knock, indicating he is demanding a showdown. This gives the other players the chance of only one more draw and then the high hand takes the pot. If the knocker wins, he collects two chips from each player who has stayed. Previously, players who figure they cannot win can escape additional losses by paying the knocker one chip. (The knocker keeps this prize even if he turns out to be holding a losing hand.)

If the knocker loses, he must pay the high hand an extra two chips.

According to the rules in some versions of the game, the victorious knocker gets additional bonuses from all losers besides the above payoffs if he holds special hands.

For a royal flush he collects four chips; for a straight flush, two chips; four of a kind, one chip; and for not drawing any cards, two chips.

This last bonus can be tricky. Bear in mind that in a five-man game, two players on average will get a pair on the deal, and roughly every four games one player will get two pairs. This should temper the idea of knocking on the basis of a pair of jacks at the outset. It should also be remembered that standing on a pair at the start means the knocker has to beat four six-card hands, since his opponents are permitted one draw. It is not recommended that a player knock at the outset with less than aces or two pairs. After a couple of go-rounds even two pairs should be regarded as not strong enough.

KNOCK RUMMY: Father of Gin
Knock Rummy is a fast form of RUMMY and the "father" of GIN. It is sometimes called Poker Rum, but that game is really just an early form of Knock Rummy.

How to play: The game is played by two to five players and in the case of two, each gets ten cards. In all other cases each player is dealt seven cards. Unlike Rummy, players do not lay down their melds but hold them in their hand. Play ends when a player draws a card, knocks on the table or announces "Knock," and then discards. At this point players separate their matched cards from their unmatched, or "deadwood," cards. Only the deadwood is counted against each player, with all picture cards counting for 10 points and the rest according to their pip value, with the ace being 1 point.

To knock, a player need not "go Rummy" or meld all his cards according to the standard rules of Rummy. The knocker wins if his deadwood count is lower than any of the other players. If the knocker wins, he gets paid the difference between his deadwood count and that of each player. If he melds all his cards he collects a bonus of 25 points from each opponent. An early rule of the game established that if another player tied the knocker's score, he was declared the winner; this has since been generally altered so that the knocker is the winner on ties. Should the knocker fail to win the game, he pays the difference between his count and that of the player with the lowest count, plus a penalty of 10 points.

No knock is permitted once the stock is reduced in cards to a number matching the number of players or lower. Instead, drawing cards continues until the stock is exhausted and all hands are melded.

Strategy: Much is made by some experts on the wisdom of when to knock. In a two-handed game it is often suggested that players knock on their first turn if their deadwood is no more than 60. On the second turn, 40 is considered a safe knock. Thereafter, the knock figure should be reduced 10 points per turn. In a game involving three players 35 is considered the highest safe deadwood count on the first round, and when there are more players, 30. After one round has been completed, the safe knock figured is reckoned at 20. After two turns, 15 is the highest logical knock count and after that it should be under 10.

However, slavish devotion to this strategy will lead to a gambler's certain downfall. Far more important is following normal Rummy sense, with observation

of discards and remembering where previously exposed cards are, being essential for successful play. It is generally not wise to hold high cards; it's better to discard them and hold low cards, even if the latter offer only limited potential for melding. Defensive play that avoids heavy losses is a key to the best strategy, so that one may pull far ahead when the cards are running right.

KNOCKING OUT: Casino and Cheater's Lingo

"Knocking out" can mean more than one thing among casino dealers. It can simply mean cleaning out a customer legitimately. But for a dishonest dealer it will have another connotation. If the dealer is cheating the house, say paying off a secret partner for nonwinning hands, he is creating a problem for himself. There is a danger that the scam will reduce the table's win rate so that his bosses will become suspicious, or at least disenchanted, about him. (Casinos do not appreciate any table that does not produce the winning edge the casino expects.)

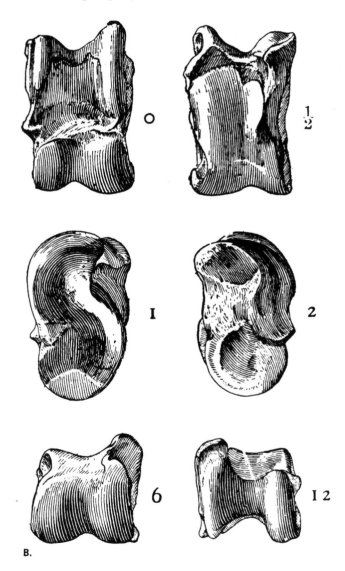

Knucklebones are the earliest form of dice. The ancient Greeks told of many legendary knucklebone contests between Aphrodite, the goddesss of love, and the god Pan, here illustrated (A) on a 4th-century B.C. mirror case. (B): The point values ascribed to the different sides of a knucklebone by ancient Mexican Indians. (Photos: N.Y. Public Library)

A.

B.

To counter this, the dishonest dealer will make it up by fleecing, or knocking out, other customers. If occasionally the dealer is caught in an errant move, he can usually convince his superiors it was an honest mistake. Since the "error" was in the house's favor, there seems little reason for them to doubt him, or to a cynical eye, even to want to doubt him.

KNUCKLEBONES: World's First Dice

Marked cubes, of which DICE are the modern form, are the oldest gambling implements known to man. While we do not know where or when the first such implements were used, knucklebones are considered to be the granddaddy of all marked cubes. Fashioned from the anklebones of sheep, they were marked with four faces and the first prehistoric shooter, it may be safely assumed, was immediately covered.

The ancient Greeks firmly believed gambling to have been an invention of the gods and many artifacts assure us that Aphrodite, the goddess of love, was addicted to knucklebone contests with the god Pan. In the *Iliad,* Homer records a quarrel involving a game of knucklebones, and, again according to many artworks, Greek wives apparently whiled away the time while their husbands were off at work or war at long games of knucklebones.

The American Indians developed the same kind of knucklebones from the animal game available to them—the moose, caribou, and buffalo.

L

LAKE TAHOE, NEVADA
See LAS VEGAS.

LANSQUENET: Banking Card Game
Lansquenet is a dead-even banking game, but in practice, in defiance of the laws of mathematics, the banker generally wins out. The game dates back to 17th-century Germany where the mercenaries of the day, the *landsknecht*, played it endlessly and frequently lost all their pay.

How to play: Two cards of different rank are turned up, one for the player (or players) and one for the banker. The player(s) places his bet on his card, and then cards from the deck are turned up one at a time. If the cards, as is likely, are of different values, they to are placed on the table and other players can bet on them as well. As soon as a card appears matching any player's card, the banker collects that money and puts the pair out of the game. If in the future additional cards of that rank turn up they too are eliminated. In the meantime play continues until the banker's card turns up, at which time he pays the board on all outstanding bets.

Lansquenet is an even game. If the banker starts off with an ace and the player with a deuce, it is an even-money proposition as to whether the ace or the deuce will turn up first. The same is true with any other value cards put in play against the ace. However, in practice, the banker has the edge. For example, the banker has an ace and, after a few cards are turned, players have placed bets on their cards—deuce, 3, 6, and queen. The odds against an ace beating any one of these cards is 50-50, but it is 4 to 1 that one of the players' cards will turn up before the ace. As a result the banker generally jumps into an early lead. The game's odds remain even if players continue to cover all new cards, but as they lose a few times their ardor cools and when the banker's ace turns up he frequently pays out less than he previously took in.

Dead-even odds do not mean that either the banker or the players can't have a long succession of wins, but in practice Lansquenet works out to the banker's advantage.

LANTERLOO
See LOO.

LAS VEGAS: America's Gambling Mecca
Las Vegas is the town the mob built. Before Bugsy Siegel, it was little more than a watering hole in the desert with a few sleazy slot-machine emporiums and some shabby gambling joints.

The first gamblers in Vegas were the Paiute Indians. When Brigham Young sent his Mormons down from Utah in 1855 to convert them, the missionaries found their magic was far less captivating than a Paiute version of ROULETTE played in the sand using bones and colored sticks. The die was already cast for Las Vegas. By 1905, Vegas was a town, but one without distinction until, in 1931, Nevada legalized gambling. Still, the gaming activity in Vegas was second rate through the 1930's until 1939 when construction of the Hoover Dam began in Boulder City. Las Vegas offered the nearest gambling spot where the construction workers could find gambling action.

This did not go unnoticed in mob circles back East—hence the eventual arrival of Bugsy Siegel. With a mob bankroll of $2 million, which grew to $4 million, which then became $6 million, Siegel built the first glittering palace in Vegas, the FLAMINGO. He also dug his own grave when the mob decided calls for additional funds were not entirely intended for construction. Bugsy became Vegas's first unofficial skimmer, and the first to be taught a lesson for it. He was assassinated.

Nevertheless Bugsy's dream of Las Vegas as one of the world's premiere gambling meccas proved right. Slowly the Flamingo turned profitable—despite its astronomical building costs. As Californians especially started making the car trek to Vegas, the mob poured money in and more and more major casinos were built. State officials set up what were described as strict rules for keeping organized crime out. Law enforcement people know who originally won that battle. Today? Perhaps the best answer comes from comedian Alan King, who said of Caesars Palace: "I wouldn't say it was exactly Roman—more kind of early Sicilian."

That hardly can be offered as proof of fact, but it does point up that mob influence in Vegas has become a matter of jest. In fact, whether the underworld is present or not is something that hardly

Welcome to Las Vegas (A) means "Place your bets." While there are considerable support services in Vegas, it's clear from the map (B) the only really important points in town are the fabulous Strip and the downtown casinos of "Glitter Gulch." (Photos: Las Vegas News Bureau)

A.

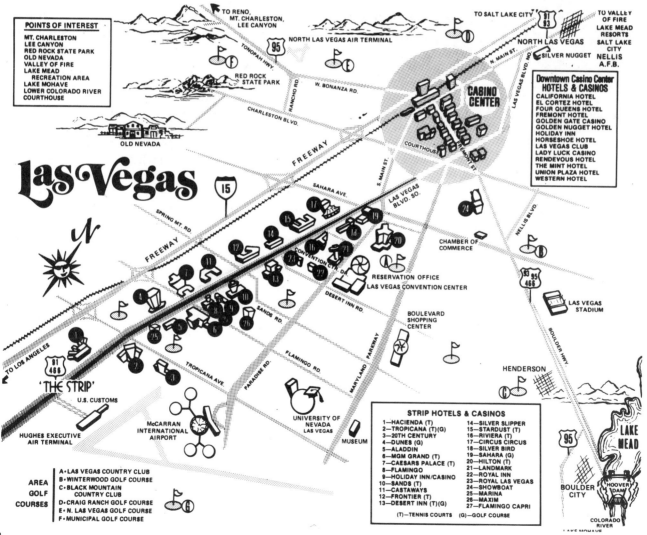

B.

A.

B.

Many seasoned gamblers actually prefer the downtown action in Vegas (A). However Vegas will always offer a gimmick such as rooftop gambling (B) or swimming pool betting action. (Photos: Las Vegas News Bureau)

bothers gamblers, who are convinced that what they get in Vegas is honest play. (Actually the public can be said to *want* to believe in the mob's presence in Vegas as it adds mystique to their visits. Not only are they bucking the gaming tables, but the underworld as well!)

More than anything else Las Vegas offers glamour, within the gambler's comprehension of the term. Some of its plusher casinos may be described variously as glittering, spectacular, tacky, or bordering on the obscene. There are the great shows that cost $25 to $40 per, depending on the star quality. You will be bowed and scraped to if you tip the maitre d' a mere $5 to $25 extra, and you will get a table accordingly. Tip nothing and he'll lead you so far to the side you'll think you're in the next casino. Walk out of the classiest casinos in town and "hooker flyers" litter the street or wink invitingly from freebie newspaper dispensers. They offer, in their own words, "the perfect way to climax your gambling stay."

None of the trappings matter a whit to the average gambler. What Vegas offers them is the illusion of

limitless choices, of non-stop action 24 hours a day, seven days a week—until the money runs out. Vegas casinos admonish gamblers to "bet with your head, not over it." If you lose you are invited to leave and come back when you have another stake. When you do, there'll undoubtedly be yet another lavish joint under construction, a new wing added perhaps where you had last stayed. "Feel free to visit your money anytime," the saying goes.

Vegas doesn't apologize for this. It operates on its own ethics. The IRS says the casinos must do certain things when making big payoffs, and the town does the minimum required. Vegas peddles the point that it always pays off instantly and in cash. Says a leading executive: "You win a million dollars, we give it all to you. We do what the government demands. We get ironclad identification and even take a color photograph of you, but then we hand over the money—no checks, all cash." Why cash? "If we give you cash, we stand a good chance of getting at least some of it back immediately."

A story is told of a gambler hitting a casino for $1 million and taking off. He returned a few weeks later and dropped a quarter of a million. The next trip he lost so much, he killed himself. The tale is repeated without any moral to be drawn, but rather just to illustrate the law of Vegas: give and take.

None of this is said to condemn Vegas, not that it would matter to the town if it were slurred. It is said to recognize, to identify its uniqueness.

When colorful old-time gambling operator Benny Binion was named by Mafia informer Jimmy "the Weasel" Fratianno as a man who'd taken out a $200,000 underworld contract for a hit on an annoying gambling figure, it hardly created a stir in Vegas, and certainly Binion himself was sublimely unconcerned. As British poet and writer A. Alvarez notes in *The Biggest Game in Town*, a penetrating study of Vegas, old Benny's friends were indignant that the owner of the famous Horseshoe would be so maligned. Binion would not do such a thing, they said. "Two hundred grand, never," one protested. "Two, maybe. In casino credits." Thus does Vegas see itself in the mirror.

Binion stands as the epitome of the town's ethics, a bad man to cross. Perhaps the favorite story told about him concerns a welsher who ran up a $100 tab at Binion's glitzy downtown establishment and refused to pay. The enraged Binion decided the welsher had no need for his clothes. He had the man stripped and flipped out on to Fremont Street stark naked.

Despite this—if not in part because of it—the Horseshoe is regarded by many as the best damned gambling joint in Vegas. There are many who say there is no better gambling joint anywhere in the world. Located in Glitter Gulch, the so-called pits of

Las Vegas, it is in the seedy downtown area that supposedly lacks the "class" of the fabulous Strip where the big hotel casinos are. But the Horseshoe is tops for gambling. Sure, sometimes the action is noisy, two-fisted, whoop-it-up, but it's all a gambler could want. The restaurant and coffee shop are plush, the furnishings rich and subdued. In its own way it offers the restraint common to the classier casinos of Europe. And betting—forget about limits, the Horseshoe will cover any bet of any size. Basically, the Horseshoe lets the player set his own limits. Whatever he bets on his first wager (even if it's outrageously high) becomes his limit. (He may start low and raise his bets without being noticed until they get well up into four figures.)

Vegas is really two different cities, the Strip and downtown. The Strip was the Hollywood Rat Pack's turf and it's where most high rollers play (though the smart ones are at the Horseshoe or another class downtown joint, the Golden Nugget). Some visitors come to the Strip and are awed by the spectacle. Others are merely mystified at what is considered "glamorous."

Scattered in between the huge hotel casinos are shabby little shopping centers, souvenir shops, and at its perimeter those eternal tiny tacky wedding chapels (one boasts a sign that blares "Dynasty's Joan Collins was married here"), with often a motel next door offering X-rated movies in all rooms. Most seasoned gamblers are truly impressed only by certain aspects of the Strip casinos. The plush high-tech horse and sports book at Caesars Palace is paradise for horseplayers. The Stardust runs a close second in this field, and both offer large-screen live telecasts from several tracks—be there by 9 in the morning to cover the New York and Florida action—as well as baseball, football, basketball, hockey, boxing, tennis, golf, and whatever else gamblers can bet on.

But for real "down home" gambling one has to head for downtown Vegas, a vulgar five-block area where chubby girls in Western outfits practically haul you into the grind joints with coupons good for free slot plays and souvenirs. There is grind joint after grind joint, given over mainly to slot play and separated only occasionally by pawnshops, bail bondsmen, and collection agencies whose signs promise quick action. However, there are also the class casinos like the Horseshoe and the Golden Nugget, the latter now the brightest, airiest, most tasteful casino anywhere in Vegas, putting to shame the gaudiness of the Strip. These casinos are the very best for betting. The great POKER games take place there, as well as at the nearby Las Vegas Club, which offers the best buys in town. The Club's hotel rooms, equal in quality to anything offered on the Strip, are less than half Strip rates, and in BLACKJACK it offers the best rules available for players. Gamblers can double down even on three or four cards and a winning hand is automatic on six cards under 21, splitting and resplitting pairs can continue indefinitely.

What about the rest of Nevada? There is always Reno, which is the place to go from Frisco if you are on a limited budget. Reno is billed as "the biggest little city in the world." After visiting Vegas you'll know what the "little" means, despite the fact that some massive expansion has been taking place there. The other important gambling center is Lake Tahoe, smaller yet than Reno but making up for it in natural beauty, grandeur, and the opportunity for outdoor activities such as skiing and boating. Of course, your average gambler never sees any of this, since he never ventures out of doors in daylight.

Certainly Harrah's Lake Tahoe deserves high-roller action as much as any casino on the Vegas Strip, but on the whole northern Nevada odds are dreadful, giving gamblers a poor shake compared to the Vegas spots. *Playboy* magazine noted in a recent survey of the worst places to gamble in America that "anyone playing blackjack in northern Nevada should be arrested for stupidity."

There are other pit stops of gambling throughout the state, but they are just on the way to Vegas. The only real competition Las Vegas faces now and in the future is Atlantic City. Until now it has been no competition at all. Atlantic City can be described as Dullsville by the Seashore. It offers only a handful of games and there is no important difference from one casino to the next, except perhaps that some are less equal than others.

Atlantic City gambling is basically a monopoly play. Since the rules are the same for each casino, players have no real freedom of choice. It's play at their rules and at their high stakes or not at all.

LAST CHANCE TAVERN: Kansas City Gambling Den

The famed Kefauver crime committee hearings of the 1950's were triggered in main measure by the corruption and gambling—as well as murders—in Kansas City, Missouri. Senator Estes Kefauver cited one gambling joint, the Last Chance Tavern, as typical of the gambling corruption there.

The Last Chance was located in a building on Southwest Boulevard, right on the Missouri-Kansas state line. In Kansas City—where corruption ran rampant under Boss Pendergast's political machine and under its successor, Charley Binaggio—no one was surprised when it later developed that Binaggio himself was a partner in the building.

After Binaggio's rubout in 1950, the Kefauver crime hearings came to town to study firsthand how corruption operates. With wry humor Senator Kefauver zeroed in on the notorious operation:

> The Last Chance was an intriguing establishment located on the border between Kansas and Missouri, with a thin wall right on the state line. When the cops from one state would come to "raid" it, the gamblers with great hilarity would shift their equipment over to the other side and carry on without interruption. Cops from both states never seemed to arrive at the same time, so everybody had a lot of fun and Binaggio's gang made a lot of money. Senator [Charles W.] Tobey did not think much of this operation. After we pried from Eddie Osadchey how the racket worked, Tobey exploded: "You know, Mr. Chairman, if I had been one of those cops, I would have gone across and brought them back and knocked them cold and said, 'Here they are in Kansas territory.'"

The Last Chance was shuttered, but no one has ever claimed that organized gambling did not continue to thrive in Kansas City.

LAST IN: Trump Gambling Game

Last In, sometimes called Lift Smoke, is a game for four, five, or six players. It is played with a 52-card deck, aces high, deuces low, and hands are dealt to contain as many cards as there are players. The last card dealt to the dealer is dealt face up, and determines trump.

Tricks, which have no particular value, are taken by the highest trump or the highest card of the suit led. The eldest hand (the player to the left of the dealer) opens and his opponents must first follow suit, after which they may trump or, if unable to follow suit or trump, discard any other card. The winner of the trick draws a card from the top of the remaining pile before leading on the next trick. No other player draws a card. This is so on all succeeding tricks as well. Unlike most gambling games of this type, the object in Last In is not to play out but to be the last remaining participant in the game.

The winner takes the kitty, and there is a new ante before the winner deals the next game. The dealer enjoys the slight advantage of being assured of a trump at the start of play (the last card dealt). However, far more important is good card sense by players to determine when and if they have the power to force their opponents to play trumps without taking the trick.

LAW OF AVERAGES MYTH
See GAMBLER'S FALLACY.

LAZY MARY
See ONE-CARD POKER.

LEBANON, Gambling in

Before Lebanon became mired down in the crosscurrents of civil and religious strife, it offered the best, most lavish gambling center in the Middle East. Beirut—"the Paris of the Middle East"—proudly claimed the crown jewel of the area's casinos, the fabulous Lido. Elegantly appointed in the Arab manner to complement its French heritage, the Lido lured the jet-setters, Greek shipping tycoons, oil sheiks, and others eager to try their luck. The gambling volume often surpassed the action at Monte Carlo, Cannes, or Deauville. The casino's gamblers were noted for their flamboyance, and their capacity for being either good losers or generous winners.

That make-believe world collapsed in the 1980's in the real world of gunfire and bomb-ravaged rubble. Yet it goes without saying that if peace ever comes to Lebanon, gambling on a grand scale will return to Beirut.

LEFTY LOUIE: Wild Poker Variation

Lefty Louie is a POKER game in which all picture cards with faces looking to the left are wild. This is an intriguing game when several decks are switched constantly during play, since picture cards vary among different makes and manufacturers. When the dealer calls the game with a deck he is familiar with, he gains something of an edge.

LEG IN POT
See LEG POKER.

LEG POKER: Multi-game Poker

Leg Poker is best played in a Draw Poker setting, although there is a variation involving STUD. In Leg Poker, the winner of a pot does not collect it; it remains on the table until he or another player wins twice, that is, wins "two legs," not necessarily in consecutive order. As a result, the pot can grow enormously over the course of a game.

The same principle can apply to any form of Stud, generally called Two-Leg Stud. In the Stud version players may be forced to stay with sucker hands (trying to fill an inside straight or a three-card flush) simply to prevent another player from winning his second leg and taking all the money. The more prudent player will not do so—if he sees some other players doing so.

Kitty LE ROY: Western Female Gambler

Along with Poker Alice and Madame Mustache, Kitty Le Roy (1850-1878) was among the top women gamblers in the old West. Born in Texas, Kitty started her public life as a jug dancer in Dallas at the age of 10. As her beauty unfolded over the next decade, she became the toast of that Texas city, occupying a place in local society somewhat comparable to Lily Langtry in Victorian England. Like Langtry, Kitty took up a stage career but she gave that up in favor of working as a FARO dealer. Cowmen and miners flocked to her table and she drew a higher commission than other dealers.

Though popular, Kitty was not considered honest, undoubtedly for good reason. But she met challenges to her veracity by becoming an expert pistol shot, and her quick draw and deliberate near-misses settled many a dispute at the gaming table. The word was that she was always armed with more than one pistol and at least a bowie knife or two. Indeed, her private arsenal, which she occasionally showed to a favored gent, consisted of seven guns and 12 knives.

Kitty was adept at making certain cards appear at Faro; she was equally talented at making husbands disappear. Her first was a gallant sport with enough gumption to let her shoot apples off his head as she galloped by on horseback. When she got interested in a wealthy German, she ran the first one out of town by suggesting she just might start missing those apples. Husband No. 2, the rich German, was given notice when his money ran out. Husband No. 3 was very short-lived. She shot him right after they met. One version was that she became annoyed at his romantic advances, another that he'd said her movements with the Faro box were most unladylike. No matter, Kitty took pity on him and married him hours before he expired.

In 1876 Kitty arrived in Deadwood, in Dakota Territory, with yet another spouse and they opened the Mint Gambling Saloon, among whose more illustrious patrons were badman Sam Bass and that lousy card player WILD BILL HICKOK. It was said that Kitty became romantically involved with both of them, among others. In 1878, presumably in a state of rage, Kitty's husband killed her and himself.

LESOTHO, Gambling in

The mountainous kingdom of Lesotho, once a British protectorate, now has a new reputation. It is where white South Africans go to do their sinning. Lesotho is convenient because it is completely surrounded by South Africa. South African whites who would not do so in their own country—and are in many cases prohibited from doing so by law—zip into Lesotho for such pleasure meccas as the Holiday Inn Casino where they can rub elbows, bend elbows, and, above all, gamble with their black neighbors.

Gambling has always been a multi-racial affair and leveler, though not in South Africa.

Joe E. LEWIS: Entertainer and Compulsive Gambler

Over the years many entertainers have been particular favorites of the casino-owning fraternity. Joe E. Lewis (1902-1971) was among the most popular because, while he drew huge salaries, he gave it back at the gaming tables.

Lewis appeared as a star performer at the plush—if illegal—Beverly Club in New Orleans, an establishment secretly owned mostly by crime kingpins Frank Costello and Meyer Lansky. Lewis frequently had to borrow money from Costello to get out of town, but always paid back his debts. When the comic died, a saddened Costello attended his funeral, much as any grieving bookmaker would on losing a meal-ticket.

The speed with which Lewis could drop a bundle made for legend in Las Vegas. Taking a shortcut across the gaming rooms could cost him a small fortune. Once Lewis was dining in a casino restaurant with an attractive woman who asked him to get her some cigarettes. Not seeing a cigarette girl in the restaurant, he jauntily made his way to the counter out in the lobby. He returned in a few minutes. When the couple finished their meal, Lewis noticed his lady friend had left the unfinished pack of cigarettes on the table. "Better take them with you, honey," he said, "they cost me $32,000."

LIAR DICE: Five-dice Poker-style Game

Not to be confused with POKER DICE, Liar Dice, or Doubting Dice, resembles POKER in any of several versions. Any number can play Liar dice, which uses five dice. Ace is high and the 6, 5, 4, 3, and 2 represent the king, queen, jack, 10, and 9. In the standard two-man game, the opponents are separated by a screen behind which they conceal their dice rolls. When there are more than two players no screen is used and players shake the dice in dice cups, turn the cup over, and deposit the dice behind the shelter of their hand.

Each player starts off with three chips of predetermined value. The first player casts his dice and then announces the value of his hand. As is the case with all subsequent players, he has the right to rethrow all or some of his dice a second or third time before announcing his hand. He is not required to tell the truth, and the player to his left, the doubter, must either call him a liar or accept the claim. If the first shooter is wrongfully accused and he turns out to have the hand or indeed one of an even higher value, the doubter must put a chip into the pot. If the shooter proves to have been a liar, he must give the doubter one chip and put another into the pot. Now the doubter becomes the shooter.

If, on the other hand, the doubter accepts the

shooter's claim, the doubter has to shoot and he *must* announce a higher hand than the first shooter. He does this even if his hand does not justify the claim. The first shooter must make a decision whether or not to accept the doubter's claim. Play continues in this fashion with each player having the right to reshoot all or some of his dice before announcing a new, higher hand. The game continues until one or the other's hand is challenged. At that point the original rules of doubting apply as to who must pay. When a player uses up all his chips, he is out of the game. The winner takes the pot and a new game begins.

Skill at bluffing is critical in Liar Dice, and the ability to confuse an opponent will prove rewarding to the astute gambler. A word of warning: playing Liar Dice with strangers is not a smart move. Liar Dice has long been a favorite game of hustlers on transoceanic and cruise ships. Shielding the dice with one's hand allows for all sorts of dice palming and DICE-CUP CHEATING.

LIAR'S POKER
See DOLLAR POKER.

LIFT SMOKE
See LAST IN.

LIVERPOOL RUMMY
See CONTRACT RUMMY.

LOCATION PLAY: Cheating Card-dealing Technique
Location play is the ideal cheating method for a card player with little or no dexterity. When the player—or locator—takes the deal, he need simply identify in order three, four, or five cards. The locator places the seconds at the bottom of the deck. As he shuffles the deck, he simply fails to mix in these bottom cards. Then he offers the deck for cutting. The "located" cards remain together in sequence. All the dealer has to do is remember the sequence. When one of these cards appears, he knows the location of the cards.

For example, the locator calls Seven-card Stud. He's located a pair of jacks, a 10 and a 7. As his second downcard he draws the 7. He now knows the player to his right has a 10 in the hole, and the two hands immediately before that player each has a hole-card jack. He now has an enormous advantage on them that frequently determines if he folds or stays and raises.

Location play is even more potent in Five-card Stud; a cheating dealer will call it in DEALER'S CHOICE if the cut tells him his cards will come out early. Often he knows in advance the next face card several players will draw. Even if he can't be sure he will win the hand he will at least know when to drop out to avoid losses.

LOLLAPALOOZA HAND: Scam and/or Top-hand in Poker
The Lollapalooza hand has a long if not always honorable history in POKER. Among the first written descriptions of it appears in John F. B. Lillard's 19th-century work, *Poker Stories*. Lillard tells of a gambling stranger who joined a game in a Butte, Montana, saloon with four prospectors. After a rather uneventful first hour, he suddenly came up with four aces at Draw Poker. The stranger stood pat on the draw and was hardly concerned when another player did also. After all, he could have nothing more than two pair or three of a kind and be trying to appear stronger, or he could have been holding a straight or a flush or a full house or even four of a kind. It didn't matter. The stranger had him beat. After some wild final betting, the stranger triumphantly showed his four aces and started to rake in the pot.

"Not so fast, sonny," his whiskered opponent said.

"What do you mean, not so fast?" the stranger said. "I've got four aces."

"Sure you do," came the reply, "but in this town a Lollapalooza beats any other Poker hand. And that's what I've got—three clubs and two diamonds."

The other players nodded earnestly.

The stranger could do nothing but abide by the odd rule. He played on patiently and finally came up with the same hand—three clubs and two diamonds, a Lollapalooza. He bet the hand to the hilt and then triumphantly announced his Lollapalooza.

His chortle of joy was cut short by the sad shaking of heads. "Sorry, pardner," the previous Lollapalooza victor said, "you should ask about the rules before you deal yourself in. The Lollapalooza can only be played once a night."

While the Lollapalooza was born as a scam it has now become an accepted custom in many private games. Late arrivals at a weekend game will sit down at the table and immediately inquire what the Lollapalooza is and ask if it has been won yet. Common in a five-card game is a Lollapalooza of one card in each suit—spades, clubs, hearts, and diamonds—with one of the cards paired. In seven-card games the hand often consists of three pairs, even though the rules otherwise limit hands to just five cards. In any event, after the first spectacular win, the Lollapalooza goes into mothballs for the rest of the game, reverting to its actual rank. And once an evening is quite enough.

See THREE-PAIR HIGH.

LOO: Old English Card Game

For several decades around 1800 Loo, or Lanterloo, was one of the favorite gambling games in England and to some extent the United States. Unlike some other card games it crossed all class lines, being played, as one observer put it, by "the idle rich and industrious poor."

It can be played in either a three-card or five-card version, although the three-card is more common. Since only three cards are dealt to each player quite a number can participate, but the best games are with six or seven. At first only the dealer antes, putting three chips into the pot. The play is for three tricks, with each player following suit if possible, otherwise trumping. There is no trump until a player is unable to follow suit, at which point he discards another card. Then the top card of the stock is turned over and its suit becomes trump. The trump is retroactive, so the card discarded on the previous trick will take it if it happens to be trump. One-third of the pool goes to the winner of each trick, and each hand that doesn't win a trick is looed and must put three chips into the next pool.

Under the rules of the game players must use their highest trumps at all times. The best hand is a flush composed of three trumps. If a player holds a trump flush he takes the entire pool without any play. In case of a tie the first flush shown wins.

The game turns into Unlimited Loo when Loo is not set at three chips (or five in a five-card version) but rather at the size of the current pot. In this version, the action can turn somewhere between mindless and limitless. No wonder one HOYLE book reported "a certain Irish Lord is reported to have lost 10,000 pounds at one sitting at half-crown [ante.]"

LOTTERIES

A lottery is any means of awarding cash or other prizes by lot, the total amount of prizes always being less than the money taken in. Without doubt lotteries are the most popular form of gambling, involving more people than any other type of wagering. Today well over 50 countries have lotteries of one type or another. They include Ireland, Great Britain, West Germany, Italy, France, Turkey, Spain, the Soviet Union, China, Poland, Thailand, Australia, and the countries of Latin America. Lotteries have had a checkered history in the United States. From 1776 until 1820 over 70 lotteries were authorized by the U.S. Congress for public works. During that period and later, many lotteries were plagued by charges of fraud. Today many states offer lotteries of one form or another to finance various public projects or activities.

Lotteries can be traced back to ancient Rome, where emperors held lotteries for their guests. Nero awarded such prizes as villas or slaves. Eccentric Heliogabalus mixed in dud prizes; some "winners" were awarded a dead dog, ostriches, or six dead flies. Augustus Caesar first conceived the idea of selling lottery tickets to his guests. That in time led him to conceive of a public lottery as a way of raising revenues for the repair of the city of Rome.

While there were undoubtedly many other lotteries in intervening centuries, the next recorded lottery was held in the town of L'Ecluse in Burgundy in 1420 when the good burghers were given the opportunity to fund the fortification of the town through wagering. In 1466 the widow of Flemish painter Jan van Eyck organized a lottery in Bruges as a way to raise funds for the poor.

By 1520 France had lotteries in five cities—Paris, Lyons, Bordeaux, Lille, and Strasbourg. In Venice and Genoa merchants held lotteries for their wares, discovering that in this way they could net more than if they sold their goods in the regular fashion. Florence's first government lottery, *La Lotto de Firenze* was held around 1528 and many other city-states followed with similar schemes to raise funds for public projects. Soon most of the Italian states had lotteries and, when Italy was united in 1870, the Italian national lottery was born. Save for wartime interruptions, the Italian lottery has been in operation ever since.

Once lotteries start up they are almost never cancelled. They have, however, incurred the wrath of the church (for a time the papacy ordered excommunication for anyone betting on certain lotteries). The results have also been altered. King Louis XIV of France once "won" a 100,000-franc prize while his queen and the dauphin garnered smaller prizes. In response to public outrage, the monarch "graciously" returned the money and asked for a new drawing.

There have been numerous scandals since. In Pennsylvania, a lottery was fixed even as it was televised by false numbering of the balls. But the fact remains, honest or crooked, lotteries are here to stay, especially since they have become an excellent source of revenue for governments all over the world, on both sides of the iron curtain.

See also LOTTERY MANIA, IRISH SWEEPSTAKES, NEW YORK LOTTERY SWINDLE.

LOTTERY MANIA

The main argument made in favor of state-run lotteries in this country is that they are honest and that the amount wagered by an individual can be small. However, as anyone who has stood in line to buy a lottery ticket can attest, the operating phrase of the previous sentence is "can be small." There are, un-

Louis XIV of France at center top of main table presiding over a royal lottery. When he, his queen and the dauphin all miraculously were winners, there was a public outcry, and the monarch "graciously" returned the prizes and called for a new drawing. (Photo: N.Y. Public Library)

fortunately, a great many people who spend a considerable amount of money on lottery tickets. It's not uncommon to see people in tattered clothing spending as much as $100 on one day's play in the thrice-weekly New York Lotto. Newspaper columnist Jimmy Breslin has constantly chastised government for essentially hustling poor people to play lotteries, including the numbers game, a massive swindle always aimed at victimizing the poor.

Sen. David Durenberger of Minnesota has criticized states for being less than forthright with their citizens about lotteries. "Nobody ever tells people how high the odds are against winning," he declares.

Generally speaking, what the states claim they give back to the bettors and what they keep is not exactly accurate. Many lottery players say that they feel they are doing a good thing in betting on the games, that the money goes for such purposes as education or to reduce a state's overall tax load, and that half the money is paid out to contestants. Actually it is estimated that for the year 1984, for example, sales of state lottery tickets exceeded $7 billion. Of this, $3 billion went to the states, more than $2 billion for administration, advertising, commissions to vendors, and other costs, and only about $2 billion to the players. And it should be added that all levels of government then immediately tax the big winners. It should also be noted that very few people actually win $1 million even when that is the payoff prize. Payment over 20 years is not exactly the same thing as $1 million up front. Getting it all, even with the heavy lump-sum tax bite, winners should be left with enough to amass considerably more money in interest. This additional income is lost in a 20-year payment play, or more accurately, it is kept by the states. Funding in this manner permits the states to exaggerate the amounts it is paying out to a winner. There is much to be said for the idea that if a Wall Street promoter represented a stock deal the way the states do their lotteries he would most likely be clapped behind bars.

What are the real chances of winning a lottery jackpot? Based on the general system of getting two bets for a dollar, if the numbers range from 1 to 30, the odds are 1 in 593,775. Most lotteries now use more numbers (which increases the chances that the jackpot will grow as no winner turns up for several games running). In a 1-40 game the odds on winning plummet to 1 in 1,919,190. At 1-44 they become roughly 1 in 3.5 million. At 1-48, they are about 1 in 6 million. And at 1-54, such as in New York's Lotto 54, the spread widens to well over 1 in 12.9 million. New York's Cash 40 offers a better chance of winning, 1 in close to 2 million, but when second or third prizes are considered, the odds are a more realizable 1 in 228. Of course virtually all of these are third-prize awards, which means that if a person plays $1 a week in a little over four years he will win a prize of about $30—give or take $10 or $20 either way, depending on how many others share it with him.

Obviously no casino, legal or illegal, in fact no mob-run numbers racket, could survive at such an enormous takeout. The states have turned hustlers, shilling their niggardly paying games out of pure necessity. Under the circumstances it is futile to criticize the states for hawking their games to the poor while knowing full well that they are hustling money being paid out, in some cases, in welfare checks. In many states the very check-cashing establishments that cash welfare checks also sell lottery tickets, a sort of one-stop banking for the poor.

The states' glib answer is that lottery income is something called a "voluntary tax" since no one is forced to buy tickets. Compulsion, however, comes in more ways than with a gun at one's back. The states have created a new class of gamblers, lottery addicts. One example is the Michigan woman who faced 24 counts of criminal fraud for cashing a half-million dollars in bad checks and using fake money orders to support her lottery habit, which frequently reached $1,000 a day for tickets. Presumably, the unfortunate woman never worked it out that her thefts alone amounted to more money than the lottery would have paid her if she'd won.

LOTTO: Bingo Predecessor
Lotto, today still popular as a parlor game in America, is generally regarded as the predecessor of Bingo. It was played in gambling houses and church socials in the United States until Bingo, a quicker game, overtook it.

Lotto was inspired by the Italian national lottery, which has been in operation in regional forms since 1528. But it is difficult to determine when Lotto itself was first played.

To play special Lotto cards, consisting of numbers in nine vertical rows and from three to five horizontal rows, are used. As in Bingo, numbers are drawn from a container in any of several fashions and play continues until a winner is determined, one who fills a horizontal row, or the entire card, or some other previously established winning pattern. Unlike Bingo, 90 numbers are pulled instead of only 75.

Prizes in games played in a gaming parlor or elsewhere outside the home are generally a portion of the ante made by all the players—less a house percentage for the operator of the game.

LOW HOLE CARD WILD: Seven-card Stud Variation
Of all the Seven-card Stud games Low Hole Card Wild has been among the most upsetting to POKER purists. Under the rules a player's lowest hole card is wild as well as any others of the same denomination in his hand. Conservative players never cared much for the game since the seventh card is also dealt down and if it turns out to be a new low card, an otherwise powerhouse hand can be destroyed. In recent years a new wrinkle has sometimes been added to make the game a bit saner. Each player has the option of getting the last card up or down. If he wants it down, he must turn up one of his two previous downcards. Otherwise he gets the card up, thus protecting his previous wild cards.

Anything can happen in Low Hole Card Wild and it is rather common to get four or five of a kind or royal flushes. The value of playing the option of last card up or down is that it makes it possible to read an opponent's hand. If, for example, an opponent has a pair showing and takes the final card up, it is generally a good indication he is protecting a hand that has three wild cards. Admittedly, he could be bluffing, but bluffing is not much of a tactic in a game in which someone is likely to have four of a kind, a hand he isn't likely to fold.

LOWBALL: Poker in Reverse

Generally speaking, the farther west one goes in the United States, the more common is the game of Lowball, which could be called POKER in reverse. The game is almost the opposite of Draw Poker in that the lowest hand wins. Lowball is highly popular in California's legal Poker clubs and may even be the second most popular game after straight Draw (Stud is not legal in these clubs).

Under the usual rules, straights and flushes do not count. Instead, the lowest possible hand is 5, 4, 3, 2, ace, which is called a bicycle, or wheel. Aces are always low and thus a pair of aces would rank lower than a pair of deuces. But it is generally very difficult to win a pot with a pair and if the pair is high, say 10's or higher, virtually impossible.

Under another set of Lowball rules, standard Poker rankings stand and the ace is always high. In this variation the best possible hand is 7, 5, 4, 3, 2, and, since straights and flushes are recognized as high hands, such a hand must be composed of mixed suits.

More important than the variation in the rules, is the ability of the player to determine the probabilities of making or improving on a good hand. The poor Lowball player may, for instance, stay with an opening hand of 3, 4, 9, and a pair of kings (in ace-low Lowball). He would discard a pair of kings and draw two cards. The good player would more likely drop out altogether. Even if he got two other low cards, he would still be 9 high—which is too high. Even an 8 high on three cards is not a good Lowball hand. Many players do not realize how difficult it is to match up three low cards with two more. It is almost as difficult as filling to a three-card straight at regular Poker. Even if the player draws two low cards there is an excellent chance that he will end up with a pair and possibly two pair. Should this happen to a player in straight Poker he might actually luck into a win, while in Lowball he merely comes to grief.

Similarly the amateur and the professional would probably have a different reaction to a hand consisting of 10, 9, 7, 4, 2. The amateur will often discard either the high card or the two highest in an effort to improve his low hand. The professional will almost always stand on such a hand, not even drawing one card, which generally would be the most he'd try for in some other hands. There is almost no percentage in trying to reduce his high from 10 to 9, at best, while risking drawing a card higher than a 10 or even worse, pairing up. Standing with a pat hand has the added advantage of frightening the opposition, which

has no way of knowing what the highest card in this "stand-pat" low hand is.

Thus the basic strategy in Lowball should be to stand with a pat hand or at most draw one card. If a player can't do either, the best move is to drop out. The strategy of the game alters when it is played in the less-popular version of Five-card Stud, since a player gets to see most of his opponents' hands.

LUMINOUS READERS: Card-marking technique

Luminous readers are cards marked by a technique promoted in Hollywood and television plots. They are almost never used by professional hustlers. In fact, it can be said that the only people making money out of these devices are the gambling supply houses that sell them to gullible amateur cheats.

The technique involves identifying red-backed cards with a very faint green pencil marks. The marks can be large because they show up only on red-backed cards and must be read through red filter—glasses with red-tinted lenses, or an eyeshade with a red visor. Some of these gambling supply houses also peddle cheap red contact lenses that can be recommended only for those wishing to ruin their eyesight. (It is true that some optometrists now supply red-tinted contact lenses for jacked-up prices ranging from $500 to $1,000, clearly indicating they know the uses to which the lenses are put.)

Still, no real professional would consider this flim-flam. Reason: no luminous reader will last long in any game. If a potential cheat shows up with a red visor or red-tinted glasses he will be laughed out of the game, or worse. Lenses might last a while, presuming they are good, but no regular cardplayers will tolerate playing with red-backed cards exclusively for long. The cry will go up for blue-backed cards instead. And suspicion will soon focus on a gambler who bets and wins big with red cards and bets and loses small with blue ones.

LUXEMBOURG, Gambling in

After the passage of an anti-gambling law in 1903, it was illegal to operate a gambling house, to permit gambling on one's premises or in one's home and to advertise any form of wagering, including publicizing gambling outside the country.

Bowing to the pressure of the needs for a tourist economy, things have changed in recent years. Now a gambling casino is within easy reach of the center of Luxembourg, the capital city, although the action seldom rivals that in neighboring France, Germany, or Belgium.

M

MACAO: Blackjack-style Game

A very popular game in the United States early in the 20th century, Macao is seldom played any longer because, despite what appear to be very attractive odds for a player, it gives the dealer a tremendous advantage.

The object of the game is to score 9 or as close to it as possible without "busting" (going over 9). After bets are placed, all players including the dealer are dealt a card face down. All cards from ace to 9 have their pip value, but the 10 and all picture cards are counted as zero. If a player draws a 7 on his first card he wins the amount of the bet. If he gets an 8 he collects double, and triple for a 9. However, the dealer does not pay off if he has a 9 or an 8 himself that is higher than the player's card. All bets are off in case of a tie.

After the cards have been faced and appropriate payoffs made to all players holding a 7 or more, those with a score of less than 7 can draw one or more cards to try for a higher total. However, they lose if they go over 9. Once they have their point, the dealer tries to top their scores.

While the rules seem to make this an easy game for a player to win, the ties cut that advantage very severely. The dealer has an enormous edge in knowing beforehand the other players' point totals so that he can decide whether or not to try to improve his own score. He will not risk going over 9 himself if he sees he is beating two out of three players. Despite the possible double or triple payoffs, gamblers have learned that Macao does not give them as much of an opportunity of winning as BLACKJACK.

MACAO, Gambling in

Macao, a Portuguese colony granted broad autonomy in 1976, is an enclave consisting of a peninsula and two islands lying about 40 miles from Hong Kong, from where most of its gambling clients come via luxury ferries and speedy hydrofoils. There are several casinos on Macao, and in the past they have been known to play cutthroat tricks to force competition out of business.

Among the games offered are ROULETTE, BLACKJACK, BACCARAT (American style), FAN TAN, CRAPS, BOULE, and SLOT MACHINES. The Chinese name for slot machines is *hack got tse lo-fu gei*, which translates aptly as "eat coins tiger game."

The odds offered in Macao are not the best. Americans are not advised to wager at CRAPS since the odds are less favorable than in the U.S. Roulette, although better than the Nevada version, does not operate under the imprison, or "halvsies," rule on the single zero but rather gives all even-money bets to the house. Fan Tan is very popular with the Chinese crowds, but the odds heavily favor the house.

Why, then, go to Macao to gamble? If you are in Hong Kong or thereabouts, it is, as the saying goes, "the only game in town."

Macao's casinos are regarded among the unfriendliest to winners. The Macao casinos love high rollers and big spenders but have a positive dislike for big winners. It is said that when someone goes on a roll, the casino's telex is sure to start clicking, checking up on him to see if he has a record as a CROSSROADER, or casino cheat. If he does, he and his suspected confederates may well be clapped into jail. It has also been alleged that trials in such cases may never be held. One group of American crossroaders got turned loose only after the payment of $100,000. They were not paid their winnings but instead were supplied with one-way plane tickets to California.

There is no known instance of this sort of treatment being accorded to winners whose records check out clean, but perhaps prudence dictates that you can be too lucky in Macao.

MADAME MUSTACHE: Famous Western Gambler

Her name was often given as Eleanor Dumont, but it was really Simone Jules. However, she has become best known as Madame Mustache (1830-1879). The sobriquet was given her late in life when what was up until then no more than a faint hairy endowment on her upper lip blossomed into a fuller mustache. Thus, popular accounts that say she was famous from her younger days as Madame Mustache are incorrect. She actually gained her true fame as a gambler in 1849 in California, where this young, handsome, French-born (apparently) woman first turned up as a card dealer. Since good women gamblers were rare then in the West, the gambling addicts flocked to her table. Her more enthusiastic profilers claim that she always gave her opponents a fair shake at the gaming tables. That accolade should be limited to her time as an honest croupier at ROULETTE at San Francisco's Bella Union. When she had socked away enough of a stake to open a house of her own in Nevada City, it was another story.

There she took the name of Eleanor Dumont and kept it until the 1870's when she became known as Madame Mustache. Her gambling saloon thrived as did her later establishments, strung out from Nevada to Montana. Some of the boys did right well at her other games but when they made a big score they would headed for Madame Dumont's table to try their luck at TWENTY-ONE or FARO. Invariably they lost. The "law of average" just didn't seem to apply to her games. But most of the boys didn't mind. They were gambling with a glamorous lady, and few thought that anyone in skirts was capable of cheating them. When enough of them did, however, the lady would decamp for some new mining town. Her story was not an uncommon one in the world of gambling. She drank a lot, loved a lot and ultimately lost her touch. Part of her appeal in the rough Western gambling saloons world was her claim that she was still a virgin. That turned out to be something of an exaggeration, and as her gambling prowess decreased, she took to making more of her money from the upstairs activities of the more obliging girls than from the downstairs action at the tables.

Then her lovers began taking her for her money, and in time she had very little left. By the time she opened a seedy joint in Bodie, California, she had gone quite to pot, physically and professionally. It was here that the Madame Mustache monicker first caught on, and some biographers even suggest that after overhearing the cruel nickname a few times she committed suicide by taking poison. This was not quite accurate. Shortly before coming to Bodie from Carson City, she had been cleaned out of her property and jewelry by her latest main man. In Bodie she used the last of her money to try to recoup against a pair of sharpers. Unfortunately, they cleaned her out, working tricks that in her sorry condition she could not even spot. After that game, she went up to her room and played her last hand, swallowing a lethal dose of hydrocyanic acid.

MAH-JONGG: Chinese Gambling Game

Mah-Jongg, is an ancient Chinese game for four players (there are also two- and three-player versions), which has gone through waves of popularity in the West. In its basic Chinese form it is a gambling game. The Western version has many "special hands," more elaborate scoring and at times extra tiles. This version—or versions to be more accurate since there are no universally acknowledged rules for the Western game—was first introduced to the West around 1900, and after World War I it took off in popularity. Mah-Jongg was a veritable craze in America by the 1920's, but faded away with the proliferation of new rules and with the growth in appeal of Contract Bridge.

Mah-Jongg, similar to the card game RUMMY, requires luck and a fair amount of skill. Gambling at Mah-Jongg takes place in Chinese communities all around the world. A tourist in Singapore or Hong Kong will soon come to recognize the sounds of shuffling tiles resounding from the back streets—or as the Chinese call it, "the twittering of the sparrows."

The game is played with 136 to 144 ivory and bamboo dominoes, or tiles. There are three suits of four sets each, one with three honors (red, white, and green); the second representing the four winds, East, South, West, and North; and the third with three sets of nine dominoes called characters, circles, and bamboos. Players must build a wall, and when one has three tiles of the same suit he calls "Pung." To get Mah-Jongg (go out) a player must draw four pungs and a pair (two tiles of the same suit).

Only the player who goes Mah-Jongg scores his hand; the losers pay him the total score rounded to the nearest 10. The dealer (prevailing wind) has to pay double, but if he makes Mah-Jongg all the players pay him double. Strategy of play is to strike a logical balance between building a hand worth a high score and going out with Mah-Jongg as quickly as possible. Because of the doubling factor, the dealer should always try to go out first. It is advisable for all players to aim to go out without trying for a big score if the game continues for a considerable period of time, which indicates that several players may well be nearing Mah-Jongg.

When playing Mah-Jongg under the more complicated Western rules, it is important to establish all the ground rules in advance in order to avoid later disputes. The best gambling game is the uncomplicated Chinese version, but it is hardly advised that a Westerner try to beat a Chinese at the game. The Chinese appreciation of the nuances of the game reflects a long-term cultural play and the average Chinese will pick a foreigner clean in rather quick order. Leave the game to the East and remember that saying about the twain.

MAINE—Legalized Lotteries

Maine law allows for several forms of state-operated lotteries as well as a Tri-State Megabucks lottery run jointly with New Hampshire and Vermont. There are the common-type "rub off" instant games in which buyers rub six latex-covered spots on a card. If three of the prize symbols match, the player wins a prize that ranges from $2 to $10,000. There is also a "Superdrawing" for $50,000 for which instant-game losers are eligible. This allows for a sales pitch that losers can become winners.

The typical three-digit numbers game is also available with payoffs at 500 to 1 for getting all three numbers in the correct order. Lesser amounts at comparable odds are offered for any-order bets. A four-digit numbers game is also offered in which the true odds for winning with four in the proper order is 1 in 10,000. Payoff is made at half the true odds, or 5,000 for 1.

See also TRI-STATE MEGABUCKS.

MALAYSIA, Gambling in

You name it as far as gambling goes, and you'll find it in Malaysia—lotteries, numbers games, slot machines, POKER, DOMINOES, DICE, horse-race bookmaking—even though most gambling is proscribed.

In 1952, all lotteries were declared illegal except those with special authorization for charitable purposes. Later "common gambling houses" were banned and police were empowered to arrest anyone found in what they believed to be a place for gambling. About the only betting that was legal were totalizator betting at race tracks in Kuala Lumpur, Ipoh, Penang, and Singapore (which is now independent from Malaysia).

The fight against illegal gambling was never won and, under a change in the law, Malaysia opened its first casino in 1971 in a luxury hotel high in the mountains east of the capital city of Kuala Lumpur. The ever-practical Malaysians determined however not to have any pauper gamblers on their hands, and the casino requires visitors to leave a deposit of $100 in local currency before entering. That money cannot be used for chips, but is merely security for the casino that guests can pay their hotel bills and get themselves back to Kuala Lumpur.

The most popular games at Malaysian casinos are ROULETTE, BACCARAT, and BLACKJACK, and there are SLOT MACHINES as well. The casinos run 24 hours a day.

Brian MALONY

See HIGH ROLLER.

MAN WHO BROKE THE BANK AT MONTE CARLO

SEE CHARLES WELLS.

MARINER: Five-dice Game

Mariner—also known by the longer name of Ship, Captain, Mate, and Crew—is a five-dice game very popular with the seamen of several countries. The scoring is referred to in nautical terms. The 6 is the ship, 5 the captain, 4 the mate. The "crew" is the score made by the remaining two dice.

Before a winning score can be compiled, the shooter must obtain a ship, a captain, and a mate. He has three throws in which to do so, and must get them in order, the 6 first. If on the first roll of the dice he gets a 6 and a 5 he may keep them both and try to get the 4 on the next roll. However, if he gets a 6-4 on the first roll, he can only keep the 6 and must roll the four remaining dice to try to get the 5 and 4. If he achieves this goal, his score becomes the total of the remaining dice. Let us say he gets 5-4-4-1 on his second roll and thus has his ship, captain, and mate. His crew is 4-1. He can stop there or he can take his third roll with one or both of these dice. Let us say he decides to keep the 4 and rolls the 1 again, getting a 3. Thus, his crew is seven.

The winner is the shooter who accumulates the highest score. Shooters who do not get 6-5-4 get zero. The winner with the highest score takes the pot. Under a rule peculiar to Mariner, if two players tie for high, the entire game is a wash and a new game is played by all participants, including those who would have otherwise lost. There may also be a second ante at this point by previous agreement.

MARK: Gambling-scam Victim

Gambling cheats refer to their victims as "marks." The term harkens back to the early days of carnivals in America; when the operator of a crooked gambling game got hold of a sucker, he'd pat him on the back warmly when the man was about to leave his counter after losing a considerable sum. On the theory that the sucker had not been cleaned out, the cheat would chalk up the palm of his hand so that when he patted the victim's back he left a chalk stain on him. This was a tip-off to other grifters along the midway that the man was an easy setup.

Such chalk-stained individuals were truly marked and so came to be called "marks."

MARTINETTI
See OHIO.

MARX BROTHERS: Gamblers Four
No mention of gambling personalities would be complete without including the Marx Brothers—Groucho, Chico, Harpo, and Zeppo. All were dedicated card players, two straight, two not so straight.

On the honest side were Groucho and Harpo. It was not publicity-department hype that Groucho was an inveterate POKER player and gained his nickname because he carried his cash around in a "grouch bag," or G-string. Harpo was an important member of the so-called "Thanatopsis Literary and Inside Straight Club," the Poker-player division of the famed Algonquin Roundtable, along with such astute players as Franklin P. Adams and Heywood Broun. A fair shot, however, could not be guaranteed in any game involving Zeppo and Chico, both of whom were noted for their abilities to communicate through ingenious hand signals.

Of the four brothers Chico came closest to being a "degenerate" gambler (see COMPULSIVE GAMBLER), and his brothers sought to protect him from his vice. Their constant worry was that Chico would survive them and, left to his own devices, would be sure to lose every penny he had. Chico did his dishonest best to keep his poke, and developed his cheating to a fine art. He even got together with a notorious underworld figure and hit man, Jimmy "the Weasel" Fratianno, and beat the El Rancho race book in Las Vegas out of thousands of dollars in a past-posting operation. Jimmy the Weasel had a special line strung to a house that overlooked the New Orleans racetrack. He would hold a line open and call Chico at the El Rancho race room. As soon as they had the result—and before the wire service flashed the results of the race to bookmakers around the country—Chico would step up and place a bet on the winning horse. One time the pair even worked their scam during the Marx Brothers' three-week engagement at the El Rancho.
See also FRIARS CLUB.

MARYLAND—Legalized Lotteries
Maryland offers two standard forms of state lotteries. One is Lotto, which in a typical form offers prizes for selecting the six correct numbers chosen from 1 to 40. The minimum jackpot is a cash prize of $200,000, but this frequently can grow into the millions. There is a random selection method by which the lottery's computer will choose six numbers for those too perplexed to make their own picks. It is possible to purchase the same selections in advance for up to a year at a time.

Numbers games are presented in both the Pick 3 and Pick 4 methods, with all payoffs at about 50 percent of what the true odds would be.

MASSACHUSETTS—Legalized Lotteries
Massachusetts has one of the most successful lottery systems in the country. It offers a myriad of games and options and frequently better payoffs than other state lotteries. The first state lottery ticket was sold in 1972; in 1984 the lottery returned close to $300 million to cities, towns, and arts councils. Its Megabucks, or jackpot game, builds from week to week until someone wins the top prize—although a minimum of $400,000 to be paid out over 20 years is guaranteed.

The state numbers game varies considerably from that in other states, allowing bets as low as 25 cents compared to a 50-cent minimum in most states. More important, the payoff is based on a parimutuel method, the sum being determined by the amount of money bet on that number. As a result, the average prize in a three-digit play in exact order works out to about $700 for $1. The payoff in other states is usually fixed at $500 for $1.

The state also has a Big Money lottery game with prizes ranging from $5 up to a chance at a $1-million drawing. Tickets are 50 cents, but players can buy a $10 ticket that is good for 20 weeks or a $25 ticket good for a year and avoid weekly visits to a selling agent.

MATCH GAME: Guessing Game of Skill
Many amateur players consider the Match Game a game of chance, while many gamblers believe it is truly a game of skill. The truth is somewhere in between, although a professional or a good player with knowledge of percentages will almost always defeat an amateur. However, when two experts compete in a head-to-head game, the result is or at least should be a tie. For that reason the Match Game is mostly used by a hustler taking advantage of an inexperienced player or players, knowledge of which fact should save the casual gambler considerable money.

How to play: Each player, from two to six, gets three matches and extends a closed fist containing from 0 to 3 matches. Each player then in turn guesses the total number of matches held by all the players, and the one guessing the correct total wins. However, no player may repeat a total previously called. The player who goes last always enjoys an advantage, because he can make certain deductions based on his opponents' guesses. This is most pronounced in a two-player game, and to alleviate this situation play goes "around the table," so that each player must be the first caller and so on. In a two-handed game, the first player to win two rounds is the victor while in multiple-player games the winner of each round drops out until only one competitor remains, and he is the loser.

Strategy: A sample play that only an unskilled player would make is holding no matches and announcing 0. His opponent, let us say, holds 1 match and since he concludes that the first player has no matches, he announces 1 and wins. The first player tipped his hand, causing his loss. Similarly, if a novice calls 6, he is holding 3. If he calls 5 he has either 2 or 3. In these cases the second player adds his number to the estimated or known number of matches and bids accordingly. If the second player has no matches and gets a call of 5, he will guess either 2 or 3 and he has an even chance of winning; at worst the game is a tie. To varying degrees the calls of 0, 1, 2, 4, 5, 6 give the second player a substantial percentage advantage. Only a call of 3 gives the first player an even chance of winning. If he has 2, for instance, and calls 3 he will win if his opponent has 1, since his opponent may not also call 3. The second player of course could just as likely have 0, 2, or 3, which would mean that the first caller has only one chance in four of being correct. At the same time, however, the first caller's bid of 3 indicates he could be holding 0, 1, 2, or 3 matches. Thus the second caller also has one chance in four of being correct. Clearly, a call of 3 remains the best for the first caller.

Much can be made of good players developing "tells" about opponents, for example, determining if a foe has a tendency to hold three matches more often than one match, etc. Superior players prefer playing defensively when they are the first caller and will simply give an impossible total, which can lead to a "no-game" and permit them to go last in the next game. An example of this tactic, known as "overcalling," would be when the first player has 1 match and calls 5, an impossible total no matter what his opponent holds. The first player cannot win but the second player has to assume that his opponent has either 2 or 3 matches. Therefore the second player makes a bid that is also incorrect and the result is the standoff the first player is seeking. If used too much, overcalling itself becomes a "tell" and can backfire as the opponent disregards what may be an overcall and calls a number consistent with his own holding and what he can deduce from the overcall.

Here are the possible overcalls depending on the first player's actual hand:

Matches Held	Possible Overcalls
0	4, 5, or 6
1	0, 5, or 6
2	0, 1, or 6
3	0, 1, or 2

From this chart it is obvious that only a call of 3 is never an overcall. While it is true that 0 and 6 represent the best overcalls, since they reveal the least information on the actual matches held, the problem is that they are likely to be suspected of being overcalls. When 0 is called by an experienced player it is obvious that he is not holding 0. If he calls 6 it is equally obvious he is not holding 3 matches. For that reason 1 and 5 make better overcalls, because there is more of a chance that they are *not* overcalls. On the other hand, 2 and 4 can be deadly overcalls, because if the second player determines the first player is overcalling, he knows precisely what his hand is. Inconsistency in play, therefore, is the key in a two-man game.

A standard strategy involves the game's obvious averages. On average, though not in actual play, each player will hold 1½ matches, and in a five-player game a player who holds 0 would do well to call 6 for the total. Unfortunately, such strategies will become obvious to good players and should not be used regularly. A far more important guideline in playing the Match Game is whether a player is winning or losing. If a player is winning, it is probable that his opponents are inferior. On the other hand, a player who is losing should not stick around waiting for his "luck" to turn. More likely, he is being out maneuvered by a smarter player. In that case, the wisest call to make is "good-bye."

MATCHING DICE: Carnival and Private Betting Game

Matching Dice is such an elementary scam it is almost unworthy of inclusion in a book on gambling, except for its popularity with hustlers and with the pigeons they suck in on the play.

As the name of the game indicates, the entire play requires just a single roll of a pair of dice with the shooter winning if he throws a pair—1-1, 2-2, 3-3, 4-4, 5-5, or 6-6. Occasionally a counter game of Matching Dice is played at carnivals offering odds of 4 to 1 to the shooter. This gives the house a horrendous advantage of 16 percent.

Serious gamblers who understand the true odds avoid the game. But perhaps more important is that the unsophisticated player is not interested either since he is sure that the 4 to 1 odds are a gouge. If such a gambler is asked what he considers to be fair odds, he will often say 8 to 1 or so. Actually, fair odds with no advantage to the shooter or fader would be 5 to 1. At 6 to 1 the shooter would enjoy an advantage of 16 percent.

Unfortunately, unknowledgeable dice players have been brainwashed into believing hardways bets (pairs) are much harder to make than is actually the case. A bar hustler's typical spiel goes: "I really should get at least 7 to 1. Go to any casino at the CRAPS table and they'll give you 7 to 1 on a pair of 2's or a pair of 5's, and they'll cough up to 9 to 1 on two 3's or two 4's. All you're giving me extra is two 1's and two 6's and they can only come out one way each. They can't change the edge very much. At 7 to 1 you'll still have the advantage." Eventually the hustler allows himself to be talked down to 6 to 1. It is not uncommon to see bar hustlers having victims standing in line to fade their action.

Of course, it was not luck but good odds that made the hustler a winner. Victims are fooled by this oranges-and-apples comparison with hardways bets in Craps, which it must be remembered is a bet on a *single pair* that must appear before the shooter makes his point in some unpaired fashion or throws a 7.

MATRIMONY: Old English Gambling Game

Matrimony, an 18th-century English card game, allows for a big payoff even when played for low stakes. Played with a 52-card pack with any number of players from two to two dozen, it uses a special table with simply divisions on it. These are "matrimony," which represents any king and queen; "intrigue," any queen and jack; "confederacy," any king and jack; "pair," any cards of the same rank; and "best," the ace of diamonds.

Bettors must wager a specified number of chips per game, but may distribute them among the various categories as they desire. Each player is then dealt two cards, one face down and one face up. If a player is dealt the ace of diamonds *face up*, he immediately sweeps all the money from all divisions on the table—provided he has a wager on the "best" pile. (Consequently, players always place one unit of betting on "best" on every deal.) If, as is likely, no one is dealt the queen of diamonds face up, the first player turns up his hole card. If he matches any of the categories listed above, he takes all the money in that particular pot. The next player then turns up his card, and so on around the table. If a late player makes a category that a previous player has won, he is simply out of luck.

The deal passes on each hand so that every player gets the opportunity to hit the categories first. Usually one or two categories are not won in a hand and those pots are carried over and continue to grow until won on a subsequent deal. Thus individual pots can grow significantly and a sweep of the table with the ace of diamonds can be extremely profitable. (The ace of diamonds in the hole has no significance other than the possibility of its being paired.)

At first blush Matrimony may seem to be strictly a game of luck, but considerable betting skill is involved. While all players will cover all categories, they should distribute their wagers according to their particular position in relation to the deal. Since "pair" is the easiest category to draw, the leader, or first player to show his cards, will have a vested interest in building that pot. The second player may well have a similar interest because, in addition to having an early shot at it on the deal, he will be first on the next deal. Players further down the order have little interest in building the "pair" pot but will have an interest in equalizing the pots.

The virtue of Matrimony is that the betting stakes can be quite small—usually it is a 10-chip basis, one on the "best" and the rest divided on the other categories—and still allow a winner to come out substantially ahead by the end of play. Although once a popular tavern game, Matrimony has not become a gambling house game, although some Nevada casinos are said to be considering it. This could be accomplished by allowing the house to deal itself a hand without an ante in any category. The house dealer would show his cards last and if the house wins any category it would be under the "imprison" rule, that is, the house takes half the pot in that category. The house would not win the "best" category. Once a game starts, new players could not enter the game until there is a sweep of "best" or they replace players dropping out. This would in the long run provide the house with a considerable cut but allow the big-stakes quality of the game to stay in force.

While many players would participate on the basis of a game of pure luck, others would participate on the basis of betting skills. The house would find no problem with this as it does with BLACKJACK counters because these players would not be competing against the house.

JED MCCADE
See MUSEUM OF DEATH.

MECHANIC'S GRIP: Cardsharp's Giveaway
If you suspect a dealer is cheating, check his grip on the deck. Assuming the dealer is right-handed, he will hold the deck in his left hand with three fingers along the long right side of the deck and his index finger at the front edge of the cards all the way over on the outer right corner. Other mechanics put two fingers at the side of the deck and two at the outer corner, but this is a less used style. Called the mechanic's grip, it allows the dealer a whole series of cheating moves: peeking at the top card on the deck; dealing from the bottom of the deck; or dealing the second card of the deck to reserve the top card for himself or for a secret partner in the game.

From time to time, any player might grip the deck in the same fashion. If you spot a mechanic's grip,

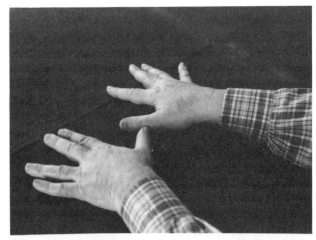

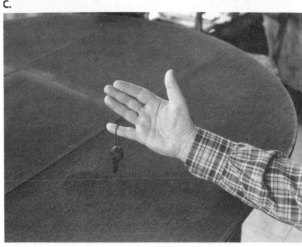

The advanced "mechanic's grip" (A) shows the index finger held loosely below the deck. Only on the actual deal does the finger go up to the right hand corner of the deck, making the grip now very difficult to spot. Card mechanics do all sorts of finger exercises (B, C, D), sometimes for 4–6 hours a day so they can nimbly control the cards. (Photos: E. Gerard)

chalk the first hold up to chance. If the dealer continues to use the grip, drop out when he's got the cards.

See BOTTOM DEALING; BOTTOM PEEKING; PEEKING; SECOND DEALING.

MELDS
See TRUMPS AND MELDS.

MEXICAN STUD
See FLIP STUD.

MICHIGAN: Stop-type Card Game
Michigan—also called (in various versions) NEWMARKET (in England), Saratoga, Chicago, and BOODLES (in the U.S.)—is played by three to eight persons with a regular pack of 52 cards plus four duplicate cards from another deck. These four cards, the "boodle cards," are an ace, king, queen, and jack, each from a different suit.

The boodle cards are laid out face up on the table. Each player must put chips on them. Under some rules, players must put an equal number of his ten chips on each; under other rules, a player may divide up his ten chips any way he likes, a few on each card, all on one, all on just two, etc.

The entire 52 cards are then dealt out and, depending on the number of players, some hands may have an extra card. An extra hand is also dealt to the left of the dealer. This hand, or "widow," is the property of the dealer and he may, at his option, exchange his own hand for it, in the hope of getting better cards. If he does not prefer to exchange, he must put it up for auction to the other players. The high bidder (if any) takes it and his own hand then becomes the widow. The widow is always faced down, and thus only one player at most knows which cards it contains.

The hand is opened by the person on the dealer's left who leads with the lowest card (deuce is low, ace high) in his hand. If he also has any cards in sequence in the same suit he plays those as well. Then the player who holds the next card in sequence picks up on the play and so on until the sequence runs to completion up to the ace or until stopped because the next card is in the widow. When the sequence is terminated, the last person to play begins a new sequence in any other suit or in the same suit, either below or above the stopped sequence.

There are two objects to the game. One is to play the cards corresponding to the boodle cards. Whenever this happens, the player takes the chips on that boodle card. Play ends when a person gets rid of all his cards, whereupon he collects one chip from each player for each card the opponent has in his hand. If any boodle cards are not matched, the chips remain on them for the next deal.

The strategy in Michigan revolves around buying the widow since the owner learns which cards are dead, that is, those in his discarded hand. If the widow goes to an auction and several players bid, the accomplished competitor will deduce there is a good chance that there are some boodle cards in the widow. However, a smart player will not give up a hand that contains no boodles if it is loaded with high cards, since that increases the chances that he will be able to play out first. Generally speaking, players try to lead with the longest suit in their hands at the start of the game, but if they hold a boodle, they should first try to steer play into that suit.
See also SPIN OR SPINADO.

MICHIGAN RUMMY: Early Variation of Five-hundred Rummy
Michigan Rummy, although identical in play to FIVE HUNDRED RUMMY, is an older game with a different method of scoring. In Michigan, each player scores his melds as he makes them. The winner is the player who "goes Rummy," laying down all his cards. He scores his melds and has the point totals of his opponents' cards-in-hand added to his score.

This is not nearly as good a game as Five-hundred Rummy because early leaders can seldom be caught and frequently can go over 500 in a couple of winning hands.
See POLISH RUMMY.

MICHIGAN—Legalized Lotteries
Probably the hallmark of any state-run numbers game is the terrific gouge made in the payoff odds—giving a mere $500 for $1 on three correct numbers in exact order when the true odds are 1,000 to 1. When the payoff is on a 3- or 6-way box, virtually all states nick the winning player for a little extra, offering only $160 or $80, respectively. Michigan, in what may be regarded as at least offering minimal respect to the

players, sticks to the half-odds principle by paying off at $166 and $83, respectively. The state follows through in the same way in its daily four-digit numbers game.

Michigan also gives lottery winners other breaks. Its instant games may not be any better bargains than those in other states, and the same applies to its Lotto game, which offers a guaranteed minimum jackpot of $1 million and grows when there are no winners. However Michigan, unlike many other states exempts Lottery prizes from state and local taxes, a most refreshing attitude and one that is common in foreign countries but not in the United States. Of course, the IRS is always waiting at the payoff window.

Revenues from lotteries go to education and for one recent year the lottery contribution came close to $138 per pupil.

MIKE: Stud Poker variation
Mike adds zing to basic Five-card Stud. It may also be used in Seven-card.

Each player is dealt two downcards and bets on them, starting with the player to the dealer's left. Single cards are dealt thereafter, all face down. The entire game is played blind and therefore open to more bluffing. A big winner might be wise to call Mike in DEALER'S CHOICE because he has the other players on the ropes financially. In any POKER game where the abilities of the players are roughly equal the big edge goes to the player with the biggest bankroll, who can raise his shaky opponents out of the game.

MILK-BOTTLE TOSS: Carnival Scam
In this popular carnival game, a counterman sets up six wooden milk bottles on a pedestal in pyramid form, three on the bottom, two above them, and one on top. Usually for 50 cents or $1 a customer is given three baseballs with which to knock the bottles completely off the pedestal. If he does so with one, two, or three throws, he wins an impressive prize. But even a major-league pitcher couldn't knock the bottles off very often when the game is gaffed, which it is at the counterman's inclination.

The Milk-Bottle Toss isn't always gaffed. Sometimes the counter-man (or a shill posing as a customer) easily knocks the bottles off. But when the bottles, the same bottles, are restacked for a customer, he often tries and tries and loses and loses— all of which proves that one shouldn't go to a carnival for a fair shake at any kind of bet.

The milk-bottle scam is a simple one. Three of the bottles are lead-weighted and three are not. When the three light ones are placed at the bottom of the pyramid, it is relatively easy to knock all the bottles off the pedestal. However, when the three lead-weighted bottles form the base, it would take three direct hits to knock them completely off the pedestal. They may fall over but will seldom fall off.

At some crooked carnivals, this game can become a major money-maker. The operator will allow a mark to win after explaining to him the fine points of Milk-Bottle Toss technique. With the bottles stacked in his favor, the mark starts to win. But when the operator suggests a money gamble, say his $50 against the mark's $25 that he can't win two out of three games the customer's "skill" deserts him, and he loses time after time. A well-heeled mark can be stripped of $100 or more in a matter of minutes. He can sometimes even be "put on the send"—going home to get more money.

MISSISSIPPI GAMBLERS: Thieving Gentry

If anyone would like to know what the average Mississippi gambler of the 19th century was *not* like, just refer to any film about that period. According to Herbert Asbury and other river historians more than 90 percent were mean, tough, slovenly dressed characters who serviced the rugged flatboat sailors of the period both ashore and afloat. They were murderous types and if they were not master manipulators of the cards, they frequently made up for their shortcomings with skilled use of the blade and gun, dispatching victims who objected to their cheating ways.

In the mid-1800's, an estimated 2,000 to 2,500 riverboat gamblers plied the American waterways. They first appeared along the Mississippi out of New Orleans just after 1800. When the first steam packets appeared on the river to cater to upper-strata society, these professional gamblers were not wanted and were frequently heaved over the side or stranded on some lonely shore or sandbar. In time, however, the boat operators realized that during a long card session, gamblers tended to spend huge sums on liquid refreshments. During one POKER game in 1858 the liquor tab for the players came to $791.50. Soon a few well-known gamblers, often done up in exquisite finery that lived up to Hollywood's otherwise false image, were welcomed aboard, and many captains held up sailing until at least one gambler was aboard.

Of course, some gamblers paid off captains for the privilege of skinning the passengers, and under those circumstances it was understood that no restriction like honest playing was necessary. According to one contemporary account on the subject it was estimated that of the 2,000-odd gamblers, there were no more than four who played it straight all of the time.

Asbury notes that Tom Ellison, a reformed cheating gambler, said in his later years: "I've seen fellows pick every card in a pack, and call it without missing once. I've seen them shuffle them one for one all through from top to bottom, so that they were in the same position after a dozen shuffles that they were in at first. They'd just flutter them up like a flock of quail and get the aces, kings, queens, jacks, and tens all together as easy as pie. A sucker had no more chance against those fellows than a snowball in a red-hot oven. They were good fellows, free with their money as water, after scheming to bust their heads to get it. A hundred didn't bother them any more than a chew of tobacco would."

Ellison recalled a planter who lost "his whole tobacco crop in one night and get up and never mind it particularly. Many a time I've seen a game player just skin off his watch and ring and studs and play them in. More often lost their goods playing in their waybills. I've seen them betting a bale of cotton at a crack, and it wasn't at all uncommon to hear an old planter betting off his Negroes on a good hand. Every man who ever ran on the river knows that these old planters used to play in their lady servants, valuing them all the way from $300 to $1,500. I saw a little colored boy stand up at $300 to back his master's faith in a little flush that wasn't any good on earth."

Most riverboat cheats operated in pairs or groups of up to half a dozen. Often, one member of a crooked combination would disembark at a stop to be replaced by another gambler coming aboard there, thus allaying any suspicions that might be building up among the victims. A common tack was for a confederate to stand in the crowd watching the game and signal his partners what cards the suckers held. This was called "iteming," and could be worked by puffing on a cigar or by scratching certain parts of the anatomy to indicate certain hands. One dandy used a walking stick as a signal, indicating various hands by the angle at which he held the stick. One of the more ingenious plays involved a spotter who played coded snatches of music on a violin while masquerading as a half-wit.

Among the legendary riverboat gamblers were CANADA BILL JONES, perhaps the greatest THREE-CARD MONTE filmflammer of all time; GEORGE DEVOL; and DICK HARGRAVES, the richest of the straight gamblers.

And there was John Powell, considered the beau ideal by his river colleagues; he was tall, handsome, nattily dressed—and honest. Well educated, he was a close friend of Andrew Jackson and Stephen A. Douglas (a noted Poker player).

Being so adept at cards, Powell was regarded by the more cynical as a logical man to go to Congress, but he rejected such overtures from politicians in his native Missouri. He did, however, take politics seriously and his advice was frequently sought by Louisiana politicos when he was ashore in his lavish home in New Orleans.

Powell's gambling successes were legendary. Once

during a three-day Poker game aboard the steamer *Atlantic,* he won more then $50,000 from a rich Louisiana planter named Jules Devereaux. In Powell's lushest years—1845 to 1858—his net was always more than $100,000 annually. Late in 1858 Powell beat a young traveling Englishman out of $8,000, which was all he had. The next day the young man came up on deck, shook hands with his fellow passengers and then blew his brains out. Powell was so shaken by the tragedy that he sent the $8,000 and the young man's luggage (he had won that as well) to his family in England and retired from the gambling tables for a full year. When he at last returned to the river, his luck and skill and his killing instinct had deserted him, and he lost his entire fortune within 12 months.

Powell died in extreme poverty a few years later, proof to other gamblers of the folly of developing a guilty conscience.

See JAMES ASHBY, GEORGE DEVOL, DICK HARGRAVES, WILLIAM "CANADA BILL" JONES.

MOHAWK INDIANS
See INDIAN GAMBLING CASINOS.

MONEY POKER
See DOLLAR POKER.

MONEY WHEEL
See BIG SIX (Wheel of Fortune).

MONTANA, Gambling in
Montana, like all the Western states, has a long history of gambling—although it wasn't legal gambling until 1973. Today the state is loaded with rather sophisticated gambling spots that attract everyone from college kids to cowboys.

POKER is the most popular game (BLACKJACK is illegal) with the pot limited to $100 for any single hand. Montana poker games vary in player composition from the amateur to the experienced professional who can make a reasonable living beating up on the weaklings rather than going head to head with others in his own league. On the other hand, a novice can find himself in a friendly game and play all night plus or minus $20.

In a sense Montana is a kind of statewide Vegas with wagering permitted on BINGO, KENO, sports pools, horse races, raffles, and Poker in such varieties as Five-card Stud, Five-card Draw, High or Low; RAZZ (six-card lowball with two down and four upcards); Seven-card Stud, High or Low; and HOLD 'EM.

MONTE BANK: Quick Money-card Game
Although SPANISH MONTE is often called Monte Bank, the real Monte Bank is a rather different and very much faster game.

The banker deals two cards off the top of the deck and turns them face up. He then draws two cards off the bottom of the deck and turns them face up as well. The two pairs are separated from each other so that players may place bets on either pair. Then the banker turns over the deck to reveal the bottom card, which is known as the "gate." If either card in the pair the player bet on is of the same suit as the gate, the player wins. Otherwise the bank collects.

In the long run the dealer has the edge. Players can make dead-even bets only when all four suits turn up among the four cards or when one pair is of the same suit and the other has one card from two other suits. In all other cases the banker has the advantage. Traditionally the banker also has an advantage of raising or lowering the betting limit, and he can reduce it when dead-even bets are available and raise it when they are not. That factor is a deadly trap for the careless gambler.

MONTE CARLO, Gambling in
Monte Carlo, in the tiny principality of Monaco on the French Riviera, is strictly a one-horse town. It may offer diversions in the fine arts, sports, and racing events, but essentially it exists for gambling.

The early history of Monaco's casinos was not inspiring. The first was built in 1856 on the initiative of Prince Florestan I who wanted desperately to attract money to his poor principality. It proved to be a flop. Bad roads and poor boat service discouraged gamblers from seeking out such an out-of-the-way place. In 1861, France annexed most of Monaco, but as a sop for this land grab agreed to build a railroad line from Nice to Monaco. Prince Charles III, for whom Monte Carlo was named, invited François Blanc, the operator of the successful German casino at Homburg, to come to Monaco to try to open a casino once again. Blanc was a former jailbird who had done time in prison along with his brother for fraud. However, he had subsequently proved at Homburg that he was a financial genius when it came to gambling houses. When Blanc offered something like $300,000 for the sole rights to a casino concession in Monaco, the prince was in no position to refuse the offer.

Blanc arrived in 1863. By 1868 he had his casino going and was luring wealthy visitors from the nearby Riviera resorts. At the time casinos were banned in France and, when it looked like they might be allowed in neighboring Italy, Blanc played hardball by secretly funding anti-gambling protests in several Italian towns. The fledgling casinos died on the drawing boards.

A whole mystique grew up around Monte Carlo, much of it true. Yes, there were a number of suicides who ended it all after losing their money at Blanc's tables. And the shrewd operator always saw to it his security people found the bodies first—and stuffed money into the pockets of the deceased.

To play at the Monte Carlo casino, players have to leave their hats, briefcases, and other articles in a casino cloakroom. In the 1920's a gang of robbers smuggled a smoke bomb into the casino, set it off and made off with several cash boxes during the panic that ensued following the explosion.

The Blanc family maintained control of the Monte Carlo casino until the 1920's when heirs sold out to outsiders. The first of several new owners was Basil Zaharoff, the notorious arms king, and much later one of the owners was Aristotle Onassis, who finally sold out his share under considerable pressure from the government.

Today Monte Carlo has three casinos rather than one. There is the beautiful old Palais on the town's main square with its sea-view picture windows. This is headquarters for the high rollers during the winter months. In the summer the action adjourns to the newer Monte Carlo Sporting Club, set on a spectacular man-made promontory overlooking the sea. The newest casino is the Vegas-style Loew's casino, which is the only one in Europe that charges no admission fees. It is loud and brassy with neon-lit slot machines that draw American tourists and junketeers like honey draws flies. (If you want to play CRAPS in Europe, you have to consider Loew's. Several casinos in France and Italy offer the game, but finding a table in action is another matter.) To open up shop Loew's had to agree not to have French games and thus not compete with the Monte Carlo casino. So Loew's is the only casino in Europe that offers an old American chestnut, BIG SIX. And there are Craps, BLACKJACK, and American ROULETTE, which can't compete with the one-zero kind, except to Americans who want some ''down home'' gambling.

The action at the three Monte Carlo casinos offers a picture of casino gambling throughout Europe. Despite all the pretensions about past glories, the Monte Carlo casinos are about the same as many others on the glitzy Riviera. It would be hard for instance to find anyone preferring them to Cannes casinos, although they are way ahead of some of the ''grind-type'' houses in Nice.

MONTEREY: Flip Stud Variation
Monterey, sometimes called Rickey de Laet, is a Five-card Stud game played according to the rules of FLIP STUD. Players are dealt two downcards and then must flip over one of the cards. This procedure continues on each succeeding round as players are dealt additional downcards. However, the card in the hole and all others of the same rank are wild for that player. This makes for a wilder game than Flip Stud and

indeed allows for smarter play, adding considerable zip to a five-card game.

MONTY: Two-card Draw Poker Variation
Monty is a variation of Draw Poker played with just two cards, high-low, with deuces wild. Players are dealt two cards singly, after which they may stand pat or draw one or two cards. Under most interpretations, the highest possible hand is two aces and the low deuce-trey. The key to the game is holding deuces since it is possible to go both high and low in the game (a pair high, deuce low).

Some gamblers knock Monty because they say playing on two cards reduces the game to pure luck. Others like the game because it offers great opportunities for bluffing. The cold-blooded consensus is that Monty is great to play with inferior opponents who stay in on bad hands, generally in hopes of stealing a low with, say, 5-6. Unlike other high-low games of POKER, where it is advisable to stay in with a potential low, Monty is not a game that is full of surprises. One should only stay on a strong high hand or a very low low hand.

MORA
See FINGERS.

MOUSE GAME: Carnival Gyp
The Mouse Game is one of the more exotic money-stealers operated at fairs and large carnivals; it is popular with the public because it seemingly can't be fixed. The fact is you can fix a mouse.

A mouse covered with a tin can is placed on a wheel and spun around vigorously. When set free, it is weaving from dizziness. Bettors wager on which of 60 numbered holes the dizzy mouse will enter. Meanwhile, the operator of the game has made a quick survey of the board to determine if more money is bet on odd or even numbers. By use of a pedal, the operator simply closes either the odd or even holes, greatly enhancing the chance the house will sweep the board by closing the mouse off from the played number. If the mouse, staggering around the holes, butts his head against a closed-off hole, it simply bounces away and heads for another opening. This hardly appears suspicious. What, after all, can be expected from a dizzy mouse?

MULTIPLICATION: Dice Bar Game
A three-dice game, Multiplication is similar to YANKEE GRAB, but offers more suspense and gives a low scorer a good chance to catch up on his final throw. As many players as want to can compete, with each making an ante to the pot. On the first cast the highest die (or one die if the high number is paired or tripled) is set aside. The shooter then throws the

remaining two dice and once again keeps the higher die and makes a final roll with the remaining die. High score wins the game and is determined by adding the totals of the first two dice and multiplying that figure by the value of the last die. Thus, a 5 and a 4 on the first two throws and a 4 on the last would total 36. It can be seen that making a 6 on each of the first two rolls won't mean much if the final die is a 1, making for a low total of 12.

MURDER: Two-card Poker

Murder is two-card STUD POKER somewhat similar to ACEY-DEUCEY but with more treacherous rules and traps. A round of betting commences as soon as each player is dealt a downcard. Then an upcard is dealt and there is another round of betting. The game is usually played high-low with a pair of aces (with one exception) being high and deuce-trey being low—in this game the ace is never low. However, two 7's is considered the best hand for both high and low and sweeps the pot.

After the players have their two cards, each player may opt for a substitute card and pays one chip (usually the amount of the initial ante) for the swap. It is dealt to him up or down depending on which card in his hand he is replacing. If the player is disappointed with his new card, he can draw another card, this time paying two chips for the privilege. He is allowed a third and final draw, but at a price of five chips—and placing murderous odds on the new card. Serious players will seldom take this risk. In fact, they will seldom take part in this game unless they are competing with rank amateurs who buy substitute cards wildly without measuring the amount of risk of money involved against the probabilities of improvement.

A typical trap is getting a 7. The amateur who draws a seven will often buy several cards, chasing another 7. The novice holding, say, a 7 and a 3 is foolish to give up the 3 in search of another 7. Assuming no deuces and no other 7's are showing, he has a one-third greater chance of getting a deuce than a 7, and with the 2 he is guaranteed the low hand. However, the amateur seldom reasons this out.

The game of Murder can truly be homicidal for the unknowledgeable.

MUSEUM OF DEATH: Anti-gambling Establishment

There have been many anti-gambling zealots in the world but none perhaps could match fanatical Jed McCade, an Australian prospector who established the Museum of Death in the outback in the latter part of the 19th century. McCade had run up a fair-sized fortune in the Australian gold rush of the 1850's as had many others. However, he saw many of those fortunes lost in the gambling saloons (there are conflicting stories about McCade losing all or just most of his poke in the same fashion), and he developed a passionate hatred for playing cards.

McCade came to believe, or at least to claim, that playing cards had first been imported into Australia on a disease-ridden ship and that every pack of cards printed thereafter had inherited some dread contamination that would kill gamblers. McCade soon discovered this theory was a hard sell to grizzled prospectors, so he took to the printing presses, grinding out pamphlets denouncing gambling as sinful. That was a line that did not work well either.

McCade turned to a more graphic approach. Through leaflets and display boxes in his pamphlets, he invited miners all over the outback to "Come to the Museum of Death."

The attraction of the museum was immense, for the miners' interest in the lurid was almost equal to their addiction to gambling. They looked with awe upon the embalmed hand of a compulsive gambler exhibited with an affidavit from a Melbourne doctor that "this is the hand of John Singest, stricken with palsy while playing three-card monte." There was also the door from an outback shack bearing the inscription "Hube Martin died here of the cupid's itch [syphilis] caught from cards 18.7.79."

For those doubters who wanted proof of McCade's claims, he offered numerous playing cards that under magnifying glass bore what McCade said were infectious bacilli. He also had on exhibit a skeleton that was identified as the remains of a man killed by cards impregnated with some aboriginal poison by murderous operators of a FARO game.

Eventually, in the grand contest between the Museum of Death and the gambling instinct, the latter won out. But McCade's establishment was remembered for decades with considerable fondness in the outback. Gamblers loved to swap stories about it, but its epitaph came in a traditional gambling line: "Shut up and deal the cards."

MUTUAL OF OMAHA: Spit Poker Variation

This game is essentially the same as OMAHA but has what is called an "insurance" gimmick. A player may draw an extra card dealt down to go along with his normal two downcards. He can use these downcards to match up with the five mutual upcards that are available to all hands. The price for this insurance is extremely high, often as much as half the pot or even the equal of the pot. Yet there are situations when buying insurance makes sense, especially if throughout the game there has not been heavy raising, indicating there is no powerhouse hand at the table.

For instance, a player has the king and jack of hearts in the hole; the common upcards are the king of diamonds, jack of spades, queen of clubs, 10 and 3 of hearts. Thus he has kings and jacks paired and has four chances of drawing another king or jack for a full house. He also has a four-card open-end straight, needing an ace or 9—eight more chances. There are also nine more chances he will get a heart for a flush. In theory he has innumerable chances for improving his hand. The fact that he is paired twice also cuts down the possibility that another player holds the same high pairs that he does.

Under these or similar circumstances, insurance becomes a viable option.

N

NAIL WORK: Marking Cards During Playing

While card cheats have come up with all sorts of methods for marking cards, there are many who say Mother Nature is best. They rely on nothing more than their fingernails. The simple pressing of a thumb or fingernail into the edge of a card will leave a telltale identification that can be seen across the table and certainly felt when the cheat is dealing. Cheats mark the card on both the top and bottom so that they can see the crease no matter which way the card is turned.

The secret to such cheating is not to mark up too many cards. POKER cheats usually mark no more than a couple of deuces. Knowing the location of these cards is critical information in DEUCES WILD (which the cheat will call consistently in DEALER'S CHOICE once he's made the marks). Even in High-Low, the marked creases can mean the edge, indicating if an opponent really has a low hand.

Some gamblers absolutely refuse to play with women, feeling they have more equipment for marking the cards with their nails. This is silly; any fingernail, long or short, can get the job done. The only good way to spot nail work is by squaring up the deck and studying the edges. The markings will stand out clearly. However, they will not be discernible to the average player out of the deck simply because he doesn't know where and what he is looking for.

NAPOLEON (OR NAP): Popular English Card Game

At one time Napoleon was so popular in England that it was virtually regarded as the national game, and it still has a fair number of proponents. The game is similar to Contract Bridge in that tricks are bid and played for.

Napoleon is played with a standard 52-card deck, with values running down from ace to deuce. Two to six people can play, although four is preferred. Each player is dealt five cards. Then each player bids—but only once each—on the number of tricks he feels he can take. Five tricks are the maximum bid. The highest bidder then dictates trump by leading with a card in that suit. Others must follow suit if possible and the highest trump wins the trick. The winner of the first trick leads to the next, in whichever suit he wishes. At all times opponents must follow suit if they can; if they cannot, they may trump or play any suit they wish. The trick is taken by the highest trump or the highest card in suit, in that order.

A Nap is a bid of five tricks but it is outbid by a Wellington, which is the same number of tricks but risks bigger losses. A bid of Blucher also is a five-trick bid but outranks a Wellington because it is under greater risk. Clearly as the English played the game, they had a clear view of Waterloo where Napoleon was beaten by Wellington, but it took Blucher to carry the day. In the bidding, it must be remembered that Wellington may not be bid until Nap has been called and Blucher is only possible after Wellington is bet. The risks in betting Blucher should be obvious; there are two other players in the game who think that they each will take five tricks. That makes ten tricks and Blucher's five makes 15, meaning there are some miscalculated views around the table.

If the bidder takes the number of tricks he bid, he collects chips from all opponents according to the following table and loses accordingly if he does not meet his goal. (There are some variations, but this is the most common payoff system.)

(Scoring is not necessary since hands end as soon as a bidder makes or loses his bid.)

Bid	Bidder Wins	Bidder Loses
Less than five	1 per trick	1 per trick
Nap	10 per trick	5 per trick
Wellington	10 per trick	10 per trick
Blucher	10 per trick	20 per trick

Some variations of the game include a bid of *"misere"* or *"null."* In bidding this ranks above three tricks but below four tricks and calls for a three-chip payoff. Under *misere* there is no trump and the bidder must *lose* all tricks to win his bid.

NEEDLE BET: Age-old Gambling Game
Needle Bet is played around the world, from cafes in Belgium to tearooms in the Orient to tough waterfront dives in New Jersey. Some say the game was brought to Europe from China by Marco Polo. More likely it arrived earlier with the Moors in Spain. The game calls for dropping a needle about one inch in length between two parallel lines ruled one inch apart. The play is lost if the needle touches or bounces beyond either line.

Contested in a series of tries, it is a fair gamble between two or more players. Today the more common bar or "friendly" bet is even money—and there are plenty of hustlers ready to offer such odds. The 18th-century French naturalist Georges Louis Leclerc, the Count Buffon discovered the probability that the needle would fall across a line rather than remain between the lines was $2/\pi$ or 2 in 3.1416. The Italian mathematician Lazzerini repeated Buffon's experiments in 1901 and deviated from the same results by only .0000003.

That's all the hustlers have had to know in 20th-century America. Offer even money with a 31% edge.

NEPAL, Gambling in
There is casino gambling in Nepal, but most gamblers there are not Nepalese. Instead they come in on bus or air charters from neighboring Pakistan and India, where there are no casinos.

In late 1987, plans were introduced to open casinos in India. However, admission is to be limited to foreigners, with an eye toward luring free-spending Arabs. This will mean that wealthy Indians will still have to fly to Nepal for their action.

NETHERLANDS ANTILLES, Gambling in
The four Dutch-controlled islands of the Netherlands Antilles—Bonaire, Curacao, St. Maarten, and Aruba—offer some of the best casino gambling in the Caribbean, especially the last two. Games are played in the relatively poor-paying Vegas style instead of the more lucrative Dutch style, using a single zero. The locals, inside and outside the casino are extremely friendly. One can count on decent advice on the games from casino employees. Only four hours from New York and two hours from Miami by air, the hotel casinos offer package deals that frequently top Vegas or Atlantic City. The islands are also free ports, so it is not uncommon to meet a high roller, who may have dropped thousands gambling, reveling in the few bucks he has just saved on liquor.

NEW GUINEA STUD: Seven-card Stud Poker variation
In New Guinea Stud each player is dealt four down cards. These are examined and then each player turns up any two. There is a round of betting and play continues as in Seven-card Stud POKER.

New Guinea can conceal a powerhouse hand and at the same time is ideal for weak-hand bluffing, such as turning up a pair of deuces to give the impression of more hidden strength. Some strategists use such a weak-hand gambit to infer power and then, if their fifth card gives them no improvement, they simply drop out, having lost only one bet.

NEW HAMPSHIRE—Legalized Lotteries
New Hampshire was the first state in the 20th century to offer a lottery, starting in 1964. There are various forms of "rub off" instant games with prizes ranging from the smallest prize, free lottery tickets, to many thousands of dollars with a grand prize of $1,000 a month for life. One popular version has been a variation of BLACKJACK, or 7-11-21. Players rub off the surface of their tickets to make numbers appear. If they add up to 7, 11, or 21, they win the amount shown on the ticket.

Other games offered include six variations of the daily numbers. In addition, in partnership with Maine and Vermont, the state offers a TRI-STATE MEGABUCKS lottery.

NEW JERSEY—Legalized Lotteries
New Jersey operates a number of traditional lottery games—three- and four-digit numbers games, instant games, and Pick-6 Lotto of the 1 to 42 variety. One innovation in its Lotto is that a randomly generated five-digit number "Bonus" is printed on each ticket. If a player matches all the digits in the precise order, he is guaranteed a minimum payoff of $250 and an entry in a bonus grand-prize drawing with a jackpot of $1 million, payable over 20 years.

Casino gambling is also legal in New Jersey—but only in Atlantic City. Outlawed in the casinos, however, is Keno, a very popular play in Nevada. Undoubtedly it is viewed as lottery competition that would hurt the state games—an irony in that Keno is one of the worst gouges on the casino scene. However, compared to the 50 percent payoff offered in the state games, casino Keno is the bargain of the century, with a mere 20 percent or so takeout.

NEW YORK STUD: Five-Card Stud Poker Variation
New York Stud is a Five-card Stud POKER game that recognizes a four-card flush hand as a winner over a single pair but as a loser to two pair. It is occasionally played in DEALER'S CHOICE games, but as a serious gambling game is surpassed by CANADIAN STUD, which also permits four-card straights as a winning hand over a pair but is a loser to a four-card flush.

NEW YORK—Legalized Lotteries
New York is the Big Golden Apple when it comes to state lotteries. It offered the first Lotto game in 1979, and its three- and four-digit numbers games have a huge take as does its "rub off" and other games. There have been occasional larger Lotto payoffs around the country, but for consistently big prizes New York ranks first. New Yorkers spend more than 1.6 billion a year on state lottery tickets, more than half of which goes into the state's revenue coffers as profit.

New York has used Madison Avenue pitches to sell its games but occasionally has been more candid about the state's offerings. For instance in 1987, John Quinn, then the state lottery's director admitted that New Yorkers were more likely to be struck by lightning—three separate times—than to win a Lotto jackpot prize. Quinn also said he considered the Lotto game as entertainment and not as gambling. But that's not the message that comes through in the state's annual $15-million lottery advertising campaign pushing Lotto sales.

"Most of our ads stress showing Lotto winners because we want our players to see that, yes, everyday people do win the lottery," a lottery spokesman said, trying to reduce the impact of Quinn's remarks. However, he noted that the actual odds of winning one of the twice-weekly multi-million-dollar Lotto jackpots are 12 million to 1.

The lottery folks then said they hadn't the vaguest idea what the odds were for being struck by lightning—either once or three times. Many of the claims New York state made in introducing its games, especially numbers, proved less than accurate. One of the principal contentions was that a legal numbers game ultimately would drive organized crime out of the racket. Now the state has admitted that the numbers game has not made so much as a dent in illegal play in New York City. In parts of western New York state, however, officials report that the underworld takes "were reduced by about 20 percent." That may be significant—but not enough to kill the racket.

Still, New York is viewed as the American state with gambling savvy. In 1987 Chinese officials visited the state to study its operations with an eye toward setting up their own lottery.

NEW YORK—LOTTERY SWINDLE
Early 19th-century lotteries in America were known for their dishonesty. A prime example was the first New York state lottery, which operated on the premise that if you let the politicians win at the game, you can steal all you desire.

The lottery operators, for a kickback from crooked players, simply fixed the lottery so that certain numbers won. Very little profit was left over to go to those supposed to benefit—the poor.

The scam was exposed in 1818 by a crusading journalist, Charles Baldwin, the editor of the *New York Republican Chronicle*, who wrote:

> It is a fact that in this city there is SWINDLING in the management. A certain gentleman in town received intimation that a number named would be drawn on Friday last and it was drawn that day! This number was insured high in several different places. A similar thing had happened once before in this same lottery; and on examination of the managers' files the number appeared soiled as if it had been in the pocket several days. . . .

Several of the lottery operators sued Baldwin for libel, and a select committee was appointed to look into the matter. The investigation discovered that one of the complainants, John H. Sickles, was a secret supplier of the lottery forms and had provided certain political figures with information in advance. By using politicians in the scam, Sickles and others assured themselves that the lottery would have governmental support. As a result of the inquiry, Baldwin was cleared and became famous as the first of New York's journalistic muckrakers. The New York lottery, along with several others around the country accused of fraud, was ended.

NEW ZEALAND, Gambling in
Horse-race betting has been allowed in New Zealand since 1837 and the country can claim the development in 1880 of the original tote, a hand-operated calculating machine. New Zealand was also the site of the first use of an electrical calculator for a tote operation in 1913. The use of the electrical totalizator spread in 1928 to France and two years later to England. In 1932, the electrical tote was adopted in America and has since developed into a complex modern-day computer operation. New Zealand deserves much of the credit for the great technological advances made in horse-race betting.

In 1950 off-track betting was legalized in a state-run operation. New Zealand is quite a betting nation, and the off-track purses provide the government with considerable revenues.

Lotteries are legal in New Zealand and they are run for welfare or educational purposes, provided they are licensed by the Ministry of Internal Affairs. Gambling houses are illegal but, bowing to public demand, the government okayed Bingo in 1959. Today it is one of the most popular wagering activities in the country.

NEWMARKET (CARDS): English Version of Michigan

Although the name of Newmarket is often used for a dice game called Yankee Grab, it is also the common English name for the card game that in America is known as MICHIGAN. In Newmarket, the widow hand is always dead and neither the dealer nor any other player may exchange his hand for it.

Very often in Newmarket, and much less so in Michigan, an arrangement can be made to play for the uncollected boodle card money on completion of a hand by simply redealing all the cards on face up. Whoever gets the appropriate boodle cards wins the chips outstanding.

See SPIN OR SPINADO.

NICK THE GREEK: Gambler and Hustler

Nick the Greek (1893?-1966) is often described as 1) America's most famous gambler and 2) the epitome of the honest gambler. The first is undoubtedly true, the second undoubtedly false. A compulsive gambler, Nick the Greek was a loser more often than he was a winner. Only successful gamblers can afford to be honest; losers cannot. Much is made of the fact that Nick was a high-stakes player and that something like $500 million may have passed through his hands at the gambling tables. Despite his gambling skills, he could be suckered by cheats—and he was not above doing a little cheating himself. In the end Nick the Greek ended up haunting those sad $5- and $10-limit games in the POKER parlors of Gardena, California. When it was suggested that he had come down a long way from the hyped-up glory days, he snapped back: "It's action, isn't it?"

Perhaps the best quotation that summarizes his life was what he said about CRAPS: "The most exciting thing in craps is to win. The next most exciting thing is to lose." It's sentiments like these that make a head shrinker's day.

Born Nicholas Andrea Dandolos in Rethymon, Crete, apparently in 1893—although it may have been several years earlier—he was the son of a prosperous rug merchant. His grandfather, a wealthy shipowner, financed his relocation to America when he was 18 with a then-fabulous allowance of $150 a week. Exhibiting an inclination for gambling, Nick followed the horses to Montreal where he was a heavy bettor on and off the track and picked up his nickname of Nick the Greek. Not without reason, the term "the Greek" tended to identify him as a gambler; it is a reputation that Greeks hold in general. Through shrewd handicapping and some very special "inside information" Nick accumulated a half-million dollars in profits and headed for Chicago.

He quickly blew his entire bankroll in the Windy City at cards and dice. That taught him that he had much to learn and he began studying the games assiduously. He became good enough to have winning and losing streaks, flush periods and pauper times. In the process he gained a "rep." There are those observers of the gambling scene who claim the powers that be in Las Vegas made Nick the Greek, promoting him for their own reasons. The town likes to have notorious high rollers in residence, since it adds to the magnificent con that "Here's an expert who makes a huge living at gambling—so you can too." The fact is no casino ever refused the Greek's action, which tells a great deal about his true ability. He was never barred from the BLACKJACK tables in the old pre-"counter" days, while many more proficient gamblers were.

Nick the Greek was often a reckless bettor, and for good reason. He was frequently backed by "marks"—men or women who financed his action. If they won, they split the profits; if they lost, Nick was merely out a bit of time. Some acerbic observers did not see him as a tower of moral stature in these situations. They have even said he was known to proposition other gamblers that he would deliberately dump some big games for a secret split of the take, with the marks left out in the cold.

He was also arrested by the FBI for conspiring to extort money from millionaire oilman Ray Ryan, an inveterate gambler. The charges against him were eventually dropped, but two of his confederates were tried and convicted. Later on victim Ryan was assassinated by the mob for complaining about being trimmed by them.

The mob in the past may well have trimmed Nick the Greek as well. He was cheated out of a half-million dollars in a scheme involving a radio-cue prompter and a high-powered telescope. The game, big-stakes GIN RUMMY, took place at the newly built Flamingo Hotel—mobster Bugsy Siegel's creation—at poolside. The Greek and his opponent were always attired in bathing suits but the cheats had concealed a small radio receiver under his opponent's trunks. A telescope placed in a room overlooking the pool was used to spy on the Greek's cards. Nick never tumbled to the scam and, because both chairs and table were riveted to the floor, he was always directly in the telescope's eye. Later on, when the skinning of Nick the Greek was exposed, Ian Fleming incorporated the gimmick in one of his James Bond books, *Goldfinger*.

Nick the Greek had a bad reputation with the pit bosses, dealers, and croupiers who had to deal with him. He was notorious for pulling minor swindles at the tables, claiming he had been shorted on payoffs or cheated on call bets that had been ignored. Unlike many other gamblers, the Greek's beefs were frequently honored because they involved small amounts of money; the casinos tolerated the petty thievery, hoping to win thousands from him—or at least from his marks.

During the final decade of his life, Nick's big-moneyed opportunities began to fade. His marks became fewer and fewer, although he still benefited from media exposure that portrayed him as a cultivated and honorable man. Nick the Greek told them this was so himself.

In the end Nick the Greek's fall to the minor leagues of the Poker parlors had to be seen as a sad ending. It represented the life of a typical gambler, one who despite his many big wins was added proof that beating the house, honestly or otherwise, is, as they say, a very tough bet.

NIGERIA, Gambling in
There is very little official supervision of gambling in Nigeria, and games abound—gambling on CARDS, DICE, sweepstakes, and LOTTERIES. There is racetrack betting in some sections of the country and a state-controlled lottery. Football (soccer) pool operators are required to be licensed to ensure they will pay off.

NINE-CARD STUD: Poker "Insanity"
A variation of POKER, nine-card stud is dealt according to the rules of Seven- or EIGHT-CARD STUD with the number of down cards decided in advance. When nine cards are dealt to players for a five-card Poker hand, it goes without saying the hands can be so outlandish that planning strategy becomes meaningless. It is best recommended as a penny-ante game. For an even zanier play, see TEN-CARD STUD.

NINE-HANDED HIGH-LOW DRAW POKER
This is an excellent five-card version of High-low Draw when there are a large number of players, up to nine. Each is dealt five cards and there is a betting round as in normal Draw Poker. Then the dealer deals two cards face down in the center of the table. Each player may discard none, one, or two cards. If he discards one card, the first centered card becomes his replacement card; if he had discarded two cards, he can make use of both centered cards.

After the two common cards are faced, there is another betting round and the showdown. Straights and flushes are considered for both high and low. Ace, deuce, 3 4, 5 would be a good high hand and a certain low winner.

As a precaution, it is wise to establish a rule that all players must place a certain color chip in front of them, indicating whether they are standing pat or discarding one or two cards. At times a player who has made one discard discovers that the second common card will help his hand considerably, and he may be tempted to "bury" one of his four cards and claim he had discarded twice. The chip ID avoids arguments.

Because two cards are the most that can be used to improve one's hand many gamblers believe most players end up going for low. This is not true. In an eight- or nine-handed game the percentages say that at least four players have been dealt a pair of some kind or perhaps more. Most of these players will be going for high. Logically only players with four low cards should stay. If they have three low cards, they really should drop on the discard. So should the holder of a low pair without four cards good for low.

This is an excellent game for the disciplined player because the pots, unlike many five-card games, tend to be large and he can drop quite often, knowing that he can easily recoup on one good hand.

NO LOOKIE
See ROLLOVER.

NO PEEKIE
See ROLLOVER.

John NORTH: Crooked Gambler
It has been said that a 19th-century operator named John North (?-1835) was the South's most dishonest gambler. That took in a considerable amount of territory, yet North may well have qualified for the title.

North, whose early life is shrouded in mystery, bossed much of the Landing, the pesthole of Vicksburg, Mississippi, where the city's army of thieves and gamblers congregated. There is no doubt that North bossed many crooked endeavors, but his main occupation and indeed love were his crooked gambling establishments. The number of Mississippians and others who lost their fortunes at North's gaming tables and crooked wheels cannot even be estimated. And despite people's desire to gamble, it became evident to many that what North was offering wasn't gambling. Inevitably, a secret force of vigilantes was organized.

In 1835 the entire South was in ferment following exposure of a bizarre plot. A criminal zealot named John A. Murrel called for criminals and slaves to seize a number of Southern cities and set up an underworld empire with New Orleans as its capital.

The scheme required the cooperation of criminal bosses in a number of cities; in Vicksburg, that boss was John North.

The plot—planned for July 4, 1835—was crushed in the criminal sections of Nashville, Memphis, and Natchez. Vicksburg was quiet, a good indication that North had backed away from the scheme. However, the vigilantes had no intention of losing out on a good thing and launched a mass attack on the "rebels" of the Landing. They hanged victims by the dozen, most of them gamblers or dealers in North's main gambling joint. North himself managed to flee but was captured the next day. Brought back to Vicksburg, he was hanged on a hill above the city, with most of the city's population in attendance.

There was much less pretense in Vicksburg than elsewhere that the hanging had anything to do with Murrel's rebellion. North's body was left swinging with a "fixed" roulette wheel tied to it. The message was heard loud and clear by the gambling sharks; it was almost a year before the hustlers came back to Vicksburg.

NORWAY, Gambling in

The opportunities for gambling legally in Norway are limited to football (soccer) pools, horse races and the state lottery. The lottery is a bit of a growth industry, with the sums wagered on the lottery tripling over a ten-year period.

This may indicate that Norwegians enjoy gambling, but if they want the real thing they must cross the water to Germany or England.

NUMBERS GAMES
See THIRTY-ONE.

NUMBERS RACKET

Despite the fact that about half the states in the country now offer legal numbers games, the illegal numbers racket thrives. Nor have the sales pitches made by the legalized lottery lobby made a dent in the action still going to the illegal operations. In fact, by endowing the legal games with the mantle of respectability, government has made it even more difficult to convince the public that it is doing something wrong in playing the underworld-dominated game. Lottery officials in New York state now admit that the introduction of lottery numbers has not reduced illegal gambling on numbers one iota in New York City. In other sections of the state, such as the Buffalo area, there has been a drop-off of 20 percent, not insignificant but hardly crippling to the mob.

According to recent estimates, at least 20 million people a day play illegal numbers games, the total take being in the billions. There are many reasons the public will not turn its back on the illegal play,

most of them financial. The payoffs in the underworld games are better, averaging 600 to 1 compared to 500 to 1 for the lottery games. Then too the IRS insists on being partners with big winners while the underworld is not much for filling out tax forms for the government. In addition, the illegal games generally allow betting on credit, which the government does not. Illegal numbers are especially popular in lower-income areas whose public, even if somewhat mistakenly, believes the games play a vital role in the community's economy. The players see local people working and benefiting from this part of the underground economy, and they feel that their money in large measure remains in the community.

The numbers racket in various forms has existed since the early 16th century when the Italian national lottery started (well before the political unification of Italy, indicating perhaps that gambling may have been more of a driving force than nationalism). Through the centuries—and most certainly in our time under Mafia control in the United States—the numbers game has been without doubt the biggest and most profitable gambling racket of all.

Numbers shops, where people go to play "the numbers," turned up in America in the 19th century. AL ADAMS, a New York operator, had about 1,000 policy shops in the city, and was one of the biggest kickback donors to Boss Tweed's Tammany Hall. Adams became known as "the meanest gambler in New York." Apparently he rigged the results not only to cheat his clients but also he could then bet heavily on the correct numbers with other operators, in order to ruin them and take over their shops. After Boss Tweed was dethroned, Adams went to prison. To assure numbers players that everything thereafter would be legit, operators switched to taking the numbers used from Treasury Department figures, released daily by telegraph and therefore presumably unfixable.

While numbers have been played in this country for over a century, the game has changed a number of times. True penny-ante numbers, the most lucrative of all, actually did not start until the 1920's. Earlier, black operators in New York's Harlem sold only 50 cent and $1 numbers tickets. Later they experimented unsuccessfully with 10-cent tickets. Over the years both Lucky Luciano and Meyer Lansky told various interviewers that Lansky was the true inventor of numbers, meaning the game that could be played for as little as a penny by inhabitants of the poorest ghettos. And indeed on the Lower East Side, then a Jewish ghetto, the numbers were referred to as "Lansky's game."

Interestingly the Chicago mob, the old Capone outfit, did not discover the numbers racket until the 1940's when Sam Giancana did some time in the federal prison at Terre Haute. A black racketeer from Chicago bragged to him about the millions he was making out of the numbers racket, even with many of his customers betting as little as one to five cents a day. When Giancana got out, the Chicago mob set about "eliminating" the black operators and took over.

Hitting the numbers means picking the right one ranging from 000 to 999, and pays off at 600-to-1 odds, so that for a one-cent bet a player gets back $6. Since the mathematical chances are 1 out of a thousand it is easy to see that the numbers racket offers greater profits to the operator than almost any other gambling game. The numbers operation therefore can easily support a bureaucracy of employees from the "banker" on down through operators, distributors, agents, and runners. The agents and runners are the ones susceptible to arrest and it is the duty of the higher-ups to see that they are immediately bailed out and if possible to put in the fix to prevent a conviction. If all else fails they are required to support the families of those in jail.

Once penny numbers took over, the black operators in Harlem embraced the game. One, the storied Madam St. Clair, became a millionaire from her numbers operation, but the members of organized crime were not about to let these black independents clean up. Prohibition beer czar Dutch Schultz masterminded a brutal invasion of Harlem, terrorizing individual banks into paying him for "protection."

Then the Dutchman simply declared their rackets all belonged to him. Those who objected were executed. Madam St. Clair once avoided Schultz executioners by hiding in a pile of coal in a Harlem cellar.

Schultz reintroduced the old Adams formula of cheating on the numbers results, which at the time had been switched to the totals of the betting pools at various racetracks. Schultz's "mathematical brain," OTTO "ABBADABBA" BERMAN, worked out a method to rig the results so that only little-played numbers won.

When Schultz was murdered by underworld associates, the numbers racket passed to the Luciano-Lansky combination with Vito Genovese appointed as overseer. Over the years probably as many murders have been committed to gain control of or hold onto the numbers racket as were done during the bloody bootleg wars of the 1920's. In many areas today, numbers money is the main source of illegal payoffs to politicians and police for protection. The new line going around is that organized crime and the Mafia are being edged out of control of the rackets in the ghettos by black and Hispanic gangsters. This is a Mafia-nurtured myth. The mob still is in charge, but as a presidential commission has determined, simply grants "franchises" to certain ethnic groups (as in the past to Poles and Jews, among others, in their ghettos) and for its cut guarantees full protection to numbers operators.

O

ODDS MAKERS: Sports-betting Experts

A Las Vegas odds maker laments: "The easiest job in the world is being a stock market analyst. You don't have to know a damned thing. You just say some stock will go up, and if it goes down, you just say you meant medium term. If that doesn't work, you really meant long term. And hey, guess what, sooner or later you are right. Stocks go up, stocks go down, sooner or later you're right. . . . In Vegas, we live and die every Saturday, every Sunday, every baseball day, every big fight night. We can only be wrong a little bit of the time. More, and we get nailed to the wall."

In the world of gambling there is no greater pressure job than being an odds maker. A successful one becomes a millionaire, a national celebrity. Jimmy "the Greek" Snyder became a network TV commentator on CBS, picking winners in National Football League games and their margins of victory.

Odds makers have operated out of various cities for different sports, but today more and more it's the "Las Vegas line" that counts. At one time the odds-making business was dominated by colorful characters with a shrewd knowledge of gambling and popular psychology, and a great gift for intuition. But today much more is demanded, and for good reason. Today's odds maker earns a handsome income because his sports judgments are almost always sound. Of one, Michael "Roxy" Roxborough, the *Toronto Star* has said, "He is paid to calculate the odds most Las Vegas bookmaking establishments give their customers and, with hundreds of thousands of dollars at stake, he has to be right. He wouldn't last long if he weren't."

Roxborough is president of Las Vegas Sports Consultants, and a power in a town where right odds make you a hero and wrong ones a bum. Even such staid publications as *The Atlantic*, have spoken of Roxborough in near-idolatrous terms: "Roxy is one of the most influential men in Las Vegas today because he supplies the line both to the Stardust, which is the first bookmaker to post odds, and to Caesars Palace, which handles the most money . . . Michael "Roxy" Roxborough wears dark, conservative suits, carries a beeper, and depends on computers and sophisticated data bases . . . Roxborough represents a changing of the guard in Las Vegas bookmaking circles. He brings an insurance adjustor's approach to a business formerly dominated by charismatic gamblers."

In the old days there were no odds makers with Roxy's peculiar background. A one-time political science major at American University in Washington, he switched tracks and studied probability theory and behavioral psychology at the University of Nevada—Las Vegas. He pursued additional studies in journalism that helped him prepare his weekly "Sports Betting" column in the *Los Angeles Herald Examiner* as well as hosting the "Stardust Line" radio show, heard Saturday and Sunday nights from 10 P.M. to midnight. Roxy also teaches college courses on race and sports book management.

The public does not appreciate what an odds maker must do under pressure-cooker conditions. When, for instance, the New York Jets won the 1969 Super Bowl by a score of 16-7, beating the Baltimore Colts who were favored by 17 points, the public chortled that the bookmakers and the odds makers didn't know what they were doing. Actually, Bob Martin, the resident Vegas odds maker at the time, was rather proud of his line. He established the Colts by 17 points because the line is not intended to pick winners or losers. The line is devised to *divide the betting public into two equal groups*, in this case bettors who thought the Colts could win by a certain number of points and those who thought they could not. The line was virtually on the button with, in fact, very little movement needed, except that the Colts finally were raised slightly (to 18 points) to keep the betting groups equal.

There were two big winners in the '69 Super Bowl. One was a brash young quarterback for the Jets, Joe Namath, who predicted loudly that his team would actually win. That prediction made him a sports celebrity known as Broadway Joe, and a future millionaire. The other big winners were the bookmakers. They booked their action at 11 to 10, which meant while they paid off the winners at $10 for every $11 they had put up, they collected $11 from every losing bettor. The "vigorish" had worked perfectly for the bookies.

Oddly, games that the public decides the bookmakers have called right can be financial disasters for the bookmakers. A case in point was the 1978 Super Bowl between the Dallas Cowboys and the Pittsburgh Steelers. The odds makers established the Steelers as a 3-point favorite. The bookies were swamped with bets on Pittsburgh. The point spread was raised to 3½ but the deluge continued. Only when the spread went to 4 points and then 4½ did Dallas money start coming in.

Pittsburgh won by four points, 38-34, and it was a bloodbath for the bookies. They lost a fortune. All the early bettors who took the Steelers at 3 or 3½ won their bets (the majority of the Pittsburgh money), and the late Dallas bettors (the majority of the Cowboys' supporters) either won their bets or broke even. This was not what the odds makers were being paid to do. They are supposed to come up with a line that divides support evenly on both sides and never moves. Men like Roxborough are paid not to be wrong.

To do so, they must keep up on everything—weather conditions, key injuries, site and time changes, team momentum, and so on. Roxy's outfit stays open during the baseball season until the last game every day, so if there is a late pitching change the organization can flash a new price line immediately.

A sports line like Roxy's is expected to be knowledgeable enough to set correct odds for special occasions such as the World Cup, off-road racing, America's Cup, the Indy 500, and golf and tennis tournaments. Sports consultants are also expected to call various sporting events "off the board" when reports indicate that the game may be crooked.

And everything is now high-tech—the sports books demand it. But inside information is still important. What if a star athlete's girl said no, or perhaps more important, said yes. Or what if the player had a run-in with some professor? What if he was dropped from the game at the last minute? These are things the odd makers have to know. Some odds makers have been hoisted on their own inside information,

however. There was the time Jimmy the Greek and two gambling buddies were privy to information about the pitcher due to pitch a key World Series game. He had been out with a lady friend the night before and never got to bed, at least not to sleep. They reasoned that he would never last through a tough series game. They plunked down $100,000 on the opposing team. Things went wrong, however. The supposedly tuckered-out pitcher, who should have fallen asleep between innings, was alert enough to pitch a no-hitter.

That's the way the odds go—even when the experts have the most intimate inside knowledge in the world.

OHIO: Three-dice Game

Ohio, sometimes called Martinetti or Centennial, is an interesting three-dice game for any number of players. It works as a private game, as a bar game, or run by a gambling club for a cut of the pot.

How to play: All that is required is a layout numbered 1 to 12, three dice, a dice cup, and individual markers that can be just different denominations of coins.

Each player rolls the three dice and the highest scorer becomes the first shooter. The object of the game is to go from 1 to 12 and back to 1 first and collect the pot.

The first shooter rolls the dice looking for a 1, which will get him started. If he does not get a 1, the next shooter takes over, and so on. Naturally the early shooters, especially the first shooter, have the edge if they hit a 1 quickly and retain the dice. The dice are also cumulatively tallied so that a player can move on. For example, if a shooter rolls 1-1-5 at the beginning, he gets the 1 position on the basis of one 1 and the 2 position on the basis of 1 plus 1. Let us say the next roll comes up 1-2-3. These dice may be considered separately so that the 3 allows him to move to the third position. Two or three dice may also be added any way possible so that the added numbers would be 3 (of no value since the shooter is already in the third position), 4, 5, and 6. Thus the player can move to the fourth, fifth, and sixth position and shoot again, looking now for a total of 7, and so on.

If the shooter rolls a total he can use but fails to notice it and passes the cup, conceding he can't play, any other player can at that point call out the number and use it if it will advance his own marker. If more than one player calls the missed number at the same time, the first one on the shooter's left has the right to it.

As already noted, Ohio is hardly a dead-even contest. The early shooter has a clear edge, and unfortunately there is a fair amount of cheating in the game. A dice-cup cheater will use his ability to roll a high score to start the game and then will roll one or more 1's on the opening play. He is now in a commanding position to take the entire game rather easily. Ohio is a game not to be played with strangers—or with friends who win consistently.

See DICE-CUP CHEATING.

OHIO—Legalized Lotteries

Over the years Ohio has been a state with a great fondness for illegal gambling activities, and legalized gambling in the form of LOTTERIES has been very well patronized.

Basically, lotteries come in the same standard forms as most other states, including various instant games that offer such top prizes as a million dollars, $1,000 a week for life (one wonders why children and grandchildren seem to do better at this than the older generations), and so on.

Numbers are the usual three- and four-number variety with payoffs around the 50 percent mark. Lotto's jackpot, with potential prizes in the millions, is the most popular state game, with four, five, and six numbers out of six producing winners. Auto-Lotto lets the computer pick your selections at random if you so wish.

Ohio's lottery profits go for primary- and secondary-school education.

OKLAHOMA RUMMY: Midwest Variation of 500 Rummy

Given its name, it's hardly surprising that for years Oklahoma Rummy enjoyed its main popularity in the Midwest. Since then it has attracted a following elsewhere in the gambling fraternity.

How to play: Oklahoma is a high-scoring wild game that still follows many of the rules of 500 RUMMY. Two 52-card decks are used and the game can be played by two to six persons, although four is the ideal number.

The eight deuces are wild so that one may make a meld, either in sequence or suit or in set by rank, with two deuces and only one other card. In addition, the player employing a wild card in a meld may later substitute the natural card for the deuce and then use the deuce to make another meld.

Players in turn may pick from the balance of the pack (the stock) or he may take the top card from the discard pile if he can meld it immediately. However, a player who takes the top discard must take the rest of the discard pile in his hand as well. Players may, before discarding, add to their previous melded cards but they may not meld cards to their opponents' melds.

Card values are figured differently than in most Rummy games. Aces, which may be high or low in

sequences, are always 15 points, the 10s through kings are 10 points, except for the queen of spades, which is 50. The 3's through 9's are all valued at 5 points and the value of the deuces is determined by the cards for which they are substituting. However, if deuces are melded as deuces, they are worth 25 points each.

If the stock is exhausted before any player has gone out, the discard pile, except for the top card that starts the new discard pile, is shuffled and reused as a stock. If all cards are exhausted including those in the discard pile, which is highly unlikely before a player goes Rummy, the game is ended and scores counted up with laid-down melds counting as pluses and cards in hand as minuses to each player's score. Normally, a player will win the hand. The losers total their points and subtract their minus points for cards in hand, which have the same value as they would have if melded. The one exception to this is the queen of spades, which costs the player caught with it 100 points.

Game is 1,000 points and some gamblers prefer to play Oklahoma Rummy for a set pot rather than for the point differences for each player. When the point differences are used, it is wise, depending upon the players' rolls, to keep the value of a point low. Otherwise the payoffs can get extremely large, sometimes more than most players anticipate.

OLD ENGLISH BLIND AND STRADDLE

See OLD ENGLISH DRAW POKER.

OLD ENGLISH DRAW POKER: Archaic game of Competing High and Low Hands

Old English Draw Poker, sometimes referred to now as Old English Blind and Straddle, used to be extremely popular in England, South Africa, and Australia. It incorporated the basic rules of POKER but made more winning hands possible to increase the betting action. Certain "low" hands were introduced as being better than certain high hands.

The highest low hand was Big Cat (sometimes called Big Tiger), which involved cards from kings down to 8 low without any pairs. Big Cat lost to a flush but beat a straight as well as all other low-ranking hands. Little Cat (or Little Tiger) rated just below Big Cat and constituted cards from 8 to 3 without a pair. Ranking just below Little Cat was Big Dog, made up of cards without any pair from ace down to 9 low. Next in line was Little Dog, a hand from 7 to deuce without a pair.

When duplicate Cat or Dog hands appeared, the highest ranking hand won, that is king, queen, jack, 9, 8 would beat king, queen, 10, 9, 8.

Eventually gamblers eschewed the game, noting that it put a premium on near-busted straights over ones that actually filled, and adopted purer Poker instead.

OLD SLEDGE

See SEVEN UP.

Big Jim O'LEARY: Chicago Gambler

Jim O'Leary, the son of the Mrs. O'Leary of Chicago Fire fame, became one of the most colorful gamblers in American history—and, in the process, a millionaire several times over. A youthful handyman for the bookmaking syndicates, O'Leary quickly absorbed gambling-house known-how and opened a gambling resort of his own. Located 23 miles from the center of Chicago in Long Beach, Indiana, the place had stockades, barbed-wire fences, alarm boxes, lookout posts for armed sentries, ferocious watchdogs, and a network of tunnels for a quick escape. Unfortunately, the distance from the Windy City discouraged gamblers from coming and the place folded.

Returning to Chicago, O'Leary opened a gambling house on South Halsted Street near the stockyards. He then set up a string of bookie operations and poolrooms. Big Jim, as he was dubbed when his stature as a gambler grew, was always taken with grandiose ideas. In 1904, he outfitted the steamboat *City of Traverse*, which was the first vessel in American history devoted entirely to gambling. About 1,000 horse-players boarded the vessel every day at noon for a leisurely cruise on Lake Michigan, usually ignoring the view. Instead they studied their form charts and bet all day until all the day's races were run. Results were flashed to the boat by wireless. The police, needless to say, were highly displeased by the *City of Traverse*. Because it was offshore on non-Chicago waters, O'Leary had the peculiar idea that the police deserved no protection money. The police didn't agree; they sabotaged his operation by scrambling the wireless messages giving the odds and results of the races and arrested passengers as they disembarked.

O'Leary abandoned ship and returned to his South Halsted Street establishment, determined to make it the premier gambling joint in the country. It was indeed one of the most lavish, complete with a restaurant, a Turkish bath, bowling alleys, and a billiards room. But its main attraction was the horse parlor, outfitted with plush couches and chairs, with servants offering refreshments and charts showing the entries and odds in every race in the United States and Canada. Action was also taken on every other kind of sporting event as well as on elections and even the weather. O'Leary once won a $10,000 bet that there would be 18 days of rain during the month of May.

Big Jim prospered, amazingly without the usual graft to the police. He once told a reporter: "I could have had all kinds of [protection], but let me tell you something. Protection that you purchase ain't worth an honest man's dime. The police is for sale, but I don't want none of them." His South Halsted Street "fortress" emphasized the point. It boasted massive iron-bound oaken doors layered over with zinc that were, Big Jim proudly proclaimed, "fireproof, bombproof and policeproof." During what came to be known as the gamblers' war of 1907, the doors withstood bomb blasts set off by O'Leary's rivals. Sometimes the police managed to breach the doors with axes and sledgehammers and at times even nabbed some of O'Leary's bookies and customers, but usually their efforts provided only comic relief. Once they stormed into the grand betting parlor and found it bare—except for a kitchen table at which sat an old man reading a prayer book. When the police regularly resorted to chopping through the establishment's inner walls searching for hidden rooms and exits, Big Jim had the walls loaded with red pepper. When the police axes penetrated the wall's zinc covering, the officers were so blinded by the pepper that several had to spend several weeks recuperating in the hospital.

When Big Jim O'Leary died in 1926, he was a multimillionaire and was as known in Chicago as the maligned family cow.

See LOUIS M. COHN.

OMAHA: Spit Poker Variation

This is a seven-card spit POKER game that derives from SEVEN-CARD MUTUAL and can actually be played by as many as 23 players. Even in a five- and ten-cent game, as it is often played, the pots can grow considerably. (It has been said that one professional football team plays this regularly for five- and ten-dollar stakes with 22 players, the starting offensive and defensive units.)

The rules differ from Mutual in that there is a round of betting after each player is dealt two downcards. Then one card at a time is turned face up in the center of the table as a spit card, meaning that it is available to all players' hands. The last card, the seventh, is also dealt up, which is at variance with Mutual in which the final card is dealt down. A player must then make up his best five-card hand from his two hole cards and the five upcards.

The guiding strategy in Omaha is to drop with the initial downcards if they are weak and disparate. For instance, a player is dealt a deuce and an 8. There is little reason for the player even to pay to see the first upcard. If it is anything higher than an 8, he will have a still weaker hand, with many players in the game at least two higher pairs are probably already in the game. And of course higher face cards will turn up later in the deal. Even if the player pairs up on the first upcard, he wouldn't have much of a hand. A pair of deuces is meaningless and even a pair of 8's isn't much.

In an odd twist to this game, it occasionally happens that several of the surviving players actually try to stand on the five face cards, hoping to split the high hand with other alert players. This is very tricky. The author once witnessed such a game—as a player who had dropped out early—in which five players remained when the five upcards constituted a full house, 9's over 8's. Since another player had dropped out early after accidentally exposing a 9 downcard, they saw it as a good chance of standing as the winning hand, since they were about a dozen cards left in the deck. Each covered the final bet only to see the last player bump the pot heavily. Was he bluffing or did he have the remaining 8's in the hole? Two of the players dropped out while two stuck it out, covering the bet. This meant that if the raiser was bluffing he would now collect one-third of the pot instead of the previous one-fifth.

But he wasn't bluffing. He had the two 8's in the hole. His hand had not been bet aggressively since the upcard 8's had fallen first and last. When the three 9's appeared, he had a stab of anxiety that someone might have a higher pair than eights or might pull it on the last card. (For a variation on this game, see MUTUAL OF OMAHA.)

OMBRE: 500-year-old Spanish Card Game

Ombre is a Spanish card game for three players introduced some five centuries ago. It soon spread throughout the world, gaining great popularity, and it is still widely played in Spain under the name of *Trefillo*, in Latin America as *Rocamber*, and it is also still in vogue in Denmark. Katherine of Braganza introduced the game to England when she married Charles II in 1662, and it had a long run in the public's favor until the appearance of WHIST. In many countries Ombre has been replaced by a derivative game, GERMAN SOLO, which offers a less eccentric valuation of the cards than Ombre.

How to play: Ombre is played with a 40-card deck, without 8's, 9's and 10's. The game is perhaps easier to master than is learning the unusual order of the cards. In the plain non-trump red suits the rankings proceed from king high, to queen, jack, ace, and then deuce upward to 7, meaning a red deuce is higher than a 7, etc. In the plain nontrump black suits the ranks go from king high straight down to deuce low. Note that the black aces are not included at all.

In trump suits that happen to be red the order of the value of the highest trump to lowest is as follows: Ace of spades *(Spadille)*, 7 *(Manille)*, ace of clubs *(Basto)*, ace *(Punto)*, king, queen, jack, and then deuce up through 6. When a black suit is trumps the order goes: Ace of spades *(Spadille)*, deuce *(Manille)*, ace of clubs *(Basto)*, and then king high down to 3.

The three top trumps, *Spadille, Manille,* and *Basto* are collectively called *Matadores*. A player holding a *Matadore,* or "Mat," may renege—refuse to play it— to a trump lead if he has no other trumps, unless a higher Mat has already been played to the trick.

Each of the three players are dealt nine cards with one player, *Ombre,* playing against the other two. Play and deal is always to the right, or counterclockwise, in the Spanish custom, so the leader is the player to the right of the dealer. He may pass or announce himself as *Ombre,* which will allow him to name trump suit and to discard any cards he doesn't want and draw replacements from the pack. If he passes, the second player can declare *Ombre,* and if he passes, the final player also can. If all choose to pass, the deal is passed and there is a new hand.

When *Ombre* is announced and he replaces his cards, the other players may in turn draw from the pack for replacements. If there are any cards left in the pack afterward, the dealer has the option of looking at the remaining cards to see what cards were not taken. If he does this, he must let the other players see those cards as well. If he does not look, they may not either.

Play begins with the player to the right of *Ombre* leading any card he wishes. The others must follow suit if they can; if they cannot, they may discard a different suit or trump the trick. The trick goes to the highest card in suit unless trumped, in which case it goes to the highest trump. The taker of a trick leads to the next.

The game is played for a pot into which each player has put three chips. Each time the deal is passed when there is no *Ombre,* each player contributes another chip. Whoever becomes *Ombre* must take more tricks than *either* foe. This is *Sacardo,* and *Ombre* takes the pot. If either opponent ties *Ombre,* this is *Puesta* and *Ombre* is required to double the pot for the next deal. If an opponent takes more tricks than *Ombre,* it is a *Codille,* and Ombre pays that player the equivalent of what is in the pot, which is then held over intact for the next deal.

If *Ombre* takes the first five tricks, he naturally has scored *Sacardo* and play ceases on the hand unless he declares he will try for *Vole,* which means he will take all nine tricks. If he succeeds, each player must pay him one-half the size of the pot; if he fails, he pays them at that rate, but his *Sacardo* win stands.

Players have one way of overriding an opponent's claim to being *Ombre*. After a player has announced for *Ombre,* an opponent may declare he will be *Ombre* "sans prendre," or *without discarding*. The original declarer can reclaim the right to *Ombre* by declaring he too is willing to forgo discarding.

Except for those areas where Ombre has remained strong after 500 years, the game is not played elsewhere, GERMAN SOLO having replaced it.

ONE-CARD POKER

This game, also known as Lazy Mary, accommodates as many players as can fit around a card table.

How to play: Since there are usually a lot of players, the game is played for both high and low. The game hand consists of one face-down card, and an ace is considered high only. Ties for either high or low split that particular portion of the pot. The bad thing about the game is that it is a card mechanic's dream. He has a range of eight cards (four aces and four deuces) that can make him a certain winner just by controlling any one of them. A particularly vicious scam involves the dealer and a confederate or two, one of whom gets an ace and the other a deuce. This permits the pair to whiplash all the other players by raising and re-raising one another. Because of the cheating danger, many sophisticated gamblers refuse to play what they regard as a one-card version of suicide.

ONE-WAY PICTURES: Cards Never to Be Used for Gambling

It is amazing how many amateur gamblers are caught in one of the most simple frauds around. This is playing with a "one-way-picture" deck, that is, cards whose backs are pictures or designs which when reversed are upside down. Yet such cards turn up in many friendly games. Admittedly, these are usually rather low-stakes games, but a cheat can make some high-stakes money with such a deck. All he has to do on his deal is arrange the cards upside down for low cards and right side up for high cards. The shuffle does nothing to alter this arrangement and he can then proceed to deal a high-low game with an unbeatable advantage.

Sometimes two or even three cheats are involved in the scam, which allows them to rearrange the cards that much easier and produces that many more crooked deals.

OPEN-HAND DRAW POKER

This variation of SHOWDOWN is frequently used to wrap up a gambling session. After an ante each player is dealt five cards *face up*, followed by a round of betting. Since all hands are exposed, only players with high hands will bet, driving the other players out of the game. All those who stay in may discard up to four cards in an effort to pull off a win.

When played at the end of a long gambling session,

and often for only one time around the table, desperation has usually set in and the big losers in the game will stay in on just about any hand. Previous big winners will stay in only if they get a good opening hand. As a result Open-Hand Draw usually creates a case of the rich getting richer or the poor getting only slightly less poor.

OPEN-HAND POKER PROPOSITION SCAM: Sucker Bet

Hustlers frequently have a tricky scam going following a game of Open-hand Poker. A hustler will suggest that he and his victim simply draw any cards they wish from an open deck and declares that after the discard he will have the higher hand, following the rules of Open-hand Poker. As an added inducement to his victim he will say that if the pigeon even ties him, he (the pigeon) wins. For giving his victim such an "edge," the hustler insists he has earned the right to go first. The proposition is often couched in belittling terms, indicating that the hustler does not think much of the pigeon's POKER sense. So little, in fact, that he may even add: "I won't even take an ace—not even a picture card on the first five cards."

The pigeon thus has been neatly set up. He figures he has a sure thing, since he will be able to draw a royal flush for himself (the highest possible hand) he can't help but come out with at least a tie.

The deck of cards is then spread out face up on the table. The hustler chooses his first card, perhaps a deuce, and then all four 10's in the deck. The game is effectively over right then and there, although the victim may not realize it. He is intent on building his royal flush—until he realized that all the 10's are gone, shutting off the possibility.

At that point the victim realizes that the best hand he can put together is a straight flush from the 9 down. The hustler now discards four cards, three of the 10's, and the deuce. He builds a royal flush to the ace from his remaining 10. Sometimes, to lure in a pigeon, the hustler will originally promise that he won't draw an ace or a picture card throughout the entire game. No problem. He simply builds down from the 10 and ends up with a 10-high straight flush, one better than the victim's 9-high.

Of course, this scam only works in Open-hand Poker, in which four discards are permitted. A shrewd gambler faced with this proposition can outflank a hustler by agreeing to play the game under standard Poker rules, in which only three discards are permitted.

This foils the hustler, who must play the four 10's and one 9 to lay the groundwork for a 10-high flush. When he does, the would-be pigeon simply draws four jacks and the 8 in the same suit as the hustler's 9. The hustler's straight flush is killed and, in fact, he can construct no higher hand than his four 10's. The so-called victim can stand pat on his four jacks.

Even if the hustler leads with just three 10's and two 9's, the smart opponent simply counters with three jacks and two matching 8's. The end result still has to be four jacks topping four 10's—provided the hustler has pledged to take no pictures.

OREGON—Legalized Lotteries

When Oregon sold its first lottery ticket in July 1985, there was a sort of mini-revolt by the public, which objected to the idea of the big prizes being payable over a 20-year period. Oregonians seemed obsessed with the idea that if they couldn't take it with them, they wanted it all in hand right away. The public didn't win out. In fact, it couldn't. The reason: money for big prizes simply isn't there, but rather is earned through an annuity setup that accumulates the interest over time on the top prize. Winners would soon discover that they were going to get a lot less than they originally thought.

The Oregon Doubler, the state's first instant game, was the usual "rub off" deal, but it had a fillip. If you got two matching prize-amount symbols and a star symbol on the same ticket your prize doubled. Based on approximately 25 million tickets being sold, there was about 1 chance in about 14 of winning a free ticket, and up to 1 in 960,000 of winning a $50,000 prize.

Megabucks, the Oregon Lotto-style game, offers the largest prizes. In standard form big winners pick the six numbers drawn from 1 to 38, getting two selections of six numbers for $1. For players too lazy to make their own selections, there is a "Quick Pick" method through which a computer selects numbers at random. There are also state game machines that allow players to go through the whole process on their own. By playing two games, a person has 1 chance in 181 of winning a prize for getting six, five, or four right numbers. The vast majority of prizes, of course, are in the four-number category.

Revenues from the Oregon lottery have been earmarked for economic development.

OVERPAYING: Stealing by Casino Personnel

When it comes to stealing from a casino, the most simple way is often the most successful. A crooked dealer at BLACKJACK, for instance, will simply overpay a confederate when he wins. This crooked partner makes it a habit of betting several chips at a time, being careful to bet in the same denomination as several other players at the table.

Let us say three other players are betting with $25 chips. The confederate does the same. When a game is completed, standard operating procedure calls for the dealer to first gather up the losing chips and then pay off the winners. The dealer will palm two or three chips from the losers and as he comes to his confederate's winning pile, he breaks these chips into even piles of five and in the process deposits the extra chips on the winning pile. Thus if he adds three chips worth $75, the crooked pair have beaten the house for $150.

This simple overpayment ploy is one that the casino's "eye in the sky," the spy system located in the ceiling, almost never can spot. It is up to the floorman to catch this thievery, but the overpayment is only done when the floorman's attention is turned elsewhere, usually at another table. The crooked player's second function is to watch the floorman and signal the dealer when no overpayment should be made.

P

PAI GOW (CHINESE DOMINOES): Casino Game

Visitors to Las Vegas are surprised and mystified to find an unusual game of dominoes being offered in many gambling establishments. The game is Pai Gow, which means "Heavenly Dominoes" in Chinese, and it is being especially targeted at Vegas' growing Asian clientele. Pai Gow is an ancient Chinese game that requires considerable skill. At present it is not surprising that most of the casino play is by Asians, but a few Westerners are also intrigued by it. Pai Gow advice books are turning up and one of the best is *Pai Gow (Chinese Dominoes)* by Michael Musante, a former Oriental games supervisor at several Nevada hotels. This is the first complete book of rules and strategy, as well as history and symbolism involved in the game. It is available from the GAMBLERS BOOK CLUB.

How to play: The game is played on a table resembling a BLACKJACK table and allows for seven seated players. The dealer mixes the special red and white dominoes face down and then, using a set of three dice, determines which player will start the bank, which passes from one player to the next. Each player and the dealer are dealt four dominoes, which they form into two separate hands, a high hand and a low hand.

The object of the game is to make the highest possible high and the lowest possible low hand and, in the process, beat the bank's high and low. If a player beats the bank both ways, he wins his bet. If he loses both ways, he loses his money. If there is a split in the results, the game for that player is a wash and no money is exchanged. The casino does not cover any bets but merely collects a 5 percent commission on all winning bets.

It is difficult to work the percentages in this game because of the variety of possible hands and the varying skills of each player (especially the banker's)

at coming up with the high and low hands. Despite these problems, there are computer scientists studying the game and trying to develop a surefire strategy for winning at Pai Gow. Considering that the game has been around for thousands of years, it seems like a truly formidable task.

Pai Gow remains a game of skill, and the edge belongs to the player with the cultural background for it.

PALMING: Sleight-of-hand Card Cheating

The BLACKJACK rules at the Golden Nugget in Atlantic City, typical of all the casinos there, stated: "Players are not allowed to touch the cards . . ." That tells it all: what really petrifies the gambling joints are not Blackjack counters but palmers. An excellent palmer, or "holdout artist," can rob a casino blind. The late gambling expert, John Scarne, once told of watching such an expert switch six Blackjack hands in a row at a Lake Tahoe casino without either the dealer or the pit boss spotting any of his moves.

However, there is really no reason for holdout men, or "hand muckers" as they're known by casino staff, to risk getting caught cheating at a casino, since it is easier for them to operate against relative amateurs at, for instance, legalized California POKER games or in private games. In private Blackjack a player has only to palm an ace and hold it until he draws a 10-point upcard. He then switches his hole card while in the process of looking at it and turns up blackjack.

Holdout men also profit from Five-card Stud; the trick here is to palm both a king and queen on previous shuffles and hold them until either picture is dealt as a face card. A palmer then switches the appropriate card into the hole and now has a commanding high pair, gaining a tremendous edge in the hand.

Another hand-mucker favorite is palming the ace

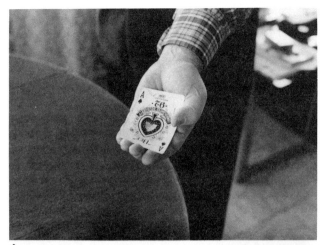

A.

B.

Palming is not an easy scam, requiring considerable dexterity and constant practice so that a desired card is slipped into the hollow of the palm of the cheat's hand, as demonstrated here with the ace of spades (A). A dealer may hold out the card on the cut and then place it atop the deck (B) where it can be dealt to a confederate or to the dealer himself after he bottom deals around the table first. (Photo: E. Gerard)

of spades when DEALER'S CHOICE is the game and CHICAGO, a version of Poker in which the ace of spades takes half the pot, is called. The cheater can raise the pot with abandon since he knows he will at worst take half the money.

Palming is not the easiest scam to work. It requires considerable dexterity, native talent, and constant practice. It takes skill to pick up the cards from the table on a new deal and slip the cards wanted into the hollow of the palm of one's hand. Holdout men of lesser talent prefer to palm only cards from their own hand, holding back a prized card when discarding the hand. When the card is palmed, it is concealed by the cheater's hand, his fingers held tightly together and flat on the table. Then the man simply draws his hand back and hides the card, perhaps in a jacket pocket as he supposedly digs for his ciga-

rettes. Or he may simply pull his chair closer to the table and, in the process, slip the card under his knee, where he can retrieve it at the proper moment. Often a holdout man works with a partner and signals him when he is either going to palm or retrieve a needed card; his partner causes a diversion at the critical moment, such as dropping a cigarette or slamming down his own cards in disgust. After the holdout man rakes in his pot, he waits for an appropriate moment when discarding a hand to get rid of the unwanted card he has secreted.

There are ways to spot the average hand mucker, especially when he keeps his hand flat with his fingers stiff and close together. If he goes to his pockets and hitches his chair around a lot—and wins—he is probably palming cards. Really talented hand muckers are much harder to spot, since they can work what is called a "rear palm" and are so good that they leave their fingers free and open. Speed is their secret, and it takes a very suspicious and watchful player to spot them. The only comforting thought for the average player is that these talented cheaters are strictly big league and seldom operate in anything smaller than games involving pots in the thousands of dollars. Expert John Scarne was adept at palming and could perform his art under the close scrutiny of a television camera without being detected. Many people shaking hands with him for the first time said that it felt like shaking hands with Jello.

A careful gambler will make it a habit to count the cards every few hands, saying, "Gee, this deck feels light." Usually the deck will be full, but the act sends a message to a hand mucker not to try anything. If the deck is counted and found to be short, the missing cards will invariably be found under the table, where they had fallen "accidentally." There will be no way to prove who had palmed the cards, but the cheat will be disabused of the idea of trying again and he will soon be off in search of less wary cardplayers.

PALMING CHIPS

There is a standard rule of thumb that can be applied to POKER pots: they seldom grow when someone other than the winner sticks his hand in them. A pot winner should be allowed to gather in his chips without help from other players. There are card hustlers galore who have invented many ways to cop chips while helping a winner out.

When a player helpfully shoves the pot toward the winner he may very well be declaring himself a secret partner, palming a big-value chip in his hand in the process. Other scam artists divert suspicion, never touching the chips with their hands, but instead using their cards to push the chips to the winner and in the process clip a chip between two of the cards.

Scam artists like to pull this when they are getting the deal and thus can easily drop the chip in their laps as they are gathering up the cards.

A more advanced method of palming chips is the "beanshooter," available from any crooked gambling equipment supplier. This is a very elementary hold-out device consisting of a gum-covered bit of leather on an elastic band that runs up the cheater's sleeve. The cheat simply holds the leather in the palm of is hand as he shoves the chips, allowing one of them stick to the gummy surface. He then releases the leather and the chip shoots up his sleeve for later retrieval.

PAN OR PANGUINGUE; Multi-deck Gambling Game

Panguingue, generally better known simply as Pan, is a card game that is widely popular in the Far West and Southwest of the United States. There are innumerable gaming clubs where the game is offered, legally and illegally. The game derives from the Spanish-Mexican game of *Conquian*; it is usually played by at least six, but preferably more, as many as 15. Generally, about eight 40-card decks (Spanish decks) are used, with the 8's, 9's, and 10's removed. In the past the kings, queens, and jacks were stripped in-stead but this is no longer popular. Originally, the value of the cards were governed by the original *Conquian* rankings, but today the standard rankings of king high down to ace low is used.

Rules and betting regulations for Pan vary by locality and according to the specific club restrictions (including whether play progresses to the left or right), but there are many rules that apply generally. The object of the game is to meld sets (cards of the same rank) and sequences (cards in the same suit in order), especially those of special value. Usually players ante two chips into a pool, and those dissatisfied with their cards can drop out with no further loss.

The dealer gives each player ten cards and turns up the top card of the remaining pack, putting it beside the pack to start a discard pile. Each player then in turn has the option of taking either the top card of the discard pile or the top card of the pack. Again, local rules govern, but in most cases a player does not take either card into his hand. If he cannot use the card from the pack he must place it on the discard pile. If he can use it, he must meld it immediately, along with the other meld cards in his hand.

Sequences must be of three or more cards, while sets may be made by different methods, and have different values. The best values would be those sets

Pan, extremely popular in the western and southwestern U.S., may be in all its versions among the world's top-played games. Above: A Pan room in Manila in the 1850s. (Photo: N.Y. Public Library)

that are of the same rank *and the same suit,* such as three 5's of clubs or four 4's of diamonds. Other sets may consist of the same rank but all different suits, such as 5's of clubs, hearts, and spades or 3's of clubs, hearts, spades, and diamonds. Three or more kings or aces can be of any suits, duplicated or not.

Melding a high or low sequence—king, queen, jack of diamonds, or 3, 2, ace of clubs—allows the player to collect one chip from each active player. If the sequence is in spades, he collects two chips.

A set of three identical cards such as three 6's of diamonds collects one chip, while if in spades, two chips. If the sets are in 3's, 5's, or 7's, they are *valle,* or value cards, and the holder collects double (two chips) for the original set of three and double again (four chips) for spades. If the three *valle* cards are all of different suits, the player collects one chip, and for a fourth card of the remaining suit, one chip.

Payment is always made as the game progresses. All other melds that are nonpaying still figure in the game. A player may "borrow" from them to make up other sequences or sets, which are "conditions"— that is, any of the above paying melds. Let us say the player has previously laid down four queens of all different suits. This has paid him nothing, but now he finds he had the jack and king of hearts. He borrows the queen of hearts from the four queens (leaving it as a viable meld of three queens), and creates a high meld of king, queen, jack of hearts, that earns him a chip from each player. If he creates this meld in spades, he would of course collect two chips from each opponent. And if at the same time he also has the 7 of spades (the next card below the jack) he would collect yet another two chips.

After any meld the player discards an unwanted card from his hand. To go out of the game the player must meld a total of 11 cards, there being no final discard. At this point he collects a chip from each active player as well as the original ante in the pot. According to the rules set by some Pan clubs, any active player who has failed to make a meld must also pay the winner two additional chips.

The game becomes more complicated and cutthroat through the principle of "forcing." An opponent may order a player whose turn it is to take the top card of the discard pile because he can lay it off on his melds. Unfortunately for that player he must do so and then discard, and in the process he may spoil his own hand, to say nothing of possibly helping the next player who may need that discard.

PANAMA, Gambling in

Many seasoned gamblers say that the best casino gambling in all of Latin America is to be found in Panama. This is probably due to the Canal Zone influence, and the presence of an American com- munity. Casinos in Panama, while not huge, are well run and supervised by the government. A gambling control board is quite knowledgeable and stresses courtesy and fairness to the customers and follows all the rules of American games. The major casinos are located in the leading hotels. Action is not in Panamian currency but rather in dollars so that Americans are not whipsawed by money-changing gouges, which is not uncommon elsewhere in Latin America.

Slots too are available and offer the best payoffs to be found below the Rio Grande.

PAR: Five-dice Game

Par is a five-dice game very much in vogue in the Midwest. Any number can play, but generally not more than six or seven do, since losses can mount if there are too many participants.

How to play: High dice determines the order of the shooters, and using a dice cup, the first man throws all five dice. The object of the game is to get the dice to total 24 or more, and the shooter may hold any number of dice he wishes and rethrow the rest. However, on each roll he must leave at least one die as part of his score. Thus if he throws 6-6-3-2-1 on his first roll, he would retain the two 6's. If he rolled the remaining dice to come up 2-1-1, he would be forced to retain the 2 and would roll the remaining dice for his final try.

If after shooting all of the five dice the player has a total under 24, he must pay the difference times the unit of betting to each player. If his total is 22 he would pay two chips (or the money amount) to all other players. If, however, he goes over 24, the surplus amount becomes his point. Let us say he hits 28, making 4 his point. He throws all five dice once and for every 4 that comes up he collects four chips (or the money amount) from all players.

This is a thoroughly honest and even-steven game, provided of course there are no dice-cup cheaters involved. Since Par tends to be a low-stakes bar game, that would not appear to be much of a danger, but one should remember that dice-cup cheaters practice their craft constantly and prefer to hone their sharpness by playing under game conditions. They do occasionally frequent bars looking for Par games to take.

See DICE-CUP CHEATING.

PARLIAMENT
See FAN TAN.

Blaise PASCAL: 17th-century Mathematician, Philosopher, and Scientist
The great French mathematician and scientist Blaise Pascal (1623-1662), together with another mathema-

The death mask of mathematician Blaise Pascal. It is perhaps ironic—or cynics might say fitting—that pictures of the mask or even replicas can be seen in some European casinos under the oft-quoted legend: "The Gambler's Friend." (Photo: N.Y. Public Library)

tician, Pierre de Fermat, established probability theory as a new branch of mathematics. Pascal's work has been a boon to successful professional gamblers, and indeed it was his work with one gambler in particular that started Pascal on his trailblazing path.

Antoine Gombaud, the Chevalier de Méré, was a very prosperous gamester, thanks to a lucrative dice game he played. De Méré bet at even money that he could roll a 6 with a single die in four tries. He made a fortune out of the simple system, which he had either figured out or guessed gave him a distinct edge. But, as the story goes, de Méré became too successful and other gamblers refused to play his game. To lure them back, he switched to a pair of dice and declared he could throw two dice and get a 6-6 within 24 tries. The good Chevalier arrived at this conclusion by simply multiplying four by 6, the total possibilities of the second die. Unaccountably, things didn't work out and de Méré was losing his cloak.

In desperation he turned to Pascal for help. Pascal, dealing with a science still in its infancy, soon con-

cluded that de Méré's figures were wrong. Pascal's method was very advanced for the time. He multiplied the odds against winning by the colog of the hyperbolic log of two, i.e., 0.693, in this case $35 \times 0.693 = 24.255$. This meant de Méré had to roll the dice 24.255 times exactly to have an even chance of winning. Obviously the gamester needed 25 rolls of the dice to get an edge of 0.745. And 26 or 27 rolls would have been more like it. Legend has it that de Méré followed through on Pascal's advice and recouped his former losses.•

Pascal's involvement in de Méré's dice problem sparked his interest in further research of similar gambling problems and he engaged in long correspondence with Fermat. Together they discovered much of the basic mathematics of probability.

Some gambling historians credit Pascal with inventing the game of ROULETTE during a monastic retreat. There is much evidence to the contrary. What can be definitely established is that Pascal did experiment with a perpetual-motion device and he did utilize a ball and wheel in his research. He apparently even called his wheel "roulette." But it was left to others to see the great gambling potential of a ball and wheel. See also SIXES AND DOUBLE SIXES.

PASS THE GARBAGE: Stud Poker Variation
How to play: Pass the Garbage is a wide-open Stud Poker game in which seven downcards are dealt to each player (six if there are eight players in the game) and there is a round of betting. Then each player picks out his three worst cards and passes them the opponent to his left. After another round of betting, each player discards two cards, leaving five in each hand. These cards are then turned up one at a time, with another round of betting on the first four.

Strategy: Pass the Garbage is often played as a high-low game. Unlike most high-low games, it is wiser to be going for high rather than low since the passing of three cards by all the players often creates chaos by pairing up a low hand. By contrast, a high hand cannot be destroyed and actually has as much chance as any other of being strengthened. Not surprisingly, Pass the Garbage is also known as Screw Your Neighbor.
See also BASKETBALL.

PASSE-DIX
See TEN.

PAST POSTING: Cheating the House
Cheating the casinos is a time-honored art form and while many inept practitioners are caught at it, the real professional does very well. The tactic is called "past posting" and is most practiced at the ROULETTE table, although it works as well in other games. The

term originally referred to the hustlers who learned the results of a horse race quickly and got a bet down with a book-maker before he learned the results of the race. Modern past posters have learned that it is much easier to past post a casino.

Watching a past poster at work is no simple task. They can strike with lighting precision. Most American Roulette wheels have only one dealer-croupier and in that second when the ball lands in a slot, he or she must look at the wheel. If the past poster can see the results faster he can suddenly push a stack of chips on some winning spot on the layout.

One of the best past posting scams involves two hustlers, one doing the betting and the other hovering near the wheel, perhaps making an insignificant bet in the process. The man near the wheel is the spotter and it's his job to watch the wheel intently—as almost every gambler does. The moment the ball plops into a number slot, the spotter signals his partner. Just as the croupier calls "no more bets," the second hustler puts a stack of chips on one of the three column bets that pay 2 to 1 odds. Past posters prefer positioning themselves at the bottom of the table, as far from the wheel as possible. This makes the column bets the most accessible. The spotter does not have to relay the actual number to his confederate. A rapid finger signal can indicate columns one, two, or three. Let us say the bettor put his money on the middle column and the winning number comes up in the first column. With a fast movement, the bettor can shift the chips to that column before the croupier's eyes leave the wheel. If, on the other hand, the second column actually wins, the bettor can simply collect the honest bet, or if he feels it's safe, slap a few more chips on his pile.

Since there are floormen behind the tables who survey the action at a few tables, the hustlers have to watch for them as well before making a move. The floormen have a way of gravitating to tables getting a lot of action, and past posters have learned how to create a diversion at another table. One way is through heavy betting, perhaps $500 or $1,000 bets going down on even money or 2 to 1 bets. Then the action is stepped up, with bets coming in all around, including some bets on the zeroes. What the hustlers create is a sense of intense betting, but it is really balanced out so that they neither win nor lose. But it does get the floormen's attention. Meanwhile back at table number one, the past posters strike.

PEEKING: Card-cheater's Tactic

The art of peeking during a card game is a subtle skill. A dealer who can peek at the top card of the pack is, of course, at a great advantage. In Stud Poker or BLACKJACK he knows an opponent's down-card and therefore knows when to bet or drop in the

Using the peek method the dealer, while ostensibly studying his own card, determines his opponent's next card will be the eight of spades. (Photo: E. Gerard)

former and when to draw in the latter. If he is adept at SECOND DEALING, he can also decide whether he should give an upcoming card to an opponent. If the card will help that player, the dealer holds back the top card and gives him the second card instead.

Peeking itself is a rather simple move for the experienced card manipulator. Many are good enough to do it while dealing one-handed. This is an effective tactic for a sharper because many unknowledgeable players think it is impossible to cheat while dealing one-handed. Actually, only one hand is used in peeking. The thumb presses down and to the left of the top card, pushing it against the fingers on the opposite corner of the deck. The top card buckles just enough for the dealer to get a glimpse of the inner corner of the card.

The games of Blackjack and Stud Poker are perfect for peeking. The other players usually are not looking at the dealer or the deck, but are busy studying their own hole cards. The dealer himself will also slump down and squint at his own hole card more than once, and in the process is peeking at the deck's top card at the same time. A peeker is hard to catch and the best defense is to watch for the so-called "MECHANIC'S GRIP," which the peeker must use in pulling the dodge. Also beware of the dealer who looks at his own hole card several times during a hand. When the alarm bell of suspicion sounds, a player should stare constantly at the deck hand. This is usually enough to inhibit a peeker, and in time he will take his deception elsewhere.
See BOTTOM PEEKING; SECOND DEALING.

PEGGING: Marking Cards

Pegging is a method cheats use to mark cards during play. If they are playing with novices, they can get away with showing up at a game with a bandage on a thumb or finger. Protruding from the bandage is the point of a small thumbtack that the sharper uses to prick certain cards in just the right spot. The idea is to "peg" the card without penetrating all the way through. A cheat might peg some of the deuces in DEUCES WILD, for instance. When dealing, he can feel the cards in just the right spot to see if a deuce is coming up.

An adept mechanic might deal seconds when he knows there is a deuce on top and reserve the prize card for himself. But it is often enough of an edge to know if any opponent has a deuce, making it easy to gauge his hand in stud.

Of course, these days a gambler with a finger bandage will attract considerable attention, especially if he is a winner, and bandages are hardly ever used now. Favored are rings that have a sharp point on the loop. Some cheats carry duplicate rings, one with the point and one without. Upon completing their pegging, they will leave the table and switch rings so that if any suspicions are aroused, the ring will be demonstrably clean.

A peg is quite discernible to a cheat who knows where to feel. A prudent player who suspects pegging will make it a habit to run his fingers over the entire backs of important cards depending on the game—deuces, aces, jacks, jokers, etc.

Edward PENDLETON: Washington, D.C. Gambling Entrepreneur

Throughout much of the 19th century Washington, D.C., may have been the gambling as well as the national capitol of the United States, with hundreds of gambling houses and rooms centered mostly in and around the Capitol. Many catered to all elements, including the low-salaried civil servants and uniformed men, but others barred their doors to all but the very wealthy and those highly-placed in government. For at least a quarter of a century Edward Pendleton's Palace of Fortune, which opened in 1832, was the gaming place of the power elite. Pendleton (?-1858) was said to have been Virginia-born, but whether wellborn or not was a matter of dispute. There is no doubt, however, that he became Washington's aristocrat of the gambling halls.

A staff of black servants at Pendleton's Palace saw to it that no patron was without "rare viands and choice wines" while they lost their money. Most patrons certainly did so, and in time Pendleton's establishment gained an appropriate nickname, the Hall of the Bleeding Heart. Members of the Cabinet and Congress frequented the Palace, and Pres. James Buchanan was often to be found challenging its FARO games. In the 1840's and 1850's the Palace was one of the few places where abolitionists and secession-

ists deigned to be seen together publicly, the gaming tables being regarded as neutral territory.

Pendleton himself became one of the city's richest and most illustrious citizens and quite a power broker. He extended credit to many political figures, lobbyists crowded around his tables eager to pay off the gambling debts of congressional losers who then saw the wisdom, said some journalistic muckrakers of the day, in supporting certain legislation. Pendleton himself, veteran journalist Perley Poore declared, "assisted in the passage of many useful bills of a private nature, involving considerable sums of money" and, he added wryly, "a broker in parliamentary notes is an inevitable retainer of broker votes."

It marked the end of an era when Pendleton died in 1858. Several leading Democrats acted as pallbearers at the funeral and the president was in attendance. It could not be estimated how many IOU's—it was said Buchanan's among them—were torn up on Pendleton's demise.

PENNSYLVANIA—Legalized Lotteries

Like Michigan, Pennsylvania is one of the few states that exempts winners of state-run lotteries from paying income tax on the prize money. This is common in Europe but rarely practiced in the United States, and indeed the IRS turns a deaf ear to any proposal to make the monies tax-free from federal income taxes. Some states look upon lotteries as a source for additional revenues even beyond income taxes as well as returning to the bettors less than half the money wagered. One "hidden" tactic is imposing the state sales tax on the tickets, with the money coming off the top before pools, expenses, and the traditional state cut.

Pennsylvania, in that sense, is one of the more advanced lottery operators. The games offered are traditional. There are the usual three-digit and four-digit numbers games. In addition, in the three-digit game, players, as they can in some other states, also can make a two-number bet on either the "Front Pair," the first two numbers in order of the three-digit winner, or the "Back Pair," the last two numbers in order of that result. A $1 bet is paid off at $50, just under 50 percent of the true odds.

Pennsylvania also offers instant "rub off" games that award such typical immediate prizes as $75,000 in cash and a shot at a super drawing for $1,000 a week for life. Pennsylvania's longtime Lotto is a 1 to 40 proposition and prizes are determined by the amount of money bet and the number of winners. The usual jackpot is usually over $1 million.

In October 1987, Pennsylvania started a Super 7 game in which 11 numbers are drawn and a winner must pick seven out of seven of these 11. Faced with the biggest prize ever in American lottery history,

Pennsylvanians bought tickets at a rate that reached 19,140 a minute, with a total of 27,662,192 $1 tickets being sold. A man and woman jointly bought the one winning ticket that brought them a $46 million jackpot. Soon this jackpot total was eclipsed by one of $115,000,000.

Revenues from the Pennsylvania lottery go to senior-citizen programs for such items as food, rent, and medical and hospital care. In a recent year, lotteries netted the state a half-billion dollars.

PENNY FALLS: Carnival Gambling Gyp

Penny Falls is the newest gyp item to appear on the carnival gambling scene in the past decade. Despite their name, these machines are seldom played for pennies, but rather for nickels, dimes, or quarters. Players are lured by a stack of coins slowly gyrating inside the glass case, looking for all the world to be ready to topple over a ledge. The player feeds coins into the machine in an effort to dislodge the coins since whatever tumbles over the ledge is his.

Almost none of the coins do, however. The machines are equipped with a side chute that retains almost all the coins for the house. Despite an extremely poor payout rate, people become fascinated with these machines and feed coin after coin into them, much as they would into a casino SLOT MACHINE. They do not get back 80 to 90 percent as they do with legal slots, however. In fact, it has been estimated the payout is generally around 10 percent. Not surprisingly, some of the more competent state authorities have cracked down on these gyp machines, but because of the huge profit margin, Penny Falls continue to proliferate.

PENNY TOSS: Worst Carnival Bet of All

You'll see it at almost every fair, carny or charitable fund-raising affair. It's called Penny Toss, although the more common games today are played for nickels, dimes, and, most often, quarters. To win all you have to do is throw a coin so that it lands in a circle or square without touching a line. All Penny Toss boards are designed to produce a 20 percent payout rate, or less. This doesn't mean a player will win 20 percent of the time but rather that his payoff will amount to 20 percent of what he invests. Compare this to almost 99 percent at casino CRAPS, 94-plus percent at American ROULETTE, and about 85 percent on the average casino SLOT MACHINE, Penny Toss, on the other hand, has the virtue, from the operator's point of view, of taking your money faster with lower overhead.

PERCENT: Casino's True Profit Margin

Because this is a book devoted to gambling, the odds in various gambling games are stated in terms of an "edge" or "advantage" held by a dealer or banker or a gambling casino. As noted in a number of entries, this so-called "house edge" is not nearly as important as it seems, and it is hardly the whole story. By and large the house edge in CRAPS works out to about 1.40 percent, meaning that in theory if in the course of a betting session a gambler wagers a total of $200, he will lose a bit less than $3. While it may be all right for a gambler figuring the odds of a game to think in that fashion, in any other sense it is arrant nonsense. Casinos do not run Craps tables to take 1.4 percent of the handle on the most important bets. If that was all that they did, the practice of skimming would not even be under discussion. The IRS could simply run long samples of the wagered amount and estimate the casino's take. The fact is, gambling casinos take in more than a dozen times their supposed edge.

Casino operators have their own terms for stating their anticipated profits. There are words like "drop" and "percent." The drop is the total amount bet at a table, similar to the "handle" at a racetrack. The key word is "percent," and that has little to do with the gambling edge they enjoy. The important thing to bear in mind is that bettors are human beings, with all the weaknesses and flaws humans exhibit. The main failing among these is loss of self-control. People may bet small at first but then, win or lose, they get reckless and bet more and more. At the Craps table they may double their money or lose it all. In the latter instance, it's "Tap City." If they win and don't walk, they will almost certainly give their winnings back. Thus, instead of looking for 1.4 percent edge from a game, the house expects every Craps table, every BLACKJACK table, every ROULETTE wheel to produce from 19 to 22 percent in profits. Those are the real odds a player bucks if he can't play under restraint. Many experts claim a gambler can use various money-management methods to keep from going broke or perhaps even retain some of his winnings. The casino is betting a gambler cannot do it and will average out losing 20 cents on every dollar he bets.

It's a pretty sure bet.

PERSIAN RUMMY: Variation of Five-hundred Rummy

Persian Rummy is a game for four players in partnership, and was once called 500 Joker Rummy. However, over the years, the game's rules and scoring have been altered so much that it should be considered a game in its own right, although its roots obviously are from FIVE-HUNDRED RUMMY.

How to play: A regular deck of 52 cards plus four jokers is used. The jokers are valued at 20 points each, but are not wild cards. They just represent cards that can be melded separately into sets of either three or four jokers. The jokers cannot be used in sequence with other cards. Aces in Persian Rummy are always valued at 15 points, but can only be used in sets of aces or in a high suit sequence such as ace, king, queen of clubs. The ace is never ranked below deuce. Scoring of points is the same as in Five-hundred Rummy, but a full set of four cards, such as four deuces, count for double, that is, three deuces would be 6 points while four deuces would be 16. Therefore it is preferable to meld sets instead of sequences. However, a player should consider taking an early sequence to "go Rummy," or laying down all his cards, rather than waiting to meld a full set, since ending the game is worth a bonus of 25 points. Conversely, there is the temptation to stay with three jokers awaiting the fourth, because this set is worth 160 points.

A game of Persian Rummy runs to two or three deals as agreed in advance, after which payment is made by the losing team on the basis of the difference in score. There can be some additional bonuses awarded the winning team. Some gamblers like to add 50 or 100 points to a winning game (not hand) score.

PERU, Gambling in

Peru has year-round horse-race betting and there is also wagering on cockfighting in many local arenas on Sundays and frequently on holidays. There is all sorts of lottery gambling, with many cities running their own contests. Bingo is legal when conducted by public welfare institutions. Most forms of private gambling games are against the law, though dice games are common enough in many private clubs.

PETITS CHEVAUX: "Horse-race Roulette"

A sort of horse-race betting game that was especially popular in the 18th and 19th centuries, Petits Chevaux was originally regarded as a sort of "poor man's roulette." It can still be found in a few French casinos and in Ireland.

In Petits Chevaux there are nine figures mounted on horses that race around separate concentric circular tracks. As the horses are brought to a stop, the one nearest the winning post is the winner. Bets are paid off at 7 to 1, producing a handsome edge for the house of 11.1111 percent. Bets can also be placed on the odd- or even-numbered horses, except for the 5, which functions as a zero in favor of the house (see ROULETTE), at even money. These even-money bets produce the same huge 11.1111 edge for the house, which explains why so many casinos were loath to drop Petits Chevaux. However, in the 20th century most French casinos finally gave up the game

mainly because near dead heats led to many messy arguments.

The casinos switched to BOULE as their new form of poor man's Roulette, and so maintain the treasured 11.1111 edge.

PIG: Single-die Game

While a simple game of luck, Pig has been used very successfully by hustlers in big-money scores, sometimes on casino junket flights. Often three or more of them hustle up a quickie dice game that can be played easily under air-borne conditions. Only one die is used and a player can throw the die as often as he wishes, adding up his point totals. The first player to reach a total of 100 is the winner. There is a kicker, of course. If the player throws a 1, his entire score is cancelled and he must pass the die and wait for its return to him in order.

But this is not exactly an equal opportunity game. The player who goes first has the best chance to reach 100 first. To compensate for this, it is often ruled that all players have a right to complete the round, in which case the highest score over 100 wins.

The reason Pig is favored by hustlers is that they can control strategy of how each scam artist will play. If the game is played as DEALER'S CHOICE, they position themselves in fourth, fifth, and sixth spot in a six-man game. Thus for three games in a row one, two, or three of them will have the advantage of playing last. Equally important, if one of them gets a good run and nears 100, he has the option of pressing his luck against getting a 1 so long as his nearest opponent is one of his secret partners.

Some scam artists, according to one junketeer specialist, take victims for thousands of dollars before they even land at their green-felt destination.

PIG (CARDS)

Pig is another example of a juvenile game gone adult as a gambling game. Let us first consider the children's version. "Books" of four cards of the same value are taken from a deck of cards to match the number of players. Thus if there are 13 players the entire deck is used. If there are five players, sets from the ace down to the 10 are used, and so on.

The cards are shuffled and four cards are dealt to each player. On a set signal each player simultaneously passes one card to the player on his left. Play continues in this fashion until one player ends up with four of a kind. He immediately puts down his hand and places a finger to his nose. On seeing that, the other players put down their cards and do the same. The last child to get his finger to his nose is "pig," and he loses the game.

In the adult version an ante is made and the money won by the player first completing the book. If two or more books turn up on the same exchange of cards, the pot is split. The game is not entirely luck. Strategy by many adult piggers calls for splitting a pair and passing one along. Then if the player re-pairs, he passes one more card from the set to the same player. He, of course, holds that third card until hell freezes over, hoping to get a new three of a kind while keeping the vital third card from his competitor. Of course, if he gets the fourth card to that book, he can pass an additional card of that value along and then hang up his opponent for the rest of the game.

Ideally, a player will get two pairs early on. This will allow him to send one of the pairs forward and hold the other pair to try for a book. He is taking a risk passing on a pair but if he survives the move, he frequently can freeze that player with a pair or three of a kind and never pass on another card in that book unless he pairs them again. Admittedly, such defensive ploys often leads to ties, since a player will only pass on a likely fourth card to a book when he makes his own set. Still, half a pot always beats losing.

PIG IN THE POKE
See SPIT IN THE OCEAN.

PIG POKER
See SHOTGUN.

PIG STUD POKER: Combination Stud and Draw Game
Although it is called Pig Stud Poker, this game is actually a combination of both Stud and Draw.

How to play: After an ante, three downcards are dealt to each player and there is a round of betting. The fourth card is then dealt face up and there is more betting, followed by a fifth card up and betting again. Then each player picks up his two face cards and adds them to his three downcards. All players continue the game as in Draw Poker, discarding as many as three cards and drawing new ones or stand-ing pat. The game is often played with wild cards and the two exposed cards gives players somewhat of a chance to gauge opponents' strength. A good player will study the upcards to assess the outlook on probabilities for his own hand, something straight Draw doesn't permit.

PINCHING: Cheating-the-casino Tactic
While most attempts by players to cheat the casino is through the art of PAST POSTING, the practice of "pinching," or, as it is sometimes called, "dragging," is by no means a lost art in those casinos that deal cards face down in BLACKJACK. Unlike past posting, in which generally chips are added to a winning bet, pinching works the other way around, removing chips from a losing or weak hand, which is in its own way winning in the long run.

The Blackjack cheat does this by using his cards to steal back a chip. He rests his hand on the table as he picks up his cards with his other hand. If the hand looks rotten, he passes the cards over his bet pile of chips and as he does so, he uses the lower edge of the cards to deftly flick the top chip from the stack so that it lands under his other hand. This is not nearly as hard as it may sound and can be successfully done when the floorman isn't looking. Frequently this pinch cheat sits at "third base," that is, to the dealer's extreme right so that he is the last to play and has more time to pull the switch. Just as frequently the cheat will have a partner who sits at "first base," that is, the first player to call for cards, and he will stall to give his partner more time and safety by holding the dealer's attention.

The chip steerer does not attempt to remove the chip under his hand immediately, waiting instead for the next hand in the hopes that it will be a good one. If it is, he will utilize a good hand-mucking move to add the chip to his betting stack.

The main idea in pinching is to lose small and win big.

PINOCHLE: Demanding Gambling Game
Many experts consider Pinochle a card game requir-ing great skill, and that the two-handed version per-haps involves more skill and strategy than any other two-handed game currently in vogue. In all its forms Pinochle is a demanding pastime requiring a good memory and strong card sense. Years of experience are a help as well.

Although Auction Pinochle, a game for three active players, is played more by gamblers, the two-handed version will be discussed in detail because the strat-egy is more clearly evident.

How to play: Two-handed Pinochle is very similar to BEZIQUE and it is played with a pack of 48 cards, running down in order from ace to 9 in all four suits—duplicated. Each player is dealt 12 cards and the next card is turned face up to determine trump suit. The rest of the deck is placed face down to partially cover the exposed card.

The object of play is to take tricks that include cards that bear a scoring value when won in a trick, and to meld certain combinations of cards that have a scoring value.

Taken in a trick, an ace is 11 points; a 10, 10 points; a king 4; a queen, 3; a jack, 2. Taking the last trick is worth 10 points. Melds, which fall into three classes, are as follows:

Class A:
ace, 10, king, queen, jack of trump suit . 150 points
king, queen of trump suit (royal marrriage) ..... 40 points
king, queen of a plain suit (common marriage) .. 20 points

Class B:
Pinochle (queen of spades and jack of diamonds)............................. 40 points
Dis (9 of trump suit) .... 10 points

Class C:
Four aces—one of each suit .... 100 points
Four kings—one of each suit .... 80 points
Four queens—one of each suit.......... 60 points
Four jacks—one of each suit............. 40 points

The nondealers lead to the first trick, and the winner of a trick thereafter leads to the next. A player is not required to follow suit to a led card. The winner of a trick takes the top card of the undealt pack (the stock) and the loser the next card.

When a player wins a trick, but before drawing a replacement card from the stock, he may lay down any of the above melds, but only one meld is allowed per turn. There are two rules that apply: 1) For each meld, at least one card must be taken from the hand and placed on the table; 2) A card previously melded is allowed to be melded again provided it is in a different class or a high-scoring meld in the same class. Thus if clubs are trump, the king and queen of clubs may be used to score a royal marriage for 40 points and the player can later add the ace, 10, and jack of clubs for a trump sequence worth 150 points. However, he may not do the reverse, first laying down the five trump cards and then attempting to make a royal marriage.

Should the dealer at the start of play turn up a dis for trump, he credits himself with 10 points. Any player holding dis may get credit for it by showing it on winning a trick. In that case he may also make another meld at the same time. On winning a trick, the holder of a dis may swap it for the exposed trump card.

When a player wins the 12th trick, he is permitted to meld, if possible, and he then draws the final face-down card. He must show this card to his opponent, who then picks up the exposed trump card left on the table.

Then the last 12 tricks are played off. From this time on a player must follow suit, if he can, to the card led. If he cannot, he must trump the trick if he holds a trump. If a trump is led, the opponent must win the trick if he can.

Melds are scored as shown, and the score for cards won in tricks are added after the hand is finished. A total of 7, 8, or 9 points is counted as 10. Each deal may be treated as a complete game with payoffs made at that time or scores may be kept until one of the players reaches an agreed-upon total.

Strategy: Pinochle is no contest if one player has more skill, experience, and an ability to remember which cards have been played. In that situation, an astute player will pretty much know what cards his opponent holds during the playing of the last 12 tricks. Because this is the case, a player leading to the last trick before the stock is exhausted will make an informed decision whether to win that trick and thus stop his opponent from melding or to lose the trick and get the exposed trump card to give him added strength in playing the final 12 tricks.

However, it is important to realize that no matter how expert a player may be, he frequently will face a situation he has not seen before. There is no such thing as "the correct play," and two different players, even at the same level of ability, will almost certainly play a hand differently. The second-guessing after a game of Pinochle is much greater than even in BRIDGE. But don't think for a moment that a novice can rely on luck to beat a superior player. Skill will win out, and quickly.

For that reason, any aspiring Pinochle player should sharpen his skills in the two-man game before going on to those involving more players, all of which have some subtle changes in rules and manner of play.

Auction Pinochle is really a game for three, but often four or five participate. When there are four players, the dealer gets no cards and the other three are the active participants for that hand. When there are five players, the second player from the dealer's left also gets no cards. Bidding and the use of a three-card widow goes to the successful bidder who buries three other cards from his original hand of 15 cards. The bidder is required to show the widow cards before putting them in his hand. He may meld before burying his three cards (which can include one or more of the widow cards).

The bidding must be opened by the player at the dealer's left and he must bid at least 200, this representing the points he will get in melds or taking and capturing high-point cards in tricks. A bidder knows he will also name trump, which greatly affects his estimate of his possible score. Succeeding bids must go up at least 10 points at a time.

There are many nuances to Auction Pinochle and to various other multiplayer Pinochle games such as Partnership Pinochle, Firehouse Pinochle, and Check Pinochle. Among the recommended books on strategies in all the variations of Pinochle are *Scarne on Cards* by John Scarne; *Pinochle Pointers* by P. Hal Sims;

How to Play Pinochle by Walter J. Zarse; and *The New Complete Hoyle* by Albert Morehead, Richard L. Frey, and Geoffrey Mott-Smith.

PINOCHLE POKER: Intriguing Hybrid Game

Many gambler regard Pinochle Poker as an excellent game, every bit as satisfying as regular POKER—but don't try to tell that to the average Poker addict. He is too prejudiced against using anything other than ordinary cards or, at worst, a stripped-down pack from the standard 52-card deck to take kindly to switching to a Pinochle deck. The saying goes: ''If you want to play Pinochle, play Pinochle. Otherwise let's play Poker.''

How to play: Pinochle Poker is played with a Pinochle pack ranking ace, king, queen, jack, 10, and 9, with all cards duplicated. Naturally five of a kind is the highest hand. Special rules apply to flushes—a flush with two pairs, beats a one-pair flush, which outranks a regular flush. Having learned that last rule, it is wise to forget it. Flushes (and straights) seldom appear, as they regularly do in DRAW or Seven-card Stud, but the point is that they are seldom good enough to win anyway.

Unfortunately, gamblers apply the standard rules of Poker to Pinochle Poker and then are disappointed when things turn sour; that can poison one's attitude toward the game. For a player who learns to appreciate the probabilities, Pinochle Poker can be a very rewarding experience.

Strategy: In the Five-card Stud version players should seldom stay if the first two or three cards fail to produce a pair. An ace-king start is not as promising as in regular Poker. Although a player could fill an ace or king, the fact is that most games are won by hands of two pairs or better. Naturally, a gambler with an early pair of aces must stay, but by the fifth card he has to be wondering why, especially if other pairs are showing. Generally, three of a kind should be bet hard, with the bettor ignoring the possible straights or flushes. Far more worrisome would be a hand showing two pairs, which is much more likely to fill than a straight or flush.

In Seven-card Stud, a full house is the minimum required winning hand. Straights and flushes are strictly drop-out hands.

In Draw, strategy plays an important role. The first rule is to absolutely ignore possible straights and flushes when drawing new cards. Chasing such weak hands should be left to the uninitiated. Staying for the draw on a pair is also risky since the improvement needed is too great. A pair that draws a second pair should fold because two pairs is a weak hand. Another frequent error of uninformed gamblers is to hold a pair and an ace kicker. Whatever the virtues

of the ace kicker in regular Poker, they disappear here. The first task of a pair is improving at least to three of a kind and it is better to have three shots at that than to be looking for a second ace, which will not help very much in itself.

Unfortunately, Pinochle Poker has simply never attracted the following its intriguing possibilities fully deserve.

PINOCHLE RUMMY
See FIVE-HUNDRED RUMMY.

PIQUET: One of the Oldest Card Games Currently Played

Piquet is among the oldest card games still widely played. Rabelais mentioned it more than four centuries ago, and it has enjoyed popularity in many countries, especially in England, Spain (where it may have originated, although the terminology is now in French), and France, where it enjoys the most support.

How to play: A 32-card deck ranking from ace high to 7 low (6's to deuces removed) is used for Piquet, which is basically a two-person game, although it can be adapted for three or four. Each player gets 12 cards, and the remaining eight are spread out face down on the table as a stock. If the nondealer has no picture cards in his opening hand, he may declare ''carte blanche'' immediately for 10 points. The dealer may also score carte blanche, but he must await his turn to claim it.

The nondealer has the right to draw one to five cards from the stock after first discarding a like number. If he does not claim all five, he still has the right to look at them and put them aside so that he may look at them later to refresh his memory of what they are. The dealer then has the right to the remaining cards in the stock, after discarding the cards he does not want. He too may study any cards from the stock he does not take and can refresh his memory about them or his discards.

That ritual being completed, the players declare various scoring combinations. First the nondealer states the number of cards in his longest suit. If the dealer does not have a longer suit, the nondealer scores 1 point for each card in his longest suit. If the dealer's suit is longer, he scores instead in the same fashion. Should they tie, they add the point values in that suit, the ace being 11, the face cards 10, and the rest having their pip value. The highest total gets the 1 point. If they both remain tied, no one scores.

The nondealer then declares his highest sequence, which is at least three consecutive cards in the same suit. Again the player with the longest sequence scores. If the two sequences are of the same length, the highest card of the sequences wins. If they are tied, no one scores. One point is awarded for each card in the sequence, but if the sequence is more than four, an extra 10 points is added. Thus a six-card sequence would be 16 points. Only the player with the highest sequence scores, and he gains the right to score all sequences he holds as well.

Then the sets are scored, with the nondealer declaring his highest set of four- or three-of-a-kind. If there are no fours of a kind, the highest three of a kind wins. Four of a kind is worth 14 points and triplets 3 points. The high set holder also claims any additional sets he has. His losing opponent may claim nothing for the category.

With the counting of all combinations now completed, the game enters the trick competition. Tricks are taken by the higher card of the suit led, and if a player has no cards in suit he discards another suit. The taker of a trick leads to the next. Ten points are awarded for taking the most tricks, but nothing is awarded if the players tie. The taker of the last trick gets 1 point. Taking all the tricks is called a *capot* and is worth a total of 40 points, but it also nullifies the 10 points for taking most of the tricks and the 1 point for taking the last trick.

Points are also awarded for leads and certain tricks. If a player leads a card above a 9, he gets 1 point, and when a player takes a trick with a card over 9, he also scores 1 point.

The scoring moves rapidly and each player must announce his point total every time it changes. If a player gets a total of 30 in declarations before his opponent scores any points, he has made *repiquet* (repic, in England and America), which is worth 60 points. If the player gets his 30 points from declarations and trick-taking together before his opponent scores, he has a *piquet* (pic, in England and America), which is worth 30 points.

The game is declared over after four or six deals, as previously agreed upon or when a player has 100 points. The winner receives the point difference over his loser's score, plus an additional 100 points. Piquet variations for more than two players follow this entry.

PIQUET—a Ecrire

This is an interesting variation of PIQUET for three players. Each player deals twice in succession, once to the player on his left and once to the one on his right. After the conclusion of the second round, each pays the difference between his hand and the other two.

PIQUET—Partnership

With four players playing in partnership, all the cards are dealt out and there is no stock. The game is played like regular PIQUET, with the scores of the partners combined.

PIQUET—Three-handed or Normand

In Three-handed, or Normand, Piquet ten cards are dealt to the competitors, leaving only two cards as a stock. The dealer has the right to them after discarding two cards. Only one player may score in each of the declaration categories, and *capot* scores 40 points as in two-handed PIQUET. However *repiquet* counts for 60, but only a score of 20 is necessary to make it. Similarly, *piquet* also scores 60, with only 20 needed. The player with the most tricks gets 10, but if two tie, each get 5 unless the third player was shut out, in which case each gets 20.

PISHA PASHA: "War"-style Gambling Game for Adults

Pisha Pasha is a two-man game that may be described as very close to the juvenile game of War. Surprisingly, it is frequently played as a time-passer by big-time gamblers. Among high rollers it is not unusual for a game to start out at a $100 a hand, with the loser having the option to raise the stakes $100 a pop after each loss. It doesn't take long to get into the thousands and for losses to mount precipitously.

How to play: Under the rules of Pisha Pasha the deck is divided equally and players turn up cards together to form individual piles until two cards of the same suit appear simultaneously. The high card takes both piles, which are put aside by the winner. Cards rank from ace high to deuce low.

When the two decks are run through, play ends, the captured cards are counted and the highest total wins the bet. This is obviously a rather mindless game, amounting to the equivalent of flipping coins or cutting for high card, but it can get addictive. That it is played so intensively may also speak volumes about the compulsions of some gamblers.

Sometimes Pisha Pasha is turned to by the first two players arriving for a weekly POKER session. It is recommended that if so played, the stakes be kept small; with a run of bad luck a player can get wiped out before the regular game starts.

PITCH: Modern Version of All Fours

Pitch is a modern game that developed out of the old English game of All Fours, or SEVEN UP, which has been played for the last few centuries. Actually, very few gamblers today concern themselves with straight Pitch but prefer Auction Pitch, so much so that it is now commonly called Pitch. It is sometimes also know as Set Back.

How to play: Cards rank from ace high to deuce low. The game may be played by two to eight players, but four is the preferred number. Each player is dealt six cards and then the player to the left of the dealer opens the bidding to determine trump suit. A bid is made from 1 to 4, based on how many points a player feels he can make. The dealer has the option of matching the bid, which is enough for him to take it. The only exception is a "smudge," which is the highest possible bid of 4 points. The dealer cannot take that bid by simply matching it.

The top bidder is known as the maker and he pitches (leads) to the first trick. The card that he leads becomes the trump suit. On all tricks a player must follow suit if he can. If he cannot, he may discard an odd suit or he may trump. The highest card of the suit led takes the trick unless it is trumped, in which case the highest trump wins the trick. The winner of a trick leads to the next trick.

Points are scored in the following manner:

High. Taken by the player who holds (and plays) the highest trump in the hand.

Low: Taken by the player who holds the lowest trump in the hand.

Jack: Taken by the player who wins a trick including the jack of trump, regardless of who holds it. Of course, in many hands the jack of trump is not present.

Game: Taken by the player who wins the highest count of "honor cards" in tricks won by each player. The honor cards are in all suits and carry the following point values: ace, 4; king, 3; queen, 2; jack, 1; and 10, 10.

If two players are tied in the game count, there is no point award for Game for that hand. Combined with a missing jack of trump, this means a hand can produce no more than 2 points. It should be apparent that when there is a smudge bid the bidder has both the jack of trump and some higher trumps or he could not make such a high bid.

Every player records his point score and if the maker fails to make his bid, he is "set back" the total points of his bid. If that puts him in a minus category, his score is circled to indicate he is "in the hole."

The game is won by the first player with 7 points, although some make the game total 9, 11, or 21. Seven is the bet winning total to use. If the maker and another player or players reach 7 on the same deal, the maker is automatically the winner. If two players, other than the maker, reach 7, the winner is determined by the order in which they get the score, the order being determined by the points coming from High, Low, Jack, and Game. This means that if player A achieves 7 after Low is reckoned and player B after Game, player A is the winner.

A player who smudges and wins his bid of 4 is automatically the game winner unless he was in the hole at the time. In that case he is allowed only the 4 points and the game continues.

The winner receives the difference in the point score between himself and each of the losers.

In traditional Pitch there is no bidding for trump, consequently no setback. The player to the dealer's left simply establishes trump with the first card he pitches.

PLACE POKER: Special-rule Stud Variation

The concept of Place Poker can be adapted to any type of game, with the second-best hand becoming the winner. It is rather difficult to come up with rules to win at this game so that the prudent gambler—if he plays what most experts look upon as a rather simpleminded game at all—simply works out the guidelines that indicate when he should drop out. If after the third or fourth card in Five-card Stud, for example, he "beats the board"—meaning his hand including his hole card tops the other players' open cards—he should drop as the potential high hand. Some addicts to Place Poker say the draw variety (see VICE PRESIDENT) allows for real strategy, a claim not many gamblers agree with.

PLAY OR PAY: Fan Tan Antecedent

While Play or Pay is often described as a variation of FAN TAN, it is really a card game that preceded it, and from which the latter was adapted. Play or Pay is still popular in some betting circles.

How to play: From three to seven players ante to the pot and all 52 cards are dealt out one at a time to each player. Those players who get one less card are required to ante another chip into the pot to equalize matters, since the object of the game is to get rid of all of one's cards.

The first player then lays down any card he chooses. Let us say he puts down the 6 of diamonds. The next player must put down the 7 of diamonds and play continues in ascending order "around the corner": 8,9,10, jack, queen, king, ace, deuce, 3, 4, and 5. Whenever a player cannot lay down the next higher card, he is required to feed the pot another chip. The player who completes a suit begins the next suit.

Strategy: This is not a game for the unskilled, and a good Play or Pay gambler will generally win when he is the eldest hand, i.e., the player who goes first. If the first player is dealt four two-card straights, one in each suit, or three two-card straights and only one card in the fourth suit, he cannot lose with correct play. For simplicity's sake let us assume a player gets the 5-6 in all four suits. He starts off leading the 6 in the first suit and controls the next suit when he plays the 5. However, in the fourth suit, if he leads with the 6, he is a sure loser, since he will play the final card with the 5. Instead, on this suit he leads with the 5, follows with the 6 and ends the game. Admittedly, the cards do not usually fall so fortuitously, but a good leader controlling only two suits can frequently win the cards if the remaining suits are reasonably close. Much practice is needed to master the strategy in what appears to be a simple game.

PLUS OR MINUS: Dealer's Choice Game
Because this game is dealt exactly like Draw Poker, some gamblers permit it in DEALER'S CHOICE even though with its points count it is certainly not POKER.

How to play: Hands are rated according to the card rankings, with the ace being 1, deuce 2, and on up to the picture cards, which are 10 points each. All red cards are plus cards and all black cards minus.

Players are dealt five cards after a betting round and discard as many as they wish, drawing replacements. There is showdown betting and the player with the highest plus total (after subtraction of the minus cards, if any) takes the pot. The game may also be played high-low, with the highest hand and the lowest hand splitting the pot.

Strategy: There are many ramifications to this seemingly simple game, and when played for high only it calls for quite different strategy than high-low does. For the prudent gambler, high only is the better game because it is much easier to read an opponents' hands. There is no doubt what a one- or two-card draw means, for example. Sometimes players will stay and draw three cards, in which case they had better have 20 points going in. Let us say a player has three red cards totaling 28 points, and there are two other players staying with four cards each. Unless the two-card draw comes up with two red cards that player should think twice about remaining in the game. Normally a player would stay in for a draw at 25 or so and drop if his score falls below 20. But in this case let us say the player draws a black 9 and a red deuce, leaving him with 21 points. He is very likely a sure loser. The odds are that one of the two one-card draws will get a red card and, since staying on four red cards almost certainly means having a point score of 25 or more, that would make the two-card draw hand a losing hand. Indeed even if both those one-card draws get black cards, one is probably a low card and will still leave that player with a score above 21. Of course a four-card draw may consist of three red cards and a black ace. This does not alter the situation much since that hand could be as high as a 29, which is still a very high score.

If high Plus or Minus is a game of strategy, high-low is less so because more players stay in and their disparate hands are harder to read. In high-low it makes very little sense to stay with two cards, and even three cards is not a good staying hand unless the point total is at least 25. A wash of a red and black card of near equal value is the likeliest result

of a two-card draw, which will put that player at a disadvantage to numerous one-card draws, complicated by the fact that he has no way of knowing if they are high or low hands. Because of this high-low mix, it is imperative to have 25 or more to draw new cards. Ironically though, once having stayed, a player generally should see the showdown bets if his final score is over 15—on the outside possibility of his being the only player going high or low.

Plus or Minus may not be Poker, but it is a thinking man's game—plus or minus some of the time.

POCHEN: Old Card Game
Pochen is an old 32-card game, perhaps of German origin, which incorporates elements of a great number of games, including what later became modern POKER.

How to play: At one time Pochen had a special layout for playing but like many old-style games in modern play, plates are now used to hold wagers on the various possibilities. There are eight sections marked Ace, King, Queen, Jack, Ten, Marriage, Sequence, and "Poche," or "Pool," and players put one chip on each section. All players are dealt as many cards as the 32-card deck (ranked aces down to 7's) will allow evenly. The next card is turned up to signify trump suit and the remaining card or cards are out of the game, which obviously alters the game possibilities.

The first call in the game is for high trump cards and the players who can show the ace, king, queen, jack, or 10 of trump suit collect the appropriate wagers. If a player shows both king and queen of trump, he also collects the Marriage section. Wherever a high card has been turned up to indicate trump, that section will remain uncollected. The players then return their trump cards to their hands and these cards no longer serve any trump purpose.

Next a Sequence play is held and players lay down their longest sequence of three or more cards in any suit they can, such as 7, 8, 9 of hearts or 9, 10, jack, queen of spades, etc. The longest sequence, if any, wins the Sequence wager. If there are two sequences of equal length, the highest card wins. If the high card is the same the contenders divide the Sequence section, with any odd chip going to the player nearest to the dealer's left.

There then follows a high-hand play utilizing some of the rules of POKER, limited to four of a kind, three of a kind, or a pair, with the highest hand winning and ties in the number of cards being ranked as in Poker. Thus, three aces would beat three kings, and so on. There is no two-pairs category in this game and often one high pair is good enough to win. The high-hand winner takes the Pool section.

This completes the section wagering, although some

sections may not have been taken. Now the players seek to play out their hands before their opponents. The person to the left of the dealer leads with any card he chooses, let us say the 8 of clubs. The other players must add to the sequence in suit, with a player unable to do so simply losing his turn. The play in that sequence continues until the ace is reached or because no one has the next card in sequence. At that point the player laying down the last card starts a new sequence. The first to play out his cards collects one chip for each card his opponents are still holding. The deal then passes to the next player and everyone contributes another chip to each section, including those that were not won on the previous hand.

There are other variations of play in Pochen, some with the final play in the form of tricks in suit, with the player taking the trick with the highest card (trumps do not apply) leading to the next trick. Again, the first player to go out collects chips from his opponents on the number of cards with which they are stuck.

Pochen is not played much today, but there is a more modern version called TRIPOLI.

POKER: The True National Pastime

For American males under 18, baseball may be said to be the national pastime. When they grow up it becomes Poker. Poker can in fact be called the true national pastime. Among card games it is far more commonly played than all forms of RUMMY combined. BRIDGE is a distant third. The popular belief is that women prefer Bridge to Poker, but every survey taken shows that more women play Poker than Bridge.

Although on the face of it Poker is a relatively simple game it requires more skill than any other card game. In fact, the range of skills is phenomenal. No other game requires such redoubtable traits as unfriendliness, nongenerosity, a lack of compassion or sportsmanship, deception, and cruelty as does Poker. Is it any wonder, then, that Poker, by most estimates, regularly involves at least 65 million Americans in more or less regular play, or that they gamble well over $100 billion annually on the game? It is played for pennies or for thousands of dollars a hand, and more often than not with cutthroat determination.

Poker is not a difficult game to learn insofar as the rules are concerned. The rankings of hands from low to high are not hard to grasp. They ascend as follows:

1. Highest card. The hand with the highest ranking card, usually an ace or king, if there is no hand with a pair.
2. Pair. Two cards of the same rank, along with three unrelated cards.
3. Two pair.
4. Three of a kind. Three cards of the same rank and two other cards.
5. Straight. Any five cards in sequence not of the same suit.
6. Flush. Any five cards of the same suit.
7. Full house. Three of a kind and a pair.
8. Four of a kind. All four cards of the same rank.
9. Straight flush. All five cards in sequence in the same suit.
10. Royal flush. The highest possible straight flush—ace down through the 10 in the same suit. (At all times an ace may be high or low in sequences.)

That's all there is to Poker—in theory. Millions of words have been written on how to play the game. It's frequently not what cards you hold but how you play them that counts. Bluffing is an integral part of the game. So too is "false carding" in Draw Poker, which is taking fewer cards than is necessary to improve one's hand, thus giving an impression of greater strength. So is the study of one's opponents to develop a "tell" on them, certain quirks in their behavior that betray their hands. Even more important is developing and projecting false tells about oneself. And most important of all is knowing when to stay in a game and when to drop—the last option being the most important element in one's game.

These factors very according to the version of Poker being played. In friendly games, "pure Poker" is recognized as consisting of just three standard versions—Five-card Draw, Five-card Stud, and Seven-card Stud—and to the true purist the seven-card version is blasphemy as well.

In Five-card Draw, the granddaddy version of them all, each player is dealt five cards after an ante. Usually certain minimal strength is required for a player to open the game, the standard being a pair of jacks or better. If no one has jacks or (for whatever reason) doesn't open, the hand is discarded and there is a new deal, usually with an additional ante. If a player opens, the other players may either drop out by not meeting his bet, or call, or raise him. To do any of these the nonopeners need not have jacks or better. They may have much better cards or merely high expectations. After all calls are made and raises and re-raises, if any, met, players may discard in order up to three cards from their hand and get replacements. The five cards they now hold represent their final hands, and starting with the opener there is another round of betting called the showdown. The opener need not make an additional bet but may prefer to check. At this time the other players may make bets and raise bets. In friendly games the opener may not check and then later raise, but in big-money games this is permitted and is a standard form of strategy. In friendly games only three raises are permitted, but there need not be any limit on raises. Friendly games might have a minimum and maximum bet, but big games might allow for "table stake," which lets a player bet as much as an opponent has in chips on the table at that point in the game.

In Five-card Stud—some call this the purest form of Poker—players are dealt one downcard and one upcard. There is a round of betting and then one by one three more upcards are given each remaining player with a round of betting after each. In small-stakes games, Five-card Stud has lost favor because the game is relatively open, with four out of five cards showing, so there is much less chance of bluffing or hiding the value of one's hand. But the game is one of skill and, if played correctly, can be an excellent money game.

Seven-card Stud has pretty much replaced the five-card version. It is dealt with two downcards and one upcard and there is a round of betting. Then three more upcards are dealt one at a time, each followed by a betting round, and then a final downcard. From these four upcards and three downcards each player uses his best five-card hand.

Naturally, the seven-card version is a more wide-open game and it can also be played high-low, which means the highest hand takes half the pot while the lowest hand takes the other half. This usually makes for some whiplash betting, with players with middling hands caught in between. Of course it is not always easy to determine whether a player is going for high or low; declarations are made in order from the last man to make a bet to the pot after all betting is completed. Players may also go for both high *and* low, using different combinations of five cards for each hand in hopes of taking the entire pot. If a player goes high and low, he must win both ways or he loses all right to any portion of the pot. Let us say he takes the high but does not have the lowest hand. He loses the high as well and the player with the next highest hand takes that half of the pot.

This, in a nutshell, represents the standard forms of Poker. There are almost endless versions of the game, such as DEUCES WILD, various spit games, and so on. They are described under their own listings elsewhere in this book.

Naturally, no short entry can deal with the nuances involved in even the standard games. But here are a few, which veteran Poker players will agree are important strategies:

1. In Five-card Stud it is never wise to play catch-up when another player has a stronger hand. Obviously, the best hand to stay on with the first two cards is a pair, one card up and the other down. Lacking that, a player should have a card either up or down that at least beats all the cards that are showing. If a player has a queen in the hole and there is a king showing, the queen should drop immediately. If a player holds a small pair, say 7's or less, and there are five or six opponents, it figures that by the time five cards are dealt, probably two opponents will also have at least a pair, and a pair under 7's will be beaten unless it is improved upon. Good players often drop with a pair of 7's showing when another player raises with nothing showing other than several high cards. Usually they have done the right thing, knowing that at least one higher pair will show up in the course of the game.

2. Because no cards are showing, Five-card Draw makes for a better bluffing or concealed game. The rules of staying or dropping are different in Draw, since players see their first five cards at once. Among good players, a player who must bet or pass early frequently doesn't open if he has jacks. If an early player does open, the shrewd players following him will generally not stay unless they have at least kings or aces.

   Another important strategy in Draw is false carding. Under this principle, which involves concealing one's strength or weakness, one should never draw as many cards as possible to improve one's hand. This means almost never drawing two cards. To do so is to develop a "tell" as a novice player. For instance, if one has three of a kind one should keep one additional card, and it doesn't matter what rank it is. Keeping this card admittedly cuts in half the chances of the player getting four of a kind, but mathematically doesn't appreciably reduce the chance of his getting a full house. Taking one card will confuse opponents because it becomes unclear what the player has. He may well have two pairs or he may have nothing but expectations, the chance of drawing either a straight or a flush.

3. One way that professionals identify a player's level of skill is by listening to him as he advises others that they should not try to fill an "inside straight." (This is a sequence of cards that needs an internal card rather than one at either end to complete a straight.) One *should never* try to fill an inside straight, but making this statement implies that trying to draw to an open-end straight is a smart play. Having four cards in sequence is not a hand one should call with. It is a *dropping hand*.

4. Misleading strategies in Seven-card Stud are plentiful, among them being that one may stay on a three-card straight or flush through the first three cards but that the failure to get the fourth card on the very next card makes it a dropping hand. In HIGH-LOW, it is generally better to be

going for low rather than high and one may remain in the game a bit longer without dropping if one has a potential low hand. A high hand must start coming together much sooner or the player should drop. The virtue in going for low is that a high hand may develop in the process, as when three low cards pair up once or twice on the next two cards. The player then has the potential for going both ways. A cardinal rule in Seven-card is never to raise on a four-card hand to build the pot. In other words, don't raise on mere expectations. This strategy can be set aside at times when the game is High-Low because this tactic under the right circumstances not only builds the pot but creates a bluffing situation that overemphasizes the player's strength.

There is a wealth of literature on Poker, some excellent, some good, some fair, and some nonsensical. One of the best recent studies on Draw Poker is *Poker Strategy—Winning with Game Theory* by Nesmith C. Ankeny, a professor of mathematics at M.I.T. Other recommended books include: *Winning Poker Strategy* by Edwin Silberstang, *Scarne's Guide to Modern Poker* by John Scarne, and *Oswald Jacoby on Poker* by Oswald Jacoby. The GAMBLER'S BOOK CLUB lists close to 100 books in its catalog on the subject.

Some books present a great deal of material on the psychology of Poker, on the ability, for instance, to pick up a "tell" that reveals how an opponent behaves when he has a good hand, when he is bluffing, and so on. Few offer advice on an important variant: how a player can foster false tells about himself. Remember, Poker is largely the art of lying, and an excellent way of doing that is to give false clues that indicate when a hand one draws is a disappointment. It's a small thing, but sometimes it can make the difference between an opponent deciding to stay or drop out of a hand. Develop such a behavior pattern and then use a non-Poker face when you really fill out your hand. It will suck your opponents in and then you can hit them squarely between the eyes. The idea is to keep one's opponents off balance.

Because the subject of Poker is so large, and many books devote little space to the many variations of the game, these are treated under individual listings. A listing of some Poker variations and subjects follows this entry. Let the purist beware, however. This is a very broad compilation, including many games that not only are not pure Poker but not necessarily Poker at all. Since, however, many carry the name of Poker and others customarily are permitted in DEALER'S CHOICE, they are also included.

The following entries describe types of poker:

Acey-Deucey
Amarillo

Any Card Wild
Any Suit Wild
Around the World
Baseball
Basketball
Bedsprings
Best Flush
Big Squeeze
Bimbo High-Low
Bing-O Draw Poker
Bingo Poker
Blind Five-card Stud
Blind Stud
Bluff
Bull Poker
Canadian Draw
Canadian Stud
Chicago
Chicago Piano
Color Poker
Color Poker With Bluff
Crisscross
Dealer's Choice
Deuces Wild
Dr. Pepper
Double-barrel Draw
Double Draw Poker
Draw Poker—Five-card buy
Draw Poker High Spades
Draw Your Own
Dutch Stud
Eight-card Stud
Elbow
English Draw Poker
English Stud
Fiery Cross
Five and Ten
Five-card Baseball
Five-card Stud—Five Bets
Flip Stud
Flip Stud with Low Card Wild
Follow Mary
Follow the King
Follow the Queen
Football
Four-card Poker
Four Forty-Four
Four-Four-Four
Gin Poker
Heinz
High-Low Poker—Five-card Stud
High-Spade Split
Hold 'Em
Hurricane
Jersey High-Low
Kankakee Seven-card Stud
Knock Poker
Lefty Louie
Leg Poker
Low Hole Card Wild
Lowball
Mike

Monterey
Monty
Murder
Mutual of Omaha
New Guinea Stud
New York Stud
Nine-card Stud
Nine-handed High-Low Draw Poker
Old English Draw Poker
Omaha
One-Card Poker
Open Hand Draw Poker
Pass the Garbage
Big Stud Poker
Pinochle Poker
Place Poker
Plus or Minus
Poker Solitaire
Poker Squares
Put-and-Take Stud Poker
Razz
Red and Black
Rollover
Seven-card High-Low Progressive Stud
Seven-card Mutual
Seven Card Poker
Shifting Sands
Shotgun
Show Five Cards
Showdown Poker
Six Card Poker (Draw)
Six Card Poker (Stud)
Six-card Stud
Sixth Card Optional
Sixty-Six
Skeets
Slippery Elmer
Spanish Draw Poker
Strip Poker
Take It or Leave It
Ten-Card Stud
Tens High Draw
Third Hand High Poker
Three-card Monte
Three-card Poker
Three Forty-Five
Three Pair High
Three-Three-Three
Twin Beds
Two-card Poker
Vice President
Whiskey Poker
Wild Widow
Woolworth
Zebra
Zombie

POKER ALICE: Female Gambler

No woman's life was more ruled by cards than that of Alice Ivers Duffield (1851?-1930), a peripatetic Englishwoman better known in the American West as Poker Alice. Professional gamblers, gold dust-laden miners, and saddle hustlers all considered it an honor to bend cardboards with Poker Alice. Her manners and idiosyncrasies made her a colorful frontier figure. She smoked long black cigars and spoke with a clipped English accent that she never lost, and while she drank hard, she never drank when she gambled and she never gambled on Sunday. When one played with Poker Alice, it was always by her rules. The Sabbath was reserved for reading the Bible, and anyone trying to lure her into a game of Poker on Sunday risked taking lead in their britches, and on at least one occasion it is known to have been fatal.

Born in England, the daughter of a schoolmaster, Alice Ivers came to the United States at about the age of 12. After a proper young lady's education in a fashionable Southern school, she moved west with her parents and married a mining engineer named Frank Duffield in the Colorado Territory. Alice was 19 at the time, and her husband was killed in a mining accident the following year. After a suitable period of mourning the young widow had to figure out how to support herself. She decided on teaching school, but soon found that she lacked the calling. She took up dealing cards in a saloon on a percentage basis. It proved a lucrative occupation for Alice who soon became the best "producer" in the establishment; she developed a dexterity that permitted her to win with stunning regularity. Poker Alice, as her name and fame grew, soon divested herself of schoolmarm decorum; she toted a gun and smoked big black cigars. She became famous for two sayings: "I'll shoot you in your puss, you cheating bastard!" and "I never gamble on Sunday."

Poker Alice was soon traveling the West, working the railroad gambling circuit, suckering fellow travelers into high-stakes card games. She took on the great card pros in other gaming establishments, and breaking the bank was her greatest pleasure. After cleaning out the house once in Silver City, New Mexico, she took off for New York and a binge of nightlife, shows, shopping, and men until she'd spent all her money—and then headed west again. In the Black Hills gold rush she dealt FARO for Bedrock Tom, working the midnight-to-6 A.M. shift when lonely prospectors were looking for action and feeling reckless.

She later settled in Creede, Colorado, and dealt cards in a saloon belonging to Bob Ford, the man who shot Jesse James. Then it was off to Deadwood, South Dakota, where she demonstrated her shooting ability one night when a drunken miner accused another dealer of cheating and came at him with a Bowie knife. Poker Alice quickly drew and shot the knife out of his hand.

Alice and a professional gambler named Tubbs were married in 1899 and they retired from the gam-

A roaming gambling lady takes a stateroom train passenger at Poker. The scene is often described as a young Poker Alice in action, but has also been identified as an early Madame Moustache as well. (Photo: N.Y. Public Library)

bling life to run a chicken farm. Tubbs died in 1910 and Alice, now close to 60, picked up her cards, cigars, and shootin' iron and headed back to the gaming tables.

She opened her own joint near Fort Meade, South Dakota. It was a gambling establishment not limited to wagering alone; the second floor featured young ladies who offered patrons other diversions. The place thrived, getting a steady clientele from the fort. However, Alice held to her old-fashioned ways. On Sundays drinks were served but there was no gambling, and the ladies upstairs rested. Since Sunday was the big day off for soldiers, it was inevitable that Poker Alice's code would not go unviolated. One Sunday night in 1920 a bunch of drunken soldiers tried to break into the place. Poker Alice fired once through a door and a soldier fell dead.

She was found guilty of the shooting, but the judge took one look at the elderly woman before the bench and announced, "I cannot find it in my heart to send a white-haired lady to the penitentiary." Once outside the courtroom, beyond the judge's surveillance, Poker Alice lit up a victory cigar.

But the Army and reform elements kept the heat on her and Poker Alice's place was finally closed. What with campaigns against gambling and prosti-

tution and later the heavy hand of Prohibition, times grew tough for Poker Alice. She finally retired to a ranch to smoke cigars and reminisce over the good old days when she could rake in pot after pot.

Poker Alice cashed in her chips in 1930.

POKER CHIPS
See CHIPS; POKER STORIES.

POKER DICE: Bar Game
Poker Dice is similar to INDIAN DICE (which is sometimes called Poker Dice incorrectly). Originally Poker Dice was played with five special dice with faces showing ace, king, queen, jack, 10, and 9, but generally regular dice are used with the 2, 3, 4, 5, and 6 having comparable values and the 1 being the ace and outranking them.

How to play: The game has many variations, but the standard one does not recognize straights and has hand values of five of a kind, four of a kind, full house, three of a kind, two pairs, and one pair. In versions in which straights are permitted, the ace may be played at either end, below the 2 or above the 6.

Poker Dice is generally played according to Draw Poker rules and players may only discard a maximum of three dice. Each player may have up to three rolls to build the best possible hand.

Betting is usually for small stakes or for drinks, and Poker Dice is pretty much an even game of luck. Indian Dice, with the 1 as a wild die, is actually a more interesting game. It offers the smart player a better chance of winning since it's a game that requires more strategy.

POKER PARLORS: Legalized Poker Rooms
The first rule of POKER playing is to beware of gambling with people you don't know. It's not a foolproof safety measure—some of your best friends could be cheats—but it is standard advice and procedure. Now square that approach with the reality of gamblers who travel all the way to Nevada and then instead of hitting the gaming tables or even the slots, head for the Poker rooms. Talk about playing with strangers! Of course the same applies to those legal Poker houses in California, Montana, and elsewhere. Gambling authority Tom Ainslie states it simply but accurately when he describes playing Poker in such places as "for pigeons only."

There are sharks who make their living at such games. Some can do it strictly on skill, while others, working alone or with partners, cheat.

The Las Vegas casinos provide Poker tables mainly as an accommodation to well-heeled customers, and make their money by charging an hourly fee or taking a percentage out of each pot. This is not a huge money-maker for the casinos, but it does bring in the high rollers who hopefully will then take their winnings to the CRAPS tables to try their luck. The Nevada casinos furnish the dealer for the Poker games. He handles the cards, cuts them and supervises the games. This eliminates one of the major sources of crookedness, since no player ever touches the deck. In California Poker rooms, where players deal the cards themselves, this represents an open invitation to card manipulators.

But other forms of cheating aren't as easily preventable. There is no guarantee that two or more players are not working together, signaling each other on what they have so that only the better hand stays and bets. Or an accomplice may raise and re-raise so that his secret partner can collect a bigger pot.

Well, you might ask, why don't casinos and Poker parlors police the games so that such cheating doesn't take place? Even if the house could do so, it really has little incentive. The house is not a participant in winning or losing. That is a matter for the players alone. The house is there for its cut. The reality is that the Poker parlor has a vested interest in *not* exposing cheats. If word got around that its tables were loaded with crooks, other players would give them wide berth.

In fairness, it should be noted that some establishments do a better job of policing their games than others. Even in California, where some managements are extremely lax, others will, upon spotting a cheater, send an employee or floor manager up behind him to give him the "brush off." This is done by unobstrusively rubbing a thumb down a cheater's back, a standard warning for a crook to leave. He generally does. Unfortunately, he also leaves with his victims' money because the parlor doesn't want to press a case against him and risk unwanted publicity.

Like to play Poker? Stay home and play it with friends. When you go to a casino, opt for a fairer shake at Craps, BLACKJACK, or some other game.
See "BRUSH OFF"; HOOK GAME.

POKER RUM: Early Form of Knock Poker

Poker Rum is an early version of Knock Poker and thus also one of the fathers of GIN Rummy. Poker Rum is distinguished from KNOCK RUMMY in that knocking is not permitted until the deadwood count is not more than 15 points. This makes the game longer than Knock Rummy by limiting the cutthroat strategy of a quick-kill game.

POKER SOLITAIRE: Gambling Game for Two or More

In Poker Solitaire each player in turn shuffles the deck and deals 25 cards face up for himself, one at a time. The cards are laid out in any order in five rows

of five cards, each forming a POKER hand. The idea is to come up with the five highest possible hands, but cards must be left in whatever position they are committed. Each player takes his turn with the deck and scores are matched and the winner collects the difference in points according to a previously agreed-upon value.

Scoring points differ greatly in England and America, as follows:

Hand	American system	English system
Royal flush	100	30
Straight flush	75	30
Four of a kind	50	16
Full house	25	10
Flush	20	5
Straight	15	12
Three of a kind	10	6
Two pairs	5	3
One pair	2	1

Of the two methods of scoring the English one is superior since it weights the relative ease and difficulties in achieving various hands under the game's rules. The American system, on the other hand, is trapped into the values of hands as they occur in regular Poker. Notice the differences in the point values, for example, for flushes and straights. The English system recognizes that with 25 cards to draw from it is relatively easy to set up flush hands and therefore the point value is sharply reduced.

Esthetics aside, however, the shrewd gambler wants to play the American way because he realizes the errors in its scoring. He will wisely concentrate on royal flushes, straight flushes, and flushes. He does not bother with straights, recognizing that even full houses are easier and more rewarding to pursue.
See also POKER SQUARES.

POKER SQUARES: Variation of Poker Solitaire

Poker Squares is a faster way to play POKER SOLITAIRE under more competitive conditions. All scoring is done exactly as in Poker Solitaire, the only difference being that all players take part in the same game using the same 25 cards simultaneously.

Each contestant gets his own deck and one player actually deals out the hand onto the table, calling out one card at a time while the other players lay out the same card. All the other participants have previously arranged their decks in suit sequence to facilitate their finding each card quickly. When the 25 cards have been dealt, each player then creates the best possible five POKER hands. The high score takes the difference in points from all losers or a pre-set pot, whichever has been agreed upon.

POKER STORIES

No encyclopedia on gambling would be complete without including several great gambling stories. And probably more tales have been told about POKER and its vicissitudes than any other game. Indeed in the 1890's there was a magazine called *Poker Chips*, which was given over to tales, some fictional and some allegedly factual, about the grand game. Like the *National Police Gazette*, dog-eared copies were sure to be found in the local poolroom and barbershop of every neighborhood or village.

Some of the tales offered as fact are morbid, as perhaps befitted accounts of great wagers lost. A typical story related the sad fate of a Mexican boy who tried to come to the aid of a professional gambler in a Phoenix saloon. The gambler had befriended the youth who sought to repay his benefactor when he spotted a tinhorn attempting to cheat by ringing in a hand of four kings.

When the boy spoke up, the cheat fatally stabbed him. The professional gambler shot the crook to death. He was touched by the youth's devotion to him, but truly wished the boy had held his silence. The gambler was holding four aces.

Probably the standby Poker story of all time is the one about the Denver bank that once made a loan of $5,000 with a Poker hand as collateral. The bank cashier arrived one morning to find four men waiting for him outside the bank. They had just come from an all-night Poker game and one of them held a sealed envelope. Inside the bank, the man with the envelope, within full view of his three companions but beyond their hearing, opened it and produced five playing cards. They were four kings and an ace. He explained to the cashier that there was $4,000 in a pot and because he was out of money his three opponents had given him a half hour to raise $5,000 for a final raise. "I can't lose," he whispered to the cashier, "because we ain't playing [straight] flushes. I want to borrow the $5,000 from the bank with this hand as my security."

The cashier, no Poker player, turned him down cold, and the gambler was leaving the bank downcast when he encountered the bank president. Apprised of the facts, the president ordered the cashier to hand him $5,000 and he accompanied the gamblers back to the Poker game. He returned minutes later with the $5,000 loan—and interest of $500.

"If you were a Poker player," he told the cashier sharply, "you'd know good collateral when you see it. Remember now, in the future four kings and an ace, flushes barred, are always good in this institution for our entire assets, sir—our entire assets!"

A story relating to Captain Tom Custer, brother of Gen. George Armstrong Custer, with whom he died in the massacre at Little Big Horn, was more than

likely true since it was repeatedly attested to by many companions. Tom Custer was acknowledged to be the best Poker player in the Seventh Cavalry, an organization renowned nearly as much for its gambling prowess as for its fighting abilities. Custer's reputation might appear remarkable since he usually played a reckless game and was noted for raising wildly on no cards at all or on the slightest of expectations. Yet he often won, and when he did it was usually for big stakes since his opponents always thought he was bluffing.

One time Custer was playing his usual crazy game, doing all the wrong things. He stayed for a two-card draw on the 6, 7, and 10 of spades. Not only that, but he raised enthusiastically.

The game was being played under strict rules that a card accidentally exposed on the original deal had to be taken, but a draw card that was faced could not. Instead, the player had to draw another card.

Custer picked up his first draw card and it was the 8 of spades. However, as he reached for his second card, it hit his hand and flipped over. The king of spades!

Custer started cursing, immediately giving away his hand. The other players all chuckled as Custer took a new card in icy silence.

Then the betting commenced and when it reached Custer he raised wildly. The other players bumped him back. They had to, since they were certain he was bluffing out of pure pique after blowing a winning hand. Custer re-raised and finally got only calls.

When the hands were revealed Custer's grim look turned to a wide smile. He had lost the king of spades and a flush and on the redraw caught the 9 of spades—for a straight flush!

A somewhat similar twist-of-fate story concerned a young man and his sister aboard a steamship headed for New York from Rio de Janeiro. The young man and an older passenger had been engaged in six days of Poker playing, with the cards going steadily against the former.

The last night out of port, the young man, having lost most of his money—all the funds he and his sister had—was desperately trying to recoup. The game was Jacks or Better and for an astonishing number of hands neither could get openers and the pot built enormously. Both players were forced to dig deeply, and the young man finally placed the last of the family funds on the table.

And still no openers. Finally the young man stood up and said, "I've heard that there's luck in a new player. If you've no objection, deal this hand to my sister."

His opponent had no objection and the sister took her brother's seat. She picked up each card one at a time and held them in such a fashion that her brother, standing directly behind her with several others, could see her hand. The first card was an ace, the second an ace, the third a queen, the fourth an ace, and the fifth an ace! The sister had four aces and a queen with the pot well over $1,000 already.

"Open it," the brother whispered.

The sister did, for $10, the limit being played. The man raised her back. She raised again. Clearly, after such a run of poor cards both players had finally gotten good hands. The raises went back and forth until the brother asked the man if he had any objection to removing the betting limit. His opponent was willing and eager.

"Bet it all," the brother told his sister.

The bet was immediately covered, and the pot was now several thousand dollars.

"Cards?" asked the older man, who was the dealer.

Then followed what can only be described as the greatest blunder in Poker history. The flustered woman threw her four aces on the table face up and answered, "Four."

Instantly the dealer flipped over her four cards.

Onlookers gasped in horror. There was nothing to be done. The sister had abandoned the four aces and had no choice but to accept the four new cards.

The brother let out a deathlike gasp and staggered for the door. Some onlookers half expected him to try to throw himself overboard.

Back at the table the stunned sister tearfully tried to explain her idiotic play, saying that in the excitement she had gotten the game confused with Old Maid, in which she would have had to discard her aces!

There was nothing to be done. The game was for table stakes and the brother and sister had invested their last penny. Almost in a trance the sister picked up the four cards that were to go with the queen she'd kept by mistake. Queen . . . queen . . . queen . . . Four queens! The sister had discarded four aces and drawn three queens—to match her lone queen.

Her opponent held a lowly full house!

Like some of the preceding stories, if this particular story is not true, perhaps it should be.

POKER—WORLD SERIES OF POKER

The World Series of Poker is held annually at Binion's Horseshoe on Fremont Street in downtown Las Vegas. Some experts regard Binion's as the best gambling joint in the country. It outdoes itself with the POKER tournament, which several other casinos try to emulate, but the Horseshoe contest remains the great granddaddy of them all.

The climax of the event is a four-day no-limit game of HOLD 'EM Poker, in which contestants put up $10,000 apiece to compete. The winner in recent years has walked out of the game with over a half-million dollars. The runner-up got about half that much and there were several lesser prizes—all sizable by the average man's standards. Media attention to the World Series of Poker has increased over the years. A California public relations firm grinds out daily press releases that make the press association wires, and television now picks up the highlights of the various events. The *Times* of London, among other leading foreign newspapers, carries the results.

Obviously, this is not a game for novices, but some high-rolling amateurs—who can beat the players in their own localities—are among those trying. Actor Gabe Kaplan is a frequent competitor and has made the final six as well as winning the 1979 Poker Classic in Reno. The names of Vegas's true Poker pros generally dominate the finalists' groupings—brilliant players like Jack Straus, Johnny Moss, Doyle Brunson, Amarillo Slim Preston, Stu Ungar, Perry Green, Crandall Addington, Pug Pearson, and others.

Contrary to public belief, true mastery of cards and knowledge of odds are not the decisive factors in these championship games. They are important and necessary, but bluffing is frequently the key. The games are played with no limit for table stakes, and players are eliminated only when they lose every chip they have. In the classic 1982 contest, Jack Straus was down to $500 on the first day and, as one observer noted, "bluffed his way back from the dead and went on to win the title and $520,000."

Numerous magazine articles have been written about this annual Poker showdown, but the most penetrating study of the game and its cast of characters can be found in *The Biggest Game in Town*, by English poet and drama critic A. Alvarez.

POLAND, Gambling in

The biggest lottery operation among the Communist bloc countries is to be found in Poland. The national lottery, *Toto Lotek*, is probably the most successful state enterprise in the country. Football (soccer) pools are second. Fifty percent of the total amount taken in goes in prizes. The balance, minus operating costs, is allotted to a special sports fund.

Some smaller lotteries are also permitted for various organizations, commercial enterprises, and institutions with a state permit. A more innovative lottery system is one based on bank savings accounts. The prizes are determined by the size of the account. The accounts pay no interest, but that accrued money is essentially used for the prizes. It has been suggested that the United States, with its low savings rate, could profit from such a lottery. The banking industry, if it bought the idea, would probably be flooded with deposits to "lottery" accounts.

Poland also offers a numbers game that is very popular. There is also horse racing, under state supervision.

POLIGNAC: Old French Gambling Game

How to play: Polignac, also called Four Jacks and Quatre Valets, is an old French game played with all 52 cards as a party game. For serious gambling it is stripped of all cards of 6 and less, leaving only the cards from ace (high) down to 7, or a total of 32 cards. This works fine for four players. If there are five or six players, the black 7's are also stripped so that there are 30 cards, or equal hands for all contestants.

The object of the game is to avoid taking jacks, each of which costs the holder 1 point except for the jack of spades, the "Polignac," which is a 2-point penalty. The player to the left of the dealer leads the first trick and thereafter the tricks are led by the player who won the previous trick. Tricks are taken by the highest card in the suit led. Players out of suit discard another card, there being no trump in Polignac.

Strategy: While Polignac is a simple game, the matter of skill comes into play when one has to decide the best card to lead after a trick has been won, and indeed whether one should win the next trick at all. Correct discarding is a key factor as well.

One of the options of play is called *capot*, under which a player can, upon examining his opening hand, declare that he will take every trick. If he succeeds, each player must contribute five chips to the pot. And since in the process of taking all the tricks he has also taken all the jacks, there is no penalty scoring in this case. If he should fail to make the *capot*, however, he pays five chips to the pot and any jacks he has taken are scored.

A set number of chips are bought at the outset by each player, and the game continues until one player loses ten chips. The pot is then claimed by the player having lost the least number of chips. This makes for an interesting and cut-throat contest since a player who is not low might try to keep the big loser in the game by playing off his jacks to the low man.

It is recommended that the visitor to France not get roped into Polignac with French gamblers who will have too much skill for the casual Polignac player.

POLISH RUMMY: Variation of Michigan Rummy

Although Polish Rummy follows the basic rules and scoring of MICHIGAN RUMMY, it deviates in the fact that a player may pick up the entire discard pile whenever he wishes without having to meld the deepest card. This rule gives the early leader an edge, which is a criticism lodged against Michigan Rummy

as well by seasoned gamblers. As a rule, gamblers who dislike Michigan Rummy really hate Polish Rummy. For these gamblers the basic game of FIVE-HUNDRED RUMMY and its more simple refinements are greatly preferred.

POLO BETTING

The concept of betting on polo may strike the average person as rather startling, but it has been going on for some time. Polo itself is based on Savlajan, a form of horse racing traced back to 6th-century Persia. It has been common through the centuries for polo players and their followers to wager on the contests, especially in such bastions of the sport as England and India. In the early 20th century the "common herd" started to get into the action at a British polo club that happened to be located near a race course. Spectators and bookies would stop by to watch polo after the racing card was concluded, and soon they were betting on such things as which team would score the next goal, whether the man with the ball would score, or on who would be the higher scorer in the game. This kind of unofficial betting still goes on today. Finally the Polo Association sought permission to set up a totalizator to accept wagering, but the British authorities denied the organization a permit. It seems the British government is determined to keep polo a "class" sport, free from the vulgarities of the betting fraternity.

POPE JOAN: Old Scottish Card Game

Pope Joan is an ancient card game that once enjoyed immense popularity in Scotland. Perhaps because the game made a politico-religious statement it is not included in some Hoyle-type books on card games. This is unfortunate since it represents a traditional elaboration of MATRIMONY as well as being the forerunner of games like MICHIGAN and NEWMARKET.

The 9 of diamonds is called the Pope in this game and since the Pope was the Antichrist as far as the Scottish reformers were concerned, it can be seen how the nickname of "Curse of Scotland" became attached, rightly or wrongly, to the card.

How to play: The game is played with a 51-card deck, the 8 of diamonds having been removed. The game originally was played on a special board, which can now only be found in museums. It consisted of a circular tray with eight compartments for the counters or chips. When Pope Joan is played today, gamblers make do with eight saucers. They are labeled: Game, Ace, King, Queen, Jack, Matrimony, Intrigue, and Pope.

All players start with the same number of betting chips and the dealer places six in the Pope (or 9 of diamonds) plate, two each in the Intrigue and Matrimony plates, and one each in the other plates. This is called "dressing the board" and each dealer in turn must do so. The game must continue until all players have been dealer an equal number of times.

The dealer then proceeds to deal out all the cards to the players, with an extra hand, or widow, being placed in the center of the table. All players must get the same number of cards so that the overage, if any, is added to a "widow" pile. The widow cards are face down and are out of the game. However, the last card is faced up to denote trump suit. If it is the Pope or the ace, king, queen, or jack, the dealer takes the chip or chips from the appropriate plate.

The leader, or player to the left of the dealer, opens to the first trick, using any card he wishes. Let us assume it is the 5 of spades. Let us assume the same player also has the 6 of spades. He places that down over the five. Then whoever has the 7 of spades will put that down, and so on, with play continuing until the end of the run to the king if possible (ace is regarded as low). The four kings, of course, represent stop cards, as is the 7 of diamonds, since the eight is not in the game. In fact, any card may be a stop card because the next card in sequence may be in the widow, or because that card may have been used earlier to start a previous sequence.

When a stop is hit, the player who has put down the last card starts a new sequence. The object of the game is to play out one's cards and when this happens, that player collects the chip or chips in the game saucer and also gets one chip from all players for every card in their hands. The player who holds the Pope is exempt from this payoff unless he has played the card during the hand. During the game any player who lays down the ace, king, queen, or jack in trump suit is entitled to that saucer. If he lays down both the king and queen in trump suit he collects the Matrimony plate. If he lays down the jack and queen of trump, he is entitled to the Intrigue plate.

The deal then passes and a new hand starts. Any plates not collected are left for the next hand and there is a further dressing of the board.

In the later development of related card games, the 8 of diamonds was restored to the deck and the Pope Joan definition removed for the play. It is easy to see how Matrimony developed as a game in this fashion, and of course variations on the use of the widow led to Newmarket and, eventually, Michigan. See SPIN OR SPINADO.

PORTUGAL, Gambling in
Gambling in Portugal—including football (soccer) and other sports pools and a national lottery—is tightly controlled by a special council. On-track totalizator gambling has been permitted on horse racing since 1956, and approval was given for opening gambling casinos in 1958.

The Portuguese casinos, except for the one at Estoril, a half hour from Lisbon, are pretty much on the dowdy side. The least charming aspect of Portuguese ROULETTE is that all even-money bets are lost on zero, making these bets virtually the same as their counterpart in Atlantic City.

The casino at Estoril is perhaps the largest casino in Europe and is one of Libson's social magnets. It has long been a favorite refuge for exiled monarchs and nobility, adding their titled presence to an already glittery clientele. There is a spectacular floor show offered on twin revolving stages that puts Vegas to shame, and a marvelous restaurant for seafood lovers.

The gambling itself, unfortunately, does not match these pyrotechnics; the casino's slots for example, offer the most miserly payoffs in Europe.

POVERTY POKER: Sociable Game Ploy
The success of a POKER session often relies on having enough players to keep the game interesting. Since players in sociable Poker sessions are usually required to buy a specified number of chips, and no more during the course of the evening (to make sure no one loses more than he can afford), many friendly gamblers allow for "Poverty Poker" to be played by any player who runs out of chips.

Often this is done on the basis of giving him another stack of chips, with the understanding that he must return any he still has at the end of the session. If he keeps on losing, obviously he will not have enough to make good and in that case the bank will be short. Should that happen all the other players will have to make good his losses, contributing equally to the deficit. On the surface this appears to be a free ride for the losing player, but it must be borne in mind that the other players have to one degree or another won his lost chips. What they have really paid for is the opportunity to have the game continue.

It happens at times that the player forced into poverty comes back as a big winner, but it really can't be claimed he did it on the other players' money. The others have the same assurance that in case they go broke they can go on playing.

Unfortunately, there are cases when the impoverished player may seem to disrupt the strategy of the game. Since he knows he can't lose he may start playing wildly, staying when he should drop, trying to fill three-card flushes or inside straights, and raising constantly in bluffs that force better hands to drop. Most down-on-their-luck players claim they have the right to do this because it is the way losers traditionally try to make a comeback.

To avoid any ruffled feelings such tactics invite many gamblers to opt for a different version of Poverty Poker. Under this method the player is given no chips at all but is allowed to stay when others players bet. He is not permitted to bet or raise, but he can stay and show his hand. If he has the high hand, he takes the pot and is back in business as an active player. Generally however, no poverty status is allowed a player who "taps out" within a half hour before the agreed-upon breakup time for the game.

John POWELL
See MISSISSIPPI GAMBLERS.

PRAYING
See GAMBLER'S PRAYER.

PRESIDENTIAL POKER PLAYING
The stories about presidential card playing are legion, the most avid players being Harry Truman and Warren Harding. Of Harding's POKER games it was said later that never was there a bigger collection of rogues around one table in the White House. Certainly, though, the classic White House Poker story was about Grover Cleveland. The Southern politician and journalist Henry Watterson has left us this memorable account of the powerful at play in a Poker game involving himself, President Cleveland, Secretary of the Navy Whitney, Sen. Don Cameron of Pennsylvania, and Speaker of the House John Griffin Carlisle:

> It chanced on the deal that I picked up a pat flush, Mr. Cleveland a pat full. The Pennsylvania Senator and I went to the extreme, the President of course willing enough for us to play his hand for him. But the Speaker of the House persistently stayed with us and could not be driven out. When it came to a draw Senator Cameron drew one card. Mr. Cleveland stood pat. But Mr. Carlisle drew four cards. At length, after much banter and betting, it reach a show-down and, *mirabile dictu,* the Speaker held four kings! "Take the money, Carlisle, take the money," exclaimed the President. "If ever I am President again you shall be Secretary of the Treasury. But don't you make that four-card draw too often." He was President again, and Mr. Carlisle was Secretary of the Treasury.

Many gamblers lament the decline of presidential Poker playing in recent years, and Speaker Tip O'Neill's memoirs include an unflattering portrait of one of the last presidents who played the game. The speaker recalled Richard Nixon as a participant in a regular Poker game when he was vice president, but one who had trouble remembering the draw and who complained whenever he lost. Later, during the

Nixon presidential years, O'Neill wrote, it occurred to him that "any guy who hollers over a forty-dollar pot has no business being president."

PROGRESSIVE RUMMY
See CONTRACT RUMMY.

PUERTO RICO, Gambling in
Puerto Rico has more casinos than any other Caribbean locale. By American standards they are not very good despite high-voltage advertising. Besides the inconveniences and dangers of getting involved in recurrent labor disputes, the prevalent feeling among seasoned gamblers is that the casino staffs in general are less than helpful to bettors and that their hands are extended much too blatantly in search of tips.

Some Americans resent the limitations on drinking at the gaming tables (overall this should be viewed as a plus), and a more stringent dress code, such as the requirement of jackets and ties for players in some casinos. "If they are going to go for European standards," one sophisticated gambler observed, "they should start by matching them on odds as well." It is a point well taken. The BLACKJACK rules and the odds at the CRAPS table do not match Vegas casinos overall, and ROULETTE is haunted by the 0 and 00 bugaboo.

True Vegas addicts also won't like the fact that the casinos aren't open 24 hours. If that is considered a plus by some, the rainy season is not. Even the most compulsive bettor can go stir-crazy when trapped in a hotel casino for hours, even days on end.

PUSH
See TAKE IT OR LEAVE IT.

PUT AND TAKE DICE: Often Crooked Dice Game
Put and Take Dice was very popular a few decades ago, but eventually the dice cheats killed the golden goose by turning so many games crooked.

How to play: The game itself is a simple enough gamble. There is a fairly sizable ante to the pot and then each participant takes turns throwing the special dice. One is usually numbered 1, 2, 3, 4, and 6; in place of the 5, there is the word ALL. The other die is marked "P" or "T" alternately on its six sides. If T appears on the roll the player *takes* from the pot the number that comes up on the other die. If ALL appears, he cleans out the pot and there is a new ante and a new game. If the P appears he does the converse, *putting* into the pot whatever the other die calls for. In this case ALL means he must match the pot.

After the game had a good run for some years, the public and the GI's in World War II came to realize that cheaters were cleaning up on the game. All they had to do was slip misspotted (such as four T's and two P's) or loaded dice into the game on their play and then slip them out on the victims' turn. By the end of the war there was virtually no more betting on the game.

PUT-AND-TAKE STUD POKER: Banking Game

It is a mystery why Put-and-Take Stud Poker is so named since it is actually a banking game that has very little to do with POKER.

How to play: The dealer banks the game and at the outset calls for an ante, say one chip, from each player. The banker himself does not ante.

Each player is dealt five upcards, after which the dealer deals himself five upcards, one at a time. As the dealer's first card—the first "put" card—is turned up, players who have one or more cards of the same denomination must ante a chip into the pot. On the second put card the ante increases to two chips. The third, fourth, and fifth put cards call for antes of three, four, and five chips. (In some higher-stakes games the ante increases at a doubling rate—one, two, four, eight, and sixteen chips.)

Once the dealer has turned up the final put card, he discards that hand and one at a time deals himself five "take" cards. On the first take card, players with cards of the same denomination take back one chip from the pot. On subsequent take cards players follow the same take-out proportions as was made on the put-in. If after the fifth take card there is still money in the pot, it goes to the dealer; if the pot is exhausted along the way the dealer must make up the difference.

The dealer enjoys an advantage in this game, based on the original ante of one chip at the beginning of the game. This is not an insignificant edge since few games vary by more than 20 chips or so, plus or minus. This makes a stake for the dealer of five or six chips a big factor. For that reason the bank should be passed regularly.

The name of the game has led to its being used at times as a final betting play after a Poker session. Custom calls for the big winner to bank a round, in theory to allow other players a chance to win back some of their losses. Most big winners magnanimously offer no resistance to the idea. Since the banker enjoys a built-in advantage, what more often happens is that the rich get richer and the poor get poorer.

PUT-AND-TAKE TOP: Crooked Betting Game

Like PUT-AND-TAKE dice, the Put-and-Take Top game is often a hoary old scam, but unlike the dice version this one just doesn't seem to die out.

How to play: The game works on the same principles as the dice version, but uses instead a special eight-sided top. The sides are usually marked P-1, P-3, P-4, P-ALL, T-1, T-3, T-4, T-ALL. There are also High and Low Tops marked in a similar fashion.

When a player spins and gets a P, he must put the number amount in the pot, with the "ALL" requiring him to match the pot. The T's call for taking money or chips from the pot, the T-ALL cleaning out the pot and ending the hand.

The tops are used in friendly bar games and can even be found at carnivals or illegal gambling houses, sometimes in a horse-race version. The carney and gambling joints tend to operate honest games. Why not, since the layouts usually allow a house edge at times approaching 40 percent.

The real danger of cheating occurs in private games since it is easy for a sleight-of-hand expert to work an honest top out of a game and substitute a gaffed one. Crooked tops come in two styles, one with "edge work" and the other with "spindle work." Edge-work tops have rounded edges on some sides and sharp edges on others. As a result the top will usually roll off the round edges and land on the sides with the sharp edges. A more sophisticated version is beveled so that if the top is spun clockwise with one's right hand (as almost everyone does), it will generally land on P. The scam artist spins the top counterclockwise and usually gets a T.

Spindle work tops come with a movable spindle. Pulled out full, the top will tend to come out on T's or in the case of High-Low tops on the high numbers. When the cheat passes the top to the next player he simply pushes the spindle down so that it will stop on a P or low number. Crooked supply houses and some "magic" shops offer such gaffed tops for sale at about 25 times the price of a legit top.

Of course, this is hardly a bar game to be played with strangers, but it frequently is. Therefore the best advice is to look over the edge work and the spindle before the start of a game, and certainly before one makes his own spin. Or one can simply always spin such a top counterclockwise. If you do that and start winning, don't count on your luck continuing. It's a fair bet that the top will soon be worked out of the game.

QUALIFY: Banking Dice Game

Qualify is a five-dice game played both socially and as a gambling house banking game.

How to play: Players may bet any amount they wish in trying to score 25 points or more. The player rolls five dice and sets aside the highest die. On the next roll he sets aside the highest die again, and so on. On no roll may he reserve more than one die.

If the shooter winds up with 24 or less, the bank takes his stake. On higher scores he wins. Offhand, 25 points may seem high for five dice, but in the vast majority of the cases shooters find they have a chance on the final die, having already reached 19 or better. About half the time players stand at 21 or more after four dice and have an even or better than even chance of winning.

Qualify gained considerable popularity as a banking game after the noted authority Ely Culbertson declared the banker enjoyed no advantage. Gamblers eventually backed off the game when they saw, contrary to Culbertson, that they lost far more than they won. The advantage to the house lay mainly among those who didn't reach 19 on four dice or got no higher than 20 by that point. This creates a house edge that approaches 20 percent.

QUATRE VALETS

See POLIGNAC.

QUINZE: Blackjack Predecessor

A predecessor to BLACKJACK, Quinze, or Quince, is a two-handed gambling game with all the same card values as in Blackjack except that the ace only has a point value of 1. The object of the game is for the player and dealer to try to approach 15 without going over.

How to play: The dealer gives the player and himself one card face down and the player can then decide if he wants another card. He may simply stand, which tells the dealer the player has no more than 10. If he draws a card it is dealt face up (in a less common version the additional card or cards are dealt face down). If the player goes over 15 he does not announce it but simply asks for no more cards. The dealer now plays in the same way, having a decided advantage since he can assess the strength of the player's hand. The totals of the player's face cards can even indicate that the player definitely is or may be over 15, in which case the dealer may opt to stand with any hand of 6 or more.

If both the player and the dealer is over 15 or the hand ends in a tie, it is a standoff and the hand is played over, often with an additional ante to the pot.

Quinze was very popular in England in the 19th century. At the fabled Crockford's Club such Quinze devotees as the Duke of Wellington, Talleyrand, Disraeli, and Bulwer-Lytton sometimes wore masks during play to hide their reactions from the scrutinizing eyes of the dealer.

In the long run Blackjack gained popularity over Quinze because of the restriction of Quinze to just two players. Modern casinos have indicated little interest in working out a form of Quinze adaptable to gambling house play, no doubt because the theory of "counting" cards, especially 10-pointers, would be even more rewarding to a player than in Blackjack.

245

R

RACING: Simple Betting Game and Bar Bet

Racing is an even-up card game that is popular in many bars and private clubs that stage racing tournaments.

How to play: A standard deck of cards is used, the four aces are laid out in a row, paired, with a card space between the pairs.

The dealer then deals a card, which he places directly below the open space between the aces. He will continue to lay out additional cards one at a time directly below the previous card so that the design of a "T" is formed. As each card is exposed, the ace of the same suit advances one card down the stem of the "T." The first ace to move eight spaces wins and collects the wagers placed on the other aces.

In "tournament" contests the usual effort in a club is to recruit 32 contestants who bet $5 apiece on the first game. Twenty-four of these will lose and the eight winners will be paid off at 14 to 5, the balance of $1 per winner being the house cut. On the second round the eight survivors bet $10 and only two players will survive. The losers end up as $4 winners overall. The two finalists now bet $20 out of their prize money and the winner ends up with a net profit of $98 and the loser comes out $22 ahead.

Bars like to run these contests, not so much for the house cut, which comes to only $16, but because during the game the players are buying lots of drinks, making Racing a lucrative house game.

RAMS: Old German Card Game

Rams is a game of German origin for three to five players.

How to play: It is played with a 32-card pack with all cards from deuces to 6's stripped out. Originally the cards were ranked high to low from king to 7, but in modern play they run from ace down to 7.

The dealer antes five chips into the pot and gives all players five cards. He also deals an extra hand face down as a "widow," and turns up the next card to determine trump suit. Players in turn have the option of exchanging their hand for the widow, but once this has been done, no more exchanges are possible. The player to the left of the dealer has the first option of play. He can place his hand face down and announce "Pass." Or he may announce "Play" and either use his hand or the widow. The remaining players then in turn decide whether to pass or play.

If all the players pass, the last player before the dealer is required to play or to pay the dealer five chips. If there is only one player willing to play, the dealer must oppose him. At all times the dealer has the option to pick up the faced trump on the table and discard one of the cards in his hand.

The first player staying in the game leads to the first trick. All others must follow in suit if possible or then trump if possible, in either case playing higher than the previous cards, again if possible. If a player can do none of these things he may discard out of suit. The trick goes to the highest card in suit unless trumped, in which case the highest trump takes the trick. Upon taking a trick, the winner takes one-fifth of the pool and then leads toward the next trick. Winners of each succeeding trick take one-fifth of the original pool as well. Should any player who stayed in the game fail to take a trick, he must put five chips into the next pot, as must the next dealer as well.

At the beginning of any hand any player may announce "General Rams," meaning he is announcing that he will win all five tricks. From that moment no one may pass, and those who have already done so must retrieve their cards and play. All players in turn can then decide to exchange for the widow unless it has already been picked up.

All players then play against the General Rams

caller, who naturally leads to the first trick. Should his call stand up, he collects five chips from each player and the pot as well. However, should he fail to win all five tricks, he must pay each opponent five chips and double the size of the pot for the next deal.

RANTER GO ROUND: Large-group Gambling Game

Ranter Go Round, which is also known as Cuckoo in a children's version, is said to be an ancient adult card game of Cornish origins.

How to play: It is played by a large group with the standard 52-card deck, cards are ranked from king high to ace low. No pot is built in advance, but each player must possess three betting units to play. The object of the game is not to be caught with the lowest card in the hand.

Each player is dealt one card down, and then Player A, to the dealer's left, starts by announcing "Stand" or "Change." If Player A stands, it means he is satisfied with the card he is holding. If he calls for a change of cards, he swaps with Player B to his left. Player B must surrender his card unless he has a king. If he does, he shows it and the exchange is cancelled. Additionally, any player passing an ace, deuce or 3, must announce it.

Play now shifts to Player B who has the right to call for change of cards with Player C (obviously he will stand on a king). Play continues in this fashion until it reaches the dealer. If the dealer wishes to exchange his card, he does so by cutting the deck and taking the top card of the cut. If the dealer does so and draws a king, he declares it and becomes the loser of the hand.

If the dealer stands or draws any card but a king, all the competitors reveal their cards and the low man is the loser and puts a betting unit in the pot. If more than one player has the same low card, each must pay the pot.

A new hand is dealt and play continues. When a player loses all three of his betting units, he retires from the game, which continues until only one player has any money left. He is the winner and takes the whole pot.

RAZZ: Casino-style Lowball Stud Poker

Razz is essentially LOWBALL Poker played in the Seven-card Stud variation. It is widely played west of the Mississippi in illegal card rooms and is popular in the Nevada casinos.

How to play: It is played exactly like Seven-card Stud, but strictly for low. Straights and flushes have no meaning, so the lowest possible hand is 5-4-3-deuce-ace. (Ace is always low.)

Razz makes a fine private game and is much pre-ferred by astute POKER players because it is easier to figure than the high or high-low version. Since players are concerned only with low, there are fewer secrets that a player's hole cards can conceal. In a high game, flushes, straights, and full houses can be very effectively concealed by the three hole cards.

Strategy: Experts tend to drop out if they don't have three low cards at the start of a hand. Few players will see a raise if the highest card of their three is more than an 8. If they are extremely tight players they won't even stay with anything higher than 7 at this stage. The only problem with such cautious play is that it compels them to drop out of nine hands out of ten. And when they do stay, it is a dead giveaway of their power. For that reason good players stay at times with a higher card, if they also have two very low ones. In fact, if a player is 9 high on the first three cards, and all others players show a higher upcard, he is sitting pretty and should bet hard to make them pay for the privilege of trying to improve their hands.

The casino version of Razz contains one oddity of play. On the opening round, the player with the highest card must open the betting even though strategy calls for him to drop. The purpose of this is to build the pot. More often than not, a low card will raise. At this point the prudent high card should immediately drop. Razz is not the sort of game in which a player should chase his forced opening bet.

Razz, like HOLD 'EM, is a rugged game for average players at the Vegas Poker tables. Some of America's sharpest players gather there looking for amateurs who chase the seventh-card rainbow.

READING GAME: Famous Illicit Crap Game

In the late 1950's and early 1960's the biggest illegal CRAP game on the East Coast (and most probably in the nation) was the so-called Reading Game, which was operated in that Pennsylvania city by the Phila-delphia mob. Every night high rollers from all over the East would gather at a restaurant in the heart of Philadelphia to be taken to the action some 50 miles away. "Luggers" in limousines would pick up the gamblers and deliver them to the million-dollar dice game played on three high-rolling "California ta-bles."

A hoodlum who boasted about it after the FBI busted the game said, "Everybody made a buck on that game. They rented their limousines from a fu-neral director, because they only used them from ten at night until seven in the morning." An insight into the free hand organized crime then enjoyed in Phil-adelphia was revealed when he added: "They even had a cop out in front of the restaurant—he'd blow a whistle like a hotel doorman to signal a limo when he had a full load coming in for the game. It looked like opening night on Broadway. The cops never touched them."

RED AND BLACK: Alleged Poker Game

Although many books on POKER call Red and Black a version of Draw Poker, it is not unusual for seasoned players to storm from the table when it is called in DEALER'S CHOICE. While many object to the fact that the game is not "pure POKER," most simply don't want to play a game they regard as basically devoid of skill with little need to estimate probabilities and potentials for improving one's hand.

How to play: Although the game is dealt like Draw Poker, the winner is not determined by Poker hands but by counting the point value in one's hand. An ace is worth one point, all pictures are ten, and all other cards have their pip value. All red cards have a plus count and all black cards are minuses. The hand with the highest plus points wins the pot. However, the game is more often played high-low, with the pot being divided between the highest plus and lowest minus hands. At times there is no minus hand, in which case the lowest plus hand gets half the pot.

Strategy: Strategy is not at a premium in this game, and the best laid plans often go awry. A player holding two black picture cards may discard three cards and then draw three red cards, ending up with a low plus score. On the theory that four red or black cards have a good chance of taking the game, some players will hold one black and one red card of as close to the same value as possible and draw three cards, hoping they are all the same color. It is a good mindless strategy in a rather mindless game.

RED DOG: Gambling Game of Skill

Red Dog, known in some circles as High-card Pool, has been the newspaperman's gambling game over the years, rather than POKER. Tales of legendary Red Dog games abound, and it has been said that a break in many an important news story was missed because pool reporters were immersed in a game with a very big pot. Police reporters are notorious for sending only one legman to cover a beat while a Red Dog game goes on. Of course he shares what he learns with the others, who all got to the telephone at the same time with the same information. Then it's back to the cards, and the news of the day is forgotten.

How to play: Basic Red Dog can be played with up to eight players who are dealt five cards each as in Draw Poker (four if there are nine or ten participants). Cards are ranked in descending order from the ace to the deuce. There is a fairly healthy ante to the pot, and after studying their hands players in turn bet from one betting unit to the entire value of the pot that they hold a higher card in the same suit than the top card of the pack. The dealer turns up the next card and the player whose turn it is wins or loses accordingly.

If the player wins, he shows only the winning card and takes his winnings from the pot. If he loses he throws in his cards after showing them to the other players and his bet is added to the pot. After all players, including the dealer, have had their chance, the deal passes to the next player and there is a new deal. Play continues in this fashion until someone wins the pot, whereupon there is a new ante and a new deal.

Strategy: As noted above, Red Dog is a game of skill, and the late players (and especially the dealer) have a monumental edge if they have the ability to exploit it. In part, of course, this is based on card memory, since the later players see all the earlier exposed cards, which helps them to evaluate their own hands and adapt their wagers to the changing situation. For instance, let us say a dealer is holding five picture cards. If some of the aces are exposed before his turn he can judge if his hand is strong enough to try to take the entire pot. Sometimes a later player or a dealer can bet the entire pot because he's figured out his hand is absolutely unbeatable.

Players sometimes know the number of cards that can still beat them, and as these dwindle the more their bet escalates. A more mechanical way to approach it is to assign a value of 14 to aces; 13 to kings; 12, queens; 11, jacks; and all other cards as per point value. If a hand adds up to 32 the player has a 50-50 chance of winning. A player holding four aces—a highly unlikely event—would be at 56 on just four cards, an unbeatable hand. Certainly a score of 50 or so would be very strong, and grow more powerful as some higher cards are exposed.

Red Dog is a simple game since the only decision a player makes is how much to bet. But it can become a staggeringly high-stakes affair after several players unsuccessfully bet the pot and fail, a not infrequent occurrence. The successful Red Dogger, however, does not have to concern himself so much with betting the pot as with simply playing strategically. He recognizes that when he leads off he is at a distinct disadvantage and tends to bet close to the minimum allowed unless he holds a very impressive hand. As he becomes a later player and especially the dealer, he figures to be betting more strongly because he is now in a more advantageous position.

In another version of Red Dog players may bet either that they can or cannot beat the deck card. This of course places an even greater premium on being able to remember cards as well as figuring percentages.

Cheating is a very real danger in Red Dog because the revelation of just one card can determine if a player wins or loses. For years Red Dog card mobs have plied their trade on steamships or planes and in the armed services. A very effective method is for three cheats to work a scam together. When any of them deals, the other two are positioned on opposite sides of the table. The dealer does not have to peek at the top card, but simply flashes a glimpse to the confederate who is the later player. Gamblers always watch the deck and the dealer, but such a subtle move is seldom spotted and arouses no suspicion because the gambler who is betting is clearly not in the line of vision. The cheat making the spot uses a coded signal to tell his partner what the card is. If his confederate cannot beat the card, he bets small. If he knows he can beat it, he bets the pot.

See also RED DOG—G.I.

RED DOG—G.I.: Variation of the Basic Game

G.I. Red Dog, a variation of RED DOG, became popular during World War II and still enjoys action. Unlike the basic game, the dealer banks through three deals—unless the pot is wiped out—and then the deal passes to the left.

In G.I. the players do not ante. Instead, the dealer, supposedly to compensate for his advantage, puts into the pot whatever stake he wishes. Then play begins. Each player is dealt three cards, which makes it most likely that most players will lose their bets and add their money to the dealer's in the pot. By the time play gets to the dealer, he has seen a considerable number of upturned cards and can figure his hand with considerably more accuracy than his opponents. (Adding to the dealer's advantage is that under some forms of G.I. Red Dog, he gets four cards instead of the three for his opponents.) The fact that the dealer has three rounds means he is

almost certain to be able to work up a good hand by the third hand. If he is fortunate enough to make a killing on the first hand, he wisely does not sweep the pot. He leaves a small amount, hoping his opponents will build it up again before it comes around to him again.

Despite the efforts to cut down the dealer's edge, the game usually enhances it, with the result that many a G.I. and his pay are soon parted.

RENO, NEVADA
See LAS VEGAS.

RHODE ISLAND—Legalized Lotteries

At latest count Rhode Island offers two instant "rub-off" games, a numbers game, and a grand Lotto game. Payoffs in the latter two games is about average compared with other states, but its instant games generally produce one winner in every 8.8 tickets. By comparison nearby Vermont and Connecticut pay out on one out of every seven tickets.

RICHMOND, VIRGINIA
See FAROBANKOPOLIS.

George "Tex" RICKARD: Honest Gambler and Boxing Promoter

George "Tex" Rickard (1871-1929) was the epitome of the honest gambling man, one who won and lost fortunes with equal abandon, and who never engaged in a single instance of cheating—rare among gamblers. He was later the leading fight promoter of the early 20th century in another field not particularly known for morality or high ethics.

Rickard cut his teeth as a gambler in the Gold-Rush Klondike in the 1890's. Rickard learned there that while money was an obvious means to an end it hardly stacked high against life itself, especially against the gun of a cheated man or the noose of angry vigilantes.

As a result, and unlike such unsavory gambling hustlers like Soapy Smith, Rickard was soon widely respected throughout the Klondike. When Nome had its fabulous gold strike, the town rocketed upward in size and men were being ambushed, robbed, and killed every day. The citizenry decided there was a need for law and order and Rickard was elected mayor. As gambling historian Henry Chavetz states in *Play the Devil*, he was "the only man everybody—honest men and crooks alike—could trust."

Rickard was born in Kansas City, Missouri, in 1871 and grew up in the saddle. From the age of 10 when his father died, he was the main support of the family. By the age of 23 he was the town marshal of Henrietta, Texas. By then gambling occupied all his nonworking hours and when he heard of fortunes

Casino Red Dog is basically a more simple play than the private game. The rules here are offered by the Frontier in Las Vegas. Few experts consider casino Red Dog attractive for the bettor.

RED DOG RULES

Red Dog dates back to the gambling halls of the early west. It's easy to play. And the action is fast and exciting.

First, place your bet. The dealer turns over two cards, face up. Aces are high, deuces are low. If the next card falls between the original two numbers, you win.

IF THE FIRST TWO CARDS ARE NOT CONSECUTIVE (Example: 5 of diamonds, 9 of clubs). Once the cards are dealt and the dealer announces the spread and the payout odds, you may raise your bet by any amount up to your original bet. The dealer then draws a third card. If its value falls between the value of the first two cards, you win.

IF THE FIRST TWO CARDS ARE CONSECUTIVE (Example: 4 of spades, 5 of hearts). There is no spread and the hand is considered a tie. You neither win nor lose.

IF THE FIRST TWO CARDS ARE A PAIR (Example: 2 of diamonds, 2 of hearts). You may not raise your bet. If the third card drawn makes three-of-a-kind, you automatically receive eleven times the amount of your original bet. If the third card drawn does not make three-of-a-kind, the hand is a tie and you neither win nor lose.

	RED DOG PAYOUTS											NO RAISES			
SPREAD	1	2	3	4	5	6	7	8	9	10	11	CONS	PAIR	3 of KIND	
PAYS	5:1	4:1	2:1	EVEN	EVEN	EVEN	EVEN	EVEN	EVEN	EVEN	EVEN	TIE	TIE	11:1	MAXIMUM PAYOFF ON ANY ONE WAGER: $11,000

being made by miners on the Yukon, he headed for Alaska. He had little trouble collecting enough in gambling winnings to open one gambling saloon after another. His place, the Monte Carlo in Dawson, offered no-limit FARO. In one 12-hour session, Tex was cleaned out of funds by four gamblers (when the house lost at Faro it had to have been a truly honest game). Without blinking any eye he offered to bet the joint on one play against $50,000. His opponents agreed, and Rickard lost.

"The place is yours, gentlemen," he announced and left.

Rickard, in true gambler style, went up and down financially several times, but wherever he was and whenever he opened a joint, the miners and other gamblers flocked to his place. Miners knew they always got a fair shake from Rickard and thought nothing of leaving their gold dust—uncounted—in Tex's care. Many was the time bleary-eyed miners would end up in Rickard's joint totally broke, reduced to mooching drinks after a little-remembered night of gambling and carousing. Frequently they had forgotten the dust they'd left with Rickard or thought in their alcoholic haze that they had reclaimed all of it—rather than just a portion of it—and then lost it at the gaming tables. Rickard would sober them up and give them their gold.

After a series of winnings and losings, Rickard built up a poke of a half-million dollars and went into a new gambling endeavour, buying up gold claims. By then the yellow was thinning out, however, and Tex lost his money.

He returned to the States, in time cutting out a new career staging boxing matches, including the first million-dollar gate in history. He built a new Madison Square Garden on the site of the old one in New York City, and with typical high-roller nerve promoted the Dempsey-Carpentier match in Jersey City before there was an arena there, using the money from early ticket sales to erect a stadium that would seat 90,000.

When Rickard died in 1929, he was saluted in two fields, gambling and prizefighting, areas in which a man's word is seldom his bond.

RICKEY DE LAET
See MONTEREY.

RIFFLE TEST: Detection Test for Marked Cards
There is a method of detecting most forms of marked cards most of the time. If that seems like a qualified statement it is meant to be, mainly because some writers on gambling erroneously claim the "riffle test" is foolproof and will catch all sorts of marked cards. This is definitely not true.

The riffle test is a simple method, one harkening

The "riffle test" will catch most forms of marked cards. Simply riffle the deck in the way those children's animated cartoon books are maneuvered to produce a moving image. When the cards are riffled, the "picture" should not "dance." (Photo: E. Gerard)

back to childhood days and those animated cartoon books in which the images move as the pages are riffled. Just do the same with a suspected deck of cards and watch the backs. Repeat the test several times, inspecting all parts of the backs carefully. If you get a moving picture effect, you know the backs have been altered.

Unfortunately, some gamblers who do the test and find nothing think there is nothing more to worry about. They are leaving themselves wide open for marked cards the riffle can't catch. One is a white-on-white method using the same white-out fluids typists use to cover their errors. When small white dots are put on the white-bordered backs of cards, they will not show up in a riffle test. Another way of achieving the white-on-white markings is with a nail whitening pencil women use on the underside of their nails. Some cheats like this method because all they have to do is doctor some of the cards just before a game or during a short break. White-on-white hustlers read these marked cards by looking for a special glare as light hits the backs of the cards. Only a player schooled in the white-on-white technique can hope to spot it.

Still, caution demands that the riffle test always be applied as a matter of course since marked cards are used more by amateur crooks than professional ones. The latter will only try it for big scores. The amateur might try it in a regular friendly game and, being an amateur, he will use the simple forms of markings that the riffle test can easily catch.

ROCKAWAY: Adult Card Gambling Game
Rockaway is a gambling game for adults, which some say developed from the juvenile game of Go Boom.

The latter is played with simpler rules and uses one deck of cards, while Rockaway utilizes two.

How to play: Each player is dealt seven cards face down and the next card is faced up in the center of the table. The remaining pack becomes a stock that players draw on as required. The player to the left of the dealer must cover the widow card with a card of the same suit or rank, or with an ace. If he cannot or does not choose to do any of these, he must draw a card or cards from the stock until he can do so. When a player covers the widow, his card becomes the widow for the next player. Should the stock become exhausted, players continue to play cards from their hand and any who cannot play simply lose their turn.

The game ends when a player discards his entire hand. Scoring is done on the basis of the cards remaining in the hands of the rest of the players. They are charged 15 for each ace, 10 for all picture cards, and the pip value for numbered cards. Of course payoffs can be made at this point to the winner, but many gamblers prefer a more level method of payoff. The losses of each player go into a pot and this continues for all additional hands. The game is completed only when all players have dealt a previously agreed upon number of times. Then the pot is divided equally among all players. Obviously, the big losers are able to recoup a portion of their contributions to the pot but, more important, a player who has done extremely well and yet lost every hand by a small margin will still come out ahead.

Strategy: Poor Rockaway players fail to grasp the strategy differences in a game in which cards are assigned point values. They view an ace, an exceptionally useful card, as merely a danger and they opt to get rid of aces too early for fear of being caught with 15 points. Certainly they need hardly rush since no one can go out for seven rounds of play at the minimum. As a rule, playing any card rather than an ace is preferable until it is time to panic when another player is down to one or two cards. Usually, a player who succeeds in hoarding a few aces can control the end of the game or, at worst, be stuck with no more than one ace, 15 points, which in a divided pot setup will still provide him with a profit in a six- or seven-man game.

ROLLING STONE
See ENFLE.

ROLLOVER: Five-card Showdown Variation

The uninitiated tend to regard Rollover, in either the five-card or seven-card version, to be strictly a game of luck, but the peculiar way the cards are played and bet makes this a very interesting game of skill, involving considerable knowledge of probabilities.

The game, also called No Peekie, No Lookie or Beat Your Neighbor, is particularly appealing in the five-card version for the expert.

How to play: Each player is dealt five face-down cards and is not permitted to look at them. The first player turns up a card. Since he has the only card showing, he is high and may bet if he wishes. More often than not, he passes and the next player now turns up a card. If it is lower than the previous player's card, he turns over one or more cards until he has a higher card or pair—in other words, a partial or whole POKER hand that is tentatively higher than the first player. There is another round of betting, and the third player then turns over one card at a time until he is high (if he turns over all five cards and does not become high man, he folds). The sequences continue until only one player remains, and he is the winner.

Let us examine a typical five-player game after each has turned up some cards. Player A, the leader, turns up a 3; Player B has a 2 and a 6; Player C, a king; Player D plays four cards and holds a pair of 7's, a 9, and a jack; Player E also runs through four cards and holds a pair of 8's, a 10, and a queen. At this point, play reverts to Player A. By then Player B has folded rather than cover the bet of Player E on his pair of 8's.

Player A is forced to turn up all his cards and cannot beat the 8's. Player C turns up a second king and has a pair of kings on two cards. He bets very heavily, trying to drive out Player D (a pair of 7's on four cards) and Player E (a pair of 8's on four cards). Player D covers the bet, but Player E folds. This is an example of Player E playing intelligently and Player D rather foolishly. Player D figures he has a pair and that if he draws another 7 (none are showing) or pairs up either his 9 or jack, he can win. He is overlooking the fact that he has only one card in which to accomplish this, and he not only must beat the kings but also the pair of 8's (Player E has not yet dropped) behind him, which have as much chance to improve as his 7's.

Player D turns over a king and loses. Player C takes the pot. Player E, who had not tried to beat the pair of kings, did the proper thing, whether or not we look at his last card. Of course he might have drawn a third 8 or improved on his two other cards, but he reasoned correctly that he had only one chance of doing so. And even if he had improved to two pair, the pair of kings had three cards to go and had three times as much chance of improving as did Player E. Obviously, Player E is the smarter Rollover player and over the course of time will probably come out ahead—and certainly win a lot of money from Player D.

Seven-card Rollover may not always be as easy to

figure out for the smart player but he may be willing to accept that drawback, knowing that poorer players will stay longer on even poorer hands.

Arnold ROTHSTEIN: Gambler and Fixer

In the 1920's Arnold Rothstein (1882–1928) was the most widely known gambler in America. His involvement, real or fanciful, in fixing the 1919 World Series—the Black Sox Scandal—had won him great notoriety. Typically, he may not have been directly implicated, but may have simply been asked to advance the money needed to bribe the players and place the bets. In what was vintage Rothstein, the gambler may have refused to get involved and then secretly laid in his own bets and made a profit of $270,000.

Rothstein in reality was much more than a gambler and a fixer; he was probably one of the spiritual fathers of organized crime in America, tutoring such future racket bosses as Meyer Lansky and Lucky Luciano. But gambling was his true love and his obsession up to the very day he was murdered.

Rothstein ran New York gambling establishments from plush parlors on Broadway to shabby little Stuss operations on the Lower East Side. He ran high-stakes floating CRAP games all along the Great White Way. He owned the Park View Athletic Club on West 48th Street, a body-building establishment. There were also private rooms where a patron could flex his muscles tossing dice and shuffling cards.

Rothstein's own betting coups were legendary. He won a half-million dollars on the first Dempsey-Tunney championship fight, and collected $800,000 on a horse named Sidereal at huge odds at the old Aqueduct racetrack on July 4, 1921. On that day Rothstein led the bookmakers astray by having some of his agents place sizable bets on the favorite while others bet steadily and heavily on Sidereal. At the last moment, the bookmakers realized they were in too heavily on Sidereal, but when they tried to lay off part of the action on other bookies, they found they too were loaded.

In his personal gambling Rothstein was said to be scrupulously honest, insisting that crooked gamblers were fools. In any event no one ever caught him cheating at dice or cards. Rothstein even made it into fictional lore, and at least two literary characters are based on him: Meyer Wolfsheim in *The Great Gatsby* and later Nathan Detroit in the musical *Guys and Dolls*.

Eventually, Rothstein, "the Brain" as he was called, self-destructed. Gambling obsessed him and he bet compulsively. He made huge bets, won some and lost more. In 1928, Rothstein played in one of Broadway's most fabulous POKER games, one that ran nonstop from September 8 to 10. At the end, Rothstein was down $320,000. That Rothstein could lose shocked the Broadway wise guys, but not nearly as much as the fact that he welshed on the debt. He declared the game had been fixed by two of his opponents, California gamblers "Nigger" Nate Raymond and Titanic Thompson.

On November 4, Rothstein sat at his customary table in Lindy's restaurant making election bets. He wagered almost $600,000 that Herbert Hoover would beat Al Smith and that Franklin D. Roosevelt would be elected governor of New York. In a few days he would have collected more than enough to pay his Poker losses. In any event, later that night Rothstein was shot to death at the Park Central Hotel—in the middle of a Poker game. The prime suspects were Thompson and Raymond, but they had convenient alibis and were never prosecuted.

The Rothstein murder was a standoff—never solved.

ROULETTE: The "Class" Casino Game

Roulette is the most glamorous of all casino games. But it is *not* made in America. Europe is the only place to play Roulette. One can while away the hours there happily, even though you may not win or lose much (if you're lucky). Roulette is, or should be, played with the pace and relaxation that is properly the mark of a laid-back yet exciting casino gambling game.

Most casino games are mindless affairs. In CRAPS you bet on the way some mindless cubes will fall; in BACCARAT, on how mindless cards may fall; and in Roulette on how a mindless little ball may or may not nestle in a slot. There's no brainpower at work here, but that hardly detracts from the beauty of the game. It has pace, excitement, and atmosphere. There's something very special about attending the afternoon races just outside Baden Baden and sipping champagne on the lawn during the runnings, and then going on to the casino where on warm summer nights there is even Roulette under the stars.

The lore of Roulette exceeds that of any other casino game. Part of the joy is watching your fellow gamblers—the bulky German clutching handfuls of 10,000-mark chips, worth $5,000 or $6,000 apiece, depending on exchange rates—while covering a layout and rushing off to do the same at another table simultaneously . . . to a young French couple who have obviously spent far beyond their means and are fast approaching panic. They and others behave on cue as though they are on loan from a Somerset Maugham story. You can philosophize with your croupier in any of several languages—German, French, Italian, English—although some will strike you (in any language) as uncertain that there is a world beyond the casino's halls. It is a world of generally civilized make-believe. The hapless industrialist

Many hold Roulette is the greatest and grandest casino gambling game of all—especially as played with glamorous touches in European casinos, if not in more sterile play in the U.S. (Photo: Las Vegas News Bureau)

holding his head as he is losing thousands, while next to him a vivacious American woman giggles happily about winning a 5-mark bet. Life is unfair, the industrialist is probably thinking, but then he gets an inspiration. He duplicates the young woman's bet on the next spin and wins. The world is right again, the social order will survive.

Now back to America, and an Atlantic City or Vegas Roulette wheel. It is impossible to play Roulette in America because the game has a 0 and 00 while the European or French version, as it is commonly called, has only one zero. If that were the sum total of the highway robbery involved it would almost be tolerable. But the difference between American and French Roulette can balloon to *four times* the European take. That's why the game has never caught on in American casinos as it has in France.

The average American or Caribbean Roulette table requires only one croupier, while in Europe several are needed to handle all the business. Let us look at the American layout. The wheel has numbered cups along the perimeter from 1 through 36, half of them

red and half black. There is also a zero and directly across from it a double zero, both in green.

Spin the wheel and let the betting begin: We bet on a single number, any of those from 1-36 or, if we wish, the 0 or 00. If we win we get paid at 35 to 1. But there are 38 possibilities and that means the house advantage is 5.26. (In Europe the payoff rate is the same, but since there are only 37 possibilities, the house edge is almost half—2.70.)

For the next several bets these house edges remain the same. When a player bets on two numbers at the same time by, for instance, placing his chips on the line between the 1 and 2, he is paid off at 17 to 1. In betting on three numbers such as 1, 2, and 3, the chip goes on the outside line of the line of the 1 or 3. If a player bets on four numbers such as 1,2,4,5 (the chips going on the intersection of the four numbers), he is paid at 8 to 1. If he bets on six numbers, such as 1 through 6 (the chip goes on the outside line between the 1 and 4 or the 3 and 6), the payoff is 5 to 1.

It is also possible to bet on groups of 12 numbers— 1-12, 13-24, or 25-36—by placing the chip or chips in the appropriate boxes on the layout. These bets pay off at 2 to 1. The same applies to betting on the vertical rows of 12 numbers.

In all these cases the American house edge is an enormous 5.26 while the European edge is about half.

There are a number of even-money bets that are possible in Roulette. One may bet on the red or black (Rouge or Noir in Europe), Low (1-18) or High (19-36) (Manque and Passe in Europe) or Even or Odd (Pair or Impair in Europe). On any of these bets a player gets back winnings equal to his bet.

However, in virtually all Nevada casinos when 0 or 00 comes up (as they will on average twice in every 38 spins), the player's bet is lost. In Atlantic City, in what may be considered an act of magnanimity, the casino only takes half the bet. In Nevada the house edge is 5.26 on even-money bets and in Atlantic City 2.63. In Europe, where there is only one 0, an *en-prison* rule is in effect on even-money bets when 0 appears. The bets are not lost but moved back to another line and "held prisoner" for the next spin of the wheel. Let us say a player has bet on the red and his bet is imprisoned. On the next spin 19 red comes out. His bet is released. He does not win anything, but his bet is returned to him. If black had appeared, his bet would have been lost. This means that on average in half the cases the rule works to the advantage of half the bettors and to the disadvantage of the other half. In effect, therefore, the 2.70 house edge applying to all other bets is effectively reduced to 1.35 percent on even-money wagers. Thus even-money bets on the French wheel end up costing about one-quarter of what they do in Vegas.

Just for a little added zinger, the American casinos have a special sucker bet that gives them an edge of 7.89 percent. Many Roulette players like to play the zero on the French wheel, either as their bet or as insurance for their even-money wagers. They frequently make it a four-number bet of 0-1-2-3. At 8 to 1, the house edge is 2.70. But the American wheel has 0 and 00, and to bet both zeros together with the first three numbers makes it a five-number bet at 6 to 1. This is the only five-number bet that can be made, but notice that if one could make seven such bets that would use up 35 numbers and leave three over out of a total of 38. This is the house edge, and it is 50 percent more than any other bet where the house edge is 5.26, or a total of 7.89 percent—the most outrageous bet to be found in Roulette anywhere.

Why don't the American casinos switch to the single zero wheel? The casinos claim that whenever they have tried to do so it has not attracted new business, but such a response may be taken with a grain of salt. What gives the casinos an acute case of anxiety is that if they go to the single zero, sooner or later they would have to go to the imprison rule or the half-refund on even-money bets, which would cut the house edge down to 1.35, lower even than the basic house advantage of 1.41 for Craps.

The casinos claim the public prefers Craps because it is a faster game, and there may be some truth to that. But it must be realized that Craps is loaded with all sorts of sucker bets as well; the casinos thrive on patrons who don't understand this and play the various options at Craps where the house edge jumps to 2.4 percent, or 2.7, or 3.2, or 4.0, and on up the scale to as high as 16.7!

That is the real reason American casinos gut Roulette—if just doesn't allow for a big enough gouge.

Of course Roulette is, like all casino games, a losing proposition but when the house edge is low you stand a much better chance of winning and thus it becomes more of a fun game.

American casinos also run the game under very arbitrary rules. Chips used in other games must be converted into special chips that are only usable at one specific Roulette table. This means you cannot hop around the casino from one table to another where you may get better "vibes." Additionally, once you sit down at a Roulette table you *must* play every game. It's like having Simon Legree as the croupier.

The knock on European casinos is that they are too stuffy and cater only to a certain class of people. That is nonsense. Like their American counterparts they'll take anyone's money almost anytime. On

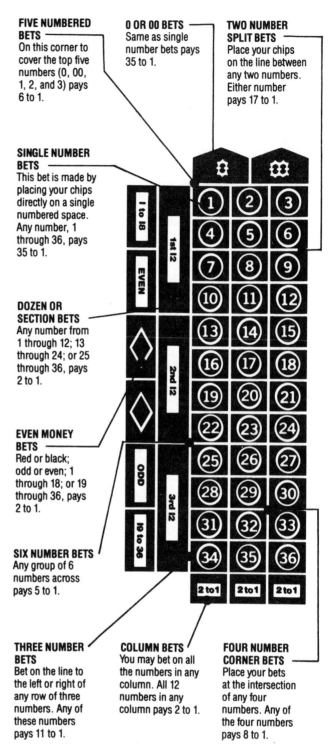

FIVE NUMBERED BETS
On this corner to cover the top five numbers (0, 00, 1, 2, and 3) pays 6 to 1.

0 OR 00 BETS
Same as single number bets pays 35 to 1.

TWO NUMBER SPLIT BETS
Place your chips on the line between any two numbers. Either number pays 17 to 1.

SINGLE NUMBER BETS
This bet is made by placing your chips directly on a single numbered space. Any number, 1 through 36, pays 35 to 1.

DOZEN OR SECTION BETS
Any number from 1 through 12; 13 through 24; or 25 through 36, pays 2 to 1.

EVEN MONEY BETS
Red or black; odd or even; 1 through 18; or 19 through 36, pays 2 to 1.

SIX NUMBER BETS
Any group of 6 numbers across pays 5 to 1.

THREE NUMBER BETS
Bet on the line to the left or right of any row of three numbers. Any of these numbers pays 11 to 1.

COLUMN BETS
You may bet on all the numbers in any column. All 12 numbers in any column pays 2 to 1.

FOUR NUMBER CORNER BETS
Place your bets at the intersection of any four numbers. Any of the four numbers pays 8 to 1.

The layout and betting procedures of American Roulette.

occasion they do go in for some old-world glitz, such as the fabulous Casino de Deauville on the Normandy coast where during the peak month of August formal wear is required and gambling is conducted with genuine gold chips. But this is not done very often.

CASINO' MUNICIPALE
CAMPIONE D'ITALIA

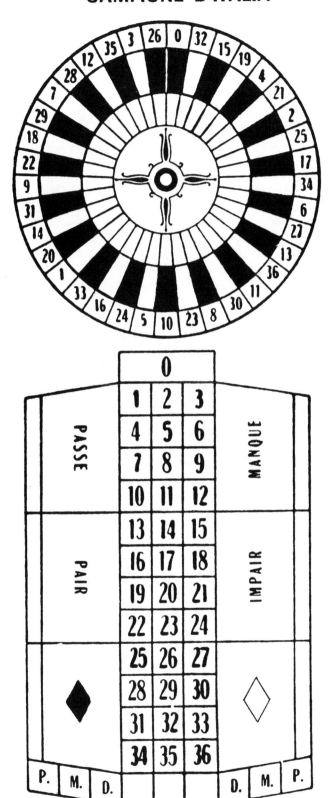

A: Wheel and layout of the Standard European table.

TABLEAU DES VOISINS

12	35	3	26	**0**	32	15	19	4
5	24	16	33	**1**	20	14	31	9
15	19	4	21	**2**	25	17	34	6
7	28	12	35	**3**	26	0	32	15
0	32	15	19	**4**	21	2	25	17
30	8	23	10	**5**	24	16	33	1
2	25	17	34	**6**	27	13	36	11
9	22	18	29	**7**	28	12	35	3
13	36	11	30	**8**	23	10	5	24
1	20	14	31	**9**	22	18	29	7
11	30	8	23	**10**	5	24	16	33
6	27	13	36	**11**	30	8	23	10
18	29	7	28	**12**	35	3	26	0
17	34	6	27	**13**	36	11	30	8
16	33	1	20	**14**	31	9	22	18
3	26	0	32	**15**	19	4	21	2
23	10	5	24	**16**	33	1	20	14
4	21	2	25	**17**	34	6	27	13
14	31	9	22	**18**	29	7	28	12
26	0	32	15	**19**	4	21	2	25
24	16	33	1	**20**	14	31	9	22
32	15	19	4	**21**	2	25	17	34
20	14	31	9	**22**	18	29	7	28
36	11	30	8	**23**	10	5	24	16
8	23	10	5	**24**	16	33	1	20
19	4	21	2	**25**	17	34	6	27
28	12	35	3	**26**	0	32	15	19
25	17	34	6	**27**	13	36	11	30
22	18	29	7	**28**	12	35	3	26
31	9	22	18	**29**	7	28	12	35
27	13	36	11	**30**	8	23	10	5
33	1	20	14	**31**	9	22	18	29
35	3	26	0	**32**	15	19	4	21
10	5	24	16	**33**	1	20	14	31
21	2	25	17	**34**	6	27	13	36
29	7	28	12	**35**	3	26	0	32
34	6	27	13	**36**	11	30	8	23

B: The guide offered by European casinos to indicate the nearest numbers to one another. Many players believe in the "neighbors theory," that every wheel is biased in some way and that numbers in certain areas will come up in greater frequency. This is not the case but the casinos are happy to oblige players who think so.

The real knock can be put on some casinos like those in Puerto Rico where dress codes are enforced and—more important—they give you the worst odds in Roulette to be found anywhere. In Europe the odds are first class, all the way.

And America? Gambling expert Edwin Silberstang called it right when he observed, "Since the game [Roulette] has such a high percentage in favor of the house . . . the only reason left to play this game is to rest one's feet."

See BETTING SYSTEMS; James BOND; Sean CONNERY; JAGGER'S SYSTEM; Charles WELLS.

ROULETTE PREDECESSORS

Today Roulette is the oldest casino game still in existence, but it was hardly the first gambling-establishment game to be played. Other wheel games preceded Roulette and it is sometimes said that two games, Hoca and E-O (for "even" and "odd"), probably are the basis for Roulette. Since these games came into prominence in the early 1700's, that would preclude the theory that French mathematician and physicist BLAISE PASCAL invented the game in 1655 while in monastic retreat, and that it was first played in a fly-by-night casino in Paris. What is clear is that Hoca and E-O both enjoyed considerable popularity for almost a century before Roulette began to make inroads in Europe.

Hoca was more the game of continental Europe; it employed a circular table with 40 pockets, or cups, around the edge. The ball was propelled by a special apparatus from the center of the table and skimmed along the rim before dropping into a stationary pocket. The house takeout was rather large, three of the pockets being marked zero, which in time led to objections from knowledgeable players. Hoca also suffered from growing suspicions that since the table pockets were stationary the ball could somehow be controlled away from the pockets that had been heavily bet.

By about 1765 Roulette was much more popular in Paris, having been heavily promoted by a police official, Gabriel de Santine, who was looking for a game that would stymie the cheats then dominating gambling in the French capital. Meanwhile in England E-O was very much the rage in fashionable resorts such as Bath. E-O consisted of a wheel with 40 cups, alternatively marked E and O, for "even" and "odd." Wagering was at even money, with the management "barring" one E and one O for the house edge. If the barred E came up, E bettors got their money back without profits but the O bettors lost. This gave the house an advantage of 2.5 percent. Some operators fattened their edge by barring two E's and two O's, doubling their advantage.

It was not the edge that eventually doomed E-O at the beginning of the 19th century but rather the fact that refugees from the French Revolution introduced Roulette, which greatly appealed to gamblers because of the variety of betting available.

ROUNCE: Modern Version of Rams

Rounce is an updating of the excellent gambling game of RAMS.

How to play: Instead of a 32-card deck a full 52-card one is used to accommodate three to nine players. The cards rank from ace high down to deuce. Players are dealt five cards and a "widow" hand dealt face down gets six cards. A player exchanging his hand for the widow follows the same rules as in Rams and then discards one of the widow cards before play commences.

Trump is turned up as in Rams, but the first player leads any card. Unlike Rams, the others are not required to play higher or to trump if out of suit. However, the winner of the first trick must lead a trump to the next trick if he holds one. The game otherwise follows the Rams rules of play and betting, but there is no "general call." As in Rams, the winner of each trick collects one-fifth of the original pot.

Rounce is a much more wide-open game, so the astute player is better off sticking to Rams since he can do better in figuring out the hands.

ROUND THE CORNER: Unusual Poker Rules on Straights

Round the Corner is a game in which the ace may be linked both the deuce and the king. Thus a straight is allowed for such cards as 3, 2, ace, king, queen. It must be borne in mind that in this game the picture cards are always regarded as being the low end of the straight. This means a straight from 5 down to the ace is 5 high and beats a 4-high straight, which runs from 4 to the king.

ROXBOROUGH, MICHAEL "ROXY"

See ODDS MAKERS.

RUMMY: Very Popular Card Game

Rummy is one of the most popular of all card games, ranking second in the United States only to POKER (BRIDGE is probably a distant third), and indeed it forms the nucleus of many games. Therefore only straight Rummy, or Rum, will be considered here while many variations, with or without the word Rummy in their names, are accorded their own categories. Chief among these would be GIN Rummy, FIVE-HUNDRED RUMMY, KNOCK RUMMY, and MICHIGAN RUMMY.

How to play: Straight Rummy is played with up to six players. When two play each gets ten cards, with three or four players seven cards, and with more, six cards. The rest of the deck (the stock) is faced down and the top card turned up beside it to start the discard pile. Cards are ranked from king down to ace. Players in turn must take either the top card of the stock or the top card of the discard pile and then discard; the discard cannot be the card just picked up from the discard pile.

The object of the game is to make melds of three

or four sets of the same rank, such as three aces or four queens, or sequences of three or more cards of the suit in order such as deuce, 3, 4 of diamonds or 10, jack, queen, king of clubs, etc. A player places these groups of cards face up in front of him. This is called "laying down," and on every play whether he lays down or not he must conclude his turn by facing a card from his hand on the discard pile. Whenever it is a player's turn to lay down he may also lay down one or more cards relating to previous melds or sequences that he or any of his opponents have laid down. Should the stock be exhausted before there is a winner, the discard pile is turned over and becomes a new stock.

The first player to lay down all his cards and make a final discard wins the game. All the other players pay him one point per pip value of each card remaining in their hands, with all picture, or court, cards counting 10 points. If a player lays down all his cards at one time, he receives double payment from the losers. This of course places a premium on holding melds and sequences in one's hand, while running the risk that the player will be caught with them if an opponent goes out first.

Rummy is a relatively simply game that has lent itself to a number of variations. The most common variations follow, each offering what some players regard as improvements on the straight game.

RUMMY—BOATHOUSE

In Boathouse Rummy a player may draw the top card of the stock and discard as usual. However, if he elects to pick up the discard, he must also take a second card, either from the stock or the discard pile. Despite the fact that he has taken two cards, however, he may only discard one.

To win, a player must lay down his entire hand at the same time. One difference in melding is that the ace may be played as a high card (above the king), or low (below the deuce), or "around the corner"—as in queen, king, ace, deuce of hearts. No matter how it's used, the ace counts for 11 points.

When a winner goes out, losers may still lay down whatever melds or sequences they have been holding and then pay off only on their remaining cards.

RUMMY—CALL

Call Rummy is played in the same manner as straight RUMMY except that, should a player unmindfully discard a card that could have been laid off on an existing meld or sequence, another player may call, "Rummy!" He then lays off the card himself and follows by making a discard from his hand. Play then reverts to the previous order. If two players make the call simultaneously, the one nearer to the discarder's left is deemed the winner of the call.

RUMMY—GAMBLER'S (OR TWO-MELD)

When it comes to playing basic RUMMY for real money, Gambler's, or Two-meld, Rummy is the variation that is preferred. This writer has witnessed some games for phenomenal stakes, including one in post-war Germany involving an army lieutenant colonel and a cook holding a special rank of master sergeant with what constituted the equivalent of three months pay for a 200-man unit. The cook won (and shortly thereafter was busted to private).

This is simple Rummy with no gimmicks other than the fact that a player must take two or more turns to meld out. Thus when he lays down cards he is serving notice that he may go out on his next turn. He may not do so, and may simply be trying to force his opponents to lay down cards so that he might be better able to gauge his own and their strengths or be able to lay down his final unmatched card to one of their melds.

The stock is only gone through once and thereafter players must take the top card of the discard pile. The game ends with a finisher, or if a player refuses to take the discard card and all possible melds are laid down, settlement is made on the basis of the man left with the fewest points against him.

RUMMY—QUEEN CITY

Queen City Rum is played exactly like regular RUMMY except that seven cards are always dealt each player and the winner must "go Rummy," or lay down his entire hand at once. This may be done with or without a final discard and settlement is made by the winner getting the point value of his own hand from all opponents.

RUMMY—ROUND THE CORNER

Round the Corner Rummy means that an ace may be high or low in the same sequence, such as king-ace-deuce, and always is counted as 11 points. Thus it uses only one of the variations of Boathouse Rummy to differ from the basic game.

RUMMY—WILD-CARD

In Wild-card Rummy, deuces are wild and may be used in any melds to fill them out. Thus a meld of king-king-deuce qualifies as three kings and 7 of spades-deuce of hearts-9 of spades represents a three-card sequence (7-8-9). To win a player must "go Rummy" by laying down his entire hand at once; he is paid for his point total by each of his opponents. All deuces are counted as 25 points no matter how they are used. To make the game even wilder, one or two jokers are sometimes added as extra wild cards and are also worth 25 points.

RUSSIA, Gambling in

By an edict put through by Josef Stalin in 1928, all private gambling was forbidden in Russia. Needless to say, not even a reign of terror could really wipe out gambling in the Soviet Union, and there have been reports from defectors who speak of apartments in big cities turned into gambling joints, frequented by industrial and party officials. To expect otherwise from a country with Russia's culture and background would be the height of gullibility. While the state runs a lottery, it has yet to match the pervasiveness or the efficiency of the Polish model.

Horse racing too is handled rather awkwardly, although there is totalizator betting. The problem is that past-performance information is scanty. Russian newspapers don't carry such intelligence and the on-track race cards list only the names of the horses, some background material on the jockeys, and sparse accounts of recent performances. Even more disconcerting to American visitors would be that some race cards consist of first a flat race, then a trotting race with driver and sulky, then another flat race, and so on. This would probably thoroughly confuse the average U.S. horseplayer, who is not used to such an eclectic approach. Does this mean there are no professional horseplayers in the USSR? Hardly. Western journalists have done interviews at the Russian tracks with regulars who never miss a day at the races, and they seem to travel from one track to another to follow the bangtails. It should be understood—as probably the Russian authorities do not—that scant racing information helps the pros and hurts the public. Some journalists have witnessed bettors with their own stopwatches and others actually measuring the wind velocity at race time. This is a crude duplication of the tactics used by the so-called "speed boys" at American tracks. These bettors develop their own past-performance charts and it can be seen why some Russian bettors might follow horses from one track to another to bet on a hot horse at the top of his form, something the locals would be unaware of.

These professional Russian horseplayers probably live in fear of glasnost—if it ever extends to publishing detailed past performances. As things stand now, they are betting against a particularly ill-informed public—and most likely cleaning up.

RUSSIAN ROULETTE: Greatest Gamble of All

Russian Roulette is the ultimate gambling game. A bullet is placed in a cylinder of a pistol, the cylinder spun and the "player" takes his chances, putting the gun to his head and pulling the trigger.

Let us look at this strictly as a gambling matter. What are the odds that a player will die on that one pull of a trigger? There are six chambers, one loaded. Odds: 1 to 5. That's probably wrong, however. Experts say that the odds are less than 1 to 5, since when the cylinder is spun, the weight of the loaded chamber should logically cause it to drop to the bottom of the cylinder.

Some physicists and screwballs might be impressed with the logic of such a "system."

S

SANDBAGGING: Treacherous Betting Tactic

Sandbagging is when a player with a strong hand checks instead of bets in order to lull opponents into a false sense of security. Then, after seeing a few bets, the sandbagger socks his opponents with a huge raise. Sandbagging is usually not allowed in friendly games, but it is considered a legitimate ploy in big-money games; in fact, experts who so entrap their rivals are complimented for having played brilliantly.

Timing in the art of check and raise is all important. Most serious bettors do not attempt to sandbag unless there are more than five other players in the game. In DRAW POKER, especially in Jacks or Better, the leader, or first bettor, might check instead of opening—even though he has two pairs or three of a kind. With six, seven, or more players, it may be assumed that one of the later players will have at least jacks and will open. If not, the first bettor will be faced with the embarrassing situation of having everyone pass and thus he would lose his hand. On the opening round in Draw it is probably wiser for an early bettor to forget about sandbagging and instead resort to "slowplay." This involves making a small opening bet that protects the pot and hopefully leads opponents to feel he is merely betting from weakness. If someone raises, the first bettor can come back with his big bet.

Even in friendly games, check and raise—or, more correctly, pass and raise—on the opening round is permitted but not allowed in subsequent betting. For instance, a player might be holding a potentially strong hand and still not have jacks or better for openers, and he is thus forced to pass. When another player opens, he is permitted to raise. This could happen if, say, a player is dealt a four-card open-end straight flush. In theory, the odds of his filling to either a straight, a flush, or a straight flush are 17 out of 47, and he could legitimately bet away on such possibilities and build the pot substantially.

SANDING: Method of Marking Cards

Sanding, or "sand work," is a method of marking cards. With a small piece of sandpaper, a cheat may scrape off a tiny part of the back pattern of several cards. This is most effective with cards that have a design that bleeds to the edge, typically Bee brand cards, but it can also be done with others.

For example, a cheat might obscure the extreme left-hand corner of each end of a card to indicate an ace. Sanding the center of each end might mark a deuce. It would be impossible to lose at any kind of POKER with aces and deuces so marked. Most cheats do not sand too many cards, however; marking just two aces and two deuces would give them more than enough of an edge. They might mark up to two deuces in different spots and leave the other two unmarked. If suspicions are aroused, examination of the cards won't turn up any consistent pattern of markings on the four deuces and two different kinds of markings could be passed off as a factory imperfection in the cards.

Ideally, sanding is done before the game, but any suspicion would then fall on the cheat because he was the one who supplied the cards. For that reason, some sanders prefer marking up cards during play. In the old days it was common for a sander to have a small bandage on one finger with a slit in the fabric for the sandpaper. The cheat drew the card over the slit and marked it.

Over the years veteran gamblers have come to view with suspicion the presence of a bandage on an opponent's finger. Nowadays it is more common for the cheat to paste a tiny piece of sandpaper on his finger or in the palm of his hand and mark up some cards. Once this is done, he discards the sandpaper or perhaps pastes another piece in position later on when he wants to do a little more sand work.

SANDWICH, EARL OF: Compulsive Gambler
The sandwich was born at a card table.

John Montagu (1718-1792), the fourth earl of Sandwich, led a public life tainted with many vices, among which gambling was certainly a minor one. But when Lord Sandwich played cards he would never dream of leaving the table for a meal. Involved once in a 48-hour card game (not much over par for him), Lord Sandwich was so caught up with the action that he ordered a servant to bring him a slice of cold roast beef between two slices of bread. Thus he was able to eat with one hand and continue to play with the other.

In time other gamblers adopted Lord Sandwich's inventive way of eating—and the "sandwich" was born.

SARATOGA: Variation of Michigan
Saratoga is the same game as MICHIGAN but requires that each player put the same amount of money or chips on each payoff, or "boodle," card. Some gamblers continue to call this variation Michigan, and specify that equal payment applies.

John SCARNE: "According to Scarne" Gambling Authority
He was seven years only when his mother caught him shuffling and stacking a deck of cards for the first time. At 11, he startled family members by studying the exposed cards played in a game and naming the remaining cards. He was constantly at the family Parcheesi set, practicing controlled CRAPS shots. He had little interest in baseball and other kids' games, preferring to study crooked card moves in front of a mirror to see whether the sleights of hand could be detected.

John Scarne (1903-1985), who was to become the world's foremost authority on games, long dreamed of becoming a great gambler. He did, and he also became known as gambling's greatest cop, putting more sharpers out of business than any law, any committee, any police force or anti-crime campaign in America. His books on cards and gambling—ripped off by many imitators—have exposed the gimmicks of card tricksters for millions of readers. His one-man war on card sharps in the service during World War II cleaned up thousands of crooked GI games. He advised the FBI and Senate committees on how to stop gambling cheats, and he was hired by the biggest legitimate casinos to help control cheating of the house from both sides of the table.

As one profiler stated, "He's been beaten up, shot at, run off the road and nearly killed by crooked

Gambling expert John Scarne, center of three men standing, watching the action at a high-stakes Baccarat game in Las Vegas. (Photo: Las Vegas News Bureau)

operators all over the country. They've offered him blondes by the dozens and bribe money in the tens of thousands to go easy on their rackets, but he's never copped out."

John Scarne was, in short, an honest gambler, precisely because he was so good. Had he had less talent, he might have been forced to work the shady side. But when a man gets as good as Scarne, he can afford to be honest and sleep well at night. It was quite a badge of distinction for Scarne to win his own special form of military "commendations" for his wartime activities. Gen. Hap Arnold, commanding general of the U.S. Army Air Force, said: "John Scarne's one-man crusade against crooked gambling in the Armed Forces during World War II saved servicemen tens of millions of dollars a month in potential gambling losses when he practically cleaned up crooked gambling in the Armed Forces single-handedly." And Adm. Ernest J. King, commander in chief of the U.S. Navy, told Scarne: "You have done a great service, both to your country and to the members of the Armed Forces."

Perhaps the best advice Scarne ever gave the average gambler was not to expose a cheat during a game. The result, he explained, could be rather violent. He made this mistake himself when he was 15 and got into his first gambling game with adults. The game was BANKER AND BROKER and he noticed that the dealer always seemed to get the highest card although his moves seemed straight. The dealer cut the cards into four stacks, face down, one for each player. Then one of the players cut a fifth stack from one of the four, which was for the dealer. Each player then turned over his stack to show the bottom card. High card took the pot.

Young Scarne started out with $8, his weekly pay, and was soon down $7. Years of practice and study had served Scarne well and he asked to shuffle the cards, any player's privilege. He had not detected any sleight of hand and concluded that the dealer had somehow gaffed the deck. What he had noticed, however, was that the dealer always cut the cards close to the top or bottom. But when a player cut the last stack for the dealer's card, he would cut the cards (as one normally would) at the middle of the stack.

As Scarne shuffled the cards, he became aware that some of them were a shade narrower than others. He realized the dealer was using "strippers." The dealer held the pack with his left hand at the center and his right hand at one end. When he pulled the deck apart, all the low cards stripped out in his left hand and all the high cards into his right. Thus when the dealer made his four stacks he could cut four piles, each with a low card on the bottom. When another player made the final cut for the dealer's card, though it was a legitimate cut he inevitably was cutting to a higher card.

Caution dictated that Scarne say nothing and simply drop out of the game. Instead, the anger of youth won out and he broke into a storm of invective, slamming down the cards and denouncing the dealer's trickery. Retrieving the deck, he showed the others how it worked, announcing in advance whether he would cut to a low or high card, and then doing so. The exposed dealer made a panicky rush for the door, but he was dragged back into the room. The dealer pulled a switchblade; another player picked up a bottle.

Young Scarne ran for it. He was a block away when he heard police sirens. He watched as the police dragged five blood-spattered men into the paddy wagon. It was a lesson Scarne never forgot. Gambling and cheating were deadly serious matters. It was important to avoid being cheated *and* to stay alive in the process.

From that moment, Scarne had nothing but contempt for gambling cheats. Did he ever cheat? Yes, in the sense that he at times "took the play away" from cheats when he caught them at their nefarious deeds. Once, after he'd hit the big time, Scarne was at Hialeah with boxer James J. Braddock. Some strangers hustled Braddock (who was a patsy for gambling cheats) and Scarne (whom they did not recognize) into a "friendly" game of POKER. The game took place in a hotel room with the two strangers, two other well-heeled men whom Scarne spotted as "shills," and three well-stacked blondes who constantly leaned over Scarne and Braddock offering drinks and glancing at their cards.

The two original card sharks went to work stacking several hands, palming cards, and signaling one another on how to bet or play. Soon Braddock was a big loser, but then the deal moved to Scarne. Suddenly Braddock got four aces while one of the crooks thought he had legitimately gotten a surefire hand of four kings. Even though Scarne dealt only one hand out of six, it was enough to make Braddock and Scarne big winners despite whatever happened on the other deals.

The crooks couldn't understand what was happening to them until "Machine Gun" Jack McGurn, the notorious triggerman for Al Capone, walked into the room. He greeted Braddock effusively and then broke into wild laughter when he spotted Scarne. He turned to the two cheats. "Out of 20,000 suckers at Hialeah," he roared, "you idiots have to pick out John Scarne to clip in a Poker game!"

If the crooks had any ill feelings toward Scarne, they had no chance to show it. McGurn had other ideas. He was on the phone, calling up every card mechanic, croupier, dice thief, and mobster in Miami, inviting them over to have Scarne demonstrate "how to really cheat at cards." Scarne could do nothing but cooperate.

Scarne's passion for cards and dice inevitably brought him into contact with gangsters. Anyone involved in gambling, either legal or illegal, will soon find himself dealing with the underworld. That was true in the 1930's and is just as true today.

Scarne left an impressive mark on gambling, and not just in the area of exposing cheats. The old saying of "according to Hoyle" was in large measure replaced by "according to Scarne," especially when one moved beyond simple explanation of rules and into the strategies involved in various plays.

Scarne also did much to deflate many of the exaggerated claims made by some BLACKJACK counters that they could teach the average gambler how to win big in casino games. Scarne challenged the leading exponents of this strategy to a game to be played for $100,000 in Las Vegas with Scarne as the dealer. The challenge was never met. Evidently the Blackjack counters decided it would be easier to beat the house than Scarne.

Of course, the gambling industry had to love John Scarne. The fact that, because of his consummate skills, he was barred from most gambling in Las Vegas made him the perfect (unwitting) shill for the gambling interests—the inference drawn by the public being that the casinos could indeed be beaten. Unfortunately, the average casino addict is not John Scarne. No one is, or ever will be. They threw away the mold after one shuffle of that deck.

SCHNAUTZ
See THIRTY-ONE.

SCHWELLEN
See ENFLE.

SCOTCH WHIST: Basic Whist Gone Far Afield
While the name of the game is Scotch Whist, it differs greatly from and should not be considered a form of WHIST. In fact, many players do not even know it by its Whist name. They call it Catch the Ten, since one of the objects is to win the trick containing the 10 of trump.

The game may be played solo by two to seven players, but is best as a partnership game for four. A deck of 36 cards is used, the 2's, 3's, 4's, and 5's being removed. The cards rank from ace high down to 6, except in the trump suit, where the jack ranks above the ace. All cards are dealt out so that, in a four-player game, each gets nine cards. With five or seven players, there is a leftover card and it is turned up as trump.

In all other games the dealer turns up his final card for trump and then takes it up before play begins. The player to the dealer's left leads to the first trick, which is taken by the highest card in suit. If a player is out of suit he may trump or discard an odd suit. If trump is played, high trump takes the trick. However, unlike Whist, tricks are not counted in Scotch Whist. The main scoring comes in capturing the high trump cards that have the following values: jack, 11 points; ace, 4; king, 3; queen, 2; 10, 10. The 10 is a key card with a high-point value, but vulnerable to the ace and all the picture trumps. Therefore an important strategy for the player holding the 10 is voiding himself of a suit so that he may take a trick in that suit with the 10 of trump. While tricks do not count in the scoring, it is still important to take them since the number of cards exceeding 18 entitles a player or side to score 1 point for each card. The first side to get to 41 wins the game and settlement is made accordingly. Again, Scotch Whist is a much better game played in partnerships with four players and when there are six players, they frequently divide into three partnerships of two each or two partnerships of three each.
See also FRENCH WHIST.

SCREW YOUR NEIGHBOR
See PASS THE GARBAGE.

SECOND DEALING: Cardsharper's Crooked Technique
Dealing the second card from the top of the deck is known as "second dealing" and a "number two man" is much prized by crooked card mobs. In private games a second dealer operating alone has a huge advantage in deciding whether to deal a particular player the top card of the deck, the identity of which he has learned by PEEKING, or the second card if he wishes to hold the top card for himself.

Dealing seconds takes considerable skill, much more than another cheating tactic, BOTTOM DEALING, which is dealing a card from the bottom of the deck. The virtue is that second dealing is much harder to spot—even by a skilled professional gambler.

The deck is held in the MECHANIC'S GRIP. The left thumb covers the farthest corner of the top card while the other fingers curl around the deck and have it fully under control. The left thumb pushes the top card over the side of the deck so that it can—or at least should—be grasped by the right hand. This is what the other players "see" happening, but actually the top card is covering the real action. The dealer has executed the two-card push-off so that the top card and the second card extend from the deck at the same time. The right fingers come away with the second card while at the same moment, the left thumb deftly pulls the top card back onto the top of the deck.

The entire move is completed with lightning speed and precision and can be spotted only occasionally by very few observers. A really good second dealer cannot even follow his own moves, and is only tactually aware that he is doing anything unusual. A good second dealer will practice before a mirror and videotape his own moves. When he himself cannot follow any untoward movements, he knows he is ready for professional play.

The only way to spot—or at least suspect—a second deal is by watching for the mechanic's grip, nearly always the sign of a crooked operator. On the other hand, good second dealers insist they can spot a second dealer themselves even while *blindfolded*. Their secret is that their hearing is atuned to the sound of a second deal. If you listen closely to cards being dealt, you can pick up the sound of a card scraping the card underneath it. When a dealer is second dealing, the scraping noise is louder because the second card is scraping against two cards at the same time. Unfortunately, few cardplayers know how to listen for such subtle sound distinctions.

There was one second dealer, a notoriously hard scraper, who covered the sound by humming Beethoven as a cover. As he dealt each card, he added suspense to the action by imitating the "bum-bum-

A second dealer in action: A: He uses thumb to squeeze back the top card of deck. B: He works forward the second card (shown here in different backing). C: He pulls out and deals the second card, retaining the top card for more appropriate use. Second dealers seldom waste their talent in small-stakes games—unless practicing. (Photos: E. Gerard)

bum-BUM'' of *Beethoven's Fifth* with each flick. Unfortunately for him, that soon developed into a "tell" and his days as a second dealer quickly ended. See BOTTOM DEALING.

SENATE DEALER: Trusted Nonplayer

The senate dealer is a hackneyed standby regarded fondly by Hollywood. He is portrayed in movies as an honest dealer used in high-stakes POKER games because he is universally trusted. In *The Cincinnati Kid* Karl Malden was a senate dealer who could manipulate the cards so that even the most sophisticated gamblers couldn't spot his action.

In fact, senate dealers actually are chosen because they *cannot* manipulate cards that well. Seasoned gamblers have an additional dependable control—the bottom line. It is within the realm of possibility that once in his lifetime, a senate dealer might deal a royal flush (1 chance in 649,740) and a four of a kind (1 chance in 4,165) on the original five cards and conceivably even on the same hand (1 chance in 2,706,167,100). But if he does that, or something similar, he has dealt his last high-stakes game.

SET BACK

See PITCH.

SEVEN AND A HALF: Blackjack Imitator

Seven and a Half is an interesting betting game similar in many respects to BLACKJACK. Like private Blackjack, the game favors the dealer who also has a way of pressing his advantage. The game is played with a 40-card deck with the 8's, 9's, and 10's removed. Ace to 7 count according to their pip value while all picture cards are valued at half a point.

After bets have been placed, each player and the dealer are dealt one card face down. The players decide in turn to stand or take an additional card or cards. The object is to reach or approach 7½ but not to go over that total, in which case the dealer wins the bet. A "natural" 7½ consisting of a 7 and a picture, wins the bet for the player and the deal as well, unless the dealer also gets a natural. A natural beats any other combination of cards that total 7½ on more than two cards. The dealer also wins all ties, as in private Blackjack.

If those advantages aren't enough, the dealer may also double all the players' bets after looking at his hole card. Thus a dealer will very likely double the bets when he gets a 7 in the hole. Some dealers even double with a picture card in the hole, playing for a 7 on the draw. Additionally, by doubling the dealer also creates the impression that he has a 7 in the hole and thus his opponents will try for a 7½ and often bust out in the process.

Some versions of private Blackjack allow the dealer to double the bets on the basis of his first downcard, but in that case any player may redouble the bets. This option is not available in Seven and a Half, where advantages of having the deal are enormous.

The best tactic of a successful player can use is betting the lowest possible amount in hopes of catching a natural and winning the deal. Playing aggressively once one is the dealer should more than make up for any previous losses.

SEVEN UP: Predecessor to Pitch

Seven Up, also known as Old Sledge in America and All Fours in England, is still played as a two-player game but has been succeeded by PITCH, especially when three or four players are involved. A regular deck of 52 cards is used, with rankings from ace high to deuce low. There is a trump suit. Each player is dealt six cards and the next card is turned up to indicate trump. Points are scored in four ways, each worth 1 point:

1. *High.* This is for being dealt the highest trump in play.
2. *Low.* This is for being dealt the lowest trump in play.
3. *Jack.* This is for winning the jack of trump in a trick.
4. *Game.* This is for taking in tricks the highest number of counting cards, with 10's worth 10; aces, 4; kings, 3; queens, 2; and jacks, 1. If the total is a tie between the players, the nondealer gets the point. (When Seven Up is played by more than two players, ties make the game point a wash.)

The nondealer (or the player to the dealer's left, if it is a larger game) has the option of refusing trump suit at the start of the hand. If he okays the trump, he announces he will stand. If not, he "begs." This puts the decision up to the dealer or the next player, who may decide to accept the trump. If he does, he says, "I give you one," which allows the nondealer to score a point and the game proceeds. On the other hand, the dealer may also refuse the trump card. In that case, the dealer "runs the cards," giving each player three more cards and turning up a new trump card. If that trump is different from the first one, there is usually no further option by the players and that suit is trump. If, however, the new trump is the same suit as the first trump, the cards are run again until there is a different trump. If the deck is run through without establishing trump, the dealer gathers up all the cards and redeals. The exception to the nonoption requirement of the second trump involves one of the players suggesting "bunch." If there is no disagreement to that, the trump is thrown out and there is a new deal.

Once trump is established—usually the second card

does become trump if the first one is not accepted—the nondealer leads to the first trick, and the opponent or opponents must, if able, follow in suit or play a trump as preferred. The winner of each trick leads to the next. At the conclusion of the hand, points are totaled and there is a new deal. The object of the game is to be the first to win a total of 7 points. Because it is possible for more than one player to go over 7 in a particular hand, the points are reckoned one at a time. The first player to get to 7 is the winner. The order is as listed earlier: high, low, jack, and game.

Some players prefer to make the winning game score 10, 11, or 12 (see ALL FIVES.)

SEVEN-CARD HIGH-LOW PROGRESSIVE STUD: Poker with Escalated Betting

This is similar to Seven-card High-Low Stud, but with an important difference. The player to the left of the dealer opens the betting for one chip after the first upcard. Naturally other players may raise on that round. On the second upcard the second player to the left of the dealer is required to start the betting at two chips. This continues with the third player opening the betting for three chips, and so on. Note that highest hands do not open the betting on any round. If the player who is supposed to open does not do so, he must fold and the next player in sequence starts the betting or folds. Some players limit the raises to the size of the opening bet on each round. Still the constant escalating of the bets on each round builds a substantial pot.

While at first blush this looks like a very wild game, it actually can build discipline for the average player. Since players know there will be no free rides on any round and that the amount of investment will grow, it forces players to evaluate their early cards more judiciously before remaining in the game. Because of the low opening bet in the first round, a player might stay for one more card without a strong hand. After that, without improvement, the weak should drop.

SEVEN-CARD MUTUAL: Spit Poker Variation

Many gamblers opt for Seven-card Mutual when there are too many players to be accommodated by more standard games of POKER. As many as 16 players can take part in Mutual, which sometimes leads to enormous pots. If a player bets judiciously and drops out early if he does not have a powerhouse hand, he figures to be a winner over the long haul.

Each player is dealt two cards down and then a card is dealt face up in the center of the table. This card is a mutual upcard for all players. A betting round ensues and then another mutual upcard is dealt. In all there are four upcards with a betting sequence after each is exposed. A final downcard is dealt to each player and there is another round of betting. Players use their three downcards and four mutual cards to create their best five-card hands, meaning that all surviving players must use at least two of the mutual cards. If a player is dealt two disparate hole cards, neither of which help each other or matches up with the mutual face card, he should drop immediately. A player who is dealt a pair of 6's in the hole to a mutual jack might stay on the hand—but a pro would drop. The jack is stronger than a 6, and if there is a big group of players there may be several pairs of jacks out there, all outranking the pair of 6's. But say the player remains in the game with the pair of 6's. The second mutual card is a 10. Now he absolutely must drop. The jack and 10 puts six potential pairs out there that beat his pair of 6's (to say nothing about likely two-pair hands or triplets). Also a jack-10 represents a potential straight; there are probably four-card straights already formed, which makes a pair of 6's all the weaker.

The best hand pairs up with the highest mutual card, since that obviously cuts down on the pair possibilities of other players. Such a hand should bet or raise early to try to force other players out. A player holding a four-card straight after the second upcard is dealt is in a poor position if the third upcard produces a pair among the upcards. This gives him only two more chances to get his straight (or flush) while it is a virtual certainty that some opponents are already holding three of a kind or two pairs. It is time for the four-card straight or flush to give up the ghost.

Seven-card Mutual is not a tortoise-and-the-hare game. The winner over the long haul is the player who runs the fastest. He stays only on real strength. A high pair after the first upcard and at least two pairs or three of a kind by the third upcard is dealt are minimum staying hands. And even a player with this much strength will only continue betting if his hand improves further. The delightful thing about Seven-Card Mutual is that most players aren't smart at the game and will seek to improve a weak hand by covering bets, a suicidal approach that makes them easy victims for the smart player.

OMAHA and HOLD 'EM derive from this game.

SEVEN-CARD POKER: Nine-card Game
Seven-Card Poker is an extension of the wildness of SIX-CARD POKER, DRAW and STUD. Seven-Card Poker gives each player nine cards from which he must use seven to form a complete POKER hand. The game is supplemented by six wild cards—the four deuces and the two jokers—which makes it easier to form a

seven-card hand. However, it must be remembered that *all* seven cards must be utilized in the hand. If, for instance, a player comes up with four aces and a pair of kings, he has a busted hand that is worth nothing.

The rankings of the winning hands are as follows: seven of a kind (seven aces would be the highest), seven royal flush (ace down to 8), straight flush, five of a kind with a pair (such as five queens and a pair of 4's), fours and threes (such as four queens and three 9's), seven-flush (such as seven diamonds, but not in sequence), seven-straight, and three of a kind with two pairs. No other combinations are possible.

At first glance it may seem impossible for players to get seven usable cards, but in a six-handed game all six wild cards are used and usually someone fills his hand.

Because there are seldom enough cards available for draw in Seven-Card Poker, the game is usually played in the form of Showdown Stud, with six cards dealt face up and three downcards. All cards are dealt immediately, but there is a final round of betting before the downcards are faced. There is no bluffing in this game insofar as a player trying to fake a seven-card hand. If he doesn't have it, he is an automatic loser.

The game is best with six players since that guarantees all the wild cards will be used. If no one can make a seven-card hand, the pot remains intact, and there is an additional ante and a new deal.

SEVEN-CARD STUD
See POKER.

SEVENS
See FAN TAN.

SHASTA SAM
See CALIFORNIA JACK.

SHELL GAME: Old Gambling Swindle
It is the baldest swindle of all, and it is much worse a bet than THREE-CARD MONTE. At least in Monte you theoretically can guess which of three cards is the correct one. You'll never guess which of three shells is hiding the pea—because none of them is.

The late gambling authority John Scarne insisted the first "thimble-rigger," as an operator of the shell Game was called, must have arrived on these shores shortly after the *Mayflower*. He was undoubtedly right, but the shell game is much older than that. It has been traced back to ancient Egypt, and Alciphron of Athens has left us an excellent description of the

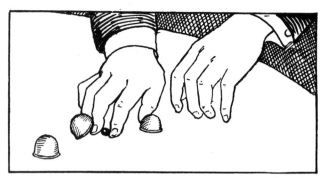

The Shell game is a crooked scam going back at least to ancient Egypt. This illustration from an old guide to gambling swindles was allegedly to inform victims but was of extreme value to professional cheats.

cups and balls, a forerunner of the shell game, in Greece in the 2nd century A.D.

In its standard play, the Shell Game can never be won by the sucker, since the pea is not under any of the shells. After the operator clearly places the pea under one shell and starts shifting all three around, he gingerly lifts the shell so that the pea is stuck between the back of the shell and the table top (generally a felt surface). He then pops the pea out between his thumb and first finger, and when he pulls his hand away, his finger covers the pea. After the sucker makes his selection and loses, the operator shoves the other two shells back toward him as he turns them over, in the process slipping the pea under one of them.

A fundamental law of the Shell Game is never to allow the sucker to win. The theory is that a loser will become more desperate and bet even greater amounts in a futile effort to get even. The greatest thimble-riggers were such 19th-century gamblers as CANADA BILL JONES, who won many a deed to a plantation with the game and whose motto was "Suckers have no business with money, anyway," and JEFFERSON RANDOLPH "SOAPY" SMITH, who won a fortune at it before he was killed by vigilantes in Alaska in 1898. There is only one recorded instance in which Smith lost in his shell shuffle. A likely appearing victim slammed a gun on the little table and then made a whopping bet. But he then said he was going to turn over the two shells that *did not* have the pea. He did and said, "I reckon there's no need to turn over the last shell." He picked up the money and left. Smith promptly folded his table and did the same.

Starting in 1843, when a reformed Mississippi gambler named JONATHAN GREEN first wrote about it, there have been numerous exposés of the Shell Game, but the racket has thrived and still can be seen at carnivals and on the grounds of racetracks. Three-card Monte is "played" regularly on the streets of

most large American cities and the Shell Game is also showing up once again. Remarkably, in New York City it appears most often on Wall Street on paydays.

SHIFTING SANDS: Flip Stud Variation
Shifting Sands is Five-card Stud played under the same rules as FLIP STUD with two cards dealt down and each player turning up the card of his choice. The same procedure is followed on each succeeding round so that a player has only one hold card at all times. The difference in Shifting Sands is that the first card turned up becomes wild for him as do all other cards of the same denomination.

SHILLS: Gambling's "Come-on" Artists
There are two types of shills, those used by illegitimate gambling joints and card mobs and those employed by honest casinos in Nevada and Atlantic City. The early form of shill lured victims into crooked card or dice games. This sort of shill, or STEERER, is still alive and well today, but most gamblers are more likely to run into the so-called "honest shill" in casinos.

Casinos do not like to use the term "shill," preferring the more antiseptic "game starter." Generally speaking that is an apt description, since the main purpose of a shill is getting a game started. Most casino players don't like to sit down at an empty table and are more comfortable when they have plenty of company. Not surprisingly, many (in fact, probably most) casino shills are beautiful young women. The rest are usually senior citizens, another type that inspires confidence in reluctant gamblers. If gramps and granny can play without getting hurt, the public feels, it must be a pretty safe gamble.

To get action started at a high-minimum ROULETTE table, as many as three shills might be brought in. They make all sorts of bets so that at least one collects a small pile of chips on every spin of the wheel. That is enough to convince observers that "this is a good table." As other (genuine) gamblers join in, the shills are pulled out one at a time to make room.

Shills are used extensively at BACCARAT, which is a very high-stakes game. Generally a shill gets at least $2,000 in $20 bills to play at the game. If one comes across a casino Baccarat game with only three or four players, it is a safe bet they are all shills. Eventually though, the shills do their thing and players take the lure. Shills are extremely poorly paid— in a major Vegas casino they may get as little as $20 a shift—and it is pretty much a public misperception that female shills hustle sexually at the tables. The casinos do not permit this. The pit bosses watching the tables constantly admonish the women to "Keep your eyes on the green" and "Don't smile."

At Baccarat a peculiar custom has sprung up among

A Baccarat table in action in Las vegas. It would be a fair guess that several of the players, more than likely the women, are casino employees—shilling or acting as "game starters." (Photo: Las Vegas News Bureau)

the more knowledgeable gamblers. These regulars tip the female shills in the same way they tip the dealers, recognizing that they are a necessary part of the casino scene. (See BACCARAT—AMERICAN.) To the outsider this appears to be a case of a winning gambler on the make. Actually it is the gamblers' recognition of the fact that the average shill finds it hard to get along on her regular pay.

From the gambler's viewpoint, however, not all shill activities are harmless. When a casino suspects a big winner of being a BLACKJACK counter, it will bring in a few shills to sit in and chatter away to break his concentration. In Nevada casinos, which offer single-deck play with some of the cards dealt down, lackadaisical shills can effectively stymie a counter by failing to turn up their downcards, making it difficult for him to keep track of the cards that have been played.

The IRS has its own problems with shills, since the government lacks the resources to keep a constant watch on them. The house does, to make sure shills are not stealing chips or money. But tax authorities maintain that shills play a key role in skimming operations, quickly cashing in big winnings that can later be greatly reduced or even recorded as a loss. The profit goes to the house, of course—not to the shill.

SHINER: Card-cheater's Device

A shiner is a small mirror device that reflects cards as they are dealt out by a crooked dealer. Originally shiners were almost exclusively worn in rings, but as experienced gamblers became aware of the ploy, cheaters tried concealing them in matchboxes or in piles of mixed coins. One of the more successful gimmicks is hiding the shiner in the bowl of a pipe that is cleaned out at key moments.

SHOOT: Banking Card Game

Shoot, sometimes called Slippery Sam, is unusual for a banking game in that the player actually enjoys an advantage over the banker. For that reason, the bank is transferred by certain rules to the next player. Unlike BLACKJACK, for instance, in which players must bet against the banker before seeing their cards,

A.

Table Reflector, very fine, our own
invention.......................... 5 00
Reflector, in seven half dollars....... 7 50
" in one half dollar.......... 2 50
" in pipe........ .... 5 00
" to work on any ring........ 2 00
" to fasten to greenbacks... 2 00
" plain..................... 1 50

A "greenback shiner" (A) fastened to a bill in the dealer's money pile permits him to read every card he deals. Page from a 19th-century crooked gamblers' catalog (B) shows the then going prices for shiners (referred to as reflectors). An excerpt from a 1912 guide offers a rundown on other shiners. (Photo: E. Gerard)

Shoot players look first and bet afterwards—a very important edge for the disciplined player.

The cards are valued as in POKER with the ace high and deuce low. The game starts with the banker putting a set amount of his money into the pot and then dealing each player three downcards. He places the balance of the deck—the stock—on the table. Only the first player may now look at his cards. He can bet a specified minimum or as much as the entire amount in the pot. The wager is that he will hold a higher card of the same suit as the top card of the stock. Since the player has at most three suits, he will lose if the missing suit turns up. However, if he holds high cards in the other three suits, he can figure precisely what the odds are for and against him.

Let us say the first player has the ace of spades, the queen of clubs, and the jack of hearts. He knows there are 31 cards in the stock that he can beat—12 spades, 10 clubs, and nine hearts. He will lose to 18 cards—two clubs, three hearts, and all 13 diamonds. The prospects are very favorable for him, and with the odds 31 to 18 in his favor he should bet, or "shoot," heavily.

Let us say after his bet, the banker turns over the top card from the stock and it is the 4 of hearts. The

the dealer who used it to read the face of each card as it was taken, face downwards, from the pack. Of late years, however, the makers of these implements have greatly improved the process of manufacture.

Poker Check Mirror. A very fine glass is set in five poker chips, and can be played at any distance from the deck, up to 20 inches. Reflector can be placed in any kind of checks, of any color desired. It is claimed that this mirror stack mixed in with the other stacks is a big success in getting the money.

Triangle Reducing Glass. This is made to set between two stacks of poker checks. It is made of very

fine glass, and can be played from four to twenty inches from edge of table, set with friction hinges so glass can be lowered or raised as required; is very light and compact, can be closed up like a book and concealed in an instant.

Pipe Reflector. This is a genuine French briar pipe, with a reflector made of the finest imported Swiss flint glass, so ar-

ranged that the glass can be put in or out at a second's time, and the player can continue to smoke.

The above illustrations are sufficient to show the many ways of securing knowledge of what the other fellow holds.

B.

player shows his higher heart and is awarded his winnings from the pot. The two exposed cards and the two unexposed cards are then discarded and the next player looks at his cards and makes his bet. He has the advantage of memorizing the two exposed cards, the 4 and jack of hearts, and he can use this information to gauge his own possibilities.

Let us say the second player feels that the odds are against him—perhaps his three cards only give him coverage of two suits—and bets small, and indeed loses. His bet is added to the pot and betting passes to the next player. If at the completion of the deal, the pot has not been exhausted—often it will increase—the banker deals another round, and if necessary a third round. At this point the banker has the option of holding the deal for another round or passing the deal to the next player and retrieving the pot, which may contain more or less than his original ante. If at any time the pot has been wiped out, the bank immediately passes to the next player, who must ante the pot all over again.

Later players in a round have a distinct advantage, provided they have the ability to remember all the exposed cards. Overall, the real secret to winning at Shoot is betting intelligently, more when the odds are favorable and the minimum allowed when they are not. Some Shoot players insist it isn't all that important to try to remember exposed cards, that together with all the unexposed cards things tend to even out. They operate on the principle that they are in the same position as the first player who has three cards and sees a stock card with no previous information. If, using this outlook, their advantage appears to be 28 to 21 or better, they bet heavily. If it's less, they bet lightly. The exposed cards, they argue, might change the overall equation one, two, or three points, but not enough to alter their bets.

SHORTING POTS: Card-cheater's Technique

Probably the most common method of POKER cheating is stealing from the pot. This can be done in two forms. One is shorting the pot by throwing in fewer chips than are called for. The other is taking out more change than is correct. Such stealing may not seem like a big deal, but a half-dozen steals an evening can make a loser into a winner.

The expert shorter learns to strike at the opportune moment, when there is some distraction that causes inattentiveness to the game on the part of the other gamblers. The arrival of another player is a typical time for the shorter to make his move. And if a beer foams up, the shorter will laugh or curse—and steal.

SHOTGUN: Draw Poker Variation

Shotgun, sometimes called Pig Poker, is Draw Poker with much more betting and speculation. Each player is dealt three cards, after which there is a round of betting. Then a fourth card is dealt, followed by another round of wagering. After the fifth card is dealt, the game continues as regular Draw Poker. In Shotgun, players who hold a three-card straight or flush and would drop out on the basis of five cards frequently are forced to stay in on the hopes of filling.

In a spectacular form of Shotgun, appropriately called Double-barreled Shotgun, the game becomes high-low and there are four additional betting rounds; after the final draw players turn up one card at a time from their hand and bet. The pot, which can get huge, is split between the high and low hands.

SHOW FIVE CARDS: Seven-card Stud Variation

Show Five Cards is a form of Seven-card Stud in which players are dealt all seven cards down immediately. Players then arrange five of the cards in the order they wish them to be exposed to reveal their final hand. After a round of betting, the dealer on a set signal orders all players to expose one card simultaneously. After the exposure of each card, there is the usual betting sequence. The fifth upcard represents the final play and showdown.

The game is played high-low, and players may well constantly shift their remaining downcards to confuse opponents or indeed change their own plans of going for high or low as the exposed cards reveal the power around the table. A player might have a pair of kings and a 9-low in his seven cards, neither a crackerjack hand for high or low so he would figure to lay out his three lowest cards early to get the drift of the game. If several other players immediately expose three of a kind or a pair—which indicates high strength—the player would go for low and lay down his final two low cards. If on the other hand the early exposures indicate no strength or pairs, the player might on his fourth and fifth turns expose his kings and hope to steal half the pot on a high pair.

The catch in this game is that all participants are trying to confuse the others. As a result the exposure of cards can get very tricky, and a player could be sadly outfoxed. Bluffing too can be very effective, and exposure of three or four low cards can force other players to shift to high so that low occasionally will be won by a picture-high low. Tight players will however stay only with an eight-low, two pair, or sometimes with a very high pair.

SHOWDOWN POKER

Showdown, sometimes called Cold Hands, is generally a game of pure luck. It is frequently played by gamblers near the end of a POKER session, usually for a final round of play. In its simplest form there is only an ante at the start and then each player is dealt a complete Poker hand face up. There is no draw and the high hand takes all. In another variety there are two separate antes, the regular one for high hand and a smaller one for highest spade.

One version of the game allows for a bit of strategy by including a draw of up to four cards. Since all cards are faced up, this can produce some varied forms of draw. For instance, a player who holds two 3's, a 4, a 5, and 7 usually would hold the pair and draw three cards. However, in this open form he might see that another player has a higher pair or even three of a kind. Knowing that, he might decide to try for the inside straight, especially if he sees that no 6's, or possibly just one of them, have appeared.

Before the draw a round of betting is permitted, and if high spade is also being played, raises are also permitted in that pot. Dropping out of either pot forces a player out of both games, which can put a player holding the ace of spades in the catbird seat. And if the ace hasn't fallen, the chances of still drawing the high spade can suck some player in for the draw.

While straight Showdown is a good way for losers to make up some ground at the end of a Poker session, the draw version can be murder for them. Seeing additional bets with a weak hand late in the game puts them in the position of playing with "scared money." A player who is winning big should call for the draw version to press his advantage.

BENJAMIN "BUGSY" SIEGEL
See FLAMINGO HOTEL.

SINGAPORE, Gambling in
In 1963, Singapore joined with Malaya, Sarawak, and Sabah to form the Federation of Malaysia, but two years later Singapore pulled out because of tensions between Malayans and ethnic Chinese, the latter being the dominant population in Singapore. Only the standard forms of gambling were allowed in Singapore—private card games, horse racing, etc. Specifically barred was casino gambling.

When Malaysia started setting up casinos in 1971, the Singapore Chinese suddenly found they could tolerate the Malayans after all and they became the most important customers of the luxurious Casino Genting near the Malaysian capital of Kuala Lumpur. The saying goes that the balance of trade on the Malay peninsula is maintained by Singapore selling goods in Malaysia and the Singapore Chinese returning a hefty portion of the money at the gaming tables. That is an exaggeration, of course, but it does show the "leveling" influence of gambling between less than harmonious parties.

A unique Oriental gambling game very popular in Singapore is *Chap ji kee,* on which millions are bet every week. The operator picks a name or number from a list and puts it in a locked box. Bettors try to guess the name or number based on a riddle that the operator offers as a clue. The clue, which Westerners would probably find very obscure, turns the gambling into a genuine sport for the players, and winners are paid off at 100 to 1. The numbers game is well played also and newspapers carry the results. Payoff is at 700 to 1, which is better than the odds offered legally or illegally in the United States.

SIX-CARD POKER (DRAW)
Six-card Poker is not SIX-CARD STUD or Draw Poker in which a player can only use five cards, but rather it is POKER played with six cards, all of which count. Traditionalists may mourn the fact, but Six-card Poker is growing in popularity. Since it is very difficult to fill a six-card hand, wild cards are a must in this game. Generally the four deuces and two jokers are wild, making the game a 54-card game.

Rankings of hands are as follows: six of a kind (six aces would be highest), six-royal flush, six-straight flush, fours with a pair (such as four kings and a pair of 3's), double triplets (such as three jacks and three 9's), six-flush, six-straight (such as 10 down to 5 in mixed suits), and three pairs.

The highest six-card hand wins the game. How-

ever, should there be no winning hand utilizing all six cards, players discard one card and the winner is determined by the best hand in regular five-card Poker.

In Draw, this highly volatile game is best limited to five players since a four-card discard is permitted. With six players, the discards are shuffled and reused if necessary.

The art in Draw is to understand which cards to hold and which to discard—a situation that can be markedly different than in regular Poker. When a player feels he must discard four cards, there is almost never a reason for him to stay in the game (an exception might be staying with just two wild cards). Even staying with three cards is a borderline call. It is very difficult to fill three more cards in trying to complete a six-card hand.

Let us assume a player holds a pair of queens, one of which is a heart, a deuce, a 4 and two other hearts (not in a sequence making a straight flush possible). His choice is drawing to the four-card flush or three queens. Experts agree he should draw to the flush (and if he has a five-card flush going in, it is no contest at all). If he gets two hearts or wild cards to fill, he has a powerful six-flush. Equally as important, if he gets only one more heart, he at least has a five-card flush, and could win if the game goes to the five-card version. The three queens offer very little chance of achieving a six-card hand and even though it might improve enough to win a five-card game (improvement would be vital because experience shows three of a kind seldom stands up when this game goes to five cards), strategy must always first be geared to filling a six-card hand.

SIX-CARD POKER (STUD)
Six-card Poker (Stud) is an alternative to SIX-CARD POKER (DRAW). Players are dealt a total of eight cards in the usual Stud manner, six of which must be used to achieve a full six-card hand. Rankings are as above in Six-card Poker (Draw). Players are under the gun to get a promising hand early or they should drop out. Some tight players fold if they aren't paired, preferably with a wild card on the first two cards down and one up. Since a total of five cards are dealt to players going the route, it becomes somewhat easier to "read" many hands. If an opponent shows two wild cards or any three of a kind, it is time for most players to drop.

Overall strategy in the Stud version of this game, however, differs from the Draw. Players should play for a five-card hand as long as they see no overwhelming indications of power in other hands. Once they have the five-card hand they can worry about the sixth card. However, the lowest staying hand should be a five-card straight. Furthermore, it should not be bet with overwhelming confidence since a six-card hand can well be concealed by an opponent's three downcards.

SIX-CARD STUD

Some Poker addicts regard Five-card Stud as "pure POKER," and Seven-card Stud as on the wild side, but even such purists admit that Six-card Stud is an intriguing and demanding game of skill. The game is Five-card Stud with an added deal of a downcard and another betting round at the end. Thus a player has two hole cards and four up cards to create a five-card hand. The virtue of the game is that it opens up the action compared to Five-card Stud, yet still gives the disciplined Poker player a big edge. The strategy for gauging the power of one's hand and whether to stay or drop remains the same as in Five-card. Good hands in Six-card Stud are still hard to come by. Two pair is a rather strong hand, and, indeed, a high pair will win a good number of hands.

SIXES AND DOUBLE SIXES: Two Longtime Dice Bets

Sixes and Double Sixes are two dice games that have been linked for centuries. It would probably be untrue to call the 17th-century Chevalier de Mere the world's first dice hustler, but the record is clear that he was very good at his game, a simple one called Sixes. De Mere bet even money that he could make at least one 6 in four rolls of a die. He had plenty of takers, and he proceeded to take them for plenty. In fact, it got so nobody would play against him.

The good Chevalier switched to a new play with a pair of dice—Double Sixes—wagering that he would within 24 rolls come up with 6-6 at least once. Much to his surprise, de Mere discovered he was now a steady loser. It was only after he consulted BLAISE PASCAL, the great French mathematician and scientist, that he learned his ideas were all wet. Far from giving himself a nice edge as he had in Sixes, de Mere was actually making himself the underdog. Pascal determined mathematically that de Mere needed a bit more than 24.6 rolls to make 6-6. At 24 rolls he got the worst of the odds, giving up an edge of 1.27. While that did not seem like much, in later centuries gambling casinos could grow rich on that sort of advantage. Pascal advised de Mere to switch to 25 rolls or more.

Still today even many seasoned gamblers make de Mere's mistake and lose their shirts. In a famous New York gambling session in the 1950's a shrewd gambling house operator named Fat the Butch lost $49,000 at Double Sixes. Like many pigeons before him, Fat used the faulty logic that since 6-6 is one of 36 possibilities on a roll of the dice, it figured to be an even-money proposition that the number would come up within 18 tries, which Pascal demonstrated was not so. Fat the Butch insisted on a big edge and was allowed 21 tries. At $1,000 a roll, Fat was out $49,000 in 12 hours when he finally tossed in the towel.

SIXTH-CARD OPTIONAL: Five-card Stud Variation

For those who find Five-card Stud—the purest form of POKER—too limited in action, Sixth-card Optional may add the spice they are seeking. After the fifth card has been dealt and a betting sequence concluded, players are permitted to exchange either their downcard or one of their face cards for a new one. Then there is another round of betting.

This is a good game for professionals to play with poorer players who are incurably optimistic. For instance, the poor player who stays for the fifth round on chances of filling an inside straight thinks that his chances of filling are twice as good if he stay for the optional card after failing to fill on the fifth card. Actually, the odds on filling with the sixth card are only slightly better than on the fifth card. If he didn't make it on the fifth card his expectations are no better than they were, and actually can be worse if one of his cards turned up on that round. And in order to stay for the optional card he must cover all the betting and raises after the fifth card, which can be very hefty. In addition, of course, players holding two pairs or three of a kind can also improve with the optional card.

Sixth-card Optional is not a game for the unthinking gambler.

SIXTY-SIX: Fast-moving Card Game for Two

Similar to two-handed PINOCHLE, Sixty-six is a dynamite-fast gambling game for two. Only 24 cards are used, the aces (high) down to the 9's (low) in all four suits. Scoring is by melding and capturing high-point cards. The ace is worth 11; 10, 10; king, 4; queen, 3; jack, 2. The dealer gives his opponent and himself six cards each, three at a time. The 13th card is faced up alongside the remaining pack (the stock) to establish trump suit.

The object of the game is to score 66 points by taking the above cards in tricks. In addition, 10 points are awarded for taking the last trick.

It is also possible to announce some points in "marriages," if the player holds both a king and queen in the same suit. He must announce the marriage by displaying these cards and leading one of them to the next trick. A nontrump marriage scores 20 points, a trump marriage 40.

The nondealer leads to the first trick, but it is not necessary to follow suit. The trick is won by the highest card in suit unless trumped. The winner of each trick leads to the next after drawing the top card from the stock. His opponent draws the following card.

A key tactic in Sixty-six is "closing" the stock, which either player may do upon taking a trick, either before or after he draws. He does this by turning the trump card face down. Thereafter no cards are drawn from the stock and the last six tricks are played under the rule of following suit if possible. If a player cannot, he may play any card he wishes, trump or not. If the stock is closed there is no 10-point award for taking the last trick. Any player who has taken a trick may exchange the trump 9 for the face-up trump card, except if he draws the 9 of trump on the last card from the stock. In this case, he must keep the 9 and the other player gets the higher trump card.

After the final trick, players add their points for captured cards and for marriages. The first player to reach 66 gets a game point. If at that stage the loser has failed to reach 33 points, he is "schneidered" and the winner gets 2 game points. If a player takes no tricks it is a "schwarz" and the winner is awarded a total of 3 game points. If a player closes the stock and fails to score 66, his opponent is awarded 2 game points. If the opponent had not taken a trick up until the time the stock was closed but still keeps the closer under 66 points, he gets 3 game points.

A player may announce during play that he has 66 points or more, and the play is closed for scoring. If his claim proves correct, he wins; if he does not have the 66, his opponent gets 2 game points.

The first player to accumulate 7 game points wins.

Less satisfying versions of Sixty-six for three or four players follow this entry.

SIXTY-SIX: Stud Poker Variation

This is SIX-CARD STUD POKER with the 6's wild. Strategy dictates the game be bet much the same as Five-card Stud with deuces (or any other denomination) wild. Many players forget that good hands are rather hard to come by in SIX-CARD STUD compared to the Seven-card version. It is important that a player not think in terms of a powerhouse hand taking every pot, as can happen in Seven-card Stud with four wild cards. Wins in this game can occur with a lonely pair, while two pairs are fairly rare since if a player has a wild card and a pair, he actually has three of a kind.

SIXTY-SIX—Partnership

Partnership Sixty-six is a four-handed game using 32 cards, the 8's and 7's being restored to the 24-card deck. Players sitting opposite each other are partners and each is dealt eight cards in groups of three, two, and three. The dealer's final card is shown to indicate

trump, and the player to the dealer's left leads to the first trick.

Unlike regular SIXTY-SIX, each player must follow suit and with a higher card if possible. If he is out of suit, he must trump if possible, and overtrump if possible when another trump has been played. Beyond that a player may discard a different suit. There is no melding in Partnership Sixty-six, and there is always an award of 10 points for taking the last trick. The rest of the scoring (without marriages) is the same as in the parent game, and the two partners pool their scores. A side making 66 to 99 gets 1 game point; for scoring 100 or more they get 2 game points; and for taking every trick, 3 game points. If both teams score 65 points (total is 130), neither side gets any game points and 1 game point is added to the winner's score in the next hand.

Game is 7 game points. In a not-too-common variation played in some areas, if a side has 6 points and gets the 10 of trump on a trick during the next hand, it gets 1 game point immediately and play stops.

SIXTY-SIX—Three-handed

Three-handed Sixty-six is really a two-handed game in which the dealer on each occasion takes a turn dealing to the other two. The dealer scores as many game points as the winner on his deal earns. The deal then passes to the next player. Game is 7 game points; however, a dealer may not get his final point on his deal but rather must score it as an active player. If the two active players tie at 65, or both make 66 or more, neither scores, but the dealer is awarded 1 game point.

SIXTY-THREE

See CINCH—SIXTY-THREE.

Elijah SKAGGS: Crooked Gambler

It is inspiring when a youngster can settle on his chosen profession early in life and make a go of it. That was what a Kentuckian named Elijah Skaggs (1810-1870) did, but alas he decided as a teenager that he was going to become the country's greatest dishonest gambler. He worked hard at his craft and left such a mark that before the Civil War the term "Skaggs patent dealer" came to mean any practitioner of fraud or deception at a gaming table.

Before he was 20, Elijah had much of the card-sharping art down pat. He could deal from the bottom of the deck or "make a pass"—the skillful exchanging of the upper and lower parts of a pack of cards—and arrange the position of cards in a deck. He got so skillful that he managed to cheat his family and friends out of $2,000, enough of a stake that he could shake off the dust of Kentucky and head for

Nashville. There he won big and at the same time picked up more card maneuvers than he'd ever dreamed of. He studied other crooked gamblers until he caught on to their tricks. If he couldn't figure them out, he'd quietly proposition them with a substantial payoff to reveal their secrets. If they refused, he threatened to expose them to their victims. That got results, and young Skaggs was willing to pay up to $2,000 for card-sharping information. While that might seem like a lot of money to some, it did not faze Skaggs, who estimated no secret he had bought netted him less than $100,000 in the long run.

Skaggs was soon traveling the Mississippi making his gambling coups, but he realized in time that there were too many sheep out there for him to fleece alone. He taught his secrets to a gang of confederates and put them to work on the riverboats. In exchange for 25 percent of the profits, these crooks played honest with Skaggs who had the foresight to have them supervised by one of his relatives. He didn't trust a relative either, but he could survey the bottom line of what each gambling crew produced, and if one fell below standards, both crew and the relative would be pulled from their beat and shifted to leaner territory.

Skaggs's biographers assert that his personal income frequently hit $100,000 a month, especially after he began to operate crooked FARO games. By the mid-1840's Skaggs was a millionaire and retired, clearly knowing it was time to go. By that time, John Morris, a 19th-century biographer wrote: ". . . the true character of his games leaked out, and a cry was raised against them throughout the country, till the name of 'Skaggs patent dealers,' as they were termed, was a synonym for all sorts of frauds and dishonesty at the gaming-table."

In the late 1850's Skaggs dismissed all his crooked dealers and announced that they were on their own, while he himself turned to the life of a gentleman planter in Louisiana, boasting 200 slaves on his plantation. During the Civil War Skaggs made his own "sucker bet," investing heavily in Confederate bonds. At war's end he was impoverished. His spirits crushed, he was incapable of returning to the profitable gaming tables, he resorted to drink and reeled off to Texas where he died a few years later in an alcoholic stupor without a dime in his pockets.

SKAT: Germany's Favorite Card Game

Skat, which dates back to the early 19th century, is the most popular card game in Germany. It was carried by emigrants to other countries including the U.S., and is rated by many players as the most scientific card game.

Skat is a game for three players that uses a stripped 32-card deck, from ace down through 7. The suits are ranked downward from clubs (high), spades, hearts, and diamonds (low). The four jacks are the highest trump cards and are ranked by the same suit order. This means the ace of trump is the fifth highest card, followed by the remaining trumps, king down to 7. In the side suits all rankings are also from ace down to 7, except for the jacks.

Broadly speaking, Skat is like EUCHRE. It involves taking tricks, trump, and the use of a widow, called the "skat." Each player cuts the deck, and the low card deals ten cards to each player, in sets of three, four, and three. After the first three cards are dealt, two cards are faced down as the skat. The player to the dealer's left is called *Vorhand,* or leader. He is followed by the *Mittelhand,* or middle hand, and then the *Hinterhand,* or end hand. Whichever of these wins the chance to name trump becomes known as the Player and the other two are the opponents.

The leader is entitled to name trump unless another player makes a bid that the leader refuses to equal. Middle hand starts by bidding, and if the leader is prepared to bid the same amount he will say "I hold." If this happens the middle hand must increase his bid until the leader drops out of the bidding by announcing "Pass." Now the end hand has the right to challenge the survivor by bidding against him. Each bidder declares for a certain number of points, without specifying what he wishes to be trump or the version of game (there are 15 of them) he will play. When the bidding is completed, the winner must declare his game.

The Player may choose to play with or without a trump suit, with or without using the skat, or by using only the four jacks as trump. He may contract to win all the tricks to make his score or contract to win no tricks at all. He may also attempt to combine many of these propositions in yet another version of the game. All these versions have a specific name and a certain point value. The final value of his hand, if he makes his score, is based on the established value he has gone after multiplied by other values that derive from the cards held or captured and the number of tricks taken.

It can be seen that Skat is a complicated game with numerous variations. To play the game properly, Americans should study the lengthy Official Rules of the North American Skat League found in *Official Rules of Card Games* edited by Albert H. Morehead. One of the most definitive studies of the game in English is *Wergin on Skat and Sheepshead* by Joseph P. Wergin, which can be purchased from the GAMBLER'S BOOK CLUB. Somewhat harder to come by are the 1906 *Skat Manual* by R. F. Foster and *Sheepshead and Skat* by Walter J. Zarse.

A word of warning: it is always risky for an "outsider" to gamble in another ethnic group's game, since these players draw on an entire cultural affinity and understanding of the play. Play Skat with a German? Why not teach him POKER and let him squirm instead?

SKEET: Freak Poker Hand

Probably the best known of the freak hands in POKER is "skeet"—a hand of mixed suits that must contain a 2, 5, and 9 with an intervening cards bracketing the 5. Thus a 9, 7, 5, 4, 2 would be a skeet. Under some rules the two "in between" cards need not bracket the five, in which case a 9, 8, 6, 5, 2 would also qualify.

Where a skeet hand is permitted in a game it ranks below a straight and above three of a kind.
See also SKEET FLUSH.

SKEET FLUSH: High-ranking Freak Poker Hand

When SKEET is permitted in a POKER game the skeet flush is a powerful hand. It consists of a flush hand that contains a 9, 5, and 2 and two intervening cards between the 9 and 2. In some circles the rules are stricter, requiring the two in-between cards to bracket the 5.

Usually a skeet flush ranks below a straight flush and above four of a kind; however others consider it the highest possible hand, outranking even a royal flush.

Like skeet, the skeet flush has had fewer and fewer adherents over recent decades and some younger Poker players have never even heard of it.

SKEETS: Optional Spit-card Poker

Skeets is an unusual version of Five-card Stud. After each round of betting the dealer may call "skeets" and deal a spit card in the center of the table. The card is not wild, but each player may use it in place of one of the five-cards in his hand. When skeets is called there is another round of betting. The dealer may call skeets three times, after dealing the first, second, and third upcards. However, the dealer may also decline to deal a spit card at any time. Generally he will not wish to call skeets when he has good cards and considers himself ahead.

Obviously, Skeets gives the dealer an advantage and as such is not suitable for DEALER'S CHOICE—unless a player can get away with it. The only fair way to play the game is to have a complete round so that each player gets a shot at the deal.

SKIMMING: "Nontaxable" Gambling Profits

"To skim" is to lift off the cream at the top and leave the milk.

The language is "casinoese." The speakers are members of organized crime. The most beautiful word in that language is "skimming." And that ex-

plains why mobsters are the greatest boosters of legalized gambling. While hundreds of thousands patronize illegal gambling houses annually, millions visit legitimate casinos. The "take" in legal gambling is proportionately much larger—even with everything apparently run strictly on the up and up.

The tax laws require that profits must be reported to the government. Skimming makes that requirement a minor annoyance to the mob, which strips away its profits before figures are given to the IRS. The money can be skimmed even before it gets to the iron-barred casino counting rooms where tax agents are on hand to observe the count. Lou Rothkopf, for years one of the secret owners of the Desert Inn in Las Vegas, once boasted to underworld cronies that the casino in its first year of operation had a reported profit of $12 million—after $36 million had been skimmed off by various means.

With some ingenious flimflam, money can even be skimmed off in the heavily guarded cages where the accountants and bookkeepers labor. It can also be done out on the floor. Perhaps a "high roller" suddenly hits a run of "luck" and wins a huge sum, taking his winnings and walking off before the tax men can descend on him for identification. Such big payoffs have a double value. It takes large chunks of money out and at the same time is great advertising for the casino, luring in other customers trying to duplicate the "high roller's luck."

There is also a less spectacular way of doing it. Shills can be pulled off their regular duties and allowed to win relatively small sums, say $500 or $1,000, which they promptly cash in. They may do this a half-dozen times without arousing suspicion. Several casino shills doing this in the course of a day can get the skim up to meaningful figures.

The skim, as perfected by Meyer Lansky, is a work of criminal art—and it is virtually untraceable. Moe Dalitz, for years the head honcho at the Desert Inn, was unsuccessfully charged with income tax evasion in 1968. A few years later, Lansky and five others who had interests in the Flamingo were accused of skimming off $30 million, probably the understatement of the year, but none of the charges could be made to stick.

According to estimates made by informers, skimming runs to about triple the reported profits or about 20 percent of the handle, which is the total amount of money bet. This adds up to a monumental problem for organized crime because all these funds have to be "moved," "laundered," or "washed"—all terms used in casinoese. Then the money has to be stashed somewhere where it can be used in a way that will avoid federal scrutiny. Again, it was Lansky who showed the boys how the money could be funneled into secret foreign bank accounts. At that point, let us say, a front man is needed to buy a casino. He goes to a bank that can't swing the deal on its own, but remarkably a Swiss bank shows up with money (guess whose) to lend to that bank. The American bank lends the money to the front who then buys a casino—and once more the skimming starts.

SKIN: Fast-moving Card Game

Skin is an even-steven gambling game. It is played among American blacks and is popular today mainly in the South and, to a lesser extent, in the Midwest. The action is fast and furious and very similar to the Italian-American game of ZIGINETTE. Skin is played with a 52-card deck. There is a theory that the name Skin derives from the fact that there is so much naked cheating in the game.

Although Skin is a banking game, small clubs and sawdust joints don't bank it but simply take a cut of the winnings.

The cards are shuffled and dealt out of a dealing box. Players bet that their card will not turn up from the rest of the deck before the banker's card does. The banker deals out a card to the first player on his *right* who decides upon seeing it if he will accept it. If he does not, the card is offered to the next player who makes a decision. The first player is out of the game until the cards come around to him again. There is generally a lot of superstition about the cards in skin and some players will not accept certain rankings because they are "unlucky." In a crooked game this offers a fine opportunity for cheating, as will be explained later.

Once a card has been accepted, the banker extracts the next card from the dealing box and turns it up. This is the banker's card. If the card is of the same rank, the cards do not count. Cards are dealt until two different cards are. Then the first playing card is dealt. If it matches either the banker's or the player's card, that player loses. If it represents a third value, that card is offered to the next player as his card, so that the banker is now competing against two cards at the same time. Bets are made within a minimum and maximum range set by the banker, who can alter it at any time. Players already active in the game may also bet their card against any other player's card, so that there is soon a mixture of action taking place. Play continues in this fashion until all players lose their bets to the banker or the banker's card turns up, at which point he must pay off all bets against him still on the table.

When honestly played, Skin offers no advantage for the banker or the player—explains why the house does not bank the game. Instead, gambling joints supply a houseman, who acts as a cutter and as a lookout to make sure all bets are properly collected. The house profit comes in one of two ways: collecting 25 percent from the player or banker winning the last bet of the deal; or collecting a flat 2 percent on each bet won by the player from the dealer or the dealer from the player.

There are many ways to cheat at Skin. The dealing box and cards may be fixed as in FARO. And the house can trim the banker. This is done on the house cut of the cards through the use of STRIPPERS, whereby all the low cards are stripped one way and the high cards stripped the other. On the shuffle the house-man ends up stripping the deck so that most high cards are, for instance, at the bottom of the deck and most low cards at the top. On any subsequent cut the relative positions are merely reversed. The house has one or two plants in the game who are signaled whether the top or bottom of the deck contains the low cards. If it is the top, these players will refuse a low card and hope for a high one. If they get it and the banker gets a low one, they make a very heavy bet since the odds greatly favor the banker's low card being matched first. Similarly, other players will probably also get a low cards and the house plants will bet against them as well with the same sort of advantage. See also FARO—CHEATING; STRIPPERS.

SLICK-ACE DECKS: Cheaters' Cards

Slick-ace decks are used in sociable games much more than most players believe. These decks, available from gambling houses for a few dollars, make it possible for a cheat to cut to the card he wishes, usually an ace. After a bit of practice, the cheater can shove the cards slightly before cutting so that the deck "breaks" just where the aces are.

Some cheaters fix their own decks by waxing selected cards. After a deck is fixed, all the cheater has to do is "shove" the deck to find the breaks. Waxed cards will slide to a break.

Slick decks have other values, especially when the scam artist is dealing Stud Poker. He can determine how many other aces or other face cards remain in the deck. Thus if an opponent shows two aces and another player has a third ace, the dealer can shove the deck slightly to see if the last ace has been dealt. If it has not, he knows the pair of aces is not three of a kind and he can bet against his opponent accordingly.

The only real defense against slick decks is watching for the player who always shoves the deck on the cut—and as a precaution to do so yourself. If you find you are playing with a slick deck, you have learned something you can turn to your advantage— if you are the conniving sort.

SLIPPERY ANNE

See HEARTS—BLACK LADY.

SLIPPERY ELMER: Five-card Stud Variation

For those who find Five-card Stud too dull a game, Slippery Elmer provides a sort of "spit" variation that makes it more exciting and allows for an extra betting round.

To play, five cards are dealt and bet on as in normal Stud Poker. The dealer then turns up an additional card that becomes a spit card. All cards of the same denomination that are held in the players' hands become wild cards, although the spit card itself has no other role in the game. The spit card thus can alter the fortunes of the hand and, to reflect this, there is another round of betting before the showdown. The introduction of a wild card at the end of play is also a great "leveler" since a player holding two pair has much less chance of getting the wild-card bonus.

The pot builds very nicely in Slippery Elmer. Players with three-card flushes or straights have good reason to stay in although they would most likely drop in regular Stud.

SLIPPERY SAM

See SHOOT.

SLOBBERHANNES: Dutch or German Gambling Game

It is not clear whether Slobberhannes, a simple game very popular in Holland and Germany, originated in Holland or Germany. It is played somewhat like the French game POLIGNAC, but the four jacks have no special meaning in Slobberhannes. The game is played with the same 32-card pack, ranking from ace down to 7, when there are the preferred number of four players. When there are three, five, or six players, the black 7's are dropped from the deck so that an equal number of cards may be dealt each player.

The first player to the left of the dealer leads any card to the first trick, and the rest of the players must follow suit if they can. They discard another suit if they cannot. There is no trump suit in Slobberhannes. High card in suit takes the trick and leads to the next.

The object of the game is *not* to take the first trick, the last trick, or the queen of clubs. Taking any of these means the player loses a point. If he takes all three points in the deal it is a "Slobberhannes" and he is penalized a fourth point. The game is over when a player is charged with 10 points, at which time he must pay all his opponents the difference between his score and theirs. Considerable skill is involved in discarding when out of suit and when positioning oneself to get rid of the queen of clubs, or avoid being forced to take it.

SLOT MACHINE GAMBLING

It's a growth industry—undoubtedly the biggest one in the gambling field. No wagering game or device has grown as consistently as slot machines, and today many American gambling casinos could not make it without slots. While the biggest concentration of slot machines are to be found in such legal havens as Atlantic City and Nevada, one can probably find illegal slots in every state of the union.

The American slot machine dates back to 1887, when Charley Fey, a skilled German mechanic in San Francisco, invented a machine that took in and paid out nickels. It quickly became popular and was set up in saloons around the city. The house takeout was usually set at 25 percent. Since gambling devices could not be patented, Fey's idea was lifted freely. In Chicago, Herbert Mills began making machines for distribution throughout the country, and by 1907 he was known as Mr. Slot Machine.

Not surprisingly, the mob moved into slots and in the 1930's the biggest Mafia operator of the machines was Frank Costello, who saturated New York City with them. Each Costello machine sported a special sticker, which protected it wherever it was set up. If a free-lancer tried to install machines without Costello stickers (whose colors changed regularly), he would be subject to attack by the mob or to police seizure. Police officers who made the mistake of interfering with the operation of Costello's machines would suddenly find themselves on foot patrol in the far reaches of Staten Island.

Costello's hold on the New York slot machine racket was secure during the corrupt administration of Mayor Jimmy Walker (1925–32). Beau James was tolerant of almost anything Costello did. When the mob chief installed step stools at some of his machines so that the tinier tots could contribute their coins, the mayor probably saw that as evidence of Costello's love for kids.

Sadly for Costello and the mob, Fiorello H. La Guardia became mayor in 1934 and waged all-out war against the slots. Costello went into court to get an injunction to prevent La Guardia from interfering with the slots, but the Little Flower ignored the orders and set out special police squads to smash up the machines around town. Costello was shocked at such blatant disregard for the law, but eventually pulled his slots out of the city. He found a new location for them, thanks to an invitation from Gov. Huey Long of Louisiana, and he set up a slot machine empire in New Orleans. It was said Long's cut from the revenues mounted into millions of dollars.

When gambling was legalized in Nevada in 1931 the slots also enjoyed fast growth there. At first, however, when the glittering casinos came into existence, the casino operators did not appreciate the slots' full potential. The machines were seen only as a distraction for the wives while husbands moved to the gaming tables for some real gambling.

It was women who built up the slots trade, and are still its mainstays today. It is not unusual to see a woman playing three machines at once, and a casual visitor who unsuspectingly steps up to a machine that a woman is playing risks a broken arm if he dares pull the arm of a one-armed bandit that is in use.

Can the slots be beaten? Certainly not the illegal ones. For instance, the machines one finds in New York City generally have a payout rate of only 50 percent, which means a slots player and his coins are soon parted. The legal casinos, however, pay off much better, from at least 83 percent on up to about 98 percent on $5 slots—that's right, $5 machines! And now $25 and $100 machines are being introduced.

A revolution is taking place in the casino business and slot machines have become a staple in even the plushest casinos. The slots have established a lucrative niche that, in some places, account for as much as 55 percent of a casino's total take. This is certainly true in the smaller casinos in Nevada and is fast becoming true in the larger ones that do not have a sizable high-roller clientele. More and more casinos are catering to the steady slots player. There was a time when casinos worried about gamblers being annoyed by the noise from the slots. Now, conversely, some casinos are starting to worry about slots players being annoyed by noisy CRAPS shooters. For instance, the Tropicana in Atlantic City has opened up "Slot City Estates," a handsomely appointed area where players can drop their coins in peace and quiet. It's a slightly elevated section of the casino, plush and comfortable and featuring 165 upscale slots, all $1 and $5 machines. And there is a steady parade of cocktail waitresses ready to supply an endless flow of free drinks.

The sales pitch by the Trop is best summed up by Harry Hirsch, the casino's vice president in charge of slots: "We're giving you an area where the machines aren't all bunched up, not over in a corner somewhere. The aisles are 12 feet wide, instead of six. And instead of having to stand up we're giving you a plush velour swiveling seat with a back. Why should you have to stand at a $5 slot machine when someone is playing $2 blackjack with a lot more comfort? You deserve to have it, too."

It may sound incredible to the average person— and to the average gambler as well—but the Trop's $1 and $5 machines don't limit players to such puny bets each time they pull the lever. The $1 machines

Many experts believe slot machine gambling will eventually become the dominant game in casinos. The headway to date is impressive. Typical is the Tropicana in Atlantic City, which offers a handsome special section for slots players. All machines are either $1 (taking up to 15 per pull) and $5 machines (taking up to five coins at once). Plush armed chairs can swivel so that players can cover two high-priced machines at the same time. (Photos: Tropicana, Atlantic City)

can take 15 coins per pull and there are $5 machines that can handle five $5 tokens per play.

Traditionally, the higher-priced the machine, the better payoff it gives. In Atlantic City, casinos are required to give a minimum return rate of 83 percent on lots. Because of competition, the casino average is up around 90 percent and the $1 and $5 machines pay back at a rate of up to 98 percent. With a 2 percent takeout, playing slots actually becomes competitive in terms of odds with most casino games—and is far better than the odds offered at ROULETTE. This too is part of the slots revolution. Figuring very conservatively, at $25 a pull, a slots player can feed a one-armed bandit at least $100 *per minute.* This means that the casino is making at least $2 a minute, or $120 *per hour per machine.* And just to show how accommodating the folks at the Trop can be, some of the plush swivel seats are positioned so that they can move back and forth to cover two machines at the same time!

At the Trop and a number of other casinos big-money slots players are starting to get the same kind of special attention and extras given high-rolling Craps, Roulette, and BACCARAT players—complimentary rooms, meals, and show tickets.

Sensitive to change, the slots business is becoming much more high tech. A Nevada company, Electronic Data Technologies, has come up with a way to identify big slot machine players. Players are provided with a card that is "read" by the machine so that their frequency of activity can be measured. This active play is rewarded with cash—much like the airlines' frequent-flier program. By 1988, nine major Nevada casinos and two in Australia had installed the system. Four more in Nevada and one in Italy have orders in. Undoubtedly, more will follow, since the slots high roller represents the new king on the casino scene.

To further lure in slots players a number of Nevada hotels have instituted a form of progressive slots called Megabucks, in which machines are linked not merely in the same casino but from hotel to hotel. A number of incredible jackpots have resulted—in one instance it was $4,998,000.

None of the other casino plays—even no-limits Craps or Baccarat—can offer these kinds of payoffs, making the potential for slots, as some of the more astute casinos are coming to realize, unlimited. Emphasis is on offering every wrinkle possible in the machines, games at which to play BLACKJACK, various versions of POKER, and even KENO. Oddly, the casino takeout for VIDEO KENO is actually lower than in the real game.

Are there any rules that can improve a slots addict's performance? Even seasoned gamblers say there are, and these are men who in the past eschewed all machine play. Some tips from the growing legions of slots players:

At Video Poker, play differently than you would at real anything-goes Poker. If you get a pair of 9's, ace, queen, jack, kill the pair and hold the three picture cards. Most machines pay off at 1 for 1 on jacks or better and there is only a 2 for 1 payoff for two pairs. It is much easier therefore to draw an ace, queen, or jack than to get a second pair or draw a third nine. And there is a reasonable possibility of filling out the straight. Confirmed slots players will always opt for holding an ace and 10 in the same suit over a low pair. Bear in mind that jackpots are awarded for royal flushes and therefore strategy should be aimed at that. Chances of an ace-10 filling to a straight are slim, but the ace could get paired, or a flush or straight filled for a respectable payoff.

It is true that there are some slot machines that are "loose"—paying off better than others, simply because they are programmed to do so. For that reason, say the experts, you should always play a machine in full view of passersby. A machine in full view of casino guests lined up to get into an eatery that clangs away with steady payoffs impresses them. After they eat, they charge out of the restaurant or coffee shop and head for the slots section. Alas, they must go far into the inner reaches to find an available machine—where there are more tight machines than loose ones. Because casinos realize that many slots players work more than one machine at a time if possible, they like to bracket a loose machine with a tight one, so that what one slot giveth the other can taketh away. The non-compulsive slots player will not hesitate to leave a poor-paying machine. If he gets a machine that is paying off, he presses his luck on that one rather than desert it because the law of averages is likely to turn against it. Similarly, slots players who refuse to give up on a tight machine in fear that if they do the next player will step right up and score after they have set it up for him, are also wrong. Even the smallest three-reel machines allow for 8,000 to over 15,000 possible combinations, and the four-reelers run from 160,000 to 390,000 possibilities, while the five reelers can come up with almost 10 million variations. The basic rule of the slots pro, therefore, is that a dead machine is just that—a dead machine.

When visiting any Nevada town, check out which casinos the locals seem to patronize to play the slots. Through years of trial and error they seem to pick out certain spots for their action. Even if they don't win, they feel they do better there. Circulating around Vegas on a recent trip, I noticed that many of the off-hours patrons at La Mirage, for example, were "neighborhood" people. With this as an indicator I decided to try my hand at Video Poker (because I like to delude myself that I only play thinking-man's games, the only slots I patronize are those featuring Poker or Blackjack). After about 30 minutes of action with a machine that seemed to pay off quite regularly, I was ahead $30, admittedly no great shakes

DROP NICKEL IN THE SLOT.		
Rewards in 5 cent Cigars.		
Royal Flush (Ace, King, Queen, Jack and Ten of either Suit)	100	Cigars
Straight Flush (all of One Suit in Rotation, as 3-4-5-6-7)	50	"
Four of a Kind	30	"
Full Hand (Three of One Kind and Two of Another)	20	"
Flush (All of One Suit, Regardless of Rotation)	10	"
Straight (All in Rotation, Regardless of any Suit)	8	"
Three of a Kind	5	"
Two Pair	3	"
One Pair (Tens or Better)	1	Cigar

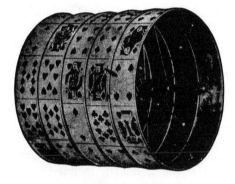

A.

Payoff list for an old-time machine quotes winnings in cigars but this was convertible to cash (A). The payoffs of 100 and 50 were purely fictional, as the unwrapped spindles of the machine illustrate (B). It was impossible to make a royal or straight flush and four of a kind was also impossible above the nines, cutting down the chances of that payoff as well.

but one that produced a much nicer feeling than one gets after losing at the gaming tables.

An additional truth about slots is that it's a myth that machines can quickly be adjusted in order to control the percentage take. To quote Walter I. Nolan in *The Facts of Slots*—probably the most honest non-shill book published on the subject—"It takes careful planning and strategic adjustments to change the percentages on conventional electro-mechanical slots." There is, Nolan notes, no magic button or switch that can turn a machine from a loser to a winner or vice versa. Of course, a casino will keep meticulous performance records on every machine, to make sure they are all performing properly. Another Nolan bit of wisdom: "It makes absolutely no difference how a player pulls the handle."

For years gamblers have considered the slot machine as the granddaddy of casino sucker play. Compared to Keno, the BIG SIX, and even games like American Roulette and many betting options in Craps

B.

it is fast becoming one of the smartest plays available, with of course a caveat on what that really means.

Frank Costello, where are you now that we need you!

SLOT MACHINE HUSTLERS: Two-armed Bandits

Despite the constant efforts of the casinos, the slot machine sections are haunted by hustlers pulling dodges on the public. At times in many casinos business is so heavy that players actually have to wait in line to get a machine. Thus, there has developed the "slot hoarder," a person who monopolizes two machines, playing very slowly until he is offered money to give up one. Usually there are two accomplices, one playing ever so slowly and another waiting nearby. He tells a likely victim that he is willing to pay for a machine and then proceeds to buy one for $10. The hoarder then offers his other machine to the victim, who if he is anxious enough, will buy also.

A classic story is told among slots hustlers of a victim who bought one of two machines—and on his second try actually hit a 250-coin jackpot. The hustler on the other machine was crestfallen until the eager victim offered to buy his machine as well for $20. "At least we took him for $30," the hustler recalled. "When we left he was plunking five coins at a clip in each machine. He probably lasted a half hour more."

So strong is the public's belief that slots can be beaten—and even tampered with—that many suckers will also buy a machine that a hustler tells them is "fixed." The hustler will inform the slots addict that he knows a casino mechanic who has doctored a machine, and that he has taken several hundred dollars out of it in the past hour. "Now we've attracted attention as winners so we'll bail out for $25. You'll win four out of every ten tries, and just hope you keep winning small prizes. One more big jackpot payoff and they'll shut the machine."

Remarkably, more than half the slots players approached with that spiel will buy. And hustlers can make four or five such hits every couple of hours. While they are doing so they are also on the lookout for other scams. Many slots amateurs do not realize that some machines retain coins for additional games unless the player presses a button to take his payoff. Hustlers pounce on such machines as soon as someone leaves.

Ironically, some slot jackpots are paid off only in part by the machine and the rest by an attendant. Some machines might only give out $100 in coins and say another $100 paid by an attendant. Frequently, some slots players will stuff more coins into the lucky machine and make another play, whereupon the balance of the jackpot is lost. Our ever-friendly hustler tries to keep the casino from enriching itself because of player ignorance. "Boy, are you lucky," they tell a sucker. "Take my advice. Take your money and get out of here. That machine won't pay off again for another month." If the unsophisti-cated player heeds this advice, the hustler waits until he or she is out of sight and then presses a button that summons an attendant for the additional payoff.

SLOT MACHINES—CHEATING

Call it "Slot Wars."

Historically, cheating at slot machines requires less talent than ringing in crooked dice to a Crap game or stacked cards into BLACKJACK. Even stealing chips requires more finesse. Then the manufacturers of one-armed bandits got wise.

Many would-be slot machine thieves take courses in slot machine maintenance at legitimate schools in Nevada and New Jersey just to learn the equipment's weak points. For a time various makes were susceptible to a number of cheating methods. A longtime favored method was "spooning," pushing a spoon-shaped device, indeed often a teaspoon, into the coin-return opening and wedging open the little trap-door leading into the payoff tray. In this fashion the machine paid off on any combination. Spooning was eliminated by the slot makers who put a couple of sharp angles on the pay chute to prevent penetration.

A special no-pay method of play was called "stringing," slipping a coin on a string or wire into the coin slot to activate play and then pulling the coin back for a free game. Another gimmick developed by the more chemically inclined cheats was to spray liquid detergent into the coin slot to get free plays. The manufacturers succeeded in halting these methods.

Perhaps the most common way of all was "rhythm play," which involved pulling the handle so as to force winning combinations to appear. This worked on a large scale for a few years after World War II when rhythm crooks discovered that some machines had wheels that made the same number of revolutions on each play. Depending on the skill of the rhythm player, it then became possible to control the number of spins of one or more wheels and thus insure a payoff.

Some rhythm players found they could control only one cherry symbol—but that was enough, since it guaranteed them eventual payoffs. For a time a group of these slot players, calling themselves the "Rhythm Boys," actually opened a school in Las Vegas to instruct players in how to beat the slots. Their fee at the time equalled the annual tuition received by a number of leading universities. And basically the pupils got their money's worth, a unique occurrence in the world of the gambling dodge. The rhythm bubble lasted for a few years and in 1949 it was estimated rhythm players took the slots for a half-billion dollars nationwide. A massive research drive by slot manufacturers finally paid off. They introduced a device called a variator that controlled the mechanism so that the spin timing varied, breaking the cheater's rhythm.

Today the biggest threat to slots comes from new techniques by means of which a cheater simply opens a machine, fixes the reels, closes it, pulls the handle and wins a jackpot. The method requires a number of conspirators who crowd around a machine while one of them, with lightning precision, decodes the machines's lock with a pick. The operation has to be swift because the aisles of the casino slot sections are patrolled by guards, change persons, cocktail waitresses—all of whom are watching for such hankypanky. Usually women are part of the crooked group and it's their job to break away from the group and stop any snoopers by sidetracking them, asking for change or directions, or claiming that another machine is not working properly.

The conspirators leave the casino and in a car outside make a key that will work on the machine whose lock was picked and any similar machine in the place. They then move back in, open and adjust a machine's reels and depart again, leaving only one person or a couple to play the machine, win and claim their jackpot.

One set of "CROSSROADERS" (casino cheats) in recent years was bossed by the late Glen Grayson. The gang was more interested in beating the CRAPS tables for huge sums, but the boys worked the slots regularly, averaging two or three hits for about a $2,500 payoff every couple of weeks. Besides the money, the slot machine hits were used to sharpen the gang's reflexes.

Slot machine openers have been countered in part by protective measures that cause a light to flash in a central control room panel whenever a machine on the floor is open. The hitch is that if the cheats move rapidly, they can open a machine and shut it before the light is noticed.

There are also advanced drilling scams, which people in the industry absolutely won't talk about. One of the most novel drilling scams in recent years involved drilling into a machine that takes one to five coins at a time. The more coins that are played, the higher the payoff. The drillers set it up so that the machine paid off at the five-coin rate even when they inserted only one coin. They played the machine on the square and had to come out ahead. They didn't win any more often than a regular player, but at five times the payoff, they stayed well ahead of the machine.

In perhaps the most high-tech development of all, some casinos now have computers that will record if the door of a machine was opened before a jackpot payoff. In a few known cases the casino's read outs showed that such tampering had taken place just prior to some six-figure jackpot hits. Still the payoffs

were made, sometimes inadvertently, sometimes deliberately. The official line, in the first instance, was that no one had noticed the readouts until a week later. Actually the real problem, reflecting the second instance, was that a casino faces the public's charge that it is "welshing" if it refuses to make a payoff on a jackpot hit. This greatly limits the effectiveness of this computer detective work—other than to identify the cheats so that they can be spotted in action in the future.

The "Slot Wars" never ended. Every scam the crooks come up with is eventually countered by the house, but the unquenchable dreams of slot machine cheats keep them in there trying for that big dishonest hit.

SLOW PLAY
See SANDBAGGING.

SMACK GAME: Matching-coin Hustle
Since matching coins is a popular gambling pastime, a description of the Smack Game is called for—not for the gambling elements involved but because it illustrates a can't-win contest in which a player becomes a hapless victim.

Frequently the Smack Game hustle is worked at train and bus stations, airports, and bars. Hustler A joins Hustler B who has already lined up a likely victim. They start passing the time matching coins for smokes or drinks. Soon they are playing for money. The game calls for each contestant to flip a coin with the odd coin the winner, such as one "heads" collecting from two "tails," etc. A replay occurs if all three coins come up the same.

When hustler A goes off to the john, Hustler B confides to the victim that A is a rotten individual and that they should take him when he returns. He suggests that they play for higher stakes and that everytime he, B, says he gets heads, the victim should say he has tails, and vice versa. Under that arrangement A can never win. The victim eagerly agrees to the strategy and they proceed to clean out A. It so "happens" that B wins most of the time and in the process collects not only from A but from the victim as well.

Hustler B and victim leave the bar in a happy frame of mind and outside B starts to split the winnings with the victim. At that moment A appears and wants to know what is going on. "You two cheated me," he screams. "You're a couple of swindlers. I'm calling the police!"

Naturally this shakes up the victim, and he tries to reassure A there was no crookedness involved. He insists, truthfully, that he didn't know B before the past hour.

"Well, if that's so" A declares, "I'll stand right here

and watch you two walk in opposite directions. Otherwise—" A starts looking around for a cop again.

B takes the opportunity to whisper to the victim he'll meet him in back of the bar in ten minutes where they will split the money. Much relieved, the victim marches off. He will show up at the rendezvous point, but B won't be there. He has already met A to cut up the victim's money.

Harold S. SMITH, Sr.: Pioneer Gaming Entrepreneur

In October 1985, "the last of Nevada's great gaming pioneers," Harold S. Smith, Sr. (1910-1985), cashed in his chips. Back when families rather than corporations owned casinos, Smith, an old-time carnival operator, opened Harolds Club in Reno in 1936. And so he became the first major casino owner in Nevada after gambling was declared legal in the Thirties.

Through the 1930's, 1940's, and into the 1950's, Harolds Club was the most famous of the Reno gambling houses. Smith and his family promoted gambling in Nevada as no one ever had before. They plastered almost every available barn wall and roof across the western United States with the slogan, "Harolds Club, Reno, or Bust!"

And the gamblers, male and female, young and old, came pouring in. They came in trains, in buses, in old cars steaming at the radiator. They even hitchhiked. Harolds Club gave them all the action they could wish for, even a game with live mice and numbered escape chutes (this was the hoary old carnival MOUSE GAME scam but Smith, it was said, ran it honestly, with no more than a healthy mathematical edge in his favor). The attitude of Harolds Club was that everybody could scrape together some money when it came to gambling and the establishment took people as they came—and with whatever they came.

The club is on what is now Reno's downtown casino row, surrounded by numerous imitators. In 1971 the Smith family sold out its holdings to Howard Hughes's corporation for $11.5 million, demonstrating what a good bet a casino can be.

Jefferson Randolph "Soapy" SMITH: Crooked Gambler

Jefferson Randolph "Soapy" Smith (1860-1898) may be the only crooked gambler whose gear for skinning suckers is preserved in a museum—Alaska's Pullem Museum in Skagway. Soapy was an incorrigible con man and gambler who worked every crooked con there was—from THREE-CARD MONTE and the SHELL GAME to marked cards, crooked wheels, and educated dice cages.

Soapy acquired his nickname from one of his famous cons. It involved selling soap to the hicks in the western cow towns, where Smith would stand on a soap box and announce that several of the bars of soap he was selling had a $10 or $20 bill inside the wrapper. The suckers would rush to buy, especially after one buyer, one of Smith's shills, waved a $20 bill and yelled he had just pulled it out of a wrapper.

A runaway from Georgia, Soapy ended up in Texas in his early teens, punching cows. He was separated from six months' pay by a shell-game artist. Far from taking it badly, he decided to learn the con himself, eventually teaming up with a venerable old con artist named V. Bullock-Taylor. When Bullock-Taylor died, Smith became the king of the con circuit throughout the West. He opened a gambling hall in Denver that never gave anyone an even break and recruited an organization that brought him virtual control of all the city's con games, including goldbrick swindles and phony mining stock. Later, Soapy moved his operations to Creede, Colorado, to get his share of the silver wealth pouring into the town. Smith became king of the rackets there with opposition only from saloonkeeper Bob Ford, Jesse James's assassin. Eventually, the story went, Soapy forced Ford to take him in as a secret partner. Ford was killed by a man named O'Kelly; some said Smith had paid for the job.

When the silver ran out at Creede, Soapy and his gang headed for the Alaskan gold fields, setting up in Skagway to trim the miners in his gambling saloon, robbing many of valuable claims. Soapy was too greedy to pass up any form of revenue. He set up a sign over a cabin that read "Telegraph Office" and charged $5 to send a telegram anywhere and another $5 to receive a reply. Miners flocked to send out messages and paid eagerly for responses, never learning there were no telegraph wires out of Skagway.

Smith's avarice ultimately ran amok. He took control of the entire town, naming his own marshal and judges. Thus no miner was ever able to make it stick that he had been gypped at Soapy's games. Finally a vigilance committee, called the Committee of 101, plastered up signs reading:

NOTICE
To all gamblers and bunco men:
We have resolved to run you out of town and make Skagway a decent place to live in. Take our advice and get out before action is taken.

Soapy laughed at such warnings and formed his own Committee of 303 to indicate his power. Losing heart, the Committee of 101 backed down. Then in July 1898, Soapy's boys robbed a miner of $2,500 in gold in a daylight mugging that sparked an instant reaction. With the leaders of the Committee of 101 in charge, hundreds of angry miners armed with shotguns and picks stormed into Soapy's saloon. Soapy tried to con his way out. The vigilantes listened for a time, then looked at each other and shot Soapy to pieces. Most of Soapy's boys were rounded up and what would have been Alaska's greatest lynching was avoided only by the arrival of U.S. infantry troops and the imposition of martial law.

When they buried Soapy, someone ceremoniously tossed three shells and a pea into his grave.

SNAIL-RACE BETTING: Slowest Gambling in the World

It started in France where they eat snails by the ton. In the 1960's the town fathers in the small Alsatian village of Osenbach came up with the idea of racing snails to raise funds for community projects. Snails, of course, are just about the slowest creatures alive and it takes a real expert to train a championship racer.

The idea caught on both with the French and the Germans across the Rhine, and today they pour into the tiny town of Osenbach in late April for the racing season. There is win and place wagering (the latter being the second and third finishers in the European style of betting) and bets can be made for as little as a franc or two, while the total handle per race can get up into the $1,000–$2,000 range. The winning bettors traditionally are rewarded with a plateful of snails as well. However, there is also considerable private betting for hard cash; $100 bets are not unusual and a bet of $500 has been recorded. Some breeders are very proud of their top snails and save them from one season to the next to bring home the bacon.

The champion snail was the Spanish-bred "Geronimo" who ran at a second snail "track" that has since opened in Murillo, Spain. Geronimo took the championship two years in succession.

Getting snails to move in winning time is no easy matter. Lukewarm water is sprinkled on the wooden course and on the snails themselves as flashlights are beamed on the creatures. This cons the snails into believing it is raining and lightning and that it is time for them to get out and romp. In addition, the town band plays loud music punctuated with loud drumbeats to simulate the crack of thunder.

For the students of racing form, it should be noted that the fastest time a snail has attained has been computed at 21.6 kilometers (about 13 miles) *per year*.

Snail trainers don't coddle nonperformers. Nonwinners, that is, snails who fail to finish first, second, or third, go straight into the cooking pot. Only the successful ones live to run another day. Horseplayers will recognize this as true improvement of the breed,

and no doubt would like to recommend some slow-running nags for a similar fate.

SNIP SNAP SNOREM
See EARL OF COVENTRY.

Jimmy "The Greek" SNYDER
See ELECTION BETTING; ODDSMAKERS.

John SOARES
See CROSSROADERS.

SONS OF HOPE: America's Millionaire Gamblers

In the earliest part of the 20th century—some would say the last stand of the freebooting rugged individualists—America boasted the richest gamblers the world had ever seen. Men like John Studebaker, Harry F. Sinclair, J. Leonard Replogle, Joshua Cosden, Harry Payne Whitney, George Loft, and others played POKER as it was never played before or since. Cosden, for instance, once raked in a pot of $875,000. Studebaker thought nothing of losing $200,000 in an evening of gambling. Known as the Sons of Hope, these and other highstakes gamblers played Table Stakes Stud with $100,000 stacks in front of them—for starters. A single blue chip might be worth as much as $10,000.

On one private railroad trip to Florida from New York, the game was wilder than usual. One of the Sons of Hope was sitting with a pair of kings back to back and bet $300,000 on his hand. An opponent with a pair of queens was contemplating calling when the millionaire with the kings had a sudden coughing fit and in the process blew over his hole card.

In the pregnant moment of silence that followed, the queens folded. The kings announced: "Dammit! I should have bought the Smith Brothers Cough Drop factory last week. This would have paid for it!"

SORTS: "Unmarked" Marked Cards

Sorts are identifiable cards that have not been marked in any fashion. The cheater goes through many decks of cards to come up with a deck of "marked" cards. Inevitably there are flaws on any brand of cards that features a full-back design bleeding to the edges. What sorters do is go through deck after deck—they regard it as an excellent investment to come up with one marked deck out of 50 or even 100 new packs—to find distinctive cards by the shape of the diamonds on the edges. Let us say a cheat finds three or four cards ranked deuce to 6 in a deck with half diamonds showing on each side. He will scour other decks looking for cards with similar distinctive markings until he has a complete set of cards from deuce to 6. He combines these with other cards featuring full diamonds on the rest of the cards and he has a beautifully marked deck of cards on which no doctoring can be found—because there is none.

The advantage of "sorts" to crooks is enormous. Imagine playing BLACKJACK and always knowing if the next card is under 6 or over 6! Knowing whether a card is high or low is also all the edge a POKER cheat needs. If the game is Five-card Stud, he knows if an opponent has a low or high card in the hole and can determine if the card aids or possibly kills his opponent's hand. In any high-low game that information is all that's necessary to figure out a majority of the hands.

Since there are no illegitimate markings on the cards, few average players can spot sorts. The cautious player automatically checks out any deck. He can do it during a game without giving himself away. As he discards, he can drop the cards "carelessly" in front of him and study their revealed backs intensely. If he notices any distinguishable differences between the backs of high and low cards and if he finds the same pattern on subsequent checks, he knows the game is "sorted." The player has two options now: he can expose the situation or, if he is the naughty kind, he might decide to turn the knowledge to his own advantage.

SOUTH AFRICA, Gambling in

The only legalized form of gambling in South Africa is horse racing, with the betting taking place through totalizators. Otherwise South Africa was, and is, very straitlaced. Gambling acts of 1939 and 1949 circumscribed virtually all other forms of gambling, declaring SLOT MACHINES and LOTTERIES, among other games, illegal. Although also illegal, private DICE and card games remain very popular with the minority whites in private games. Apartheid has long been ingrained in South Africa's attitudes toward gambling, and as one guide book notes, "All colored people are forbidden to gamble in any way."

The laws "protecting" blacks from the perils of wagering also have stunted white South Africans' recreational needs. Consequently they are drawn to casinos across their borders to do their sinning, particularly in black Lesotho and Swaziland, where they eagerly share the gambling tables with numerous blacks. Gambling has always had a political morality of its own.

See LESOTHO, GAMBLING IN; SWAZILAND, GAMBLING IN.

SPAIN, Gambling in

During the Franco years the Spanish government complained bitterly that the people were spending more than one-tenth of their total income on illegal gambling on bullfighting and cockfighting. That official sentiment hardly stopped the action. And after the grim Franco years, gambling has come back with a vengeance in a country that loves to gamble on anything—bulls, cocks, horses, dogs, and so on, legally or otherwise.

Card gambling approaches a national pastime and gambling casinos have been legalized in recent years and have sprouted up everywhere. Among the best is the Casino de la Toja at El Grove, and another is the Casino Castillo de Perelada, located in an imposing castle near Gerona. Visitors to Madrid need only go 17 miles beyond the capital to find the Casino Gran Madrid at Torrelodores. Besides the casinos at Gerona, Barcelona and the eastern coast boast casinos at or near San Pedro de Ribas, near Alicante, Valencia, and Palma among others. A visitor will have about as much difficulty finding a gaming table in Spain as he would getting a bottle of sherry.

SPANISH DRAW POKER: 32-card-deck Game

Whenever only two, three, or four players are available for a POKER session, some gamblers choose Spanish Draw and SPANISH STUD. These games are played with a stripped-down deck of 32 cards, aces through 7's. Strategies on the draw change considerably from the 52-card game, and the gambler who adjusts his thinking accordingly has a huge edge on other players who play the game like any other version of Poker.

For instance, the chances of filling an open-end straight improve considerably as does the improvement possibilities of a hand consisting of a pair. Conversely, chances of filling a four-card flush go way down. Thus, when a player has a hand consisting of a four-card flush and a pair, he should draw three cards, holding only the pair.

Five players can be accommodated in this game by shuffling and reusing of the discards if necessary.

SPANISH MONTE: Near-even Betting Game

Spanish Monte is at times referred to as Monte Bank, but it should be remembered there is another game of the same name that has some similarities to Spanish Monte.

The game, which is played mostly by Hispanics in the United States, is an even proposition in private play. A bettor selects one of four faced-up cards and says it will show up before one of the three other cards. Let us say the four cards are an ace, king, queen, and jack. The player says the ace will appear before the king. He places his money or chips on the ace with the king slightly covered as well. This signifies he prefers the ace to the king.

The dealer deals two cards from the bottom of the deck face up and then two from the top of the deck. The player makes his bet, and other participants may copy his bet or bet on any of the six possible combinations of two cards. After all bets are down, the dealer turns the deck face up and then starts dealing one card at a time from the pack. If the top card matches either the dealer or the player, that person wins. The dealer keeps taking cards from the upturned pack until all bets are settled.

Spanish Monte is most often played as a house-run game in private clubs in the Southwest. The house does not cover the action but only supervises the game for a cut. The houseman supervises the betting and makes sure all bets are paid correctly. If a player wins a bet on the first hand dealt from the pack, the house takes 25 percent of his winnings as its fee. If the dealer wins, the house takes nothing and the rest of the game is dead even. This works out to a house percentage of .0156. Some houses split this cut with the dealer so that the latter enjoys an advantage over the player of .0078. Without this slight edge, there would be no incentive for anyone to take the deal.

Other clubs demand a bigger cut; 25 percent of the winnings of the first player to collect is appropriated and split with the dealer. This greatly enhances the dealer's edge, and under these circumstances gamblers should fight for the deal—which is determined by a cut of the cards and passed at the completion of a game. In the long run if a player makes extremely small bets and then sets a high limit and, more important, a high-low bet if permitted, when he is the dealer, he can tilt the percentages in his favor. This doesn't mean the tactic will negate a bad run of luck for the dealer, but over time consistent play in this manner will result in a better return for the intelligent player.
See MONTE BANK.

SPANISH STUD POKER: 32-card-deck Game

Like SPANISH DRAW POKER this game is played with a stripped deck of 32 cards, minus the 2's, 3's, 4's, 5's, and 6's. Because of the altered probabilities in filling certain hands in a 32-card deck compared to a 52-card deck, player strategies are different.

Staying on a three-card flush is extremely foolish, and even if the player gets a fourth flush card, he is still in a weak position, especially if other players hold one or two cards of the same suit. On the other hand, a four-card open-end straight is extremely powerful. In a four-player game, such a straight with none of the missing cards showing has an almost even chance of filling. Smart play in this game is to bet into a possible flush but to check to the open-end straight.

SPIDER SYSTEM: Zany Roulette Betting Method

It has been used in Monte Carlo, as well as in Las Vegas, Atlantic City, and elsewhere. It is called the Spider System, whereby a ROULETTE player imprisons a spider in a match box that has been painted half red and half black on the inside. The gambler generally gives the box a good shake and after a while opens it, betting then on the red or black, according to the spider's position.

Not surprisingly, casinos tend to discourage the system. The Spider system gets a big play in Puerto Rico and other island paradises during the rainy season when spiders abound.

SPIN OR SPINADO: Variation on Numerous Card Games

Spin or Spinado is often described differently in various Hoyle-type guides and is played dissimilarly in various areas. Strictly speaking, there really is no such game as Spin, which is merely an adaption to a number of other card games. In some cases, these games are still referred to under their regular name. Thus it would be more accurate to speak of Spin or Spinado as Spin Pope Joan, Spin Michigan, Spin Boodles, Spin Newmarket, Spin Saratoga, and so on.

In all these games the Spin variant is that the ace of diamonds is wild, a factor that can greatly alter the strategy of the game being played.

In MICHIGAN, NEWMARKET, BOODLES, or SARATOGA, this means the player holding the ace of diamonds may use it to end any sequence he wishes. Then he can switch to another sequence where he holds a boodle card or to block another player's chance to cash one.

Spin is also adapted to the rules of POPE JOAN, and in other versions it becomes a less complicated version of the game with only three money pools: Intrigue, Matrimony, and Game. In addition to the 8 of diamonds all four deuces are removed from the game. In this Pope Joan version the dealer contributes 12 chips to the Matrimony pool and six each to Intrigue and Game while other players give three chips to the Game pool. The winner of a hand not only takes the Game pool but is not required to contribute to the Game pool on the next hand, unless he is the dealer in which case he must meet all the requirements of the dealer.

SPIT IN THE OCEAN: Popular and Varied Poker Game

There are many variations and alternate rules to Spit in the Ocean. However, the most widely accepted version of the game is a form of Draw Poker with a wild-card denomination.

How to play: After an ante each player is dealt four cards and then the dealer centers a "spit" card on the table. This card represents the fifth card in each player's hand and is wild, as are all others of the same denomination. The game is played like Draw Poker except that the players hold only four cards and may discard any or all of them to improve their hands.

Strategy: a special strategy is involved in Spit. If, for instance, the spit card is a 4 and a player is holding a 2, 4, 7, and queen, he has three queens. In Spit, three of a kind is not a powerful hand. Consequently the player will discard three cards, including the queen, and keep only the 4. That way he has three chances to pick up another 4, which would give him four of a kind. Giving up the queen means little since he will automatically draw another card for at least a three-of-a-kind hand. It generally takes a flush or better to take the pot in Spit.

In a tamer version of Spit, known in some areas as Pig in the Poke, only the upturned card is wild and others of the same rank are just ordinary cards. There are literally dozens of gambling games that are variations or descendants of basic Spit.

Some of these games, which may be called line games in some circles, include AMARILLO, BED-SPRINGS, CRISSCROSS, ELBOW, FIERY CROSS, HOLD 'EM, MUTUAL OF OMAHA, OMAHA, SEVEN-CARD MUTUAL, SPIT, NO CARD WILD, and WILD WIDOW.

SPIT IN THE OCEAN, NO CARD WILD: Tamest of the Spit-family Games

Spit, No Card Wild is the tamest of all varieties of SPIT IN THE OCEAN, and one that takes considerable skill to win at consistently.

How to play: Following an ante, each player is dealt four downcards, after which the dealer centers a "spit" card, the fifth card in everyone's hand. Unlike Spit in the Ocean, neither this card nor others of that rank are wild. After a round of betting, play continues as in normal Draw Poker with the discarding and drawing of up to three cards. There follows a final round of betting, and then the showdown. Each player still has only four cards in his hand and cannot escape the common spit card.

Strategy: Ideally, before the draw a player will be holding another card of the spit's denomination and be paired, but unfortunately many players allow the spit card to dominate their hands. Thus if the spit card is a 7 many players will hold, say, a 5 and 8, hoping to get a straight. The trouble with this is that other players are doing the same thing, reducing everyone's chances of pairing up. The smart gambler will view the spit card as nothing more than a kicker. If he does not have an opening pair, or a four-card flush, or an open-end straight there is little reason to stay in the game.

SPOIL FIVE: Irish "National Game"

A famous old trump game, Spoil Five is often described as an Irish "national game." It is fairly close to other trump-type games, but Spoil Five never made it off the Emerald Isle—mainly because of the eccentric play and card ranking.

How to play: Spoil Five can be played by two to ten players, but it is best as a contest of skill with five or six. Each player is dealt five cards and the next card is turned up to determine trump. The 5 of trump suit is always the highest trump, with the jack of trump second. The third highest trump, regardless of trump suit, is the ace of hearts. When hearts are trump the remaining values descend from king to deuce. When diamonds are trump the values run from the 5 of diamonds, jack of diamonds, ace of hearts, ace of diamonds and then down from the king to the deuce. When a black suit is trump, the values rank differently, descending from 5, jack, ace of hearts, ace, king, queen, and then deuce *upward* to the 10. Thus, with a black suit trump the deuce is higher than the 10 while in a red suit trump the 10 is higher than the deuce.

Rankings of the cards in nontrump suits also vary. For red suits the values go from king high down to the deuce in hearts (the ace of hearts is always a trump), and from ace high in diamonds. In the black suits the values descend from king, queen, jack and then upward from the ace to the 10. In plain suits this means that while the 10 of diamonds beats the ace of diamonds, in clubs or spades the ace tops the 10.

Once these rules have been absorbed, players may start the game. All players make an ante to the pool and then on each deal the dealer is required to add a chip to the pool whenever the pool is not won. Once the pool is taken, all players ante one chip to start a new pool.

The object of the game is to win three tricks while preventing other players from doing the same. When no one wins the three tricks (a "spoil") the deal moves left to the next player. If a player wins the first three tricks he can claim the hand and the pool unless he declares "jinx." This means he will try to take the two remaining tricks. If he fails to take them, he loses the pool and the deal passes for a new hand. If he succeeds in taking the spoil, he not only takes the pool but each player must also pay him the original ante again.

The player to the left of the dealer leads to the first trick and the winner of each trick leads to the next. However, rigid rules are applied to the allowable play. These are as follows:

1. If the turned-up card to determine trump is an ace, the dealer can "rob" it, exchanging any card

in his hand for it. The dealer must do this before the first trick is led. He places his discard under the undealt pile without revealing it to his opponents.

2. If a player has been dealt the ace of trump, he is also entitled to take the turn-up in exchange for a discard of his choice. He does this on his turn and his discard is handed face down to the dealer and not revealed.

3. If trump is led to a trick, a player must follow suit if he can unless his only trumps are the 5 and jack or the ace of hearts. The player is then exempt from following suit, that is, he may renege and discard out of suit. However, a player may not renege the ace of hearts if the 5 or jack of trump is led, and the jack of trump must be played if the 5 is led.

4. If a plain suit is led, other players may follow suit or trump as they wish, but they may not discard from another plain suit if they can follow suit or trump.

Strategy: Reneging is an important part of strategy in Spoil Five. It is important to save a single high trump for later use against an opponent who has taken two tricks. When it looks certain that a player will get three tricks, some shrewd players renege in hopes that the player will declare for jinx only to be frustrated when hit with the winning trump.

In a five-person game, three out of five hands are spoiled. In the vast majority of three-trick wins, the power is always high trump strength rather than high strength in nontrump suits. The best strategy is to lead trumps at the earliest opportunity and it is always wise to play the best card to a plain suit lead—provided no other high card has been played first.

There is a modern form of Spoil Five known as FORTY-FIVE that does not involve the spoil principle.

SPOOKS: Blackjack Cheaters
Gambling casinos have learned the hard way that they must watch out for "spooks" around the BLACK-JACK tables. Like FRONT LOADERS, spooks concentrate on spotting a Blackjack dealer's downcard. Under the rules in many Nevada casinos, dealers cannot look at their downcard unless they have either an ace or a 10-point card showing, which means the dealer might have a blackjack that sweeps the table. Since the dealer's upcard will be one of these two cards approximately two times out of five deals, this means cheating players using spooks have a chance of gaining an overwhelming edge in almost 40 percent of all games.

The key to spooking is that the spook does not take part in the game. He is, in fact, sitting at another Blackjack or ROULETTE table or even at a nearby slot machine. Blackjack tables are arranged in back-to-back rows so that usually the best position for a spook is in another Blackjack game. The spook is betting the house minimum, perhaps as little as a dollar or two or possibly as much as $5. His confederate in the important game is betting in the hundreds.

Blackjack dealers are instructed to peek at their hole card very carefully, shielding it from prying eyes. The spook has positioned himself where he can get a quick glimpse of the card. Most players find it hard to believe that anyone could possibly see the dealer's hole card, but spooks are highly trained to do so and need only a fraction of a second to identify a card. Many have sharpened their visual acuity with the use of a TACHISTOSCOPE, a machine that flashes images of cards for split-second intervals. A good tachistoscope-trained spook can correctly identify a card under casino conditions more than 95 percent of the time.

The spook signals the game player through a movement code. Naturally the casinos are acutely aware of the spooking play and whenever a Blackjack player starts winning big, the pit boss will start searching for a spook at a nearby table. Spooks generally avert suspicion by transmitting their signals through a relay person, someone completely out of position to be a spook. The relay person flashes the signal to the player in the big game, who never looks directly at the spook. In a skillful spooking setup, the housemen will finally conclude that the player is not part of a cheating operation but just having a remarkable run of luck.

STATE STREET CRAP GAME: Famous Mob Operation
The underworld has been involved in both legal and illegal gambling operations for decades. When it runs a game, one may be very sure of one thing: it will not be held up, or, if it is, there will in due course be the requisite number of corpses turning up in abandoned cars. Mob-run CRAP games are huge money-makers and the boys do not look kindly on any free-lance operations that disrupt the steady intake.

One of the most successful crap operations that ran for years was Brooklyn's State Street Crap game, which somehow never came to the official attention of the law. It was located in a building just off the corner of State and Court streets in busy downtown Brooklyn. No nickel-and-dime setup, it attracted men of considerable wealth and quite often police brass and politicians, in time making them beholden to the underworld when they took big losses.

The mob runs gambling setups not only for the vig, or cut, they take out of the game but also for the loansharking of designated "shylocks" who circulate among the players, fists full of money, making loans at only 20 percent—per week. The Brooklyn game demonstrated just how interrelated these mob dealings were. For instance, the shylocks at the game were agents of Abe "Kid" Reles and Pittsburgh Phil Strauss, the two most important hit men of Murder, Inc., the national crime syndicate's assassination arm. Reles and Phil were never paid for doing mob killings; their reward was the State Street operation. It has been estimated that the play each night exceeded $100,000—during the Depression years—and the shylock profits alone were $1,000 to $2,000 a night. Druggists, liquor store proprietors, clothing merchants, doctors, dentists, and shoe manufacturers were found to be paying incredible amounts of "or else" interest. In a manner of speaking, the crapshooters were bankrolling the operations of Murder, Inc.

When Reles started singing to the authorities in 1940, the State Street game was closed, a loss almost as troublesome to the mob as was the exposure of Murder, Inc. Still, the revenues from the game and from others started with its profits provided much of the money used to finance mob investments in Las Vegas.

STEER JOINT: Crooked Gambling Establishment

A steer joint is a crooked casino, or a supposed private game in a hotel room or private house. Here victims are fleeced by various means, such as fixed gambling equipment or dishonest dealers. But much as their victims pay through the nose, the steer joints are not nearly as profitable as might be imagined. Besides having to pay for protection, the steer joint coughs up considerable overhead in salaries for shills, the gambling cheats, and the STEERERS who guide the victims to the game.

Unless the house scores big on a number of well-heeled victims, it can become a losing proposition. Ironically, many of these operations often turn honest because it cuts down on their expenses considerably, since they don't have to hire the dice and card mechanics whose dishonest services do not come cheap. As an illegal casino gets known as an honest house, its patronage inevitably increases, with not only customers being guided there but also the locals, professional gamblers, and even their own dealers playing the games.

STEERER

A steerer is an agent, male or female, who "steers" a victim to a crooked gambling game or house. Often the steerer is a woman who allegedly is taking a male MARK to her room in a hotel. But then she mentions a private game where her mark can do better than at a hotel casino since there is no house percentage taken out of the pot by the management. That may be true but such crooked operators don't need that minor skim when the game utilizes fixed dice or various card-cheating gimmicks.

The steerer, who may also be a cab driver, bartender, or supposed chance acquaintance, gets a cut of whatever the mark loses.

STRING GAME: Carnival Hustle

"You have to win, folks, every time," the carnival pitchman chatters. "You pay your dollar and pull your string. Win a big prize and it's yours for a buck. You can't lose." And so suckers are drawn into the classic String Game carnival hoax. And, sure, everybody's a winner. Admittedly not all the prizes are big ones—many are cheap pens, flashlights, balls, and the like—but many are worth much more than a dollar. There are portable radios, wristwatches, even a small TV. The operator proves to you that you can win a big prize if you pull the right string, demonstrating this conclusively by tugging on all the strings in front of a collar into which the strings are threaded. This causes all the prizes to elevate, showing they can be won.

Now you pull a string coming through the collar and win—a nothing prize worth no more than 15 or 20 cents. But you are satisfied; you had your shot at a biggie. You may even be tempted to try again . . . and again . . . and again for a prize, but you keep right on getting the valueless items.

The truth is you can't win big at the String Game, because the operator doesn't believe in gambling with his money. The game is gaffed in a simple way. Not all the strings are threaded through the collar for the player to pull on. Only the cheapies come through. The ends of the string for the big prizes terminate inside the collar.

Yes, everybody wins at the String Game—especially the carney operator.

STRIP POKER: The Ultimate Gambling Game

There are those who insist that Strip Poker is the highest stakes game in cards, but that may be a matter of perspective.

The rules of the game are simple: the play is usually Draw Poker without an ante or additional betting. After the draw all players expose their hands and the worst POKER hand of all is required to remove an article of clothing. The game continues as far as is mutually agreeable.

One HOYLE-type guide suggests two basic rules for enhanced enjoyment of the game:

1. Play in mixed company.
2. Play during a heat wave.

STRIPPED DECKS: Pack of Fewer than 52 Cards

To pick up the pace of POKER and other card games without introducing wild cards, many players "strip the deck" of certain suits. Generally in a 40-card deck, the 2's 3's, and 4's are stripped. Still faster action is possible with a 32-card deck, which means removing the 5's and 6's as well.

In many gambling clubs in England Five-card Stud is played with a 32-card stripped deck, and for heavy stakes. In the so-called Italian deck, the 8's, 9's, and 10's are removed.

STRIPPERS: Special Cards for Cheating

Strippers are specially trimmed cards that allow gambling cheats to control almost any kind of game.

The most usual form of strippers are "belly strippers" in which most cards in the deck are trimmed about a 32nd of an inch on both the vertical sides. The remaining cards, for instance four deuces, are trimmed the same amount but only at each end, so they protrude ever so slightly in the middle—or at their "bellies." When a cheat wants to, he can square the deck on its end, and then pull his hand along the long sides of the deck and strip away the four deuces. Other decks are stripped with the bellies cut in. In other decks, *all* cards are trimmed—say, the low cards at the ends and the high cards in the middle. This is valuable in such games as ZIGINETTE and SKIN where it is possible to cut most of the low or high cards to the bottom of the deck. In BANKER AND BROKER the dealer cuts the deck several times to provide stacks of cards for several players and himself. In this game the dealer can control whether there is a low or high card at the bottom of each pile. (For that reason, in Banker and Broker, the dealer should not be allowed to set up his own pile. He

A "stripper" deck permits a cheat to pull from a deck whichever cards that have been trimmed in the proper fashion. In this case the aces are the only cards that have been stripped. (Photo: E. Gerard)

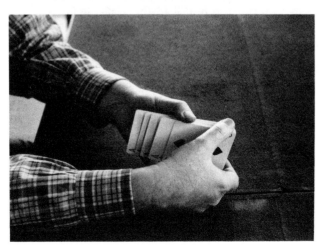

should be required to deal several piles and take the pile that no other player picks.)

The only sure way to detect Strippers is to check the deck or decks in play by squaring them against the table and looking and feeling the sides to make sure they are all flush.

STUSS: Faro Variation

Stuss, often called Jewish Faro, is a simplified version of FARO. Generally it is found in illegal gambling joints today, mainly because the layout and betting are less complicated than Faro, and gamblers seem to trust the game more than FARO. This may often be misplaced trust since all the cheating methods involved in Faro are readily adaptable to Stuss, and most certainly have been. There is no "coppering" in Stuss, meaning that unlike in Faro players may not bet on any cards to lose.

Overall, Stuss is a better game for the house. The last four cards in the dealing box are automatically retained and do not come into play. While the bank loses the opportunity to gain a 16-plus percentage edge on the last four cards, the rules of Stuss let it collect in other ways. The last four cards are turned over and if they are matched with any bets on the layout, these are collected by the house. Additionally, in "splits" (ties), when a pair shows on the same turn, the house takes the entire wager, instead of half as in Faro.

Like Faro, it is arguable what the house edge is in Stuss. Gambling expert John Scarne put it at 6 percent while others would probably make it higher. In any event, a 6 percent take out is enormous for a gambling game if the player entertains any hopes of beating the house.

SUBS: Chip-stealing Tactic

The next time you visit a gambling casino, notice the dealers' ties. They may be bow ties, string or leather ties, or very narrow ties—but they won't be wide ties. Dealers also do not wear shirts with French or ruffled cuffs. Reason: Many a dealer in the old days got rich by stealing $100 chips from the house and concealing them in a hidden pocket in the back of the tie. This pocket—or any secret pocket used to hide a chip—is called a "sub."

In many casinos a dealer also wears an apron over his trousers, which one would think is intended to cut down on wear and tear on them since they constantly rub against the edge of the table. Actually, it is to keep the dealer from getting to his pockets easily and dropping in chips. Some casinos even go so far as to insist all trouser pockets be sewn closed.

Nevertheless, all these preventive measures have not eliminated subs. Some crooked dealers sew two aprons together and use the opening in the double apron as a giant sub. It is best, however, to drop only one chip into a double apron; additional chips might click together as the dealer goes off duty.

Some ingenious dealers have been known to develop more imaginative Subs, such as wearing two pairs of undershorts sewn together at the bottom. The waistband of the outer pair of shorts is attached to the inside of the crook's trousers by velcro and his shirt is tucked between the two shorts, creating a super Sub. In addition, the legs of the shorts form two separate pockets so that chips can be dropped down each leg.

This information about Subs may seem of small consequence to the casino patron since the dealer is stealing from the house. However, many dealers are concerned about stealing so much that their table will net a below-average return. A crooked dealer will try to make up the house's losses by shortchanging the players on a payoff or simply "overlooking" an occasional winner.

Sometimes crooked dealers or croupiers may steal so much that they can't short the public enough to make up for it. In France in the late 1970's, a scandal rocked the Nice casino scene when 20 croupiers were arrested for stealing $4.5 million in chips at the rate of $4,000 a night.

SURE COP: Chip-stealing Chemical
If you can get hold of a crooked gambling supply catalog you may find reference made to a product called "Sure Cop" or "Check Cop." When the heat picked up on such gambling supply companies in the 1960's, the crooked ones dropped all descriptions of Sure Cop (or Check Cop) from their catalogs. But gambling cheats knew what it was: an adhesive chemical liquid that is smeared on the palm of the hand. During a game, the cheat may be very helpful when a pot is won by another player and he will shove the coins or chips toward him. In the process, a chip sticks to his palm.

Some cheaters see no need to purchase these preparations; they have their own do-it-yourself methods. They simply cook up a piece of adhesive tape and scrape the gummy substance onto their palm. It is just as effective a method.

SWAZILAND, Gambling in
Swaziland is one of the most recent nations to legalize gambling casinos. The Swaziland Spa opened in 1966 and did a thriving business from the start, with customers flown in by the casino from South Africa and Mozambique. First-class entertainment is offered the money crowd, which may be slightly out of place in a country where 46% of the population lives in absolute poverty.

The most popular games are ROULETTE (one zero)

and the Chemin-de-fer version of BACCARAT. BLACK-JACK has become very popular, so much so that there is action on the game during most casino hours, something that is not always true in some European casinos.

SWEAT
See CHUCK-A-LUCK.

SWEDEN, Gambling in
Sweden as a betting nation is far ahead of neighboring Norway. There is wagering on horse races, soccer matches, and the national lottery. Sweden was in the forefront of sports betting with such gimmicks as having bettors pick the winners of five games. Swedes are strong bettors on horses and there is on-track betting as well as off-track betting through bookmakers. Because of the long football off-season during the Swedish winter, betting switches to British soccer matches.

The Swedes are virtual trailblazers in betting on tennis, permitting bookmakers to do business in such places as King's Hall in Stockholm for matches. However, if the bookmakers want to shout out their odds they are required to remain outside the building.

SWEDISH RUMMY
See EIGHTS.

SWITCHER: Crooked-dice Manipulator
A gambling house stickman who can replace legitimate dice for crooked ones is known in the trade as a "switcher." A crooked gambling joint will employ a switcher as a stickman in what is normally an honest game. If the house is having a bad run, the switcher will be signaled to put in some "six-ace flats" for a time. These are percentage dice that allow any number to be thrown but not in the correct percentages, and seriously cut down the chances of "right" bettors.

Ten or 12 games with these crooked dice will generally put the house in the black again, and the switcher will get the signal to go back to the honest cubes. In very special situations after a big bettor makes his point, the switcher might get instructions to put in some "bust-out" dice on which certain numbers cannot be rolled. For instance, let's say the shooter's point is 10. When bust-outs are put in the game, the 10 is impossible to roll. One die will have two 1's, two 2's, and two 3's. The other die will have two 4's, two 5's, and two 6's. Shooting these dice the 10-point cannot be made and the 7 will inevitably come up very quickly, usually within a roll or two. The shooter loses. Bust-outs are not easily spotted if they are left in a game only for a few rolls. Unless one has a mirror to view dice from the far side only, legitimate numbers will be visible to any onlooker—that is, every number from 1 to 6.

A good switcher knows how to get bust-outs in and out of a game rapidly. He rakes in the legitimate dice with his long curved stick after they have rolled against the board, picks them up and makes the switch. He then tosses the shooter the crooked dice. Once the shooter loses, the switcher deftly rakes in the dice and just as deftly brings the honest dice back into play. In the heat of the game, it would take an unusually cool bettor to detect the switch.

One story often told among crooked gambling-house operators concerns a switcher who was brought into a Saratoga, New York joint. The proprietor hired him on reputation alone. Because the switcher arrived late in the evening, there was no time for the casino owner to "audition" his man. He threw him right into action. The owner himself took up the payoff post, and it wasn't long before a high roller came along and plunked down a $2,000 bet. After the big bettor rolled his point, the owner signaled a switch and the switcher immediately put in bust-outs. He was so good at his move that the owner never noticed the switch being made. The shooter rolled and did not 7 out immediately. The owner panicked, figuring the switcher had not picked up his signal. He signaled again. The switcher picked up the signal and, although it didn't make sense to him, followed orders and put the honest dice back in the game.

The shooter made his point and walked out with the house's $2,000. The angry owner called the switcher into his office, read him out and fired him. The switcher denied missing the signal and said he had put the bad dice in and taken them out when he got the second signal. "Listen, when I switch dice, nobody can see my action," he said.

He then demonstrated how he had done it and the awed owner never spotted a thing. This did not, however, get him his job back. "You're fired anyway," the owner declared. "When anybody switches dice in my game—I want to know it."

SWITZERLAND, Gambling in

You have a better chance of going snow-blind in Switzerland than of losing your money gambling. The Swiss are more interested in sure things, like getting interest on money in the bank. At least that's the way it goes for the Swiss in Switzerland.

It is illegal to operate a private lottery or to run a casino in Switzerland, and you won't find the gambling machines that are common in German bars and cafes.

The exception to the gambling law is BOULE, a bald-faced swindle common in France. The French version of Boule is an outrage, with an 11.1111 percent rake-off. That is based on paying on numbers at 7 to 1 instead of true odds of 8 to 1. The Swiss Boule rooms (sometimes called casinos, but actually part of a restaurant, nightclub, cafe, or conference center complex) cut the payoffs of 6 to 1 on the numbers so that the house edge is 22.2222.

Still, it's hard to fault the Swiss attitude about gouging on Boule since the government takes about a quarter of all profits to help victims of national catastrophes such as avalanches, floods, fires, or train crashes. Football (soccer) pools are legal and LOTTERIES are run in various cantons, but their profits then go to charity and public works.

Switzerland, with all that numbered-account money floating around, is virtually surrounded by casinos on its borders with Austria, France, Germany, and Italy. Campione, on an Italian island next to Lugano, is a veritable a Swiss colony. The restaurants and cafes on Campione quote their prices in Swiss currency, the public telephone operates with Swiss coins, and the casino gambling is conducted with Swiss money. Divonne, not the best known of all the French casinos, is about 11 miles from Geneva, and frequently does the biggest annual business of any French casino, topping Cannes, Deauville, and, one suspects, possibly even Monte Carlo.

SYSTEMS

See BETTING SYSTEMS.

T

TABLE STAKES: Optional Poker Rule

In Table Stakes (or Freeze-Out) POKER, each player may only bet the amount of chips he has on the table at the beginning of a hand. Usually there is a requirement at the start of a game as to the minimum that must be put on the table (sometimes, although rarely, there is also a maximum). Table Stakes sometimes works in favor of the player and sometimes against him. Player A can assess the number of chips Player B has and then decide if he should be afraid of his hand. If Player B does not have too many chips, Player A does not have to "respect" him too much, even if his hand looks powerful, since Player B cannot bet more than he has on the table. As a result, it is wise to keep a fair amount of chips on the table and add to it if necessary before a hand. In that way the player protects himself in the event he gets a powerhouse hand. He is also open to heavy betting against him since an opponent can announce "I tap you," meaning he is betting all his opponent has on the table.

Even though a player may run out of chips, he cannot be forced out of the game entirely. If a number of players still want to bet more, they set up a subsidiary, or side, pot. The player who has "tapped out" continues to get his cards and competes for the original pot only. Thus, it is conceivable to have two winners—the tapped-out player taking the original pot and the highest hand of the remaining players taking the side pot.

See also TAPPING OUT.

TACHISTOSCOPE: Card-cheater's Training Device

Every gambling cheat is so devoted to his technique that he will study endlessly to perfect his scam, card manipulation, or whatever. Card spotters, whose specialty is to sneak peaks at opponents' cards, are just as dedicated. Casino "front loaders," who try to position themselves to get a look at a BLACKJACK dealer's downcard, have only a brief moment to see the card as the dealer perhaps raises it a fraction too high before slipping it under his upcard. It is not easy to read a card with only that sort of quick glance. This is similarly true with POKER players in private games. Few will expose their hands completely but will often inadvertently expose a new card as they put it in their hand, again only for an instant.

A good card spotter is attuned to that moment to what appears to other players with untrained eyes as a mere blur. Card spotters, and especially front loaders, practice for hours learning to identify cards when they get only a brief look at them. Many train themselves with a tachistoscope, a machine that flashes images at split-second intervals. In time a spotter can learn to identify a 4 of diamonds, a jack of spades, or an 8 of hearts when they are seemingly not even exposed, while another player will see absolutely nothing given the same opportunity.

See FRONT LOADERS; SPOOKING.

TAKE IT OR LEAVE IT: Five-card Stud Variation

Take It or Leave It, sometimes called Push or Forward Pass, is a form of Five-card Stud. A good DEALER'S CHOICE game, it offers a built-in advantage for the dealer at the end of the game.

The principle of Take It or Leave It is to dispose of unwanted cards by pushing them along to the player to the left. Each player is dealt one card down as in normal Five-card Stud, but then the leader, or first player, is dealt an upcard. He has the option of keeping that card or passing it on to the next player. If he passes it on, he is dealt another face up card that he must keep. The second player then decides if he wants the face card he's received or he can opt for a new one from the deck by passing along the card himself. If a player does not get a card passed forward, he gets a card from the deck and may keep that card or pass it along and get a new card. When the cards reach the dealer he can take his first face card or simply throw it out of the game and take a new card.

After each round there is a betting session, as in Five-card Stud. After the fifth card is dealt and betting finished, all players have a right to discard their hole card and draw another from the deck. At this stage that the dealer has a distinct advantage because he draws after seeing what all the other players are up to. The leader, having to draw first, is at the greatest disadvantage. Because the game favors the dealer at the draw stage, a player should try to call it for his own deal. But if the player at his right calls it, he should drop out after the first face card unless he gets a pair, in which case he can remain in the game as long as he beats the board in so far as the other players' up cards are concerned. The game is often played high-low, so the leader should consider staying on a good low hand as well, especially with an ace in the hole and a low card up. While the dealer enjoys an advantage on the final draw in high-low, he should, if he can, call the game strictly for high since that allows him to "read" more easily the draw action of the other players.

TAPPING OUT: Poker Betting Rule

Tapping out occurs when a POKER player has put all his table money or chips into the pot and is unable to bet further. Under the rules, the player is permitted to play for the pot as it exists up till then with all additional bets by other players going into a side pot, with the high hand among them taking that pot. The tapped-out player remains in contention for the original pot and if he has the top hand among all the players, he wins that pot.

The rule is not popular with all Poker players, many of whom feel some gamblers abuse the tapping-out feature to stay out of a big-betting sequence while remaining safely in the game. Some tapped-out players have a knack for leaving the table after losing and returning shortly, claiming to have borrowed some money. To cut down on this ploy, a general rule is that a player is allowed only one tap-out during an entire Poker session.
See also TABLE STAKES.

TEAR-UP

See HOT SEAT GAME.

TEN: Ancient Dice Game

Ten can be traced back to the Roman Empire. Perhaps the most popular of their dice games, it is, according to some experts, probably the game the soldiers played for Christ's garments at His crucifixion.

Played with three dice, Ten has very simple rules. Any number can play and each player in turn becomes the banker for a game. One of the players, usually to the left of the banker, throws the dice. If the total of the three dice is less than 10, he and all other players lose their wagers against the bank. If the total is 10 or more, the banker loses and must pay off all bets.

Under these rules, the players will wipe out the banker over the long haul. While there are 81 ways to make the points of 3 through 9, there are 135 possibilities to roll 10 or more. To make the game even, the total of 10 would have had to be shifted to the banker's favor, offering 108 possibilities for the banker and 108 against.

The Romans hadn't the benefit of the science of probability. Yet even after the mathematics of the games were clearly spelled out, the addiction to Ten continued. Spread by Caesar's legions into Gaul, the game prospered as Passe-dix into modern times. In Italy the game is called Talus, in Turkey Zarf, and in Britain, Spot, Dicey, Roll-ten, or Birdie. Just as CRAPS is the American national dice game, Ten, or Passe-dix, is a favorite throughout much of Europe. While American soldiers in World War II played Craps, French and British soldiers played Ten.

Today some sophisticates insist on shifting the 10 score to the banker, but more games are played among friends under the original skewed terms. In theory, the fact that the banker role shifts on each game should equalize matters, but hustlers can always find a way to keep the edge as a player. In a cafe in Belgium (dice box and dice are kept on the counter in most Belgian cafes for the convenience of patrons) a waiter had the tactic down to a fine art. Since he could not sit down and play, he obviously could not be banker. Instead he jumped into a game whenever he passed the table, doubling his bet after a loss. In the end he had to come out far ahead, with odds of 135 to 81 in his favor.

TEN-CARD STUD: "Freak" Poker

Ten-card Stud represents the ultimate in silly POKER. It is played according to the rules of Seven- or Eight-card Stud, usually with two cards down, followed by six up-cards, dealt one at a time, and then two more downcards. It is impossible to get much of a handle on opponents' hands, and the value of the winning hand can vary widely although with ten cards, straights and flushes turn up very often. The game is often played by children with little or no betting. Gamblers who are always on time often play Ten-card for nickel-and-dime limits while awaiting the arrival of others. However, some gamblers refuse to play in these "warm-up" games, claiming the blizzard of cards tends to cloud their grasp of probabilities once they get down to serious Poker.

TENNIS GAMBLING

Tennis, many gambling experts contend, is the coming sport for real betting action, even though it violates the one human vs. one human element that gamblers traditionally shy away from. (There is a great misapprehension that BOXING is a big betting sport; it is not.)

As tennis gains in popularity, interest in betting on the matches increases. The possibility of tennis wagering extends to other countries as well. Some French bookmakers will work up odds now on matches at the Tennis Club de Paris for a steady client. Sweden has allowed bookmakers on the premises of Stockholm's King's Hall, although if they wish to shout out the odds they are required to remain outside. In England, a bookmaker has even applied for permission to set up for business at Wimbledon. The request was turned down by the English Lawn Tennis Association, but eventually the organization may have to alter its stand.

Part of the reason for this has been the Las Vegas sports books, which recently have shown interest in the game. Vegas's initial interest was sparked by an event that was really only a hustle, by that sublime hustler Bobby Riggs. In the early 1970's Riggs, long over the hill for men's competition, came up with the wild idea of challenging the top women players. First he took on Margaret Court in a singles match and defeated her in what he and the press labeled the "Battle of the Sexes." What Riggs did was psych Court out with all sorts of upsetting or off-putting tactics, the last of which was showing up on the court with a bunch of roses for his opponent. Court was so flustered that she lost her cool and was beaten by the aging Riggs.

Immediately there was great interest in Riggs and his challenge to the leading female player of the day, Billie Jean King. Arguments raged over whether he could beat her because of the superior physical strength of a male player over a female, especially when Riggs threw in his psych-out tactics. Bookmakers could not resist grabbing the hot action and Riggs was established as a 5 to 2 favorite.

In the end the psyching out was done by King who appeared on court riding a litter carried by male "slaves," carrying under her arm a "male chauvinist piglet," which represented Riggs. In the match King proceeded to take apart Riggs's game and won with ease. However, Riggs had gained new fame and fortune from the exposure and, incidentally, had put tennis on the gambling map. Even though the bookies were wrong in their judgment of the Riggs-King

match, they found they had tapped a gambling lode, one that lured in people who never bet on other sporting contests. It's 10 to 1 that there will be more wagering on tennis ten years down the pike than there is now.

TENS HIGH DRAW: "Thinking Man's Silly Poker"

The "Thinking Man's Silly Poker," Tens High Draw is a seemingly wild game that is actually a strategic one—especially when played in DEALER'S CHOICE. The rules are simple enough: Any hand of a pair of 10's or higher is disqualified. The winner holds the highest hand remaining. Thus a pair of 9's is the highest possible hand, and in fact any low pair can be considered a genuine power. In a variation of the game, two pairs, three of a kind, or even four of a kind are permitted, provided the cards are all below 10 value. Straights and flushes are not permitted in this version.

In the basic game, players with low pairs avoid the draw and stand pat. If they hold a low pair and a high pair they are forced to discard the high pair and run the risk of pairing high again, or picking up a second pair, or adding to their original low pair, all of which will cause them to lose. Players holding no pairs generally hold their low cards and discard the others, but they must take care not to hold four cards towards a straight, since filling would cause them to lose.

The dealer enjoys a slight advantage by being able to judge the strength of other players by their discards. If no player stands pat—indicating they do not have a low pair—and the dealer holds an ace, he may stand pat in hope of winning the pot with the high card. He has a reasonably good change of doing so, especially if there are no more than three opponents remaining in the game.

In the more complicated version in which two low pairs, etc., are permitted, a player may try to improve his low pair, but must take care to do it in a way that does not risk getting a high pair hand. Thus a player holding a pair of 8's and a king, queen, jack is forced to stand pat since drawing three cards (or even one or two cards) could produce a high pair. If, on the other hand, the three cards accompanying the pair of 8's are 4, 9, and king, he can safely discard the king and hope for another 8, 4, or 9. It is important to remember that a low pair is quite powerful to begin with and no risk is worth taking that could jeopardize such a hand.

THAILAND, Gambling in

In the 20th century Thailand has been ambivalent on gambling activities, outlawing such games as SLOT MACHINES, BACCARAT, BINGO, and POKER, but allowing betting on horse races, LOTTERIES, DOMINOES,

MAH-JONGG, and even fish fighting. Oddly, the country outlawed gambling on "sports" involving cruelty to animals, such as TORTOISE RACING (in which fires are set on the animals' backs to hurry them along), but permits betting on COCKFIGHTING.

THANATOPSIS LITERARY AND INSIDE STRAIGHT CLUB

One of the most storied groups of gamblers in America was the Thanatopsis Literary and Inside Straight Club. This group of literary lights and men of letters played a wicked game of POKER in New York City every Friday night from the 1920's to the 1940's. The game was for high stakes and played cutthroat, but probably the most important contribution participants were required to make to the game was scintillating humor and wit, easy for a group that included Franklin P. Adams, Bob Benchley, Heywood Broun, and Harpo Marx.

On that point Adams (F.P.A.) was always in the forefront. One sunny Saturday morning at 11 o'clock, as the members of the club staggered out to the street unshaven and red-eyed, Adams spotted a young cherub in the care of his governess. Shaking his head, he boomed out to his fellow gamblers so that the governess could hear: "Imagine, keeping a child that age out until this hour!"

THIRD-HAND HIGH POKER

Generally a DEALER'S CHOICE game, Third-hand High Poker has recently enjoyed a growth in popularity among serious gamblers. Perhaps the best version is played in Five-card Stud. The third highest hand wins the pot; the two highest hands are eliminated. Since in the five-card format, players get to see four of their opponents' cards, they can get a handle on relative strengths. Usually a player with an extremely weak hand will tend to drop out early, often a sad mistake since paired hands and even the appearance of an ace will cause other players to fold. The game is best when played with seven or eight players, and frequently by the fifth card only two or three players remain making the lowest hand the winning one.

Third-hand High has betting strategies all its own, and players who master them earn an enormous advantage. One general rule: when a player has four cards and is low on board, he should bet aggressively to force other players out. If he maintains his low position with the fifth card, he should bet even heavier. Despite the name of the game, low hand usually ends up top dog.

One seasoned player reports he often calls the game on every round at Dealer's Choice and wins 40 percent of the time, an impressive statistic in a seven-player game, especially allowing for paired hands that force an immediate dropout. Chances are the player is exaggerating a bit when he claims a 40-percent win record, but once a gambler latches onto a successful gambit, he sees it as a wonder of the ages.

THIRTY AND FORTY (TRENTE ET QUARANTE): High-stakes Casino Game

Trente et Quarante, or Thirty and Forty, is a French card game that is very popular in Monte Carlo, some of the larger French casinos, and most especially in the Italian casinos. Like BACCARAT, Thirty and Forty is a game of pure chance with players having no options but to place bets, all of which are even-money affairs.

Six packs of cards are mixed together. The ace counts for 1, all numbered cards have their equivalent point number and all picture cards are 10. The croupier or dealer (tailleur) deals out a row of cards until the total value adds up to between 31 and 40. As soon as a total reaches that range, the row is complete. The first row is the noir, or black row. Let us say the cards dealt out are:

Five of diamonds, king of spades, deuce of spades, 3 of clubs, 5 of hearts, and king of hearts. This would give the black row a total of 35.

Now the dealer starts a lower row, the rouge, or red row. The cards dealt are:

Seven of clubs, 5 of spades, 9 of diamonds, 3 of hearts, 3 of spades, 10 of clubs. This totals 37.

The winning row is the one that comes closest to 31, so that in this case the black or first row is the winner, and all players who have bet on noir win.

In addition to black and red bets, the players may also bet on whether the first card of the first row is the same color (couleur) as the winning row. If that is the case, couleur wins. If it is not the case, bets on the opposite color (inverse) win. In the example above, the first card dealt was the 5 of diamonds. Since the black row won with the lower points, this means inverse wins and couleur loses.

All these four bets are even-odds affairs and by themselves offer no advantage to the house. The casino gets its edge when certain ties result. Should both the black and red rows end up with the same point total, the game is considered void. The single exception is a tie score of 31. In this case the house in some European casinos takes one-half of all bets wagered. In other casinos, probably the majority, an "imprison" rule is followed with the stakes either being "freed" or entirely taken by the bank, depending upon the results of the next game. The results for the casino are the same over the long haul. Half the players will get their wagers back and half will lose the entire amount.

To avoid having their bets imprisoned or half appropriated, players may insure their stake by paying

1 percent of it. Such insurance must be paid in advance and the stake must be appropriately marked. The insurance is very lucrative for the house. (Some gambling books claim that there are casinos that charge as much as 5 percent for insurance, a claim some Thirty and Forty addicts confirm. However, an extensive recent survey of European casinos did not bear this out. And it would seem that it hardly makes sense for casinos to kill the golden goose by making the gouge too obvious.)

Trente et Quarante is not an inexpensive game to play. For instance, at the Casino Municipale in Venice, Italy, the minimum bet is 50,000 lire and the maximum 2 million lire. Allowing for possible shifts in exchange values, this would put the minimum bet at about $40 and the maximum at about $1,600. At other casinos both the minimum and maximum bets are much higher.

Since the game is one that attracts high-stakes bettors it is rather surprising that many of them fail to realize that this game offers a bigger house advantage than the straight money bets in European ROULETTE or Baccarat, running from 1.35 percent at Roulette down to just a tad over 1.00 percent at Baccarat on many bets. By comparison the house cuts itself in for about 1.50 percent at Trente et Quarante, and selling insurance jacks up the edge considerably.

Most addicts of the game do not grasp the fact that ties at 31 occur 3.3 times more frequently than ties at 40. Frequencies of ties at the other numbers become statistically closer as the score totals decline from 39 to 32, but ties at 31 are still the most prevalent.

Why, then, are Trente et Quarante tables always crowded with bettors? The reason is simple. The games move along much more rapidly than Baccarat and especially Roulette, where the time "wasted" for payouts slows the action considerably. Thus a gambler sojourning in Europe may play Thirty and Forty if he wants his action fast and furious.

But remember. The faster the action, the faster a player will be tapped out.

THIRTY-ONE

Thirty-one, sometimes known as Schnautz, is a card game that can accommodate a large number of players but is best played with at least four.

The object of the game is to use a three-card hand to total 31 points in one suit. The player coming closest to 31 collects the pot. Cards are ranked 11 for the ace, all picture cards are 10, and all other cards get their numerical worth. Each player is dealt three cards and then three cards are dealt face up as the "widow." Beginning at the dealer's left, each player may take one card from the widow and put a card from his hand in its place. This continues until one

player knocks, thinking he has the best hand, or indeed has 31. For instance, an all-hearts hand consisting of an ace, a jack, and a 10 would total 31. Players may also try to achieve three of a kind, such as three 7's. All three-of-a-kind hands are valued at 30½ points. When a player knocks, all other players have the right to make one more play before the hands are totaled and the winner determined.

A player may knock at any time, even before the exchange of cards, in which case no other player is permitted to exchange any card with the widow. Early in the game it is wise to knock even with only a fairly high hand such as queen, 9, 4, for 23, before other players have much chance to improve their hands.

The big danger in Thirty-one is playing in a crooked game. Two scam artists sitting next to each other can easily control the game with one of them feeding the other the suit he signals he needs. There have been cases of stings run by four or five crooks trimming one or two suckers. The crooks prefer sitting next to each other and can rig matters so the victim doesn't even get a chance to play before being knocked out of a big-ante hand.

THIRTY-ONE (NUMBERS GAME): Bar Hustler's Favorite

There are many varieties of games especially played in bars that are not really gambles but rather outright cons, although someone with a scientific bent might prefer calling them "mathematical games." Sharpers are especially fond of a card hustle called Thirty-one, at which they claim to win 99 percent of the time. The game can be found in Paris neighborhood cafes, London pubs, and American saloons. The proponents of the game are outright hustlers in any language. It is folly to get into a numbers game because it is not a gambling contest with elements of luck complemented by an element of strategy. If a game is *all* luck or *all* strategy, the astute gambler can gain no advantage, and therefore should not allow himself to be hustled.

Thirty-one is simplicity itself. All the cards from ace up to 6 are laid out in six vertical rows by their pip value (the ace is counted 1). Each player takes up one card at a time with the totals added cumulatively, and the player who gets the total up to (or closest to) 31 without going over wins the bet.

Let us say the victim leads with an ace, the sharper plays a deuce—and for all practical purposes has already won the game. Let us say the victim leads with a 4; the sharper counters with a 6, establishing the pattern to win the game. These are not empty suppositions. The problem with playing a numbers game is that a sharper is working from a fixed formula while the victim is not.

The basic rule to follow in Thirty-one is that since the draws are limited to one to six, the winning combinations to reach 31 are composed of sevens. To get to 31 the winner has to get to 24 before that. To get to 24, he must be at 17, and prior to that 10, and before that 3. Of course if the 3 is passed on the first play the target becomes 10 and the sharper can hit that if the card led is a 4, 5, or 6. If the victim leads with a 3, it is relatively simple for the sharper to take control. Sooner or later the sharper will take over at one of the key plateaus and then he cannot be stopped. Usually, sharpers play with opponents who don't grasp the 3-10-17-24-31 strategy. If they do, it makes no difference unless the victim understands *all* the ramifications of the game. And there are many. Generally speaking, the sharper gains control of the game *whenever* the victim starts. Finally some shrewd outsider who has been watching the play for a long time and has figured out the key sequences will offer to bet the sharper and will also insist that the sharper lead.

What he does is play a 5, and the shrewd outsider counters with another 5 and holds the advantage. The sharp plays a 2, and the outsider bounces back with yet another 5 for 17 and controls again. Undeterred, the sharper plays another 2 and the outsider follows with another 5 for 24 and control again. The sharper follows once more with a 2 and the outsider reaches for a 5—only to find there are no more. (That there are four of any one rank is one of game's tricky ramifications.) The score now stand at 26 and the not-so-shrewd outsider can't play a 6 because that will put him over. And any lower card he chooses will be countered by a card that will make 31.

Actually there are very involved ways to lead with an ace or deuce by which the leader can also win, but sharpers never bother with them since the 5-lead is such a simple one.

Earlier it was stated that sharpers claim they win at this hustle 99 percent of the time. The one exception is the opponent who understands how to play the 5-opener gambit. This does not mean the sharper loses any money. He simply argues that in fairness each should take turns leading—and the result will be at worst a standoff, causing the sharper to pack up his cards and head for another bar where suckers abound.

The odds of 99 wins against an occasional standoff are hard to beat.

THIRTY-SIX: Dice Form of Blackjack
Although the scoring is different, the dice game thirty-six is very similar to BLACKJACK.

One die is used after each player puts an ante into the pot, a preliminary throw of the die is made to determine the order of play. Low man rolls first.

Then players throw the die and continue to throw it until they get as near to a total of 36 without going over it. Players who go over 36 are busted and lose. The winner of the game is the player who scores 36 or the highest total short of that. This means a player should throw the die when he has 32 but stop at 33 or higher, since at 33 the odds are 50-50 at busting on another toss. Ties split the pot.

The advantage lies with the players throwing late in the game. They know they must throw again even at 33, 34, or 35 if an earlier player has a higher total. The opening toss of the die normally settles the matter, but as many bar games are becoming DEALER'S CHOICE, it is now customary for the "dealer" to play last in whatever game he calls.

Although most bar games are even propositions, most players fail to take advantage of calling a "smart" game, such as Thirty-six. The player who does has to benefit over the long haul.

THREE FORTY-FIVE: Eight-card Stud Variation
This is an eight-card game of Stud in which all 5's are wild. Three cards are dealt down, followed by a betting round. Then four cards are dealt up, with a betting sequence after each. Finally a fourth down-card is dealt and there is the final betting. The lowest likely winning hand is generally a straight, and players having a straight or flush on the first five cards should bet the hand solidly in an effort to drive out the others. If the straight or flush comes late in the hand, however, it should not be bet aggressively because chances are it is no longer a strong hand.

Of course a hand with, say, two wild cards is more powerful than the same hand with all "natural" cards, since opponents have been deprived of half of the wild cards. Thus hands with wild cards merit much stronger betting.

THREE-CARD MONTE: Gambling Con
For more than a century, Three-card Monte operators have, without real variation, cheated one generation after another of gullible victims. Every few decades the street hustle enjoys a stunning revival as a new crop of suckers discovers it. The last wave of Three-card Monte scams developed in the late 1970's as practitioners of the craft flooded most big American cities. On almost any weekend as many as a half-dozen games may be in progress at one time, for example, on New York's fashionable West 57th Street from Fifth Avenue to Carnegie Hall.

The idea in Three-card Monte is to guess which of three face-down cards is the queen, avoiding picking one of the accompanying aces. It looks simple enough: the dealer shows the winning card (the queen), then does a fast shuffle and places the three cards face down; pick a card and put your money on it. The

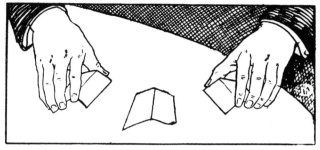

Three-card Monte is a come-on con game using shills who make it appear an easy game to beat. However when the "pigeon" plays, he invariably loses.

average victim will watch for a time and feel confident he has spotted the correct card every time. Other players try and win—or lose. These losing efforts are particular exasperating to the potential victim, who *knows* he spotted the correct card. What he *doesn't* know is that all these players, winners and losers, are shills who are trying to coax outsiders to play. When an outsider does play, the dealer becomes extremely adept at his craft and lays the cards out in a way that not only prevents the sucker from spotting the queen but makes another card appear to be the queen.

The variations to the swindle are endless. A victim may suddenly notice that the corner of the queen is bent so that it can be easily identified. When the victim bets, the quick-fingered dealer uses a talented pinkie to first straighten that corner and fold a losing card instead. Sometimes a victim will spot a correct card and try to put down $20 on it. The dealer will put the stall on him, insisting the minimum bet has to be $40. While the victim hesitates, a shill slaps $40 on a losing card and the dealer then tells the honest player, "Sorry, only one card can be bet a game." Should the victim complain that his bet was down first, the phony bettor insists his was. The dealer will throw up his hands in feigned disgust and say, "I don't know whose bet was down first, so all bets are off."

At other times a shill will yell out, "Cops!" and the dealer and shills flee the scene. It has even happened that a victim has found himself standing by an upended cardboard box with three cards on it and money in his hands, being hassled by police who insist he is a Monte operator!

A final word of warning: regardless of how it may appear, *everyone* collecting money from a dealer is a shill. It is against his principles for a Monte gyp ever to let a sucker win a bet, not even a small one on the theory that he will then bet big. Gyps take no chances that a sucker will walk away with any of their money. Besides, the gyp artists have found that losers are more likely to come back for more action—out of frustration or simply trying to get even. If you are

ever watching a Monte scam in operation and someone sidles up to you and points out the shills and tells you how it works, don't listen to him. Especially if he says the two of you can work together to beat the game, that he'll stand behind the dealer and signal you which is the correct card. He's a shill too.

See GEORGE DEVOL; WILLIAM "CANADA BILL" JONES.

THREE-CARD MONTE: Poker variation

The card game called Three-card Monte, a shortened version of POKER known also as Three-card Stud (and in some circles as Three-toed Pete), bears no relation to the street and carnival scam of the same name. The game has an ante that is followed with the dealing, one at a time, of first a downcard and then two upcards, with a round of betting after each card. Seventeen players can be accommodated, but the game is better with fewer than 10.

Traditional Poker values of the five-card game do not apply here. The following sequence of high hands often applies: 1) straight flush, 2) three of a kind, 3) flush, 4) straight, 5) pair, 6) high card. An alternate rule, not without logic, ranks three of a kind ahead of a straight flush. A high card is often good enough to win in a three-card game.

THREE-CARD POKER: Draw Variation

This is the draw version of THREE-CARD MONTE, or Three-card Stud. Players get three cards and may discard and draw one or two cards. There is an ante and rounds of betting before and after the discarding.

In another version of the game, players keep their first three cards and after a round of betting must draw an additional two cards. Only three of the five cards can be used in the showdown, however. Values of the hands are ranked as they are in Three-card Monte.

THREE-CARD STUD

See THREE-CARD MONTE.

THREE-HANDED BRIDGE

See CUT-THROAT BRIDGE.

THREE-PAIR HIGH: A "Lollapalooza"

Occasionally a bastardized game of POKER is played in Six-, Seven-, or Eight Card Stud versions that lets a player figure in a sixth card in the showdown if that card gives him three pairs. Such a hand is reckoned higher than even a royal flush and wins the pot.

Three-Pair High has never been very popular with serious Poker players, but it has won favor as a LOLLAPALOOZA hand. This is a hand that is allowed only to the first player in a game to get one and automatically wins the pot. For the rest of the session the so-called Lollapalooza has no more than its regular strength. Actually Three-Pair High does build pots early in the evening. Anyone having two pairs is forced to stay in search of the Lollapalooza, since the player can also end up with a "lower hand" like a full house. Big-stake players seldom will permit the hand.

THREE-THREE-THREE

This is a SIX-CARD STUD Poker game dealt three cards up, three cards down and all 3's are wild. Betting starts after two cards are dealt down and one up. The final card is the last downcard. One denomination of wild cards in a six-card game does not necessarily produce really powerful hands all the time. Three of a kind wins quite often, but the catch is that, with only three cards exposed, it is not always easy to gauge opposing players' hands. As a result many seasoned players stay only on a strong two pair or low three of a kind. Aggressive betting is not advised unless the player's hand is at least three aces.

THREE-TOED PETE

See THREE-CARD MONTE.

TIP THE TEE: Poolroom Hustle

Here's a sucker bet that turns up at some carnivals and in pool halls or bars with pool tables for the customers. A golf tee is placed on the table. Three pool balls are arranged in a triangle around it, one ball in front of the tee and the other two behind, all three balls touching.

The suckers are bet they cannot knock down the tee by shooting a cue ball that scatters the three balls. The hustler has a sure thing here; a law of physics make it impossible for the tee to be knocked over. When the cue ball strikes the front ball, the impact is shifted to the other two balls so that the entire force is deflected around the golf tee, and it remains standing.

After collecting several bets, the hustler puts up money that he can perform the feat, and he does so. All he or a confederate has to do is rack up the balls quickly so that two of them are not quite touching. The law of physics is repealed and the hustler wins again.

TOPS

See PUT AND TAKE TOP.

TRENTA-CINQUE: Fast-moving Italian Card Game

Trenta-Cinque, a gambling game very popular in Italy and among Italian-Americans, is played by four gamblers with an Italian deck (a 40-card pack without 8's, 9's, and 10's). Cards are valued according to their pips—an ace is 1, deuce 2, etc., with all pictures counting 10. Each gambler is dealt nine cards, after an ante of five chips into the pot. The last four cards are faced down on the table as a "widow." Players may then pass or bid up to five chips that they have the highest count of cards in a single suit. If the bids are tied, the winning bidder is the one with the highest count in his suit.

The triumphant bidder adds his chips to the pot and takes the widow. If the four-card widow totals 35 or more, regardless of suit, he takes the pot. Otherwise, he loses his bid and the pot stays for the next deal. Any player who remains in the bidding to the end and can show an original hand without a face card or a hand of king, queen, jack in the same suit collects two chips from each opponent.

Trenta-Cinque is not a game of strategy but one of luck. Nevertheless, one should hardly risk five chips on less than four cards that offer an appreciable point score, although a score of 30 is sufficient if all the cards are pictures.

TRENTE ET QUARANTE

See THIRTY AND FORTY.

TRICKS

See TRUMPS AND MELDS.

TRIMS: Marked-cards Technique

As is true with most marked cards, trims are less used in big-stakes than in the amateur games. Trims are cards with white borders that are literally trimmed down the edges of one lengthwise side. This is done to mark selected cards, very often the low cards.

There was a time when trimming was a sophisticated enough dodge to fool most amateur gamblers. Nowadays, however, trimming is too blatant even with the most casual of players—unless the deck is moved in for one game and out again before the action is spotted. If trims are left in play it would not be long before even the most gullible player would lay a trimmed card over an untrimmed one and notice the difference.

The trimmers do have an answer for this that's good enough to keep them in business. *All* the cards are trimmed. The low ones on one side and the high ones on *both* sides. The cards with the double trim have half as much taken off on each side so that the width of all cards remain the same. It makes the narrow margin a little harder for the sharpers to discern, but then again they should suffer a bit of eyestrain for the money they make.

TRIPOLI: Modern Version of Pochen

Tripoli is a modern version of POCHEN, played with a full 52-card deck instead of the 32-card one used for the latter. The game is for four to seven players. An equal number of cards are dealt to all, and the leftovers are set aside as "dead." Instead of designating trump suit to collect from the various sections as they appear in Pochen (Ace, King, Queen, Jack, 10, and Marriage), hearts are fixed as the vital suit. The Sequence section is won by another suit only, usually spades. The high hand, or "Poker" phase, is won by the best five cards in a full modern POKER hand, not limited as in Pochen to four of a kind, three of a kind, and pair. The final phase is won as in Pochen by sequences of cards being laid down in ascending order to the ace, or the highest card possible if that card has been played earlier or is in the "dead" pile. The player laying the last card in the sequence then starts another, and play continues until one player goes out. Settlement is again as in Pochen.

Tripoli's chief virtue over Pochen is that fewer cards are exposed in the early phases of play so that more of the action in the final "stop" portion is subject to strategy by the more astute gambler.

TRI-STATE MEGABUCKS: Three-state Lottery

In the first multistate lottery the states of Maine, Vermont, and New Hampshire joined forces to offer a lottery game with a pool none of the states figured to build on their own.

In the lottery as first constituted, players must pick six numbers from 1 to 30, and winners who get them all right share the top prize. Those picking five of six get $100 and four of six receive $10. It frequently happens there are no first-prize winners, in which case the pool is carried over to the following week.

Additionally, the Vermont public has the right to buy a "season pass" in the form of a 26- or 52-week subscription, and the numbers selected are eligible automatically week after week. The lottery commission notifies these winners if they win prizes.

TRODMORE RACE SYNDICATE: Classic Horse-Betting Swindle

In 19th-century England it was traditional for small race meetings to be held on bank holidays. On the August Bank Holiday of 1898 a syndicate of swindlers executed one of the most original and outrageous coups in the history of horse racing. They garnered more than a quarter of a million dollars betting on horses that never lived, in races that were never run, at a track that didn't exist.

The great swindle started when the editor of *The Sportsman*, a racing newspaper, received a press release on the letterhead of the Trodmore Race Club of Trodmore, Cornwall, announcing the inauguration of the Trodmore Races with the first events to be held on the August Bank Holiday. This was hardly unusual; many small race meetings were scheduled for such holidays and sometimes these meets amounted to only one, two, or three days of racing for the entire year. Being a newspaper of record for the racing gentry, *The Sportsman* was faced with the problem of covering the Trodmore Races, since inevitably there would be some betting action with the bookmakers on them. The English had a way of getting action on any race meeting, no matter how obscure.

The editor's problem was solved when some days before the meet a well-dressed gentleman appeared at the publication's offices and explained that he was on his way to Trodmore. He agreed to wire back the names of all winning horses and other pertinent track information for the customary fee. The problem resolved, the newspaper printed the names of all entries at Trodmore. Just before the time of the first race, bookmakers all over London got considerable action on the Trodmore Races, accepting the program odds published in *The Sportsman*. At the end of the day, *The Sportsman's* special correspondent, true to his word, wired in the results and payoff odds.

Several bookmakers discovered that they had booked heavy bets on "winning" horses, and one bookie in particular noted that he had been hit very hard on a horse called Reaper who had "paid off" at 5 to 1. Since he had never heard of Reaper, he decided to check up on its registry. He discovered there was no horse registered under that name. Furthermore, he also discovered there was no such place as Trodmore. And there was no such racetrack at Trodmore—or elsewhere.

An investigation showed the bookmakers had been shorn with neat efficiency. They had been lulled out of any suspicions because they had gotten many bets on several horses in the same race, but the winning bets always totaled more than the combined losing bets. What became known as the Trodmore Race Syndicate had simply made up its own results, set the odds and collected the winnings, disappearing with more than $250,000 in a legendary day at the races that never was. And *The Sportsman's* special correspondent who had forwarded the results to the newspaper never showed up to collect his fee for services rendered.

TROTTING-RACE BETTING

"Trotting horses, or standardbreds, are a coming thing in horse racing, though they still have a long way to go to equal the interest generated by the sport of kings [thoroughbred horse racing]." This quote, taken from a gambling guide written in 1981, is far from accurate. Trotting is in a sad state of decline.

Virtually no bookmaker will take any bet of appreciable size, if any at all, on any trotting race. The reason: the "fix." Trotting racing is perceived by many to be dishonest. There is a much-quoted saying by a bookmaker that "I might take action on a night's trotting race if I was invited to the rehearsal that afternoon." It is a sweeping indictment of the game, told in what may be too-broad brush strokes, but one that must be measured against bookmaker reaction, the ultimate test of a betting sport's integrity.

In December 1987 *Sports Illustrated* reported: "In the past 10 years the harness racing industry in California has suffered a 50% decrease in both attendance and wagering, and some of the financial crisis can be attributed to a credibility crisis." The previous September, the *Los Angeles Herald Examiner* reported that a trotting-horse trainer estimated that one race per night was fixed at Fairplex Park in Pomona. The *New York Post* published a full-page story by racing expert Bill Finley under a headline: "CLEAN UP HARNESS FILTH! Scandals give sport black eye." Finley wrote: "Harness racing is a sport run by lenient racetrack management, overseen by a powerless racing commission and overrun with drivers whose track records are soiled by serious offenses."

In the grand old days, trotting was considered a fine and fair activity. Millionaire William H. Vanderbilt, in relaxed moments, personally raced his pacers at New York's Jerome Park. Today, disgruntled fans have ripped down fences and set fire to them at trotting tracks when a more-than-questionable race has been run. A number of drivers are suspended annually for what is called "lack of effort" and a newspaper exposé showed that a leading driver in California had previously run afoul of racing officials in Massachusetts, Ohio, New York, Pennsylvania, Delaware, and New Jersey. Comments the *New York Post*, "Imagine the American League employing a ballplayer after he was banned by the National League for betting against his own team. Then you'll understand what goes on in harness racing."

In 1988, a suspicious race at Yonkers Raceway in New York came under intense investigation. Seven of the eight drivers involved were suspended (the other one was the winner). In triple wagering (picking the three top finishers in the exact order) it was estimated that a $3 ticket should have returned $1,000 to $1,500. The winner was an 18-to-1 long shot who led for the entire race. The favorite came in second, and a 6-to-1 entry was third. The payoff came to only $192, because, according to *Sports Illustrated:* ". . . there was an inordinately large amount of money bet on the winning combination at off-track betting locations. Jim Michaels, the presiding judge at Yonkers, says that even while the race was in progress

he and the two other judges were questioning the performances of the drivers. 'Then when the price went up, the small triple payoff confirmed our suspicions that there was something wrong with the race,' says Michaels."

No one really believes that trotting racing will disappear in America, but the prospects of major reforms are limited as well. Serious gamblers—those without inside information—will ignore the trotters and the betting handle will continue to dip, as the attendance is made up more and more of a novice betting public that bets on numbers rather than form.

Despite this, there still are profitable harness tracks in the country. One of the most successful is the Meadowlands in New Jersey. Of the track's bettors, *Playboy* magazine noted: "The Northern New Jerseyans at Meadowlands come to eat and play lucky numbers and have yet to learn which end of the horse eats."

Hugh TROY: Practical Joker and Bet Hustler

Muralist and illustrator Hugh Troy (1906–1964), whose practical jokes and exploits are immortalized by H. Allen Smith, was a betting man, and one who never lost a wager when it concerned his bizarre tricks. Troy was said to have bet $500 that he could get a preposterous poem he'd written published and credited to him by *The New York Times*. When he exhibited his terrible verse he had no dearth of takers on the wager. What his challengers failed to understand was that Troy only bet on sure things. He'd already figured out a surefire scheme.

Using the phony identity of "Miss Julia Annsbury, of Auburn, N.Y.," Troy wrote the newspaper's Sunday book section, seeking aid in identifying some verse that had "haunted [me] since long-gone childhood." It concerned, so the bogus Miss Annsbury said, a gypsy girl taken sick on the trail and abandoned there by her compatriots. A few weeks passed and the book section published a response to Miss Annsbury's missive. The letter was signed "Poetry Lover, Rahway, N.J." and was, of course, Troy once again.

"I happen to remember the poem Miss Annsbury seeks," Poetry Lover announced cheerfully. "It is by Hugh Troy, and if memory does not fail me, its last lines run like this:

> So we leave her,
> So we leave her,
>   Far from where her swarthy
>   kindred roam,
> In the scarlet fever,
> In the scarlet fever,
>   Convalescent home."

As the saying goes, Troy laughed all the way to the bank.

TRUMPS AND MELDS

Virtually all card games fall into two main categories—trumps and melds. There are many card games in which certain cards may be "trumps"—actually a slang derivation for the word "triumph"—and players in these games can win "tricks." The taking of a trick was the original meaning of "trump." Later, the word applied to cards or suits that were more powerful than the others in some games. But many trump games do not utilize trump cards.

A trick represents the cards, often four, that are played and won in a round. Contract Bridge and the WHIST series of games are in this group. Other games belong to the "meld" family, in which specific combinations of cards are formed. POKER and the various forms of RUMMY are typical melding games. There are also games that combine in various ways both the principles of tricks and melds. Among these games are PINOCHLE and PIQUET.

TUNK: Cross Between Gin and Knock Rummy

Tunk is a game that falls somewhere between GIN and KNOCK RUMMY. Deuces are wild. The game is best played with two to four players who are dealt seven cards each. The next card is turned up alongside the remaining deck. Each player has the option in turn of drawing from the pack or taking the upcard. He then discards as in Knock Rummy. However, a player cannot knock unless the count of his unmatched cards gets down to 5 points, as in Gin. The player may use deuces when needed to make sets of three or four of a kind or to meld sequences in suit of three or more cards. All sets must have two "natural" cards, thus 10-10-deuce-deuce is possible but not 10-deuce-deuce.

After the knocker has laid down his hand, other players get one more opportunity to draw, meld, and lay off on the knocker's hand, unless he matched it entirely. The player's unmatched cards are then scored against them. If any of them scores lower than the knocker, the knocker's count is doubled against him.

The deal is passed and a new hand begins with players eliminated as their scores reach 100. The pot goes to the last remaining player.

The game may be played with more than four, using two decks. However, the four-player limit is usually preferred.

TURKEY, Gambling in

It is relatively easy to gamble in Turkey at CARDS, BACKGAMMON, and other DICE games. There are also a number of gambling casinos and clubs where the more traditional big-time gambling games may be played—ROULETTE, BACARRAT, CRAPS, etc. Traditionally, Turkish gambling entrepreneurs play cutthroat with their competition, and are reputed to use dirty tricks to get them out of business. One casino is known to have hired a team of American CROSSROADERS (professional cheats) to sabotage a new casino that was sapping some of its business. The crooks went to work on the casino's Craps tables and through the use of doctored dice took the establishment for $400,000. It was enough to put the casino into bankruptcy.

It has been said that Turkish casinos can be among the worst losers in the world, but in truth it is hard to find a casino management that enjoys paying off on big hits. The trouble with some Turkish casinos is that they are undercapitalized and go into shock when hit hard. What they prefer is drawing a steady supply of jet-setters, royalty, the wealthy, and those eternal affluent Arabs who will lose steadily with the best of grace. That's the way it usually goes but, says one international gambler, "The Turks have never understood why it doesn't happen that way all the time."

TWENTY-NINE: Fast-moving Card Game

Today Twenty-Nine is generally regarded as a family or children's game, which is in itself an unusual development. There are a number of family or juvenile games that have developed into gambling games, but very few that have evolved the other way. Yet as long ago as the 19th century there was mention of Twenty-Nine both in news accounts and criminal memoirs as a high-stakes game.

The rules are rather simple. All cards are numerically valued, with suits of no consequence. All face cards are 1 point and other cards get their spot value. There are four players, and those sitting opposite each other are partners.

The deck is dealt out completely. The first player plays a card and the next player adds another to it, announcing the total points of the cards. The third player does the same, and play continues until the trick is taken by the team bringing the total to exactly 29.

A new trick is then started. Whenever a player cannot add a card without pushing the total over 29, he has to pass. If the last trick fails to reach 29, these cards are nullified. The winning team is determined by the total number of cards collected rather than the tricks taken.

Conversely, as a family game, the number of tricks taken are now the winning factor.

The demise of Twenty-Nine as a gambling game is probably explained by the fact that cheating by partners was so easy. Only the most elementary code for signaling was necessary since only point value counted. Partners would merely have to know that they controlled a few denominations and they could then keep their opponents from making 29. A cheater, knowing he and his partner controlled the 6's, would simply get the total of 23. The opponent between them would either have to play a low card, giving the other cheater a good shot at closing out at 29, or pass, which would allow the cheating partner to play his vital 6.

Presumably widespread cheating along these lines, and the flare-ups that followed, convinced serious gamblers to leave Twenty-Nine to the kids.

TWENTY-ONE (DICE)
This is a gambling game popular in bars in many parts of the United States as well as England and Europe, especially France.

How to play: Any number can play and only one die is used. A player rolls as many times as he wishes to get as close to a total of 21 without going over. He may stop whenever he wishes and the player at or closest to 21 is the winner. Ties usually split the pot, but if the two or more players agree, there can be a playoff game.

Twenty-one is usually played with an ante of one coin or chip. Players who go over 21 are required to pay a penalty of a chip to the pot.

Strategy: Many players, especially the early shooters, tend to stop with too low a score, allowing later players to have the advantage of an easy target to exceed. Bear in mind that 18 has a 50-50 chance of being improved upon on the next throw, and early players should have at least 18 before stopping. Even at 18 another throw is almost always advisable, since a 3 will make the player a certain winner.

Later players have a natural advantage, which is only partially offset because they are more likely to go over and have to feed the pot. This happens when a late player has a 20 and must match an earlier player's 21 or automatically lose. Still, since he has only one chance in six of getting a 1, he should drop out if there are fewer than ten chips in the pot or he is betting at a disadvantage. The fact that late players tend to go over 21 more often eliminates only part of the disadvantage the early shooter is under. Thus, to equalize the odds, it is important that the die pass to a succeeding shooter in every new game.

TWENTY-SIX: Tavern Tournament Dice Game
There was a time back in the 1950's when it would have been difficult to find a Midwestern tavern where a dice game called Twenty-six was not the rage. Today, after legal crackdowns, the game is not as popular, although many establishments still offer it as a way to beef up earnings. A player chooses a point from 1 to 6 and tosses ten dice from a cup a total of 13 times. The object is to make his point 26 or more times. Most Twenty-six operators have a special score sheet providing all the rules and pay-offs.

Scoring varies from place to place, but a typical payoff is 3 to 1 for making one's point 26 to 32 times, no easy feat since the mathematical odds are that it will come up only 21.666 times. For an even harder goal, a score of 33 or more, the payoff is about 7 to 1. With odds like that, the house has an edge of approximately 24 percent. Other little gimmicks are sometimes thrown in, such as 3- or 4-to-1 odds for a score of 11 or less and 2 to 1 for an exact score of 13. Such "losing" scores are even harder to make than a winning figure of 26, and so they don't make much of a dent in the house take. If the house wanted to be fair, it would pay 4-to-1 odds for a score of 26 or more and 18 to 1 for 33 or more.

Taverns use the game as a way to hold patrons and if a "tournament" is well attended, the establishment will sell quite a few drinks during the time of play required. Generally players ante up a dollar or so for the bet against the tavern and a separate ante with that pot going to the highest score, whether or not anyone reaches 26. Thus, there is always a consolation winner. Meanwhile the house takes in its percentage and also moves the booze.

See also FOURTEENS.

TWIN BEDS: Wilder Version of Bedsprings
Twin Beds may be described as BEDSPRINGS run amok. Bedsprings calls for ten cards in the center of the table to be turned up in two rows of five and any top-and-bottom row pair of cards may be chosen as a player's possible cards along with the five in his hand. This makes a sort of Seven-card Poker.

Twin Beds also allows for the turning up of ten cards, but generally in a different order. First one from the top row is turned, then one from the bottom row, and so on. However, after all cards have been turned up, each player may use five cards from either the top or bottom row in conjunction with the five cards in his hand. Thus this is a sort of Ten-card Poker, and the fact that players can choose between two sets of five cards makes it even wilder than "normal" Ten-card.

While some gamblers might wonder what constitutes the usual winning hand in this game, the real question is what is the serious gambler doing betting money in a zany game like this.

Carrying the insanity even further, there are several versions of what is called Twin Beds Gone Wild in which certain cards, such as the last card in each row and all others like it, are wild.

TWO-CARD POKER

Sometimes called Frustration, Two-card Poker is played like Draw Poker except that hands are limited to two downcards. There is an ante (as there is in all two-card forms of POKER) and a round of betting, after which players may stand pat or draw one or two new cards in place of the originals. A round of betting then follows, and the showdown. The highest possible hand is a pair of aces. Flushes and straights have no standing.

To give the game more variety, it is often played with deuces wild and high-low at the same time. Aces count either as high or low, thus making ace-deuce or deuce-deuce winners both ways, as a pair of aces and one-two. Ties, of course, split their portions of the pot.

This game is often called Hurricane in Europe, but in America HURRICANE has different rules.

TWO-DECK PROPOSITION BET: Card Hustler's Delight

The Two-deck Proposition bet has long been a gold mine for card hustlers. All they need is two decks of cards set side by side after thorough shuffling. They announce they are willing to bet that in turning over one card in each deck simultaneously that the same card in each deck will turn up simultaneously at some point. For instance, the two kings of diamonds (one from each deck) will be turned over together. It is a proposition most gamblers think is a reckless bet. Considering that there are 52 cards in each deck the likelihood of identical cards appearing seems remote.

Most pigeons eagerly accept an even-money bet, convinced that they have a huge edge. In fact, the hustler has everything going his way. Mathematically the hustler will be proved right in five games out of every eight. The hustler could give 3-to-2 odds and still make money.

There is a gambling legend that a card hustler once took department store tycoon Bernard Gimbel for $5,000 with this scam. After losing five $100 bets in a row Gimbel was said to have worked it out that the odds were really against him, but he was unable to get out of the game. It was being played as a $5,000 freeze-out, meaning both players had put up that sum of money in advance and had to keep betting $100 a pop until someone won the full $5,000. They played two and one-half hours before the inexorable 5-to-3 true odds ground Gimbel down.

See FREEZE-OUT PROPOSITION.

TWO-DICE KLONDIKE
See BEAT THE DEALER.

TWO-LEG STUD
See LEG POKER.

TWO-PACK RUM
See COON CAN.

U

UNDER AND OVER SEVEN: Carnival Gambling Game

It is nearly impossible to find Under and Over Seven (sometimes called Over and Under) in any legal gambling casino—not even the most grasping casino operative would dare offer a game with such highway-robbery odds against the player. However, the game is a staple at honky-tonk gambling joints, carnivals, fairs, Las Vegas nights, and even religious fundraisers. To the uninitiated, the payoffs look good and many players can't understand why the operator doesn't go broke, since he appears to be giving "even odds."

How to play: The game is played with two dice and either a dice cup or an hourglass device similar to the kind used in playing CHUCK-A-LUCK. Bettors can make three types of bets on a simple layout (which can even be chalked on the pavement by hustlers): That the dice will add up to less than 7, more than 7, or 7 exactly. If the bet is made on either under 7 or over 7, a payoff is made to the winner at even money. If the player bets on 7, the winning payoff is 4 to 1.

Since the odds on hitting over or under 7 are exactly the same, the casual player is brainwashed into believing that the bank has no advantage. The catch is, of course, the number 7, the highest mathematical result in a throw of the dice, since it will come up on average six out of 36 times. When 7 appears, the bank wins all "over and under" bets. This makes over-and-under bets an enormous 16.67 percent house advantage. Of course the bank has to pay off on any 7 bets at the same time, but here too it pays off at only 4 to 1 when the correct odds should be 5 to 1. This shortchanging of the player works out to the same 16.67 percent house advantage, making Under-and-Over Seven a classic sucker game.

The game is recommended only for masochists, or if you want to play it at a religious Las Vegas night, simply chalk up your losses to charity (but don't expect the IRS to buy that one).

URUGUAY, Gambling in

When on a gambling jaunt, tourists would be wise to check out the currency situation in a number of countries, especially those in Latin America and typically in Uruguay. Uruguay is a nation much addicted to football (soccer) and there is considerable action, lottery and otherwise, on the sport. The economic differences between rich and poor are as striking in Uruguay as anywhere in South America. For the super-rich there is casino gambling and, of course, this action is available to foreigners.

However, their is a catch for winners. In much of Latin America the countries are wallowing in currency-exchange problems and it is virtually impossible for an amateur to get gambling winnings out of the country. One of the world's most dedicated ROULETTE players, Paddy O'Neil-Dunne, relates in his book *Roulette for the Millions* of winding up in a Montevideo casino loaded down with huge profits in pesos, at a loss as to how to take the money home with him. He finally decided he would not be able to do so and writes, "There was a limit to the number of gins I would drink there, so I found satisfaction in donating my winnings to a home for crippled children."

Kenneth S. USTON: Famed Blackjack Counter

In the murky world of BLACKJACK counters, Ken Uston (1935–1987) was the David who stood up to Goliath, the gambling casinos. It was he, in the revered name of Blackjack counting, who sued the Atlantic City casinos and won a verdict that ordered them to accept bets by Blackjack counters. Some observers, however, always felt that Uston, like other counting experts, won far less than he claimed to. Some outright cynics even had the effrontery to say that *all* the money Uston made out of Blackjack came from writing books on how to beat the game and not actually from beating it. Uston did turn out a total of 16 books in all—on Blackjack, video games, and personal computers.

A Phi Beta Kappa graduate at 20 from Yale with a master's degree from Harvard, Uston was a former stock-broker who served as a senior vice-president of the Pacific Stock Exchange in San Francisco for six years. Then he heard the siren call of the Blackjack tables in the 1960's. He gained such notoriety that in the end he was barred from the card tables in Nevada, Atlantic City, and most of Europe.

In the process he was lionized by such moneyed organs as *The Wall Street Journal.* The popular press fell in love with the idea of his use of disguises to try to crash the casinos, and some other counters later tried to do so in drag. In one of his books, *The Big Player,* Uston related how he would dash madly from one card table to another pretending to be drunk, to justify his erratic betting pattern, the mark of a Blackjack counter. When quizzed by casino officials, he bemoaned the fact that he once had lost $30,000 at a sitting. This supposed propensity for losing produced a magical change on the part of many casinos, and, so he said, he was given (free) room, board, and entertainment (including hookers), in hopes that he would duplicate his run of bad luck.

In 1981 Uston successfully challenged the rights of the Atlantic City casinos to stop him from gambling; the Appellate Division of the New Jersey Superior Court ruled that he and other counters had been illegally discriminated against. (Uston never won in the Nevada courts, which as one wag put it, has never acknowledged that the Bill of Rights applies to anyone other than the gambling casinos.)

It did not prove to be the end of Blackjack in Atlantic City. A few protective measures, such as the use of eight decks instead of four (since cut back to four, in some cases) kept the Blackjack tables humming, so much so that today the game is a much bigger money-maker in Atlantic City than before the court ruling.

Uston had done the casinos an inestimable service not because he did or did not offer proof that Blackjack could be beaten but in fostering the belief in the public that it was possible. About a year after the dispute, Resorts International, the specific casino Uston had sued, hired him to shill for it in television commercials and to show off the disguises he had used to gain access to the Blackjack tables.

Uston, of course, insisted he'd made a fortune at counting, but later on he allegedly lost most of his money in California real estate deals. For the last year of his life, Uston, who died in October 1987, worked on a computer project to help Kuwait track billions of dollars in investments. It apparently had not occurred to him to recoup at the Blackjack tables—where so many of his readers were still trying to make their fortunes.

V

VERMONT—Legalized Lotteries

Vermont's legalized lottery activities have not produced huge amounts of money, not surprisingly considering the state's size. In 1984 the Vermont lottery did however add $1.25 million to the state's general fund. Vermont offers a three-digit and a four-digit game with a payoff rate of about 50 percent, which, as is true in most states, is below the payoff average made by underworld-run numbers games. Additionally, of course, big prizes are subjected to tax withholding.

The state also offers an instant "rub off" game in various forms. On average, one in every seven tickets is a winner, although the overwhelming majority are only for a $2 minimum. The maximum score in a typical game, roughly 10 out of 183,000 winning tickets, is for $10,000, the top prize.

In an effort to bring in more revenues, Vermont has joined Maine and New Hampshire in the nation's first three-state lottery.

See TRI-STATE MEGABUCKS.

Denmark VESEY: Lottery Winner and Slave

Despite the notoriety given big-money lottery winners today, easily the most prominent winner of a lottery in America was a black slave named Denmark Vesey (1767–1822) who won $1,500 in the "east Bay Lottery" in 1800 and bought his freedom from his master for $600. He refused to be manumitted to Africa, having other plans. Included was a long-contemplated plot to foment an uprising of all slaves in Charleston, South Carolina, with the hope that the rebellion would spread throughout the slave-holding South.

Vesey converted some 9,000 slaves to his secret plan, which was to be put into effect in 1822. However, a few slaves turned informers and the betrayed Vesey was apprehended on the eve of the planned uprising that called for the slaughter of all slaveholders in Charleston. Vesey and his top aide, Peter Poyas, and 33 slaves were hanged and 43 others banished. As gambling historian Henry Chafetz observes in *Play the Devil*, "Had Vesey's insurrection succeeded, it would have been the bloodiest aftermath of a lottery in American history."

Not surprisingly, many local lotteries in the South subsequently sought to bar slaves from purchasing tickets.

VICE PRESIDENT: Place Poker Variation

Vice President is the draw version of what is called PLACE POKER, which is any game in which the second-best hand wins the pot. Most games of Stud played under these rules produce situations that can alter too radically—with a player who thinks he is second-best suddenly facing a situation in which the presumed high player drops out, forcing him into the top position. Place Poker addicts insist Vice President allows for more reasoned strategy, such as that a player with a low pair, preferably deuces, or an unpaired hand with an ace-high should stand pat. Players with high pairs will most certainly break their pairs but the odds are that at least one will still re-pair, allowing the deuces or ace-high to come in second best. If two players stand pat on the draw, later players should probably drop out. A possible exception would be a hand consisting of a pair of aces, king, 7, 5. The player would probably do best discarding an ace and hoping not to re-pair. He would be assuming one of the two pat hands has a low pair and the other an ace-high, but he is figuring that his ace, king would still make him second best.

Some gamblers agree there is some merit to this strategy, but shy away from all forms of Place Poker, saying, "Why not just play some POKER instead?"

VIDEO KENO: Slot Game

It is a cardinal rule that all slots games are among the worst gambles that can be found in a casino, and that those games patterned after a real game have an additional built-in disadvantage for the player. That is not true of Video Keno, which is based on the game found in most Nevada gambling houses. Real KENO has a 20-25 percent house edge while Video Keno has only a 15 percent disadvantage. Does that make the video form the preferred version? The answer is positively not. The sad fact is that while you will almost certainly be a loser at Keno, you will be much more likely to lose your shirt at the slots version.

As in Keno, a card appears on the video screen with the numbers 1 through 80. The player simply marks off from one to ten numbers with a provided light pen and when he has completed his selections (he is able to erase selections before he completes his play), he presses the "Start" button. The machine then selects a total of 20 winning numbers at random. These are compared with the player's selections and his hits, if any, are tallied. The payoff prizes are determined according to a set schedule. Rest assured that the payoffs hardly reflect the true odds. For instance, picking ten numbers out of ten is a nine million-to-one shot. The payoff will not be made accordingly, not even if the player wins a progressive jackpot that requires playing five coins.

As a matter of fact, Video Keno is about the worst slots play of all, by comparison, an 85 percent payout rate is about the worst a player can do in a legitimate casino on any machine. Alongside Video Keno, Video Poker is a true game of skill.

However, as previously started, the real knock on Video Keno is that it is worse on the player's bankroll than playing regular Keno. That game is little more than a lottery, a leisurely sort of game that some casino addicts use for their loose bills while resting from table play. The lure is the admittedly longshot chance of getting a big payoff for a tiny bet. The logic is the same as playing any of the current legal state LOTTERIES. The odds are against the player in all these games and, as a matter of fact, at a 25 percent takeout, casino Keno is better than the public lotteries.

Why then knock Video Keno with a payoff record better than regular Keno? The answer involves the speed of play. A game of casino Keno takes seven or eight minutes to play and one can wager as little as 70 cents. In Video Keno the game can be completed in as little as one-one hundredth the time. Thus in the same time frame a player figures to lose 25 percent of 70 cents compared to 15 percent of say 100 quarters. As much as casinos love customers to play Keno, they adore them patronizing the slots version. The payoff is so much greater for the house.

VIDEO POKER

See SLOT MACHINES.

VIG OR VIGORISH: The House Edge

Vigorish is a gambler's term for the house edge on any bet or game. Originally the term applied to the game of Bank Craps as booked by John Winn, the first CRAPS bookmaker. Early in this century Winn started booking Crap games in alleys in New York City around East 14th Street. Bettors could bet either with or against the dice and Winn paid off, minus 25 cents on a $5 bet and 50 cents on a $10 bet.

Eventually other gamblers saw that Winn was making a fortune with his way of operating and began booking Crap games themselves instead of playing. Soon the idea of a 5 percent charge swept the country and hundreds of Craps bookmakers set up shop. Illegal casinos adopted the system and made so much money that they could eliminate the use of crooked percentage dice. The new order was popular with dice players who considered a 5 percent charge reasonable in exchange for a fair shake.

Finding their income coming in so strong, bookmakers took the word vigor and added a syllable to make "vigorish." Later the word was frequently shortened to "vig" and came to mean any game in which a house edge existed whether in the form of a percentage takeout on the bet or one hidden in the mathematics of the game.

Bookmakers like to use the word vigorish rather than "edge" because many amateurs do not understand the meaning of the former, and would pick up on edge as indicating they have a less-than-even chance.

VINGT-TROIS: For-pigeons-only Game

The thesis that European casino games, and especially the French ones, give bettors more attractive odds than do grasping American establishments is not always true. ROULETTE is a better game played under the standard European rules of one zero, but the French have come up with so-called "poor man's roulette" games that can only be described as sucker traps. BOULE is considered the kingpin of such outrageous games and Vingt-trois is little more than a variation of Boule.

Vingt-trois uses a wheel with 27 cups. It is like a Roulette wheel but is capped by a plastic dome and operated by controls outside the dome, so that the croupier neither handles the ball nor the wheel. The 27 cups on the wheel are numbered from 1 to 14.

Numbers 1, 2, 3, and 4 appear only once, and if one bets and wins on any of these numbers the odds are paid off at 23 to 1. Numbers 5, 6, 7, 8, 9, 10, and 11 have two pockets each and a win on any of them is paid at 11 to 1. Numbers 12, 13, and 14 appear three times each and the payoff on them is 7 to 1.

There are also the standard forms of even-money betting, with number 13 taking the place of zero in Roulette. Since Roulette in the same casino penalizes even-money bettors with only one zero out of 37 possibilities and Vingt-trois has three 13's out of a total of 27 possibilities, it does not take an Einstein to figure the odds in favor of the house are enormous. In fact, the house edge on all bets runs to a ruinous 11.1111 percent (more than some casino one-armed bandits in the States), which makes it a virtual certainty that no extended play at Vingt-trois can result in a gambler coming out on top.

One of the more pathetic sights at the Vingt-trois table is seeing a system player trying to beat the bank on even-money bets. Since the house edge at Roulette is a mere 1.35 percent on all even-money propositions, one can conclude an even-money bettor will go broke eight times faster at Vingt-trois than at Roulette. And since time between plays at Vingt-trois can be quicker, there being fewer payoffs, a fool and his money are even more quickly parted.

VIRGINIA—Legalized Lotteries

Almost annually in the 1970's and 1980's the Virginia state legislature voted down proposals to institute a state lottery. In November 1987 the voters finally approved such a plan, which made Virginia the twenty-eighth state to offer a lottery. Approval came despite the opposition of church groups, the governor, and the former governor. Most voters said they favored the lottery because they believed it would prevent a tax increase.

Generally, voters will approve a lottery but usually will vote down casino gambling. The real reason: many worry that casino gambling will cause severe hardship for habitual gamblers, but that the lottery is a minor-stakes affair. Of course they are voting down small takeouts and voting for big takeouts—lotteries invariably take out 50 percent or more—but who is to say the public is wrong.

WASHINGTON, D.C.—Legalized Lotteries

Residents of the District of Columbia are not eligible to vote for members of Congress, but they are allowed to "vote" on daily and weekly LOTTERIES. There are two-digit, three-digit, and four-digit numbers games, drawing players from noon to night. The latter two games are drawn in the evening house while the two-digit game, the Daily Double, caters to lunchtime bettors with a drawing at 1:30 P.M. The three- and four-digit games have fixed prize amounts with a return in about the 50 percent range compared to true odds. The Daily Double, however, is a pari-mutuel play with prizes determined by the numbers of winners. Tickets cost $1 and bettors select any pair of digits from 00 to 99. A winning selection must have both numbers right but in either order. Persons who pick one number correctly are entitled to a free play in the next game.

Instant games of the "rub-out" type change regularly and usually pay from $1 to $10,000, with odds on winning some prize working out to about 1 in 6. Five nonwinning tickets may be submitted for a shot at a large compensatory jackpot prize.

WASHINGTON (state)—Legalized Lotteries

Income from various lottery games in Washington go to the state's general fund. The typical LOTTO game with numbers from 1 to 40 operates under the same general conditions as in most states. The jackpot prize is guaranteed to be at least a half-million dollars and it can grow into the millions. Chances of winning a first prize is 1 in 3,838,380 per play; for second prize (five right out of six) it is 1 in 18,816 per play; and third prize (four right out of six) 1 in 456 per play. Overall, the odds of winning some prize is 1 in 445.

Washington's Triple Choice is a typical three-digit

numbers game with the usual approximate 50 percent payoff compared to true odds.

The third form of play is various "rub-out" games, a typical one offering payoffs from $2 (1 chance in 13.61) to $10,000 (1 in 300,000). Chances of winning some prize is 1 in 8.52, fairly good for a game without $1 payoffs.

WAVING: Marking Cards During Play

A good card cheat does not have to depend on marking cards before a game, and he does not even have to use such methods as nailing or pegging, which leave telltale signs of cheating. Instead, the cheater will rely on a method that arouses far less suspicion, that of "waving."

During play the cheat skillfully bends the card he wants to identify over one finger and under another. The movement, which is very fast, leaves a "wave" in the card. A wave near the end of a card may indicate a deuce, one in the middle may identify an ace, and so on. Such waves don't attract too much attention in the average game since many players are very rough or nervous in handling cards and frequently bend their entire hand.

In many games two decks are used, one in play. The other from the last go-round is passed on to the next dealer who can "wash" the cards while the current dealer is preparing for the current hand. This allows a good wave man to fix one deck after another. Even when a deck is tossed out of the game in favor of a new one, the cheat will have his waves back in action in no time.

If waving is suspected, one should square up the whole deck and look at the edges. The waves will show clearly. When two decks are in play, this detection method can be used during the washing period without raising an undue clamor. That dealer can then request a new pack and keep a sharp eye out for the ginger moves that make waves.

Charles WELLS: "The Man Who Broke the Bank at Monte Carlo"

The key fact to remember about Charles Wells (1841–1926), immortalized in song as "The Man Who Broke the Bank at Monte Carlo," was that he did not. Nobody ever has.

What this roundish, bearded, bald little Cockney swindler did was break the bank several times of one of the casino's tables. Wells, not long out of Her Majesty's prisons for confidence rackets, showed up in Monte Carlo in July 1891 with the equivalent of a $2,000 stake. He hit the ROULETTE table and seemed to be playing some sort of system involving the low numbers. Numbers 1 and 2 came up quite frequently and he was always on them. Pretty soon he wiped out the bank at the table and it had to be shut down to be replenished. Wells soon broke it three more times. Within 11 hours he broke the table's bank a dozen times. His phenomenal streak lasted two more days and at one point he won 23 out of 30 spins, not all on individual numbers, but the chips just piled up. It is estimated he beat the casino for at least $200,000. A few months later Wells was back and repeated the entire procedure, walking off with another $200,000.

The casino had detectives watch him, experts checked the wheel, and croupiers were interrogated, but no evidence of fraud turned up. Other gamblers charted Wells's method of play, but it proved too erratic for them to trace his system. Wells became world famous and for that matter so did the Monte Carlo casino, and droves of would-be casino-busters headed for Monaco to duplicate the little Cockney's exploits. They did not.

Still, everyone was singing the tune written in Wells's honor. And when Wells showed up again in 1892, this time by yacht with a beautiful model in tow, it looked like he was primed for a third fabulous repeat. He wiped out the table a half dozen times, but then suddenly he started to lose—and lose and lose.

Rich backers in England wired him more money and he kept on losing. So, sans yacht and lady friend, Wells headed back for England and permanent retirement from Roulette gambling. He spent his remaining years working various swindles that put him in prison a number of times. In 1922, near the end of his life, Wells confessed he'd not had a system at all but had simply bet without any pattern, relying on instinct and luck. He'd had an incredible run of luck in '91. In '92, however, Wells had come back to Monte Carlo with a system all worked out. *That's* when he lost.

WEST VIRGINIA—Legalized Lotteries

West Virginia's Lottery is hardly distinguishable from those in many other states, but in November 1987 it achieved a bit of notoriety highly unlikely to be featured in the state's advertising hype for its gambling games. Seventy-seven-year-old Clarence Kinder spun a wheel and won a televised state lottery for $50,000. It was, said his stepdaughter, "the greatest day of his life." Happily, he laid plans to buy a house.

The next day the lucky winner, still in throes of celebrating his big win, died of a heart attack.

WHEEL OF FORTUNE

See BIG SIX (WHEEL OF FORTUNE).

WHISKEY POKER: Sociable Gambling Game

The name Whiskey Poker derives from the fact that the game undoubtedly originated as a sociable game in American lumber camps to decide who bought the drinks. In fact, *American Hoyle,* published in 1880, says: "The game is often played for refreshments."

How to play: Each player gets five downcards as in Draw Poker but the dealer also deals an extra hand just before his own. This goes in the center of the table and the first player has the option of exchanging his own hand for that hand, passing, or knocking, which means he is prepared to stop the game and have a showdown, with the high man taking the pot. If that player (or any subsequent player) exchanges hands blindly, his former hand is laid face up on the table as a widow. Subsequent players now have the option of picking up the entire widow, exchanging one card from it for one in their hands, knocking for showdown, or passing (however no one may pass two times in a row).

If no one takes the faced-down hand by the time it reaches the dealer, he must turn them face up and make his own decision—as any player would concerning the exposed widow. Knocking must be done *before* exchanging a card with the widow, and following the knock all players get one more shot at the widow before the showdown.

High man takes the pot. Usually the low man must also match the pot. This is the carryover from the original version of Whiskey Poker whereby the low man buys the drinks.

Strategy: Today Whiskey Poker is played mostly as a straight gambling game, much preferred by good gamblers who find it very difficult to lose at the game. They realize the key strategy is very defensive in nature, geared not so much at winning as not losing. The good gambler understands that if he can avoid losing the wins will take care of themselves, and he should come out ahead. He recognizes that it is very dangerous to try for a flush or straight because if he is caught short by a knock, he will almost assuredly have the low hand. Of course, he might hold a four-card flush or straight as long as his hand contains a pair at the same time. However, as play develops, he is always ready to abandon the possible straight or flush to better his hand in any other way, or even to prevent later players from exchanging a card he knows they need.

WHIST: Forerunner of Bridge

Whist, originally called Whisk, was the game that Edmond Hoyle made famous, and vice versa. However, Hoyle was not the first to write about the game. That honor, although that may be not quite the word for it, belongs to one Richard Seymour, Esq., as he named himself in his 1734 work *The Compleat Gamester, for the Use of Young Princesses.* Seymour described a version of Whist, but spent very little time on the rules or legitimate strategy. He was much more concerned with explaining to noble young ladies how to win by every means possible, from peeking to hand signals.

Perhaps Seymour thought he was doing right because almost up until that time Whist had been considered more of a "downstairs" game to be played by the servants than an "upstairs" game for their employers. Whist, as an upper-class game, was born in the famous Crown Coffee House where Lord Folkestone and his friends met and played the game. They, together with Hoyle, eventually introduced it to fashionable society. During the 18th and 19th centuries Whist became the most-played game in the English-speaking world, and it was not until around 1900 that it finally lost its leading position to BRIDGE.

How to play: All rules applying to the deck, partnership, preliminary cuts, and deal are similar to those in Bridge. Thirteen cards are dealt to each of four players except that the dealer leaves his final card face up on the table, temporarily establishing trump. The player to the left of the dealer leads to the first trick and the trick is taken by the highest in suit, unless a player without suit trumps it instead. If so, highest trump takes the trick. If a player can neither follow suit nor trump, he may discard any other card.

After the first trick the dealer picks up his trump card and puts it in his hand. There is no bidding in Whist, and since every player plays his own hand there is no dummy as in Bridge. Partners simply try to take as many tricks as possible. All tricks after the first six taken by a partnership count for one point. Game score is 7 under the laws of the American Whist Congress and 5 in England. The ace, king, queen, and jack of trump are known as "honours"; any side dealt all four of them scores 4 points, and for any three, 2 points. However, if at the start of a

deal a partnership already has a score of 4 points, it cannot score for honours. Object of the game is to win a rubber, two out of three games.

Strategy: There are many gambits recommended since Hoyle's day that remain valid under almost all conditions. Generally the second player should play low and third player high. Also when a player holds five or more trumps it is advisable for him to lead a trump.

Other variations of basic Whist follow, not including SCOTCH WHIST and FRENCH WHIST which, despite their misnomers, are so far from basic Whist that they deserve their own listings.

WHIST—Bid Whist

Bid Whist is a very popular variation of the basic game. The entire deck is dealt out face down and instead of turning up trump, that suit is decided by bidding. The player to the left of the dealer starts off by indicating how many tricks he thinks he can take, provided he can name trump suit, and leads the first trick. Each player has one bid, but it must always be higher than the previous bid or he must pass. In what is called Auction Whist, bids continue until there are three successive passes. After the highest bid is determined, play continues as in regular WHIST.

WHIST—Boston and Boston de Fontainebleau

Boston was a very complex version of WHIST and now survives in the more simple game of Solo Whist. Boston gained great popularity around the time of the American Revolution, but diluted the Whist character of the game to some extent by incorporating rules from other games of the period. One was that the turn-up of a card to make trump was made from a separate deck.

Boston de Fontainebleau was another variation that allowed bidders always to name suits when bids were made for the same number of tricks. The suits ranked upward in value: spades, clubs, hearts, and diamonds.

WHIST—Cayenne

It is odd how many WHIST addicts speak almost lovingly of the Cayenne version of the same, and then never seem to play it. As a result Cayenne is virtually extinct today. Under the rules of play the final card is turned up, not for the purpose of naming trump, but to set the values of the suits in that deal. The dealer chooses the trump suit after consulting his hand. He may if he chooses call no-trump, or "nullo" (see WHIST—NORWEGIAN).

Thus, while the game is extinct, it can be seen in the context of anticipating the modern game of BRIDGE in that it established no-trump and fixed suit values. It also established another precedent, one that permitted the dealer to take none of the acts mentioned above but instead "bridge" the bid to his partner, the act that gave Bridge its name.

WHIST—Contract Whist

Contract Whist is a combination of two games, WHIST and Contract Bridge. The bidding and scoring in Contract Whist are the same as in Contract Bridge, the only difference being that there is no dummy and all four players participate in each hand.

WHIST—Dummy Whist

Dummy Whist is for three players, with the low cut determining who plays opposite an exposed dummy for the first rubber. The second-lowest on the cut inherits the dummy for the second rubber, and so on. Dummy is not exposed until after the opening lead.

WHIST—German Whist

German Whist is a two-player game with the standard 52-card deck. Each player gets 13 cards and the next card is faced up on the pack to indicate trump. The nondealer leads and the dealer follows suit if he can; if he cannot, he may trump or discard another card. The winner of the first trick takes the exposed card from the pack, thus gaining a trump while the loser takes the next card. Thereafter the winner of each trick leads to the next. When all the cards in the pack are exhausted, play continues from the players' hands until they are played out. The player taking the most tricks collects the previously-agreed units of betting on the difference between their totals.

WHIST—Norwegian

A partnership game for four, Norwegian Whist is a form of no-trump WHIST. Beginning at the dealer's left, each player is accorded a chance to bid either a "grand" or a "nullo." A bid of grand means the player will take seven of the 13 tricks, while nullo means he will lose at least seven tricks. If the first three players pass, the dealer is required to make a bid, but as soon as a bid is made by any player, play begins. Each trick goes to the highest card of whatever suit is led.

When the bid is a grand, the player to the bidder's right makes the first lead. When it is a nullo, the player to his left leads first. When grand is made, the bidding partnership scores 4 points for each trick over six but if the bidders fail, their opponents score 8 points for each trick they take over six. In a nullo matters are reversed. The bidder's side is awarded 4 points for every trick over six lost. But if the bidder loses the contract by winning seven or more tricks, the opponents get 8 points for each odd trick won by the bidder's side.

The game is usually for 50 points.

WHIST—Solo Whist

While four persons play Solo Whist, there are, as the name indicates, no partnerships but each plays for himself. However, there can be a temporary exemption to the no-partnership procedure. Trump, unless changed later in the bidding, is determined by the dealer turning up his final card, which he takes into his hand before playing to the first trick. The player to the left of the dealer speaks first on a bid and bidding continues until there are three passes in a row. If a player passes, he must continue to pass on each go-round. Each bid must overbid the previous one. The bids, from lowest to highest, are as follows:

Proposal. Player contracts to win eight tricks if another player *accepts,* agreeing to be his partner for that particular deal—5 points.

Solo. Bidder undertakes to win five tricks, playing alone, with the trump as turned up—10 points.

Misere. Contracting to win no tricks, alone with no trump—15 points.

Abundance. Contracting to win nine tricks alone, bidder setting trump—20 points.

Abundance in Trumps. Same as Abundance, using the turned-up trump—20 points.

Spread (or *Open Misere*). Contracting to win no tricks, playing alone, no trump, with bidder's cards exposed—30 points.

Slam (or *Declared Abundance*). Contracting to win all tricks alone, with the privilege of naming trump and leading to the first trick—40 points.

As previously stated, a player normally may not reenter the bidding but he may state an acceptance to a bidder's proposal. If no bids are made, the deal passes. One variation is that in that case "Grand" is declared and played. This is a no-trump hand and the player taking the last trick must pay all other players at the rate of a Solo settlement.

Settlements are made in red or white chips, a red chip being worth five whites. The settlement rates for all but Proposal is as follows, with successful bidders collecting from each player and unsuccessful ones paying opponents at the same rate:

Solo	2 red
Misere	3 red
Abundance	4 red
Abundance in trumps	4 red
Spread	6 red
Slam	8 red

In the case of Proposal, the successful bidder and his partner win one red each, the losers each contributing one chip. Losses are paid at the same rate.

The white chips are used for overtricks and undertricks. If the bidder makes more tricks than necessary, he picks up a white chip for each additional trick. If he fails by more than one trick, he pays each opponent a chip for each additional trick.

See WHIST—BOSTON AND BOSTON DE FONTAINEBLEAU.

WHITE-ON-WHITE MARKED CARDS
See RIFFLE TEST.

WHITE'S CLUB: Early English Casino
Opened in the 17th century, its name still perpetuated on the London gambling scene today, White's Club is among the most storied of all casinos. The club attracted the greatest titled nobles of the day, and tales of their incredible gaming losses are legion. Some of the zaniest bets of all were made at White's. Members bet on births, marriages, how long a government ministry would last, now many members of Parliament would die by year's end, the identity of a mistress, and they even ran pools on the day some of their own ailing members would die. A typical entry in the club's wagering book reads, "Lord Montfort wagers Sir Jon Bland one hundred guineas that Mr. Nash outlives Mr. Cibber."

The aristocratic young scamps even laid bets as they wandered down the road from White's to Mrs. Comyns's brothel on whether or not they would contract venereal disease on that occasion. Biographer Henry Blythe has noted, "One member even wagered that he would, and then went to a great deal of trouble to discover a pox-ridden young harlot who could ensure that he won his bet."

Horace Walpole once described in a letter some wild action at the club: "A man dropped down at the door of White's; he was carried into the house. Was he dead or not? The odds were immediately given and taken for and against. It was proposed to bleed him. Those who had taken odds that the man was dead protested that the use of a lancet would affect the fairness of the bet; he was therefore left to himself and presently died—to the great satisfaction of those who had bet for that event."

Clearly, at White's the bet was the only thing.

WILD WIDOW: Spit in the Ocean Variation
Wild Widow is a Draw Poker game that is not quite as wild as SPIT IN THE OCEAN. Each player is dealt four downcards and then a card is faced in the center of the table. Unlike Spit in the Ocean, this card does not become the fifth card for all players. Like Spit, however, this card indicates the wild card for the hand so that the other three cards of the same denomination are wild. Thus hands in Wild Widow do not have to be quite as powerful as in Spit in the Ocean, or even in a four-wild-card game such as DEUCES WILD. In the latter, three aces is looked upon

as the average lowest winning hand whereas in Wild Widow a player may generally figure any fairly high three-of-a-kind set as worthy of play. It should be kept in mind that in any three wild-card game (and, of course, in a four wild-card game even more so) the chances of getting three of a kind is greater than getting two pairs. Therefore two pair should be viewed as a very weak hand—especially since the player does not have a wild card. A player whose three-of-a-kind hand is composed of one or two wild cards should regard his hand as all the more powerful since he has deprived his opponents of much of their chances of getting wild cards.

Wild Widow is played exactly like Draw Poker, with a discard and draw. There is a round of betting after the first four cards and the showing of the wild card. There is another round of betting after the fifth card is dealt, and another after the draw.

The game can also be played with no draw, in which case there are only two rounds of betting.

WILSON RANGERS: Civil War Gamblers' Military Unit
They were perhaps the dandiest unit in the Civil War. What else could an outfit be if composed entirely of Mississippi riverboat gamblers? There were those in the South who felt that if they had more outfits like the so-called Gamblers Cavalry, the Confederacy would have been unbeatable. Actually a better nickname for the unit, officially the Wilson Rangers, would have been the "Gambling Fourflushers."

Most of the riverboat gamblers of necessity abandoned the steamboats with the outbreak of the Civil War, and most being southerners they sought refuge and action in New Orleans. At the outbreak of hostilities these cardsharp dandies thought it would be smart public relations to form a military unit that would keep them out of real campaigning. Thus the Wilson Rangers were born and one newspaper, the *True Delta*, glowingly reported, "A finer-mounted troop of cavalry, we think, can hardly be found anywhere in the South than the Wilson Rangers of this city. . . . From what we have seen of them at drill, we judge them to be a valuable support to our army of gulf coast defense."

However, a different portrait of the gallant outfit was told by George Devol, one of the most-storied rogues of the river, in his autobiography, *Forty Years a Gambler on the Mississippi:*

> I was a member of the company. We armed and equipped ourselves, and the ladies said we were the finest looking set of men in the army. . . . When we were ordered out to drill (which was every day), we would mount our fine horses, gallop out back of the city, and the first orders we would receive from our commanding officer would be "Dismount! Hitch

horses! March! Hunt shade! Begin playing!". . . . in less than ten minutes there would not be a man in the sun. They were all in the shade, seated on the ground in little groups of four, five and six; and in each group could be seen a little book of tactics (or at least it looked like a book at a distance). We would remain in the shade until the cool of the evening, when the orders would be given: "Cease playing! Put up books! Prepare to mount! Mount! March!" When we would get back to the city, the people would come out, cheer, wave handkerchiefs and present us with bouquets; for we had been out drilling in the hot sun, preparing to protect their homes from the Northern invaders. . . . The citizens called us their defenders; and we did defend them, so long as there was no hostile foe within five hundred miles of them.

Unfortunately for the gamblers cavalry, it was ordered to active service in April 1862 when Union forces attacked by water and land. "As we went through the streets," Devol recounted, "the ladies presented us with bouquets, and cheered us; but there was but little cheer in that fine body of gamblers."

The Rangers rode forth about six miles when a Federal ship loosened a salvo at them. That was the end of the Wilson Rangers as the doughty gamblers retreated at double speed. "When we got back to the city," Devol said, "we dismounted without orders . . . cut the buttons off our coats, buried our sabers, and tried to make ourselves look as much like peaceful citizens as possible; for we had enough of military glory, and were tired of war."

More accurately, they were following the old gamblers' axiom: never buck the odds.

Michael WITTKOWSKI: Big Lottery Winner

With the growth of legal LOTTERIES in the United States Michael Wittkowski's claim to fame proved fleeting, but he was at the time the winner of $40 million, the greatest single lottery prize in North American history. Despite the fact that he received a first check for $1.5 million after taxes and would get nearly $2 million a year for the next 20 years, Wittkowski announced he was going to keep right on working at Delux Check Printers in Chicago. "If I quit, all I have to do is sit around and count my money."

A year later, in 1985, and some 20 pounds heavier, Wittkowski quit. But he did miss his pals at the print shop, he said.

WOOLWORTH: Wild Form of Seven-card Stud

A variant of POKER, most often in the Seven-card Stud version, this is an insanely wild game in which both the 5's and 10's are wild. However, when a player gets a 5 face up, he must ante an extra five chips into the pot or fold. The face-up 10 will cost the player 10 chips. No penalty is involved for 5's or 10's dealt face down. Cards are dealt as usual in normal seven-card-stud fashion, with the first two and seventh cards dealt down. A smart gambler will call for this game at DEALER'S CHOICE if he is contending with unsophisticated players who tend to stay in almost any kind of game to the bitter end, hoping to improve poor hands. The reality of this game is that anything under four of a kind seldom takes the pot.

In another variety of the game a player dealt a face-up 10 is knocked out of the game. A player holding a face-up 5 gets no penalty and does not have to ante up any extra chips. If no 10's are showing and a smart player has a nothing hand after getting three or at most four cards, he will drop; not only is he faced with covering additional bets with a weak hand but he risks getting a 10 to add expensive insult to injury.

Y

YABLON
See IN-BETWEEN.

YANKEE GRAB: Dice Bar Game
This is a rather simple three-dice game also known as Going to Boston and Newmarket, as it is more commonly known in England.

How to play: As many players as wish can play and each antes an equal amount to the pot. On the first cast the highest of three numbers is set aside (in case of a double or triple number only one die is set aside). Then the player shoots the remaining two dice and once more sets aside the high die. He then rolls the one remaining die and his score becomes that number plus the total of the two dice previously set aside. The highest cumulative score takes the pot.

For a more interesting variation of this basic game try MULTIPLICATION.

YUGOSLAVIA, Gambling in
There are more gambling casinos in Yugoslavia than in any other communist country. It was the late Marshal Tito's dream to salvage his country's economy by turning his resort coast into another Monaco. It has long been alleged that the marshal had no objection at all to wooing hard currency with American casino-operating expertise, and that meant employing the mob. It is known that a big racket conference in the Mexican resort of Acapulco in the early 1960's attended by such gangland stalwarts as Meyer Lansky and Chicago's Sam Giancana discussed how best to help Tito out. Lansky sent his people and mob money into the Adriatic country as well as cash from the mob's chief Cuban ally, Fulgencio Batista, who was eager to invest his secret funds with the type of people he had previously fought in Cuba. It was proof once again that gambling makes the strangest bedfellows.

The standard travel guides recommend such casinos as those in Dubrovnik ("The Pearl of the Adriatic") and to the north and south of that vacation paradise, and others in Belgrade, Split, Bled, and the island of Krk. Particularly recommended is Sveti Stegan where one may rake in the dinars in a luxurious casino with capitalist trappings as decadent as any in the West.

More discriminating gambling experts do not think highly of Yugoslavian casinos, however. They find the action at CRAPS undependable, with the limits mostly too small to allow for a good streak or effective system play. They also describe the payoffs on the slot machines as among the lowest in the world for legalized action.

One casino expert advises visitors "to see the sights and forget about the casinos." It may be sage advice, in the light of recent seizures of crooked gaming equipment by international authorities. It was suspected the rigged material was Yugo bound.

Z

ZEBRA: Seldom-played Form of Draw Poker

How to play: Zebra is a rather limited form of Draw Poker in which only "zebras" count as winning hands. A zebra is any five cards of alternating colors and descending ranks, such as 8 of clubs, 7 of hearts, 6 of spades, 5 of hearts, and 4 of clubs. An ace may be played high or low. The zebra with the highest card takes the pot. Since all other POKER hands are eliminated, the pot can grow substantially. However, because of the limited form of play, Zebra is not too popular a game.

ZIGINETTE: Italian-American Money Card Game

Ziginette is Italy's number one money card game and as such is heavily played by Italian-Americans. In many big cities the game is operated in clubs said to be dominated by the mob. The game itself is little more than a modern and highly popular version of LANSQUENET using a 40-card so-called Italian deck, with the 8's, 9's, and 10's stripped.

How to play: While Ziginette is a banking game, the house does not bank it. There is a cutter at the table who runs the game for each player, who in turn becomes the banker-dealer. The cutter settles bets and takes out a 10 percent house cut from the dealer's winnings.

The deck is shuffled and placed face up in a metal card box that allows only one card to be extracted at a time. The dealer takes two cards from the box, leaving the third card visible. The first two cards become players' cards—usually there are seven or eight contestants in the average game—and players can bet on either or both of them. The object is for bettors to wager on cards that the dealer fails to match before matching his own card. The dealer's card is the exposed card in the box. (All three cards must be of different values or a "no play" is called, requiring a new shuffle.)

Once all bets are placed, the dealer withdraws his card from the box and places it before him. In the process he has revealed a new card. Let us assume the players' first two cards were king and queen and the dealer's card an ace. If the new card is also an ace, the players would win all their bets. If it is a king or queen, the dealer would win all the bets on that particular card.

Most likely it would be none of the above but a card of yet another value. Let us say it is a jack. This also becomes a players' card and any bettor who wishes can put money on that card as well. Play continues in this fashion until the dealer's card is exposed, whereupon he must pay off all outstanding bets. In practice several new cards will become players' cards before the inevitable end occurs, and at times the dealer may collect many bets before he finally loses.

When he does, the cutter pays off the winners and totals up the dealer's previous winnings, deducts the house cut of 10 percent, and then supervises the passing of the deal to the next player. The cutter has many responsibilities, such as settling whose money was on which cards if there is a dispute. During the actual game he also weeds out "dead cards." These are cards that have been matched already. Obviously when a king is matched there are still two other kings left in the deck. These cannot, however, come into play. If the third king, for example, became a players' card there would be only one more in the deck as opposed to three of the dealer's card. The players would then hold an enormous advantage on such a card.

Ziginette is a dead-even game, a fact confirmed by the house's refusal to bank the game. The odds are even on the order of first appearance of any particular players' card and the dealer's card. However, in practice, as is true in the relatively defunct game of

Lansquenet, the dealer has a certain advantage. If a number of additional cards come into play it figures the dealer will win on a certain number of them before his card appears. For the players to maintain their equality in the odds they must keep betting all fresh cards. If their ardor cools, as can happen, the dealer could well end up taking in much more than he ultimately pays out.

However, in the final analysis only the house is a certain winner, with its cut from the dealer's winnings. The mob likes such a sure thing, and will therefore run a number of such games. If independents are running the game, it is also a safe bet they are paying for the privilege.

ZIONCHECK: Original Form of Contract Rummy

Zioncheck is sometimes used as an alternate name for CONTRACT RUMMY, but more accurately it is the original form of the game. It is played exactly like Contract Rummy but only the first five deals of that game are played, followed by the betting settlement.

ZOMBIE: Draw Poker Variation

Zombie is dealt and played just like Draw Poker except that a zombie, or temporarily "dead hand" is also dealt.

How to play: Betting and dropouts occur as in normal Draw and on the showdown the high hand is determined. However, that player is not necessarily the winner since the second highest hand is still in contention. This player now discards his hand and takes up the zombie. He may draw to improve the zombie, and he is at a slight edge now because he knows the cards he must beat. The high hand between the two, the original winner and the zombie, takes the pot.

While the original high hand may sometimes end up losing to the zombie, bear in mind that the pots tend to be larger overall as weaker hands usually stay in longer in hopes of at least being second best. Overall, original winners may take fewer pots but those that they do take will be bigger—with no additional investment on their part.

GLOSSARY

This glossary is intended to cover important gambling terms that may or may not appear in the text but which the reader will encounter in normal gambling activity. Emphasis is given to gambling "slanguage" so that "ace" is identified as a playing card but also as the 1 spot on a die or $1 in wagering jargon.

abandon: To give up a hand or deal.

above: A gambling casino's earnings as recorded in its bookkeeping ledgers.

above the line: In Bridge, the scoring of premiums.

accommodation arrest: A prearranged police raid on an illegal gambling joint or game to demonstrate to the public that officials are supposedly enforcing the laws.

accumulator: A cummulative bet in British horse racing, for which the American term is parlay. The bettor chooses horses in two or more races and if he wins a bet, that money is wagered on the next race.

ace: The highest ranking card in many games, especially Poker; the 1 spot on a die; $1 in wagering jargon.

ace kicker: An ace held along with a pair of another value in Draw Poker, a tactic frowned upon by many experts.

a cheval A split bet on two adjacent numbers on the layout in European Roulette.

across the board: A bet in horse racing in which a gambler places a bet on win, place, and show, collecting if the horse finishes first, second, or third.

action: Betting activity (see entry).

active player: The player who bets the most against the dealer in Chemin de Fer. He is dealt the cards and retains some options on whether or not to draw another card.

Ada from Decatur (or eighter from Decatur): The 8 point in Craps.

advertise: In Gin, Five-hundred Rummy, etc. to discard a card in the hope of luring an opponent to discard one of a similar rank or suit.

African dominoes: Dice. So named because the blacks along the Mississippi did so much to popularize the game of Craps.

agent: A person who takes lottery or numbers bets; the accomplice of a crooked casino employee who poses as a player in a plot to cheat the house.

alibi store: A fixed carnival game of skill in which the player cannot win, although the operator eggs him on with seemingly good advice.

also ran: A horse that finishes out of the money, i.e., not first, second or third. It also applies to any loser in any game.

anchor man: A player who sits to a Blackjack dealer's extreme right and is the last to act on his hand before the dealer. In a crooked house game, he will decide to hit or stand depending on whether or not such a play will improve the dealer's hand.

ante: A stake placed into the pool or pot before any other action in a gambling game, especially Poker.

(the) arm: A gambling operation backed or under the protection of organized crime.

around the corner: A card game procedure that permits the ace to link the lowest and highest cards in a sequence, such as queen, king, ace, deuce, three, etc.

auction: Bidding toward establishing trump in a game. In Chemin de Fer, the bidding to determine who will be the banker.

back in: In Poker, to bet after first checking.

back line: In Craps, the Don't Pass area on the layout, thus a back-line bettor is betting against the shooter.

backer: A person financing a game or staking a gambler.

banco: An old-time gambling scam (see entry); in Chemin de Fer, a bid by a player to cover the banker's entire wager.

bank: The house or dealer who pays off.

bank craps: A casino game in which, unlike private Craps, players bet against the house rather than against one another.

banking game: Any gambling game in which players compete against the house rather than one another.

bankroll man: The same as a backer, meaning the person who finances a gambling game or scheme.

base dealer: A card cheat whose specialty is dealing cards off the bottom of the deck. (See BOTTOM DEALING.)

beanshooter: A holdout device, especially for cards, worn on the arm.

belly joint: A crooked carnival game, especially a wheel game, which the operator fixes by leaning his stomach into the counter.

below the line: In Bridge, the entry of trick scores.

bet: A wager on the outcome of any play or game.

bet blind: To bet without looking at one's cards, especially in Poker.

bet the pot: To bet an amount equal to the money already in the pot, or kitty.

bevels: Dice that have been rounded on one or more sides so that the cubes tend to roll off these sides to the flat sides, thus making some numbers more likely to come up.

bicycle: In Lowball Poker, the lowest possible hand—5, 4, 3, 2, ace.

bid: In many games, an offer to take a certain number of tricks or points.

Big Dick: In Craps, the 10 point.

Big Eight: In Craps, a foolish even-money bet on a Craps layout that an 8 will be rolled before a 7. The same bet can be made elsewhere on the layout at more favorable odds.

big order: In bookmaker parlance, a big sports bet, often as much as $50,000.

Big Six: In Craps, a foolish even-money bet on a layout that a 6 will be rolled before a 7. The same bet can be made elsewhere on the layout at more favorable odds.

bird dog: An informer who finds easy games or victims for gambling hustlers.

bite: A gambler's request for a loan—seldom a good bet.

black line work: A method of identifying picture cards by scratching along the line that borders the face of all picture cards. The cheat can feel the mark as he deals the cards and knows when an opponent is holding high cards, vital information in games played for "low."

blanket roll: In Craps, a cheating controlled roll of the dice on a blanket or other soft surface.

blister: A tiny mark on the back of a playing card so that it can be identified by a cheat, especially when dealing.

block-out work: A technique for marking the designs on the backs of playing cards so they can be identified.

bluff: In Poker, an attempt to force other players out of the game by making a huge bet not justified by the cards in hand.

book: In Bridge or Whist, the fist six tricks that must be taken in before any score is made; to take racing or sports bets.

book, bookie, bookmaker: An establishment or individual that accepts wagers on the outcome of races and sporting events.

box: In Gin, a score for winning the deal; in the Numbers game, making a bet on all combinations, i.e., boxing 123 means winning on any of the six possible results: 123, 132, 213, 231, 312, 321.

boxcars: In Craps, a roll of 12.

boxman: A casino employee who is in charge of the Craps table.

box numbers: In Craps, the place numbers of 4, 5, 6, 8, 9, and 10.

bricks: Crooked dice that have been shaved so that some sides have more space than others.

bug: A clip that can be attached to the underside of a card table to hold cards secretly removed from the deck; in slot machines, a device that prevents certain combinations from appearing.

bunch: To give up or abandon the deal; to gather cards prior to shuffling; in Auction Pitch, an offer by the dealer to play the hand at a bid of 2 or to have a new deal at the opponent's option.

bust: In Blackjack, taking too many cards so that a player's hand goes over 21 and automatically loses no matter what the dealer does afterward.

bustout joint: A gambling house or special game in which honest players are cheated.

cackle: Dice jargon for pretending to shake the dice while holding them in a special finger grip so that they actually do not tumble in the hand.

call: In many games, especially Poker, to match the amount bet by an opponent.

call bet: In Craps, to make a bet without actually putting up the required money, generally prohibited in casino play.

caller: In Bingo, the person calling out the numbers as they come up.

card counter: In Blackjack, a player who tries to keep track of the cards already played to determine when the deck is against the dealer.

card sense: A term used to describe a good card-player, one who understands the percentages and plays correctly.

carpet joint: A slang term used to describe a luxury gambling casino, as contrasted with a "sawdust joint."

carre: In Roulette, the French term for betting on four numbers on the layout that form a square, for example, 1,2,4,5.

chalk: The favorite, especially in horse-race betting.

check and raise: In Poker, a cutthroat method of betting by which a gambler pretends weakness to coax a bet or bets out of opponents, and then the gambler raises. Considered fair play in big-money games, but often not permitted in more friendly games.

chippy: An inexpert gambler or sucker. The same as pigeon (See MARK entry.)

circled game: A game in which the sports book reduces the normal betting limit.

closed cards: Cards that are dealt face down.

closed poker: Any game of Poker in which no cards are revealed until the showdown, especially in Five-card Draw.

cognotte: In Baccarat, the slot in the table into which the bank's winnings are dropped. In Chemin de Fer, it is used for the bank's cut.

colonne: In European Roulette, a bet on a complete column of 12 numbers running the length of the layout.

column: The American term for *Colonne.*

come-out: In Craps, the first roll after the shooter has won or lost.

cooler: In card games, especially Poker, a pre-arranged deck of cards that is switched into a game by a cheat or cheaters. (See COLD DECK.)

coup: One complete round or play of a game, the term being most commonly used in Roulette and Baccarat. In betting parlance, a successful wager.

cover: When the favorite wins a sporting event by more than the required number of points.

crimp: In card cheating, putting a small bend in a card so that it can be located later in the deck. This can be used so that a confederate of a crooked dealer can cut the deck in an appropriate spot or, indeed, often to cause an innocent player to make the cut at that point.

crosseyes: In Craps, the English term for a throw of 3 with dice.

croupier: A casino employee in charge of operating a Roulette table, although the term is also used for the dealer in games of Baccarat.

cut: In cards, dividing the deck into two or more piles and rearranging them in a different order; in some gambling house games, the percentage charge made by the house against the winners in some games of Baccarat or Craps, etc.

cut-edge dice: Crooked dice with some edges cut at a 45-degree angle and others at usually 60-degrees, which greatly affects the roll.

daily double: In race betting, a combination bet on the results of two races, generally the first two on the card, in which both winners must be picked or the wager is lost.

daub: Usually a paste but sometimes a special fluid used by cheats to mark cards during a game.

dead ace: A die in a crooked game that has been doctored so that the 1 will come up more often than it normally would.

dead card: A card that has been already played and discarded or one that may not be brought into play.

Under the rules in many Poker games a card inadvertently exposed is automatically dead and is out of the game, even though the player receiving it is willing to take it.

dead number dice: Dice doctored so that a number will come up more often than average. The most common is the "dead ace."

deadwood players: Persons who hang around a gambling game but do not play, often because they lack the resources.

deuce: In cards, the 2; in dice, the 2-spot on a die; in money talk, $2.

dice chute: A plastic tube used to drop the dice in some gambling games, supposedly to cut the cheating possibilities compared to those when dice are thrown by hand or with a dice cup.

dice degenerates: Players who lose consistently at Craps. The dice gambler's term for one form of compulsive gambler.

dime: Wagering jargon for $1,000.

do bettor: A dice player who bets that the shooter in Craps will win.

dog: In sports betting, the underdog; in common parlance, any losing race horse a gambler has bet on.

don't bettor: A dice player who bets that the shooter in Craps will lose.

dollar: Wagering jargon for $100.

door pops: Mis-spotted dice that will make 7 or 11 on every roll. Cheaters must move such mismarked dice in and out of a game very quickly to avoid suspicion.

double deuces: Crooked dice that have two deuces, the extra one in place of a 5.

double-number dice: Any dice that have two of the same number on opposite sides. Those with two deuces are called "double deuces," those with two 5's "double fives," etc.

doubling down: In casino Blackjack, a player may double the size of his bet after receiving his first two cards. However, under casino rules he will receive only one more card.

doubling up: To double the size of one's bet over a previous wager. This is called for under many betting systems, sometimes after a loss and sometimes even after a win.

doubter: A player in a number of dice games, such as Liar Dice, who must either challenge or concede the shooter's claim on the point value of his hidden throw.

downcard: A card dealt face down so that only the cardholder may see it, such as the hole card or last card dealt in many games.

dragging: A cheater's technique of slipping chips off a bet after the game is in progress. (See PINCHING.)

draw: To get a new card or cards upon discarding from one's hand.

driller: A slot machine thief who drills holes in a slot machine to make it pay off.

drop: A place where numbers runners deliver their action to a controller; in cards, to withdraw from a hand by not matching the bet.

drop shot: A dice cheat's method of controlling the fall of one of the two dice he rolls.

dump shot: The technique used by a dice mechanic to control the roll of one of two or more dice rolled from a dice cup.

ear: A cheating technique in cards of bending a corner of a card so that it can be identified or located. Used in the Three-card Monte scheme to lure in a sucker by making it appear spotting the winning card is a cinch. The operator then picks up the cards and straightens that ear while bending a corner on a losing card instead.

edge: The mathematical advantage held by the bank or the casino in a gambling game. This is called the house edge.

eighter from Decatur (or Ada from Decatur): The 8 point in Craps.

eldest hand: The cardplayer on the dealer's left.

electric dice: Gaffed dice loaded with steel slugs, which will react to an electromagnet installed in a dice table or under a counter.

en prison: In European Roulette, the imprisonment of all chips bet on even-money chances when zero appears. The chips are won or lost by the player depending on the outcome of the next roll.

english: The spinning or sliding action put on dice by an expert manipulator.

entry: In horse racing, two or more horses in the same event with a common owner or trainer. In such cases, with a few exceptions, the horses are considered a common interest and a bet is decided on the performance of any of the animals.

exacta: In horse racing and other events, a bet in which one picks the winner and runnerup in a race in the exact order of finish.

exotics: Any unusual wagers in a sports bet such as exactas, trifectas, teasers, parlays, etc.

face card: The picture cards—jack, queen, king.

fader: A Craps player who covers the shooter's bet.

false opener: A Poker player who opens the betting illegitimately by not having met the requirements, i.e., in Jacks-or-Better, opening on a lesser pair.

field bet: In Craps, a layout bet that wins if 2, 3, 4, 9, 10, 11, or 12 appears on the next roll. This bet greatly favors the house, but is sometimes improved by the substitution of the 5 for the 4; in racing, the coupling of several horses of different interests in a single betting unit, usually all horses beyond the first 11 entries.

first base: In Blackjack, the player to the dealer's extreme left, the first player to get cards and the first to play the hand.

first dozen: In Roulette a bet at 2 to 1 odds on the first 12 numbers: 1-12.

first flop dice: A combination bet in American Roulette on 0, 00, 1, 2, and 3. The payoff rate greatly favors the house and is the worst bet on the layout for the player.

fix: To illegally influence the result of a game or contest; to pay authorities bribes to allow a gambling operation.

flag: Signaling a confederate in a crooked game.

flash: Expensive prizes used as a come-on at carnival games. They are almost never won by the public.

flashing: A cheating method used by a casino Blackjack dealer to let a confederate see the top card of the deck before he draws.

flat joint: A term used for any dishonest gambling house or game.

flat passers: Fixed dice that have the 3-4 sides of one die and the 6-1 of the other cut down. As a result the numbers 4, 5, 9, and 10 will turn up much more frequently.

flats: Fixed dice that have been shaved so that two sides have more surface area than the four others. Also called "bricks."

floating game: An illegal gambling game that moves from one location to another to avoid police detection.

floorman: A roving casino supervisor who checks that all the games are being operated according to the house rules.

flopping the deck: A cheating-the-casino scam whereby a dishonest dealer turns the deck over in midgame so that previously used cards come back into play.

free ride: In Poker, a situation where all players "check" in a round so that no bets are added to the pot.

front line: In Craps, the layout area where Pass bets, the most common in the game, are made.

front loader: An inept Blackjack dealer who inadvertently flashes his hole card to an opponent as he deals.

fruit machine: An English term for slot machine, coined because so many of them display cherries and the like.

G joint: Any crooked game or gambling house. The G stands for "gaff."

gaff: Any cheating device or gimmick for fixing cards, dice, or wheels.

glim: Any sort of mirror that allows a cheat to see an opponent's cards as he deals them. (See SHINER.)

going south: Secretly removing cards, dice, money, chips, etc., from a game in a scam.

goulash joint: A bar or restaurant that permits gambling games in a back room.

Greek shot: A difficult controlled roll of the dice that must hit a wall. When done correctly, the dice will hit one atop the other so that the bottom die does not roll over. Only experts can pull this off.

grifter: A gambling cheat or con man.

grind joint: A gambling house or casino that relies on low-limit bettors and a huge number of players to operate profitably.

half-time action: Legal sports books in Nevada and illegitimate ones elsewhere often post new odds at half-time for the balance of a football game. Many gamblers will bet the new odds or point spreads to protect their original wagers, hoping sometimes to win both ways.

handicapper: An expert who studies, rates, and/or wagers on races and other sporting events.

handle: The total amount of money bet at a casino or racetrack, frequently being the same money, previously bet and now in the hands of new owners.

handmucker: An expert card cheat who can switch cards by palming and other methods to get a winning hand.

hard way: In Craps, throwing the same number on each die to achieve a point, such as 2-2 to get 4, 3-3 to get 6, etc.

hedging: Betting on the opposing team or side of your original wager in order to reduce the size of the original wager or to try to "middle" (see definition) the game.

high-low pick-up: A Blackjack cheating method whereby the discards are picked up alternately: a high card, then a low card, etc. After a superficial shuffle, the cards will remain in that basic order.

high-low splitters: Gaffed dice with one die bearing the numbers 1, 2, and 3 twice and the other 4, 5, and 6 twice. This will produce a huge number of 7's. A crooked house will also switch in such dice when a player has made a big bet on the field, which is almost impossible to get with these dice.

hit: In Blackjack, to deal a player another card as he tries to get closer to 21.

hits: Any dice fixed to favor the shooter in Craps or a similar game.

holdout man: A card cheat expert at switching cards by palming and other methods to get a winning hand. Same as Handmucker.

hole card: A card that is dealt face down, such as in Stud Poker.

hook: A ½ point in a bet on a sporting event, such as the Giants being favored over the Redskins by 3½ points. This eliminates the possibility of a tie bet.

home-court advantage: Recognition that sports teams generally perform better at home than on the road.

hop: In Craps, any bet that is determined on the next roll of the dice.

horn: In Craps, a hop-bet combination that is won if the next roll produces a 2, 3, 11, or 12.

house limit: The maximum bet permitted by a casino, frequently lifted for big bettors.

house numbers: The 0 and 00 in Roulette, since the casino derives a profit against all even-money bets. However, they may be bet on singly or in combination with other nearby numbers.

ice: Money paid by illegal gambling operations and cheats for protection.

impair: In European Roulette, a bet on the odd numbers.

in-betweeners: In a number of card games, cards that fall in rank between two other cards determined by various methods, which take on special value.

in the money: In horse-race betting, a horse that finishes first, second, or third.

information: A term generally attributed to horse-race betting and involving "inside dope" that a horse is ready to win. The result does not always confirm the tip.

inside bets: In Roulette, wagers placed on the numbers, singly or in combination, rather than on outside bets (Red-Black, Odd-Even, or High-Low).

inside straight: In Poker, four cards in broken sequence toward a five-card straight, i.e., 9, jack, queen, king. As a general rule, it is not wise to try to fill such a straight.

insurance: In Blackjack, an optional bet that the dealer has Blackjack if his upcard is an ace. If a player buys such insurance and the dealer has Blackjack, the player collects 2 to 1 on his insurance bet. In a number of other gambling games in which a tie results in a loss for the player, he may also buy insurance against that event. In all cases the odds offered for insurance make it an excellent bet—for the house.

jackpot: The highest payout made by a slot machine.

jackpots: In Poker, a game of draw requiring a pair of jacks or more to open. The term is commonly used in England today, the more common term in the U.S. being Jacks or Better.

jeton: A gambling token used in French casinos in lieu of cash.

joker: An extra card supplied with a deck of 52 cards, which can be assigned special value, such as being wild or the highest trump. Some card games involve the use of two jokers.

juice joint: A crooked Roulette or dice game that is controlled by electromagnets.

kibitzer: The hanger-on at a gambling game who watches instead of playing.

kicker: In Poker, an odd or unneeded card held in Draw to mislead opponents.

kitty: A pool, which goes in whole or in part to the winner of a hand or round of betting.

knave: An old-fashioned word for the jack, although it is still widely used in England.

knock: In many card games, to end a hand or make a special announcement by knocking on the table or simply stating so.

knock out: A casino term for wiping out a gambler, especially a high roller.

ladderman: A casino employee who sits on an elevated chair overlooking the gaming tables looking for cheats and to correct dealer's errors.

lame: A bookie's customer who is unable to pay his playing losses.

late line: Revised betting odds offered on sporting events to adjust to the wagering patterns.

lay off: When a bookmaker finds he has too much money bet on one outcome in an event, he will pass on some of the disproportionate bets to another bookmaker.

laying the odds: To bet against the dice in Craps, by taking the short end of the odds if necessary, such as putting up 2 against 1 that the shooter will not make the 4 point.

laying the points: To bet on the favorite in a sporting event by giving up points.

laying the price: To bet the favorite by laying money odds.

lead: In cards, to play the first card at the start of a trick.

leaker: An inept gambling cheat, such as one who gives away his moves by letting a palmed card show between his fingers.

letting it ride: Leaving the original bet and its accumulation of profit in place in hopes of making an even greater profit by winning again.

light work: Marking cards with very fine lines.

line: The current odds or point spread on a particular sporting event.

line game: Any "spit" game of Poker, that is, a game in which cards faced up on the table are mutual or spit cards and are used to supplement the cards in the player's hands.

line work: Adding small markings such as spots, curlicues, or a lengthened line to the backs of playing cards so they can be read by a cheater.

Little Dick: In Craps, the 4 point.

Little Joe (or Little Joe from Kokomo): In Craps, the 4 point.

loaded dice: Dice weighted down in various ways to affect the numbers that come up.

location play: A technique of memorizing the sequence of a number of cards so that when they come up again, the cheat will know the order of likely appearance of several cards to follow.

long game: A card game in which all the cards are dealt out at the beginning.

long shot: An unlikely winner, especially in horse racing, which will carry long odds.

lugger: A person who delivers a group of gamblers to a game.

machine: Any type of cheating device worn on the person or attached to a table that is used to hold certain cards in a game out of play until needed.

maiden: Any race horse that has never won a race.

manque: Betting Low in European Roulette, that is, on numbers 1-18.

marked cards: Any cards used by cheats that in some way are altered or soiled to reveal their identity.

marker: In casino gambling, a coin or slug or chip used to indicate the player's bet or his tab; an IOU.

martingale system: A wagering pattern used mostly in Roulette that calls for doubling the bet after each loss. Generally this results in several small wins and one gigantic loss.

mechanic: A gambling cheat accomplished in sleight of hand.

Memphis dominoes: Dice.

Mexican standoff: A betting session that results in either negligible winnings or losses.

Michigan bankroll: A money roll consisting of a large denomination bill wrapped around a large number of $1 bills—much favored by gambling hustlers.

middle: When both sides of a point spread win. For example, a gambler bets on the Giants to win by 3 points over the Redskins. Later the odds go up to 6 points and he now bets the Redskins. The final score is 14-10 Giants, and the gambler wins both bets.

middle dozen: In Roulette, a wager made on the middle column of 12 numbers on the layout.

misdeal: An irregularity on the deal that requires a reshuffling and a new deal of the cards.

misses: Fixed dice that make more 7's than point numbers or produce more missouts than passes. In all cases, such dice work against the shooter.

mitt man: A sleight-of-hand card cheat who specializes in palming and switching cards.

monkey: A really easy victim, more so than even the usual mark, or pigeon.

morning line: The early odds established on the horses in a race.

mucker: Same as mitt man, above.

mudder: A horse on whom the odds shorten if the track turns sloppy or muddy because it is considered to be a better runner under such conditions.

mutual cards: In Poker, "spit" cards that are faced up in the center of the table and are common cards that may be used to supplement the cards players hold in their hand.

nail nicking: Marking a card during play by putting a small dent on the edge with a fingernail.

natural: In Craps, a 7 or 11 on the first roll; in Blackjack, 21 on the first two cards; in Baccarat, an 8 or 9 in two cards; in wild-card games, a top hand without the use of wild cards.

neighbors: In Roulette, the numbers that are in proximity on the wheel.

New York Craps: A form of Craps more popular in the eastern section of the United States in which a player pays a 5 percent charge on his bets.

newspaper line: The approximate odds on sporting events as listed in many newspapers.

nickel: Wagering jargon for $500.

ninety days: The 9 point in Craps.

no dice: A disallowed roll of the dice, frequently because they failed to hit a wall or did not land straight.

noir: In European Roulette, Black.

number two man: A cheating dealer adept at dealing the second card from the top.

OTB: Off-track betting, as permitted in betting parlors in New York State.

Odds: The probabilities of an event occurring expressed in a ratio of the unfavorable chances to the favorable chances.

odds-on favorite: In horse racing and other sporting events, a betting favorite that is regarded so strongly that it will pay off at less than even money.

off the board: A sports event on which bookmakers will not accept bets, often because the result is considered certain or there is fear that the play will be dishonest.

one-armed bandit: A slot machine.

one-eyed jacks: The jacks of hearts and spades. Often these are played as wild cards in Deuces Wild Poker, so that there are six wild cards in the game.

one-roll bet: In Craps, a wager that will be decided on the next roll of the dice.

open craps: A banking Crap game in which side bets among the players are permitted on the point number.

open-end straight: A four-card sequence in Poker in which either the card below or above in rank will complete a straight; e.g., 3, 4, 5, 6, where either a deuce or a 7 will complete a five-card straight.

openers: The strength of a hand needed to open a Poker pot, frequently a pair of jacks or better.

outside: In Roulette, any bets placed outside the table layout of the boxes for the 37 or 38 numbers.

overlay: In betting, a development in which the odds are greater than they should be.

painter: A card cheat who daubs the cards during the game to be able to identity them.

pair: In European Roulette, a bet on Even.

parimutuel: A method of gambling on races in which all bets are pooled and the winners paid off according to the number of winners, minus a standard track deduction.

parlay: A cumulative bet in which all the monies won on one wager are automatically bet on another.

pass: In Craps, when the shooter wins on the initial throw of the dice (hitting a 7 or 11) or makes his point on a subsequent roll.

pass line: In Craps, an area on the table where players can bet that the shooter will pass.

passe: In European Roulette, a bet on High numbers, 19-36.

passers: Fixed dice that produce more passes than regular dice.

past posting: Making a bet on any game, but especially with a bookmaker on a horse race, after the bettor has secretly discovered the result.

pat hand: In Poker, a dealt hand that cannot be improved upon by drawing any additional cards.

P.C.: In casino parlance, short or "percentage" or the advantage the house enjoys on a particular wager. Same as house **edge.**

P.C. dice: Crooked dice that give a cheat the advantage but do not guarantee a win every time.

penny ante: Any gamble made for extremely small stakes.

pepper: A victim of gambling cheats who is judged to be extremely "green."

percentage dice: The same as **P.C. dice.**

perfects: Casino-quality dice that are true cubes to a tolerance of 1/5,000 of an inch.

Philadelphia layout: The first Bank Craps layout that gave gamblers the opportunity to bet with or against the shooter.

photo finish: In horse racing, a very close finish that requires a photograph and even several blowups to determine the order of finish.

Picasso: The same as **painter.**

pick 'em: A bet on a sporting event in which neither side is favored. Bettors, however, will be required to put up $11 to win $10 or even $6 to win $5, etc.

picture cards: The court, or face, cards in a deck—jack, queen, king.

pigeon: A victim in a gambling scam.

pit boss: A casino supervisor in charge of a table or, more commonly, several tables.

place bet: In race-horse betting, winning wager on a horse that runs either first or second (in Europe it may be the first two, three, or four horses, depending on the number running); in Craps, a bet that a point number will win or lose.

plain suit: In cards, any suit that is not trump.

point numbers: In Craps, when a 4, 5, 6, 8, 9, or 10 is rolled by the shooter, it becomes his point and he must repeat it before a 7 appears.

pot: The total money or chips in a pool to be taken by the winning player or players.

pot is right: Phrase indicating all players in a game have contributed properly to the pot.

price: The line established by a bookmaker.

punter: In America, usually a horseplayer; in Britain, any bettor; in European Baccarat, a big player, especially one who usually bets against the bank.

push: A tie or standoff. In most casino and bookmaker play, all such bets are cancelled.

queer: Counterfeit money, a real danger in private gambling games and especially at crowded Crap tables.

quinella: A form of betting especially in racing that is similar to exacta betting, except that a bettor must pick the first two horses that cross the finish line in *either* order.

raffle: A lottery.

raise: In Poker, betting more than the previous player and forcing all opponents to match the higher wager or drop out of the game.

renege: To fail to follow suit or trump when one is able to.

revised line: Same as **late line.**

Revoke: Same as **renege.**

rhythm play: A method used by some slot machine players to try to control the reel combinations that show by carefully timing the pull of the handle.

riffle: A method of shuffling cards by dividing the deck in two and intermingling the two sections.

right bettor: In Craps, a player who bets with the shooter.

ringer: A horse- or dog-racing scam in which a faster animal is substituted for the one named to run.

rip: Switching dice by a cheater.

roper: A hustler who recruits victims for a gambling scam. (See STEERER.)

rouge: In European Roulette, a bet on Red.

round the corner: See **around the corner.**

round robin: A parlay method of betting involving two or more teams in all possible two-team parlay combinations. For example, a three-team round robin of ABC can produce three separate two-team parlays: AB, AC, and BC.

rubber: The winning of two out of three games by one side, especially in Bridge or Whist.

rubiconed: In Piquet and other games, to be beaten before reaching a certain score.

rug joint: A plush gambling house. The same as a **carpet joint.**

runt: In Poker, a hand of less than one pair, its value being determined by its highest card.

sabot: In Europe, the term for a dealing shoe. See SHOE.

salle privee: A private salon in a European casino reserved for high-stakes games.

sand work: A method of marking the backs of cards with very fine sandpaper.

sawdust joint: An unpretentious gambling house, usually with very low minimum bets.

schmeiss: In Klaberjass, a declaration that is a proposal to accept the turned-up card as trump or to abandon the deal.

schneider: In Gin, a shutout; in Skat, the failure of one side to win 31 or more points in a play.

score: A big gambling win; a big gambling scam win.

scratch sheet: A daily publication devoted to race entries along with probable odds for most racetracks in the country. Vital for bookmaker operations.

set: In many card games, such as Rummy and Piquet, a valid meld or three or more cards of the same rank or the same suit in sequence; in Bridge, the defeat of the contract; in Dominoes, the first bone played.

seven out: In Craps, when a shooter rolls a losing 7 before he makes his point.

shapes: Dice that have been cut down in some fashion so that they are no longer cubed and favor certain numbers.

sharper: Any kind of card cheat or superior player taking advantage of near-novices.

shimmy: American slang term for Chemin de Fer.

shoe: A box used in gambling houses for dealing cards because it is considered more likely to be an honest method.

shooter: In Craps, the player who is throwing the dice.

short shoe: A Blackjack dealing shoe with a number of cards removed from the deck or decks used, greatly altering the percentages against the player.

showdown: The revelation of players' hands in games such as Poker after the final bets have been made.

side: When one side of a betting proposition wins and the opposite side ties—a sad result for the bookmaker.

side game: A less important and relatively lightly played game in a casino, such as Big Six or Red Dog.

shylock: A money lender who haunts private gambling games to stake players who have gone broke. The interest charged is horrendous—often 6 for 5 overnight or 5½ for 5 the same day.

six-ace flats: Shaved dice that give the 1 and opposite 6 side more surface area so that they will come up more often. This works to the shooter's disadvantage.

sixaine: In European Roulette, the term for a six-number bet.

sixty days: In Craps, the 6 point.

sleeper: A wager left on a table by a forgetful gambler; in Roulette, a number that has not come up for a very long time.

slick cup: A dice cup with a polished inside surface to facilitate the effectiveness of loaded dice.

slide shot: A dice mechanic's technique for controlling the roll of one or two dice.

slow play: In Poker, the technique of a bettor making a small bet as an opener; then if he is raised, he can come back with a large re-raise.

slug: In cards, a group of cards arranged by cheats for a desired result. Care in shuffling is required to guarantee they are not disarranged; in slot machine play, a false coin or chip used to get a play.

snake eyes: In Craps, a 2.

splash move: A cunning ploy by gambling cheats who run through a cheating method without actually doing it—to see if any suspicions are aroused.

spit: A gambler's very small bankroll.

spit card or game: In poker, cards that are faced up on the table for the mutual use of all the players to supplement the cards in hand.

splitting pairs: In Blackjack, a rule that permits players dealt a pair to split them and use them as the first card in two separate hands with the amount of the original stake on each hand.

spooning: A slot machine cheating method by a player using a spoon-shaped device to bring about a payoff.

square: In Roulette, a bet on four connected numbers. Also called a corner bet and *carre* in Europe.

stand: In Blackjack, a decision by a player not to take an additional card.

standoff: A tie; in most gambling situations, it usually results in a no-bet situation, although under some rules in some games the house wins.

stiff hand: In Blackjack, a card total of 12 to 16, which may well bust if an additional card is taken.

stock: In cards, that portion of the pack which is not dealt out, but which may be used later during the same deal.

stud: A form of Poker in which four cards are dealt up with one down (in Five-card Stud) or three down (in Seven-card Stud).

street bet: In Roulette, a bet on a row of three numbers across.

stringing: A sometimes successful technique of slot machine cheats who insert a coin on a string into the machine and pull it back up, getting a free play.

taking odds: In Craps, when a bettor supplements his bet with one at true odds against the shooter's point.

taking the odds: To bet the underdog in consideration of receiving money odds.

taking the points: To bet the underdog in consideration of receiving points.

teasers: Special sports bets in Nevada casinos involving two or more teams. The established point spread is further modified to the gambler's benefit by an established number of points for each game, i.e., additional points are either added to the underdog or subtracted from the favorite. All teams selected in a teaser combination must win by a margin as adjusted by the teaser point spread.

tell: In Poker, a nervous reaction by a player that gives his opponents information about the cards he is holding; in cheater's jargon, an inept scam move that gives away the fact that a swindle is in the works.

thimble rigger: A description for the operator of a Shell Game scam, going back to the time when thimbles were used instead of shells.

third base: In Blackjack, the seat to the extreme right of the dealer.

toking: The custom by happy gamblers of tipping the workers at a casino table.

topping the deck: A skillful move by an expert card cheat to palm off the top of the deck on the cut.

tops and bottoms Gaffed dice that bear only three numbers, two of each.

totalizator: The machine that calculates the payoffs in race betting according to the money bet.

tote: The same as **totalizator.**

transversale plein: In European Roulette, a three-number bet. The same as a **street bet.**

trick: In Bridge and similar games, the round of cards played singly by each player, forming a group won by the highest card.

trump: A card or suit that ranks higher than all other cards.

Twenty-one: Blackjack.

twin double: A form of exotic betting at some racetracks in which a bettor must pick the winners of four designated races.

under the gun: In Poker, the player who must bet first; in card games in general, the player to the left of the dealer.

underdog: An individual or team in a sporting event judged to have a less than 50-50 chance of winning.

underlay: When the odds offered by sports books appear to be lower than they should be.

upcard: Cards that are dealt face up so that all players can see them.

wash: In betting, breaking even, as when a tie results so that there is no exchange of money. In other instances a win bet by a gambler is canceled out by a losing bet he makes. (Of course, he is hoping for a different result, such as winning both ways or winning one way and tying the other.)

waste pile: Discard pile in Solitaire gambling games.

way bet: In Keno, a ticket marked to combine number bets in various ways.

weight: Cheater jargon for loaded dice.

welsher: A gambler who fails to pay off on his gambling losses.

wheel: In Lowball, the lowest possible hand of 5, 4, 3, deuce, ace. Also called a **bicycle.**

whip shot: A sleight-of-hand move by a dice thrower so that dice thrown from the hand strike a table area with a flat spinning movement and the controlled numbers remain on top.

widow: In many card games, a special setting aside of one or more extra cards, which may later be brought into play by a player.

wild card: In many card games, a card(s) that is given the power to represent other cards in suit and value.

wired: In Stud Poker, a pair of cards back to back, one faced up and the other down, so that the value is concealed from other players; in cheater's jargon, said of a casino hustler who wears a hidden computer to assist him in beating the house at various games, including Blackjack and presumably Roulette.

wise guy: In sports-betting circles, a handicapper or bettor who is considered sophisticated, well-informed, and, most important, successful.

wrong bettor: In Craps, a gambler who bets on the Don't Pass line, that is, against the shooter. Also called a back-line bettor.

yard: Gambler's jargon for $100.

zombie: A gambler who betrays no outward emotion, either when winning or losing heavily.

BIBLIOGRAPHY

GAMBLING—HOW-TO, HISTORY, BIOGRAPHY

Ainslie, Tom, *Ainslie's Complete Hoyle*. New York: Simon & Schuster, 1975.

Arnold, Peter (ed.), *The Book of Games*. New York: Exeter, 1985.

Asbury, Herbert, *The Barbary Coast*. Garden City, N.Y.: Garden City Publishing, 1933.

———, *The French Quarter*. Garden City, N.Y.: Garden City Publishing, 1938.

———, *Gangs of New York*. New York: Alfred A. Knopf, 1928.

———, *Gem of the Prairie*. New York: Alfred A. Knopf, 1940.

———, *Sucker's Progress: An Informal History of Gambling in America from the Colonies to Canfield*. New York: Dodd, Mead, 1938.

Ashton, John, *The History of Gambling in England*. Montclair, N.J.: Patterson Smith, 1969.

Barnhart, Russell T., *Gamblers of Yesteryear*. Las Vegas: GBC Press, 1983.

Barron, Mike (Pitcher), *A Professional Gambler Tells How to Win*. Las Vegas: Gambler's Book Club, 1972.

Beebe, Lucius, *The Big Spenders*. Garden City, N.Y.: Doubleday, 1966.

Chaftez, Henry, *Play the Devil*. New York: Clarkson N. Potter, 1960.

Custer, Robert and Harry Milt, *When Luck Runs Out*. New York: Facts On File, 1985.

Demaris, Ovid, *The Last Mafioso*. New York: Times Books, 1981.

Devol, George H., *40 Years a Gambler on the Mississippi*. New York, 1892.

Eisenberg, D., U. Dan and E. Landau, *Meyer Lansky: Mogul of the Mob*. New York & London: Paddington Press, 1979.

Gosch, Martin A. and Richard Hammer, *The Last Testament of Lucky Luciano*. Boston: Little, Brown, 1974.

Green, Jonathan, *Gambling Exposed*. Montclair, N.J.: Patterson Smith, 1973; rep. of 1857 ed.

———, *Secret Band of Brothers*. Philadelphia: T.B. Peterson, 1858.

Guild, Leo, *The World's Greatest Gambling Systems*. Los Angeles: Holloway House, 1973.

Hammer, Richard, *Playboy's History of Organized Crime*. Chicago: Playboy Press, 1975.

Hutchens, John (ed.), *The Gambler's Bedside Book*. New York: Taplinger, 1977.

Jacoby, Oswald, *How to Figure the Odds*. Garden City, N.Y.: Doubleday, 1954.

———, *Oswald Jacoby on Gambling*. Garden City, N.Y.: Doubleday, 1963.

Katcher, Leo, *The Big Bankroll: The Life and Times of Arnold Rothstein*. New York: Harper, 1958.

Katz, Leonard, *Uncle Frank: The Biography of Frank Costello*. New York: Drake, 1973.

MacDougall, Michael (Mickey), *Don't Be a Sucker!* New York: Malba Books, n.d.

MacDougall, Michael and J.C. Furnas, *Gamblers Don't Gamble*. Garden City, N.Y.: Garden City Publishing, 1939.

Morehead, Albert H., Richard L. Frey and Geoffrey Mott-Smith, *The New Complete Hoyle*. Garden City, N.Y.: Doubleday, 1964.

Ortiz, Darwin, *Gambling Scams*. New York: Dodd, Mead, 1984.

Quinn, John Philip, *Fools of Fortune*. Chicago: G.L. Howe, 1890.

———, *Gambling and Gambling Devices*. Las Vegas: GBC Press, 1979; reprint of 1912 ed.

Rosa, Joseph G., *They Called Him Wild Bill*. Norman: University of Oklahoma Press, 1974.

Sarlat, Noah (ed.), *Sintown U.S.A.* New York: Prime, 1952.

Scarne, John. *Scarne's Encyclopedia of Games*. New York: Harper & Row, 1973.

———, *Scarne's New Complete Guide to Gambling*. New York: Simon & Schuster, 1986.

Shampaign, Charles E., *Handbook on Percentages*. New York: Casino Press, 1976; reprint.

Sifakis, Carl, *The Encyclopedia of American Crime*. New York: Facts On File, 1982.

———, *The Mafia Encyclopedia*. New York: Facts On File, 1987.

Silberstang, Edwin, *The New American Guide to Gambling & Games*. New York: NAL, 1987.

———, *Playboy's Book of Games*. New York: Galahad, 1972.

Snyder, Jimmy, *Jimmy the Greek*. Chicago: Playboy Press, 1975.

Thackrey, Ted, Jr., *Gambling Secrets of Nick the Greek*. New York: Rand McNally, 1968.

Waller, George, *Saratoga: Saga of an Impious Era*. Englewood Cliffs, N.J.: Prentice-Hall, 1966.

Wykes, Alan, *The Complete Illustrated Guide to Gambling*. Garden City, N.Y.: Doubleday, 1964.

NOTE: Possibly the most comprehensive book of rules listed above is by Morehead et al. Recommended for novices because of their clarity are Ainslie and Arnold, while Jacoby, MacDougall, Silberstang, and Snyder are somewhat stronger on insight and with opinionated views. In this vein Scarne remains in a class alone, always combative in his beliefs, but extremely informative, especially on dishonest play. The most updated cheating information is offered by Ortiz.

CASINOS AND CASINO GAMBLING

Ainslie, Tom, *How to Gamble in a Casino*. New York: Simon & Schuster, 1987.

Alvarez, A., *The Biggest Game in Town*. Boston: Houghton Mifflin, 1983.

Atti, David Michael, "Dealing on the Las Vegas Strip," audiotape interview, Special Collections, University of Nevada, Las Vegas; 1978.

Braun, Julian H., *How to Play Winning Blackjack*. Chicago: Data House, 1980.

Collver, Donald, *Scientific Blackjack & Complete Casino Guide*. New York: Arco, 1979.

Demaris, Ovid, *The Boardwalk Jungle*. New York: Bantam, 1986.

Einstein, Charles, *How to Win at Blackjack*. Las Vegas: GBC Press, 1979.

Friedman, B., *Casino Games*. New York: Golden Press, 1973.

Feinman, Jeffrey, *Casino Gambling*. New York: Arco, 1981.

Fielding, Xan, *The Money Spinner: Monte Carlo and Its Fabled Casino*. Boston: Little, Brown, 1977.

Goodman, Mike, *How to Win*. Las Vegas: Holloway, 1963.

Griffin, Peter A., *The Theory of Blackjack*. Las Vegas: GBC Press, 1981.

Harrison, Dennis R., *Win at the Casino*. New York: Ballantine, 1984.

Humble, Lance and Carl Cooper, *The World's Greatest Blackjack Book*. Garden City, N.Y.: Doubleday, 1980.

Ionescu Tulcea, C., *A Book on Casino Blackjack*. New York: Pocket Books, 1983.

———, *A Book on Casino Craps*. New York: Van Nostrand, 1981.

Irwin, Bruce, *The Winner's Edge*. Toronto: Collins, 1983.

Lewis, Oscar, *Sagebrush Casinos*. Garden City, N.Y.: Doubleday, 1953.

Linn, Edward, *Big Julie of Vegas*. Greenwich, Conn.: Fawcett, 1975.

Miller, Len, *Gambling Times Guide to Casino Games*. Secaucus, N.J.: Lyle Stuart, 1983.

Nolan, Walter I., *The Facts of Baccarat*. New York: Casino Press, 1984.

———, *The Facts of Blackjack*. New York: Casino Press, 1984.

———, *The Facts of Craps*. New York: Casino Press, 1984.

———, *The Facts of Keno*. New York: Casino Press, 1984.

———, *The Facts of Roulette*. New York: Casino Press, 1984.

———, *The Facts of Slots*. New York: Casino Press, 1984.

O'Neil-Dunne, Patrick, *Roulette for the Millions*. Chicago: Henry Regnery, 1971.

Ortiz, Darwin, *Darwin Ortiz on Casino Gambling*. New York: Dodd, Mead, 1986.

Patterson, Jerry L., *Blackjack: A Winner's Handbook*. New York: Putnam, 1981.

Patterson, Jerry L. and Eddie Olsen, *Break the Dealer*. New York: Putnam, 1986.

Patterson, Jerry L. and Walter Jaye, *Casino Gambling*. New York: Putnam, 1983.

Polovtsoff, General Pierre, *Monte Carlo Casino*. London: S. Paul, 1937.

Puzo, Mario, *Inside Las Vegas*. New York: Grosset & Dunlap, 1977.

Reese, Terence, *Winning at Casino Gambling*. New York: NAL, 1979.

Reid, Ed and Ovid Demaris, *The Green Felt Jungle*. New York: Trident Press, 1963.

Revere, Lawrence, *Playing Blackjack as a Business*. Secaucus, N.J.: Lyle Stuart, 1973.

Riddle, Major A. and Joe Hyams, *The Weekend Gambler's Handbook*. New York: Random House, 1963.

Scarne, John, *Scarne's Guide to Casino Gambling*. New York: Simon & Schuster, 1978.

———, *Scarne's New Complete Guide to Gambling*. New York: Simon & Schuster, 1986.

Silberstang, Edwin, *Playboy's Guide to Casino Gambling*. New York: Putnam, 1980.

———, *The Winner's Guide to Casino Gambling*. New York: NAL, 1981.

———, *Winning Casino Craps*. New York: David McKay, 1979.

Skolnick, Jerome H., *House of Cards*. Boston: Little, Brown, 1978.

Soares, John, *Loaded Dice*. Dallas: Taylor, 1985.

Stuart, Lyle, *Casino Gambling for the Winner*. New York: Ballantine, 1979.

Thorp, Edward O., *Beat the Dealer*. New York: Random House, 1962.

Turner, Wallace, *Gambler's Money*. Boston: Houghton Mifflin, 1965.

Uston, Ken, *Ken Uston on Blackjack*. Secaucus, N.J.: Lyle Stuart, 1986.

———, *Million Dollar Blackjack*. Secaucus, N.J.: Lyle Stuart, 1982.

Wilson, Allan N., *Casino Gambler's Guide*. New York: Harper & Row, 1970.

NOTE: Especially recommended for novices are the W.I. Nolan books, which are clear, incisive and, with a virtue not found too often in the field, non-shill in character, making no dubious claims for great rewards. For interesting color, background, and insight, see especially Alvarez, Linn, O'Neill-Dunne, Scarne, Soares and, above all, Ortiz. On Casino Blackjack Thorp must be regarded as the counter's bible, but this book should be compared with the critical observations made in *Scarne's New Complete Guide*. Wilson should in turn be studied for criticisms of Scarne.

DICE

Becker, Bruce, *Backgammon for Blood*. New York: Avon, 1975.

Frey, Skip, *How to Win at Dice Games*. North Hollywood, California: Wilshire, 1976.

Garcia, Frank, *How to Detect Crooked Games*. New York: Arco, 1977.

Jacoby, Oswald and John R. Crawford, *The Backgammon Book*. New York: Bantam, 1980.

Kiely, Jack, *Hot Dice: How to Leave the Table a Winner*. Lynn, Massachusetts: Sunnyside, 1986.

Scarne, John, *Scarne on Dice*. Harrisburg, Pennsylvania: Stackpole, 1974.

NOTE: The literature on backgammon is enormous but certainly the Jacoby-Crawford work stands out as a bible on the subject. Similarly, Scarne's contribution on dice games is the definitive work in that field. However, all the "Hoyles" and how-to guides listed in the sections on GAMBLING—HOW-TO, HISTORY, BIOGRAPHY and CASINOS AND CASINO GAMES, as well as titles specifically on casino craps in those sections, can be consulted for a wealth of information on all sorts of dice play.

CARDS

Ankeny, Nesmith C., *Poker Strategy—Winning with Game Theory*. New York: Basic Books, 1981.

Beal, George, *Playing-Cards and Their Story*. New York: Arco, 1975.

Chatto, William Andrew, *Facts and Speculations on the Origin and History of Playing Cards*. London: 1848.

Dawson, Laurence (revised by), *Hoyle's Card Games*. London: Routledge and Kegan Paul, 1979.

Dowling, Allen, *The Great American Pastime*. South Brunswick, N.J.: A.S. Barnes, 1970.

Ewen, Robert B., *The Teenager's Guide to Bridge*. New York: Dodd, Mead, 1976.

Frey, Richard L., *According To Hoyle*. Greenwich, Connecticut: Fawcett, 1956.

Gibson, Walter, *Hoyle's Modern Encyclopedia of Card Games*. Garden City, N.Y.: Doubleday, 1974.

———, *Pinochle*. Secaucus, N.J.: Castle Books, 1974.

———, *Poker*. Secaucus, N.J.: Castle Books, 1974.

Goren, Charles H. *The Fundamentals of Contract Bridge*. New York: Pocket Books, 1955.

———, *Goren's New Bridge Complete*. Garden City, N.Y.: Doubleday, 1985.

Green, J.H., *Gambler's Tricks with Cards, Exposed and Explained*. New York: Dick & Fitzgerald, 1859.

Jacoby, Oswald and James Jacoby, *Jacoby on Card Games*. New York: Pharos, 1986.

Jacoby, Oswald, *Jacoby on Poker*. Garden City, N.Y.: Doubleday, 1947.

Jones, Henry "Cavendish," *The Laws of Ecarte*. London: Thomas De La Rue, 1897.

———, *The Laws of Piquet*. London: Thomas De La Rue, 1901.

Keller, John W., *The Game of Draw Poker*. New York: Frederick A. Stokes, 1887.

Lemming, Joseph, *Games & Fun with Playing Cards*. New York: Dover, 1980.

MacDougall, Samuel Davis (Michael), *Danger in the Cards*. Chicago: Ziff-Davis, 1943.

Majax, Gerard, *Secrets of the Card Sharps*. New York: Sterling, 1977.

Morehead, Albert S. (ed.), *Official Rules of Card Games*. New York: Ballantine, 1986.

Preston, "Amarillo Slim" with Bill G. Cox, *Play Poker To Win*. New York: Grosset & Dunlap, 1973.

Reese, Terence and Anthony T. Watkins, *Secrets of Modern Poker*. New York: Sterling, 1964.

Scarne, John, *Scarne's Guide to Modern Poker*. New York: Simon & Schuster, 1980.

————, *Scarne On Cards*. New York: NAL, 1973.

Sheinwold, Alfred, *First Book of Bridge*. New York: Barnes and Noble, 1952.

Silberstang, Edwin, *Winning Poker Strategy*. New York: David McKay, 1978.

Truscott, Alan, *Contract Bridge*. New York: Bantam, 1982.

Wallace, Frank R., *Poker: A Guaranteed Income for Life*. New York: Crown, 1977.

NOTE: Many more books that deal heavily with cards are to be found in the section on GAMBLING—HOW-TO, HISTORY, BIOGRAPHY, and in the case of Blackjack under CASINOS AND CASINO GAMES. Within this present heading *Scarne On Cards* gives the most inside information on various games. Gibson is the most comprehensive, while his separate works on Pinochle and Poker are noteworthy for their card-by-card approach. On Poker Scarne, Silberstang, Jacoby, and Ankeny offer the most insights. Truscott's contribution on Bridge is probably the best for beginners. For Bridge cheating, one should refer particularly to *Scarne's New Complete Guide* in the HOW-TO section.

SPORTS BETTING

Ainslie, Tom, *Ainslie's Complete Guide to Thoroughbred Racing*. New York: Simon & Schuster, 1979.

————, *Ainslie's Encyclopedia of Thoroughbred Handicapping*. New York: William Morrow, 1978.

Banker, Lem and Fred Klein, *Lem Banker's Book of Sports Betting*. New York: Dutton, 1986.

Buchele, W.J., *Greyhound Racing Guide*. Bonita Spring, Florida: no publisher listed, 1968.

Patterson, Jerry L. and Jack Painter, *Sports Betting: A Winner's Handbook*. New York: Putnam, 1985.

Scarne, John, *Scarne's New Complete Guide to Gambling*. New York: Simon & Schuster, 1986.

Silberstang, Edwin, *The Winner's Guide to Sports Betting*. New York: NAL, 1988.

NOTE: The above selections offer a background to the field of sports betting. Scarne is especially valuable as an overview of betting on various sporting events. "How to win" advice appears in some of the selections as well as in many of the overall guides listed under GAMBLING—HOW-TO, HISTORY, BIOGRAPHY. In addition, a great many books and magazines cover specific systems plays of dubious value. A common practice in how-to horse-race betting involves developing a "system" that works for an extended period of a week, two weeks, or a month at one or more tracks. It is not difficult for a resourceful writer to produce a "winning" system after studying the results of a series of races. He simply keys in on a few big winners, finds some common thread in their past performances, and allows hit-or-miss results on other races to produce enough random wins to make the betting pattern productive over several days. Then as the results founder in later races, he devises some "exceptions to the rules" or "special situations" to continue on the profitable path. Unfortunately, when the reader continues the betting pattern he will need many more "exceptions" and "special situations" to keep from becoming a loser.

MISCELLANEOUS

Adler, Bill, *The Lottery Book*. New York: William Morrow, 1986.

Berndt, Fredrick, *The Domino Book*. Nashville, Tennessee: T. Nelson, 1974.

Fenton, Robert S., *Chess For You*. New York: Grosset & Dunlap, 1975.

Forster, R. R., *Dice and Dominoes*. New York: 1897.

Granville, Joseph E., *How to Win at Bingo*. West Nyack, N.Y.: Parker, 1977.

Horowitz, I.A., *All About Chess*. New York: Macmillan, 1971.

NOTE: For offbeat gambling games such as bar plays, coin games and carnival action consult Ainslie and Scarne in the HOW-TO section.